AMERICAN GOVERNMENT
PRINCIPLES AND PRACTICES

TURNER   SWITZER   REDDEN

GLENCOE
McGraw-Hill

Lake Forest, Illinois   Columbus, Ohio   Woodland Hills, California   Peoria, Illinois

Send all inquiries to:
Glencoe/McGraw-Hill, 936 Eastwind Drive, Westerville, Ohio 43081

ISBN 0-02-823896-6 (Student Edition) ISBN 0-02-823897-4 (Teacher's Annotated Edition)
Printed in the United States of America

5 6 7 8 9 10 027/046 04 03 02 01 00 99

Authors

Mary Jane Turner has been a social studies teacher at both the secondary school and university levels. She has a B.A. in Political Science and Economics, an M.P.A. in Public Administration, and a Ph.D. in Political Science. In addition, she has done graduate study in education. Formerly a Staff Associate at the Social Science Education Consortium and Associate Director of the Center for Civic Education, Dr. Turner is presently Director of Curriculum and Senior Education Advisor for the Close Up Foundation.

Kenneth Switzer has been a classroom teacher in the United States and Colombia, South America, where he was a Peace Corps volunteer. He received B.A. and M.A. degrees in Social Science Education from the University of Northern Colorado, a Spanish language certificate from Universidad Javeriana in Colombia, and M.A. and Ph.D. degrees in Political Science/International Studies from the University of Denver. Dr. Switzer has been a curriculum developer and teacher trainer at the Center for Teaching International Relations, Center for Research and Education, and Social Science Education Consortium, as well as a consultant for the National Assessment of Educational Progress. Currently, he is an associate of Step Up Projects, a business consulting firm, and a freelance writer.

Charlotte Redden received her B.A. degree in Social Science Education from Indiana State University. Following graduate study in Urban Studies/Public Administration at the University of Southern California, she received M.A. and Ph.D. degrees in Political Science/International Studies from the University of Denver. Dr. Redden has worked in city planning, been an analyst for the Census Bureau and a senior policy/budget analyst for the Governor of Colorado, and served as Associate Executive Director for Finance for the Colorado Commission on Higher Education. She also has been an evaluation consultant for the National Assessment of Educational Progress, and a finance/operations director of American operations for several investors. Currently, she is a management consultant to the public and non-profit sectors, a community activist, and a freelance writer.

Consultants

Curriculum Consultant

Dr. Raymond B. McClain
Director, Division of Social Studies
Pittsburgh Public Schools
Pittsburgh, Pennsylvania

Content Consultant

Professor Dennis Dresang
Department of Political Science
LaFollette Institute of Public Affairs
University of Wisconsin-Madison
Madison, Wisconsin

Unit Reviewers

Suzan C. Harrison
Social Studies Chairperson
Marshall High School
Marshall, Texas

W. Bruce Laetsch
Social Studies Chairperson
George Washington High School
Indianapolis, Indiana

Martha C. Rao
Social Studies Teacher
Presentation High School
San Jose, California

Albert L. Jones
Social Studies Teacher, Department Chairperson
West Side High School
Gary, Indiana

Linberg Rollins
Teacher
Richmond Public Schools
Richmond, Virginia

D. William Tinkler
Coordinator of Secondary Social Studies
Fulton County Public Schools
Atlanta, Georgia

Preface

American Government: Principles and Practices is a practical study of the American political system. The program develops students' awareness of the principles of American government by presenting ideas simply and developing them logically. Ideas are reinforced through a readable narrative, complete with examples, and through a wide variety of precisely executed graphs, charts, tables, diagrams, and maps.

American Government: Principles and Practices is designed to inform students about the American system of government. The text moves logically from the foundations of American government to citizen involvement in the political process, government at the national level, state and local governments, and, finally, to government at the international level.

The text itself is divided into 8 units and 28 chapters. Each unit opens with two colorful photographs visualizing the unit theme, a unit introduction that discusses how these photographs relate to the topic of the unit, and a listing of the chapters within the unit. Each chapter begins with a photograph illustrating the chapter topic, a list of chapter objectives, and a Civic Participation Journal. The Civic Participation Journal serves to develop the chapter theme and to promote student interest. Each chapter centers on a topic basic to an understanding of American government and the American political system. Concepts, developed in the narrative, are reinforced by a variety of photographs and graphic art. Concept terms appear in boldface type and are defined or explained in the margins.

Four types of special features are interspersed throughout the chapters. CASE STUDIES present government-related issues that have already been decided. ISSUES present opposing viewpoints on a topic of debate in today's political system. PROFILES focus on the lives of individuals who have made a difference in shaping our nation's political structure. COMPARISONS detail various aspects of comparative government.

Each major section of the text concludes with a series of review questions that check student understanding of important facts. Each chapter concludes with a summary that concisely highlights key points in the chapter. At the end of each chapter appears a Chapter Review that contains Building Vocabulary, Reviewing Facts, Analyzing Facts, and Evaluating Ideas sections. Every chapter also contains a Thinking Skill that helps students develop a specific critical thinking skill.

Each unit in *American Government: Principles and Practices* concludes with a Unit Review that contains Review Questions covering the content of the unit and a list of Suggested Readings for students who would like to read more about a specific topic covered in the unit. In addition, each unit also concludes with a Building Citizenship Competency skill that teaches students a specific skill they need to fulfill their responsibilities and protect their interests as citizens.

An Appendix at the end of the text provides full-color maps of the United States and the world, a Glossary containing all the boldface terms in the text, and a comprehensive Index covering all major topics discussed in the text.

CONTENTS

Government

UNIT
SEVEN State and Local Governments .. 510

Government

ILLUSTRATIONS

Government

Prologue

This is a book about American federal, state, and local governments. To some people, government is a complex array of bureaucrats, agencies, and regulations. To others, it is an administrative organization set up to identify, define, and resolve problems. Still others see it as a major source of public goods and services. Whatever view, it is important to know what American government is, how it works, how it affects lives, and how one can become a part of it.

To understand how something really works, you usually have to go back to the beginning. *American Government: Principles and Practices* will show you the basics of American government so that you can understand how and why certain things are done. In addition, it will describe the world of the federal government in Washington, D.C., your state government, and your local government, and will explain how these governments work separately and together. It will also discuss how our government works with other governments of the world.

American government is a very broad topic. It is impossible to learn everything about it all at once. But it is possible to learn something about what your government does, how it is organized, and how decisions are made. When you have completed *American Government: Principles and Practices,* you will understand a great deal about American government, how it affects you personally, and most important, how you can be a part of making it work on the national, state, and local levels, and even on the international level.

FOUNDATIONS OF GOVERNMENT

Government is a process that involves many people everywhere—including you. As you look at the world, you will notice the many different kinds of government that exist today. However, in spite of these differences, most of us have a common desire to participate in and shape the decisions made at all levels by our particular government.

In the United States, we have a democracy—a form of government in which the people rule. Our democracy has its orgins in events that took place more than 200 years ago. In the picture on the facing page, Americans celebrate one of the early events in our government's history—the 200th anniversary of the inauguration of our first President, George Washington.

In other parts of the world, people are still struggling to create for themselves the kind of government that we now enjoy.

Chapter 1

What Is Government?

There are now over 5 billion people living in our world. We live in conditions that range from poverty to plenty, from violence to peace, from bondage to freedom. What causes such diversity in the way world neighbors live? One of the causes is an institution called government.

More than 250 million of Earth's people live in our nation, the United States. We, too, lead diverse lives, yet we are held together by some common threads. As a people we believe in "liberty, equality, and justice for all," familiar words that underlie the very essence of our lives. And we are united by one powerful and lasting document—the Constitution. If life in America were a game, the Constitution would be the instruction sheet that comes in the box. And it is we, the players, who have written the rules. Through this document, we have tried to form a government that serves the needs of all people. Although it is a goal that we have not fully attained, it is one that has provided hope to Americans for over 200 years and has been an inspiration to other people around the world.

★ ★ ★ ★ ★

Chapter Preview

TERMS TO KNOW
government, nation-state, sovereignty, unitary government, federal government, federalism, confederate government, direct democracy, political system, democracy, representative democracy, parliamentary democracy, presidential democracy, monarchy, dictatorship, totalitarianism, fascism, communism, economic system, capitalism, laissez faire, socialism

READ TO DISCOVER
- why we have government and what they do.
- the different forms of government.
- how power and authority are organized in political systems.
- the different kinds of economic systems.

Civic Participation Journal

Interview at least three people who have graduated from high school and have jobs. Ask them to describe the impact that government—on the federal, state, and local levels—has on their lives. What needs does government serve? If people are dissatisfied with government, how can they work to change it? Keep a tally of your interview results.

1 The Meaning of Government

What, really, is government? A political scientist would probably say it is a political authority, whether laws, institutions, or officials, that rules the areas under its control. An American struggling to raise three children might view government as a "lifesaver" that provides a job at the local post office, transports the children to and from school, and feeds them lunch. You, on the other hand, might think of government as a vague body of politicians that passes laws in Washington, D.C. While all these views are correct, government is much, much more. Perhaps the best way to understand government is to look at where it exists.

Governments exist to serve citizens. But where, actually, are governments found? You probably have a student government that handles issues in your school. City and state governments each make decisions for *their* residents. But, the largest group served by a government is the body of people living within a **nation-state,** or country.

Today all nation-states share certain features. Each is made up of a group of people that lives within definite territorial boundaries. Each has a government made up of political and administrative institutions. All have **sovereignty**, the right to govern their people.

Each nation-state is different. The number of persons living within each varies, ranging from several thousand in Luxembourg to hundreds of millions in China and India. The size of the territory of each also varies, from the few square miles of Liechtenstein to the incredibly vast expanse of Russia. And, just as nation-states vary in both size and population, they also vary in how they are governed.

At this point, you might be asking yourself, "how does all this concern me?" Your government has, in fact, been set up to address your concerns.

What Needs Do Governments Serve?

In the United States one federal government, 50 state governments, and over 85,000 local governments each serve a variety of needs. Among other things, these governments provide mail delivery, sewage disposal, police protection, and education. Political scientists believe that all governments, not just those in our nation, meet three general kinds of needs.

nation-state made up of a body of people who live within particular territorial boundaries and who have a government and sovereignty over all the people within the boundaries

sovereignty the supreme power to govern all the people living within a nation-state or country's boundaries

Roads like this one make up the vast system of transportation that our government helps to maintain. But governments work to provide other services for their people, as well. What are some of the ways in which our government serves your needs?

MANAGE ENVIRONMENT

One service of government is to manage the environment of people living in groups. You have interests and goals that may compete with those of others. Magnify this competition among the number of people living in your city, state, or country, and conflicts arise. So, in a social environment, there is a need for government to control behavior and maintain peace.

SOLVE PROBLEMS

A second need that governments meet is to provide a way to solve problems that individuals cannot solve alone. You, for example, cannot provide protection from outside attack, establish a system of trade, or build and maintain roads by yourself. All of these require a group to work together. Government provides a way to achieve group cooperation to address these problems.

PRESERVE CULTURE

A third need is to preserve a common culture, or the language, values, customs, and religious beliefs of the group. Once people who share the same culture have formed a group, they want to assure that their culture will be continued and supported. Government is the institution that is able to do this.

How Do Governments Serve Needs?

The needs that governments face are by no means small. How, for instance, do governments actually accomplish the feat of managing the environment? In this and other services, governments have general functions that allow them to get the job done.

PASS LAWS

Of all government functions, making and enforcing laws is the most apparent. Governments pass laws to regulate traffic, prevent crime, standardize time, and control pollution, among other things. Any institution may have rules for its members, but government's laws are binding on *all* the citizens in the society.

SET GOALS

A second function of government is to set social goals by making public policy. This policy can be a set of laws, ideas, or practices whose aims are to make society better. Public policies are sometimes described with slogans so that people can better remember and identify with them. Slogans such as Franklin Roosevelt's "New Deal," Lyndon Johnson's "War on Poverty," or Ronald Reagan's "Zero Tolerance for Drugs," described policies that outlined social goals and changes that these Presidents hoped to bring about.

DISTRIBUTE BENEFITS

A third function is to decide how to distribute the rewards and benefits of society. Some benefits, such as paved streets, parks, and college scholarships, are easy to identify. Other benefits are less visible but just as vital, such as the guarantee of equal protection of the laws. Some of these benefits are distributed evenly. For example, everyone benefits when their government ensures national security, a stable system of money, and a strong economy. But other benefits are unevenly distributed. A new highway, for instance, may help one particular community, but not someone living a hundred miles away. Likewise, a new tax law may benefit only certain taxpayers.

What Are the Origins of Government?

While political scientists agree that governments are necessary, they do not always agree on how government began and how it got its authority. Over the years, four separate theories have been proposed to explain government's origin and sovereignty.

EVOLUTION

The evolutionary theory suggests that governments developed from the family unit. According to this theory, in ancient times the head of the family made the rules, decided the family goals, and distributed the resources. Eventually families banded together into clans, which later joined to form tribes. Nations, in turn, emerged over the centuries from these tribes. Today's governments, then, carry out the same basic functions the heads of families in ancient times once did.

FORCE

According to the force theory, one strong person or group simply claims an area and grabs control of the people living in it. A good example is the development of feudal estates in Europe after the fall of Rome.

DIVINE RIGHT

The theory of divine right was used during the Middle Ages to justify the power of the monarchs. At that time kings and queens claimed that their right to rule came directly from God and was passed on to their descendants. Thus their power was hereditary and absolute.

SOCIAL CONTRACT

The last of the four theories—the social contract theory—was developed in opposition to divine right. In the 1600s some political philosophers began to argue that free persons unite voluntarily to form a contract allowing themselves to be ruled. This idea was originally proposed by Thomas Hobbes, an English philosopher who believed that once a free people enter into such a contract, the government has absolute power to rule as it wishes. John Locke, a later English philosopher, carried this theory further. He said that the people, who are the source of all rights and power, contract with the government for their own benefit. But, when the government stops serving the people, they have a right to break the contract.

Theories of the Origin of Government

Evolutionary Theory
Force Theory
Divine Right Theory
Social Contract Theory

Figure 1–1

Section Review

1. What are the three needs that governments meet?
2. What do governments have the power to do?
3. What are the four theories proposed to explain the origin of government?
4. **Challenge:** Do you agree with Thomas Hobbes? Explain.

2 Structure of Government

The sovereignty of a nation-state is usually divided among a central government and various subdivisions. How these levels relate to each other determines whether the government is classified as federal, unitary, or confederate.

Federal Government

The United States has a **federal government**. This means that the national government has certain powers, and each of the 50 states has others. This division of powers was established by the Constitution to protect the individual states against one strong national government. Why were we so afraid of concentrating power in one area? The development of this federal system was, in part, a reaction against the strong monarchies and centralized governments that existed in Europe when our Constitution was being written.

Besides our country, about 30 other nation-states, including Canada, Mexico, and Switzerland, have federal governments. **Federalism** seems to work best in large nations like these or in nations where people have incredibly diverse or conflicting needs. Since state or regional governments are closer to the people, they can be more responsive to state or regional needs than a faraway central government. Solving state problems at the state level also frees the national government to deal with issues of broader concern. Solving problems at this level, though, also means that laws are less uniform throughout the nation. The type of services available to you may vary considerably from those received by a person who lives across the state border.

Here, the California flag flies along with the flag of the United States. Because power is held by the individual states as well as our central government, we are said to have a federal form of government. What are some other countries with federal governments?

Unitary Government

In a **unitary government**, the central government may or may not choose to create lesser governments and to delegate power to them. In practice, such local units as provinces, cities, or towns are set up mainly to carry out the policies of the central government. But the power of the central government may not be sweeping. Often it is limited by a written constitution, by unwritten law based on custom, and by what was done in the distant past.

Unitary government is the most common form of government structure in the world today. The national governments of France, Great Britain,

unitary government form of government in which power is held by the central government

federal government form of government in which power is shared by a national government and state or regional governments

federalism principle of government in which the power of government is shared between the national government and state or regional governments

The North Atlantic Treaty Organization (NATO) is similar, in many ways, to a confederate form of government. What are two examples of confederate governments of the past?

confederate government alliance of separate and independent states

and Israel are organized in this way. So are all local governments in our nation. As you will learn later, your city exists only because your state government allows it to.

Confederate Government

A **confederate government,** also known as a confederation, is a cooperative group of individual states that give the central government the power to deal with matters of common concern. These may include such issues as defense or foreign relations. Generally all of the member states have to agree to any action taken by the central government. They can strip the government of its authority at any time. They also can separate from the group if they choose.

The United States has had two unsuccessful experiments with confederate governments in the past. One was the government of the new American states from 1781 to 1789 under the Articles of Confederation. The other was the Confederate States of America set up in 1861 when 11 southern states withdrew from the

Union and established their own government.

Several present-day *international* alliances, however, do have some features of confederations. For example, nation-states may send representatives to a joint governing body to achieve some common goal. For some alliances, like the North Atlantic Treaty Organization (NATO), the purpose is to provide cooperative security or defense. For others, like the European Union (EU), the intent is to provide better economic and trade relations among all of the member states.

Section Review

1. Why is federalism best suited to a large or populous country?

2. What is the most common type of government structure?

3. How is the central government limited under a confederacy?

4. **Challenge:** In your opinion, do the advantages of a federal system outweigh the disadvantages? Explain.

3 Political Systems

A **political system** is made up of many different elements. The formal political system of the United States, for instance, includes the Constitution; state constitutions; city charters; the executive, legislative, and judicial branches of all levels of government; administrative agencies; and political parties. To understand this or any other political system, you need to know not only what its parts are but how the parts work together. Who has the power to make decisions? How *much* power do decision-makers have, and how do they use it? The answers to these questions vary, depending on the form of government.

Rule by the Many

The form of government most familiar to Americans is **democracy**. In a democracy, the government reflects the will of the majority. The United States, Mexico, Canada, Japan, and France are all democracies, and, as such, they all have basic beliefs in common. According to Carl Becker, a noted political historian, one of those basic beliefs is in "the worth and dignity and creative capacity of the individual."

In addition, democracies also recognize the equality of all human beings. Democratic societies allow their citizens freedom of public discussion and dissent. But most importantly, they believe that government exists only by the consent of the citizens.

DIRECT DEMOCRACY
Historically, democracies have not been common. Even today true democracies are outnumbered by other forms of government. But democracy as a form of government began long ago. In its purest form, **direct democracy** was practiced in Athens and other ancient Greek city-states. In fact, the term democracy stems from this period. Originally it meant that the people themselves made the laws, set the goals, and distributed the social benefits of the government. This was usually done in a public meeting. Direct democracy is still found at some town meetings in New England and in some of the smaller territorial divisions in Switzerland. The important thing is that in ancient times and today, rather than being outside their political system, the people are the key that makes the system work. They *are* the government.

REPRESENTATIVE DEMOCRACY
Another form of democracy is **representative democracy**. Under this system, also known as indirect democracy, the people express their will by electing representatives to conduct the business of government for them.

direct democracy form of democracy in which the majority vote of all citizens makes the laws governing them

political system all practices by which the people of a country carry out their political activities and achieve their goals of government

democracy form of government in which political power is held by the people

representative democracy form of democracy in which elected representatives run the business of government

Citizens practice direct democracy at this New England town meeting. Where did the idea of direct democracy begin?

CASE STUDY: COMPARISON

A COMMON HERITAGE

Although Great Britain and the United States have a common political heritage, each established a different form of government. Great Britain has a unitary government and practices parliamentary democracy. In this kind of democracy, the executive branch is responsible to the legislative and the legislative to the voters. As a unitary government, Parliament is the final authority, with local government its administrative arm. The United States, on the other hand, has a federal government and practices presidential democracy. Yet, even with this difference, their common political heritage is apparent when looking at the ways each limits the power of its leaders.

The Framers of the Constitution were well aware of the struggles to limit the monarch's power that had gone on in Great Britain from before the Magna Carta was signed in 1215 through the time the Bill of Rights was adopted in 1689. There was no question that Britain offered a powerful example of how a monarch's absolute power could be diminished.

The Framers, however, fearful that a strong executive could too strongly influence an aristocratic legislature, chose not to follow the British form of government. Instead, they turned to a federal form of government headed by a President who was not a part of the legislative branch.

In the American system the Constitution delegates certain powers to the national government and reserves others to state governments. It also delegates specific powers to the executive branch represented by the President and others to the legislative branch represented by Congress. Although each is elected separately, both are responsible directly to the voters. Congress has two houses—the Senate and the House of Representatives. Although both major political parties—the Democratic and the Republican—try to gain control of both houses and the executive,

it really is not necessary that Congress and the presidency be held by the same party.

In the British system, the present monarch, Queen Elizabeth II, has powers that are strictly limited by custom. For the most part, her role is ceremonial and the actual governmental authority rests with the two houses of Parliament—the upper house, known as the House of Lords, and the lower house, known as the House of Commons. Membership in the House of Lords is hereditary, while members of the House of Commons are elected by the voters.

Two major political parties—Conservative and Labour—compete in the House of Commons to control a majority of seats. The party that gains the majority names a prime minister to head the executive branch. The prime minister then forms a cabinet and chooses an administration from members of that party. When the other party gains a majority, it repeats the process and forms its government.

1. Do you think a unitary form of government would work in the United States? Why or why not?
2. What advantages do you see to having a government in which both the legislative and executive branches are of the same party?

Westminster Palace, shown here, houses Great Britain's Parliament. Although very similar to our own, the government of Great Britain is different in many ways. What are some of these differences?

These representatives are responsible to the people and can be voted out of office by the people. The opinions of the citizens guide the elected officials, and laws are made in public sessions. Thus, all citizens are responsible for making sure that their elected officials truly represent them. Although it means the same as representative democracy, historically Americans have used the term *republic* to describe this system.

Today there are two major forms of representative democracy—presidential and parliamentary. Their differences are based on who actually makes the law and who carries it out.

In a **presidential democracy**, the branch of government that makes the law and the one that carries it out are separate. In the United States, for example, the Constitution gives the power to make the law to the Con-

gress and the power to carry out the law to the President. Thus, the President cannot enact laws and Congress cannot carry out or enforce the laws it has enacted. You might think it would be more efficient for one branch to "do it all." But this separation of powers has a distinct advantage. It ultimately protects your freedom by making it virtually impossible for one branch to become so powerful that it grasps total control of the government.

In a **parliamentary democracy**, the separation of powers is a bit murky. The branch that carries out the law is made up of a prime minister and a cabinet. This group of advisors, however, are also members of the Parliament, the branch that enacts the law. Because of this, there is an overlapping relationship between the two branches of government.

parliamentary democracy form of representative democracy in which the law-making and law-enacting branches of government overlap

presidential democracy form of representative democracy in which the law-making and law-enacting branches of government are separate

What Is Government? 13

Monarchy

monarchy form of government headed by a single leader who generally has inherited his or her title

dictatorship form of government in which absolute power is held by one individual or a small group

totalitarianism belief that government should control all groups and individual behavior to promote the good of the state

Another type of government is one in which a single person rules. The most common form of this type of government has been a **monarchy.** Historically, most monarchies have been *absolute* monarchies, in which a king, queen, emperor, empress, or tsar held all power to rule. These rulers based their dominance on the claim that their right to exercise supreme power came from God. A modern-day example of an absolute monarch is the king of Saudi Arabia.

Most modern monarchies, however, are *constitutional* monarchies in which the powers of the monarch are strictly limited by constitutions. Under this system, many monarchs serve only as ceremonial heads of state. The governments of their countries are actually democracies in which the real rulers are chosen by the people. The monarchs of Great Britain, Sweden, Norway, and the Netherlands are constitutional monarchs.

Authoritarian Systems

Under some systems of government, the state rather than the people holds ultimate authority. Governments like this are known as authoritarian, and there are several types, based on who holds the power and how much power they have.

DICTATORSHIP

One type is a **dictatorship.** More often than not, the person or group in control—the dictator—gains supreme power to rule by using force, either through a military victory or the overthrow of another dictator. For example, this was how Fidel Castro came to power in Cuba. The dictator's word is law, and the goals and well-being of the government are considered more important than those of the citizens. It is a form of government under which the conditions of life vary widely. In some cases, the people may have some freedoms, while in others they have none at all. People may have a high standard of living or may barely survive in poverty. It all depends on the will and actions of the dictator.

TOTALITARIANISM

Another type of authoritarian system is **totalitarianism.** Under a totalitarian system, the power of the state is unlimited. As in all authoritarian systems, the needs of the state come before the needs of individuals. The government has total control over the

Germany's Adolf Hitler led his country into World War II. His regime is an example of the Fascist form of government. What characteristics are common to Fascist rule?

lives of the people, and all citizens must work for the common goals established by the government. Two forms of this kind of government are fascism and communism.

Under **fascism,** people are allowed to own property, but they have no power to govern themselves. The government's power is absolute, and the dictator is thought incapable of error. The government denies that humans are equal, and certain ethnic groups are thought to be superior to others. Often rigid ideas exist about proper male and female roles as well. The military is idealized, and the mark of the patriot is willingness to fight for the "Homeland." Any and all means— including lies, violence, and war—are acceptable if they further the goals of the state. Examples of this form of government were found before and during World War II in Italy under Benito Mussolini and in Germany under Adolf Hitler.

Under **communism,** the central government and the Communist party control all economic and political life. Any person holding an important position inside or outside the formal governmental system must belong to the party. The political system is used to put economic plans into effect. In theory, the goal of a Communist system is to toss aside government completely and achieve a stateless society in which citizens would work according to their abilities and be paid according to their needs. But, in practice, this has never been achieved, not even in the former Soviet Union. While the Soviet Union called itself a Communist system, in the past it had been a dictatorship and an oligarchy, a government by the few. Currently, however, the people in many of the republics of the former Soviet Union are being allowed a greater voice in choosing their leaders.

Section Review

1. What are the two major forms of democracy? What group holds political power in each?

2. What is the difference between an absolute and a constitutional monarchy?

3. What do all authoritarian systems of government have in common?

4. **Challenge:** In what ways are the governments of Great Britain and the United States similar? How are they different?

fascism political philosophy that exalts nation and race above the individual

4 Economic Systems

Working hand-in-hand with each political system is an **economic system.** Factories, farms, mines, banks, stores, transportation systems, communication networks—they are all part of it. In short, the economic system is an organized way of providing for all the material wants and needs of its people.

A nation's political and economic systems are so closely linked that sometimes it is hard to tell where one begins and the other ends. More often than not, changes in one will bring about changes in the other. Simply put, governments determine which economic policies will be practiced. The economic system, in turn, determines the answers to such questions as who owns the means of production (natural resources, industry, and so on), who will share in what is produced, and who is employed and at what salary. Perhaps most important, an economic system outlines what you, as a consumer, can decide versus what the government decides.

communism totalitarian system of government in which the state controls in large measure the economic and social life of the society

economic system all the ways in which people's material needs and wants are met, through the production, distribution, and exchange of a nation's goods and services

Franklin D. Roosevelt is often considered one of our greatest Presidents. As President, Roosevelt summarized Americans' expectations of their system of government. What are these four expectations?

capitalism economic system in which the means of production, distribution, and exchange of goods and services are privately owned

laissez faire policy based on a minimum of government interference in business or economic matters

Today there are three major economic systems—capitalism, socialism, and communism. In each of the three systems, government is involved in some way. The amount of government involvement, however, varies widely among the three systems and among the nations that use those systems. In actual practice, no nation today is totally capitalistic, communistic, or socialistic. All are mixed to some degree.

Whatever form of government a country may have, its citizens expect certain things of both the political and the economic system. When Franklin D. Roosevelt was President of the United States, he identified American expectations of the two systems:

Equality of opportunity for youth and for others.
Jobs for those who can work.
Security for those who need it.
The ending of special privilege for the few.

The preservation of civil liberties for all.
The enjoyment of the fruits of scientific progress in a wider and constantly rising standard of living.

Roosevelt summed up his statement with these words:

These are the simple, basic things that must never be lost sight of in the turmoil and unbelievable complexity of our modern world. The inner and abiding strength of our economic and political systems is dependent upon the degree to which they fulfill those expectations.

Capitalism

Capitalism grew out of a theory known as **laissez faire,** French for "to allow to do." One of its best known advocates was an eighteenth-century economist named Adam Smith. As he saw it, when it came to trade, business, or industry, government should take part only in activities that private business could not carry out at a profit.

FREE ENTERPRISE
Capitalism, then, is based on free, or private, enterprise. The means of production can be owned by one person or by many. Capitalists believe that businesses exist to earn a profit and that workers need and want to receive the greatest return for their labor. As a result, "competition" is the underlying force in a capitalist economy. Laborers compete for limited jobs. Business owners compete to produce goods or services that can be sold for profit on the open market. This competition, say capitalists, forces businesses to produce the best products at the lowest costs. This, in turn, results in many sales and, thus, a high profit.

In a capitalist economy, there is no set price for any particular product. Rather, the price of a product depends on how many buyers demand that particular good or service and how many sellers supply it. The price, in other words, changes according to supply and demand. And as the price changes, so does the level of profit.

This philosophy is most evident in the American economy. Even though there is some government regulation, we are closer to pure capitalism than most other economies in the world.

MIXED ECONOMY

The United States has what is known as a mixed economy. In it, our government regulates some aspects of the economy while allowing other parts to compete for profit without government interference. The government, for instance, regulates many private businesses through controls such as a minimum wage law, build-ing codes, and pure food and drug regulations. It also regulates institutions that offer public goods and services, such as schools and banks. In addition, the government provides many social welfare programs for the needy or for those who cannot compete in the labor force. Social Security, for example, guarantees an income for retired people.

Still, most of the decisions directing the daily course of activity in our economy are made freely, without government involvement. Individuals known as entrepreneurs take financial risks to establish business enterprises with the intent of making a profit. As long as there is competition among these suppliers, the government tries to stay out of the way.

Capitalism can exist under different forms of government. But it is especially compatible with a system like democracy that values the worth of the individual.

At shopping malls like this one in Australia, businesses compete with one another for profit. How do supply and demand influence profit under a capitalist economic system like that of Australia or the United States?

Open markets like the one pictured here were popular in the former Soviet Union. However, such free enterprise would not be allowed under a pure Communist economy. Why is this true?

socialism economic system in which the government owns or controls some of the means of production and determines the distribution of some of the output

Socialism

A socialist economic system also can exist under different forms of government, including democracy. But under **socialism,** only some means of production are privately owned and operated. The government, on the other hand, usually owns and manages such basic industries as coal, steel, transportation, and public utilities. As socialists see it, an economic system should work for the benefit of all members of society, and wealth should be distributed fairly evenly. For this reason, they generally urge high taxes on the wealthy to support such social programs as education, health care, and welfare for the poor. In addition, instead of depending on supply and demand to guide the economy, resources are allocated according to a plan drawn up by the central government. Sometimes the government tries to get businesses to agree to the plan volun-

tarily. Other times it passes laws to force them to follow the plan.

In some nations with a socialist economic system, the people can vote on which industries the government will control. That is what happened in Sweden. In that country, mining, transportation, and some manufacturing industries are under the direct control of the government, as are the welfare and health care systems. In Sweden, the government went to great lengths to promote socialism. In the 1990s, however, Sweden started to cut taxes and eliminate some public jobs in a move toward a market system.

Communism

Unlike the economic systems of capitalism and socialism, communism only exists where there is a Communist government. Under a pure Communist economic system, society as a whole owns all means of production, distribution, and exchange, and there is no private property. Nor are there wages, rents, interests, or profits. People work according to their abilities and are paid according to their needs. The value of any product is set by the amount of labor needed to produce it, and the workers, not the business owners, reap the benefits. And where does government fit in? It directs the economy at first to make sure that everyone works and behaves in a way that furthers Communist goals. But after the goal of economic equality is reached, government no longer is needed and can be discarded.

Much of this economic system is theory based on a work known as *The Communist Manifesto,* which came to light in 1848. Written by Karl Marx and Friedrich Engels, it emphasized the importance of economics in understanding history and social conditions.

Although many nations have experimented with Communist economic systems, no country has ever put all of the principles of communism into practice. Today, the only nations that have Communist systems are the People's Republic of China, North Korea, and Cuba. Most other Communist nations, such as Poland and the former Soviet Union, abandoned communism in the early 1990s. Today in those nations, governments are working to move their economies toward market systems. In Russia, for example, many of the industries and much of the real estate have been transferred to private owners. In addition, the people now have a voice in the government and elect representatives to a legislative assembly. Although some people in the formerly Communist nations oppose the changes in their economies and governments, the nations have continued to institute reforms.

Section Review

1. Governments determine which economic policies will be practiced. What do economic systems determine?

2. What are the three major economic systems?

3. How are resources allocated in each economic system?

4. **Challenge:** In your opinion, what are the advantages of a capitalist economic system?

Summary

1. The largest group served by a government today is the body of people living within a nation-state.

2. According to political scientists, government developed to provide social controls, solve problems individuals could not solve alone, and preserve a common culture.

3. Government is made up of political and administrative institutions that have the power to make and enforce laws, decide on goals, and distribute rewards and benefits.

4. Government's origin and source of power has been attributed to four different theories—the evolutionary theory, the force theory, divine right, and the social contract theory.

5. There are three separate classifications of government—federal, unitary, and confederate.

6. Governments can be classified according to who holds the power to govern and who may take part in that power.

7. In a democracy, the people hold the power to govern, either directly or through representatives, while in other political systems a few individuals or a single individual rules.

8. In addition to a political system, all nation-states have an economic system.

9. The three main kinds of economic systems in the world today are capitalism, socialism, and communism.

Chapter 1 Review

★ Building Vocabulary

1. Define the words and terms that follow:
   a. government
   b. political system
   c. totalitarianism
   d. economic system

2. Write a paragraph using the words and terms that follow:
   a. capitalism
   b. socialism
   c. communism
   d. mixed economy

★ Reviewing Facts

1. What characteristics, or features, do all nation-states have in common?
2. What three functions does government fulfill?
3. Why do people living in groups need some form of government?
4. How do political scientists think government developed?
5. Into what three types can government be classified?
6. In what ways is a unitary government different from a federal government?
7. What elements make up the formal political system of the United States?
8. In what ways is a presidential democracy different from a parliamentary one?
9. In what ways is a totalitarion government different from a democratic one?
10. What are the major characteristics of capitalism? Socialism? Communism?
11. Out of what theory did capitalism grow?
12. Why does democracy usually conflict with Communist economic practices?

★ Analyzing Facts

1. One of the services governments provide is the distribution of the rewards and penalties of the society. In what ways might the manner in which this is done affect you and your family?

2. What do you think governments ruled by one person, a few persons, and many persons might have in common?

3. What do you think the Greek philosopher Aristotle meant when he said, "The human is by nature a political animal"?

4. What aspects of the American economy, if any, are similar to those of a socialist economy?

★ Evaluating Ideas

1. Which of the three functions of government discussed in the chapter do you think is the most important? Explain.

2. Provide arguments to support or refute the following claim: a dictatorship is as well-equipped to serve the needs of the people as a democracy.

3. One of the reasons governments were formed was to preserve the common culture. What do you think the American government should do to promote a common culture as the United States becomes more diverse with the immigration of peoples from very different cultures?

4. Do you think a unitary form of government could work in a large country? Why or why not.

5. Do you think the goals of a democracy can be compatible with those of a totalitarian nation? Explain.

Using Your
Civic Participation Journal

Review the tally that you kept during your interview for your Civic Participation Journal. Working with two of your classmates, create a paragraph summary of your interview results. Your summary should include the major needs and services the interview subject cited. Summaries should also detail ways that citizens can work to change government policies.

6. Do you agree with former President Jimmy Carter's statement "America did not invent human rights. In a very real sense, human rights invented America"? Explain.

7. William Jennings Bryan once said, "The humblest citizen of all the land, when clad in the armor of a righteous cause, is stronger than all the hosts of error." What do you think he meant?

★ Critical Thinking
Distinguishing Between Facts and Value Claims

A *fact* is a statement that can be proved by such evidence as records, documents, or unbiased historical sources. A *value claim*, on the other hand, is a statement that may contain some truth but also includes personal opinion. For example, the statement "The Centerville High School basketball team defeated all its opponents and won the state basketball title" is a fact. You can check this fact in the record books, on the sports pages of the newspapers, or even by asking someone who actually saw the final game. But the statement "The Centerville High School basketball team would not have won the state title if the forward from Lancaster High School had been able to play" is a value claim. It is based on the writer's beliefs about the playing ability of the Lancaster forward. The statement cannot be proved by facts and leaves room for you to disagree with the statement.

Explanation The guidelines that follow will help you to distinguish between facts and value claims.

1. Ask yourself what idea the writer wants you to accept.
2. Determine what statements or arguments the writer is using to make or support his or her point.
3. Ask yourself how or where the statements can be verified.

Practice Look at the following pairs of statements to see why one statement in each pair is considered a fact and the other a value claim.

Government is made up of political and administrative institutions that have many powers. (Fact: can be verified by reading books by political scientists and by observing how governments are organized.)

Great Britian has a better system of government than France. (Value claim: expresses only writer's belief about the two systems.)

The unitary form of government is the most common in the world today. (Fact: can be verified by consulting documents describing world governments.)

Federalism is the only form of government suited to an industrial society. (Value claim: no data to support the statement; based upon the writer's personal opinion.)

Communism is an economic system in which the means of production, distribution, and exchange of goods and services are owned by the society as a whole. (Fact: can be verified in a dictionary.)

Communism is a better economic system than capitalism. (Value claim: no proof available; based on personal bias.)

Divine right is the basis for the governments that have provided the greatest benefits for the people. (Value claim: expresses writer's opinion about governments based on divine right.)

Divine right was used during the Middle Ages to justify the power of monarchs. (Fact: can be verified by consulting documents on history and government.)

Independent Practice Read the Case Study on page 12. With a partner, write five factual statements and five value claims based on the information presented. State why each is a fact or a value claim.

Chapter 2

Foundations of American Government

Our government is based on principles that we value and have cherished for more than 200 years. One such principle is that government exists only by the will of the people. Another is that we have certain rights that government cannot take away. These and other principles and ideas form the foundation of American government. *Why* our government is based on these ideas is the theme of this chapter.

Chapter Preview

TERMS TO KNOW
royal colonies, veto, proprietary colonies, charter colonies, repeal, ratify, bill of rights, legislative branch, executive branch, judicial branch, unicameral, bicameral, suffrage

READ TO DISCOVER
- the principles and ideas behind American democracy.
- the events that led to the Declaration of Independence.
- the meaning and importance of the Declaration of Independence, the state constitutions, and the Articles of Confederation.
- the struggle of developing and ratifying the Constitution of the United States.

★ ★ ★ ★ ★

Civic Participation Journal

You probably belong to several organizations in your school or community. These organizations undoubtedly have constitutions—often called by-laws. Study one of these constitutions. Contact the officers of the organization and find out how these constitutions can be changed. Outline the procedure in your journal.

1 A Common Heritage

Our nation's colonial period was a critical time in the development of our government. It was during these early years that a tradition of self-government was established. One example of self-government during this time was the Mayflower Compact, in which the Pilgrims pledged to govern themselves. Part of it reads:

We whose names are underwritten . . . covenant and combine ourselves together into a civil body politick, for our better ordering and preservation, and furtherance of the ends aforesaid; and by virtue hereof do enact, constitute, and frame such just and equal laws, ordinances, acts, constitution, and offices, from time to time, as shall be thought most meet and convenient for the general good of the colony. . . .

Sites like this are reminders of Greece's past. What ideas did Americans borrow from the ancient Greek civilization?

The idea of self-government in the colonies grew partly as a result of circumstances. England was an ocean away, and its leaders were too involved with problems there to supervise the colonies strictly. Almost out of necessity, the colonists began to develop their own ideas about the best way to govern.

Similar backgrounds united the colonists. Most had shared the same problems and dangers as they struggled to carve a good life in a new land. They also shared a common respect for liberty and freedom. Most were Christians and, though they came from different countries, they had all been subject to British rule. Most of the colonists had read the same books and were well aware of political theories from the past. Indeed, we were not the first to think about or practice such ideas as democracy, limited government, and protection of individual freedoms. These hallmarks of the American system grew out of a heritage that goes back as far as ancient Greece and Rome.

Early Influences

Some of the first ideas about democracy developed in Athens, a city-state in ancient Greece. As early as 500 BC, Athenians practiced direct democracy. Through majority vote, the citizens themselves passed laws and decided common goals. And Athenians believed all citizens were equally qualified to govern. For this reason, public officials were chosen by lot, a practice like drawing straws. Although no copies exist today, the early Greeks also had written constitutions, which laid out the basic structure of their government.

Later, such democratic principles as sovereignty, majority rule, equality, and written constitutions became part of the Roman Republic. But instead of practicing direct democracy, the Romans elected representatives to govern. When the American colonists set up their system, representative democracy was already a well-known principle of government.

Another principle, that of limited government, also had been written about extensively. Cicero, a noted lawyer, orator, and writer in Rome, considered a variety of ways to limit the power of government. He finally decided that the best way was to combine some of the elements of monarchy, aristocracy, and democracy into one government. Cicero reasoned that each element should have sufficient power to do its own work as well as have enough power to keep the other elements from becoming too strong. Our system with its single executive and two-house legislature draws heavily from Cicero's ideas.

The notion that a limited government is a preferable form of government was supported in a different way during the Middle Ages. At that time, there were many who believed there was a law that was more powerful than the laws of any government. Some believed this law came from God. Others believed it was natural law. Whatever its source, many thought this "higher" law prevented a government from exercising total power and control over people. In short, the principle that governments do not have unlimited powers was well established by the 1700s.

The Philosophers

Although the colonists were aware of the political ideas of ancient times and the Middle Ages, they were more strongly influenced by some of the thinkers of the 1600s and 1700s. Two English philosophers, Thomas Hobbes and John Locke, and a French philosopher, Charles-Louis de Montesquieu, were of particular importance.

Both Hobbes and Locke theorized that, before government existed, people lived in a "state of nature," in which every person had the right to do as he or she pleased. Hobbes contended that these situations always led to violence and chaos because the weak could not protect themselves from the strong. He concluded that in a state of nature "the life of man [is] solitary, poor, nasty, brutish, and short." Hobbes believed that a government in which a ruler enjoyed absolute authority over the people would stop such conflict. This authority would come from a social contract in which the people would give up those rights they enjoyed in a state of nature and accept any legal rights the ruler was willing to grant.

Although Locke, like Hobbes, believed that people have natural rights and sovereign power, he did not believe that people set up government with a social contract. Rather, they contracted to establish a society. Then, they entered into a sort of trust relationship with government, which had as its main purpose the protection of their rights. Locke believed that rights such as the right to life, liberty, and property cannot be taken away. In fact, if government does not uphold them, the people have a right to change the government.

Just as the ideas of natural law and natural rights influenced the colonists, so did other ideas about the workings of government. Montesquieu characterized government as having three functions. It makes laws, enforces them, and interprets them. By separating these functions among different branches of the government, Montesquieu reasoned, no single branch, ruler, or group would become too strong.

Colonial Governments

Our system of government was also shaped by the colonial governments that the early Americans experienced. There were three different types of colonies in our nation.

ROYAL COLONIES

By 1775, 8 of the 13 colonies (Georgia, Massachusetts, New Hampshire, New Jersey, New York, North Carolina, South Carolina, and Virginia) were **royal colonies**. The British crown directly ruled all royal colonies. In each, the Crown appointed a royal governor and a council, known as the upper house, and the colonists elected an assembly, called the lower house. The governor and members of the council usually did what the British leaders told them to do. But this often led to conflict with the colonists in the assembly, especially when officials tried to enforce tax laws and trade restrictions. Colonists also resented the governor's power to **veto** laws passed by the colonial legislatures.

PROPRIETARY COLONIES

The **proprietary colonies**, Delaware, Maryland, and Pennsylvania, were ruled by proprietors, individuals or groups who had been granted the land by the Crown. Although still subject to the Crown, proprietors were generally free to rule as they wished. They appointed the governor and members of the upper house of the legislature, while the people elected the lower house.

CHARTER COLONIES

Connecticut and Rhode Island, the **charter colonies,** were established by groups of settlers who had been given a charter, or a grant of rights and privileges, by the Crown. These colonists elected their own governors and the members of both houses. Although the Crown had the right to approve the governor's appointment, the governor could not veto the acts of the legislature.

WHAT THE COLONISTS LEARNED

Drawing from their experience, the colonists developed certain ideas about government. Because some governors enforced unpopular policies without colonists' consent, many colonists thought the power of the executive branch should be limited.

Also, the idea that there should be a way to check the power of the governor grew. Through its power to control tax money, the lower house was able, at times, to modify unreasonable demands by the governor. Some legislatures even refused to pay the governor's salary until concessions were made. The colonists learned that controlling taxes and funds were effective tools. Consequently, they believed those powers should remain with the legislative branch as a check on the executive.

The colonial judicial system was much like Great Britain's. It guaranteed the right to trial by jury, the right to post bail, and the right to face one's accuser. Colonists considered these ''natural rights'' and believed that they should be protected.

Section Review

1. What important ideas did the Greeks and Romans contribute to our form of government?

2. What were the three types of colonies in colonial America?

3. **Challenge:** How did the early colonists' experiences affect their ideas about the roles of the different branches of government?

---

royal colonies colonial settlements under direct control of the British Crown

veto refuse to approve

proprietary colonies colonial settlements that were ruled by a group or individual under a grant from the Crown

charter colonies colonial settlements established by groups given a charter by the Crown

2 The Road to Independence

As relations between Great Britain and the colonies frayed, American patriot Thomas Paine wrote in *Common Sense*:

The sun never shone on a cause of greater worth. 'Tis not the affair of a city, a country, a province, or a kingdom, but of a continent. . . . 'Tis not the concern of a day, a year, or an age. Future generations are involved in the contest, and will be affected to the end of time by what is happening now.

Eventually, the conflict ended in our separation from Great Britain. What led to such a bitter conflict?

Economic Factors

During the 1700s Great Britain was one of several European powers that practiced mercantilism, an economic policy that measured a nation's strength and power by the amount of wealth that its government could accumulate. A nation grew wealthy by selling more products than it bought and stockpiling the gold and silver it earned. And a nation such as Great Britain that could count on colonies for profit had an advantage over those countries that had no colonies.

The American colonies supplied Britain with raw materials for its factories and was a market for the sale of its goods. This arrangement was profitable for the British, and, not surprisingly, they began to believe the

Major Milestones Along the Road to American Independence

British Policy of Mercantilism

Increased Taxation Without Representation

Stamp Act Congress

Committees of Correspondence

Boston Tea Party

Intolerable Acts

First Continental Congress

Declaration and Resolves

Second Continental Congress

Declaration of Independence

Figure 2-1

colonies existed only for the economic well-being of Britain.

But, ruling the colonies and making mercantilism work was a difficult task. To complicate matters, from the late 1600s to the mid-1700s, much of Great Britain's time and resources were taken up with war. With the Crown's attention diverted, the colonists could easily ignore orders issued from across the Atlantic. In addition, they began to believe that laws passed in their own assemblies were fairer and better suited to life in America. But after winning the French and Indian War in 1763, Britain swung its focus onto the colonies.

The Crown needed a way to finance its heavy war debts. Since the colonists benefited from being part of the empire, the British reasoned, the colonies should help maintain it. Therefore, the British decided to enforce existing laws more strictly and to pass new laws forcing the colonists to trade only with Britain. Also, the colonists were to pay a larger share of the cost of keeping British troops in America.

When Britain, under King George III, levied a series of taxes on the colonies in the 1760s, a serious issue was raised. The colonists thought of themselves as British citizens and believed they should be treated as such. They resented additional taxes being imposed by Parliament, especially since it had no representatives from the colonies. For this reason they believed Parliament had no right to tax them at all. Opposition to British policies spread quickly, and the cry "no taxation without representation" echoed through the colonies.

The Colonists Unite

The Stamp Act of 1765, requiring the colonists to buy special stamps for newspapers, legal documents, and business agreements, met with particularly bitter opposition. Colonial leaders asked representatives from all the colonies to meet to coordinate their protests over this form of taxation. In 1765 delegates from nine colonies traveled to New York City with "protest" in mind.

This meeting, called the Stamp Act Congress, approved the Declaration of Rights and Grievances, which claimed that colonists had the same rights as British citizens in England. It also said that colonial assemblies had the sole right to tax the colonies and called for **repeal** of the Stamp Act and other taxes. To support the Declaration, many colonists boycotted, or refused to buy, British goods.

The Stamp Act Congress was not the first time the colonies had met for a common purpose. In 1754 representatives from seven colonies met in Albany, New York, to discuss problems of trade and defense. Even at that early date, Benjamin Franklin had presented a plan to unite the colonies under a single government, subject to the Crown. Although colonial legislatures refused to accept it, certain ideas outlined in the Albany Plan appeared years later in the Articles of Confederation and the United States Constitution.

While the Stamp Act eventually was repealed, the British government continued to search for new ways to raise revenue in the colonies. In turn, the colonists continued to resist acts passed by Parliament that they considered unjust. The protest was led by groups called Committees of Correspondence, and by the early 1770s, one could be found in every American colony.

Boycotting was only one act of protest; there were others. In 1773 a group of colonists disguised as Indians dumped a cargo of tea into Boston

repeal do away with or withdraw

The *Pennsylvania Journal* published this depiction of the Stamp Act in 1765.

During the Boston Tea Party, colonists in Boston dumped tea overboard into Boston Harbor as a way of protesting unfair treatment by the British. What happened to the Port of Boston as a result of this act?

Harbor to protest British domination of trade. John Adams said of the Boston Tea Party:

This is the most magnificent Movement of all. . . . This Destruction of the Tea is so bold, so daring, so firm, intrepid and inflexible, and it must have so important Consequences, and so lasting, that I can't but consider it an Epocha [significant event] in History. . . .

As resistance continued to grow, Parliament passed several laws designed to punish the colonists. The most important of these closed the port of Boston to all shipping until the tea was paid for and increased the power of the royal governor of Massachusetts. To the colonists, these laws were the "Intolerable Acts," and they increased the colonists' determination to defend what they believed to be their "natural" rights.

The First Continental Congress

After passage of the Intolerable Acts, the legislatures of Virginia and Massachusetts called for a meeting to discuss ways to respond. In September 1774, 56 delegates, representing all of the colonies except Georgia, met in Philadelphia in an assembly now called the First Continental Congress. After weeks of debate, it adopted the Declaration and Resolves. Addressed to King George III, the document demanded repeal of the Intolerable Acts and affirmed that the colonists had the right to "life, liberty, and property."

To apply pressure on Great Britain, the Congress asked colonists to continue to boycott British goods, and groups were set up to enforce restrictions on trade with the British. The delegates also agreed to hold a second

Carpenter's Hall in Philadelphia was the site of the First Continental Congress. What document resulted from this meeting?

3 A New Nation Is Born

The Declaration and Resolves did nothing to improve the situation in the colonies. If anything, it grew worse. More and more British soldiers landed on our shores as the colonists secretly gathered arms. Then on April 19, 1775, shots rang out at Lexington and Concord in Massachusetts. Less than three weeks later, the Second Continental Congress convened in Philadelphia to address the problems facing the colonies.

The Second Continental Congress

Delegates from all 13 colonies attended the Congress. Among its first actions was to organize an army and appoint George Washington commander in chief. The Congress also arranged to issue currency, borrow money, buy supplies, and negotiate with foreign countries. As a result of its actions, the Second Continental Congress became America's first national government, and though it had no constitutional basis, it remained in control for six years.

The Declaration of Independence

The most dramatic act of the Congress was to **ratify** the Declaration of Independence on July 4, 1776, officially severing the colonies from Great Britain. Sentiment favoring independence had been growing ever since fighting had broken out. In June 1776, Richard Henry Lee of Virginia had presented a motion for independence to the Congress, stating that the colonies ". . .are, and of right ought to be, free and independent states."

meeting in Philadelphia in 1775 if conditions had not improved. The assemblies of each of the colonies, including Georgia, eventually ratified the actions of the First Continental Congress.

Section Review

ratify approve or confirm

1. How did the relationship between the British government and the American colonies change after 1763?

2. What was the Stamp Act Congress?

3. What did the First Continental Congress do?

4. **Challenge:** In your opinion, did Parliament have the right to tax the colonists? Why or why not?

Although the task of writing a formal statement of independence was given to a committee, the Declaration was almost solely the work of Thomas Jefferson.

The Declaration did more than formally declare independence from Great Britain; it also set out many of the ideals Americans valued:

We hold these truths to be self-evident, that all men are created equal, that they are endowed by their Creator with certain unalienable Rights, that among these are Life, Liberty, and the Pursuit of Happiness. . . . That to secure these rights, Governments are instituted among Men, deriving their just powers from the consent of the governed; that whenever any Form of government becomes destructive of these ends it is the Right of the People to alter or to abolish it, and to institute new Government, laying its foundation on such principles and organizing its power in such form, as to them shall seem most likely to effect their Safety and Happiness.

Although the Declaration affirms the right of the people to change or abolish the government if it does not serve them, it also states that this action should not be taken lightly. In fact, the people should consider such a step only after long and serious suffering. For this reason, more than one-half of the document is devoted to their grievances against Great Britain's abuses. The signers of the Declaration wanted everyone to clearly understand *why* the colonists were taking such drastic action.

As news of the Declaration spread, it rallied support and boosted morale in the colonies. The sentiments expressed in the document had an important impact *outside* the colonies as well. Many people in England and other European countries began to believe that the colonists had valid reasons for declaring independence. As a result, support grew for the colonists' position and the ideas they expressed.

The New States in Transition

Thus far, you have read about events that were happening throughout the colonies as a whole. Yet what was going on in each colony was equally important. In 1776 Congress asked the soon-to-be-states to organize their governments, and each moved quickly to adopt a state constitution.

These constitutions held similar ideas about government. For instance, each stated that the people are the only source of the government's power. This belief was supported by the fact that each state constitution, except that of Massachusetts, was

Benjamin Franklin, John Adams, and Thomas Jefferson are shown working on an early draft of the Declaration of Independence. What ideas did this document promote?

DOCUMENT: DECLARATION OF INDEPENDENCE

When in the course of human events, it becomes necessary for one people to dissolve the political bands which have connected them with another, and to assume among the powers of the earth, the separate and equal station to which the laws of nature and of nature's God entitle them, a decent respect to the opinions of mankind requires that they should declare the causes which impel them to the separation.

We hold these truths to be self-evident, that all men are created equal, that they are endowed by their Creator with certain unalienable rights, that among these are life, liberty, and the pursuit of happiness. That to secure these rights, governments are instituted among men, deriving their just powers from the consent of the governed; that

whenever any form of government becomes destructive of these ends, it is the right of the people to alter or to abolish it, and to institute a new government, laying its foundation on such principles, and organizing its powers in such form, as to them shall seem most likely to effect their safety and happiness. Prudence, indeed, will dictate that governments long established should not be changed for light and transient causes; and accordingly all experience hath shown, that mankind are more disposed to suffer, while evils are sufferable, than to right themselves by abolishing the forms to which they are accustomed. But when a long train of abuses and usurpations, pursuing invariably the same object, evinces a design to reduce them under absolute despotism, it is their right, it is their duty, to throw off such government, and to provide new guards for their future security. Such has been the patient sufferance of these colonies; and such is now the necessity which constrains them to alter their former systems of government. The history of the present King of Great Britain is a history of repeated injuries and usurpations, all having in direct object the establishment of an absolute tyranny over these states. To prove this, let facts be submitted to a candid world.

He has refused his assent to laws, the most wholesome and necessary for the public good.

He has forbidden his governors to pass laws of immediate and pressing importance, unless suspended in their operation till his assent should be obtained; and when so suspended, he has utterly neglected to attend to them.

He has refused to pass other laws for the accommodation of large districts of people, unless those people would relinquish the right of representation in the legislature, a right inestimable to them and formidable to tyrants only.

He has called together legislative bodies at places unusual, uncomfortable, and distant from the depository of their public records, for the sole purpose of fatiguing them into compliance with his measures.

He has dissolved representative houses repeatedly, for opposing with manly firmness his invasions on the rights of the people.

He has refused for a long time, after such dissolutions, to cause others to be elected; whereby the legislative powers, incapable of annihilation, have returned to the people at large for their exercise; the state remaining in the meantime exposed to all the dangers of invasion from without and convulsions within.

He has endeavored to prevent the population of these states; for that purpose obstructing the laws for naturalization of foreigners, refusing to pass others to encourage their migration hither, and raising the conditions of new appropriations of lands.

He has obstructed the administration of justice, by refusing his assent to laws for establishing judiciary powers.

He has made judges dependent on his will alone, for the tenure of their offices, and the amount and payment of their salaries.

He has erected a multitude of new offices, and sent hither swarms of officers to harass our people, and eat out their substance.

He has kept among us, in times of peace, standing armies without the consent of our legislatures.

He has affected to render the military independent of and superior to the civil power.

He has combined with others to subject us to a jurisdiction foreign to our constitution, and unacknowledged by our laws; giving his assent to their acts of pretended legislation:

For quartering large bodies of armed troops among us;

For protecting them, by a mock trial, from punishment for any murders which they should commit on the inhabitants of these states;

For cutting off our trade with all parts of the world;

For imposing taxes on us without our consent;

For depriving us, in many cases, of the benefits of trial by jury;

For transporting us beyond seas to be tried for pretended offenses;

For abolishing the free system of English laws in a neighboring province, establishing therein an arbitrary government, and enlarging its boundaries so as to render it at once an example and fit instrument for introducing the same absolute rule into these colonies;

For taking away our charters, abolishing our most valuable laws, and altering fundamentally the forms of our governments;

For suspending our own legislatures; and declaring themselves invested with power to legislate for us in all cases whatsoever.

He has abdicated government here, by declaring us out of his protection and waging war against us.

He has plundered our seas, ravaged our coasts, burned our towns, and destroyed the lives of our people.

He is at this time transporting large armies of foreign mercenaries to complete the works of death, desolation, and tyranny, already begun with circumstances of cruelty and perfidy scarcely paralleled in the most barbarous ages, and totally unworthy the head of a civilized nation.

He has constrained our fellow citizens taken captive on the high seas to bear arms against their country, to become the executioners of their friends and brethren, or to fall themselves by their hands.

He has excited domestic insurrections among us, and has endeavored to bring on the inhabitants of our frontiers, the merciless Indian savages, whose known rule of warfare is an undistinguished destruction of all ages, sexes, and conditions.

In every stage of these oppressions we have petitioned for redress in the most humble terms;

our repeated petitions have been answered only by repeated injury. A prince, whose character is thus marked by every act which may define a tyrant, is unfit to be the ruler of a free people.

Nor have we been wanting in our attention to our British brethren. We have warned them from time to time of attempts by their legislature to extend an unwarrantable jurisdiction over us. We have reminded them of the circumstances of our emigration and settlement here. We have appealed to their native justice and magnanimity, and we have conjured them by the ties of our common kindred to disavow these usurpations, which would inevitably interrupt our connections and correspondence. They too have been deaf to the voice of justice and consanguinity. We must, therefore, acquiesce in the necessity which denounces our separation, and hold them, as we hold the rest of mankind, enemies in war, in peace friends.

We, therefore, the representatives of the United States of America, in General Congress, assembled, appealing to the Supreme Judge of the world for the rectitude of our intentions, do, in the name and by authority of the good people of these colonies, solemnly publish and declare, that these united colonies are, and of right ought to be, free and independent states; that they are absolved from all allegiance to the British Crown, and that all political connection between them and the State of Great Britain is and ought to be totally dissolved; and that as free and independent states, they have full power to levy war, conclude peace, contract alliances, establish commerce, and to do all other acts and things which independent states may of right do. And for the support of this declaration, with a firm reliance on the protection of Divine Providence, we mutually pledge to each other our lives, our fortunes, and our sacred honor.

John Hancock, **President**

New Hampshire
Josiah Bartlett
William Whipple
Matthew Thornton
Massachusetts
Samuel Adams
John Adams
Robert Treat Paine
Elbridge Gerry
New York
William Floyd
Philip Livingston
Francis Lewis
Lewis Morris
New Jersey
Richard Stockton
John Witherspoon
Francis Hopkinson
John Hart
Abraham Clark
Pennsylvania
Robert Morris
Benjamin Rush
Benjamin Franklin

John Morton
George Clymer
James Smith
George Taylor
James Wilson
George Ross
Delaware
Caesar Rodney
George Read
Thomas M'Kean
Maryland
Samuel Chase
William Paca
Thomas Stone
Charles Carroll, of Carrollton
Rhode Island
Stephen Hopkins
William Ellery
Connecticut
Roger Sherman
Samuel Huntington
William Williams
Oliver Wolcott

Virginia
George Wythe
Richard Henry Lee
Thomas Jefferson
Benjamin Harrison
Thomas Nelson, Jr.
Francis Lightfoot Lee
Carter Braxton
North Carolina
William Hooper
Joseph Hewes
John Penn
South Carolina
Edward Rutledge
Thomas Heyward, Jr.
Thomas Lynch, Jr.
Arthur Middleton
Georgia
Button Gwinnett
Lyman Hall
George Walton

In CONGRESS, July 4, 1776.

The unanimous Declaration of the thirteen united States of America.

When in the Course of human events, it becomes necessary for one people to dissolve the political bands which have connected them with another, and to assume among the powers of the earth, the separate and equal station to which the Laws of Nature and of Nature's God entitle them, a decent respect to the opinions of mankind requires that they should declare the causes which impel them to the separation.

We hold these truths to be self-evident, that all men are created equal, that they are endowed by their Creator with certain unalienable Rights, that among these are Life, Liberty and the pursuit of Happiness.—That to secure these rights, Governments are instituted among Men, deriving their just powers from the consent of the governed,—That whenever any Form of Government becomes destructive of these ends, it is the Right of the People to alter or to abolish it, and to institute new Government, laying its foundation on such principles and organizing its powers in such form, as to them shall seem most likely to effect their Safety and Happiness. Prudence, indeed, will dictate that Governments long established should not be changed for light and transient causes; and accordingly all experience hath shewn, that mankind are more disposed to suffer, while evils are sufferable, than to right themselves by abolishing the forms to which they are accustomed. But when a long train of abuses and usurpations, pursuing invariably the same Object evinces a design to reduce them under absolute Despotism, it is their right, it is their duty, to throw off such Government, and to provide new Guards for their future security.—Such has been the patient sufferance of these Colonies; and such is now the necessity which constrains them to alter their former Systems of Government. The history of the present King of Great Britain is a history of repeated injuries and usurpations, all having in direct object the establishment of an absolute Tyranny over these States. To prove this, let Facts be submitted to a candid world.

He has refused his Assent to Laws, the most wholesome and necessary for the public good.

He has forbidden his Governors to pass Laws of immediate and pressing importance, unless suspended in their operation till his Assent should be obtained; and when so suspended, he has utterly neglected to attend to them.

He has refused to pass other Laws for the accommodation of large districts of people, unless those people would relinquish the right of Representation in the Legislature, a right inestimable to them and formidable to tyrants only.

He has called together legislative bodies at places unusual, uncomfortable, and distant from the depository of their Public Records, for the sole purpose of fatiguing them into compliance with his measures.

He has dissolved Representative Houses repeatedly, for opposing with manly firmness his invasions on the rights of the people.

He has refused for a long time, after such dissolutions, to cause others to be elected; whereby the Legislative powers, incapable of Annihilation, have returned to the People at large for their exercise; the State remaining in the mean time exposed to all the dangers of invasion from without, and convulsions within.

He has endeavoured to prevent the population of these States; for that purpose obstructing the Laws for Naturalization of Foreigners; refusing to pass others to encourage their migrations hither, and raising the conditions of new Appropriations of Lands.

He has obstructed the Administration of Justice, by refusing his Assent to Laws for establishing Judiciary powers.

He has made Judges dependent on his Will alone, for the tenure of their offices, and the amount and payment of their salaries.

He has erected a multitude of New Offices, and sent hither swarms of Officers to harrass our people, and eat out their substance.

He has kept among us, in times of peace, Standing Armies without the Consent of our legislatures.

He has affected to render the Military independent of and superior to the Civil power.

He has combined with others to subject us to a jurisdiction foreign to our constitution, and unacknowledged by our laws; giving his Assent to their Acts of pretended Legislation:

For Quartering large bodies of armed troops among us:

For protecting them, by a mock Trial, from punishment for any Murders which they should commit on the Inhabitants of these States:

For cutting off our Trade with all parts of the world:

For imposing Taxes on us without our Consent:

For depriving us in many cases, of the benefits of Trial by jury:

For transporting us beyond Seas to be tried for pretended offences:

For abolishing the free System of English Laws in a neighbouring Province, establishing therein an Arbitrary government, and enlarging its Boundaries so as to render it at once an example and fit instrument for introducing the same absolute rule into these Colonies:

For taking away our Charters, abolishing our most valuable Laws, and altering fundamentally the Forms of our Governments:

For suspending our own Legislatures, and declaring themselves invested with power to legislate for us in all cases whatsoever.

He has abdicated Government here, by declaring us out of his Protection and waging War against us.

He has plundered our seas, ravaged our Coasts, burnt our towns, and destroyed the lives of our people.

He is at this time transporting large Armies of foreign Mercenaries to compleat the works of death, desolation and tyranny, already begun with circumstances of Cruelty & perfidy scarcely paralleled in the most barbarous ages, and totally unworthy the Head of a civilized nation.

He has constrained our fellow Citizens taken Captive on the high Seas to bear Arms against their Country, to become the executioners of their friends and Brethren, or to fall themselves by their Hands.

He has excited domestic insurrections amongst us, and has endeavoured to bring on the inhabitants of our frontiers, the merciless Indian Savages, whose known rule of warfare, is an undistinguished destruction of all ages, sexes and conditions.

In every stage of these Oppressions We have Petitioned for Redress in the most humble terms: Our repeated Petitions have been answered only by repeated injury. A Prince, whose character is thus marked by every act which may define a Tyrant, is unfit to be the ruler of a free people.

Nor have We been wanting in attentions to our British brethren. We have warned them from time to time of attempts by their legislature to extend an unwarrantable jurisdiction over us. We have reminded them of the circumstances of our emigration and settlement here. We have appealed to their native justice and magnanimity, and we have conjured them by the ties of our common kindred to disavow these usurpations, which, would inevitably interrupt our connections and correspondence. They too have been deaf to the voice of justice and of consanguinity. We must, therefore, acquiesce in the necessity, which denounces our Separation, and hold them, as we hold the rest of mankind, Enemies in War, in Peace Friends.

We, therefore, the Representatives of the united States of America, in General Congress, Assembled, appealing to the Supreme Judge of the world for the rectitude of our intentions, do, in the Name, and by Authority of the good People of these Colonies, solemnly publish and declare, That these United Colonies are, and of Right ought to be Free and Independent States; that they are Absolved from all Allegiance to the British Crown, and that all political connection between them and the State of Great Britain, is and ought to be totally dissolved; and that as Free and Independent States, they have full Power to levy War, conclude Peace, contract Alliances, establish Commerce, and to do all other Acts and Things which Independent States may of right do.— And for the support of this Declaration, with a firm reliance on the protection of Divine Providence, we mutually pledge to each other our Lives, our Fortunes and our sacred Honor.

John Hancock

Button Gwinnett
Lyman Hall
Geo Walton.

Wm Hooper
Joseph Hewes
John Penn

Edward Rutledge.

Thos Heyward Junr.
Thomas Lynch Junr.
Arthur Middleton

Samuel Chase
Wm Paca
Thos Stone
Charles Carroll of Carrollton

George Wythe
Richard Henry Lee
Th Jefferson
Benj Harrison
Thos Nelson jr.
Francis Lightfoot Lee
Carter Braxton

Robt Morris
Benjamin Rush
Benj. Franklin
John Morton
Geo Clymer
Jas. Smith
Geo. Taylor
James Wilson
Geo. Ross
Caesar Rodney
Geo Read
Tho M:Kean

Wm Floyd
Phil. Livingston
Frans. Lewis
Lewis Morris

Richd. Stockton
Jno Witherspoon
Fras. Hopkinson
John Hart
Abra Clark

Josiah Bartlett
Wm Whipple
Saml Adams
John Adams
Robt Treat Paine
Elbridge Gerry
Step. Hopkins
William Ellery
Roger Sherman
Sam el Huntington
Wm Williams
Oliver Wolcott
Matthew Thornton

approved either by the people's representatives in the legislatures or by special conventions. In Massachusetts the constitution was submitted directly to the people for approval.

Each of the state constitutions also limited the power of its government. At the same time, there was so much concern about protecting the rights of the people that seven states included a special section called a **bill of rights**. These included the right to trial by jury, the right to worship as one chooses, and the right to speak out against the government.

All of the constitutions established three separate branches of state government: legislative, executive, and judicial. But while each branch had its own area of responsibility, the branches were not considered equal in power. The **legislative branch** was given the most power. The **executive branch** was the most limited because of the colonists' experience with royal governors. And state constitutions typically called for the **judicial branch** to include a state supreme court and a system of lower courts. Many of the ideas expressed in the new state constitutions were eventually incorporated into the United States Constitution.

The Articles of Confederation

Once independence had been declared, the Continental Congress began to prepare a formal plan of government. On November 15, 1777, Congress approved a plan known as the Articles of Confederation. Its purpose was to provide a way for the states to

. . .enter into a firm league of friendship with each other, for the common defense, the security of

their Liberties, and their mutual and general welfare. . . .

At this time, most Americans were more loyal to their state than to a national government. Their experiences under the British had made them extremely wary of a strong central government. It is not surprising, then, that the powers of the states were well protected under the Articles of Confederation:

Each state retains its sovereignty, freedom and independence, and every Power, Jurisdiction, and right, which is not. . .expressly delegated to the United States. . . .

Under the Articles, no provision was made for either an executive or judicial branch. The legislative branch held supreme power. Duties normally carried out by the executive branch were performed by legislative committees. Judicial matters were left largely to the states and their court systems.

The legislature was a **unicameral**, or one-house, Congress. States selected their delegates each year in a manner decided by each state. Regardless of population or land size, each state received one vote in Congress. At least nine votes were needed to approve most important matters, and a unanimous vote was required to change the Articles.

In this confederation, the states gave certain powers to the national government. These included the power to declare war, make peace, direct foreign affairs, build and equip a navy, request troops from the states, coin money, regulate weights and measures, establish post offices, and manage affairs with Indians.

Yet, some vital powers were not granted to Congress. It could not tax either the states or the people or

bill of rights special sections in the United States and state constitutions that list the rights government cannot deny

legislative branch branch of government that makes law

executive branch branch of government that carries out or puts law into effect

judicial branch branch of government that interprets the law

unicameral a one-house legislature

regulate trade among the states. Neither could Congress force the states or the people to obey its laws. As you can imagine, these limitations eventually caused problems for the new nation.

WEAKNESSES

The confederate plan made it difficult to develop loyalty to the national government. Delegates to Congress were chosen and paid by the states, and they were instructed in their actions by their state legislatures. As a result, most were more concerned with protecting their state interests than with solving national problems. Furthermore, important decisions required 9 of the 13 states to agree. Convincing 9 independent state delegations to agree on anything was hard enough, but amending the Articles, which required the consent of *all* 13 states, was next to impossible.

Many of the biggest problems facing the new government were economic. Because it could not tax, Congress could not pay its debts or support new programs. American merchant ships, for example, were at the mercy of pirates because the government could not afford to build a navy to protect them.

The paper money issued by the new government had no gold or silver to back it up. As a result, continental currency had little or no value. The phrase ''it's not worth a continental,'' which means something is worthless, comes from this time. Adding to the problem was the fact that each state still printed its *own* money. Since much of it also was nearly worthless, debts were unpaid, prices rose, credit disappeared, and trade plummeted.

Another weakness of the national government was that it lacked the power to regulate commerce and settle conflicts between states. Thus ''economic wars'' broke out between the states. New York, for example, levied taxes on goods coming from

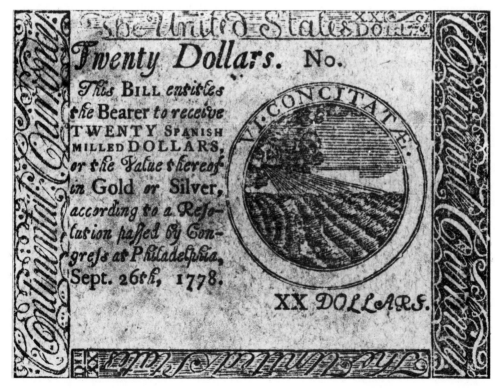

Shown here is a $20 bill in continental currency. Why did this currency have very little value?

Strengths and Weaknesses of the Articles of Confederation

Accomplishments
Treaty of Paris
  Land Ordinance of 1785
    Northwest Ordinance of 1787
      Foundation for Constitution
      Weaknesses
        Absence of sovereign power in national government
          Absence of uniform currency
            Absence of efficient amendment process
              Absence of executive and judicial branches of government

Figure 2-2

Connecticut and New Jersey. In return, Connecticut refused to trade at all with New York, and New Jersey retaliated by taxing a lighthouse built on its land by New York.

Not having an executive or a judicial branch also crippled the new nation. The legislative committees of Congress never performed the tasks of the executive well. Moreover, the lack of a judicial branch meant there was no national court system to settle disputes between the states.

Finally, Congress had no power to force the states to obey national laws. Some states, for instance, even negotiated treaties with foreign countries, although this was forbidden by the Articles. These problems caused general discord, and many Americans were concerned as they watched the nation's prestige slip away, abroad and at home.

By 1784 the nation was in such disorder that George Washington described the confederate plan as ". . .a half-starved, limping government, that appears to be always moving upon crutches, and tottering at every step." More and more people began to believe that a stronger central government was needed.

ACCOMPLISHMENTS

In spite of its weaknesses, the government under the Articles accomplished some important things. The Revolutionary War was fought and won and the Treaty of Paris, marking the end of the war, was negotiated in 1783. The Land Ordinance of 1785 and the Northwest Ordinance of 1787 also were passed. These Ordinances provided for administration of the vast lands west of the Appalachians that opened for settlement after the war. This system also set up a plan to organize areas that would years later become part of the United States.

Moreover, the Constitution is, no doubt, more workable and effective than it would have been had the Articles *not* been tried. Our leaders had found out what worked, as well as what did not. And many of these same leaders eventually met again—this time to write the Constitution.

Section Review

1. What basic principles and values of American government are found in the Declaration of Independence?

2. What branches of government were established by the state constitutions?

3. What were the major accomplishments of the Articles of Confederation?

4. **Challenge:** In your opinion, why was the Articles of Confederation an unworkable plan of government? Explain.

4 The Constitutional Convention

As the economy crumbled and other problems grew, representatives from Maryland and Virginia met in 1785. Later, there were sessions held at Mount Vernon. The original purpose of the meetings was to settle disputes over navigation of the Potomac River and Chesapeake Bay. The meetings were so productive, though, that the Virginia assembly invited *all* the states to come together to discuss ". . .a federal plan for regulating commerce."

Then, in the summer of 1786, an incident sparked concern not only for trade between the states, but for the continued existence of the nation. An uprising in Massachusetts led by Daniel Shays, a Revolutionary War officer, tried to prevent that state from collecting debts. Shays and his followers were farmers, almost bankrupt from their debts and the state's high taxes. Although the state militia regained control, the likelihood of other armed revolts became a very real threat. Many Americans became fearful that more violence and disorder would occur unless economic conditions improved.

Five states did send delegates to an interstate convention in 1786. But lacking representation from the other states, they accomplished little. They did, however, call for another meeting to be held later in Philadelphia.

And as national conditions grew worse, support for a convention increased. In February 1787, Congress called upon all the states to attend a convention ". . .for the express purpose of revising the Articles of Confederation." The meeting in Philadelphia went far beyond what it was convened to do. Rather than amend or modify the Articles, the delegates devised a document that is today the oldest written constitution.

Delegates

When the convention opened in Philadelphia in May 1787, 55 delegates from 12 states were elected to take part. Only Rhode Island, where feelings were strong against the creation of a more powerful central government, did not send a delegation.

Although the delegates had varied backgrounds, they were more alike than unlike. All were white males. Most were lawyers, planters, or merchants who were active in politics. Most also had college educations or professional training, and although many were not wealthy, none were poor.

In 1786, Daniel Shays led a revolt in which the Springfield, Massachusetts, courthouse was seized. What was Shays protesting?

Most of the delegates were also fairly young, especially in light of their length of service and experience in government and politics. About two-thirds of the delegates were under the age of 50. Many of the most prominent, James Madison, Alexander Hamilton, Edmund Randolph, and Gouverneur Morris, were only in their 30s. Jonathon Dayton of New Jersey was the youngest at 26; Benjamin Franklin, at 81, was the oldest.

Most of the delegates were well-known leaders, nationally as well as in their home states. Among those who traveled to Philadelphia was George Washington, who had led the Continental army to victory over the British. He was 55 years of age and at the height of his popularity. The feelings of the people toward him were those of awe and devotion. Persuading Washington to attend, much against his will, was felt to be essential to the success of the Convention. Similarly, the attendance of Benjamin Franklin was important.

Franklin, who was widely respected as an inventor, scientist, writer, and diplomat, did not contribute a great deal to the debates. His presence, however, added to the prestige of the event. Other notables included John Dickinson of Delaware, John Rutledge and Charles Cotesworth Pinckney of South Carolina, Rufus King of Massachusetts, William Paterson of New Jersey, Roger Sherman of Connecticut, and James Wilson of Pennsylvania, who was considered by Washington one of the wisest men at the Convention.

In describing the delegates as a whole, one American newspaper called them "the collective wisdom of the Continent." Thomas Jefferson, in Paris at the time, called them "an assembly of demi-gods." But not everyone agreed with such high praise of the delegates' abilities. One observer wrote, "Some of the characters. . .are of small consequence, and a number are suspected of being. . .public [debtors]. . . ."

In 1787, a meeting of 55 delegates resulted in the creation of our United States Constitution. Each of the 13 states was represented, with the exception of Rhode Island. Why did Rhode Island choose not to be represented?

PROFILE: JAMES MADISON

FRAMER OF THE CONSTITUTION

By the age of 36, James Madison was an experienced and respected leader, already having served in the Virginia Assembly and in Congress. In addition to his experience, Madison's study of ancient governments, political philosophy, and the American government during the colonial and confederation periods prepared him to play a major role at the Constitutional Convention.

Although the Virginia Plan, which was mostly Madison's work, starts with the statement: *Resolved that the Articles of Confederation ought to be so corrected and enlarged as to accomplish the objects proposed by their institutions—namely, "common defence, security of liberty and general welfare. . .",* it was never Madison's intention simply to revise the Articles. He believed a new document should be written, one that would put greater power into the hands of a stronger, more consolidated government.

The Virginia Plan not only reflects Madison's genius as a political thinker and writer, it also demonstrates his skill as a practical politician. If some new plan had not been presented, the delegates would likely have revised the Articles and not moved directly to the creation of a different form of government.

Madison's leadership during the convention and his meticulous notes of all the proceedings have earned him the title "Father of the Constitution." These notes, published four years after his death, are the major source of information about the convention debates and issues.

During the winter of 1787-1788 Madison, Alexander Hamilton, and John Jay wrote *The Federalist,* a series of 85 essays that explained and defended the Constitution against Anti-Federalist criticisms. These classic political essays appeared in the New York newspapers under the pseudonym "Publius." The struggle to secure ratification of the Constitution was difficult, and the Federalist papers made a significant contribution to its success.

Perhaps the major Anti-Federalist criticism was that the pro-

posed Constitution lacked a bill of rights. The Federalists agreed finally to add a bill of rights when the Constitution was approved and the new federal government under President Washington was established. Madison, a leading member of the House of Representatives, was instrumental in adding the Bill of Rights, the first 10 amendments to the Constitution, in 1791.

Despite his contributions, Madison remained modest about his accomplishments. To an admirer who referred to him as *the* writer of the Constitution, Madison replied that he did not deserve such credit because the Constitution "was not, like the fabled Goddess of Wisdom, the offspring of a single brain. It ought to be regarded as the work of many heads and many hands."

Although the Constitution may have been Madison's greatest accomplishment, he continued to play a major role in the new government. In 1801 he was appointed secretary of state, and in 1809 James Madison became President of the United States.

1. What might have been the result if the delegates had started out only revising the Articles of Confederation?
2. Madison asked Edmund Randolph, governor of Virginia, to present the new plan. Why do you think he might have done this?

Although the truth may lie somewhere in between, certainly all of the delegates were aware of the seriousness of their task. Most of the delegates were practical, experienced politicians. And more important, they believed in a central government strong enough to overcome the difficulties emerging under the Articles.

Many colonial leaders who preferred a *weak* central government did not attend. Patrick Henry said he "smelt a rat" and refused to go. Others, like Samuel Adams, John Hancock, and Richard Henry Lee, were not elected to serve.

Convention Proceedings

Soon after the convention opened, George Washington was unanimously elected to preside over the meeting. Each state delegation received one vote, and only a majority vote was required to pass a proposal.

The delegates agreed that all debates should be held in secret. In this way, everyone could discuss issues fully without fear of public pressure.

It also made compromising and negotiating easier.

A secretary was chosen to keep a written record of the proceedings. Yet most of what is known today about the Constitutional Convention comes from the detailed notes of James Madison.

The delegates used many different ideas about government to guide their deliberations. Each was important to the new plan they hoped to create. The first plan for a new government was called the Virginia Plan. Although largely the work of James Madison, it was presented to the convention by Edmund Randolph, a delegate from Virginia, in May 1787.

VIRGINIA PLAN

The Virginia Plan provided for three branches of government: legislative, executive, and judicial. The national legislature, Congress, was to be **bicameral**. Each state would have a certain number of members in each house, decided either by the population of the state or the amount of money the state contributed to the national treasury. Members of the

bicameral a two-house legislature

George Washington, pictured here with Alexander Hamilton and Gouverneur Morris, was elected to serve as leader of the Constitutional Convention. Why, do you think, was Washington selected for this role?

lower house, or House of Representatives, were to be elected by the people. Members of the upper house, or Senate, were to be selected by the House from a list of candidates chosen by the state legislatures.

Congress would also have the power to choose an executive branch, consisting of one member, and the members of the judicial branch. The executive and the judicial, acting together, could veto acts of Congress. The veto, however, could be overridden by a vote of the two houses. It was also proposed that this plan of government would be easier to amend, or change, than the Articles of Confederation.

The proposed method of representation was the subject of heated debate, especially among delegates from the smaller states. They felt they would be at a disadvantage if the number of representatives were based on population or financial contributions. Since representatives would choose members of the other two branches, the large states could dominate all branches of the national government. A New Jersey delegate concluded the only way to make this plan of representation fair would be if all state boundaries were erased and new ones drawn in 13 equal parts.

NEW JERSEY PLAN

In June 1787, the small states suggested a counterproposal to the Virginia Plan called the New Jersey Plan. Although it too proposed a government of three branches, it differed from the Virginia Plan in several important respects. The legislative branch would remain unicameral as it was under the Articles. Each state, regardless of size, would receive one vote in Congress. An executive branch, consisting of more than one person, as well as the judicial branch,

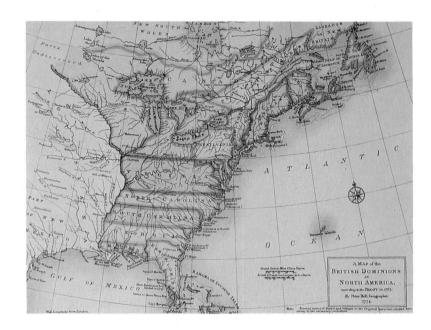

would be chosen by Congress. Other powers would be granted to Congress, including the power to tax and to regulate interstate and foreign trade.

COMPROMISES

Although each plan had its supporters, the delegates did agree on certain issues. Most of the delegates, as a result of their experience under the Articles, believed that the central government should have enough power to operate effectively. Many were also beginning to think it was better to separate the branches rather than to place any of the branches under the control of the others.

Very shortly after the convention opened, it was obvious that the delegates would have to compromise to settle specific issues. The first compromise was suggested by Roger Sherman of Connecticut and is called the Connecticut Compromise. Because of its importance, it is also known as the Great Compromise. In it, the delegates agreed the national legislature should be bicameral. The Congress would be made up of an upper house (Senate) and a lower

This map shows the British colonies that later became the United States. Why, do you think, was the method of states' representation of such importance to the Framers of the Constitution?

house (House of Representatives). Approval by both houses would be required to pass laws.

The question of representation was also answered. Elements demanded by both the large states and the small states were included in the compromise. Each state would be represented by two senators in the upper house. Representatives in the lower house would be chosen based on each state's population. Since members of the lower house were to be chosen directly by the people (rather than indirectly by a state legislature), it was decided that all money bills, taxes, and appropriations would originate in this house. Thus, the Great Compromise resolved the most serious conflict facing the convention, the question of representation.

A second compromise, called the Three-Fifths Compromise, grew out of conflicts between the northern and southern states. Since population figures determined how many members a state would have in the House of Representatives, the southern states wanted enslaved persons to be included in determining the number of representatives each state could have. Northern delegates objected. They said enslaved persons were treated as property and should not be counted. The compromise stated that three-fifths of the number of enslaved people could be counted for representation and for taxing purposes.

suffrage right to vote

Northern and southern states also disagreed on other issues. The southern states were unwilling to allow the national government to regulate commerce. Since the southern states depended on selling their farm products overseas, they feared that the national government might place high taxes on these exported goods. They also feared that Congress might forbid the slave trade.

After much debate, a commerce and slave trade compromise was reached. It gave the national government power to regulate interstate and foreign commerce, but it could not tax exports. A small tax was permitted on slaves entering the country. Otherwise, the government could not interfere with the slave trade for 20 years, until 1808. A provision requiring that all treaties be approved by at least a two-thirds vote of the Senate was also included in the compromise. This was to prevent a small majority from approving trade treaties that would harm certain sections of the country.

Compromise was also reached on several other issues regarding the executive. One compromise was that the chief executive, the President, would serve a four-year term. How to select the President was also a hotly debated issue. Ideas ranged from election by the people or by the state legislatures, to election by Congress. Some delegates had feared that the people were not qualified to directly elect a President, and others felt an election by Congress would make the President too dependent upon the will of the lawmakers.

The method used today, the electoral college system, was agreed upon as a compromise. This plan allowed the people to vote for electors who, in turn, selected the President.

The question of **suffrage** was left to each state because the delegates who wanted to broaden suffrage to include more citizens and those who preferred to limit it could not agree. After all the issues had been debated and all the compromises were reached, a new plan of government had been created.

Struggle for Ratification

The document agreed upon was called, quite simply, the Constitution

ISSUE: CONSTITUTIONAL CONVENTION

SHOULD THERE BE A CONSTITUTIONAL CONVENTION?

Since the Constitution was adopted in 1789, many people have wanted to hold conventions to amend or change the Constitution. Historically, people have called for conventions to address controversial problems of their day, such as slavery or electoral reform. Yet, there has been only one constitutional convention. Although the Constitution has been amended 27 times, all of the changes have been proposed by Congress.

Beginning in the late 1970s, interest in a constitutional convention began anew with political leaders and interest groups, concerned about the size of the federal government, spearheading this movement. They have called for a national convention to write an amendment that would require Congress to balance the federal budget and limit government spending. Even if the needed two-thirds (34) of the states ask Congress to hold the convention, other questions persist. The formal requests for such a convention differ from one state to another. It is not even clear at this time if Congress must accept them; it is possible the Supreme Court would have to rule on this issue. Another consideration is that, if a convention were to be held, any and all amendments passed would have to be sent back to the states for ratification.

Opponents of a convention believe that it would bring far greater risks than benefits. They are concerned because there are no guidelines about how convention delegates should be chosen, or whether one or several issues could be discussed. They fear that delegates might only represent the interests of certain groups, leaving others without a voice. Opponents also worry that major amendments might be proposed and passed in the heat of the moment. Such a process, they fear, would not encourage careful thought or calm debate and could harm the political system. Opponents are particularly concerned that some groups might try to weaken the Bill of Rights, and, thus, weaken individual freedoms.

Supporters of a constitutional convention argue that Congress seems insensitive to public opinion on issues relating to government spending and the federal budget. Holding a convention, they feel, would force Congress to listen. They maintain that, above all, a constitutional convention would restore the idea that the people have a right to improve their government when they feel it is not responding to their needs. Such a gathering, they contend, would not threaten the political system or individual rights. Rather, they believe a constitutional convention, by allowing the people to participate more directly in their government, would strengthen the democratic system.

1. The Constitutional Convention was called for the purpose of amending the Articles of Confederation. The delegates drafted a new document. Would you be fearful this might happen a second time? Why or why not?

2. What are some issues you think might be important enough to warrant calling a new convention? Explain.

RATIFICATION OF THE CONSTITUTION

DATE	STATE	FOR	AGAINST
December 7, 1787	Delaware	30	0
December 12, 1787	Pennsylvania	46	23
December 18, 1787	New Jersey	38	0
January 2, 1788	Georgia	26	0
January 9, 1788	Connecticut	128	40
February 6, 1788	Massachusetts	187	168
April 28, 1788	Maryland	63	11
May 23, 1788	South Carolina	149	73
June 21, 1788	New Hampshire	57	47
June 25, 1788	Virginia	89	79
July 26, 1788	New York	30	27
November 21, 1789	North Carolina	194	77
May 29, 1790	Rhode Island	34	32

Figure 2-3

of the United States of America. From the convention, it was sent to the Congress of the Confederation. On September 28, 1787, the Congress sent it to the states. According to Article VII of the new Constitution, nine states had to ratify it before it could go into effect. Yet, ratification did not occur quickly or easily. Two groups emerged: those who favored ratification were known as Federalists, and those who argued against it were called Anti-Federalists.

FEDERALISTS

The Federalists believed a strong central government was the best way to preserve the people's freedoms and rights. They admitted the Constitution was not perfect, but they argued that it would solve most of the problems created by the Articles and could be amended if necessary. Such well-known members of the convention as George Washington and Benjamin Franklin favored ratification. Others such as James Madison, Alexander Hamilton, and John Jay wrote a series of articles in which they presented the Federalists' ideas. In the last article of *The Federalist*, Hamilton wrote:

A Nation, without a National Government, is in my view, an awful spectacle. The establishment of a Constitution, in time of profound peace, by the voluntary consent of a whole people, is a [wonder], to the completion of which I look forward with trembling anxiety.

ANTI-FEDERALISTS

The Anti-Federalists were suspicious of a strong central government. Although they agreed the Articles needed to be revised, they wanted fewer changes than those the Constitution provided.

Some of the leaders of the American Revolution were Anti-Federalists. Patrick Henry, Samuel Adams, and George Mason now led the movement against ratification. They believed the new government would destroy the rights of states and the freedoms of the people. Amos Singletary, a member of the Massachusetts legislature and an Anti-Federalist, spoke of his fears of the Constitution in this way:

. . .if anybody had proposed such a constitution. . .[during the American Revolution], it would have been thrown away at once. . . .moneyed men, that talk so finely,. . .expect to be the managers of this Constitution,. . .and then they will swallow up all of us little folks.

One of the Anti-Federalists' strongest arguments was that the Constitution needed a bill of rights similar to those included in most of the early state constitutions. The Federalists finally agreed and promised to add such a bill as soon as the new Constitution was approved and the new government was organized. It is doubtful the Constitution could have been ratified without this promise.

THE STATES VOTE

It took nearly three years for all the states to ratify the Constitution. Each state held a convention to approve the document. By June 21, 1788, nine states had approved it, enough for acceptance. But Virginia and New York were not among the nine. Because of their size and wealth, most Americans believed these two had to approve if the government were to succeed. It was not until Virginia and New York had accepted the Constitution that arrangements were made for setting up the new government.

Section Review

1. Why was the Constitutional Convention called?

2. What was the provision for representation in Congress under the Virginia Plan?

3. What promise did the Federalists make to win Anti-Federalists' votes?

4. **Challenge:** In your opinion, what would have happened if the Constitution had not been ratified? Explain.

Summary

1. During the colonial period, the colonists developed a tradition of self-government while still under the control of the British crown.

2. The main ideas that are part of the American form of government grew out of the common heritage of the English colonists. This heritage was influenced by the early Greeks and Romans, as well as philosophers of the 1600s and 1700s.

3. After 1763, Britain passed new laws to control the colonies. The colonists resisted those laws with protests and boycotts because they considered the laws harmful to their economic interests.

4. The First Continental Congress was a meeting of representatives from 12 of the 13 colonies to discuss ways to deal with the British. Hostilities continued and led to open rebellion.

5. The Second Continental Congress was the governing body for the rebelling colonies. It proclaimed the Declaration of Independence, directed the new states to organize their governments, and drew up a plan of national government.

6. The Declaration of Independence set out many of the basic principles and values of American government.

7. The national government organized under the Articles of Confederation was a weak union, with no executive or judicial branches, in which each state had an equal vote in the national legislature.

8. Government under the Articles of Confederation was unable to handle many important tasks. Dissatisfaction with the Articles led to a Constitutional Convention to draw a new plan of government.

9. Although the delegates to the Constitutional Convention agreed about basic issues, there were disagreements that were resolved by compromising.

10. After much debate between Federalists and Anti-Federalists, the Constitution was ratified by all 13 states.

Chapter 2 Review

★ Building Vocabulary

Imagine that these terms from Chapter 2 are correct answers to eight questions on a vocabulary test. Write the eight questions.

1. veto
2. royal colonies
3. ratify
4. bicameral
5. proprietary colonies
6. charter colonies
7. suffrage
8. unicameral

★ Reviewing Facts

1. What was the importance of the Mayflower Compact?
2. In what ways were the colonists' backgrounds similar?
3. What contributions to American ideas of government came from ancient Athens?
4. What is meant by a "state of nature"?
5. How did royal, proprietary, and charter colonies differ?
6. Why did colonists believe Parliament had no right to tax them?
7. How did colonists respond to the Intolerable Acts?
8. What did the Second Continental Congress do?
9. What ideas of government did all of the state constitutions include?
10. What powers were granted to the national government under the Articles of Confederation? What powers were withheld?
11. What did the Constitutional Convention of 1787 do?
12. Which states supported the Virginia Plan? The New Jersey Plan?
13. What was the Connecticut Compromise?
14. What did Anti-Federalists want the Constitution to include?

★ Analyzing Facts

1. Why did the Second Continental Congress adopt the Articles of Confederation?
2. If the central government under the Articles of Confederation had been given the power to tax and to regulate trade, do you think the Constitution would have been necessary? Explain your answer.
3. Why was Shays' Rebellion a signal to the new nation that its government was faltering?
4. The Constitution has been called a "bundle of compromises." Why do you think the Framers compromised over so many issues?
5. Which constitutional compromise do you think was most important to the future of the United States? Why?
6. In what ways, do you think, would your life be different today if the American colonies had never declared independence and fought against Great Britian?
7. In your opinion, what was the most important reason for establishing a strong central government under the Constitution of the United States? Explain your answer.

Using Your

Civic Participation Journal

Review the outline that you kept during your study of a constitution for your Civic Participation Journal. Work with three of your classmates to compare your notes and present a summary of your findings to the class. You should explain to the class how the organizations you studied can amend their constitutions.

★ Evaluating Ideas

1. Why do you suppose colonial leaders basically modeled their new state and national governments after the British system, even though they had rebelled against British rule?

2. Do you consider the truths that were listed by Thomas Jefferson in the Declaration of Independence to be "self-evident"? Explain.

3. If the Constitutional Convention were held today, whom would you choose as delegates from your state?

4. Had you been alive in 1787, would you have supported the Anti-Federalists or the Federalists? Explain.

★ Critical Thinking
Making Inferences

An inference is an unstated conclusion or deduction based on directly stated information. To be valid, an inference must follow logically from the information provided.

Explanation Sometimes a speaker or writer will simply provide information and expect you to make your own inferences from that information. At other times you will be expected to identify inferences already hidden in spoken or written material. When you are identifying inferences, you should ask yourself the following questions.

1. What information has the speaker or writer stated directly? What has he or she only implied?

2. What conclusions has the speaker or writer made directly? Does he or she make any other conclusions that are not directly stated?

3. What conclusions can I reach that are not made, directly or indirectly, by the speaker or writer?

4. Do the inferences that I make, or the inferences of the speaker or writer, seem to be logical deductions from the information that is provided?

Practice Suppose a friend shouts, "I see smoke. There's a fire!" He implies no other information and makes no inferences about what is burning. It could be the leaves in your neighbor's yard, the cookies you left in the oven, or your house. Nor has he provided enough information for you to infer what is burning. The only valid inference you can make is that somewhere there is a fire and that your friend has seen the fire.

Suppose, however, that your friend says: "I see smoke. There's a fire! Let's call the fire department." This statement implies that he knows what is burning and makes two inferences—that whatever is burning should not be on fire and that it is serious enough to call the fire department. However, you still do not have enough information to know if his inferences are valid. Nor can you make any additional valid inferences of your own.

Independent Practice Study the cartoon below. It was drawn by Clay Bennett and appeared in the *St. Petersburg Times* in 1993. It won an award as one of the best editorial cartoons for 1993. What inferences can you make about the artist's attitudes toward the economy?

Chapter 3

The Constitution and the People

Our Constitution is a living, breathing document created for the people by people with vision. They knew things would not always stay as they were at that moment. So they stayed away from specifics and made it open-ended enough for each of the many generations that would follow to interpret it according to their needs and values. It affects you, your family, and your friends every bit as much as it affected those people 200 years ago because it outlines the ideals of your government and describes how they should be achieved.

★ ★ ★ ★ ★

Chapter Preview

TERMS TO KNOW

limited government, constitutionalism, constitutional supremacy, rule of law, popular sovereignty, separation of powers, checks and balances, unconstitutional, judicial review, civil rights, separation of church and state, probable cause, search warrant, petition, double jeopardy, self-incrimination, due process of law, bail, poll taxes, discrimination, precedents

READ TO DISCOVER

- how the Constitution of the United States is organized and what principles it contains.
- what changes have been made in our Constitution since it was drafted, and how they came about.

Civic Participation Journal

Interview people in your community to learn how they think the Constitution affects their lives. When you develop your interview questions, you may wish to have a copy of the chart on page 63 to show people. Many of them might not be aware that these amendments are in the Constitution and directly affect their lives. Keep a tally of your results.

1 Organization

When you sit down to read the Constitution, the first words you see are these:

We, the People of the United States, in order to form a more perfect Union, establish Justice, insure domestic Tranquillity, provide for the common Defense, promote the general Welfare, and secure the Blessings of Liberty to ourselves and our Posterity, do ordain and establish this Constitution for the United States of America.

This is the Preamble, and it tells you what our forebears who wrote the Constitution in the name of all Americans expected to accomplish through the new government of the nation. They followed this up with the main body of the document—seven articles that focus on the major aspects of government. The next sections take a closer look at both the Preamble and the main body.

This early poster encouraged Americans to serve their country by joining the armed forces. Besides protection from attack, what are some goals that our government works to achieve?

The Preamble

Here, in this introduction, are the goals and purposes of the federal government. But what do these goals mean? What did the Framers of the Constitution hope to accomplish?

At the time the Constitution was written, there were disagreements among the governments and people of the states. The leaders who met in Philadelphia to draft the Constitution hoped to end these conflicts by establishing "a more perfect union" made up of satisfied and loyal citizens. They knew that to do this the new government had to develop and foster cooperation among the states. The experiences under the government the Articles of Confederation had established had shown that the states were not at all unified. The Framers of the Constitution hoped to eliminate disunity and promote unity. This goal of promoting unity among a diverse group of citizens is still very much a goal of our government today.

Another goal of government stated in the Preamble to the Constitution is to "establish justice." Although perfect justice has never been achieved, government strives toward this goal by stressing fair treatment, respect for individual rights, and equality of opportunity.

To "insure domestic tranquillity," the many governments at the local, state, and national levels act to make sure their citizens are protected and secure. Laws against criminal acts are made to protect you. Such services as fire and police protection help make your community, state, and nation a more peaceful and better place in which to live.

And just as all governments act to ensure peace within their boundaries, our national government is supposed to protect us from attack. For this

reason, it "provides for the common defense" by maintaining the military, making treaties, and engaging in diplomacy with other countries.

To "promote the general welfare" is a goal that centers on protecting and improving the quality of our lives. To accomplish this, we have such things as a system of stable currency, social security, clean air and water standards, and fair labor laws.

To "secure the blessings of liberty" means that people must, to a certain extent, be free to do as they wish. Protecting the liberty of individual citizens also implies that the government is limited in how far it can go to carry out its other purposes. Actions by the government that infringe on basic human rights are prohibited under our system. The government, for instance, cannot take away an individual's property without paying for it, even for such a worthwhile purpose as building low-cost homes for the elderly. Similarly, the government cannot keep someone from expressing an unpopular viewpoint under the guise of protecting domestic tranquillity.

The Main Body

The seven major articles that make up the main body of the Constitution are divided into smaller sections. Take Article I, for instance, which has 10 sections. It is often considered the most important article because it sets precise limits on the powers of government. It focuses on the legislative branch, laying out the requirements for becoming a member of Congress, explaining the process by which laws are enacted, and describing the duties of Congress. Section 8 lists the powers given to Congress. Powers denied to Congress are listed in Section 9 of Article I.

Article II deals with the executive branch. It explains the way the President and Vice President are chosen and details the powers, duties, and obligations of the two posts. Article III describes the judicial branch of the government. This article provides for

As Americans, we see the Statue of Liberty as a symbol of our freedom. Why must our government limit its activity in order to protect this freedom?

a Supreme Court and defines the kinds of cases the Court can hear.

Relations among the states and between them and the national government are covered in Article IV, while Article V describes the ways in which the Constitution may be amended. Public debts, the supremacy of national law, and oaths of office are discussed in Article VI. Finally, Article VII describes the ratification process that put the Constitution into effect.

Over the years, 27 amendments have been added to the original document. The first 10, known as the Bill of Rights, were ratified in 1791. The remaining 17 were ratified between 1795 and 1992. The amendment process, however, is still going on today.

Section Review

1. What is the purpose of the Preamble?
2. Into how many articles is the Constitution divided?
3. **Challenge:** In your opinion, which of the six goals of American government as listed in the Preamble is the most important? Explain.

2 Principles

We believe that the Constitution is the highest law of the land and are willing to abide by it. For these reasons we can say that as a country, we practice **constitutionalism**.

However, just because a nation has a constitution does not mean that it practices constitutionalism. In some nations, constitutions give no rights to the people nor place any limits on the government. In others, people's rights may be listed in a constitution, but the government ignores it and the limits it imposes. In 1989, for instance, General Manuel Noriega of Panama invalidated an election that would have given control of the government to his opponents. So, even though Panama had a constitution, it did not have a constitutional government. A true constitutional government protects the natural rights of its citizens, limits how citizens can be treated, and recognizes that there are areas of people's lives that should not come under governmental control.

Our Constitution is a contract between us and the government. It is based on fundamental principles that establish the powers and responsibilities of government as well as *our* rights and duties as citizens.

LIMITED GOVERNMENT

One of these principles is the idea of **limited government**. The Constitution clearly lists what the national government can and cannot do. In the first nine amendments, for instance, Congress is forbidden to pass laws that infringe on or take away certain individual freedoms. Similarly, the Tenth Amendment provides that all powers not granted to the national government nor denied to the states are reserved to the states, or to the people.

CONSTITUTIONAL SUPREMACY AND RULE OF LAW

Article VI, Section 2 states that the Constitution, laws, and treaties of the United States are the highest laws of the land. This refers to another basic principle, **constitutional supremacy**, which means that the Constitution and *national* laws are superior to state constitutions and state laws. Constitutional supremacy is linked to another basic principle, **rule of law**. These two, taken together, assure that our

limited government principle by which the government is given the power to do only certain things

constitutionalism powers of the person or persons running the government are limited by a set of laws that they must obey

constitutional supremacy principle of American government that the Constitution is the supreme law of the United States

rule of law principle that both the ruler and the ruled are bound by the same laws and have the same rights to equal treatment

rights are protected and that the power of government officials is limited.

POPULAR SOVEREIGNTY

Popular sovereignty is another limit on the power of government. Government gets its authority from the people and functions only with their consent. The Preamble expresses this principle in the phrase, "We the people. . .do ordain and establish this Constitution for the United States of America." Other provisions in the Constitution explain how we are to elect public officials to represent us. These provisions also support the principle of popular sovereignty.

SEPARATION OF POWERS

The Framers of the Constitution chose to spread out or separate power. To accomplish this, they divided power among three branches of government:

legislative, executive, and judicial. Each branch's duties correspond to certain functions that are important in any system of government. This **separation of powers** is unlike some democratic systems where the power of government is often concentrated in the legislative branch.

Article I of the Constitution gives Congress the power to make laws. Article II gives the executive branch the power to enforce and administer these laws. In Article III, the judicial branch is given the power to interpret the laws and apply their provisions in court cases.

CHECKS AND BALANCES

The Framers also believed it was important for each branch of government to be able to check the powers of the other two. This is called the

popular sovereignty principle that the people hold the supreme power to govern

separation of powers principle by which power is divided among the legislative, executive, and judicial branches

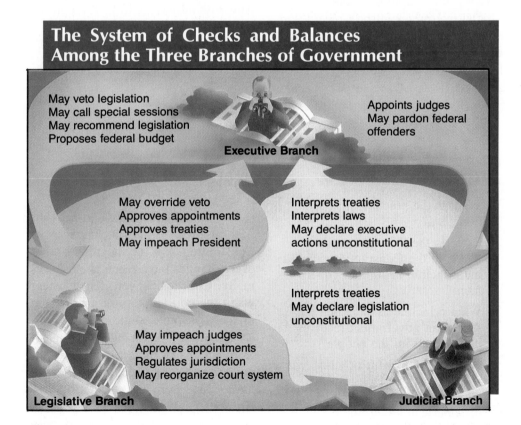

The System of Checks and Balances Among the Three Branches of Government

May veto legislation
May call special sessions
May recommend legislation
Proposes federal budget

Executive Branch

Appoints judges
May pardon federal offenders

May override veto
Approves appointments
Approves treaties
May impeach President

Interprets treaties
Interprets laws
May declare executive actions unconstitutional

Interprets treaties
May declare legislation unconstitutional

May impeach judges
Approves appointments
Regulates jurisdiction
May reorganize court system

Legislative Branch

Judicial Branch

Figure 3-1

principle of **checks and balances**. For example, Congress makes the laws. But this power is checked by the President, who can veto them. Yet Congress, with a two-thirds vote, can repass the law over such a veto. The Supreme Court can declare laws passed by Congress and signed by the President to be **unconstitutional**. The President, however, appoints the members of the Supreme Court, and the Senate must approve them. The President negotiates treaties with other countries. But, again, this power is checked by requiring Senate approval. Figure 3-1 on page 55 illustrates this system of checks and balances.

JUDICIAL REVIEW

It was not until after the Constitution was ratified that the principle of **judicial review** was incorporated into our system. Because we have judicial review, the Supreme Court is the official interpreter of the Constitution and has the final say in deciding what the Constitution means. The Court has the power to declare as unenforceable any laws that the justices decide are unconstitutional.

Section Review

1. What is the practice of constitutionalism?

2. How do the first nine amendments to the Constitution support the principle of limited government?

3. What principle assures that the American government receives its power from the people?

4. **Challenge:** In your opinion, why is a system of checks and balances important to the workings of American government?

3 The Changing Constitution

As a people, we can take great pride in the fact that ours is the oldest written national constitution still in operation. Why has it survived? One reason is that it lays out just the general provisions of government and leaves the details of day-to-day operation to those who run the government. Requirements for running a government change as conditions change. A constitution that is too specific would have to be constantly amended so that government could react to those changes.

Another reason our Constitution has survived is that its language is very broad. This allows it to be interpreted in ways to make it fit the situation at hand. Again, this has helped keep the Constitution up-to-date without having to go through the formal amendment process.

Finally, our Constitution has survived because it is flexible. It provides us, through step-by-step amendment procedures, with a way to change it. But such changes cannot be made *too* easily. Because of this flexibility, the Constitution has given us a government that is stable yet responsive to changing social conditions.

The formal amendment process has been used 27 times to change the Constitution. For the most part, however, changes have come about informally. Changes happen, for instance, when the courts interpret a provision of the Constitution and apply it to a certain situation. Changes also result from actions of the other branches of government. In addition, changes have come from custom and usage. No matter how the change has come about, though, it has affected only

PROFILE: JOHN MARSHALL

EQUALITY FOR THE SUPREME COURT

The present relationship among the executive, legislative, and judicial branches was not well-established when John Marshall became the fourth Chief Justice of the United States in 1801. The third branch of government, the judicial, was not considered on a par with the other two branches. In fact, the Supreme Court was so poorly regarded that it was difficult to convince qualified people to serve as Supreme Court justices. After a few brief years, however, the prestige of the Court had grown so much that John Marshall said that he would rather be Chief Justice than President of the United States.

Born in a sparsely-settled region of Virginia in 1755, Marshall grew up on his father's farm and had little formal education. During the Revolutionary War, he fought in the colonial army. After the war, he studied law on his own. Following a brief period of study at the College of William and Mary, he began to practice law in 1781.

It was not long before Marshall was recognized as an excellent attorney. Virginians thought so highly of him that he was chosen to be a member of the state legislature. Drawing on his experiences as a representative, lawyer, and soldier, Marshall became more and more convinced that the United States needed a strong central government. When the Constitution was submitted to the Virginia legislature to be ratified, Marshall helped lead the fight to adopt it.

In his talks and writings, Marshall made it clear that the nation needed an effective judiciary, one that had the power to review the acts of states. Without a strong judiciary, Marshall noted, the states could ignore the idea that the Constitution is the supreme law of the land. Marshall believed, as well, that the Framers intended the judicial branch to have the power to decide whether the actions of the other two branches were consistent with the principles of the Constitution. In

short, he thought that judicial review was an important and crucial part of limiting the power of government.

As Chief Justice, Marshall went about the task of establishing the power and prestige of the Supreme Court. In the case of *Marbury v. Madison* (1803), he declared unconstitutional a law passed by Congress. In *Fletcher v. Peck* (1810), the Court ruled that a state law was unconstitutional. In another case, *McCulloch v. Maryland* (1819), Marshall ruled that when state and federal powers conflict, the federal powers are stronger. These and similar cases that have followed have been critical factors in creating our present system of government.

1. In your opinion, what might have happened if the judicial branch had not assumed the power of judicial review?
2. Three important precedents were set forth by the Supreme Court under John Marshall: the right to declare the acts of Congress unconstitutional, the right to declare the acts of states unconstitutional, and the supremacy of national laws. In your opinion, which of the three is the most important? Why?

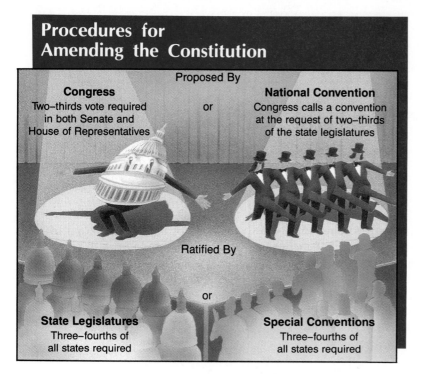

Procedures for Amending the Constitution

Proposed By

Congress
Two–thirds vote required in both Senate and House of Representatives

or

National Convention
Congress calls a convention at the request of two–thirds of the state legislatures

Ratified By

or

State Legislatures
Three–fourths of all states required

Special Conventions
Three–fourths of all states required

Figure 3-2

those aspects that deal with governing the nation. The guarantees of personal freedoms have remained unchanged.

Formal Changes

The authors of the Constitution knew that as society and conditions changed, the needs of the people would change. For this reason, they provided two ways to propose, or suggest, amendments to the Constitution and two ways to ratify them.

PROPOSING AMENDMENTS

The first method of proposing amendments, and the only one used to date, is by a two-thirds vote of both houses of Congress. The second is by a national convention, which would be called at the request of the legislatures of two-thirds of the states.

RATIFYING AMENDMENTS

After an amendment has been proposed, it must be ratified, or approved. Again, two methods are provided. The first is by approval of the legislatures of three-fourths, or 38, of the states. The second is by approval of ratifying conventions called by Congress to make this decision. This method—used only once, to ratify the Twenty-first Amendment—is much more costly because a special election for delegates to the conventions must be held. Figure 3-2 depicts the different ways of amending the Constitution.

A state may ratify an amendment after it has voted against it. However, once a state approves an amendment, there is some question as to whether it can change its mind and "unratify" it. This matter has never been brought before the Supreme Court.

The Framers of the Constitution did not impose any time limit for a proposed amendment to be ratified. Congress in recent years has, however, set a seven-year limit, during which states must act if they intend to ratify. The proposed Equal Rights Amendment failed to be approved by the required 38 states in the time allowed.

Since 1789, more than 9000 amendments have been proposed. Of these, only 26 have been ratified. Some of these, like those that make up the Bill of Rights, further protect or expand the rights of the people. Others make changes in the powers of the federal and state governments or are intended to make government more effective.

The Bill of Rights

What kinds of protections does the Constitution and its amendments give us? The basic ones are the right to think and act differently from others; the right to have equal protection of the laws; the right to own property; the right to enjoy America's economic, political, and social resources;

and the right to be protected against unreasonable actions by the government. These kinds of protections are among the **civil rights** and liberties we enjoy and are found in the Bill of Rights. These ten amendments are summarized in Figure 3-3.

FIRST AMENDMENT

This amendment provides five protections for us: freedom of religion, freedom of speech, freedom of the press, the right to assemble, and the right to petition the government.

What exactly do these provisions mean? First, they mean that we may worship or not worship as we please. We may select any religion we choose without fear that the government will punish or penalize us for our choice. In addition, the government cannot establish an official or "state" religion. These last two ideas together form the basis of what is often referred to as the **separation of church and state**.

The amendment allows us to speak freely, even to criticize the government and its officials. Similarly, the press is free to print controversial opinions about the workings of government. The Framers of the Constitution recognized that, for democracy to work, citizens must be free to hear different and controversial points of view and to discuss their ideas with others.

Neither freedom of speech nor freedom of the press, though, is completely unlimited. Speech that is obscene or unfairly harms someone's reputation is not allowed. News reports that purposefully present unjust accusations about a person are not

civil rights freedoms granted by law

separation of church and state principle in the Constitution that religion and government are to be kept separate

AMENDMENTS 1 TO 10	
Amendment 1	Guarantees freedom of religion, of speech, and of the press, and the right to assemble peaceably and to petition the government.
Amendment 2	Guarantees the right to organize state militias and to bear arms.
Amendment 3	Prohibits quartering soldiers in private homes in peacetime and limits it in time of war.
Amendment 4	Prohibits the unreasonable search and seizure of persons and property without a valid warrant.
Amendment 5	Requires a grand jury for serious criminal charges; prohibits military trials of civilians; prohibits double jeopardy; prohibits forcing accused persons to testify against themselves; guarantees that no one may be deprived of life, liberty, or property, without due process of law; prohibits government taking private property for public use without just compensation.
Amendment 6	Guarantees the right to a speedy trial by jury in criminal cases; to know all charges; to question and obtain witnesses; to have counsel.
Amendment 7	Guarantees a jury trial in most civil cases.
Amendment 8	Prohibits excessive bail and fines and cruel and unusual punishment.
Amendment 9	Assures people that they may have other basic rights in addition to those mentioned in the Constitution.
Amendment 10	Guarantees that rights not given to the federal government, nor denied to the states, are reserved to the states or to the people.

Figure 3-3

Protection of Our Rights

The Bill of Rights

Powers of Government

Rights of Citizens

Figure 3-4

probable cause reasonable grounds for suspicion based on evidence from a good source

search warrant official document that describes in detail the place being searched, the object being sought, or the person suspected of a crime

petition request for a specific course of action

double jeopardy guarantee that a person may not be tried again for the same crime

self-incrimination forcing a person accused of a crime to testify against himself or herself

allowed. And stories that might jeopardize the security of the nation during wartime may also be prohibited.

Another thing the First Amendment provisions give us is the right to peaceably assemble. This means that we can meet together, demonstrate, or march in support of our ideas. You can even **petition** the government if you disagree with what it is doing. These rights are important because, as citizens in a democracy, we must have ways to tell our representatives how we feel about government policies.

SECOND AMENDMENT

The Second Amendment guarantees us the right to keep weapons. It also prevents the national government from seizing weapons from state militias or the National Guard. The British had tried to do this in colonial

times, and many feared that an unlimited government might try to do so again. This amendment, however, does not prevent the *states* from regulating the sale and use of firearms. States may require weapons to be registered or may prohibit possession of machine guns and assault weapons.

THIRD AMENDMENT

The Third Amendment prevents the government from requiring us to house, or "quarter," soldiers in our homes during peacetime. Although this protection may not be meaningful today, it was created as a reaction to Britain's policy of quartering soldiers in the homes of colonists.

FOURTH AMENDMENT

You are protected, under the Fourth Amendment, from unreasonable searches and seizures by the government and law-enforcement officials. "Unreasonable" is the key word. Although the government must be able to protect us from the actions of criminals, it must do so in a legitimate way. There must be **probable cause,** and government officials usually must first get a **search warrant**.

FIFTH AMENDMENT

Protections for persons accused of crimes are listed in the Fifth Amendment. No one can be tried for a serious crime unless a grand jury believes there is enough evidence to bring the accused to trial. Further, a person who is found innocent of a crime cannot be placed in **double jeopardy**, or tried again for the same crime. A third protection is a guarantee against **self-incrimination**. In other words, you cannot be forced to testify against yourself in court.

Finally, the Fifth Amendment forbids the national government the

CASE STUDY: AMENDING THE CONSTITUTION

THE AMENDMENT THAT REFUSED TO DIE

The letter that follows was written in early 1989 to the Speaker of the House of the Washington State Legislature by 10 members of the U.S. House of Representatives. It was written in response to the public outcry when Congress tried to raise the salaries of those serving in the three branches of the national government.

Dear Mr. Speaker:

In 1789 Congress proposed the following amendment to the United States Constitution:

Article II. No law varying the compensation for the services of the Senators and Representatives shall take effect, until an election of Representatives shall have intervened. Introduced by James Madison, 1789

This amendment was one of 12 proposed at the time; the ten that were ratified became the Bill of Rights. The salary amendment was never ratified and is still

pending before the states. Your state is one of 24 that have not acted to ratify this amendment. We are writing to urge you to take up this issue at the first opportunity and ratify the amendment.

We believe that the current system of setting congressional salaries must be changed. Under current law, a Commission on Executive, Legislative, and Judicial Salaries is appointed every four years to recommend salaries for Members of Congress and other top government officials. After being approved by the President, any change goes into immediate effect unless Congress votes to reject it. This system puts Members of Congress in the difficult position of voting on whether to grant themselves an immediate pay increase. The result, as we are all too well aware, is the picture of an ineffective Congress seeking to avoid accountability to the public that elects it.

The 1789 amendment would delay any increase in pay until after an election, thus allowing the public to know at the time of election the salary to be paid to Congress for the next term in office. This is critical if we are to keep the public's trust in Congress and in our ability to deal with the congressional salary issue in a responsible manner.

Article V of the Constitution does not specify any time limit

within which ratification of a proposed amendment must occur. In recent years Congress has typically put a time limit on amendments. . . .

Currently twenty-six states have ratified the amendment; the required number is 38. We hope you agree that this is an important issue and one needing immediate action. Please do what you can to have the 1789 amendment ratified in your state during the current legislative session.

Sincerely yours,
Timothy J. Penny
David E. Skaggs
Dan Schaefer
Les AuCoin
Hank Brown
Lamar S. Smith
John Miller
Robert K. Dornan
Nick Joe Rahall, II
Ben Erdreich

In May 1992 Congress ratified the Twenty-seventh Amendment. The amendment states that any increase in the salaries of members of Congress will take effect in the next session of Congress.

1. Given the social and economic changes that have occurred in the past 200 years, is the fact that this amendment was first proposed in 1789 reason for concern? Why?
2. Do you favor the amendment? Why or why not?

The Constitution and the People 61

power to deprive any person of life, liberty, and property without **due process of law**. As a result of Supreme Court rulings, two kinds of due process have developed—procedural and substantive.

Procedural due process requires the government to use fair procedures in enforcing laws. At first, this protection applied mostly to criminal cases. Now, it is also used in such situations as government committee hearings and hearings before a school board to expel a student. *Substantive* due process requires that the laws under which government acts be fair. This simply means that the laws must be constitutional.

SIXTH AMENDMENT

Like the Fifth Amendment, the Sixth Amendment deals with the rights of persons accused of crimes. Under this amendment, any person accused of a crime has a right to a "speedy and public trial" by an impartial jury. However, the trial cannot be so speedy that the person does not have time to prepare an adequate defense. In addition, persons accused of a crime must be informed of the charges, are entitled to a lawyer, and may require witnesses to testify in their behalf.

SEVENTH AMENDMENT

This amendment deals with civil cases, which most often involve a dispute over a contract or some sort of damage to an individual or group. In such cases, the right of trial by jury is guaranteed if the value of the controversy exceeds $20.

EIGHTH AMENDMENT

The Eighth Amendment completes the list of rights of citizens accused of crimes. The courts cannot set excessive **bail** for a person accused of a crime. Neither can they impose exces-

sive fines on persons found guilty of a crime. Finally, the amendment forbids cruel or unusual punishment.

NINTH AMENDMENT

The Ninth Amendment states that we have many more rights than just those listed in the Constitution. These are no less important than the ones listed and cannot be taken away by the government. One such right, that of "privacy," has been the source of great debate in recent years. Others include the right to join political groups, the right to campaign for public office, and the right to travel freely around the country.

TENTH AMENDMENT

The role of the states in the American federal system is defined in the Tenth Amendment. It provides that all powers not specifically given to the national government, nor prohibited to the states, belong to the states or to the people. Among other duties, then, the states have primary responsibility for the safety, health, and education of the people.

Amendments After 1791

The amendments passed after 1791 have addressed a number of issues. Some have strengthened the power of the people by increasing the number of those who are entitled to vote. Others have extended people's rights. And some have modified or changed the structure of government. Figure 3-5 summarizes these amendments.

ELEVENTH AMENDMENT

The Eleventh Amendment (1798) prevents citizens of one state or a foreign country from suing another state in a federal court. It partially changed Article III, Section 2 of the Constitution. Under this amendment, people may sue a state only in a *state* court and under state laws.

TWELFTH AMENDMENT

This amendment (1804) was adopted to prevent a recurrence of what happened in the election of 1800. Aaron Burr, who was running for Vice President, received the same number of votes as Thomas Jefferson, who was running for President. This happened because the electors voting for them had followed the rules of the day: they had placed both names on the presidential ballot, but with the intention that the runner-up, Burr, would be Vice President. Instead, a tie resulted. The Twelfth Amendment requires that separate ballots be used in voting for President and Vice President.

AMENDMENTS 11 TO 27	
Amendment 11	Requires that when the government of a state is sued by a citizen of another state or of a foreign country, the case must be tried in the courts of the state being sued. (1798)
Amendment 12	Requires the members of the electoral college to vote for President and Vice President on separate ballots. (1804)
Amendment 13	Forbids slavery in any part of the United States or lands under its control. (1865)
Amendment 14	Grants citizenship to former slaves; defines the rights of citizens; guarantees privileges and immunities of citizens; makes the due process of law provision of the Fifth Amendment applicable to the states; requires states to provide the equal protection of the law to all citizens within their jurisdiction. (1868)
Amendment 15	Guarantees the right to vote regardless of race, color, or previous condition of servitude. (1870)
Amendment 16	Permits Congress to levy a federal income tax. (1913)
Amendment 17	Provides for the direct election of United States senators by the people in the states they represent. (1913)
Amendment 18	Outlaws the making, selling, or transporting of alcoholic beverages. (1919)
Amendment 19	Grants women the right to vote. (1920)
Amendment 20	Changes the inauguration date for the President and Vice President from March 4 to January 20; provides that the terms of newly elected members of Congress shall begin on January 3, when Congress begins its annual session. (1933)
Amendment 21	Repeals Prohibition (Amendment 18). (1933)
Amendment 22	Forbids the President from being elected for more than two terms. (1951)
Amendment 23	Gives voters in Washington, D.C., the right to vote for President and Vice President. (1961)
Amendment 24	Abolishes the poll tax as a requirement of voting. (1964)
Amendment 25	States the procedures to be followed in the event of the death, removal, resignation, or disability of the President; provides for the appointment of a Vice President. (1967)
Amendment 26	Gives the right to vote in federal elections to men and women 18 years of age or older. (1971)
Amendment 27	Delays congressional pay raises until session following passage. (1992)

Figure 3-5

CIVIL WAR AMENDMENTS

Because they were passed, in part, to resolve certain issues that were important during the Civil War, the Thirteenth, Fourteenth, and Fifteenth Amendments are sometimes called the Civil War Amendments. The Thirteenth Amendment (1865) ended slavery. Thus, it guarantees a free and voluntary labor force.

The Fourteenth Amendment (1868), which was originally passed to give formerly enslaved persons legal rights, defines citizenship. American citizens are "all persons born or naturalized in the United States and subject to the jurisdiction thereof." This amendment also forbids any *state* from depriving you of life, liberty, or property without due process of law. A powerful amendment, it is the basis for making many of the guarantees listed in the Bill of Rights apply to the states.

The Fifteenth Amendment (1870) gave formerly enslaved males the right to vote. It prohibits both the national *and* state governments from

denying you the right to vote on the basis of your race or color.

SIXTEENTH AMENDMENT

With passage of the Sixteenth Amendment (1913), Congress was given the power to levy an income, or direct, tax on individuals. Since that time, income taxes have become the major source of federal revenues.

SEVENTEENTH AMENDMENT

The Seventeenth Amendment (1913) modified some of the sections of Article I by changing the method of electing United States senators. They now are elected directly by the people instead of by state legislatures.

EIGHTEENTH AMENDMENT

Also known as the Prohibition Amendment, the Eighteenth Amendment (1919) prohibited the "manufacture, sale, or transportation of intoxicating liquors." Since so many people believed the government had no business "legislating their morals," enforcing it was difficult.

NINETEENTH AMENDMENT

This amendment (1920) granted women the right to vote. Although several western states had allowed women to vote in state elections as early as 1869, it was not until 1920 that women were given the right to vote in national elections.

TWENTIETH AMENDMENT

The Twentieth Amendment (1933) is also known as the Lame Duck Amendment. It set January 3 as the day new sessions of Congress would begin and January 20 as the day the President and Vice President would begin new terms in office. Previously, defeated members of Congress, so-called "lame ducks," could serve for four months following their defeat. Many people criticized lame duck Congresses because they did not reflect the will of the voters. This

Posters like this one show support for the Prohibition Amendment. Why was this amendment hard to enforce?

amendment also provides for presidential succession in case of the death or disability of a President-elect.

AMENDMENTS 21 TO 27

The Twenty-first Amendment (1933) repealed national prohibition established by the Eighteenth Amendment. It is the only amendment that has repealed a prior amendment.

The Twenty-second Amendment (1951) limits a President's term of office. He or she now may serve a maximum of two full terms or not more than ten years.

Voting rights are the subject of the Twenty-third and Twenty-fourth Amendments. The Twenty-third Amendment (1961) granted citizens of the District of Columbia the right to vote for President and Vice President. The Twenty-fourth Amendment (1964) abolished **poll taxes** in national elections. Such taxes were used in certain states to prevent African Americans from voting.

The Twenty-fifth Amendment (1967) clarifies the issue of presidential succession. It states that the Vice President assumes the office of President should it become vacant. The amendment also provides for the Vice President to become acting President should the President become disabled. Finally, it outlines how the office of Vice President should be filled if it becomes vacant.

The Twenty-sixth Amendment (1971) lowered the voting age in all elections to 18, thus extending the vote to a larger group of citizens.

The Twenty-seventh Amendment (1992) is the last amendment. It states that any salary increase for members of Congress will take effect in the subsequent session of Congress.

Informal Changes

As our needs have changed, our leaders have acted to modify and

In 1954, the Supreme Court determined that "separate but equal" facilities for people of different races was unconstitutional. How does the case of *Brown v. Board of Education of Topeka* show the power of the Supreme Court?

expand the Constitution. Many changes have taken place by the amendment process. Yet there are many more informal ways in which the Constitution has been changed.

JUDICIAL INTERPRETATION

One of these is through judicial interpretation. Justices have interpreted the principles of the Constitution so that they apply to current situations. In 1954, for instance, the Supreme Court changed its interpretation of the equal protection clause of the Fourteenth Amendment, which prohibits **discrimination**. Since 1896, the Court had held that "separate but equal" facilities for people of different races were *not* discriminatory and, therefore, were constitutional. But in the case of *Brown v. Board of Education of Topeka,* the Court outlawed "separate but equal" public schools as discriminatory and unconstitutional. Thus, the Court acted to change the way in which the Constitution, in this case, the Fourteenth Amendment, was to be understood. Decisions such as these set **precedents** for other legal cases.

poll taxes special taxes paid as a qualification to vote

discrimination action based on prejudice

precedents court rulings that serve as guidelines for making future decisions

ACTIONS OF CONGRESS

Another way our Constitution has been defined and expanded is by actions of Congress. The Constitution gives Congress a long list of powers. Among these, for instance, is the power to regulate interstate commerce. If Congress decides that a policy interferes with the free flow of interstate commerce, it can pass laws against the policy.

Racial discrimination was one such policy. In 1964, Congress passed the Civil Rights Act, making it illegal to discriminate in "hotels and motels, restaurants, lunch counters, movie houses, gasoline stations, theaters, and stadiums." The Supreme Court upheld the act, reasoning that those who are discriminated against are kept from traveling freely among the states. Thus, racial discrimination interferes with interstate commerce.

Still other changes have come about through congressional action. The Constitution does not establish executive departments, agencies, or regulatory commissions. Yet, to help the President carry out the work of the executive branch, Congress has provided for such bodies. In addition, Congress established the entire federal court system, with the exception of the Supreme Court.

ACTIONS OF THE PRESIDENT

Presidents have also modified the Constitution. Such strong Presidents as George Washington, Abraham Lincoln, Franklin D. Roosevelt, and Harry Truman have expanded the powers of the presidency. For example, to prevent the nation from being split apart after the secession of the southern states, Lincoln began marshalling resources for the war effort without a formal declaration of war by Congress. In similar fashion, Truman involved the United States in the Korean conflict without formal congressional action.

Presidential action also helped define presidential succession. When President William Henry Harrison died in 1841, there was a question about whether Vice President John Tyler would become President or merely carry out the duties of the office. Tyler made it clear that he was indeed President—a view no one challenged successfully. All Vice Presidents succeeding to the office upon the death of a President have taken the same position. The Twenty-fifth Amendment finally made this procedure "official."

Woodrow Wilson started the presidential practice of offering legislative programs and budgets to Congress. As a result, the President has become a key legislator as well as the chief executive. Other presidential initiatives also have developed into precedents that have increased the power of the presidency.

ACTIVITIES OF POLITICAL PARTIES

Still other informal changes have come through the activities of political parties. Although the Constitution calls for the election of officials, it does not explain how these officials are to be chosen. Political parties are the mechanism that has been established to accomplish this. The political party system has made it possible for more people to participate in government. This, in turn, has made the government more responsive to the wishes of the people.

CUSTOMS AND TRADITIONS

Customs and traditions have influenced the way our government operates. President Franklin D. Roosevelt

George Washington

sought to increase the number of Supreme Court justices from 9 to 15. Yet, he was not able to gather support for his plan, largely because there was a "tradition" of nine Supreme Court justices.

There had also been a tradition whereby a President served a maximum of two terms. This tradition was broken when Franklin D. Roosevelt was elected for four terms. Following Roosevelt's death, though, so many people believed in the soundness of the two-term tradition that the Twenty-second Amendment to the Constitution was ratified.

Section Review

1. Why has the Constitution been able to survive so well?

2. By what two methods can an amendment be ratified?

3. What are the five freedoms the First Amendment guarantees?

4. What does the Tenth Amendment define?

5. **Challenge:** In your opinion, should the process to ratify an amendment be simplified? Explain.

Summary

1. The Constitution of the United States contains 7 major articles and 27 amendments.

2. The Preamble to the Constitution explains the goals of the people and purposes of American government.

3. Articles I through III describe the powers and duties of the legislative, executive, and judicial branches of the government.

4. Article IV describes relations among the states, and Article V provides for an amendment process.

5. Article VI deals with such issues as the supremacy of national law and oaths of office, and Article VII sets up the procedures for ratification.

6. The Constitution is a contract between the people and government that is based on fundamental principles. It establishes the powers and responsibilities of government as well as the rights and duties of citizens.

7. The fact that a country has a constitution does not necessarily mean that it has a constitutional form of government.

8. The people of the United States hold sovereign power in the American system of government.

9. Basic principles found in the Constitution include limited government, constitutional supremacy, rule of law, popular sovereignty, separation of powers, checks and balances, and judicial review.

10. The Constitution has changed as the needs of the people changed.

11. Formal changes in the Constitution have been made through the amendment process.

12. Informal changes have taken place through judicial, congressional, and presidential action, the action of political parties, and custom and usage.

Chapter 3 Review

★ Building Vocabulary

The definitions of several vocabulary words found in this chapter are listed below. First, number your paper from one to seven. Then, next to each number, write the word or words being defined.

1. principle by which the government is given the power to do only certain things
2. contrary to the Constitution
3. principle by which each branch of government can check the powers of the other branches
4. rights and freedoms guaranteed to all citizens
5. idea that government must follow fair and lawful procedures in its dealings with individuals
6. court rulings that serve as examples for making future rulings
7. official document that describes in detail the place being searched, the object sought, or the person suspected of the crime

★ Reviewing Facts

1. How is the Constitution of the United States organized?
2. Explain how governments that have written constitutions may not have a constitutional form of government.
3. In what ways does the Constitution limit the powers of government?
4. Who holds sovereign power in the United States?
5. What basic principles characterize the American system of government?
6. How has the Constitution been changed informally through the years?
7. What three characteristics of the Constitution have helped it to survive?
8. What does the Fourth Amendment prohibit?
9. Describe how protection against unfair treatment by the government has been provided in the Fifth Amendment?
10. Other than the Bill of Rights, how many amendments have been added to the Constitution? For what three reasons have most of them been added?

★ Analyzing Facts

1. Explain how the Constitution helps to promote the general purposes of government cited in the Preamble.
2. The principle of checks and balances was built into the American system of government. Do you think this has caused too much conflict between the branches? Why or why not?
3. Why did the Framers give most powers of the federal government to the legislative branch?
4. Other than the Bill of Rights, which amendments do you think have been most important? Why?
5. How does the Constitution help to unify the United States?
6. In your opinion, how could a trial be so speedy that it would be unfair to the accused?

★ Evaluating Ideas

1. Louis D. Brandeis, who served as an associate justice of the Supreme Court, once said: "I would not amend the Constitution. I would amend men's social and economic ideas." Do you agree or disagree with Brandeis's statement? Explain your thinking.

Using Your
Civic Participation Journal

Review the tally that you kept during your interview for your Civic Particpation Journal. Change the tally to a chart form and present your chart to the class.

2. The Constitution has been changed informally as well as formally. What would be the consequences of allowing change only through the amendment process?

3. Why should accused criminals be allowed protection by the Bill of Rights?

★ Critical Thinking
Evaluating Primary and Secondary Sources

A primary source is an account of an event by someone who experienced it, witnessed it, or was actually involved in some way. A secondary source is an account of an event by someone who was not directly involved. Primary sources are always first-hand accounts. Secondary sources use information taken from primary sources or from other secondary sources. While biographies and interviews are secondary sources, autobiographies and eyewitness accounts are primary sources.

Explanation   Professional researchers usually prefer to use primary sources over secondary sources because primary sources put them in direct touch with the events being studied. However, even primary sources can be unreliable sometimes. The following guidelines will help you evaluate information from primary and secondary sources.

1. Determine if your information is from a primary source or a secondary source. If from a primary source, determine how long after the experience the information was given. If much time has passed, the writer may not be able to remember everything accurately. If from a secondary source, determine where the writer got the information. Did the writer use reliable primary sources or depend on other secondary sources without going back to original accounts?

2. For either primary or secondary sources, decide whether or not the account has been influenced by emotion, opinion, or exaggeration. What is the purpose of the account? Is the writer emotionally involved with the topic? Does the writer show any biases that might distort the accuracy of the

information? Could the writer have any reasons for not being completely truthful? Knowing the writer's background and credibility may help.

3. Look for documentation, evidence to support the account given. You also can evaluate a source by looking at other accounts to see if they agree with your source.

Practice   This passage about the Constitution can be evaluated by using the guidelines above.

> *I see in this instrument a great deal of good. . . . There are indeed some faults . . . but we must be contented to travel on towards perfection, step by step . . . and hope that a favorable moment will come for correcting what is amiss in it.*
> *(Thomas Jefferson, 1788)*

Since this is a quote from Jefferson, it is a primary source. Because it was written soon after the Constitution, it probably shows his early views about the Constitution better than anything he wrote later in his life. Since he writes of "faults" and "correcting," his emotions and opinion influence his account, so it is not useful as a source of facts about the Constitution.

Independent Practice   Using the same guidelines, determine if the following passage is a primary or secondary source and evaluate its value as a source for a term paper on Thomas Jefferson.

> *Although he was not a Framer of the Constitution, many of his ideas can be found in the document. Yet biographers of Jefferson, who have studied his writings, prove that he wisely feared the great power granted to the new government. His fears certainly have come true today.*

DOCUMENT: UNITED STATES CONSTITUTION

Preamble

We the People of the United States, in order to form a more perfect union, establish justice, insure domestic tranquility, provide for the common defense, promote the general welfare, and secure the blessings of liberty to ourselves and posterity, do ordain and establish this CONSTITUTION for the United States of America.

The Preamble is an introduction that explains why the Constitution is necessary and lists the purposes and goals to be achieved.

Article I Legislative Branch

Section 1 Congress

All legislative powers herein granted shall be vested in a Congress of the United States, which shall consist of a Senate and House of Representatives.

Section 2 House of Representatives

1. The House of Representatives shall be composed of members chosen every second year by the people of the several states, and the electors in each state shall have the qualifications requisite for electors of the most numerous branch of the state legislature.

2. No person shall be a Representative who shall not have attained to the age of twenty-five years, and been seven years a citizen of the United States, and who shall not, when elected, be an inhabitant of that state in which he shall be chosen.

Section 2 sets the House terms at two years, provides for the popular election of Representatives, and sets the qualifications that must be met to hold the office. The term "electors" here means voters.

3. Representatives and direct taxes shall be apportioned among the several states which may be included within this Union, according to their respective numbers, which shall be determined by adding to the whole number of free persons, including those bound to service for a term of years, and excluding Indians not taxed, three-fifths of all other persons. The actual enumeration shall be made within three years after the first meeting of the Congress of the United States, and within every subsequent term of ten years, in such manner as they shall by law direct. The number of Representatives shall not exceed one for every thirty thousand, but each state shall have at least one Representative; and until such enumeration shall be made, the State of New Hampshire shall be entitled to choose three; Massachusetts, eight; Rhode Island and Providence Plantations, one; Connecticut, five; New York, six; New Jersey, four; Pennsylvania, eight; Delaware, one; Maryland, six; Virginia, ten; North Carolina, five; South Carolina, five; and Georgia, three.

In regard to income taxes, the direct tax requirement was voided by the Sixteenth Amendment. The 3/5 reference to slaves was cancelled by the Thirteenth and Fourteenth Amendments.

Since a state's representation in the House is based on its population, a census has been taken every 10 years, beginning with the first in 1790. The current size of the House—435 members—was set by law in 1929. Since then, there has been a reapportionment of seats based on population shifts rather than an addition of seats.

4. When vacancies happen in the representation from any state, the executive authority thereof shall issue writs of election to fill such vacancies.

A vacancy in the House is filled through a special election called by the state's governor.

5. The House of Representatives shall choose their Speaker and other officers; and shall have the sole power of impeachment.

Selecting House officers is strictly by party vote. Only the House may impeach, or charge, federal officials with not carrying out their duties. Military officers are not subject to impeachment. Nor are members of Congress, since either house can expel its own members if it sees fit.

Section 3 Senate

1. The Senate of the United States shall be composed of two Senators from each state, chosen by the legislature thereof, for six years; and each Senator shall have one vote.

This paragraph establishes that each state will have two Senators and sets the senatorial term at six years. Selection of Senators by state legislatures was ended with the adoption of the Seventeenth Amendment.

2. Immediately after they shall be assembled in consequence of the first election, they shall be divided as equally as may be into three classes. The seats of the Senators of the first class shall be vacated at the expiration of the second year, of the second class at the expiration of the fourth year, and of the third class at the expiration of the sixth year, so that one-third may be chosen every second year, and if vacancies happen by resignation, or otherwise, during the recess of legislature of any state, the executive thereof may make temporary appointments until the next meeting of the legislature, which shall then fill such vacancies.

Paragraph 2 provides for one-third of the membership of the Senate to be chosen every two years. A state's governor can fill a vacancy in a state's Senate seat by temporary appointment until the next general election.

3. No person shall be a Senator who shall not have attained to the age of thirty years, and been nine years a citizen of the United States, and who shall not, when elected, be an inhabitant of that state for which he shall be chosen.

Like those for the House, the only constitutional requirements that must be met for membership in the Senate deal with age, citizenship, and residency.

4. The Vice-President of the United States shall be President of the Senate, but shall have no vote, unless they be equally divided.

The Vice-President is the presiding officer of the Senate. The Vice-President may (but is not required to) vote only when there is a tie vote on a bill or issue.

5. The Senate shall choose their officers, and also a President *pro tempore,* in the absence of the Vice-President, or when he shall exercise the office of the President of the United States.

6. The Senate shall have the sole power to try all impeachments. When sitting for that purpose, they shall be on oath or affirmation. When the President of the United States is tried, the Chief Justice shall preside; and no person shall be convicted without the concurrence of two-thirds of the members present.

The Senate sets the date for trial and provides the accused with the ''articles of impeachment'' (a copy of the formal charges). The accused has the basic legal rights of any person on trial.

7. Judgment in cases of impeachment shall not extend further than to removal from office, and disqualification to hold and enjoy any office of honor, trust, or profit under the United States; but the party convicted shall nevertheless be liable and subject to indictment, trial, judgment, and punishment, according to law.

Punishment is limited to removal from office and, if the Senate chooses, being barred from holding office in the future. But a person who has been impeached can still be tried in court for any crimes committed.

71

Section 4 Congressional Elections and Meetings

1. The times, places, and manner of holding elections for Senators and Representatives shall be prescribed in each state by the legislature thereof; but the Congress may at any time by law make or alter such regulations, except as to the places of choosing Senators.

Until 1842 Congress set no election regulations. That year it required members of the House to be elected from districts in states having more than one Representative rather than at large. In 1845 it set the first Tuesday after the first Monday in November as the day for selecting presidential electors. In 1872 it set the same day in even-numbered years as the date for congressional elections.

2. The Congress shall assemble at least once in every year, and such meeting shall be on the first Monday in December, unless they shall by law appoint a different day.

The opening date was changed to January 3 by the Twentieth Amendment. A new Congress begins on that date of each odd-numbered year and continues for two years.

Section 5 Congressional Powers and Duties

1. Each house shall be the judge of the elections, returns, and qualifications of its own members, and a majority of each shall constitute a quorum to do business; but a smaller number may adjourn from day to day, and may be authorized to compel the attendance of absent members, in such manner, and under such penalties, as each may provide.

Each house has the power to exclude, or to refuse to seat, a member-elect. Until 1969, each house viewed its power to judge qualifications as the power to set informal standards beyond the specified constitutional qualifications of age, citizenship, and residency. In 1969 the U.S. Supreme Court in *Powell v. McCormack* limited Congress's power to judgment of constitutional qualifications only.

Technically, to conduct business, 218 members must be present in the House and 51 in the Senate. The quorum rule is seldom enforced, however, in handling of routine matters.

2. Each house may determine the rules of its proceedings, punish its members for disorderly behavior, and, with the concurrence of two-thirds, expel a member.

Each house sets its own rules. There are a few unique ones. Under the "seniority rule," committee chairmanships go to the majority party member who has served the longest on the committee. Under "senatorial courtesy," the Senate will refuse to confirm a presidential appointment if a Senator from the appointee's state and of the same party as the President objects to the appointment. In the House, debate is usually limited to one hour per member, whereas in the Senate, a member can hold the floor indefinitely.

Though both houses can censure or expel members for misconduct, both have rarely been used.

3. Each house shall keep a journal of its proceedings, and from time to time publish the same, excepting such parts as may in their judgment require secrecy; and the yeas and nays of the members of either house on any question shall, at the desire of one-fifth of those present, be entered on the journal.

In addition to the journals, a complete official record of everything said on the floor, as well as the roll call votes on all bills or issues, is available in the *Congressional Record* published daily by the Government Printing Office.

4. Neither house, during the session of Congress, shall, without the consent of the other, adjourn for more than three days, nor to any other place than that in which the two houses shall be sitting.

Neither house may recess for more than three days without consent of the other, nor may it conduct business in any place other than the Capitol.

Section 6   Privileges and Restrictions of Members

1. The Senators and Representatives shall receive a compensation for their services, to be ascertained by law, and paid out of the Treasury of the United States. They shall in all cases except treason, felony, and breach of the peace, be privileged from arrest during their attendance at the session of their respective houses, and in going to and returning from the same; and for any speech or debate in either house, they shall not be questioned in any other place.

To strengthen the federal government, the Founders set congressional salaries to be paid by the U.S. Treasury rather than by members' respective states. Originally, members were paid $6 per day. Annual salaries began in 1857, when members were paid $3000 per year. As of 1995, salaries were $133,600 for Senators and Representatives. Members also receive other numerous monetary benefits.

The "immunity" privilege is of little importance today. It was included as a safeguard against the British colonial practice of arresting legislators to keep them from performing their duties. More important is immunity from slander and libel for anything said officially on the floor of either house or published in official publications.

2. No Senator or Representative shall, during the time for which he was elected, be appointed to any civil office under the authority of the United States, which shall have been created, or the emoluments whereof shall have been increased during such time; and no person holding any office under the United States shall be a member of either house during his continuance in office.

A person cannot serve as a member of Congress and hold another government office at the same time. A member of Congress also cannot hold any office established by Congress or receive any increased salary for an office that may have been approved during the time that member served in Congress.

Section 7   The Legislative Process

1. All bills for raising revenue shall originate in the House of Representatives; but the Senate may propose or concur with amendments as on other bills.

All money bills must begin in the House. Money bills include two types—tax bills for raising revenues and appropriation bills for spending funds.

2. Every bill which shall have passed the House of Representatives and the Senate shall, before it becomes a law, be presented to the President of the United States; if he approves, he shall sign it, but if not he shall return it, with his objections, to that house in which it shall have originated, who shall enter the objections at large on their journal, and proceed to reconsider it. If after such reconsideration two-thirds of that house shall agree to pass the bill, it shall be sent, together with the objections, to the other house, by which it shall likewise be reconsidered, and if approved by two-thirds of that house, it shall become a law. But in all such cases the votes of both houses shall be determined by yeas and nays, and the names of the persons voting for and against the bill shall be entered on the journal of each house respectively. If any bill shall not be returned by the President within ten days (Sundays excepted) after it shall have been presented to him, the same shall be a law, in like manner as if he had signed it, unless the Congress by their adjournment prevent its return, in which case it shall not be a law.

Paragraph 2 of Section 7 outlines the basic requirements for enacting legislation. These are: (1) bills must be approved in like form by both houses, (2) bills must be submitted to the President for signature, and (3) bills must be approved (signed) by the President. Vetoed bills must be returned to Congress with objections for reconsideration. They can be enacted into law by a two-thirds vote of both houses. Should the President fail to sign a submitted bill within 10 days, it automatically becomes law unless Congress has adjourned. If Congress has adjourned, then the bill fails to become law (pocket veto). Unlike some governors, the President cannot veto certain items in a bill.

3. Every order, resolution, or vote to which the concurrence of the Senate and House of Representatives may be necessary (except on a question of adjournment) shall be presented to the President of the United States; and before the same shall take effect, shall be approved by him, or being disapproved by him, shall be repassed by two-thirds of the Senate and House of Representatives, according to the rules and limitations prescribed in the case of a bill.

The Framers included this paragraph to prevent Congress from passing joint resolutions instead of bills to avoid the possibility of a presidential veto. A bill is a draft of a proposed law, whereas a resolution is a formal expression of opinion or intent on a matter.

Section 8   Legislative Powers

Most of Congress's legislative powers are found in this section.

The Congress shall have the power:

1. To lay and collect taxes, duties, imposts, and excises, to pay the debts and provide for the common defense and general welfare of the United States; but all duties, imposts, and excises shall be uniform throughout the United States;

Congress may tax only for public purposes, and it must exercise its power with respect to all other constitutional provisions. In addition, it can levy a variety of taxes.

Taxes must be uniform—the same rate—throughout the country. That is, the federal excise on tires must be the same in Florida as it is in Illinois.

2. To borrow money on the credit of the United States;

When need arises, Congress can borrow funds. The most common means of borrowing is through the sale of bonds. There is no constitutional limit on the amount Congress can borrow, though Congress has placed a ceiling, which it periodically revises, on the amount the federal government can go into debt. This clause, extended by Clause 18 of this section, is the basis for Congress's power to create a national banking system.

3. To regulate commerce with foreign nations, and among the several states, and with the Indian tribes;

Congress has exclusive power to control foreign and interstate commerce. Like its taxing power, Congress's commerce power has expanded over time and today is quite broad. Congress can exercise control over not only the buying, selling, and transportation of goods, but also the means by which they are traded. And it can use its power to encourage, promote, and protect, as well as to prohibit, restrain, and restrict commerce.

4. To establish a uniform rule of naturalization, and uniform laws on the subject of bankruptcies throughout the United States;

Naturalization is the process by which immigrants become citizens. Uniform rules adopted by Congress include legally being admitted to the United States; age, residency, and education requirements; and an oath of allegiance to the United States to renounce allegiance to any foreign power. Bankruptcy is the process by which debtors are relieved of debt obligations when they cannot pay in full. Bankruptcy is subject to both federal and state regulations.

5. To coin money, regulate the value thereof, and of foreign coin, and fix the standard of weights and measures;

The U.S. monetary system is based on the decimal system, with dollars as the base unit. Congress adopted the English system of weights and measures as a national standard in 1838.

6. To provide for the punishment of counterfeiting the securities and current coin of the United States;

Counterfeiting is punishable by a fine up to $10,000 and/or imprisonment up to 15 years.

7. To establish post offices and post roads;

Since colonial times, the postal service has been a government monopoly. Until 1970, it operated as an executive department. That year Congress established it as an independent agency, headed by an 11-member board of governors.

8. To promote the progress of science and useful arts, by securing for limited times to authors and inventors the exclusive right to their respective writings and discoveries;

The works of authors are protected by copyrights, which today extend for the life of an author plus 50 years. The works of inventors are protected by patents, which vary in length of protection from 3 1/2 to 17 years. Patents are obtainable on process as well as products.

9. To constitute tribunals inferior to the Supreme Court;

This clause gives Congress the power to create the federal court system under the Supreme Court.

10. To define and punish piracies and felonies committed on the high seas, and offenses against the law of nations;

Though piracy was a common practice in colonial times, cases today are quite rare. Congress does have the power, however, to protect American ships on the high seas as well as individuals traveling on American ships.

11. To declare war, grant letters of marque and reprisal, and make rules concerning captures on land and water;

Only Congress can declare war. But the President can, as commander in chief, use the armed forces as much as he chooses. Presidents have used the armed forces abroad without a declaration of war on over 100 occasions. The power to commit troops to battle, however, was limited by the War Powers Act of 1973.

Letters of marque and reprisal, authorizing private parties to attack enemy vessels in time of war, have been forbidden under international law since 1856.

12. To raise and support armies, but no appropriation of money to that use shall be for a longer term than two years;

The restriction of funding was intended to ensure the army would always be subject to civilian control.

13. To provide and maintain a navy;

Rules and procedures for the navy are similar to those for the other armed services.

14. To make rules for the government and regulation of the land and naval forces;

Under this provision, Congress has established the uniform Code of Military Justice.

15. To provide for calling forth the militia to execute the laws of the Union, suppress insurrections, and repel invasions;

Militia refers to the National Guard, the citizen soldiers of each state. It can be called into federal service by either Congress or the President.

16. To provide for organizing, arming, and disciplining the militia, and for governing such

part of them as may be employed in the service of the United States, reserving to the states respectively the appointment of the officers, and the authority of training the militia according to the discipline prescribed by Congress;

When called into federal service, the National Guard is subject to the same rules and regulations that Congress has set for the armed services.

17. To exercise exclusive legislation in all cases whatsoever over such district (not exceeding ten miles square) as may, by cession of particular states, and the acceptance of Congress, become the seat of the government of the United States, and to exercise like authority over all places purchased by the consent of the legislature of the state in which the same shall be, for the erection of forts, magazines, arsenals, dock-yards, and other needful buildings;—and

In order to check state interference and to avoid interstate jealousy, the Framers provided for a national seat of government outside of any state—the District of Columbia.

18. To make all laws which shall be necessary and proper for carrying into execution the foregoing powers, and all other powers vested by this Constitution in the government of the United States, or in any department or office thereof.

This provision is the basis of Congress's implied powers. Any implied power, however, must be related to an expressed power and must be constitutional in all other respects.

Section 9   Powers Denied to Congress

1. The migration or importation of such persons as any of the states now existing shall think proper to admit, shall not be prohibited by the Congress prior to the year one thousand eight hundred and eight, but a tax or duty may be imposed on such importation, not exceeding ten dollars for each person.

This paragraph contains the compromise the Framers reached regarding regulation of the slave trade in exchange for Congress's exclusive control over interstate commerce.

2. The privilege of the writ of habeas corpus shall not be suspended, unless when in cases of rebellion or invasion the public safety may require it.

The writ of habeas corpus is a court order to release or to bring an individual before the court to determine if that person is being legally held in detention. It is intended to prevent persons from being imprisoned for no reason. The writ may be suspended only during wartime. It has rarely been suspended—most significantly during the Civil War and in Hawaii during World War II. The Hawaiian suspension was later held unconstitutional in *Duncan v. Kahanomoku*.

3. No bill of attainder or *ex post facto* law shall be passed.

A bill of attainder is a law that declares an individual or group guilty and provides punishment without a trial. An *ex post facto* law is one which prescribes punishment for an act committed before the law was passed.

4. No capitation, or other direct, tax shall be laid, unless in proportion to the census or enumeration herein before directed to be taken.

A capitation tax is a direct tax imposed on individuals. The income tax, authorized by the Sixteenth Amendment, is the exception to this prohibition.

5. No tax or duty shall be laid on articles exported from any state.

The prohibiting of the taxing of exports was part of the Commerce and Slave Trade Compromise.

6. No preference shall be given by any regulation of commerce or revenue to the ports of one state over those of another; nor shall vessels bound to, or from, one state be obliged to enter, clear, or pay duties in another.

This prohibition prevents Congress from favoring one state or region over another in the regulation of trade.

7. No money shall be drawn from the treasury, but in consequence of appropriations made by law; and a regular statement and account of the receipts and expenditures of all public money shall be published from time to time.

This paragraph ensures legislative control of the nation's purse strings. That is, the executive branch cannot spend money without authorization by Congress.

8. No title of nobility shall be granted by the United States: And no person holding any office of profit or trust under them, shall, without the consent of the Congress, accept of any present, emolument, office, or title, of any kind whatever, from any king, prince, or foreign state.

The prohibitions listed here were intended to prevent creation of a monarchy and the bribery of American officials by foreign powers. Acceptance of a title can be grounds for expatriation, or giving up citizenship.

Section 10   Powers Denied to the States

1. No state shall enter into any treaty, alliance, or confederation; grant letters of marque and reprisal; coin money; emit bills of credit; make any thing but gold and silver coin a tender in payment of debts; pass any bill of attainder; *ex post facto* law, or law impairing the obligation of contracts, or grant any title of nobility.

The powers listed here belong solely to the federal government or are denied to both it and the states. The restrictions on the states were designed, in part, to prevent an overlapping in functions and authority with the federal government that could create conflict and chaos.

2. No state shall, without the consent of the Congress, lay any imposts or duties on imports or exports, except what may be absolutely necessary for executing its inspection laws; and the net produce of all duties and imposts, laid by any state on imports and exports, shall be for the use of the treasury of the United States; and all such laws shall be subject to the revision and control of the Congress.

If states were permitted to tax imports and exports, they could use their taxing power in a way to weaken or destroy Congress's power to control interstate and foreign commerce. Furthermore, the power to tax could result in conditions similar to those under the Articles of Confederation.

3. No state shall, without the consent of Congress, lay any duty of tonnage, keep troops, or ships of war in time of peace, enter into any agreement or compact with another state, or with a foreign power, or engage in war, unless actually invaded, or in such imminent danger as will not admit of delay.

There are exceptions to some of the prohibitions listed here. For example, states can maintain a militia. But a militia's use is limited to internal disorders that arise within a state unless the militia is called into federal service. States can enter into interstate compacts regarding problems that require joint or regional action. But these compacts require the approval of Congress.

Article II   Executive Branch

Section 1   President and Vice-President

1. The executive power shall be vested in a President of the United States of America. He shall hold his office during the term of four years, and, together with the Vice-President, chosen for the same term, be elected, as follows:

Though the Constitution confers certain powers and duties on the President, growth of presidential power has come from two sources — (1) conferred by an act of Congress, and (2) concluded by the President as the result of actions taken as chief administrator, chief executive, chief diplomat, or commander in chief.

Until the Twenty-second Amendment, there was no constitutional restriction on the number of terms a President could serve.

2. Each state shall appoint, in such manner as the legislature thereof may direct, a number of electors, equal to the whole number of Senators and Representatives to which the state may be entitled in the Congress; but no Senator or Representative, or person holding an office of trust or profit under the United States, shall be appointed an elector.

The number of presidential electors is determined by a state's representation (Senators and Representatives) in Congress. No member of Congress or federal officer may be an elector.

3. The electors shall meet in their respective states, and vote by ballot for two persons, of whom one at least shall not be an inhabitant of the same state with themselves. And they shall make a list of all the persons voted for, and of the number of votes for each; which list they shall sign and certify, and transmit sealed to the seat of the government of the United States, directed to the President of the Senate. The President of the Senate shall, in the presence of the Senate and House of Representatives, open all the certificates, and the votes shall then be counted. The person having the greatest number of votes shall be the President, if such number be a majority of the whole number of electors appointed; and if there be more than one who have such majority, and have an equal number of votes, then the House of Representatives shall immediately choose by ballot one of them for President; and if no person have a majority, then from the five highest on the list the said house shall in like manner choose the President. But in choosing the President, the votes shall be taken by states, the representation from each state having one vote; a quorum for this purpose shall consist of a member or members from two-thirds of the states, and a majority of all the states shall be necessary to a choice. In every case, after the choice of the President, the person having the greatest number of votes of the electors shall be the Vice-President. But if there should remain two or more who have equal votes, the Senate shall choose from them by ballot the Vice-President.

Coupled with the previous paragraph, Paragraph 3 outlines the original method of selecting the President and Vice-President. It has been replaced by the method outlined in the Twelfth

Amendment. It should be noted, however, that there has been considerable change in the machinery created by the Founders. For example, they did not foresee the rise of political parties, the development of primaries and conventions, or the broadening of democracy whereby the presidential electors would be elected by the people rather than chosen by state legislatures.

4. **The Congress may determine the time of choosing the electors, and the day on which they shall give their votes; which day shall be the same throughout the United States.**

In 1845, Congress set the first Tuesday after the first Monday in November of every fourth year (leap year) as the general election date for selecting presidential electors.

5. **No person except a natural-born citizen, or a citizen of the United States, at the time of the adoption of this Constitution, shall be eligible to the office of President; neither shall any person be eligible to that office who shall not have attained to the age of thirty-five years, and been fourteen years a resident within the United States.**

This paragraph provides the only constitutional qualifications to be President. Though not expressly stated, the qualifications to be Vice-President are the same, since the Vice-President could succeed to the office of President.

6. **In case of the removal of the President from office, or of his death, resignation, or inability to discharge the powers and duties of the said office, the same shall devolve on the Vice-President, and the Congress may by law provide for the case of removal, death, resignation, or inability, both of the President and Vice-President, declaring what officer shall then act as President, and such officer shall act accordingly, until the disability be removed, or a President shall be elected.**

Until the adoption of the Twenty-fifth Amendment, which expressly provides for the Vice-President to succeed to the presidency, succession was based on a precedent set by John Tyler in 1841. In 1947 Congress provided for an official line of succession in cases when there is no Vice-President to qualify.

7. **The President shall, at stated times, receive for his services a compensation, which shall neither be increased nor diminished during the period for which he shall have been elected, and he shall not receive within that period any other**

emolument from the United States, or any of them.

Originally, the President's salary was $25,000 per year. The President's current salary of $200,000 plus a $50,000 taxable expense account per year was enacted in 1969. The President also receives numerous fringe benefits including a $120,000 nontaxable allowance for travel and entertainment, and living accommodations in two residences, the White House and Camp David.

8. **Before he enter on the execution of his office, he shall take the following oath or affirmation:— "I do solemnly swear (or affirm) that I will faithfully execute the office of President of the United States, and will, to the best of my ability, preserve, protect, and defend the Constitution of the United States."**

The oath of office is generally administered by the chief justice, but can be administered by any official authorized to administer oaths. All Presidents-elect except Washington have been sworn into office by the chief justice. Only Vice-Presidents John Tyler, Calvin Coolidge, and Lyndon Johnson in succeeding to the office have been sworn in by someone else.

Section 2 Powers of the President

The President's powers can loosely be categorized under executive, legislative, diplomatic, military, and judicial.

1. **The President shall be Commander in Chief of the army and navy of the United States, and of the militia of the several states, when called into the actual service of the United States; he may require the opinion, in writing, of the principal officer in each of the executive departments, upon any subject relating to the duties of their respective offices, and he shall have power to grant reprieves and pardons for offenses against the United States, except in cases of impeachment.**

Though the President is not an active field commander, all military personnel are subordinate to the President. This provision ensures civilian control over the military.

The provision that the President "may require the opinion. . ." is the constitutional base for the Cabinet.

Like his other powers, the President's judicial powers are limited. Presidential clemency is limited to those accused or convicted of federal crimes.

2. He shall have power, by and with the advice and consent of the Senate, to make treaties, provided two-thirds of the Senators present concur; and he shall nominate, and by and with the advice and consent of the Senate, shall appoint ambassadors, other public ministers and consuls, judges of the Supreme Court, and all other officers of the United States, whose appointments are not herein otherwise provided for, and which shall be established by law; but the Congress may by law vest the appointment of such inferior officers, as they think proper, in the President alone, in the courts of law, or in the heads of departments.

The President is the chief architect of American foreign policy. He or she is responsible for the conduct of foreign relations, or dealings with other countries. All treaties, however, require approval of two-thirds of the Senators present.

Most federal positions today are filled under the rules and regulations of the civil service system. Most presidential appointees serve at the pleasure of the President. Removal of an official by the President is not subject to congressional approval. But the power can be restricted by conditions set in creating the office.

3. The President shall have power to fill up all vacancies that may happen during the recess of the Senate, by granting commissions which shall expire at the end of their next session.

Presidential appointments requiring Senate approval are made on a temporary basis if the Senate is in recess.

Section 3 Duties of the President
He shall from time to time give to Congress information of the state of the Union, and recommend to their consideration such measures as he shall judge necessary and expedient; he may, on extraordinary occasions, convene both houses, or either of them, and in case of disagreement between them with respect to the time of adjournment, he may adjourn them to such time as he shall think proper; he shall receive ambassadors and other public ministers; he shall take care that the laws be faithfully executed, and shall commission all the officers of the United States.

Today the President is the chief designer of the nation's major legislative programs. Presidential recommendations are put forth in the State of the Union Address, the federal budget, and special messages dealing with specific proposals.

The provision to "receive ambassadors . . ." is the constitutional basis of the President's power to extend and to withdraw diplomatic recognition of a foreign government.

All military commissions, that is, appointments as officers in the armed forces, require presidential authorization and congressional approval.

Section 4 Impeachment
The President, Vice-President and all civil officers of the United States, shall be removed from office on impeachment for, and conviction of, treason, bribery, or other high crimes and misdemeanors.

Presidential appointees can be removed by the impeachment process as well as being asked to resign by the President.

Article III Judicial Branch

Section 1 United States Courts
The judicial power of the United States shall be vested in one Supreme Court, and in such inferior courts as the Congress may from time to time ordain and establish. The judges, both of the Supreme and inferior courts, shall hold their offices during good behavior, and shall, at stated times, receive for their services, a compensation, which shall not be diminished during their continuance in office.

Section 1 creates a national judiciary. Congress established the national court system in 1789. Today there are 11 judicial circuits, with a court of appeals in each, and 98 judicial districts. At least one district with a district court is found in every state. Congress has also designed other constitutional courts.

Federal judges are appointed by the President with Senate approval and nearly all hold office during good behavior for life. Originally, judges' salaries were $3500 ($4000 for the chief justice). In 1995, Supreme Court justices were paid $164,100 (the chief justice $171,500); Court of Appeals judges $141,700; and District Court judges $133,600.

Section 2 Jurisdiction
1. The judicial power shall extend to all cases, in law and equity, arising under this Constitution, the laws of the United States, and treaties made, or which shall be made, under their authority;—to all cases affecting ambassadors, other public

ministers, and consuls;—to all cases of admiralty and maritime jurisdiction;—to controversies to which the United States shall be a party;—to controversies between two or more states;—between a state and citizens of another state;—between citizens of different states—between citizens of the same state claiming lands under grants of different states; and between a state, or the citizens thereof; and foreign states, citizens or subjects.

Jurisdiction is the right of a court to try a case. Federal courts have jurisdiction over a case because of its subject matter or the parties involved. Since the adoption of the Eleventh Amendment, however, a state cannot be sued in federal court by a resident of another state or a citizen of a foreign country.

2. In all cases affecting ambassadors, other public ministers and consuls, and those in which a state shall be party, the Supreme Court shall have original jurisdiction. In all other cases before mentioned, the Supreme Court shall have appellate jurisdiction, both as to law and fact, with such exceptions, and under such regulations as the Congress shall make.

The Supreme Court has both original and appellate jurisdiction. However, the vast majority of cases the Supreme Court hears are on appeal. Its decisions are by majority opinion.

3. The trial of all crimes, except in cases of impeachment, shall be by jury; and such trial shall be held in the state where the said crimes shall have been committed; but when not committed within any state, the trial shall be at such place or places as the Congress may by law have directed.

All persons accused of committing a crime for which they can be tried in federal court are guaranteed the right of trial by jury in a federal court in the state where the crime takes place.

Section 3   Treason

1. Treason against the United States shall consist only in levying war against them, or in adhering to their enemies, giving them aid and comfort. No person shall be convicted of treason unless on the testimony of two witnesses to the same overt act, or on confession in open court.

Treason is the only crime specifically defined in the Constitution. This is to prevent its use against persons who criticize the government. Treason can only be committed during war. The charge

can be levied against American citizens, at home or abroad, and resident aliens.

2. The Congress shall have power to declare the punishment of treason, but no attainder of treason shall work corruption of blood, or forfeiture except during the life of the person attained.

The families or descendants of a person convicted of treason cannot be punished for the actions of the traitor. Although death is the maximum punishment, no person convicted of treason has ever been executed by the United States.

Article IV   Relations Among the States

Section 1   Official Acts

Full faith and credit shall be given in each state to public acts, records, and judicial proceedings of every other state. And the Congress may by general laws prescribe the manner in which such acts, records, and proceedings shall be proved, and the effect thereof.

States must honor the laws, records, and court decisions of other states. Regarding judicial proceedings, there are two exceptions. (1) One state does not have to enforce another state's criminal code, and (2) one state does not have to recognize another state's grant of a divorce if legitimate residence was not established by the person obtaining the divorce.

Section 2   Privileges of Citizens

1. The citizens of each state shall be entitled to all privileges and immunities of citizens in the several states.

In other words, a resident of one state may not be discriminated against unreasonably by another state.

2. A person charged in any state with treason, felony, or other crime, who shall flee from justice, and be found in another state shall, on demand of the executive authority of the state from which he fled, be delivered up, to be removed to the state having jurisdiction of the crime.

The process of returning a fugitive to the state where a crime has been committed is known as extradition. Most requests are routinely processed, but the Constitution does not absolutely require that a fugitive be surrendered. A governor can refuse to honor the request for extradition if it will result in an injustice to the fugitive.

3. No person held to service or labor in one state, under the laws thereof, escaping into another, shall in consequence of any law or regulation therein, be discharged from such service or labor, but shall be delivered up on claim of the party to whom such service or labor may be due.

This provision applied to fugitive slaves. It was cancelled by the Thirteenth Amendment.

Section 3   New States and Territories

1. New states may be admitted by the Congress into this Union; but no new state shall be formed by the junction of two or more states, or parts of states, without the consent of the legislatures of the states concerned as well as of the Congress.

Only Congress can admit states to the Union. New states are admitted on the basis of equality with older states. The general process is outlined by the Northwest Ordinance of 1787.

Though a new state cannot be carved out of an existing state without its consent, there has been one unusual exception. West Virginia was admitted in 1863 after Virginia had seceded from the Union, and Congress held that the 40 counties of western Virginia that remained loyal to the Union constituted a "legal" government.

Texas provides another interesting case. It was the only state that was an independent republic at the time of its admission and the only state admitted by joint resolution rather than by an act of Congress. In addition, by terms of its admission, Texas could subdivide itself into five states, if it so chooses.

2. The Congress shall have power to dispose of and make all needful rules and regulations respecting the territory or other property belonging to the United States; and nothing in this Constitution shall be so construed as to prejudice any claims of the United States, or of any particular state.

Congress has the power to control all property belonging to the United States. It can set up governments for territories, establish national parks and forests, authorize reclamation projects, and exercise eminent domain (taking of private property for public use through condemnation).

Section 4   Protection of the States

The United States shall guarantee to every state in this Union a republican form of government, and shall protect each of them against invasion; and on application of the legislature, or of the executive (when the legislature cannot be convened) against domestic violence.

Though the Constitution does not define "republican form of government," the Supreme Court has held it to mean one in which the people choose their own representatives to run the government and make the laws in accord with delegated power.

The federal government can use whatever means are necessary to prevent foreign invasion and to put down domestic violence.

Article V   Amendments

The Congress, whenever two-thirds of both houses shall deem it necessary, shall propose amendments to this Constitution, or, on the application of the legislatures of two-thirds of the several states, shall call a convention for proposing amendments, which, in either case, shall be valid to all intents and purposes, as part of this Constitution, when ratified by the legislatures of three-fourths of the several states, or by conventions in three-fourths thereof, as the one or the other mode of ratification may be proposed by the Congress; provided that no amendment which may be made prior to the year one thousand eight hundred and eight shall in any manner affect the first and fourth clauses in the ninth section of the first article; and that no state, without its consent, shall be deprived of its equal suffrage in the Senate.

This article sets up the methods for amending the Constitution—two of proposal and two of ratification. To date, all amendments have been proposed by Congress, and only the Twenty-first has been ratified by convention instead of by state legislatures. There is one prohibition against change—that is, no state can be denied its equal representation in the Senate.

Article VI   General Provisions

1. All debts contracted and engagements entered into, before the adoption of this Constitution, shall be as valid against the United States under this Constitution, as under the Confederation.

This provision assured the nation's creditors that the new federal government would assume the existing financial obligations of the country.

2. This Constitution, and the laws of the United States which shall be made in pursuance thereof; and all treaties made, or which shall be made, under the authority of the United States, shall be the supreme law of the land; and the judges in every state shall be bound thereby, anything in the Constitution or laws of any state to the contrary notwithstanding.

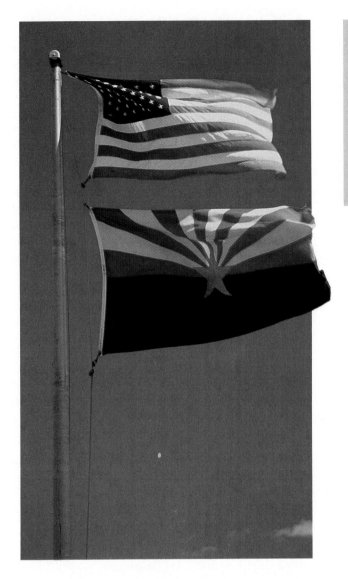

This is known as the ''Supremacy Clause'' and guarantees the federal law will take priority over state law in cases of conflict. To be valid, however, any law must be constitutional.

3. The Senators and Representatives before mentioned, and the members of the several state legislatures, and all executive and judicial officers, both of the United States and of the several states, shall be bound by oath or affirmation to support this Constitution; but no religious test shall ever be required as a qualification to any office or public trust under the United States.

Almost all government officials must affirm or take an oath to uphold the Constitution. No religious qualification can be set as a requirement for holding public office.

Article VII   Ratification

The ratification of the conventions of nine states shall be sufficient for the establishment of this Constitution between the states so ratifying the same.

To become operable, nine states were required to ratify. Delaware was first and New Hampshire ninth, but not until Virginia (10th) and New York (11th) ratified was the Constitution assured of going into effect.

Done in convention by the unanimous consent of the states present the seventeenth day of September in the year of our Lord one thousand seven hundred and eighty-seven, and of the independence of the United States of America the twelfth. In witness whereof we have hereunto subscribed our names.

Of the 55 delegates who attended the Constitutional Convention, only 38 signed the document. The 39th signature—that of John Dickinson—was written by George Read at Dickinson's request. Elbridge Gerry of Massachusetts and Edmund Randolph and George Mason of Virginia refused to sign. Thirteen delegates left the convention prior to its end. Rhode Island sent no delegates to the convention.

George Washington, **President and Deputy for Virginia**

New Hampshire
John Langdon
Nicholas Gilman

Massachusetts
Nathaniel Gorham
Rufus King

Connecticut
William Samuel
* Johnson*
Roger Sherman

New York
Alexander Hamilton

New Jersey
William Livingston
David Brearley
William Paterson
Jonathan Dayton

Pennsylvania
Benjamin Franklin
Thomas Mifflin
Robert Morris
George Clymer

Thomas FitzSimons
Jared Ingersoll
James Wilson
Gouverneur Morris

Delaware
George Read
Gunning Bedford, Jr.
John Dickinson
Richard Bassett
Jacob Broom

Maryland
James McHenry
Daniel of St. Thomas
* Jenifer*
Daniel Carroll

Virginia
John Blair
James Madison, Jr.

North Carolina
William Blount
Richard Dobbs
* Spaight*

Hugh Williamson

South Carolina
John Rutledge
Charles Cotesworth
* Pinckney*

Charles Pinckney
Pierce Butler

Georgia
William Few
Abraham Baldwin

Attest: *William Jackson,* **Secretary**

Amendments

The first ten amendments are known as the Bill of Rights. They were proposed by Congress during its first session and were adopted in 1791. Originally, the prohibitions limited only the federal government. But many of the guarantees have been extended against state action by the ''Due Process'' clause of the Fourteenth Amendment.

Amendment 1   Freedoms of Expression
Congress shall make no law respecting an establishment of religion, or prohibiting the free exercise thereof; or abridging the freedom of speech, or of the press; or the right of the people peaceably to assemble, and to petition the govern-

The First Amendment protects five basic civil liberties—freedom of religion, of speech, and of the press and the rights to assemble peacefully and to petition for redress of grievances. Like all civil rights, however, these liberties are not absolute; they must be exercised in a manner relative to the rights of others.

Amendment 2   Right to Keep Arms
A well-regulated militia being necessary to the security of a free state, the right of the people to keep and bear arms shall not be infringed.

The right to keep and bear arms is not free from government restriction. The federal government and the states can and do regulate the possession and use of firearms, such as requiring the licensing of guns and prohibiting the carrying of concealed weapons.

Amendment 3   Quartering of Troops
No soldier shall, in time of peace, be quartered in any house, without the consent of the owner, nor in time of war, but in a manner to be prescribed by law.

Like the Second Amendment, this amendment was designed to prevent what had been common practice by the British during the colonial period. It is of little importance today, even though Congress could authorize the boarding of troops in private homes during wartime.

Amendment 4　Searches and Seizures

The right of the people to be secure in their persons, houses, papers, and effects, against unreasonable searches and seizures, shall not be violated, and no warrants shall issue, but upon probable cause, supported by oath or affirmation, and particularly describing the place to be searched, and the persons or things to be seized.

This amendment prohibits unreasonable searches and seizures. Similar to the Second and Third Amendments, it was designed to prevent actions similar to British colonial practices in the years preceding the American Revolution.

Searches and seizures authorized by court warrants are permissible. To be proper, a warrant must be issued by a judge, there must be good reason for its use, and it must describe in specific terms the place to be searched and the person or thing to be seized. Evidence secured by an improper search and seizure is inadmissible in any court. Also, the police do not need a warrant for a search and seizure if they are a witness to a crime or are in pursuit of a criminal. Nor do they need one to search a movable object, such as a car, since it could vanish while a warrant is sought.

Amendment 5　Rights of the Accused

No person shall be held to answer for a capital, or otherwise infamous crime, unless on a presentment or indictment of a grand jury, except in cases arising in the land or naval forces, or in the militia, when in actual service in time of war or public danger; nor shall any person be subject for the same offense to be twice put in jeopardy of life or limb; nor shall be compelled in any criminal case to be a witness against himself, nor be deprived of life, liberty, or property, without due process of law; nor shall private property be taken for public use, without just compensation.

The Fifth Amendment protects the legal rights of people in criminal proceedings. No person may be brought to trial for a felony without first being charged with a specific crime by either a presentment or indictment of a grand jury.

No person may be tried for the same crime twice. But there are exceptions to the prohibition against double jeopardy. For example, if a person commits an act that violates both federal and state law, that person can be tried for that crime in both federal and state courts.

Persons may not be forced to give testimony against themselves. However, the prohibition against self-incrimination does not bar voluntarily testifying against one's self. The protection applies to any proceedings where testimony is required, including congressional hearings.

Due process involves the "how" and "what" of government action. Thus, there are two forms. In procedural due process, the government must act fairly in its relations with people. In substantive due process, it must proceed under fair laws in its dealings with people.

Government cannot take private property for public use without payment of a fair market price.

Amendment 6　Criminal Proceedings

In all criminal prosecutions, the accused shall enjoy the right to a speedy and public trial, by an impartial jury of the state and district wherein the crime shall have been committed, which district shall have been previously ascertained by law, and to be informed of the nature and cause of the accusation; to be confronted with the witnesses against him; to have compulsory process for obtaining witnesses in his favor, and to have the assistance of counsel for his defense.

The Sixth Amendment protects the procedural rights of people in criminal proceedings.

The right to a speedy and public trial was provided to prevent a person from languishing in jail or being tried by a secret tribunal. But a trial must not be so speedy as to prevent time for preparing an adequate defense nor so public that the trial is not fair.

A person must be informed of the charges for an arrest. After being arrested, an accused is brought before a judge for arraignment, a determination if formal charges by a grand jury will be sought.

The right to confront witnesses guarantees an accused the right to cross-examination. A witness can be compelled to testify by means of a subpoena.

Though a person can act as his or her own counsel, all persons accused of a crime are entitled to counsel. If a person cannot afford counsel, the government must provide one. The right to counsel includes during questioning by police as well as during trial.

Amendment 7　Jury Trial in Civil Cases

In suits at common law, where the value in controversy shall exceed twenty dollars, the right of trial by jury shall be preserved, and no fact tried by a jury shall be otherwise re-examined in any court of the United States than according to the rules of common law.

This amendment deals with certain guarantees in civil law in federal courts. Civil suits involve disputes between individuals or groups. The government may or may not be a party in a civil suit. If the value in controversy exceeds $20 in a civil case, the right of trial by jury is guaranteed. Most states also guarantee jury trial in civil cases in which the controversy exceeds $200.

Amendment 8   Excessive Punishments

Excessive bail shall not be required, nor excessive fines imposed, nor cruel and unusual punishments inflicted.

Bail is set by the court at the time of arraignment. Failure to appear for trial is grounds for forfeiting the bail to the government. Bail can be, and often is, denied for those accused of capital offenses such as murder.

For it to be unconstitutional, a punishment must be both cruel and unusual. Like bails and fines, a punishment must not be unreasonably severe in relation to the crime. Rarely have bails, fines, and punishments been contested as violating the Eighth Amendment, since most are imposed in accordance with what is prescribed by law.

Amendment 9   Unenumerated Rights of the People

The enumeration in the Constitution of certain rights shall not be construed to deny or disparage others retained by the people.

All the rights of the people have not necessarily been listed in the Constitution. This amendment protects these unenumerated rights.

Amendment 10   Reserved Powers

The powers not delegated to the United States by the Constitution, nor prohibited by it to the states, are reserved to the states respectively, or to the people.

The Tenth Amendment safeguards the reserved powers of the states. But with the adoption of the Fourteenth Amendment, a state's reserved powers, particularly its police powers, are subject to closer scrutiny.

Amendment 11   Suits Against States

The judicial power of the United States shall not be construed to extend to any suit in law or equity, commenced or prosecuted against one of the United States by citizens of another state, or by citizens or subjects of any foreign state.

Under Article III, Section 2, the clause ''between a state and citizens of another state'' was interpreted to mean not only that a state could sue citizens of another state, but that citizens of another state could sue a state. The states objected because they viewed this concept as weakening state sovereignty and they refused to be sued in federal courts. In 1793, in *Chisholm v. Georgia*, the Supreme Court ruled that such suits could be brought. Immediate agitation against the ruling led to the adoption of the Eleventh Amendment in 1798. According to the amendment, citizens of another state or of a foreign country must sue a state in its courts in accordance with its law.

Amendment 12   Election of President and Vice-President

The electors shall meet in their respective states and vote by ballot for President and Vice-President, one of whom, at least, shall not be an inhabitant of the same state with themselves; they shall name in their ballots the person voted for as President, and in distinct ballots the person voted for as Vice-President, and they shall make distinct lists of all persons voted for as President, and of all persons voted for as Vice-President, and of the number of votes for each, which lists they shall sign and certify, and transmit sealed to the seat of the government of the United States, directed to the President of the Senate;—the President of the Senate shall, in the presence of the Senate and House of Representatives, open all the certificates and the votes shall then be counted;—the person having the greatest number of votes for President, shall be the President, if such number be a majority of the whole number of electors appointed; and if no person have such majority, then from the persons having the highest numbers not exceeding three on the list of those voted for as President, the House of Representatives shall choose immediately, by ballot, the President. But in choosing the President, the votes shall be taken by states, the representation from each state having one vote; a quorum for this purpose shall consist of a member or members from two-thirds of the states, and a majority of all the states shall be necessary to a choice. And if the House of Representatives shall not choose a President whenever the right of choice shall devolve upon them, before the fourth day of March next following, then the Vice-President shall act as President, as in the case of the death or other constitutional disability of the President.—The person having the greatest number of votes as Vice-President, shall be the Vice-President, if such number be a majority of the whole number of electors appointed, and if no person have a majority, then from the two highest numbers on the list, the Senate shall choose the Vice-President; a quorum for the purpose shall consist of two-thirds of the whole number of senators, and a majority of the whole number shall be necessary to a choice. But no person constitutionally ineligible to the office of President shall be eligible to that of Vice-President of the United States.

Adopted in 1804, the Twelfth Amendment changes the procedure for electing the President and Vice-President as outlined in Article II, Section 1, Paragraph 3.

To prevent the recurrence of the election of 1800 whereby a candidate running for Vice-President (Aaron Burr) could tie a candidate running for President (Thomas Jefferson) and thus force the election into the House of Representatives, the Twelfth Amendment specifies that the electors are to cast separate ballots for each office. Other changes include: (1) a candidate must receive a majority of the electoral votes cast rather than votes from a majority of the electors, (2) a reduction from five to the three highest candidates receiving votes among whom the House is to choose if no candidate receives a majority of the electoral votes, and (3) provision for the Senate to choose the Vice-President from the two highest candidates if neither has received a majority of the electoral votes.

The Twelfth Amendment does place one restriction on electors. It prohibits electors from voting for two candidates (President and Vice-President) from their home state.

Amendment 13   Slavery

Section 1. Neither slavery nor involuntary servitude, except as a punishment for crime whereof the party shall have been duly convicted, shall exist within the United States, or any place subject to their jurisdiction.

Section 2. Congress shall have power to enforce this article by appropriate legislation.

Adopted in 1865, the Thirteenth Amendment ended slavery in the United States. It also prohibits the binding of a person to perform a personal service due to debt. Not all involuntary servitude, or forced labor, is prohibited, however. In addition to imprisonment for crime, the Supreme Court has held that the draft is not a violation of the amendment.

This amendment is the first adopted to be divided into sections. It is also the first to contain specifically a provision granting Congress power to enforce it by appropriate legislation.

Amendment 14   Rights of Citizens

Section 1. All persons born or naturalized in the United States, and subject to the jurisdiction thereof, are citizens of the United States and of the state wherein they reside. No state shall make or enforce any law which shall abridge the privileges or immunities of citizens of the United States; nor shall any state deprive any person of life, liberty, or property, without due process of law, nor deny to any person within its jurisdiction the equal protection of the laws.

Section 2. Representatives shall be apportioned among the several states according to their respective numbers, counting the whole number of persons in each state, excluding Indians not taxed. But when the right to vote at any election for the choice of electors for President and Vice-President of the United States, representatives in Congress, the executive or judicial officers of a state, or the members of the legislature thereof, is denied to any of the male inhabitants of such state, being twenty-one years of age, and citizens of the United States, or in any way abridged, except for participation in rebellion, or other crime, the basis of representation therein shall be reduced in the proportion which the number of such male citizens

shall bear to the whole number of male citizens twenty-one years of age in such state.

Section 3. No person shall be a Senator or Representative in Congress, or elector of President or Vice-President, or hold any office, civil or military, under the United States, or under any state, who, having previously taken an oath, as a member of Congress, or as an officer of the United States, or as a member of any state legislature, or as an executive or judicial officer of any state, to support the Constitution of the United States, shall have engaged in insurrection or rebellion against the same, or given aid or comfort to the enemies thereof. But Congress may by a vote of two-thirds of each house, remove such disability.

Section 4. The validity of the public debt of the United States, authorized by law, including debts incurred for payment of pensions and bounties for services in suppressing insurrection or rebellion, shall not be questioned. But neither the United States nor any state shall assume or pay any debt or obligation incurred in aid of insurrection or rebellion against the United States, or any claim for the loss or emancipation of any slave; but all such debts, obligations and claims shall be held illegal and void.

Section 5. The Congress shall have power to enforce, by appropriate legislation, the provisions of this article.

Adopted in 1868, the Fourteenth Amendment is one of the most important. It is the basis for numerous Supreme Court decisions, particularly relating to civil rights.

Until its adoption, the Constitution contained no definition of citizen, despite the fact that ''citizens'' are mentioned in numerous provisions. In addition to defining citizenship and extending it to blacks, Section 1 prohibits states from denying privileges and immunities of citizenship to any

citizen. The guarantee of due process was intended to prevent states from denying blacks their civil rights. The guarantee of equal protection of the laws prohibits states from making unreasonable distinctions between different groups of people in laws or executive actions.

Section 2 abolishes the three-fifths compromise as worded in Article III, Section 2, Paragraph 3. It was meant to force the Southern states to allow blacks to vote or have their representation proportionately reduced in the House of Representatives.

Section 3 was aimed at punishing the leaders of the Confederacy. By 1872, most were permitted to return to political life, and in 1898, amnesty was granted to all still living.

Section 4 also dealt with matters related to the Civil War. It validated the debt of the United States, prohibited assumption of any of the Confederate debt, and prohibited payment for any loss resulting from freeing of the slaves.

Amendment 15 Black Suffrage

Section 1. The right of citizens of the United States to vote shall not be denied or abridged by the United States or by any state on account of race, color, or previous condition of servitude.

Section 2.The Congress shall have power to enforce this article by appropriate legislation.

Adopted in 1870, the Fifteenth Amendment replaced Amendment 14, Section 2 in guaranteeing blacks the right to vote, that is, the right of blacks to vote was not to be left to the states. It denies to Congress or to any state the power to deny anyone the right to vote because of race, color, or previous condition of servitude. Yet, despite this prohibition, blacks were denied the right to vote by many states by such means as poll taxes, literacy tests, and white primaries. Not until the 1960s did Congress take firm action to enforce the guarantee of this amendment.

Amendment 16 Income Tax

The Congress shall have power to lay and collect taxes on incomes, from whatever source derived, without apportionment among the several states, and without regard to any census or enumeration.

Adopted in 1913, the Sixteenth Amendment provided an exception to the restrictions placed on direct taxation by Article II, Section 2, Paragraph 3 and Section 9, Paragraph 4. Like the Eleventh Amendment, it was adopted to reverse a Supreme Court ruling. Although there had been a temporary income tax during the Civil War, the tax's constitutionality was not tested until it was reinstated by the Wilson-Gorman Tariff Act of 1894. The Court held that it was unconstitutional since it was a direct tax imposed without apportionment or regard to enumeration in *Pollock v. Farmer Loan and Trust Company*. A great period of national growth at the turn of the twentieth century, however, prompted Congress to propose a way to pay for the tremendous growth in government expenses.

Amendment 17   Election of Senators

Section 1. The Senate of the United States shall be composed of two senators from each state, elected by the people thereof, for six years; and each senator shall have one vote. The electors in each state shall have the qualifications requisite for electors of the most numerous branch of the state legislatures.

Section 2. When vacancies happen in the representation of any state in the Senate, the executive authority of such state shall issue writs of election to fill such vacancies: Provided, that the legislature of any state may empower the executive thereof to make temporary appointments until the people fill the vacancies by election as the legislature may direct.

Section 3. This amendment shall not be so construed as to affect the election or term of any Senator chosen before it becomes valid as part of the Constitution.

Adopted in 1913, the Seventeenth Amendment provided for the direct election of Senators by the people and replaced their method of selection as outlined by Article I, Section 3, Paragraphs 2 and 3.

The governor of a state can fill a vacancy by calling a special election or, if authorized by the state legislature, by making a temporary appointment until the next general election.

Amendment 18   National Prohibition

Section 1. After one year from the ratification of this article the manufacture, sale, or transportation of intoxicating liquors within, the importation thereof into, or the exportation thereof from the United States and all territory subject to the jurisdiction thereof for beverage purposes is hereby prohibited.

Section 2. The Congress and the several states shall have concurrent power to enforce this article by appropriate legislation.

Section 3. This article shall be inoperative unless it shall have been ratified as an amendment to the Constitution by the legislatures of the several states, as provided in the Constitution, within seven years from the date of the submission hereof to the states by the Congress.

Adopted in 1919, the Eighteenth Amendment prohibited the manufacture, sale, and transportation of alcoholic beverages throughout the United States. This amendment was the first to specify the method of ratifying and to set a time limit on ratification. It also was the first to provide for enforcement by both Congress and the states.

Amendment 19   Women's Suffrage

Section 1. The right of citizens of the United States to vote shall not be denied or abridged by the United States or by any state on account of sex.

Section 2. Congress shall have power to enforce this article by appropriate legislation.

Adopted in 1920, the Nineteenth Amendment established the right of women to vote on a nationwide basis and indirectly established the right of women to hold public office. Prior to its adoption, some western states did allow women to vote. Wyoming (in 1869) was the first.

Amendment 20   Change of Terms, Sessions, and Inauguration

Section 1. The terms of the President and Vice-President shall end at noon on the 20th day of January, and the terms of Senators and Representatives at noon on the 3rd day of January, of the years in which such terms would have ended if

this article had not been ratified; and the terms of their successors shall then begin.

Section 2. The Congress shall assemble at least once in every year, and such meeting shall begin at noon on the 3rd day of January, unless they shall by law appoint a different day.

Section 3. If, at the time fixed for the beginning of the term of the President, the President-elect shall have died, the Vice-President-elect shall become President. If a President shall not have been chosen before the time fixed for the beginning of his term, or if the President-elect shall have failed to qualify, then the Vice-President-elect shall act as President until a President shall have qualified; and the Congress may by law provide for the case wherein neither a President-elect nor a Vice-President-elect shall have qualified, declaring who shall then act as President, or the manner in which one who is to act shall be selected, and such person shall act accordingly until a President or Vice-President shall have qualified.

Section 4. The Congress may by law provide for the case of the death of any of the persons from whom the House of Representatives may choose a President whenever the right of choice shall have devolved upon them, and for the case of the death of any of the persons from whom the Senate may choose a Vice-President whenever the right of choice shall have devolved upon them.

Section 5. Sections 1 and 2 shall take effect on the 15th day of October following the ratification of this article.

Section 6. This article shall be inoperative unless it shall have been ratified as an amendment to the Constitution by the legislatures of three-fourths of the several states within seven years from the date of its submission.

Adopted in 1933, the Twentieth Amendment changed the start of congressional terms (from March 4 to January 3) and presidential and vice-presidential terms (from March 4 to January 20) following general elections.

It is known as the ''Lame Duck'' amendment because it shortened the time between the general election and the date newly elected officials took office and eliminated ''lame ducks'' (defeated Representatives and Senators) from continuing to serve in Congress for four months during a new session that previously began in December.

The amendment also provides for presidential succession in case of death or disability of a President-elect.

Amendment 21 Repeal of National Prohibition

Section 1. The eighteenth article of amendment to the Constitution of the United States is hereby repealed.

Section 2. The transportation or importation into any state, territory, or possession of the United States for delivery or use therein of intoxicating liquors, in violation of the laws thereof, is hereby prohibited.

Section 3. This article shall be inoperative unless it shall have been ratified as an amendment to the Constitution by conventions in the several states, as provided in the Constitution, within seven years from the date of the submission hereof to the states by the Congress.

Adopted in 1933, the Twenty-first Amendment repealed national prohibition established by the Eighteenth Amendment. It is the only amendment that has repealed a prior amendment. And it repealed national prohibition but not all prohibition. States still maintain their power to prohibit the manufacture and sale of alcoholic beverages. Note also that the transportation of liquor into a ''dry'' state is a federal crime as well as a state crime. The Twenty-first Amendment is also the only amendment to date to be ratified by state conventions rather than by state legislatures.

Amendment 22 Presidential Tenure

Section 1. No person shall be elected to the office of the President more than twice, and no person who had held the office of President, or acted as President, for more than two years of a term to which some other person was elected President shall be elected to the office of the President more than once. But this article shall not apply to any person holding the office of President when this article was proposed by the Congress, and shall not prevent any person who may be holding the office of President, or acting as President, during the term within which this article becomes operative from holding the office of President or acting as President during the remainder of such term.

Section 2. This article shall be inoperative unless it shall have been ratified as an amendment to the Constitution by the legislatures of three-fourths of the several states within seven years from the date of its submission to the states by the Congress.

Adopted in 1951, the Twenty-second Amendment limited the number of terms to two that a person can be elected as President. Thus, it formalized the two-term tradition established by Washington, which was broken by Franklin Roosevelt.

Notice that it is possible under certain conditions for a person to serve more than two terms. Lyndon Johnson, who assumed the Presidency following the assassination of John F. Kennedy in 1963, was eligible to run for reelection in 1968. Had he run and won, he could have served 9 years, 1 month, and 28 days. Note, too, the amendment was not applicable to Harry Truman, President at the time of ratification.

Amendment 23   Presidential Electors for D.C.

Section 1. The District constituting the seat of government of the United States shall appoint in such manner as the Congress may direct:

A number of electors of President and Vice-President equal to the whole number of Senators and Representatives in Congress to which the District would be entitled if it were a state, but in no event more than the least populous state; they shall be in addition to those appointed by the states, but they shall be considered, for the purposes of the election of President and Vice-President, to be electors appointed by a state; and they shall meet in the District and perform such duties as provided by the twelfth article of amendment.

Section 2. The Congress shall have power to enforce this article by appropriate legislation.

Adopted in 1961, the Twenty-third Amendment provided for the choosing of electors for the District of Columbia. Until its adoption, residents of the District were excluded from voting in presidential elections. By the wording of the amendment, the District is limited to three electors, the same number as the least populous state. If the District were a state, it would be entitled to four electors based on its probable representation in Congress.

Amendment 24   Prohibition of Poll Tax

Section 1. The right of citizens of the United States to vote in any primary or other election for President or Vice-President, for electors for President or Vice-President, or for Senator or Representative in Congress, shall not be denied or abridged by the United States or any state by reason of failure to pay any poll tax or other tax.

Section 2. The Congress shall have power to enforce this article by appropriate legislation.

Adopted in 1964, the Twenty-fourth Amendment prohibits both the federal government and the states from denying a qualified voter the right to vote in federal elections for failure to pay any tax. The amendment did not prohibit states from imposing a poll tax as a voting qualification in state and local elections. However, the Supreme Court held the poll tax to be a denial of the "Equal Protection" clause of the Fourteenth Amendment and, therefore, unconstitutional in *Harper v. Virginia State Board of Elections* in 1966.

Amendment 25   Presidential Succession and Disability

Section 1. In case of the removal of the President from office or his death or resignation, the Vice-President shall become President.

Section 2. Whenever there is a vacancy in the office of the Vice-President, the President shall nominate a Vice-President who shall take the office upon confirmation by a majority vote of both houses of Congress.

Section 3. Whenever the President transmits to the President pro tempore of the Senate and the Speaker of the House of Representatives his written declaration that he is unable to discharge the powers and duties of his office, and

until he transmits to them a written declaration to the contrary, such powers and duties shall be discharged by the Vice-President as Acting President.

Section 4. Whenever the Vice-President and a majority of either the principal officers of the executive departments, or of such other body as Congress may by law provide, transmit to the President pro tempore of the Senate and the Speaker of the House of Representatives their written declaration that the President is unable to discharge the powers and duties of his office, the Vice-President shall immediately assume the powers and duties of the office of Acting President.

Thereafter, when the President transmits to the President pro tempore of the Senate and the Speaker of the House of Representatives his written declaration that no inability exists, he shall resume the powers and duties of his office unless the Vice-President and a majority of either the principal officers of the executive departments, or of such other body as Congress may by law provide, transmit within four days to the President pro tempore of the Senate and the Speaker of the House of Representatives their written declaration that the President is unable to discharge the powers and duties of his office. Thereupon Congress shall decide the issue, assembling within 48 hours for that purpose if not in session. If the Congress, within 21 days after receipt of the latter written declaration, or, if Congress is not in session, within 21 days after Congress is required

to assemble, determines by two-thirds vote to both houses that the President is unable to discharge the powers and duties of his office, the Vice-President shall continue to discharge the same as Acting President; otherwise, the President shall resume the power and duties of his office.

Adopted in 1967, the Twenty-fifth Amendment clarifies Article II, Section 1, Paragraph 6. Until its adoption, the assumption of the office of the President by the Vice-President because of vacancy was based upon the precedent set by John Tyler following the death of William Henry Harrison in 1841. The Twenty-fifth Amendment clearly states the Vice-President assumes the office of President should it become vacant. The amendment also provides for the Vice-President to become Acting President should the President become disabled.

The Twenty-fifth Amendment also provides for filling the office of the Vice-President by presidential appointment and congressional approval should it become vacant. Gerald Ford is the first person to be appointed Vice-President by a President, with Nelson Rockefeller being the second. Ford also became President following Nixon's resignation. Thus, he is the only person to hold both offices having never been elected to either.

Amendment 26   Eighteen-Year-Old Vote

Section 1. The right of citizens of the United States, who are eighteen years of age or older, to vote shall not be denied or abridged by the United States or by any state on account of age.

Section 2. The Congress shall have power to enforce this article by appropriate legislation.

Adopted in 1971, the Twenty-sixth Amendment lowered the voting age to 18. Note, however, that the amendment does not prohibit any state from allowing citizens less than 18 to vote if it so chooses. Thus, the amendment does not, in fact, establish a minimum voting age.

Amendment 27   Restraint on Congressional Salaries

No law, varying compensation for the services of Senators and Representatives, shall take effect, until the election of Representatives shall have intervened.

Ratified in May 1992 the Twenty-seventh amendment ensures that any increase in the salaries of members of Congress will take effect in the subsequent session of Congress.

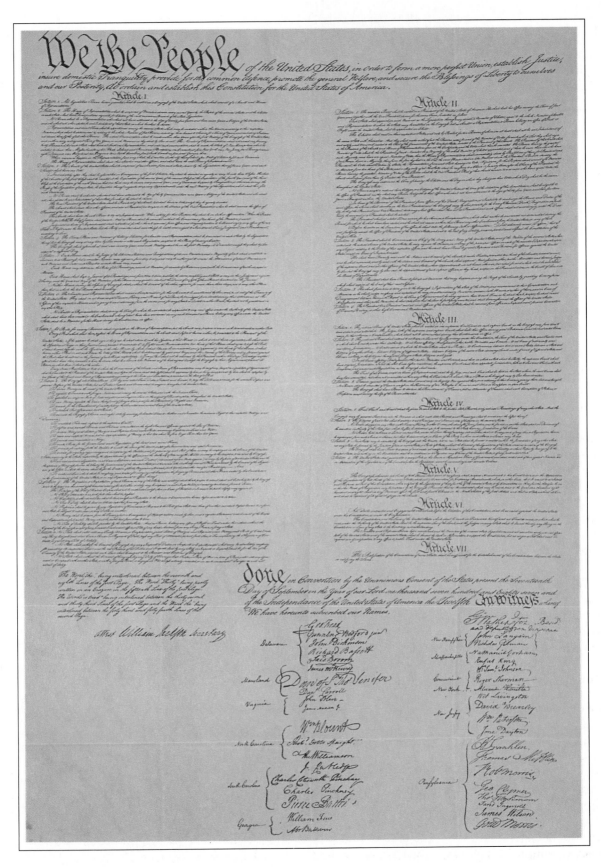

Chapter 4

American Freedoms

We live in a free society because we have the right to believe what we choose and to express our views and ideas, no matter how unpopular or uncommon they are. However, it is one thing to believe in these principles and quite another to put them into practice. Our democratic system can only be preserved when we assert our rights and exercise them vigorously. It is just as important that we affirm the freedom of others to exercise their rights. For unless we can say that the rights of *every* individual are protected, the rights of *no* individual are safe.

★ ★ ★ ★ ★

Chapter Preview

TERMS TO KNOW
civil liberties, secular, pure speech, speech plus, symbolic speech, libel, slander, actual malice, seditious speech, treason, press, prior restraint

READ TO DISCOVER
- why civil liberties and civil rights are important to us.
- the meaning of freedom of religion and freedom of assembly and petition.
- the meaning of freedom of speech.
- why freedom of the press is important in a democracy.

Civic Participation Journal

Contact a representative of a local organization that works to ensure equal rights for all Americans. You might choose the NAACP or the Anti-Defamation League, for example. Ask your contact what work the organization does in your community and if they need volunteers. Note what you learn about the organization in your journal. You may also wish to serve as a volunteer. If so, keep notes on your activities.

1 Civil Liberties and Rights

You may have heard a politician, a newscaster, or a group's spokesperson use the terms ''civil rights'' or ''civil liberties.'' If you had to define either of these terms, could you do it? Perhaps you could, but probably you would find it hard, if not impossible, to do so. The reason is that, although most people use these terms interchangeably, they do not mean the same thing.

Civil liberties are freedoms that we possess that government may not infringe upon. The freedom to worship as we choose is one civil liberty. The freedom to express our ideas and views openly and freely is another.

Civil rights, on the other hand, are protections we are granted by consti-

civil liberties Individual freedoms the government must not interfere with; includes freedom of religion, speech, press, assembly, and petition

The Bill of Rights was added to the Constitution in order to guarantee our personal liberty. But most of the rights that we enjoy are not listed in the Constitution. What are some of these rights?

tutions or statutes. For instance, the Constitution protects us against unreasonable searches and seizures. One type of statutory civil right protects individuals against discrimination on the basis of race, color, religion, sex, or national origin. Civil rights, then, are protections that government must uphold or provide.

Keep in mind, however, that there are some limits to our individual liberties and rights. For instance, you may exercise your right to free speech without restriction—so long as doing so does not interfere with the rights and liberties of others.

History

You have already read about many of the challenges that confronted the Framers of the Constitution. One of the biggest was how to limit government's power so that it did not interfere with people's rights and liberties. The Framers made a start by including a number of protections in the original draft. But to many Americans, this was not enough. They wanted our Constitution to spell out the fundamental rights of the people.

BILL OF RIGHTS

In response, the First Congress added the Bill of Rights—the first 10 amendments to the Constitution—in 1791. Even so, most of the civil rights and liberties that we enjoy are not listed either in the Constitution or in its amendments. And yet these freedoms are protected. How can this be so? The simple answer is that the Ninth and Tenth Amendments provide this protection. The Ninth Amendment, for instance, states that we have other rights in addition to those that are listed. Similarly, the Tenth Amendment makes it clear that

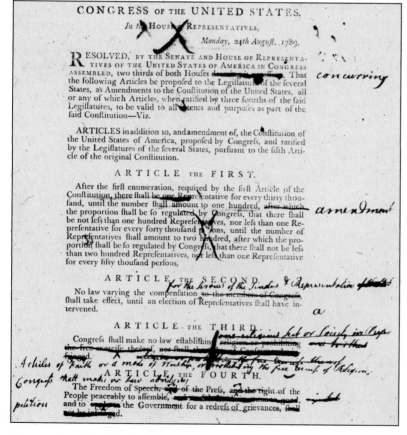

the powers not given to the national government nor prohibited by the states automatically belong to the states or to the people.

You may remember that one of the most bitter objections to colonial rule was that the power of the British government seemed to be unlimited. So, most Americans wanted to be sure that the power of their new national government would be limited by law. There was less certainty, however, about the power of the state governments. In 1833, in *Barron v. Baltimore,* the Supreme Court considered whether the individual freedoms listed in the Bill of Rights were restrictions on state governments as well as on the national government. The issue was whether, when it diverted streams from their natural courses and made Barron's wharf unusable, the city of Baltimore had deprived Barron of property without due process of law. Barron argued that the city had vio-lated a clause in the Fifth Amendment, one that prohibits taking private property for public use without just compensation. The Court ruled against Barron on the grounds that the Bill of Rights restricts only the national government, not the states.

FOURTEENTH AMENDMENT

To further define American freedoms, the Fourteenth Amendment was adopted in 1868. Included in this amendment was the clause that no state could "deprive any person of life, liberty, or property, without due process of law." Many people interpreted the clause to mean that state and local governments, as well as the national government, were under the same restrictions outlined by the Bill of Rights. In 1873 the *Slaughterhouse Cases* became the first to test this position. A Louisiana state law had created a monopoly in the slaughterhouse business. Those parties

The Protection of Our Civil Liberties and Civil Rights

The People

Judicial Branch

Executive Branch

Legislative Branch

Figure 4–1

squeezed out by the monopoly argued that the law violated their right of due process and equal protection of the law as guaranteed in the Fourteenth Amendment. The Supreme Court, however, ruled that protecting individual rights against state laws was a state responsibility and outside the power of the national government.

Not until 1925, in *Gitlow v. New York,* did the Supreme Court reconsider the meaning of the Fourteenth Amendment and its relationship to the Bill of Rights. In the *Gitlow* decision, the Court announced:

We may and do assume that freedom of speech and of the press—which are protected by the First Amendment from abridgement by Congress—are among the fundamental personal rights and liberties protected by the due process clause of the Fourteenth Amendment from impairment by the states.

By coupling First and Fourteenth Amendment protections, the Court affirmed that neither the national nor state governments may take away many of the rights protected by the Bill of Rights. Eventually, other First Amendment guarantees were brought within the protection of the Fourteenth Amendment.

Protectors

The Constitution serves as the primary safeguard of our civil liberties and rights. But it takes citizens and government working together to ensure that the Constitution works as intended. It is Congress's responsibility to pass laws that do not encroach upon our civil liberties. It is the executive branch's responsibility to protect our rights when it makes and carries out public policy. And it is the duty of the courts to protect our civil

rights. The role of the courts is critical because they interpret what the Constitution means and apply the law in real cases.

The ultimate responsibility of ensuring that the system works as it should, however, falls to each one of us. If we want our system to work, we should vote, express our views to elected representatives, and bring cases to court when our rights are in jeopardy. As Judge Learned Hand, one of the nation's most respected jurists, once noted, "Liberty lies in the hearts of men and women; when it dies there, no constitution, no law, no court can save it."

Section Review

1. What is the difference between civil liberties and civil rights?

2. Why is the Fourteenth Amendment important?

3. How are our civil liberties and civil rights protected?

4. **Challenge:** How can citizens be involved in protecting civil liberties and civil rights?

2 Freedom of Religion

The first liberty guaranteed in the First Amendment is freedom of religion. Placing this liberty first reveals how strongly the Framers believed in the right of people to practice, or not to practice, any religion they choose.

Separation of Church and State

The First Amendment has an Establishment Clause, which Thomas Jefferson referred to as a "wall of

Freedom of religion is guaranteed to Americans under the First Amendment. This amendment has an "establishment clause," creating a "wall of separation between church and state." Why, do you think, did the Framers of the Constitution include this clause?

separation between church and state." The clause forbids the government to "establish" an official religion. Yet, it does not require that the government ignore religion. Nor does it mean that government leaders are not allowed to be religious. In fact, the relationship between government and religion in the United States has always been a friendly one. Nearly all contributions to churches and religious sects, for instance, are free from taxation. Even our money is stamped with the words "In God We Trust."

The first ruling by the Supreme-Court on the Establishment Clause came in *Everson v. Board of Education,* 1947. The Court upheld a New Jersey law that allowed that state to provide busing for students attending parochial, or church-related, schools. It ruled that the law was meant to provide for the safety of the students and therefore benefited them rather than the school. The *Everson* ruling affirmed the Establishment Clause in the sense that states should not support one religion over another. The ruling also set the precedent that not all forms of state and federal aid to church-related schools are outlawed by the Constitution.

RELEASED TIME

Other cases tried under the Establishment Clause had to do with the issue of "released time," or time when students can be released during public school hours for religious instruction. The Supreme Court ruled in *McCollum v. Board of Education,* in 1948, that public classrooms and facilities could *not* be used for religious instruction. But four years later, in *Zorach v. Clauson,* the Court approved a similar program, the difference being that instruction was given *off* school grounds. Merely accommodating students' schedules for religious instruction, the Court decided, did not mean any special consideration was being given to religion.

In *Lemon v. Kurtzman,* 1971, the Court developed a three-part test to determine whether a particular state law violated the Establishment Clause. First, the law must have a **secular** purpose. Second, it must

secular nonreligious

Here, school buses wait to pick up students from a parochial school. What are some Supreme Court cases dealing with religion and education?

have the effect of neither inhibiting nor advancing religion. Third, it must not foster excessive government entanglement with religion. The test was applied in the case of *Witters v. Washington Commission for the Blind,* 1987. The Court ruled that spending vocational rehabilitation funds on ministerial training for a blind man did not violate the Establishment Clause because the funds were offered to a qualified person, not to a particular religion. The state was not significantly "entangled" by administering the law.

SCHOOL PRAYER

A controversial issue that has often come up is prayer in public schools. The Court has ruled many times that devotional exercises cannot be introduced into school curricula, although for years many public schools began the day with a prayer and the Pledge of Allegiance. In *Engel v. Vitale,* 1962, the Court declared unlawful even a voluntary non-denominational prayer designed by the New York Board of Regents for the public schools. Further, in *Abington School District v. Schempp* and *Murray v.*

Baltimore School Board, 1963, laws in Pennsylvania and Maryland requiring Bible reading or the recitation of prayer were struck down. A Kentucky law requiring the Ten Commandments to be posted in all public school classrooms also was rejected in *Stone v. Graham,* 1980. And in *Wallace v. Jaffree,* 1985, the Court struck down an Alabama law requiring a daily one-minute period of silence for "meditation or voluntary prayer." This ruling, however, did not affect laws in 25 states that promoted silent meditation so long as prayer was not suggested.

What do these rulings mean? First, it is not unconstitutional to pray in a school building or in any other place. Second, the Constitution does not outlaw the study of the Bible or religion as part of a secular program of public schools. What is considered unconstitutional, though, is the encouragement by school authorities of prayer, devotional exercises, or reading of the Bible for religious purposes. Reactions to the rulings have been mixed. While some individuals and groups staunchly support the Court's decisions, others have campaigned for a constitutional amendment that would allow voluntary prayer in schools.

AID TO PAROCHIAL SCHOOLS

You are already aware that the *Everson* case in 1947 permitted states to provide busing for parochial school students. Since then, more than two-thirds of the states have tried to provide some form of aid to parochial schools. State aid in the form of transportation, textbooks, and student lunches has been ruled constitutional, but paying for audiovisual equipment, teacher salaries, and field trips is not. The Supreme Court has tried to differentiate between public aid to students and public support of religion. Any approved aid must meet the test established in *Lemon v. Kurtzman*.

A state-aid issue with a different twist was debated in *Muller v. Allen*, 1983. The Court upheld a Minnesota law that permitted parents with children in school—whether parochial, private, or public—to take a state income tax deduction for costs of tuition, textbooks, and transportation. Parents paying for parochial and private instruction stand to benefit more from this tax break. But because these benefits could be requested by all citizens, the Court ruled that no particular religion was being favored.

OTHER SEPARATION ISSUES
Not all Establishment cases deal with education. The Supreme Court also has ruled on whether public celebrations of Christmas violate the separation between church and state. In *Lynch v. Donnelly*, 1984, for instance, the Court decided that the city of Pawtucket, Rhode Island, could include a nativity scene as part of the town's Christmas display. In 1989, however, the justices ruled in *Allegheny County v. Greater Pittsburgh ACLU* that placing a nativity scene inside the main entrance of a county courthouse violated the Constitution. At the same time, the Court upheld the placement of a Hanukkah symbol next to a Christmas tree in front of a public building a block from the county courthouse. The difference was that the nativity scene included no nonreligious symbols of the season. And since it was placed directly in the entrance of a government building, the scene implied endorsement of the Christian religion.

Some people believe that because prayer is not allowed in public schools, it should not be allowed in public government meetings. Meetings of Congress and many state legislatures are opened with prayers offered by chaplains paid with public funds. The Court addressed this issue in *Marsh v. Chambers*, 1983. In its ruling, the Court distinguished between legislative prayers and school prayers. It argued that prayers have always been offered in legislative bodies in the United States and that mature legislators are not likely to be influenced by a suggestion that one religion is preferable to another. Therefore, legislative prayers do not violate the Establishment Clause.

Free Exercise of Religion

Also included in the First Amendment is a clause forbidding laws to "prohibit the free exercise of religion." This Free Exercise Clause protects our right to believe and worship as we wish, or the right not to believe at all. But there is a distinction between beliefs and conduct.

Reactions to Court decisions on school prayer have been mixed. What is considered unconstitutional in this type of case?

"...and if it isn't unconstitutional."

In *Wisconsin v. Yoder,* the Supreme Court ruled that Amish students could not be forced to attend school beyond the eighth grade. Why, do you think, did the Court make this decision?

Generally, the Court has taken the position that individuals have an absolute right to believe what they wish, but they do not have an absolute right to act in any way they wish.

LIMITS TO FREE EXERCISE

The Free Exercise Clause was first tested in *Reynolds v. United States,* 1879. Reynolds was a Mormon who had two wives, a practice known as polygamy. Even though polygamy was encouraged by Reynolds's religion, he was convicted under a federal law that prohibited the practice. The Court ruled that practicing polygamy went beyond mere belief; it was an action that was a crime. Reynolds's beliefs were protected but not his criminal act.

In other cases, too, the Court has permitted individuals to worship as they wish so long as their conduct does not infringe upon the health, safety, and morals of the general public. In *Jacobson v. Massachusetts,* 1905, the Court upheld state laws requiring vaccination of school children even though the practice was forbidden by some religious groups. On the other hand, the Court has struck down some government actions because they violated the Free Exercise Clause. In *Wisconsin v. Yoder,* 1972, the Court ruled that Amish

children could not be forced to attend school beyond the eighth grade. This decision was based on the group's long-established tradition of self-sufficiency, which they felt would be threatened by their children's exposure to modern education.

THE FLAG SALUTE ISSUE

The Free Exercise Clause was again called into question with the flag-salute issue. In *Minersville School District v. Gobitis,* 1940, the Court upheld a Pennsylvania school's act of expelling two students for refusing to salute the American flag. The children were Jehovah's Witnesses, a religious group that believes saluting a flag is immoral. The Court ruled that requiring a flag salute was not an infringement on the children's religious freedom, but only an attempt to promote patriotism. But three years later the decision was reversed in *West Virginia State Board of Education v. Barnette,* when compulsory flag salutes were ruled unconstitutional. The Court said, in part, that "No official. . .can prescribe [dictate] what shall be orthodox in politics, nationalism, religion, or any other matter of opinion or force citizens to confess by word or act their faith therein."

Section Review

1. What three guidelines were established to determine whether a particular law violates the Establishment Clause?

2. Why is prayer allowed in legislative bodies but not in public schools?

3. **Challenge:** In your opinion, does the Free Exercise Clause protect citizens' free exercise of religion? Explain.

3 Freedom of Speech

Free speech lies at the heart of our democracy. It allows us to express opinions and to disagree with the government without fear of retaliation. It also protects those of us who state unpopular opinions.

Freedom of speech is also intended to protect our right to hear controversial or alternative ideas and opinions. The idea here is that we cannot vote wisely or well, assess the quality of governmental actions, or make decisions about public issues unless we have access to all points of view.

The Nature of Speech

The First Amendment protects some types of speech to a greater degree than others. **Pure speech** may occur in private homes or in public places such as shopping malls or parks. Government control over pure speech is extremely rare. **Speech plus,** on the other hand, may be regulated by government. For example, workers on strike may patrol a business site, march in a parade, give speeches, or carry signs. But the law might prevent them from blocking sidewalks, harassing passersby, or endangering the safety of pedestrians.

Freedom of speech also includes **symbolic speech.** While Americans were held hostage in Iran in 1980 and 1981, for instance, many citizens at home practiced symbolic speech by wearing yellow ribbons. This was a nonverbal sign of hope and support for the hostages. The Supreme Court has ruled that some forms of symbolic speech are acceptable while others are not. As a form of symbolic protest against the Vietnam War, for example, some people burned their draft cards. The Court outlawed this in *United States v. O'Brien,* 1968. But in *Tinker v. Des Moines,* 1969, the Court accepted the wearing of black armbands by students who were protesting against the war.

A more recent case involving symbolic speech has raised a storm of protest and controversy. In *Texas v. Johnson,* 1989, the Court ruled five to four that Gregory Lee Johnson's act of burning the American flag at the Republican National Convention was not unconstitutional. Because the action occurred during a political convention, the Court maintained it was protected as symbolic speech.

Tests of Free Speech

While all types of speech merit some protection, the justices of the Supreme Court often have disagreed on what "some" actually means. Their challenge has been to balance the legitimate interests of individuals with society's need to maintain public order. Various tests or guidelines for use in deciding such cases have been developed.

pure speech expression of an opinion before a willing audience

speech plus speech that is accompanied by such actions as demonstrations or parades

symbolic speech nonverbal communication through the use of symbols

Mary Beth Tinker wore a black armband to school to protest the Vietnam War. The Supreme Court upheld her right to self-expression. What antiwar action was held to be unconstitutional?

CLEAR AND PRESENT DANGER

One test, that of "clear and present danger," was developed in 1919 during *Schenck v. United States*. Charles Schenck was convicted during World War I for printing and distributing pamphlets that urged men to resist the draft. Although he argued that he was exercising his right of free speech, the Court countered that urging resistance to the draft posed a "clear and present danger that. . .will bring about. . .evils that Congress has the right to prevent."

Justice Oliver Wendell Holmes came up with the classic example of "clear and present danger" when he contended that "the most stringent protection of free speech would not protect a man falsely shouting 'Fire!' in a crowded theater." Although this test has not been used recently by the Supreme Court, state courts continue to use it.

TENDENCY

Another test came from *Gitlow v. New York,* 1925. Benjamin Gitlow had broken a state law by circulating anti-government literature. The Supreme Court upheld his conviction on the grounds that speech could be restricted if it had a "tendency" to lead to illegal action. In effect, the ruling allowed legislatures rather than courts to assume the primary responsibility for determining when speech might be restricted to prevent an illegal action.

BALANCING

Another test that has been promoted is the "balancing" test. This requires the Court to balance the rights of individuals to freely express their opinions against the need to maintain order and tranquillity.

INCITEMENT

Finally, there is the "incitement" test. Similar in some ways to "clear and present danger," this test holds that speech can be prohibited only when it is intended to incite or actually produce immediate lawlessness. For instance, a speaker could be punished for urging people to burn down a building with the clear expectation that they would do so.

As a general rule, though, the government's power to regulate what people say is limited. Reasonable regulations may be placed on the time, place, or manner of speech. Cities can require permits for distributing handbills, using sound trucks, or holding protests. When and how a peaceful demonstration or rally is held also can be regulated. But the government cannot favor some ideas or groups over others, no matter how unpopular their views may be.

The Balance Between Government and the Rights of the Individual

Public Safety   Free Expression

Figure 4–2

Unprotected Speech

Some forms of speech are not protected by the First Amendment. In these cases the government does limit what can be said.

DEFAMATORY SPEECH

One form of speech that is unprotected is defamatory speech. To be considered defamatory, a statement must damage another person's reputation or influence others not to associate with him or her. There are two kinds of defamation, **libel** and **slander.** To be considered as either of these, the statements must be untrue with the intent to do harm. Furthermore, actual harm must have occurred. It is interesting to note that the states, not the national government, have laws regarding defamation.

In 1964 the Court ruled in *New York v. Sullivan* that public officials cannot collect damages for remarks made against them unless they can prove the statements were made with "reckless" disregard for accuracy. Private individuals, then, have an easier time winning their cases, but they still are required to prove there was **actual malice.**

FIGHTING WORDS

Speech that attempts to provoke a fight also is not protected by the First Amendment. "Fighting words" were defined in *Chaplinsky v. New Hampshire,* 1942, as those having "a direct tendency to cause acts of violence by the persons to whom, individually, the remark is addressed."

SEDITIOUS SPEECH

A third form of speech limited by government regulation is **seditious speech.** Although not as obvious a threat as acts of spying, sabotage, or **treason,** this kind of speech is restricted because it relates directly to national security.

The Smith Act was tested in 1951 in *Dennis v. United States.* Eugene Dennis (third from left) was one of several members of the Communist party whose convictions were upheld in this case. What was the purpose of the Smith Act?

As early as 1798, Congress took steps to curb seditious speech when it passed the Alien and Sedition Acts. These acts made it a crime to utter false or malicious statements against the government with the intent to do it harm. But so many people opposed the acts, believing they handed too much power to government, that eventually they were repealed.

Later Congresses, however, passed other sedition laws. During World War I, the Espionage Act of 1917 was passed, again making it a crime to write or say anything negative about the government. In 1940 Congress passed the Smith Act, which outlawed the teaching of or advocating the forceful overthrow of the government or even organizing or joining a group with such a goal in mind. The Smith Act was tested in *Dennis v. United States,* 1951, a case that upheld the

libel printed defamatory statements

slander spoken defamatory statements

actual malice publishing of a false statement with the knowledge that it is false and with the intent to do harm

seditious speech speech that advocates overthrowing the government or resisting lawful authorities

treason betrayal of the nation of which one is a citizen

convictions of several leaders of the Communist party. That decision was modified in *Yates v. United States,* 1957, when the Court said that the Smith Act could be applied only to those who teach or advocate an *action* to overthrow the government, rather than a belief. The Court allows people to speak freely regarding their political opinions so long as they do not use force to achieve their goals.

press all types of printed media, as well as radio, television, and movies

Section Review

1. What are four examples of symbolic speech?
2. To what degree is each type of speech protected by the First Amendment?
3. What kinds of speech are not protected by the First Amendment?
4. **Challenge:** Do you agree with the Court's ruling in *Texas v. Johnson,* 1989? Explain.

prior restraint censorship of material before it can be read or viewed by the public

Throughout our nation's history, the freedom of the press has been protected. Here, a group of reporters try to interview a subject for a story. How, do you think, does freedom of the press affect all Americans?

4 Freedom of the Press

The writers of the Constitution believed that liberties relating to free speech also extended to the **press.** The Framers firmly believed the press should be reasonably free to publish information and opinions both for and against the government. Today the press remains the principal means of informing citizens about the government and issues of the day.

Prior Restraint

To help protect the rights of free expression, the Supreme Court has often ruled that material cannot be censored *before* it is expressed. In other words, there can be no **prior restraint,** except in rare instances. The Court has specifically outlined the situations that would allow the government to restrain what is printed. This may happen, the Court holds, only if the publication would cause serious and irreparable harm, if no other course of action would prevent the harm, and if only prior restraint would keep the harm from happening.

The first major case dealing with prior restraint was *Near v. Minnesota,* 1931, in which the Court ruled unconstitutional a Minnesota law that prohibited the publication of ''malicious, scandalous, and defamatory'' magazines. And in 1971, another important decision was reached in *New York Times v. United States.* Better known as the *Pentagon Papers* case, the *New York Times* published secret government documents revealing details of the United States' involvement in the Vietnam War. Arguing that printing these documents would harm national security, the government sought a court order to stop their publication. But the Court disagreed, ruling that the possible threat to national security was not great enough to outweigh the constitutional guarantee of freedom of expression. Thus, the government could not stop the *New York Times* from printing the material.

Not only national media are affected by freedom of the press. School newspapers, too, have sought the protection of the First Amendment. In *Hazelwood School District v. Kuhlmeier,* 1988, the Court gave public school administrators wide authority to censor school newspapers and other school-sponsored activities. In these situations, the Court ruled, school newspapers are part of the school curriculum. Therefore, administrators have the right to censor speech that promotes "conduct inconsistent with the shared values of a civilized social order."

The Press and the Courtroom

Sometimes the right of the press to report freely conflicts with the right of an accused person to a fair trial. The Supreme Court decides on a case-by-case basis how to protect these conflicting rights.

In 1954, Dr. Samuel Sheppard was convicted of murdering his wife. But the Supreme Court overturned his conviction because, during the pretrial coverage, the media had written and broadcast so many lurid details about his life that he was not able to receive a fair trial. Eventually he was retried and found not guilty.

If judges feel pretrial publicity may get out of hand and prevent a fair trial, they have a number of options. They may move the trial to another location, restrict the conduct and number of reporters in the courtroom, or isolate witnesses and jurors from the press. But these preventions must not

Dr. Samuel Sheppard was convicted in 1954 of murdering his wife. His conviction was overturned because the Supreme Court believed his case had been too widely publicized. How do judges sometimes try to prevent pretrial publicity?

go too far. In 1979, for instance, when a judge tried to prohibit the press from reporting on a pretrial hearing in Nebraska, the Court ruled the "gag order" unconstitutional. That same year, though, the Court decided in *Gannett Co., Inc. v. De Pasquale* that the press and the public *could* be barred from pretrial hearings if the trial judge strongly believed that publicity would hurt the defendant. For the next year, hundreds of trials became off-limits to the public and the press. Finally, in *Richmond Newspapers, Inc. v. Virginia,* 1980, the Court held that criminal trials are a public event and must be open to the public and the press.

Other Issues

Freedom of the press also has been tested occasionally when a legislative committee, court, or grand jury has asked a reporter to identify his or her source of information. Reporters have contended that they have the right to

Here, newspapers arrive for distribution to local stores and newsstands. To protect our access to the news, reporters are often guaranteed the right to keep their sources confidential. From what source do reporters gain their right to confidentiality?

keep that information confidential. In several cases, though, the Court has ruled that the First Amendment does not give reporters this right—that only Congress and the states can give it. Today, more than one-half the states give reporters some degree of protection for confidentiality.

OTHER MEDIA

New censorship issues arose with the development of new forms of media. Radio and television probably are the most restricted forms of communication because they use the airways, which are public property. Access to the airways can be gained only by obtaining a license from the Federal Communications Commission (FCC), which likewise can revoke licenses of stations who break FCC regulations. A station, for example, could be penalized for airing an X-rated adult film during prime time. But the FCC does not have the power of prior restraint and cannot tell stations ahead of time what they can air.

Films, too, are treated somewhat differently than printed material. At one time nearly every state and many local communities had review boards that previewed films before allowing the public to view them. In *Burstyn v. Wilson,* 1952, however, the Court

ruled that films were protected from censorship by the First and Fourteenth Amendments. Even so, the Court decided in *Teitel Film Corporation v. Cusack,* 1968, that a state or local government *can* ban a film if it is proven, at a judicial hearing, to be obscene.

OBSCENITY

Who decides what is or is not obscene, and on what do they base their decision? To illustrate how unclear the issue is, one justice said he could not define obscenity, but, he allowed, "I know it when I see it." In *Miller v. California,* 1973, the Court did try to set guidelines for judging whether works are obscene. First, would the average person in the community find that the material appeals to purely sexual interest? Second, does the work lack serious literary, artistic, political, or scientific value? And finally, does the work offensively describe sexual conduct specifically outlawed by state law? Since standards and interpretations used to judge obscenity are not the same among states, communities, and individuals, at times the Supreme Court has had to overrule specific acts of censorship.

Section Review

1. Why has the Supreme Court traditionally protected freedom of the press?

2. In what ways may freedom of the press and the right of a person to a fair trial conflict?

3. Why are radio and television stations regulated?

4. **Challenge:** In your opinion, why is it difficult to censor obscenity in a democracy?

5 Freedom of Assembly and Petition

Since people often assemble to make or hear a speech, freedom of assembly often coincides with freedom of speech. The Constitution protects our right to peacefully assemble in public and private to express our views on public matters. Likewise, we may organize into such groups as political parties and interest groups. The freedom to write letters, circulate petitions, lobby, picket, parade, and demonstrate to make our views known also are protected.

Regulation

The First Amendment clearly states that any assembly should be peaceable. Peaceable assembly does not include the right to cause a riot, block a public street, or place anyone in danger. Thus, many local and state governments have had to create ordinances regulating some gatherings of people. In cases challenging these laws, the Supreme Court has sometimes supported them and sometimes struck them down.

Generally, the Court has agreed that it is reasonable to make and enforce rules covering the time, place, and manner of assemblies. Such authority is considered necessary to protect public property and maintain peace and order. For example, in *Cox v. New Hampshire,* 1941, the Court upheld a local ordinance requiring a permit for a parade on public streets. In response to Cox's argument that the ordinance was a violation of freedom of speech and assembly, the Court disagreed, stating that the purpose was not to restrict unpopular views but to keep the streets clear for pedestrians and traffic.

Unpopular Ideas

Our right to express or listen to ideas, unpopular as well as popular, is protected. However, it has always been difficult for law enforcement agencies and the courts to deal with

These protesters exercise their rights to peacefully assemble and to express their views. Under which amendment is the right of assembly protected?

ISSUE: CIVIL LIBERTIES

LIMIT FREEDOM OF SPEECH AND ASSEMBLY?

In 1977, when the anti-Semitic American Nazi party announced plans for a Fourth of July rally and march through the Chicago suburb of Skokie, the residents were outraged. About one-half of Skokie's population was Jewish, many of them survivors of the Nazi death camps of World War II or relatives of people who died in the camps. Skokie officials feared that a march by the American Nazi party would attract a counter-demonstration and that it could possibly lead to confrontation, violence, and property damage.

In an attempt to prevent the march, the city council passed a variety of ordinances, and the city attempted to obtain a series of court injunctions. Finally, Skokie officials relented and told the Nazis they could march if they ob-

tained a parade permit. But the officials set the fee for the permit at $300,000. The Nazis objected and took the city of Skokie to court. They claimed that the permit's high cost had the effect of denying them their right to free speech and assembly.

The American Nazi party was assisted in court by the American Civil Liberties Union (ACLU), an organization that champions a wide variety of cases where such freedoms are involved. According to ACLU lawyers, the Nazis had a right to hold their march and rally, despite the unpopularity of their beliefs and actions. The attorneys cited Supreme Court Justice Oliver Wendell Holmes, who in 1919 said that the Constitution must protect "freedom for the thought that we hate."

Opponents of the Nazis responded that to permit the rally and march was not protecting freedom but allowing it to be exercised irresponsibly. To support their argument they, too, quoted Justice Holmes, who once wrote that even "the most stringent protection of free speech would not protect a man in falsely shouting 'fire' in a theatre and causing a panic."

The Nazis won their court case against the city of Skokie when a judge in the United States Court of Appeals agreed that so costly a parade permit interfered with the

Nazis' right of free speech. But despite their court victory, the Nazis decided to march elsewhere. Although the subsequent march and rally attracted few supporters, it did produce a large counter-demonstration.

The confrontation between the city of Skokie and the Nazis illustrates the increased concern with rights and freedoms that grew out of the civil rights movements of the 1950s and 1960s. It intensified debate over the question of how a nation founded on principles of freedom and harmony can resolve conflicts arising from differences in race, nationality, background, or belief. Several weeks after the Skokie incident, a sociologist quoted in *U.S. News and World Report* suggested one answer to this question when he observed that "a more egalitarian society inevitably requires more government regulation."

1. Why did Skokie officials object to the American Nazi party parading in their town?
2. Do you think there should ever be limits on freedom of speech and assembly? If yes, when? If no, why not?
3. Do you agree that "a more egalitarian society inevitably requires more government regulation"? Explain your answer.

the expression of unpopular ideas in the context of the right to assemble. The reason is that such assemblies are the most likely to result in disturbance of the peace or violence.

For example, in 1950, Irving Feiner of New York was arrested after his remarks criticizing public officials incensed a crowd almost to the point of rioting. Upholding his conviction in *Feiner v. New York,* 1951, the Court set the precedent that the police may break up assemblies to preserve the peace. But in *Edwards v. South Carolina,* 1963, the Court overturned the conviction of 150 black students, ruling that it was not the students, but the audience, who disturbed the peace. While protesting discrimination in a peaceful demonstration, the students were enveloped by a hostile crowd.

In their rulings, the courts have tried to be as reasonable as possible in deciding time, place, and manner of restrictions of assemblies. Some public areas traditionally viewed as off-limits to demonstrations, such as airports, libraries, and schools, have been ruled open so long as ongoing programs were not disrupted. But other areas, such as prison grounds, areas surrounding courthouses in which trials are being held, and military bases, cannot be used.

Section Review

1. What kinds of laws regarding assembly may state and local governments pass?

2. In what instances may police break up an assembly of people?

3. **Challenge:** In your opinion, why are the rights of assembly and petition important?

Summary

1. The idea that the government should protect the people's civil liberties and civil rights is derived from the Constitution, the Bill of Rights, the Fourteenth Amendment, and Supreme Court decisions.

2. American civil liberties and civil rights are protected by all branches of government and by the active participation of all citizens.

3. Freedom of religion is protected by the Establishment Clause and the Free Exercise Clause in the First Amendment.

4. Major issues of the Establishment Clause have concerned released time, school prayer, and government aid to parochial schools.

5. Pure speech, speech plus, and symbolic speech are protected by the First Amendment; defamatory and seditious speech are not.

6. The Supreme Court has developed guidelines and tests to help decide cases involving free speech.

7. Major issues involving freedom of the press concern prior restraint, pretrial publicity, and confidentiality of a reporter's sources.

8. While people may organize into groups, the time, place, and manner of such assemblies may be restricted.

Chapter 4 Review

★ Building Vocabulary

The definitions of several vocabulary words found in this chapter are listed below. First, number your paper from one to ten. Then, next to each number, write the term being defined.

1. nonreligious
2. speech that is accompanied by such actions as demonstrations or parades
3. spoken defamatory statements
4. censoring material before it is viewed by the public
5. speech that advocates overthrowing the government or resisting lawful authorities
6. printed defamatory statements
7. all types of printed media, as well as radio, television, and movies
8. betraying the nation of which one is a citizen
9. First Amendment freedoms
10. nonverbal communication through the use of symbols

★ Reviewing Facts

1. Where are the individual liberties and rights of Americans defined?
2. Which branch of government attempts to balance individual liberties and rights against people's rights and government's needs?
3. In addition to the Bill of Rights, what amendments make guarantees for citizens?
4. What serves as the primary safeguard of American civil liberties and civil rights?
5. How does the First Amendment of the Bill of Rights provide for the separation of church and state?
6. Why is federal aid to parochial schools such a controversial issue?
7. How and when has the Supreme Court limited the free exercise of religion?
8. What types of free speech are protected by the First Amendment?
9. What are the criteria for establishing libel and slander?

10. Why is the public expression of unpopular ideas difficult for the courts to deal with?

★ Analyzing Facts

1. Confidentiality has always been considered an important right for journalists. There have been cases, however, where reporters were jailed for not revealing their sources in a court of law. Do you think reporters should be required to name their sources? Explain.
2. Deciding between free expression and the right of society to protect itself has been a difficult task for the courts. How would you limit free expression without jeopardizing the civil rights of individuals?

★ Evaluating Ideas

1. The information in this chapter illustrates that the feedoms listed in the First Amendment are not absolute. Would you consider making any of those freedoms absolute? Explain.
2. Benjamin Franklin said, "They that can give up liberty in order to obtain a little temporary safety deserve neither liberty nor safety." Do you agree? Why or why not?

Using Your

Civic Participation Journal

Review the entries you made in your Civic Participation Journal when you contacted a local human rights organization. Work with five of your classmates to compare notes and develop a summary report of what the organizations do. Present your report to the class and encourage classmates to pursue volunteer opportunities in the organizations.

★ Critical Thinking
Asking Effective Questions

Effective questions are questions designed to obtain specific information and that provide the information desired. The ability to ask effective questions is a key to acquiring information or knowledge.

Explanation   To ask effective questions of people or of written sources requires some preparation. It is not as easy a skill as it appears to be. Frequently, when we do not obtain the information we need, it is because we have consulted the wrong sources or asked the wrong questions. There are four steps you should take before you ask questions:

1. Determine exactly what you want to find out?

2. Determine what persons or written materials you should consult.

3. Decide what questions you should ask.

4. Decide how you should ask the questions.

Practice   You could use these four steps to find out exactly why students are so unhappy about cafeteria lunches.

1. You already know that your classmates are generally discontented about cafeteria food. You want to determine exactly what it is about the food that makes them unhappy.

2. From what resource do you think you would be most likely to obtain this information—your school principal, the parents, the cooks, or the students who eat in the cafeteria every day? Students are your best source because they are the ones complaining about the food.

3. Next, you must decide what questions to ask. You would not learn what you want to know if you ask about the way the cafeteria is decorated, if it is too noisy, if students have enough time to eat, or even if lunches cost too much. You would find out what you want to know, however, by asking your classmates what their general

opinions are of the food served in the cafeteria; what cafeteria foods they liked best and least; or what items they would like added to the menu.

4. In deciding how you should ask your questions, there are two things you should consider. First, you should decide if you want to ask your questions directly in person, or if you want to prepare a written questionnaire. Also, you must be sure to ask your questions in a way that does not show personal bias nor influence the answers you receive.

Independent Practice   You also can apply the four steps for asking effective questions to written and visual materials. To practice this technique, review the issue *Limit Freedom of Speech and Assembly?* on page 110 of this chapter and study the cartoon below about the Ku Klux Klan in the 1991 Louisiana elections. Determine how you would apply these steps to gathering information about the confrontation between the American Nazi party and the city of Skokie and between the Ku Klux Klan and the voters. Decide exactly what else you want to know about this issue, determine where you can find out about it, and then design questions that will obtain the information.

Chapter 5

Due Process and Equal Protection

All citizens of the United States are entitled to due process of law. But just what does this mean? For one thing, it means that many of the guarantees listed in the Bill of Rights protect people accused of crime. But why should the rights of people who may be criminals be so protected? Although there are many answers to this question, perhaps the most important is that the rights of people accused of crime are meant to protect all Americans—the innocent as well as the guilty. Finally, due process helps us respect the law itself. When we know that the law is fair, we are more likely to abide by it and respect those who enforce it.

Chapter Preview

TERMS TO KNOW
writ of habeas corpus, bill of attainder, ex post facto law, probable cause, exclusionary rule, capital punishment, rational basis, suspect classification, segregate, desegregation, de jure segregation, de facto segregation, affirmative action programs, reverse discrimination

READ TO DISCOVER
- your rights under due process of law.
- how equal protection of the law is guaranteed.

★ ★ ★ ★ ★

Civic Participation Journal

As you study this chapter keep track of local trials reported in your community's newspaper. Note how each trial provides examples of how in the United States anyone accused of a crime has certain rights that must be protected.

writ of habeas corpus
order from a court to a law enforcement agency to release a person held in jail to determine whether he or she has been legally detained

bill of attainder legislative act that declares a person guilty and gives out punishment without a court trial

ex post facto law law that punishes someone for a crime committed before the act was considered a crime

1 Rights of the Accused

Four of the first eight amendments spell out the procedures that must be followed when a person is accused of a crime. And even before these amendments were law, the Constitution included safeguards that protected those accused of or charged with a criminal act. Article I, Section 9, Clause 2 forbids the government to suspend the privilege of the **writ of habeas corpus** ''unless when in cases of rebellion or invasion the public safety may require it.'' Clause 3 states that ''no **bill of attainder** or **ex post facto law** shall be passed.''

Over time, the Supreme Court has applied the principle of due process of law to different situations. As a result, two kinds of due process have developed—procedural and substantive.

The principle of due process of law means that proper procedures must be followed when arresting and trying suspected offenders. What two classifications of due process have developed over the years?

Procedural due process requires that government use fair procedures in enforcing the law. At first, this protection applied mostly to criminal prosecutions. Now it is also used in such situations as government committee hearings and local school board hearings. Substantive due process, on the other hand, requires that the laws under which government acts be fair. This means that the laws must be constitutional. In short, procedural due process limits the way in which government's power may be used, while substantive due process limits what government can control.

Searches and Seizures

The Fourth Amendment of the Constitution provides that:

The right of the people to be secure in their persons, houses, papers, and effects, against unreasonable searches and seizures, shall not be violated, and no warrants shall issue, but upon probable cause, supported by oath or affirmation, and particularly describing the place to be searched, and the persons or things to be searched.

This means that while the police are allowed to search persons or property for criminal evidence, they must do so in a legal and orderly way. Most of the guidelines for conducting searches and seizures have been developed over the years by the Supreme Court.

This task, however, is not an easy one. The Fourth Amendment is open to various interpretations, and courts have come to very different conclusions about what its provisions mean. A number of important issues continue to be discussed, including: what is an ''unreasonable'' search? In what ways does it differ from a reasonable one? What constitutes ''probable

Here, law enforcement officers search for illegal drugs. In some cases, officers do not need a warrant in order to conduct a search like this. When is a search warrant not needed?

cause''? And does the amendment, which was written in 1789, still apply to cases today?

WARRANTS

When law enforcement officials arrest a person, they do not need a search warrant to search that individual for evidence. But if there is no arrest, search and seizure of property may be conducted only after a valid warrant has been obtained.

A warrant is valid only if it meets certain conditions. It must be issued by a judicial officer, show **probable cause,** and describe the place to be searched and the items to be seized. It also must be served, or presented, within a reasonable time, by officers who properly identify themselves. Finally, the search and seizure must not exceed the scope of the warrant. For instance, an officer who has a warrant to search an automobile would not be allowed to inspect the contents of a briefcase found in the trunk.

Under what conditions is a search warrant not necessary? You have already learned that one is not needed when an arrest is made, but there are other times as well. A person may consent to being searched without a warrant, and evidence in ''plain

view'' may be seized without one as well. If police are chasing a suspect, they may enter a building without a warrant. They can also search if they feel it is a matter of public safety to do so, or if they feel evidence will be removed before they can obtain a warrant.

EXCLUSIONARY RULE

What happens when evidence is seized in an improper search? The Supreme Court ruled in *Weeks v. United States,* 1914, that such evidence cannot be used to obtain a conviction. The **exclusionary rule**, as it is now called, at first applied only to federal cases, but in 1961 it was extended to apply to cases in state courts.

The deciding case was *Mapp v. Ohio*. In that case, police officers, without a warrant, had forcibly entered the home of Dollree Mapp, whom they suspected of illegal gambling. They found no evidence of gambling during the search, but they did find obscene pictures and books. Later, Mapp was tried and convicted of possessing these materials. The Supreme Court overturned Mapp's conviction, ruling that obtaining evidence without a search warrant went

probable cause reasonable grounds for suspicion based on evidence from a good source

exclusionary rule court standard stating that evidence seized in an improper search cannot be used to obtain a conviction against the Fourth Amendment. Such evidence could not be used in court—even in a state trial.

The exclusionary rule has been controversial. Critics contend that criminals should not go free because police erred. In two 1984 cases, the Supreme Court decided that there is a "good-faith exception" to the exclusionary rule. In these cases, the Court ruled that evidence seized under a warrant later found to be invalid could still be used in court so long as the police had acted in "good faith." In short, the police believed they had a valid warrant. In a third case, the Court ruled that evidence illegally obtained could be used in court if it were proven that the evidence would "inevitably" have been discovered by lawful means. These rulings have been praised by law enforcement officials.

CHANGES IN PROCEDURES
Two additional rulings in the late 1980s, both dealing with suspected drug offenders, also modified search and seizure guidelines. In 1988 the Court ruled that police were within their rights in obtaining a warrant to search a house after they discovered drug equipment in trash bags outside the house. The evidence in the trash bags constituted reasonable grounds for suspicion. And, since the bags were outside the house, they were neither private nor protected. Then, in 1989, the Court upheld an arrest in which police in a helicopter spotted marijuana plants in a suspect's yard.

During the late 1980s the Court also dealt with the legality of certain kinds of drug tests in the workplace. Some legal experts contend that urine and drug tests constitute a search, so persons who are to be tested should be protected against illegal search and seizure. But in a ruling in 1989, the Court held that drug tests were legal for a group of railroad workers who had questioned whether they could refuse to take the tests. Such tests, the Court noted, were justified because the workers were responsible for the safety of the people on the trains.

The issue of searches and seizures has also been raised in cases involving electronic surveillance. The Court had ruled in 1928 that a warrant was not required for an agency of the government to wiretap a telephone. In 1967 this decision was overturned when the Court ruled that a wiretapped phone

The Supreme Court has determined that a government agency must have a search warrant before wiretapping a telephone conversation. On what basis did the Court make this decision?

conversation was something that could be seized like any other belonging. As such, a warrant was needed to set up a wiretap. Today, any form of electronic surveillance must meet guidelines established by Congress.

Fair Trial Protection

Just as the Fourth Amendment sets up guidelines for searches and seizures, the Fifth and Sixth Amendments set up general principles for fair trials. The Fifth Amendment, for instance, guarantees protection from double jeopardy. This protection, however, is not absolute. Since both federal and state laws prohibit kidnapping, a person accused of this crime can be tried in both state and federal courts. Similarly, a single act can result in the violation of several laws, and an offender could be tried separately for each violation. In addition, double jeopardy does not prevent a retrial when a jury fails to reach a decision or when an appeals court determines that legal errors were made in the original trial.

SELF-INCRIMINATION

The Fifth Amendment also guarantees protection from self-incrimination. Unlike many systems, the American system of justice does not require the defendant to prove innocence. Instead, it requires the prosecution, or the government, to prove guilt. Americans believe that it is unfair to force defendants to help the government prove their guilt by testifying against themselves. In an 1897 ruling, the Supreme Court held that use of an involuntary confession in federal courts was also prohibited by the Fifth Amendment. A confession is considered involuntary if it is obtained by tricks or force, or if a suspect is promised benefits or leniency in re-

turn for a confession. In 1964 this rule was applied to state courts as well.

The most far-reaching interpretation of protection against self-incrimination occurred in two Supreme Court cases in the 1960s. In the first, Danny Escobedo was arrested on a murder charge. During police interrogation, he asked several times to see his lawyer, but his requests were denied. Eventually, he made several incriminating statements that led to his conviction. In *Escobedo v. Illinois,* 1964, the Court ruled that Escobedo's Fifth Amendment right to protection against self-incrimination had been denied. The Court reasoned that had an attorney been present, a right provided by the Sixth Amendment, Escobedo might not have incriminated himself. The *Escobedo* case marked the beginning of judicial regulation of police interrogations.

In 1966, in *Miranda v. Arizona,* the Court went further and set strict

The Supreme Court decided that Danny Escobedo, shown here with his lawyer, was denied his Fifth Amendment right against self-incrimination. What was the effect of the decision in *Escobedo v. Illinois?*

Due Process and Equal Protection   119

Clarence Gideon is shown here with the book based on his story. In recent years, other Court cases have focused on the right to effective counsel. What two conditions must be met to claim adequate counsel?

guidelines for police questioning. The police, it ruled, must inform suspects that they have a constitutional right to remain silent, that any statement they make can be used against them as evidence, and that they have a right to have an attorney present during questioning. Critics contend that the *Miranda* decision has, in effect, tied the hands of police. In several cases since *Miranda*, however, the Court has relaxed some of its restrictions. In a 1984 ruling, the Court held that police do not have to read suspects their rights if doing so would endanger public safety.

Nonetheless, the Court refused for many years to recognize other exceptions. In fact, in *Berkemer v. McCarty*, 1984, the Court extended the *Miranda* ruling to cover minor misdemeanor arrests. It ruled that suspects in custody for any crime, no matter how minor, must be told of their rights. The only exception is people stopped for ordinary traffic violations.

Then in the late 1980s, the Court began to recognize certain limits on the *Miranda* ruling. In *Oregon v.*

Elstad, 1985, it held that if suspects confess *before* being informed of their rights, prosecutors can still use another confession obtained *after* the suspects were told about their rights. One year later, in *Moran v. Burbine,* the Court found no legal fault with deceit by police who kept a suspect's lawyer from him during interrogations. Then in *Colorado v. Spring,* 1987, the Court indicated that the Constitution does not require that suspects be aware of all the consequences if they waive their *Miranda* rights.

RIGHT TO COUNSEL

In addition to protecting individuals from double jeopardy and self-incrimination, the laws of the United States provide other protections for those accused of crime. The Sixth Amendment, for instance, guarantees every person the "assistance of counsel." At first this right applied only to defendants in federal court, cases of crimes punishable by death, and cases that had "special circumstances." For many years there were no established guidelines to define what special circumstances were.

Finally, in 1963, in *Gideon v. Wainwright,* the Court clarified this issue. After his arrest for robbing a pool hall, Clarence Gideon stated that he could not afford an attorney and asked the court to provide one for him. His request was denied, and he was convicted and imprisoned. While serving his sentence, he studied law books and filed his own appeal with the Supreme Court. In a unanimous decision, the Court ruled in favor of Gideon, noting that any person ". . .who is too poor to hire a lawyer, cannot be assured a fair trial unless counsel is provided. . . . Lawyers in criminal courts are necessities, not luxuries." Gideon got a new trial and this time, represented by an attorney, he was acquitted.

Other cases have focused on the right to "adequate," or effective, counsel. Justice Sandra Day O'Connor noted two conditions that must be met to claim inadequate counsel. For one, the defendant must show that the lawyer's performance "fell below an objective standard of reasonableness." For another, he or she must show that "there is a reasonable probability that, but for the counsel's unprofessional errors, the result of the proceeding would have been different."

TRIAL BY JURY

The Sixth Amendment guarantees the right to a jury trial. In 1930, the Supreme Court defined the requirements for the jury in a federal case. One, it must consist of 12 persons. Two, it must be advised on legal issues by a judge. And three, its verdict must be unanimous.

The Sixth Amendment also guarantees the right to a speedy trial. A trial cannot be so delayed that evidence or witnesses are lost, but neither can it be so speedy that the defendant's counsel does not have time to prepare an adequate defense. Although judges can place some restrictions on who may observe a trial, the trial must be public. In 1987, the Supreme Court indicated that the Sixth Amendment also guarantees defendants the right to confront witnesses face to face.

Bail and Punishment

The Eighth Amendment provides that bails must not be excessive. A 1951 ruling established that the amount of bail should be related to the seriousness of the crime, the ability of the accused to post bail, and the criminal record of the accused.

The Eighth Amendment also prohibits cruel and unusual punishment. Although most Americans believe torture, whipping, or similar forms of punishment have no place in their society, many feel differently about **capital punishment.** This issue was addressed in 1972 by the Supreme Court in a group of cases called by the lead case, *Furman v. Georgia.* When the Court ruled that in these cases the death penalty was unconstitutional, it voided all of the existing state death penalties. The reason they were voided was that they gave almost unlimited discretion to judges or juries in deciding whether or not to impose a death penalty. After the *Furman* ruling, 35 states enacted laws that they thought would satisfy the Court's objections. Some simply made the death penalty mandatory for

capital punishment death penalty for conviction of a serious crime

An accused person may be released from jail when bail is posted, as pictured below. What is the Eighth Amendment restriction regarding bail?

POST BAIL BOND HERE

The death penalty is a controversial issue among Americans. Many favor extended prison terms as an alternative. What are some Supreme Court cases dealing with the death penalty?

certain crimes, such as killing a police officer. Others set up a two-stage process: a trial to decide guilt or innocence, and a separate hearing according to strict guidelines to determine an appropriate sentence. Both kinds of laws were tested in the Supreme Court, and mandatory death penalties were found to be unconstitutional. But, in 1976, in *Gregg v. Georgia,* the two-stage process was found to be constitutional.

Since then, other death penalty cases have been brought before the Court. Reaction to the Court's rulings has varied. Civil rights groups, in particular, were critical of two decisions, one in 1984 and the other in 1987. In 1984 the Court ruled that a state does not have to guarantee that a death sentence imposed in one case is consistent with the punishment imposed in similar cases. In 1987 it ruled that although studies show that

racial bias may determine who receives the death penalty, defendants would have to prove that bias personally denied them a fair trial. In 1988, however, when the Court struck down laws in eight states that allowed the death penalty for juveniles who were less than 16 years old when they committed their crimes, activists applauded the ruling.

Section Review

1. What five characteristics constitute a valid search warrant?

2. What are two exceptions to the exclusionary rule?

3. What guidelines were established by *Miranda v. Arizona?*

4. **Challenge:** Why do you think the Court provides exclusions?

2 Equal Protection

Originally, the equal protection clause of the Fourteenth Amendment was written to protect newly freed slaves. Today, however, it is used more broadly to prevent discrimination between persons or groups. The first section of the amendment reads:

All persons born or naturalized in the United States, and subject to the jurisdiction thereof, are citizens of the United States and of the state wherein they reside. No state shall make or enforce any law which shall abridge the privileges or immunities of citizens of the United States; nor shall any state deprive any person of life, liberty, or property, without due process of law, nor deny to any person within its jurisdiction the equal protection of the law.

With this amendment the term ''citizen'' was defined for the first time. At the same time, the amendment forbids states to deprive citizens of their constitutional rights or to deny them equal protection of the law.

Meaning

Equal protection of the law does not mean that everyone must be treated exactly the same. Government must sometimes classify, or group, people into categories to achieve legitimate government goals. But not everyone always agrees with these classifications. So when laws involving them are challenged, the courts must decide if a particular classification denies the persons so grouped their rights to equal protection of the law.

The Supreme Court uses two tests to determine if a classification is reasonable. The first is the **rational basis** test. If a rational basis is shown, there is no denial of equal protection, and the classification stands. For example, no state allows persons under 18 to vote. This is permitted because it is rational to assume that persons under 18 will not have the education and maturity required to vote. But there would be no rational basis for classifying coal miners as unqualified to vote, so such a classification would not be constitutional.

The second test is the **suspect classification** test. In 1973 the Court stated that a suspect class is one that has historically suffered disabilities, been subjected to purposeful unequal treatment, and been placed by society into a position of such political powerlessness as to require special judicial protection. Included in this category are racial and ethnic minorities and women. The judiciary looks long and hard at laws involving a suspect classification to determine whether they are *absolutely* necessary to achieve an important public purpose.

rational basis relationship between the classification of a group of people and the public purpose of the classification

suspect classification grouping made on the basis of race, sex, or national origin

No state allows young people under the age of 18 to vote. Why is such discrimination acceptable under our laws?

Pictured is a "separate" facility where African Americans and whites were treated unequally. The case of *Plessy v. Ferguson* affirmed that "separate but equal" facilities were constitutional. Why did Justice John Harlan disagree with the decision of the Court?

Development

While the Declaration of Independence said that "all men are created equal," until the Thirteenth Amendment was adopted in 1865, slavery existed in the United States. Even the ratification three years later of the Fourteenth Amendment, which granted citizenship and due process rights to formerly enslaved persons, did not stop African Americans from being treated differently from most white Americans for many years.

SEGREGATION

segregate separate by race

After the adoption of the Thirteenth and Fourteenth Amendments, many states passed laws clearly intended to separate, or **segregate,** the use of such facilities as hotels, restaurants, parks, schools, and transportation. But since under the American legal system, the constitutionality of a law cannot be tested until the law is broken and its legality is tested in

court, it was not until 1892 that these laws were challenged.

In 1892 a group of Louisiana citizens decided to challenge a state law that required railroads to provide separate railway cars for African American passengers. One of the citizens, Homer Plessy, boarded a train in New Orleans and seated himself in a railway car reserved for whites. When the conductor ordered him to move to the other car, he refused. Plessy was arrested and later convicted of breaking the law.

Four years later, in *Plessy v. Ferguson,* the Supreme Court upheld the conviction on the grounds that segregation in public places was constitutional if "separate but equal" facilities were available. Justice John Harlan, the lone dissenter in the case, insisted that "our Constitution is color-blind, and neither knows nor tolerates classes among citizens." Despite this, the majority opinion established the separate-but-equal doctrine, which became widely used as the basis for racial segregation in other areas of life.

One of the first areas in which segregation was challenged was education. In 1938, the Court held in *Missouri ex rel. Gaines v. Canada* that refusal to admit an applicant to a state law school solely on the basis of race was a denial of equal protection. The state of Missouri, which did not have a law school for African Americans, offered to pay the plaintiff's tuition at any of the neighboring state university law schools, but he refused this offer. Equal protection according to the Court required an equal education at a facility within the state's borders.

Then in *Sweatt v. Painter*, 1950, the Court found that the separate law school provided for African Americans in Texas was not equal in quality to the school for whites. After the ruling, qualified African Americans were admitted to the law school at the University of Texas.

Although the Supreme Court gradually moved away from the separate-but-equal doctrine in the area of education, it was not until the 1950s that a case entirely reversed the precedent set in *Plessy*. It all came about when Mr. and Mrs. Oliver Brown of Topeka, Kansas, wanted their daughter, Linda, to attend a school a few blocks from their home instead of one for African Americans, which was 21 blocks away. In 1954 the Supreme Court ruled in that case, *Brown v. Board of Education of Topeka*, and similar cases filed from Delaware, South Carolina, and Virginia, concluding that:

In the field of public education the doctrine of ''separate but equal'' has no place. Separate educational facilities are inherently unequal.

Linda Brown stands in front of the school that refused to admit her ten years earlier. How did her famous case, *Brown v. Board of Education of Topeka*, affect public education?

DESEGREGATION

desegregation elimination of separation by race

de jure segregation segregation that is a result of law

de facto segregation segregation that results from housing patterns and the practice of assigning students to neighborhood schools

The *Brown* decision supported the concept of **desegregation** in public schools. But recognizing that complex problems were involved, the Supreme Court did not order immediate desegregation. Then, one year later, it ordered desegregation to proceed "with all deliberate speed," and the federal district courts began to take an active role in supervising the process. Soon **de jure segregation** no longer existed in public schools. To back their decision, the courts cited the rational basis test. In other words, there was no relationship between the classification (segregation of African American students) and a legislative public purpose (public education).

Even this and later attempts did not put an end to **de facto segregation.** Attempts to eliminate it have included redrawing school district lines, reassigning pupils, and busing students from racially segregated neighborhoods. The Supreme Court first sanctioned busing as a method to combat de facto segregation in 1971. Through the years, however, busing has met with widespread, sometimes violent, opposition. It remains a complex issue for the courts today.

SIGNIFICANT CIVIL RIGHTS EVENTS

1863	President Lincoln's Emancipation Proclamation committed the nation to ending slavery.
1865	The Thirteenth Amendment put an end to slavery.
1868	The Fourteenth Amendment granted citizenship to formerly enslaved persons.
1870	The Fifteenth Amendment guaranteed African Americans the right to vote.
1915	*Guinn v. United States* outlawed the "grandfather clause" that had kept many African Americans from voting.
1920	The Nineteenth Amendment granted women the right to vote.
1941	The Fair Employment Practices Commission was established by President Roosevelt to end discrimination in hiring defense industry workers.
1944	*Smith v. Allright* declared white primary elections unconstitutional.
1948	President Truman issued an Executive Order to desegregate the armed forces.
1954	*Brown v. Board of Education of Topeka* declared de jure segregation of public schools unconstitutional.
1955	The Montgomery Bus Boycott marked the beginning of the nonviolent, civil disobedience phase of the civil rights movement, led by Dr. Martin Luther King, Jr.
1957	President Eisenhower ordered troops to Little Rock, Arkansas, to enforce the desegregation of Central High School.
1964	The Civil Rights Act of 1964 forbade discrimination in public accommodations and by employers and unions in interstate commerce. It also banned employment discrimination on the basis of sex.
1965	The Voting Rights Act enabled the federal government to enforce the Fifteenth Amendment.
1971	The Twenty-sixth Amendment granted eighteen-year-olds the right to vote.
1971	*Swann v. Charlotte-Mecklenburg* ruled that busing of students can be used as a means of removing de facto segregation of public schools.
1978	*Regents of the University of California v. Bakke* banned the use of specific racial quotas where no previous racial discrimination has been found.
1980	*Fullilove v. Klutznick* ruled that affirmative action programs with specific racial quotas could be used if intended to remedy effects of past discrimination.

Figure 5-1

The Civil Rights Movement

As can be seen in Figure 5-1, desegregation of public schools was only one aspect of a nationwide struggle for racial equality. Among the methods that were employed early in the struggle to end segregation were "sit-ins," boycotts, and marches. The best-known leader of the movement's early days, Dr. Martin Luther King, Jr., personally led many marches and demonstrations and urged using the courts and legislation to achieve the desired ends. But even his peaceful tactics were often met with violence.

Congress responded to the civil rights movement by passing legislation to guarantee equal protection. The most important piece of legislation was the Civil Rights Act of 1964, which was based on the power of Congress to regulate interstate commerce. It made discrimination illegal in all public accommodations affecting interstate commerce, including such public places as restaurants, hotels, and theaters, and prohibited discrimination in employment practices and labor unions. The major provisions of this act are shown in Figure 5-2.

Equal Protection in Other Areas

The Supreme Court has applied the equal protection clause of the Fourteenth Amendment in other areas as well. One is the rights of women. Though the Constitution makes no reference to males or females, there have been many laws classifying women differently from men. But since the intent of most of these laws was to protect women's rights in the labor market, the Court usually ruled

CIVIL RIGHTS ACT OF 1964

Forbids discrimination
—based on race, color, religion, national origin, and, in the case of employment, sex.
—in places of public accommodation (motels, restaurants, gas stations, e.g.).
—in employment opportunities in any industry that affects interstate commerce.
—in voter registration.
—in programs using federal funds.

Provides for or authorizes
—establishment of a Community Relations Service.
—national government to bring suits to desegregate schools and public facilities.
—making the Civil Rights Commission a permanent body.
—the withholding of federal funds for noncompliance with the act's provisions.

Figure 5-2

that the laws did not violate the equal protection clause.

WOMEN'S SUFFRAGE

At first the struggle for women's rights in the United States concentrated on the right to vote. In fact, a proposed constitutional amendment to allow this was introduced in every session of Congress from 1878 to 1919. It was not until 1920 that it finally became law as the Nineteenth Amendment to the Constitution. No longer could any state deny the right to vote to persons because of their sex.

SEX DISCRIMINATION

Other areas involving women's rights took longer to change. One of the earliest sex discrimination cases came before the Supreme Court in 1948. It involved a Michigan law restricting barmaid licenses to wives and daughters of bar owners. The Court ruled in favor of the law on the grounds that it preserved family unity and safeguarded the morality of women. Even

In 1987, Rotary International was required to open its doors to women. What argument did Rotary International use to advocate an all-male organization?

affirmative action programs government programs designed to end the effects of past discrimination by helping disadvantaged groups

reverse discrimination treating minorities differently from others in order to make up for past discrimination

as late as 1961, the Court validated classification based on gender by ruling that women did not have to serve on juries if they were needed at home.

The changing role of women in American society finally led the Court to begin overturning laws that, among other things, denied women equal treatment in the workplace and equal access to club membership. In *Reed v. Reed,* 1971, the Court struck down an Idaho law that gave automatic preference to men over equally qualified women in the appointment of estate administrators. Another leading case was *Frontiero v. Richardson,* 1973. In that case, the Court overturned a federal law that treated the spouses of male and female members of the armed services differently in terms of benefits.

Then in *Board of Directors of Rotary International v. Rotary Club*

of Duarte, 1987, another issue was raised. Rotary International, an all-male service organization made up of nearly 20,000 chapters worldwide, dropped the Rotary Club in Duarte, California, because it had admitted women. The Duarte chapter sued the parent body, arguing that under state law, it was illegal to bar women from the organization. Rotary International argued that its members had the right to associate with whom they pleased. The Supreme Court unanimously held that Rotary must allow local chapters to admit female members in California and other states that have laws guaranteeing equal rights in public accommodations. There have been cases, however, where the Court has allowed classifications based on gender. For instance, in 1981 the Court upheld Congress's power to require men, but not women, to register for the draft.

AFFIRMATIVE ACTION

Although many discriminatory practices against minorities are prohibited today, the effects of years of discrimination remain. One government remedy is the use of **affirmative action programs**. The goal of these programs is to make the work force reflect the makeup of the general population more accurately. By law some employers must make special efforts to hire or promote women and minority group members. But while many people believe that affirmative action is needed to repair the damage caused by past discrimination, others contend that these programs promote **reverse discrimination**.

The first major reverse discrimination case tried by the Supreme Court was *Regents of the University of California v. Alan Bakke,* 1978. Bakke, a white male who was twice denied admission to the University of

California's medical school, claimed he was a victim of racial discrimination. In admitting new students, the school reserved a certain number of places for minority group members. But Bakke's test marks were higher than those of the minority students admitted under the program. The Court ruled that Bakke should be admitted but also said that the University had the right to maintain a selection program that considered race as one factor.

Other recent Supreme Court decisions have supported the use of quota systems in corporate training programs and in awarding federal contracts to minority businesses. For instance, the Kaiser Aluminum and Steel Corporation instituted a training program that reserved one-half of all training positions for minorities. The United Steel Workers of America labor union had agreed to the quota system used. Brian Weber, a white worker, was rejected from the program while African American workers with less seniority were accepted. On appeal, in *United Steel Workers of America v. Weber,* 1979, the Supreme Court upheld the company's affirmative action program, saying that it did not stop the advancement of any one group.

In 1980, the court decided another major case dealing with affirmative action. A section of the Full Employment Act of 1977 had set aside a portion of federal grant money for minority businesses. In *Fullilove v.*

Affirmative action programs have been criticized as promoting reverse discrimination. Here, Alan Bakke graduates with his medical degree. What did the Court rule in the case of *Regents of the University of California v. Alan Bakke?*

COMPARISON: LEGAL SYSTEMS

LAW IN OTHER CULTURES

Each society has rules by which it lives. Every government establishes formal rules, called laws, to control the behavior of people living under its authority and to carry out its policies. But what are the origins of these rules, and why do laws differ so markedly from society to society?

Over the centuries, some political philosophers have claimed that there is a universal morality, an unwritten law for all people and societies that operates for the maximum good of the individual and society. They argue that this "natural law" exists above and apart from the "positive law" formally enacted by government and enforced by definite penalties.

To test this idea, a famous legal anthropologist, E. Adamson Hoebel, surveyed much of the literature about law and legal practices throughout the world. Although he found great variation in what different societies consider to be crimes, Hoebel also discovered certain behaviors that

are universally outlawed. Generally, these are acts that threaten the survival of individuals or groups within a society or the society itself. For example, in every society, laws against murder guarantee the lives of its people. All societies also protect the right to personal property with laws against its theft or destruction or other behaviors that threaten property rights.

But Hoebel also found that in some cultures certain crimes are considered more serious than they are in other cultures. Public drunkenness, for example, is a particularly serious crime in Egypt. On the other hand, Botswana reserves its strongest legal penalty for cattle rustling.

According to Hoebel, a nation's laws and legal system can only be explained by understanding its history and culture. Such understanding should include consideration of outside influences important in the development of that society, its attitudes about the

origin of law, the structure and operation of its legal system, and its deeply held traditional beliefs.

The strong legal sanctions in Botswana against cattle rustling most likely developed out of its need to maintain adequate food supplies. In an area where food shortages occur frequently, stealing cattle would have serious consequences, making it a major crime.

In many Islamic countries, all law is believed to have divine origins, so to disobey the law is much the same as disobeying God. Egyptian and Saudi Arabian laws regarding public drunkenness are a case in point. Alcoholic beverages are banned by the religious teachings of Islamic culture and are absolutely forbidden by the laws of both countries.

By Western standards such laws may appear too harsh and the penalties too severe. But by the standards of the societies and cultures in which these laws operate, such controls on behavior seem necessary and appropriate.

1. What evidence in this passage argues against the existence of a "natural law" that governs all societies?
2. Name some laws in the United States that are not universal but that are specific to American culture.
3. What other kinds of laws can you think of that are so common they might be considered universal?

Klutznick, 1980, the court held that this policy was constitutional. This decision supported the authority of Congress to redress past racial discrimination through the use of quotas in the awarding of federal contracts.

However, in *Firefighters Local Union v. Stotts,* 1984, the Court ruled that workers with seniority could not be laid off to protect minorities and women who were hired under affirmative action plans. Many people believe this ruling will affect future affirmative action programs.

Section Review

1. What are two tests used to determine whether a classification is reasonable?

2. In what case was the separate-but-equal doctrine overturned?

3. How have women been denied equal protection of the law?

4. **Challenge:** In your opinion, is de facto more difficult to deal with than de jure segregation?

Summary

1. Due process of law is guaranteed by the Constitution.

2. The Supreme Court plays a major role in defending the due process rights of individuals accused of crime.

3. Four guarantees of due process listed in the Constitution are the writ of habeas corpus, right to a jury trial, prohibition of bills of attainder, and prohibition of ex post facto laws.

4. Procedural due process guarantees that government will follow fair and lawful procedures. Substantive due process requires that the law itself must be constitutional.

5. The Supreme Court has developed guidelines for conducting proper searches and seizures.

6. The Fifth and Sixth Amendments have several guarantees for a fair trial. Among these are protection against double jeopardy and self-incrimination, and the right to counsel.

7. The equal protection clause supports the idea of equality of all people set forth in the Declaration of Independence.

8. State and federal governments are not permitted to set up classifications of people without a legitimate governmental purpose.

9. Constitutionality in equal protection cases is determined by applying two tests, rational basis and suspect classification.

10. Segregation violates the equal protection clause of the Fourteenth Amendment.

11. The case that originally made segregation legal was *Plessy v. Ferguson.*

12. The case that made segregation illegal was *Brown v. Board of Education of Topeka.*

13. The Supreme Court has also applied the equal protection clause to end discrimination against women and to support affirmative action programs.

14. One reaction to affirmative action is reverse discrimination.

Chapter 5 Review

★ Building Vocabulary

Use the terms you studied in this chapter to complete the following statements.

1. Death penalty for the conviction of a serious crime is called ____ ____.
2. ____ ____ is a grouping made on the basis of race, sex, or national origin.
3. ____ is the elimination of separation by race.
4. A law that punishes someone for a crime committed before the act was a crime is a(n) ____ ____ ____ ____.
5. ____ ____ is reasonable grounds for suspicion based on evidence from a good source.
6. A(n) ____ ____ ____ is a legislative act that declares a person guilty and gives out punishment without a court trial.
7. To separate by race is to ____.
8. A(n) ____ ____ ____ ____ is an order from a court to a law enforcement agency to produce a person held in jail.
9. Government programs designed to remedy the effects of past discrimination by helping disadvantaged groups are ____ ____ ____.

★ Reviewing Facts

1. What four guarantees of due process are in the Constitution but not in the Bill of Rights?
2. What are the major differences between procedural and substantive due process?
3. What is meant by the exclusionary rule?
4. In what ways does the Fifth Amendment guarantee a right to a fair trial?
5. How did the *Escobedo* case further protection of the accused against self-incrimination?
6. What rights does the Sixth Amendment provide?
7. What is meant by adequate, or effective, counsel?
8. Why did the Supreme Court strike down death penalty laws in *Furman v. Georgia?*
9. On what power did Congress rely in passing the Civil Rights Act of 1964?

10. Why were many laws originally passed classifying women for different treatment?
11. What is the purpose of affirmative action programs?

★ Analyzing Facts

1. People who are against affirmative action programs often say that such programs promote reverse discrimination. Do you agree or disagree? Explain.
2. Judge Learned Hand said, "Liberty is advanced only by rule of law." Based on what you know about civil rights and civil liberties, do you think this statement is valid? Why or why not?
3. Governments often pass laws that classify people in order to achieve a public policy in which the government has a legitimate interest. What might be some constitutional classifications? What public interest would be served?

★ Evaluating Ideas

1. Because of high technology, electronic surveillance has become easier to use. In your opinion, should evidence gained through electronic surveillance, such as bugs and wiretaps, be used in courts to convict someone? Should the type of case be taken into consideration? Explain your answers.

Using Your
Civic Participation Journal

Review the notes in your Civic Participation Journal about trials in your community. Construct a chart based on your notes. Your chart should show what rights of the accused were being protected in each case you studied.

2. When someone "takes the Fifth," it is usually to avoid self-incrimination. In your opinion, when this occurs is the accused using a legal right to hide the truth?

3. Civil rights for the accused have evolved over the years in various Supreme Court cases. In your opinion, should accused criminals be entitled to such protection? Explain.

★ Critical Thinking
Identifying Irrelevant
Information

There are two kinds of information—relevant and irrelevant. Relevant information is directly related to the topic or idea you are reading or talking about and helps you to better understand it. Irrelevant information can be interesting and accurate, but it does not add anything useful to your understanding of the topic or help you decide about it. In fact, it may even hinder your ability to make a decision by confusing you.

Explanation The following guidelines will help you distinguish relevant from irrelevant information in written or visual material.

1. Study the material and determine the topic or main idea.

2. For each statement in the material or part of the illustration, decide if it is directly related to the main idea. Does it define, explain, illustrate, serve as an example, or describe a cause or effect of the topic?

3. Any statement or part of the illustration that does not do one of the things named in guideline 2 is irrelevant information, even if it is interesting and accurate.

Practice The following passage contains both relevant and irrelevant information. As you read the paragraph, each statement is identified as relevant or irrelevant based on the main idea, which is John Marshall's concern about the Supreme Court's lack of power.

The present relationship among the executive, legislative, and judicial branches was not well-established when John Marshall became the fourth chief justice in 1801. [*relevant-explains*] The third branch of government—the judicial—was not yet co-equal with the other two branches. [*relevant-explains*] Born in a sparsely-settled region of Virginia in 1755, John Marshall grew up on his father's farm and had little formal education. [*irrelevant*] In 1781, following a brief period of study, he began to practice law. [*irrelevant*] Marshall was fearful that without an effective judiciary—one that had the power to review the acts of the states—the supremacy clause of the new Constitution might be ignored. [*relevant-illustrates*] He thought that judicial power was an important part of limiting the power of government. [*relevant-cause*] As chief justice, Marshall went about the task of establishing the power and prestige of the Supreme Court. [*relevant-effect*]

Independent Practice For further practice, study the photograph below. It shows a family of immigrants in their New York City apartment in the late 1800s. Imagine that you are doing a term paper on living conditions in urban areas. What parts of the photograph would provide relevant information? In what ways would the photograph be irrelevant if you were describing middle-class life-styles?

ONE REVIEW

REVIEW QUESTIONS

1. How are the purposes of government in general, as outlined in Chapter 1, set forth in the Preamble of the Constitution?

2. What is the government's role in capitalist, socialist, and Communist economic systems?

3. In what ways do the Bill of Rights and other constitutional amendments protect and guarantee human rights?

4. In what ways was the government set up by the Constitution stronger than that established under the Articles of Confederation?

5. What is the role of judicial review in the American system of checks and balances?

6. The Constitution of the United States is the oldest written national constitution in operation. Why, do you think, has it survived?

7. What powers does the Constitution of the United States give or deny to the states alone, to the national government alone, and to both?

8. How has the relationship between the national government and the states changed over the years?

9. Why has the judicial branch been the most active branch of government in the protection of citizens' rights?

10. How has the Supreme Court been able to justify federal and state aid to parochial schools?

11. In what ways are pure speech, speech plus, and symbolic speech different?

12. What decision did the Supreme Court make in *Furman v. Georgia,* 1972? What was the reaction of many states?

13. In your opinion, what are some problems in overcoming de facto segregation, and how can these problems be resolved?

14. Different Supreme Court justices have suggested a range of "tests" by which to determine whether or not a particular speech should be protected. What are those tests, and how might they produce varying results?

SUGGESTED READINGS

1. Friendly, Fred W., and Martha J. H. Elliott. *The Constitution: That Delicate Balance.* New York: Random House, 1984. Explains the history of 16 major Supreme Court cases.

2. *The Great Voyage: Two Hundred Years of the Constitution.* Special Issue, *The New York Times Magazine,* September 13, 1987. Contains a series of articles about aspects of the Constitution that relate to American life today. One of these is a story of a high school newspaper's First Amendment fight.

3. Hentoff, Nat. *The First Freedom: The Tumultuous History of Free Speech in America.* New York: Delacorte Press, 1980. Examines past struggles and present-day conflicts as they relate to the history of young people.

4. King, Martin Luther, Jr. *Stride Toward Freedom: The Montgomery Story.* New York: Harper & Row, Publisher, Inc., 1958. Traces the development of Dr. King's ideas about nonviolence and describes the 1955 bus boycott in Montgomery, Alabama.

5. Lewis, Anthony. *Gideon's Trumpet.* New York: Random House, 1964. Describes the fight of Clarence Earl Gideon for his right to legal counsel.

6. Price, Janet R., Alan R. Levine, and Eve Carey. *The Rights of Students.* Carbondale, IL: Southern Illinois University Press, 1987. Describes students' rights under present law and offers suggestions about how these rights can be protected.

ACQUIRING AND USING INFORMATION

We all need to be able to acquire and use information in order to understand what is going on around us. Young children might need information about how to get to a new playground or whom to call in an emergency. Teenagers might want to know how to apply for a job or who is a good car mechanic. Adults could need to know how to vote on a referendum or whether to lower property taxes. Indeed, knowing how to acquire information is particularly important for us, as citizens, because it is impossible to make decisions concerning public issues or to make judgments about governmental action without such a skill.

The information we acquire comes from a variety of sources. Newspapers, books, magazines, radio, television, family, and friends are just a few. All of these sources of information enlarge our understanding of the political world around us. However, acquiring information is sometimes easier than knowing how to use it.

To use information, we first must organize it and determine how different pieces of information are related. We then can make sense of the information and develop a point of view, draw conclusions, make decisions, or simply understand something more clearly.

The following exercise will help you develop your skills in acquiring and using information about government.

1. Your task is to link governmental actions to constitutional authority by examining laws that were passed and important events that occurred in the administration of George Washington and Thomas Jefferson.

2. To accomplish the task, you need to acquire information on what laws were passed and what events occurred during Washington's and Jefferson's administrations and what the source of constitutional authority was for the law or action. You also need to decide what are the best sources of this information. Since you will need historic information, your best sources probably include a history or government text or an encyclopedia.

3. Next, to organize your information, set up three columns on a large sheet of paper. In the first column, list two important events and laws passed during the administration of George Washington and two events and laws passed during that of Thomas Jefferson.

4. In the second column, briefly state how the government handled the event and why the law was passed.

5. In the last column, list the source of the government's authority for its action. If you need extra help, check the Preamble to the Constitution and Articles I and II of the Constitution.

6. Based on the information you have acquired and organized, draw a conclusion about how problems were resolved by the national government during the administrations of George Washington and Thomas Jefferson.

Unit 2

CHOOSING GOVERNMENT LEADERS

We the people of the United States, *choose* our leaders to represent us at every level of our government. This selection process occurs in some form every year throughout our land. It often involves many steps before the final goal of electing a candidate to office is reached

On the national level of our government, the President of the United States is the most important official who is chosen by voters. The process of selecting a President occurs every four years and reaches its midway point with the naming of candidates at major political party conventions. The photo on the facing page shows Democrats celebrating Bill Clinton's nomination as their presidental candidate for the 1992 presidental campaign.

Whether at the national, state, or local level, elections require the participation of as many citizens as possible in order to be truly democratic. The kind of leaders we have depends on the choices we make on election day.

Chapter 6

Citizenship

Of the hundreds of thousands of people from such diverse countries as Vietnam, Guatemala, and Afghanistan who flee their homelands and try to get into the United States, only a limited number are allowed to enter and become citizens. In this chapter we will take a closer look at why so many people throughout the world regard American citizenship as a cherished prize.

★ ★ ★ ★ ★

Chapter Preview

TERMS TO KNOW

allegiance, jus soli, jus sanguinis, naturalization, denaturalization, expatriation, electorate, register, deported, aliens, immigrants, resident visa, refugees, resident aliens, temporary visiltors

READ TO DISCOVER

- who is or may become a United States citizen.
- the rights and responsibilities of American citizens.
- how voting is both a right and a responsibility of citizenship.
- the diverse origins of past and current immigrants to the United States.

Civic Participation Journal

Find two people in your community who are naturalized American citizens. Interview them to learn their country of origin, why they wanted to become citizens, and what procedure they had to follow in gaining citizenship. Keep notes on your interviews in your civic participation journal.

1 The Citizen

Being a citizen is a matter of rights, duties, and responsibilities between an individual and a nation. The citizen owes **allegiance** to his or her nation, which, in turn, gives the citizen all the rights and protection of the law.

Citizens' rights are spelled out in the Constitution and in federal and state laws. One right is simply to live in the United States. We also have the right to vote, hold public office, and travel freely throughout the states.

As American citizens, we have the legal duty to support the government by obeying the laws, paying taxes, serving on juries, and defending the nation whenever necessary. Citizenship responsibilities also extend to actions that are *not* legally required but are vital to the welfare of the nation, such as voting and helping to solve public problems.

Who Is a Citizen?

In the early days of the Republic, citizenship was more of a state issue than a national issue. The Constitution did not define who was or was not a citizen. But by the mid-1800s, the rising number of immigrants and the end of slavery led to a nationwide policy. In 1868 the Fourteenth Amendment defined citizens as:

All persons born or naturalized in the United States, and subject to the jurisdiction thereof, are citizens of the United States and of the state wherein they reside.

The definition also noted the two ways in which a person may become a citizen—birth and naturalization.

CITIZEN BY BIRTH

The vast majority of Americans are citizens simply because they were born in the United States. Under **jus soli,** ''law of the soil,'' those born in

allegiance   loyalty to a country

jus soli   right to citizenship in the country where one is born

The Fourteenth Amendment established a nationwide policy for determining citizenship for immigrants such as the ones shown here. What are the two ways in which a person might become a United States citizen?

the United States are automatically American citizens. American "soil" means not only the 50 states and the District of Columbia, but also American territories, Puerto Rico, U.S. military bases overseas, and even official U.S. ships and aircraft. The law holds true whether a child's parents are American citizens or not. One exception is children of foreign diplomats based in the United States. They do not automatically become American citizens.

Another exception was Native Americans. They did not attain American citizenship until the 1900s even though their ancestors had lived on American soil for thousands of years before the first European colonists arrived. This made sense at the time the Constitution was written because individual Native American groups were thought of as separate nations. But over the decades, as settlers forced the Native Americans off their land and onto reservations, the Native Americans became no more than wards, or dependents, of the U.S. government. Finally in 1924, partly as a reward for Native American participation in World War I, Congress passed a special law granting citizenship to all Native Americans.

A person may also become an American citizen at birth under **jus sanguinis**, or "law of blood." Anyone born in a foreign country to parents who are both American citizens, one of whom has lived in the United States, is automatically an American citizen. But if only one parent is a U.S. citizen, that parent must have lived in the United States at least 10 years for the child to have U.S. citizenship.

NATURALIZED CITIZENS

People who live in the United States but are not citizens by birth must go through the legal process of **naturalization** to obtain American citizenship. Article I, Section 8 of the Constitution gives Congress the power to control naturalization. The first federal naturalization law, passed in 1790, allowed any free white person who had lived in the United States for two years to become a citizen. The law had long-term effects on immigration. For one thing, prejudice against nonwhite persons was highly evident. It was not until 1870 that "persons of African nativity, or persons of African descent," could become naturalized citizens. For another, the law opened the way for a tremendous growth in population during the 1800s since citizenship became much easier to obtain.

Today, the laws on naturalization are stricter. To be eligible for citizenship, a person must have lived legally in the United States for five years and be at least 18 years old. After formally filing for citizenship, applicants must show they are of good moral character and have a working knowledge of both the English language and American government. They must then appear before a judge and swear:

This cartoon by Joseph Keppler shows that many people who demanded restricted immigration in the late 1800s were, themselves, immigrants. From where did the "new" immigrants come?

jus sanguinis right of blood, or right to the citizenship of one's parents

naturalization process by which immigrants become American citizens

denaturalization process by which a naturalized citizen loses citizenship

I hereby declare, on oath,. . .that I will support and defend the Constitution and laws of the United States of America against all enemies, foreign and domestic; that I will bear true faith and allegiance to the same; that I will bear arms on behalf of the United States. . .and that I take this obligation freely without any mental reservation or purpose of evasion; so help me God.

Upon taking this oath, applicants and any of their children younger than 18 and living in the United States become naturalized American citizens. As naturalized citizens, they have all the rights and responsibilities of other citizens, except that they may not become President or Vice President of the United States.

In recent years nearly 200,000 individuals have become new citizens annually. Naturalization usually is an individual process. But, in a few cases Congress has extended naturalized citizenship status to groups of people. In 1917, for instance, all the residents of Puerto Rico were made citizens of the United States. The most recent mass naturalization occurred in 1977 when the native residents of the Northern Mariana Islands in the Pacific Ocean were granted American citizenship.

LOSS OF CITIZENSHIP
Just as there are a number of ways to become a U.S. citizen, there are also several ways in which citizenship may be lost. One way is **expatriation,** which is a voluntary act. This might happen when an American leaves the United States, settles in another country, and decides to become a citizen there.

Citizenship may also be lost involuntarily. In extremely rare cases involving treason against the federal government, for instance, the govern-

expatriation loss of citizenship by renouncing or denying allegiance to one's country

electorate the group of eligible voters

ment can take away citizenship. Another way the government can take away citizenship is by **denaturalization**. A naturalized citizen who joins a subversive group or whose application for citizenship was obtained through fraud may be denaturalized and forced to leave the country.

Section Review

1. What are some of the rights and responsibilities of American citizenship?
2. What qualifications must be met before an immigrant may petition for citizenship?
3. According to the Fourteenth Amendment, who is a citizen of the United States?
4. In what three ways can American citizenship be lost?
5. **Challenge:** What, do you think, is the relationship between allegiance and citizenship?

2 Rights and Responsibilities to Vote

The essence of citizenship in a democracy is the right of the people to choose who will govern them. The people's power to control government is exercised by voting. The right to vote differs from other rights such as freedom of speech or freedom of religion, which are spelled out in the Constitution.

Voting is a privilege enjoyed *only* by those citizens who meet certain qualifications set by the states. Those who qualify are called the **electorate**. Over the years the definition of the electorate has changed. The evolving role of a citizen is clearly outlined in the history of who holds the power, that is, who may vote.

Early Voter Qualifications

The Constitution was intentionally silent on voter qualifications, and it was left to the states to decide who could and could not vote. As a result, when the nation was new, few Americans were allowed to vote. In general, voters were white males who owned a certain amount of property and paid taxes. Later, as civil rights were added to the Constitution and public attitudes changed, more citizens were allowed to vote.

RELIGION

From the earliest colonial years, religion was sometimes a qualification for voting. A number of colonies were settled by religious groups, and usually the dominant religious group wanted to have its views reflected by the electorate and the government. But over the years, separation of church and state became a more widely accepted idea, and by 1810 religious beliefs were no longer used as a qualification for voting in any state.

PROPERTY AND TAXES

In the late 1700s and early 1800s, only men who owned property, such as houses or land, could vote. Even in the states where the voting requirement was payment of taxes, this had much the same effect since most taxes were on property. The reasoning behind this was that only men who had a substantial interest at stake—their property—should have the opportunity to elect government leaders.

Yet as the nation changed, ideas about voting also changed. The Jacksonian democracy of the 1830s carried the message that ''every man'' mattered, not just the rich or elite.

These citizens are exercising their right to vote. In our nation's earliest days, how were voter qualifications decided?

Cities grew, immigration rose, and settlers populated the frontiers. All these elements added momentum to extending the voting right to more men.

Only in the South did broad property or tax requirements persist. In Virginia, for instance, property ownership laws continued until 1852. Today, property ownership is rarely a criterion for voting, usually only in certain local elections on matters that affect only property owners.

After the Civil War, another form of tax—a poll tax—arose as a voting requirement in many southern states. The main purpose of the poll tax was to keep newly freed blacks from voting. At the same time it prevented many poor white men who could not pay the tax from voting as well. The Twenty-fourth Amendment to the Constitution, ratified in 1964, outlawed the payment of any tax in order to vote in federal elections. Two years later, the case of *Harper v. Virginia*

State Board of Elections extended this provision to include state elections when the Court ruled that the poll tax as a condition for voting in any election is unconstitutional.

RACE

Before the Civil War, only white males could vote. African Americans, Chinese Americans, and Native Americans were excluded from the electorate until 1870 when the Fifteenth Amendment was passed removing race as a voting qualification.

The Fifteenth Amendment guarantees that states cannot deny the right to vote to anyone because of "race, color, or previous condition of servitude." Still, measures were devised to keep African Americans from voting. For instance, seven southern states added "grandfather clauses" to their constitutions. An individual was eligible to vote only if his father or grandfather had voted before 1867. Since most African American southerners had been enslaved, few African Americans qualified. Finally, the Civil Rights Acts of 1957, 1960, and 1964, as well as the Voting Rights Act of 1965, ensured full access to voting, regardless of race. In signing the 1965 act, President Lyndon Johnson said, "Today is a triumph for freedom as huge as any victory that's ever been won on any battlefield."

GENDER

Until the 1900s, most women were not allowed to vote either. This meant that the majority of adult citizens in the nation had no voice in electing those who governed. When women's rights leader Susan B. Anthony voted illegally in 1872, she had the following to say:

Friends and Fellow-citizens: I stand before you under indictment for the alleged crime of having voted in the last presidential election, without having a lawful right to vote. . . . I not only committed no crime, but instead simply exercised my citizen's right, guaranteed to me and all United States citizens by the National Constitution beyond the power of any State to deny.

Demonstrations like this one helped American women gain the right to vote. Which constitutional amendment assures women of the right to vote?

Anthony argued a position that ultimately would prevail. As she pointed out, the Constitution did not prohibit women from voting. On the other hand, however, it did not say they should be allowed to vote.

The political struggle to win women's suffrage was first organized in 1848 at a Women's Rights Convention held at Seneca Falls, New York. Women faced stiff opposition when it came to changing men's minds and convincing them that women were fit to share voting responsibilities. In 1869 the territory of Wyoming gave women the right to vote. A few states then followed Wyoming's example. Yet, 50 years later, only half the states had extended the right to vote to women, even in a few elections. The struggle lasted until 1920, when the Nineteenth Amendment to the Constitution was approved. This amendment provided that no state could deny the right to vote to any citizen ''on account of sex.''

LITERACY AND LANGUAGE

Literacy, the ability to read and write, was a requirement for voting in 18 states as late as 1970. In these states tests were given to ensure that all voters could read, write, and understand English. In theory, these tests were supposed to make sure that voters understood enough of the issues to vote intelligently. In practice, however, they resulted in denying voting rights to many members of certain immigrant, ethnic, and racial groups. In 1970 an amendment to the Voting Rights Act ended literacy as a voting qualification.

Five years later another amendment took this same act a step further by requiring that registration and voting be carried out in other languages as well as in English. It was designed to help citizens who do not read or speak

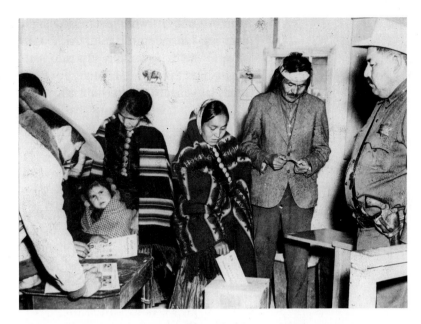

These Navajo cast their ballots in a 1951 election. In the following years, full voting access was to be extended to everyone. What legislation was to bring this about?

English to exercise the right to vote. As a result, 30 states that had a high percentage of non-English-speaking citizens were required to make additional voting provisions available. In California, for instance, ballots are printed in Chinese as well as in English. Hawaii uses Pilipino—and Japanese—language ballots. Spanish-language ballots are provided in New York, California, and Texas, and in 24 other states, voters may use Native American language ballots.

An apparent backlash to these and similar legal requirements has appeared in a number of states recently. The ''Official English'' movement seeks to have English declared the only language for official government business, including voting. Supporters of this movement say that having several languages prevents the sharing of political culture and causes misunderstandings in government and in elections. Opponents argue that citizens should be allowed to exercise their rights in whichever language they are most comfortable. Although several states have already adopted English as their official state government language, this does not overturn the federal laws requiring ballots in other languages.

Current Voter Qualifications

Today the states may not violate the Constitution or pass unreasonable laws that deny any person the right to vote. Within these limits, however, states can and do set certain other voter qualifications.

AGE
In most states, 21 was long considered the minimum age for voting. Only Alaska, Georgia, Hawaii, and Kentucky allowed younger citizens to vote. All the other states, however, had to change their requirements in 1971 with the adoption of the Twenty-sixth Amendment, which declares that no state may deny the right to vote to any person who is at least 18 years old. However, the Twenty-sixth Amendment leaves open the possibility that a state might set an even lower voting age if it so chooses.

CITIZENSHIP
The Constitution does not mention citizenship as a qualification for voting. In fact, in the 1800s and early 1900s, some western states allowed people who were not citizens to vote. Today, all states require a person to be a citizen of the United States before he or she may vote. The prevalent view is that people who show a strong interest in the nation by becoming citizens will reflect this interest in their votes.

RESIDENCE
Each state also has a residency requirement for voting. That is, a person must have lived in a state and local community for a certain period of time before being allowed to vote. Residency requirements arose from the idea that people who are closely connected to a place will be best able to vote on decisions that affect their local area.

The Voting Rights Act, however, prohibits states from requiring a person to live in an area for more than 30 days before being allowed to vote in presidential elections. In addition, most states require a residency of 30 days or less to qualify to vote in any state or local elections. Some, how-

This young woman votes for the first time in 1971. What amendment made it possible for 18-year-olds to vote in the 1971 election?

ever, require only that a voter be a legal resident of the state and do not have a fixed period of residency.

REGISTRATION

Every state except North Dakota requires citizens to **register** before voting. Registration is used to determine who is eligible to vote on election day. The registration lists prevent such fraud as a person showing up at different polling places and voting more than once.

According to the Voting Rights Act, voters may register for presidential elections up to 30 days before the election takes place. In most state and local contests, registration typically ends 28 to 30 days before election day. This allows election officials time to compile the voter lists used on election day.

For those who vote regularly, registration remains in effect so long as certain information, such as current address, is correct. If a person moves, then it is necessary for him or her to reregister. Most states have rules that automatically cancel registration if a person fails to vote. For instance, in some states, anyone who misses a general election must reregister. Other states, including New York and Ohio, eliminate the names of everyone who fails to vote in a four-year period.

Largely because of a major movement among the states, it is easier to register today than ever before. In most states voters now have a choice of locations where they may sign up. Special temporary voter centers may appear before election time at shopping centers, libraries, and even grocery stores. Some states allow motor vehicle departments to register voters at the time they get driver's licenses. And 25 states allow registration by mail at the voter's convenience.

Volunteers like these help to verify that each voter has been registered. Although voting has been made easier, some restrictions still exist. What are some of these restrictions?

RESTRICTIONS

Although laws may differ from state to state, each state has laws that disqualify certain people from voting. People who have been legally judged mentally incompetent may not vote in any state. And most states deny the right to vote to persons who have been convicted of serious crimes or election fraud. A few states also disqualify people for such other reasons as being dishonorably discharged from the military. All of these laws are difficult to enforce.

register act of reporting to a local registration office to give officials such information as name, age, and address in order to vote

Section Review

1. What were some early qualifications for voting?

2. Who may vote in elections today? Who may not?

3. Why must most citizens register before they may vote?

4. **Challenge:** Do you think election ballots should be made available in languages other than English? Why or why not?

ISSUE: CITIZENSHIP RESPONSIBILITIES

A NATIONAL YOUTH SERVICE PLAN

What are young people's responsibilities to their nation? Should some kind of civilian or military service be expected?

Most young people probably have strong opinions about such questions, which are at the center of debate about a national youth service plan. According to a recent Gallup poll, 83 percent of Americans supported the idea of national service for young people.

Given the widespread support, several models have been suggested for a national youth service plan. One proposal calls for a Citizens Corps of 1 million high school graduates to provide day care, work in literacy programs, and staff shelters and hospices. Volunteers would receive about $100 per week.

Skeptics doubt that young people would willingly enter a youth service program. Citing problems encountered in recruiting an all-volunteer military, they doubt that

enough capable volunteers could be found. They also think it would make military recruitment more difficult.

The idea of a national youth service plan found an avid supporter in President Clinton. When Clinton gave his first Inaugural Address on January 20, 1993, he called out to young Americans to give "a season of service." Many wondered what Clinton meant and who would be eligible.

Clinton believed that Americans had to start giving before they could receive. He proposed a national service program that would send young people from all areas of the country into communities to serve others. In return, participants would receive limited financial assistance to complete their education after high school.

Even before Clinton began talking about national service, widespread support for such a program came from both political parties, schools and universities, and community organizations. Marian Wright Edelman, president of the Children's Defense Fund, sees national service as a way to provide hope for disadvantaged youths. "Volunteer work will develop their self-esteem," she says, "and will demonstrate that they have options for the future." Senator Edward Kennedy of Massachusetts believes a successful youth service program can move the country "out of the 'me' generation" and into the "generation of service to others."

Kennedy believes young people will serve if it is presented throughout their education as a responsibility of citizenship.

While not everyone believes a national youth service plan is the best way to encourage young people to fulfill responsibilities of citizenship, many agree with Edelman that young people should be taught that "service is the rent we pay for living."

Congress passed Clinton's National Service program September 8, 1994. Clinton signed the bill on September 21.

Clinton had hoped to give students $10,000 a year. The final bill offered $4,725 a year for up to two years of service to individuals 17 years old or older who performed community service. The awards had to be used for educational purposes within five years of completing a term of service.

Further, the bill required that participants be chosen on a non-discriminatory basis, without regard to political affiliation. Information about National Service was to be available through high schools, colleges, and other placement officers.

1. What does Edelman mean by calling service the "rent we pay for living"? Do you agree? Explain.
2. What might be the disadvantages of the National Service program?

3 The Noncitizen

Those people living in the United States and its possessions who are not citizens are not allowed to vote in U.S. elections. A small group of people called nationals, for instance, owe allegiance to the United States and are entitled to its protection, but they may not vote or hold national office. Most nationals live on small American islands, such as American Samoa.

Aliens

The largest group of residents who are not American citizens are called **aliens**. The federal government has the power to decide how many aliens may stay in the United States. Although aliens are guaranteed most of the rights that citizens enjoy, their legal status determines how long they may remain in the United States, whether they may work here, and if they may apply for citizenship.

Some aliens are **immigrants** who want to settle permanently in the United States. To do this, they need a special **resident visa.** Many aliens who want to stay in the United States have come here to escape poverty, danger, or political persecution. For instance, a six-year airlift of **refugees** from Cuba, beginning in 1965, brought 260,000 refugees to America. In 1980 a boatlift brought in another 125,000 Cubans. After one year with legal refugee status they are considered **resident aliens**.

Another classification of aliens includes tourists, business people, students, ambassadors from other countries, and anyone else who does not intend to stay in the United States permanently. Visas for **temporary visitors** are granted for a specific period of time, depending on the purpose of the visit.

Noncitizens may be **deported** for a number of reasons. Among these are staying longer than their visas allow or committing a crime. The most common, however, is entering the United States illegally.

Illegal Aliens

More than 1 million illegal aliens are deported from our country each year. Since the early 1970s, the number of aliens who illegally enter the country each year has skyrocketed. These illegal aliens come into the United States for many different reasons. Some come to escape extreme poverty and to find work, but they may or may not want to live permanently in the United States. Other illegal aliens intend to remain in the United States, but, because of the limited number of resident visas issued by the American government, they could not enter legally. Most illegal aliens enter the United States for the same reasons that legal aliens do: to be with family, to obtain better jobs, to get a better education for their children, or to gain political freedom.

It is impossible to know how many illegal aliens live in the United States, since they obviously do not want their status known. But, it is estimated that from 3 million to 10 million persons now live illegally within the United States' borders. Most come from Mexico, but other nations of origin include El Salvador, Nicaragua, the Philippines, and Ireland.

In 1986 Congress passed the Immigration Reform and Control Act in an attempt to deal with the large number of illegal aliens. The law was designed to allow many illegal aliens to become legal residents. The results are examined in the Issue on page 153.

deported forced to leave a country

aliens citizens of another country who live in the United States

immigrants persons who travel to a country with the intention of living there permanently

resident visa authorization from the government to remain in a country

refugees persons who flee from one place to another to find protection and safety

resident aliens aliens who live in the United States on a permanent basis and enjoy the same rights as citizens except for voting and holding public office

temporary visitors noncitizens who do not plan to stay in the United States permanently

Section Review

1. What is the difference between a refugee and an immigrant?

2. What are three examples of non-immigrants, or temporary visitors to the United States?

3. **Challenge:** In your opinion, how might the government deal more effectively with the problem of illegal aliens?

4 Patterns of Immigration

Between 1607 and 1643, about 50,000 people arrived in America from Europe. By the time of the Revolutionary War, there were nearly 2.5 million people in the colonies. Most were from England, but about 40 percent came from a host of other nations. Among this number were nearly 500,000 enslaved Africans brought unwillingly to the colonies. The United States, then, is a land of immigrants. Today almost all Americans trace their origins to immigrants. Only Native Americans have a claim to being native to the land for thousands of years.

Push-Pull Forces

Between 1840 and 1860, more than 4 million Europeans immigrated to America. In the 20 years that followed, 5 million more Europeans arrived. Most were from northern Europe, primarily England, Ireland, Scotland, and Germany. This torrent of immigrants was caused by economic forces pushing the migrants from Europe and pulling them toward the United States. They left Europe for many reasons. For one, there were many more people than there were jobs. For another, small farmers and artisans were unable to compete with newly mechanized large-scale competitors. Natural disasters, such as the famine in Ireland that caused thousands to flee or starve, contributed to the push.

Revolution and religious persecution also contributed to the push force. In 1848 unsuccessful revolutions rocked Germany and Austria-Hungary, producing many political exiles. Many Quakers and members of the Dutch Reformed Church left their homelands seeking religious freedom. For those seeking political freedom, the words of the Chinese scholar Confucius rang true: "There is good government when those who are near are happy and those far away desire to come."

American economic prosperity provided the pull to attract immigrants. Laborers were needed to work in new industries and to settle the expanding frontiers. Many states even set up aggressive advertising campaigns. By 1860, 33 states and territories had opened immigration offices to attract foreigners. For example, in 1872 the Board of Immigration in the territory of Colorado issued this advertisement:

Those who are restless in their old homes, and who seek to better their condition, will find greater advantages in Colorado. . . . The young should come here to get an early start on the road to wealth, and the old would come to get a new lease of life. . . .

Letters from immigrants in the United States to relatives and friends in the "old country" told of high wages and vast, available lands. Thus, America represented a new opportunity that millions grasped with the greatest expectations. As Figure 6-1 shows, immigrants came in many different eras and from many different parts of the world.

New Wave of Immigrants

During the 1880s the pattern of immigration shifted from northern Europe to southern and eastern Europe. From Italy, Russia, Greece, Poland, Romania, and Turkey thousands of people came streaming to America. By 1896 more had come from those nations than from northern European countries. Most of these new immigrants entered New York Harbor, passing the newly erected Statue of Liberty. The poem by American writer Emma Lazarus inscribed on the statue beckoned them:

"Keep, ancient lands, your storied pomp!" cries she
With silent lips, "Give me your tired, your poor,
Your huddled masses yearning to breathe free,
The wretched refuse of your teeming shore.
Send these, the homeless, tempest-tossed, to me,
I lift my lamp beside the golden door."

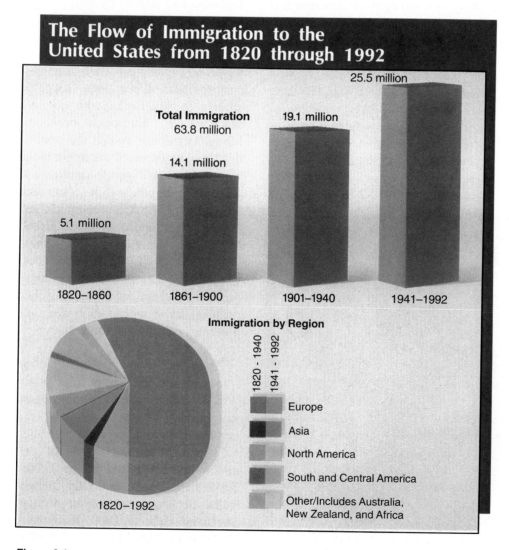

The Flow of Immigration to the United States from 1820 through 1992

Total Immigration
63.8 million

25.5 million
19.1 million
14.1 million
5.1 million

1820–1860   1861–1900   1901–1940   1941–1992

Immigration by Region

1820 - 1940
1941 - 1992

Europe
Asia
North America
South and Central America
Other/Includes Australia, New Zealand, and Africa

1820–1992

Figure 6-1

Nearly 9 million people came to the United States between 1901 and 1910, the highest number for a single decade in history. More than 2 million came from Italy and another 1.5 million from Russia.

Again, dramatic economic forces at work in their homelands lent a great push to the new immigrants. For millions, persecution also played a role. Political persecution against Greeks living in Turkey and harsh religious persecution of Russian Jews, for instance, helped swell the immigrant ranks.

The new immigrants contributed a vitality and strength to America that allowed the United States to become an industrialized nation. Many furnished cheap, unskilled labor, while others lent business skills to new industries. Since there was less land available to these later immigrants, most worked in the industrial cities of the East and Midwest. For example, in 1900, three-fourths of Chicagoans were foreign born.

During the time when so many immigrants were moving into the United States from the East Coast, other groups were joining from the West. The Treaty of Guadalupe Hidalgo, signed in 1848, transferred all of present-day California, Arizona, New Mexico, and parts of other states to the United States. This meant that some 75,000 Mexicans living in those areas became American citizens. Also, large numbers of Chinese and Japanese entered the United States from the West. By 1870 more than 100,000 Chinese were living in California, and more than 90,000 Japanese had arrived by 1910.

With the waves of new immigrants came growing resentment. Some Americans feared the new immigrants would take their jobs. Then, too, their customs and appearances appeared strange to Americans with northern and western European heritages. Many Americans voiced the opinion that these newcomers would not blend in and become "good Americans." As the new immigration continued, calls for restrictions mounted, and Congress responded by passing laws to regulate immigration. The Chinese Exclusion Act of 1882, for instance, was designed to stop Chinese immigration. Another law barred unskilled persons, those with certain diseases, illiterates, criminals, and anarchists from entry.

Fearing a flood of immigration from war-ravaged Europe after World War I, Congress enacted the Quota Act in 1921. New immigrants of a particular nationality were restricted to 3 percent of the people of that nationality who lived in the United States in 1910. Several later changes made the law even more restrictive. So, from 1920 to 1960, there were fewer immigrants than in the early years of the century.

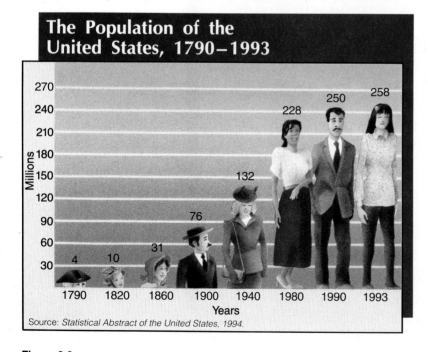

The Population of the United States, 1790–1993

Millions

270
240
210
180
150
120
90
60
30

4 — 1790
10 — 1820
31 — 1860
76 — 1900
132 — 1940
228 — 1980
250 — 1990
258 — 1993

Years

Source: *Statistical Abstract of the United States, 1994.*

Figure 6-2

ISSUE: IMMIGRATION

IS OUR IMMIGRATION LAW WORKING?

In February 1989, while 500 Central American refugees waited in camps in Harlingen, Texas, for asylum in the United States, Harlingen officials shut down the local office of the Immigration and Naturalization Service (INS). The refugees, still unable to leave the camps to look for work, were moved 25 miles to continue their wait in Port Isabel. Harlingen Mayor Bill Card said that the action was a message to Washington.

That message seems at odds with the one Americans traditionally have sent to the world from the base of the Statue of Liberty— "Give me your tired, your poor." But Americans have long had difficulty agreeing on a policy to make good on this promise while safeguarding their economy and quality of life.

Since the turn of the century, major immigration policy has been revised five times, most recently in 1986. That law, the Immigration Reform and Control Act, was in response to the influx of illegal immigrants that began in the mid-1960s, and that by the mid-1980s created an illegal alien population of over 6 million. Many Hispanics illegally crossed the border from Mexico. Illegals from British Commonwealth nations often entered through Canada. Others arrived as students or tourists and stayed after their visas expired.

For the first time, the 1986 act penalized employers who hired illegal immigrants. Lawmakers reasoned that if illegals could not find work in the United States, they would not come here. The act also established an amnesty program to allow illegal aliens who entered the country before 1982 to stay.

The effectiveness of the 1986 law has been widely criticized. Although illegal immigration fell at first, experts say it has risen again. The law's supporters respond that the rise is not due to any legal flaw. Representative Charles Schumer of New York, who helped write the law, claims the INS has not had the resources to enforce the law. "So far," he says, "the law really has not been given a fair test."

Some critics attack the amnesty program. They doubt that the 3 million illegal aliens who applied for amnesty will get adequate education to pass the test required to become permanent residents. They also claim that there was not enough publicity for the program.

Other critics claim that the law's employer penalties create a new class of indentured servants. Nearly 3.5 million illegals, not eligible for amnesty, have not gone home. Trapped in their 1986 jobs and unable to get other work, they risk abuse by employers.

Yet another issue is the priority system for legal immigrants to the United States. Currently, family members of recent arrivals have preference. Europeans, including 100,000 Irish illegals in the United States, claim that this discriminates in favor of Asians and Hispanics. But in 1988, when the Soviets loosened emigration restrictions on Jews and the Reagan administration offered them 7000 slots reserved for Asians, advocates for Cambodian and Vietnamese immigrants were outraged. Unrest throughout the world has made immigration a global problem.

Controversy over immigration policy is expected to be a topic of debate in Congress in the 1990s. Many analysts believe Congress must look more deeply at the problem than ever before. Developing a policy that acknowledges America as a haven but protects its economy will be a challenge.

1. What message did the Texas mayor send to the federal government? Why?
2. Do you agree that immigration is a global problem? Explain.

Present Immigration

The 1980s and early 1990s saw a major influx of immigrants in the United States. In 1992 about 974,000 people immigrated to the United States. Asian and Latin American nations are the source of the vast majority of recent immigrants.

Prior to 1990, immigration was largely governed by the Immigration Reform Act of 1965 that limited immigration to 270,000 persons per year. Although no nation could send more than 20,000 immigrants in any one year, there were no other restrictions based solely on national origin. Preference was shown, however, for immigrants related to American citizens, such as brothers and sisters, or adult children of U.S. citizens. Preferred status was also given to workers with special skills that were needed in the United States. Figure 6.3 at the bottom of this page notes these preference categories.

In 1990 Congress passed a sweeping revision of the 1965 law. The new law was designed to once again take the countries of origin into account and to admit more highly skilled and educated immigrants.

For most of United States history, the majority of immigrants came from Europe. The 1965 reform, however, resulted in higher levels of immigration from Asia and Latin America than ever before in American history. By 1990, 85 percent of immigrants to the United States were coming from these two regions.

The Immigration Act of 1990 significantly revised United States immigration policy. It established a limit on immigrants from any single country to no more than 7 percent of the annual visas the United States grants. It also established a "Transition Diversity Program." This program was designed to encourage immigration from any country that had been adversely affected by the 1965 law.

Section Review

1. What is meant by the "push-pull" factors of immigration?

2. What caused the growing resentment toward immigrants in the 1880s?

3. Where did the majority of immigrants to the United States come from prior to 1990?

4. **Challenge:** What are some advantages and disadvantages of being a nation of immigrants?

The Preference System Governing Immigration to the United States

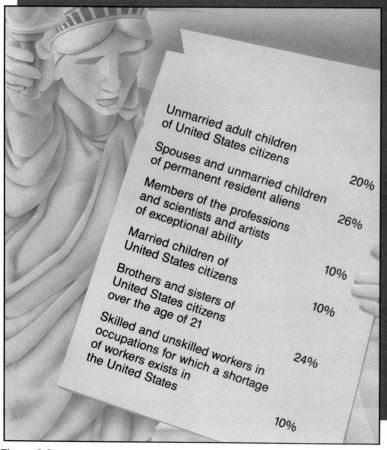

Unmarried adult children of United States citizens
Spouses and unmarried children of permanent resident aliens ... 20%

Members of the professions and scientists and artists of exceptional ability ... 26%

Married children of United States citizens ... 10%

Brothers and sisters of United States citizens over the age of 21 ... 10%

Skilled and unskilled workers in occupations for which a shortage of workers exists in the United States ... 24%

10%

Figure 6-3

1. Rights of American citizens include the right to vote, to hold public office, and to travel freely.

2. Duties of American citizens include the duty to pay taxes, serve on juries, and obey the laws. Responsibilities of citizens include voting and taking part in political affairs.

3. The Fourteenth Amendment states that all persons born or naturalized in the United States and subject to its jurisdiction are citizens of the United States.

4. To petition for citizenship, an immigrant must have lived legally in the United States for five years and be at least 18 years old.

5. American citizenship can be lost by committing certain crimes (such as treason), by expatriation, and by denaturalization.

6. When the United States was first established, the right to vote was restricted by religion, property ownership, tax payment, race, gender, and age.

7. Today, states set voter qualifications based on citizenship, residence, age, registration, and certain other requirements.

8. Aliens are citizens of another country who live in the United States.

9. Aliens are guaranteed certain rights held by citizens.

10. Foreign diplomats, tourists, business people, and students are examples of temporary visitors in the United States.

11. Job opportunities and a chance for a better living attract most illegal aliens to the United States.

12. Certain factors, such as economic forces, natural disasters, and persecution, served to ''push'' people out of Europe and into the United States. Other factors, such as the need for workers, the chance to make a better living, the abundance of land, and political freedom, served to ''pull'' people from Europe to the United States.

13. From the 1880s until the eve of World War I, the ''new'' immigrants came by the millions from eastern and southern Europe.

14. In 1882 the United States began to restrict Chinese immigration.

15. The national government has the responsibility to develop immigration laws.

16. The immigration laws passed during the 1920s were designed to limit immigration from Europe and to set up a national origins quota system. Under this system, the number of persons from a country who could legally enter the United States each year was to be based on a percentage of the number of people from that country in the United States in 1910.

17. Most recent immigrants to the United States have come from Asian and Latin American nations.

Chapter 6 Review

★Building Vocabulary

Study the following list of vocabulary words from this chapter. Imagine that these terms are correct answers to 10 questions on a vocabulary test. Write the 10 questions.

1. naturalization
2. resident aliens
3. register
4. allegiance
5. jus soli
6. refugees
7. expatriation
8. jus sanguinis
9. electorate
10. resident visa

★Reviewing Facts

1. How does the Fourteenth Amendment define a citizen of the United States?
2. How can a child born of foreign parents be automatically an American citizen?
3. How can a person born in a foreign country become a citizen of the United States?
4. What rights do native-born citizens have that naturalized citizens do not have?
5. How can native-born citizens lose their American citizenship?
6. How have voter qualifications changed since the founding of the nation?
7. What qualifications must a person meet in order to vote in the United States?
8. What groups of people, other than citizens, live in the United States?
9. Why are some people living in the United States called nonimmigrants, or temporary visitors?
10. Why do people from other countries still want to immigrate to the United States?
11. What are the rights of aliens in the United States?
12. What were some of the "push" and "pull" forces of immigration?

★Analyzing Facts

1. Should the United States government refuse to allow criminals, the mentally impaired, subversives, and illiterates to legally enter the United States? Why or why not?
2. If you had been a member of Congress in 1882, would you have voted for or against the Chinese Exclusion Act? Why?
3. Immigrants who came to the United States before the 1880's tended to be accepted more readily than many of those immigrants who entered after the 1880's. Why, do you think, was this so?
4. Do you think that the number of illegal aliens in this country poses an economic threat to the United States? A political threat? Why or why not?
5. Do you think the increase in categories of citizens eligible to vote has influenced elections? Explain.

★Evaluating Ideas

1. It has often been said that for every right there is a responsibility. On a sheet of paper, write down in one column the rights of American citizens. In a second column, write down a citizen's corresponding responsibility for each right listed. Did you list a right for which there is no corresponding responsibility? If so, explain.

Using Your
Civic Participation Journal

Review the tally that you kept during your interview for your Civic Participation Journal. Working with three of your classmates, create a paragraph summary of your interview results. Your summary should describe the major reasons the interview participations wanted to become American citizens. You might also wish to invite one of the respondents to class to describe the complex process of naturalization.

2. Citizens may voluntarily reounce citizenship, but should citizenship be taken away from a person involuntarily? Would you change the laws on the loss of citizenship? Explain.

3. Should the law of jus soli be changed to deny citizenship to those born in the United States to parents who are illegal alilens? Why or why not?

4. If you could make one reform in the electoral process, what would that reform be?

5. In your opinion, who currently is allowed to vote who should not be allowed? Who currently is not allowed to vote who should be? Justify your opinions.

★ Critical Thinking Identifying Assumptions Statements

An ambiguous statement is one that can be interpreted in a variety of ways. It can be confusing, twisted, or contradictory. Whether written or spoken, the meaning is not clear. Ambiguity can extend to our feelings about issues, and it also can be expressed through actions that we take.

Explanation We have all heard ambiguous statements, and we all use ambiguous language from time to time. Sometimes we do it deliberately if we think making our position clear might upset someone. Other times ambiguous statements occur when we are uncertain because we have inconsistent, unclear, or mixed feelings about something. Ambiguous feelings are not necessarily bad. In fact, many experts in the field of thinking believe that a tolerance for ambiguity is healthy since it is all around us. The trick is to be able to recognize it.

To determine if a statement you hear or read is ambiguous, ask yourself if the statement's meaning is unclear. If it is, can the statement be interpreted in more than one way? If your answer is "yes" to these questions, you have identified an ambiguous statement.

Practice The following statement about the attitudes of American citizens toward their government were made by Richard Nixon when he was a candi-

date for President of the United States. The ambiguities are identified for you:

> *"We want you to fell perfectly free to criticize us or this place, but want you to remember that there are limits to any criticism."* [This statement is twisted and contradictory. How can you be "perfectly free" to criticize if there are "limits" to that criticism?]
>
> *"It's time for some honest talk about the problem of order in the United States. Let us always respect, as I do, our courts and those who serve in them; but let us also recognize that some of our courts in their decisions have gone too far in weakening the peace forces against the criminal forces in this country."* [The meaning of this statement is unclear. Is the speaker critical of the courts or does he support them? His statement could be interpreted either way.]

Independent Practice Many colleges and universities have adopted "anti-harassment" policies to protect the rights of minorities. Identify why the following policy statement is ambiguous:

> *This institution supports the principles of equality, free expression, and tolerance of differences. Therefore, anyone who makes demeaning remarks about the race, religion, sex, or sexual preference of others will be disciplined by the university.*

The question of ambiguity comes up easily and frequently when we deal with First Amendment rights under the United States Consitution. In 1989, in *Texas v. Johnson*, the Supreme Court in a 5-4 decision upheld a protestor's right to burn the American flag as an exercise of free speech. Chief Justice William Rehnquist wrote a dissenting opinion which stated in part:

> *One of the high purposes of a democratic society is to legislate against conduct that is regarded as evil and profoundly offensive to a majority of the people.*

What ambiguities exist in the chief justice's statement?

Chapter 7

Political Behavior

Even before you opened this book, you already had opinions about your government. And your opinions are likewise reflected in your *actions* toward government. If you have positive feelings toward your government, for instance, you may be anxious to turn 18 years old so you can cast your vote. But other Americans may *never* vote, no matter what their age. On what do Americans base their beliefs about the system that governs them? In other words, what shapes the political behavior of American citizens?

★ ★ ★ ★ ★

Chapter Preview

TERMS TO KNOW
political culture, political socialization, political efficacy, disenfranchised, public opinion, propaganda, opinion poll

READ TO DISCOVER
- how you, as an American, learn about politics.
- the voting patterns of our nation's citizens.
- the role public opinion plays in a democracy and how public opinion is measured.

Civic Participation Journal

Contact your local Board of Elections or the local office of the League of Women Voters. Ask them for information for your community's voter registration qualifications and participation rates. Also ask what the offices are doing to encourage more people to participate in elections. These organizations often use volunteers, and you might ask if they could use your help. Keep a tally of what you learn in your journal.

159

1 Learning About Politics

Almost everyone holds certain opinions about politics and government by the time they enter high school. Take a moment to think about *your* views concerning our nation's system. Where has this knowledge come from? What influenced your thinking? You, of course, learned some of this information from previous classes in school. The rest is picked up from other influences in your life, such as family, friends, television, and the culture and environment in which you've been raised or in which you now live.

political culture   part of American culture focusing on politics and government

Political Culture

While we, as Americans, come from an incredible array of backgrounds, we do have much in common. Among other things, we see ourselves bound by common hopes and values. This is certainly true in the area of politics and government. For example, most of us share a belief in the values of liberty, equality, civic duty, and the rule of law. We also share such traditions as respect for the Constitution and Independence Day. And we recognize such symbols as the flag, the eagle, and even the image of the astronauts on the moon. All these ideas are features of the American **political culture,** which, like other parts of the culture, pass down from one generation to the next. The timelessness of one American tradition, the Fourth of July celebration, is evident in the following passage, written by Lillian Eicher in 1924:

On this day flags are hung from all the windows, industry temporarily ceases—and the nation celebrates all over again the triumph over oppression and the great note of freedom. . . . It has been customary, on every recurring Independence Day, to commemorate the great occasion by shooting off firecrackers and making a great din, in the manner of those who first celebrated the triumph.

In addition to these types of symbols, our political culture includes many of the fundamental ideas of government itself. Phrases such as "No taxation without representation," "states' rights," and "due process of law" voice some of these principles. And people often utter the phrase, "It's a free country, you know," even though they may not have politics in mind when they say it. Other practices, such as civilian election of the President or paying taxes, are also accepted as part of our nation's political culture.

Another keystone of this culture is the democratic view of political tolerance, or a willingness to let everyone

Parades like this one, celebrating the 1989 inauguration of President George Bush, reflect our political culture. What are some other symbols of this political culture?

take part. Even groups that oppose democratic values, such as the Ku Klux Klan and the Communist party, are given the right of free speech and the right to hold demonstrations.

Yet occasionally, a challenge to American political culture may arise. One issue, for instance, centers on whether burning an American flag in protest should be against the law. The belief that the flag is a symbol of the nation and must be treated with respect is part of American culture. But freedom of speech and the right to protest also are vital aspects of that culture. Political values, then, may be shared, but conflicts may occur on *how* those values should be put into actual practice.

Our government is, in fact, very stable because of the common features of America's political culture. But stability does not mean that the government remains static. New laws, procedures, and, of course, different elected officials are constantly introduced as our needs or demands change. But through all of this, the government itself remains stable, supported by a shared political culture.

Political Socialization

Americans in general hold similar political values, but Americans as individuals hold a vast number of different political attitudes. The process of learning political facts and opinions, known as **political socialization,** is ongoing. It begins early in your childhood and continues for a lifetime. And your whole environment contributes to the process.

INFLUENCES

Your family usually plays the most important role in your political socialization. Family-taught attitudes remain remarkably strong throughout a person's life. Children pick up basic attitudes about government from their parents and other family members. Ideas such as ''Government tries to help us,'' or ''All politicians are rotten,'' often are accepted by children without question. For some, the opinions formed in childhood never change. For others, early opinions evolve over time or through personal experiences. For instance, after four of his high school friends died from drugs, Dave Duerson, football star of the Chicago Bears, decided to work

political socialization
process of learning opinions and facts about politics

By burning their draft cards, these men are protesting United States involvement in the Vietnam War. How does the process of political socialization help us to develop our feelings about certain issues?

ISSUE: VOTER REGISTRATION

SHOULD VOTER REGISTRATION BE EASIER?

In 1992 only about 23 percent of all eligible voters in the United States voted for Bill Clinton for President. So how did he win the election? He won because only slightly more than 60 percent of all eligible voters cast ballots. ''And we're supposed to have representative government?'' asks Nancy Neuman, president of the League of Women Voters. In non-presidential years, turnout is even worse—only 38.7 percent in the 1994 election. In local contests, it is sometimes as low as 10 percent. Indeed, the United States has the lowest voter participation of any democracy in the world.

How can participation be increased? Some reformers urge changes in voter registration laws. Many complicated registration requirements were enacted in the late 1800s to prevent new immigrants, freed slaves, and the poor from voting. Today, many observers claim, these same restrictions are keeping the poor, the disabled, and the mobile from registering and voting. Says the director of Common Cause in Florida, Bill Jones, ''It's easier to get a fishing permit or a lottery ticket than it is to register to vote.''

A proposal recently debated in Congress would ease registration requirements by allowing people to register when they apply for or renew their driver's license, by mail, or at unemployment offices. The idea is strongly supported by such citizens groups as Common Cause and the League of Women Voters. Although registration reforms traditionally have been opposed by Republicans, who fear that most of the new voters would favor the Democrats, this proposal has now won their support. Recently Republicans also have become concerned about the especially low voter turnout among people aged 18 to 24. They now believe many of these young people would be Republicans—if they voted.

Over half the states already allow mail-in registration. Some, like Colorado, use a mobile voter registration system, taking registrars to supermarkets and shopping centers before elections. Other states have considered allowing voters to register closer to election day, so people who move shortly before an election would not lose their opportunity to vote.

Supporters claim the results of reforms have been positive. In Ohio, 70,000 voters registered in the first six weeks after registration requirements were eased. In New York, 10,000 registered in two weeks following a change in the law.

But not everyone thinks easing voter registration is the answer to low voter turnouts. A study done by political analyst Arthur T. Hadley in the late 1970s showed that only 6 percent of nonvoters failed to vote because of difficult registration procedures, hard-to-find polling places, or because they had moved close to election day and could not meet residency requirements.

Nor did Hadley's data show that registration reform encouraged voter participation. In fact, in 10 of 18 states that allowed mail-in registrations during the 1970s, the increase in nonvoting actually exceeded the national average.

As new voter registration reforms are enacted at state and national levels, observers will be watching to see if more Americans will, in fact, end up at the polls.

1. Describe one of the proposed changes in voter registration procedures and give an example of a person such a change would help.
2. What reasons can you think of why voter registration has not increased turnout on election day?

162

with students to help them avoid the same fate.

What you learn in school also affects your beliefs. Throughout these years, you are exposed to more and more points of view. Your opinions are likely to change, or at least become more complex, as they are influenced by teachers, textbooks, club activities, and friends. After you are out of school, political messages continue to bombard you. As adults, you are expected to vote on many candidates and issues, and you become more aware of political activities that directly affect you. You may pay more taxes, join the military, and apply for a license or government loan. All of these activities affect attitudes toward government and politics.

More than likely, your political socialization is also influenced by the media. Radio, television, and the press launch political messages continually. These are aired in the forms of newscasts, editorials, debates, and advertisements about public figures and issues. Political discussions with coworkers, friends, neighbors, and even strangers also help shape your ideas. Memberships in political parties, labor unions, or civic groups contribute to your outlook, too.

Over time, these and other adult experiences influence, refine, or change your political opinions. During the 1960s and 1970s, for example, many college students made headlines by leading protests against the Vietnam War. After the war ended, students responded to changing political conditions in different ways. Many returned to less activist beliefs. Others sought new ways to bring political change. Tom Hayden, once a high-profile protestor, was later elected to the California legislature. Just as you go through other changes in a life-

Tom Hayden continued his work for political change when he became a member of the California legislature. What are some other actions that may reflect our political socialization?

political efficacy feelings of effectiveness in politics

time, then, your ideas about politics and government also may change.

POLITICAL EFFICACY

Since it is such a gradual process, most of you are not aware that political socialization is taking place. Nor might you be aware that it has a direct effect on your feelings of **political efficacy.** Put another way, do *you* feel you can make a difference in government? Some people are socialized to believe that "you can't fight city hall," making no attempt to even approach the "system." Other people are socialized to trust that their actions *can* be effective and lead to changes important to them. Feelings of political efficacy are vital in a democracy. Without citizen participation, Americans and citizens of other democracies would lose their government "of the people, by the people, and for the people."

Section Review

1. What are some of the features of our political culture?

2. What are some factors that influence political socialization?

3. Why are feelings of political efficacy important in a democracy?

4. **Challenge:** In your opinion, how do your friends affect your political socialization?

2 Political Activities

All United States citizens can participate in political activities if they choose. Some citizens jump in with enthusiasm. Others take part occasionally, and still others never participate. Some political activities, such as voting, occur in a formalized fashion. Others happen quite informally, such as complaining to friends about potholes in the street.

Voting Behavior

Voting is a very common and familiar political action because elections are relatively frequent and usually widely advertised. Yet voting depends a great deal on personal attitudes and the type of election.

VOTER TURNOUT

It is surprising that voter turnout in the United States is relatively low compared to other democracies. Historian William Munro once said:

It all goes to prove what a strangely perverse creature the American citizen is. Refuse him the right to vote, and he would take up arms to wrest it from his rulers. But give this right to him freely, and he tucks it away in moth balls.

Before they can vote, qualified citizens must register. Figure 7-1 illustrates just how many people register and how many actually vote in national elections. Note that a lot more people *register* to vote than actually go to the polls and cast their ballots on election day. Both registration *and* voting figures have climbed somewhat in recent years. Some observers credit the increase to large-scale voter registration campaigns. Others note that the "baby boom" generation—the huge numbers of people born in the decades after World War II—began voting in larger numbers as they grew older.

VOTING PATTERNS

Voter turnout is most often influenced by the type of election that is being held. As Figure 7-2 shows, more people turn out for presidential elections every four years than for congressional races held every two years. And even if they are on the same ballot, more people vote for a presidential candidate than for those running for Congress. This reflects the importance Americans place on the office of the President.

This pattern holds true for executive offices on state and local levels,

Political Participation in National Elections, 1976–1994

Percent of Voting Age Population

1976* 1978 1980* 1982 1984* 1986 1988* 1990 1992* 1994

*Presidential Election Year

— Percent who reported that they registered to vote

— Percent who reported that they voted

Source: *Statistical Abstract of the United States, 1994.* Committee for the Study of the American Electorate.

Figure 7-1

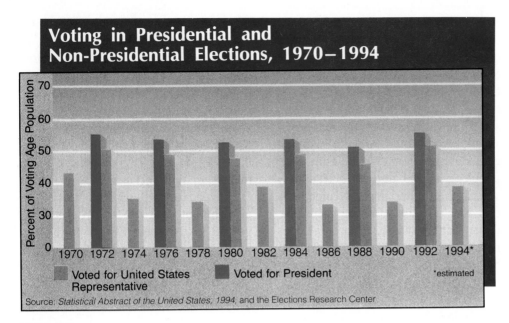

Voting in Presidential and Non-Presidential Elections, 1970–1994

Percent of Voting Age Population

1970 1972 1974 1976 1978 1980 1982 1984 1986 1988 1990 1992 1994*

◼ Voted for United States Representative   ◼ Voted for President   *estimated

Source: *Statistical Abstract of the United States, 1994*, and the Elections Research Center

Figure 7-2

too. More people vote for governor than for state legislators. And more seem to care about who wins a mayoral race than a city council seat. Even though voter turnout varies among states and regions, the more important the office is perceived to be, the more likely it is that people will vote. In the same way, voter turnout is high when *issues* that seem important or controversial, such as tax increases, are on the ballot. Thus, the higher the stakes, the more time and energy citizens will spend on voting.

INDIVIDUAL VOTERS

Those people who vote regularly, no matter who or what is on the ballot, share certain general characteristics, which are described in Figure 7-3. It seems that people who are white, college-educated, live in the North or the Midwest, or are over 45 years old are more apt both to register and to vote. Conversely, people who are nonwhite, have only an elementary education, live in the South or West, or are younger than 24 are less like-

ly to vote. Gender, too, is beginning to make a difference as women now turn out in higher proportions than men.

It is very important you understand that the voter profiles just described apply only to large groups of people, not necessarily to any specific person. Millions of young voters, for instance, do indeed go to the polls. But compared to their percentage in the entire electorate, this group votes less.

NONVOTERS

Since the act of voting is completely voluntary, what does it matter if some people choose not to vote? It has been said, "Tell me who won't vote, and I'll tell you who will win the election." Nonvoters, in fact, can make a big difference in election outcomes. Whether they know it or not, nonvoters have the potential to be an extremely powerful group.

Figure 7-4 shows the percentage of people who voted in presidential elections. In 1924, for example, only 44 percent of eligible voters actually cast their ballots. Even in the extremely close race between John Kennedy and Richard Nixon in 1960, fully one-third of the potential voters stayed home. In every presidential election since 1924, it turns out, the number of people who voted *for* the winning candidate was *less* than the number of people who did not vote. Had they voted, they could have changed the outcome of each of those races! To make matters worse, Figure 7-4 does not even show the whole picture because it does not take into account the "partial nonvoters." These are the people who go to the polls and vote for a few candidates or vote on a single issue but ignore many other items on the ballot.

Why is it that some people do not vote? Although there are many reasons, some common themes may be found. Many nonvoters are apathetic; they just do not care or believe that their vote will make any difference. Others are truly alienated or hostile to government and refuse to get involved. Still others do not vote because their religion forbids it. And in any election, there are some citizens who are considered **disenfranchised**.

disenfranchised deprived of the legal right to vote

POLITICAL PARTICIPATION IN HOUSE ELECTIONS 1980 AND 1994

	1980		1994	
	% Voting Democratic	% Voting Republican	% Voting Democratic	% Voting Republican
Sex				
Male	49	51	46	54
Female	55	45	54	46
Ethnic Origin				
White	48	52	42	58
African American	87	13	88	12
Hispanic American	72	28	70	30
Age				
18–29	55	45	54	46
30–44	49	51	48	52
45–59	53	47	51	49
60+	51	49	51	49
Region				
East	52	48	52	48
Midwest	50	50	44	56
South	54	46	45	55
West	49	51	59	41
Education				
Not high school graduate	60	40	68	32
High school graduate	55	45	52	48
Some college	47	53	47	53
College graduate	48	52	49	51

Source: *The New York Times*, November 13, 1994

Figure 7-3

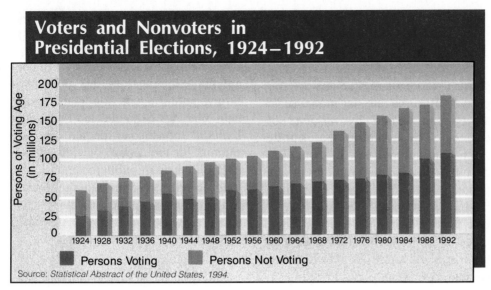

Voters and Nonvoters in Presidential Elections, 1924–1992

Persons of Voting Age (in millions)

1924 1928 1932 1936 1940 1944 1948 1952 1956 1960 1964 1968 1972 1976 1980 1984 1988 1992

■ Persons Voting   ■ Persons Not Voting

Source: *Statistical Abstract of the United States, 1994.*

Figure 7-4

Some of these people may be too ill or physically handicapped to get to the polls, and others, such as convicted felons, are legally restricted from voting. Finally, some nonvoters simply cannot make up their minds about how to vote. This indecision may be caused by insufficient information or by too much information, especially contradictory messages, that creates confusion. Avoiding the polls seems the best recourse for these persons.

Other Political Activities

There are many other ways to participate in government besides voting. Some political activities are such a common part of life that many of us take part without even realizing it. Talking about a current issue with a friend or trying to persuade others how to vote are frequent political activities. So are signing petitions, writing letters to officials, or giving money to candidates. Other activities are less common, such as distributing election materials door-to-door, testifying at public hearings, or working for a political party or candidate.

Even less common is the act of running for elective office.

But whatever your level of interest or commitment, there are many political outlets to pursue. And fortunately, many citizens feel a duty to do so. As Senator Robert Kennedy said:

When you have a democratic system in which every view can be expressed [through political activity], there is also a great responsibility imposed on the individual. This is a tremendous freedom that has been granted us. But we have to have the responsibility to exercise it properly.

Section Review

1. In what kinds of elections is voter turnout the highest?

2. What is a partial nonvoter?

3. Into what categories can nonvoters be grouped?

4. **Challenge:** What personal characteristics, do you think, may influence a person's political participation?

3 Public Opinion

Never doubt that your individual political actions and opinions are important. But imagine the influence of an opinion shared by *millions* of citizens! The influence that **public opinion** has on politics, in particular, depends on its distribution among people. Often, the larger the group holding an opinion the more weight that opinion carries. Public opinion, then, is a powerful tool that can ultimately influence our nation's leaders and government policies.

Public opinions exist on many different issues, from raising a sales tax to buying more buses for public transportation to deciding on the proper use of nuclear energy. In order to be elected, candidates try to know how the public feels about such issues. Once in office, government leaders continue to feel the effects of public opinion as they receive letters, petitions, or phone calls from voters. Even the highest levels of government are not exempt from this pressure. Strong public opposition to the Vietnam War, for example, led President Lyndon Johnson to decide against running for reelection.

Differences in public opinion have long played a role in guiding American government. Such diversity has added new ideas and spread political power among different groups.

Shaping Public Opinion

Many factors are involved in shaping public opinion. The same forces that sway *your* political attitudes—family, friends, the media, and so on—are at work influencing large groups of people as well. Public opinion is also shaped by what is happening at the moment. If the world is at peace and the economy is strong, public opinion may be nonvocal or at least subdued. But it tends to be a bit more vocal if the world is in crisis or the economy is crumbling. Take, for example, the notion that our government is responsible for national defense. This notion usually does not change, but public opinion on nuclear warheads versus conventional army troops may change over time, depending on the situation of the world at large.

Finally, public opinion is formed by the individuals and groups who actually *work* to shape it. These may include our national leaders, political parties, interest groups, or even members of a neighborhood committee against litter. These people use mass communication to reach the public. And this reach is vast when you consider that 98 percent of Americans own at least one radio and television,

public opinion point of view about a public issue held by a large number of people

TECHNIQUES OF PERSUASION

Bandwagon
Try to convince others that everyone else is behaving in a certain way and that they should do the same. In other words, they should "get on the bandwagon."

Card Stacking
Present only those facts that seem to prove your point. Ignore the other side of the issue.

Glittering Generalities
Use general, high-sounding terms, such as "peace" and "freedom."

Name Calling
Appeal to fears and biases by labeling others "reactionary," "radical," "redneck," or other such terms.

Plain Folks
Try to gain the support of "common people" by appearing to be just like they are.

Testimonial
Have a celebrity to support an issue, regardless of how much he or she knows about the issue.

Transfer
Use positive symbols, such as the flag or Uncle Sam, to support an issue.

Figure 7-5

not to mention all the newspapers, magazines, billboards, bumper stickers, and so on that confront us daily.

Using mass communication, then, opinion leaders attempt to sway political attitudes through the use of **propaganda.** These techniques of influence may appeal to your emotions or reason, present all of the facts or none, and inform or mislead. And while propaganda comes in many forms, some of which are outlined in Figure 7-5, its overriding goal is to persuade you and other citizens to think a certain way.

In nations where speech is restricted, propaganda is very powerful and can be used to control the people. But in a democracy, where free speech is guaranteed, it is up to you to listen to and analyze many different points of view. You need to ask yourself: Who is trying to change my opinions, and why? What are they trying to convince me of? What propaganda techniques are they using? And what *aren't* they telling me?

Measuring Public Opinion

Opinions vary in their strength or intensity. Strong opinions are voiced on both sides of such issues as abortion or gun control. But matters such as government aid for cancer research lead to low levels of intensity of public opinion. In a nation with millions of citizens, how can anyone—especially our government officials—know what public opinion is on a single topic? To be effective, public opinion must be measured.

Elections are viewed as one measurement. The number of votes cast for a candidate or an issue reflects public opinion. But elections are not a totally accurate measurement because only those opinions of the people who voted are tallied.

Another way of measuring public opinion is through an **opinion poll.** Polls often are conducted by professional organizations such as the Gallup Poll or the Harris Survey. The most accurate polls ask unbiased

The members of these two groups are expressing different opinions about a subject. Demonstrations such as these are one indicator of public opinion. What are some ways in which public opinion can be measured?

propaganda techniques of writing, speaking, or reporting used to persuade persons to hold a certain attitude

opinion poll survey of the opinions of a certain group of people

CASE STUDY: PUBLIC OPINION POLLS

DO POLLS MEASURE PUBLIC OPINION?

"Do you support a constitutional amendment prohibiting abortion?"

"Do you support a constitutional amendment protecting the life of the unborn?"

When 67 percent of the people polled answered "no" to the first question, "pro-choice" activists claimed public support for their views. But, they were less eager to accept the results of another survey in which 50 percent of those polled answered "yes" to the second question. Why the apparent contradiction? One possible explanation is that some people against abortion may also oppose dealing with it by constitutional amendment.

The wording of questions is a factor that can dramatically influence the outcome of opinion polls. For example, when asked if we spend "too much, too little, or about the right amount on welfare," only 22 percent of the respondents said "too little." But when "assistance for the poor" was substituted for the word "welfare" in the question, the number of respondents who picked the "too little" response increased to 61 percent.

There also are other reasons for looking carefully at poll results. For instance, the respondents in a poll may not be representative of the larger group being sampled. Before the 1984 presidential election, for instance, a pollster found that people who were at home on the first call were less likely to vote for Ronald Reagan than were those who had to be called back. Reagan supporters, it turned out, spent less time at home. Without those callbacks, the results would have been quite different.

A similar sampling bias created one of the worst mistakes in polling history. Based on its poll, the *Literary Digest* predicted that the Republican candidate, Alf Landon, would win 57 percent of the vote in the 1936 presidential election and defeat President Franklin D. Roosevelt. Instead, Roosevelt won by a landslide. The poll had used phone directories and automobile registration records to select its samples. But in 1936, people with phones or cars usually were more prosperous—and more Republican—than the average voter.

Another problem pollsters encounter is sometimes called the "ignorance factor." Since some

people are embarrassed to admit that they do not have an opinion about an issue, they will give an answer just to conceal their ignorance. One study to measure the size of the "ignorance factor" found that one-third of those polled expressed an opinion about a "law" that did not even exist.

Yet, polls can affect government. Public policy, and those who make it, are influenced by public opinion. Election outcomes can be affected. For example, when so many candidates run for an office that the media cannot cover them fully, decisions about news coverage may be based on poll results. Those receiving less coverage may then have difficulty staying in the race because citizens are sometimes discouraged from voting when polls show one candidate far ahead of another.

The problems of public opinion polling, and its consequences, demonstrate that poll results should not be taken at face value. Public education may be needed to make people more suspicious about measurements of "public opinion" until more is known about how the numbers were obtained by the pollsters.

1. State three reasons that polls may produce biased results.

2. Give one example of a problem that results from inaccurate or biased polling data. How could that problem be solved?

questions and use scientific methods to select a random sample. By asking certain questions, these polls measure how sweeping an opinion is across the nation. And by asking the same questions over a number of years, they can judge whether an opinion is stable. The disadvantage of polls is that they usually ask ''yes'' or ''no'' questions, which fails to measure the intensity of feeling for the candidate or issue.

Furthermore, not all polls are scientific or accurate. A radio station, for instance, may ask its listeners to phone in their opinions on a certain issue. The station then reports the results, which are not really valid because listeners of one station may not necessarily represent *all* citizens.

Opinion polls also may be skewed by the wording of the questions asked. A question like ''Would you rather choke on more air pollution or ride beautiful new subways?'' would provoke a far different response than the question, ''Do you want to pay $200 more per year in taxes to buy a new subway system?'' If the pollster were in favor of a new subway system, the first question might be asked. But if he or she opposed the new subway, the wording on the poll might resemble the second question.

Ultimately, polls are just best guesses as to what people are thinking. The information obtained from them may be simplified or wrongly interpreted. While some polls are better than others, all are subject to change as public opinion changes. Often, leaders base their actions on poll results, a risky practice as no poll can capture the variety of opinions.

Section Review

1. What factors commonly shape public opinion?

2. Why are elections not accepted as an accurate measurement of public opinion?

3. What methods do opinion polls use to obtain reliable results?

4. **Challenge:** Do you think the opinions of nonvoters should be considered by elected officials? Why or why not?

Summary

1. Americans share a common political culture, which adds stability to our government.

2. Political socialization is a lifelong process of learning about politics and government from family, school, the media, and adult experiences.

3. People who feel politically effective are likely to be involved in government.

4. The number of Americans who vote is low compared to other democracies.

5. The type of election and voters' general characteristics influence voter turnout.

6. Nonvoters have the potential to be a powerful group. People who fail to vote may be apathetic, alienated, disenfranchised, or undecided.

7. Public opinion is a powerful tool that ultimately can influence government policy.

8. Public opinion is shaped by the same factors that influence individual opinions, as well as by world events and propaganda.

9. Elections and opinion polls help measure public opinion.

Chapter 7 Review

★ Building Vocabulary

Study the following vocabulary terms and write two paragraphs about political behavior in the United States. All seven terms must appear in your paragraphs.

1. political culture
2. political socialization
3. political efficacy
4. disenfranchised
5. public opinion
6. propaganda
7. opinion poll

★ Reviewing Facts

1. How does American political culture contribute to the country's political stability?
2. When and how does political socialization take place?
3. How do your political attitudes affect your level of political activity?
4. When is voter turnout commonly the highest? The lowest?
5. What personal characteristics are common to people who are most likely to vote?
6. What has been the result of low voter turnout in presidential elections since 1924?
7. Why do some people decide not to vote?
8. Other than voting, what are the most common political activities?
9. What are some well-known techniques of influencing government leaders?
10. What are two common measurements of public opinion?
11. What kinds of answers do most public opinion polls seek?
12. Why are some public opinion polls not completely accurate?

★ Analyzing Facts

1. What effect does political tolerance have on a nation's political culture?
2. How has the political culture of your family been passed from one generation to another?
3. How have your political attitudes changed over time?
4. In your opinion, why do more people register to vote than actually do vote?
5. What techniques of influence do you think are most common in U.S. politics today?
6. Do you think public officials should base their decisions on public opinion? Why or why not?

★ Evaluating Ideas

1. What could you do to become more politically effective in your school? In your community?
2. If you were working for a political candidate, how would you try to convince nonvoters that they should vote for your candidate?
3. If you were a candidate in a school election, what techniques of influence would you use? Explain.

Using Your
Civic Participation Journal

Review the notes in your Civic Participation Journal on voter registration qualifications and participation rates in your community. Write a two-paragraph essay in which you propose ways to boost the participation rate. Remember that you may not suggest ways that would interfere with individual rights and freedoms.

4. Assume that there is a proposed school activities fee. How would you deliberately word a poll question so the results would show opposition to the fee? Support for the fee?

★ Critical Thinking Hypothesizing

Hypothesizing is the process of forming a number of tentative answers to a question or problem that might explain or solve it. A hypothesis is only a preliminary explanation. In a sense, hypotheses are "educated" guesses. They must be accepted, rejected, or modified as the problem is investigated and evidence is gathered.

Explanation To hypothesize, you must first be clear on exactly what the problem is. One way is to make the problem into a question. Suppose that you want to go out with your friends but you have no money. You might ask yourself: "Why don't I ever have money when I need it?"

Next, list your hypotheses, or tentative answers to your question. These will serve as guides in your search for information or evidence to explain your problem. In the example, you might formulate the following three hypotheses about your money problem: (1) you do not work enough hours on your part-time job; (2) you are a poor saver; (3) you spend money too freely.

As you investigate the problem, you should test each hypothesis against the information you gather. In the example, if you follow a tight budget, you could reject your second hypothesis. If you cannot work more hours on your job, you would alter your first hypothesis. If you have no regular savings plan, such evidence would support your hypothesis that your financial problem is due to your being a poor saver.

Practice Hypothesizing can be applied to the study of American government. Suppose you were asked to predict voting behavior based on the 1994 election. First, clarify and focus the problem by changing it into a question. (*What kinds of people are most likely to vote?*) Next, make hypotheses that might answer the question. *(young people would be likely to vote because of their energy, enthusiasm, and the novelty of voting; educated people would be likely to vote because they are aware of the issues)* Gather information about this problem from the "Political Participation Profile" on page 166. Finally, test the hypotheses against the information and accept, reject, or alter them as explanations. *(Reject the hypothesis about young people because the evidence demonstrates they are the least likely to vote. Accept the hypothesis about educated voters because the evidence shows that voting increases as education level increases.)*

Independent Practice Review the chart below and hypothesize about voter turnout in the next three presidential and non-presidential elections.

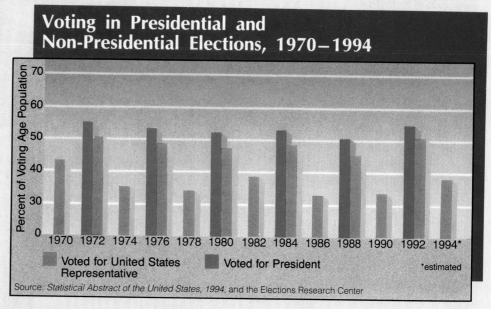

Figure 7-2

Chapter 8

Political Parties

Government has to do with you—you, as a citizen. Each one of you has ideas about what you want our government to be. And each of you working alone can make a difference, even in a country as large and as varied as ours. Yet by working *together* with others in a political group, you can have a much greater impact. Today there are many different ways for you to become involved in the democratic process. One of these, the political party, is the subject of this chapter.

★ ★ ★ ★ ★

Chapter Preview

TERMS TO KNOW
political parties, multiparty system, coalition, one-party systems, two-party systems, patronage, nominate, party platforms, plank, third parties, Independents, national chairperson, national convention, national committee, precinct

READ TO DISCOVER
- what political parties are and what they do.
- how political parties in the United States developed.
- the role of party members in a democracy.
- how political parties are organized.

Civic Participation Journal

Contact your local Republican or Democratic headquarters. Explain that you are a student trying to learn more about volunteer opportunities with the local organizations in the community. Ask how they use volunteers and what you as a student might do to help. Also ask if they have any brochures that they might mail you. Record what you learn in your journal.

These Thomas Nast cartoons popularized the Republicans' elephant and the Democrats' donkey as political symbols. What do political parties do?

1 What Are Political Parties?

Many citizens would like to be involved in helping government make decisions. Most of us, in fact, demand a say in decisions that affect us. **Political parties** are formed with such a demand in mind. Citizens organize into political parties for the purpose of winning elections, controlling government, and thus influencing government decisions.

Types of Party Systems

Most nations have one or more political parties. But the exact role parties play differs with each nation's political system.

Traditionally, the former Soviet Union and the People's Republic of China, for example, allowed only one party to exist—the Communist party. In **one-party systems** such as these, opposition arises only within the party itself. Party leaders dictate policy and hand down decisions. While elections do occur, candidates generally run unopposed.

Most countries, however, allow more than one party. The United States, Great Britain, Canada, and Colombia, for example, have **two-party systems.** Power is shared between the parties, sometimes equally, sometimes not. Sometimes there are smaller parties as well. The advantage is that voters in countries with two-party systems are given a choice.

A third option is the **multiparty system.** In Italy, France, and Israel, for example, political power is shared among many parties. Voters have a wide array of choices, but a single party rarely is strong enough to dominate elections. It often becomes necessary for several parties to form a **coalition** in order to govern.

What Political Parties Do

Working within a party is one way for you to take part in the government. Depending on your interests and time, you can participate in many ways.

In the United States, the most important of the party's roles include nominating and electing candidates,

organizing government, and monitoring the party in power.

NOMINATE AND ELECT CANDIDATES

How does the United States, with 250 million citizens, begin to choose leaders for its thousands of local, state, and national public offices? Parties play a critical role in this task, because it is their job to **nominate** people to run for office in elections. In fact, state election laws have long recognized the dominant role parties play in selecting candidates. For instance, an Oregon law of 1905 reads:

The method of naming candidates for elective public offices by political parties. . .is the best plan yet found for placing before the people the names of qualified and worthy citizens from whom the electors may choose the officers of our government.

A party nominee should represent the views of the party as well as be able to rally widespread interest among party members and voters. Once nominated by a party, the candidate then campaigns against the nominees of other parties for general public support.

Most of us are well aware of election campaigns when television, radio, magazines, and newspapers are flooded with party messages. During campaigns, parties encourage citizens to become involved in the political process. Often this is done by sponsoring voter registration drives and rallies, distributing campaign literature, and telephoning voters to encourage support of their candidates. Active party members are the key to success in all of these campaign tasks.

ORGANIZE GOVERNMENT

After campaigns and elections are over, the winning political party be-

Here, party members show support for their candidate. Why is the strong support of party members important in the nomination and election of a political candidate?

patronage practice in which elected individuals select other party members to fill government positions

gins its second function—the important, but less visible, task of organizing government. To do this, elected officials at all levels of government must appoint others to help them govern. Often, they select people through **patronage;** that is, the elected official acts as the "patron" to those who are hired.

Historically, patronage was a source of party strength. The more jobs that could be filled by partisan, or party, appointment, the more votes a party could count on. Laws eventually were passed, however, to reduce the number of patronage jobs, and civil service laws were passed to ensure that only well-qualified people,

nominate select a candidate to run for office

regardless of their party membership, were hired for government positions. Thus, party ties are not considered for many government jobs today.

Yet at the highest levels of government, there still are many patronage positions. It is estimated, for instance, that after his 1980 election, Republican President Ronald Reagan replaced about 3000 Democrats with Republicans. These included Cabinet members, top advisers, and important administrators. All elected officials, from the President down to city mayors, naturally want to know that the people closest to them are loyal, agree with their ideas, and will cooperate to make sure that government runs smoothly. Then, too, these relatively few positions usually are awarded to people who have worked hard in getting the candidate elected or contributed large sums of money to the campaign.

But party loyalties among elected leaders also serve a larger organizational purpose in government. The Democratic Governors' Conference, for instance, brings together Democratic governors to discuss state and federal policies and plan party strategies. Party allegiance unites officials in the different branches of government as well as officials of local, state, and national government.

Party connections also can provide some candidates with another benefit, sometimes called "coattail politics." In this case, candidates with wide appeal often draw votes for party candidates running for other offices. For instance, a popular presidential candidate who wins heavily in a state could give the local, state, or congressional candidates of the same party a real boost. Strong candidates for mayor or governor also can have long "coattails" that other candidates may ride.

To avoid this partisan-type voting, some people have suggested that elections for Congress and the President be held on a different date than elections for state and local offices. This, they argue, would minimize coattail politics and ensure that all candidates are elected on their own merits. Opponents of this idea contend that more elections would cost the taxpayers more money and that combining various elections raises voter interest and voter turnout.

MONITOR THE PARTY IN POWER

But what about the party that loses in an election? It, too, has an important function. The defeated party, known in Great Britain as the "loyal opposition," acts as a "watchdog" to monitor the ideas and activities of the winning party. It guards against abuses and reports other viewpoints, new information, and even scandals to the public. In this way, the defeated party acts as a *check* on the operations of government. Party organizations act as watchdogs on their own party members as well. Parties want their elected officials to do a good job because if voters believe they are not, other candidates within the party may suffer in their attempts to be elected.

Section Review

1. What three types of political party systems are important today?

2. What functions do political parties carry out in government?

3. What purposes does party loyalty serve?

4. **Challenge:** As an American, how do you interpret the term "loyal opposition"?

2 America's Political Parties

Political parties are not mentioned in the Constitution. In fact, many early leaders were against having parties at all. President George Washington had this to say in his Farewell Address in 1796: "Let me now. . .warn you in the most solemn manner against the baneful effects of the spirit of party." What Washington and others feared was that political parties would lead to competition, corruption, and inefficiency in government. How, then, did the system of political parties develop?

A Two-Party System

The nation's first political parties can be traced to the 1780s and the debate over the Constitution. Two factions emerged at that time, Federalists and Anti-Federalists. The Federalist party was America's first political party. Led by Alexander Hamilton, it supported the Constitution. The Anti-Federalists fought against approval of the Constitution. Once the Constitution was ratified, they lost their reason for being, and their unity started to evaporate. The Federalist party, on the other hand, accomplished its goal of ratifying the Constitution, but it could not maintain a strong following. After Federalist President John Adams was defeated in his bid for reelection in 1800, the party declined and soon disappeared.

The strongest opposition to the Federalists was organized by Thomas Jefferson, the successful presidential candidate of 1800. His supporters took the name Democratic-Republicans. The party was so popular that, for a few elections in this "Era of Good Feelings," they ran unopposed.

From the 1780s to the present time, Americans have been involved in political parties. This campaign memorabilia helps to illustrate our political past. How did political parties begin in the United States?

THE DEMOCRATIC PARTY

By the 1820s, the Democratic-Republicans had split into many factions. Andrew Jackson took the splinters, reshaped the party as the Democratic party, and in 1828 won the presidency. Many beliefs of today's Democratic party can be traced to Jackson's ideas. He believed that more citizens should be active in government and help decide public policy. He was especially concerned with the plight of the common people. "The humble members of society—the farmers, mechanics, the laborers," he said, "have a right to complain of the injustice of their government." His ideas became known as "Jacksonian democracy," and his party dominated national government during the first half of the 1800s. But by 1860 the Democrats were successfully challenged by a new party that had been founded in 1854—the Republicans.

THE REPUBLICAN PARTY

The Republicans were not the first party to oppose the Democrats. The Whig party, led by Henry Clay and Daniel Webster, had elected two Presidents, William Henry Harrison in 1840 and Zachary Taylor in 1848. But the Whigs had fallen apart in the 1850s, divided by the issue of slavery. Meanwhile, the Republican party grew. Over time its beliefs were broadened to appeal to farmers, laborers, and business groups. It ran its first presidential candidate in 1856 and in 1860 elected its first President, Abraham Lincoln. From then until 1932, the party virtually controlled national politics. Over these years the Republicans gained the name "GOP," or "Grand Old Party."

The 1932 victory of the Democratic candidate Franklin D. Roosevelt began a balancing of the two parties in national politics. Since then, the presidential race has been won by six Democrats: Franklin D. Roosevelt, Harry Truman, John Kennedy, Lyndon Johnson, Jimmy Carter, and Bill Clinton. The Republicans have had five presidents: Dwight Eisenhower, Richard Nixon, Gerald Ford, Ronald Reagan, and George Bush. The Republicans and Democrats, then, have wrestled for political power for more than 135 years. Neither, however, has ever dominated American politics.

Today's Political Parties

Since the time of the Federalists and Anti-Federalists, there have been two dominant political parties in America. One reason there are only two at a time has to do with election laws. In some nations, more than one person can win in each district. This encourages smaller parties because their candidate does not have to come in first to win.

But in the American system, only one person wins per district. Certain electoral rules make it hard for third-party candidates to get on the ballot,

President Abraham Lincoln, pictured here, was an early Republican leader. How did the Republican party gain popularity in the 1800s?

and it is very hard for them to come in first. Voters hate to throw away their votes for someone not likely to win. In this way, the two-party system is reinforced.

COMPARING THE PARTIES

Voters nowadays seem to have a tendency to balance power between the Republican and Democratic parties. Each party tries to appeal to a wide range of people. Each has an ideology broad enough to allow variations within the party. And since Americans share a common political culture, the two parties appear more similar than dissimilar. Former Alabama Governor George Wallace even said, ''There's not a dime's worth of difference between Democrats and Republicans.'' Although this is an exaggeration, the similarity in views holds true on some broad issues.

Yet, there are differences between the parties, particularly when it comes to specific issues or programs. While they may have the same goal, they often differ on how to reach it. For instance, although both parties agree that government should provide for the general welfare of the people, one party may want to set up employment projects, while the other one wants to cut taxes.

One way of finding differences between the parties is to read their **party platforms.** Party members are not required to agree with every **plank** of their platforms. Since it is impossible to please everyone, the platforms are designed to encompass the majority views of each party.

In a very general sense, Republicans are viewed as being somewhat conservative in government. They favor strengthening the power and responsibilities of the states while limiting the national government's role in the economy. Democrats, on the other

1994 Republican Contract With America

As Republican Members of the House of Representatives and as citizens seeking to join that body we propose not just to change its policies, but even more important, to restore the bonds of trust between the people and their elected representatives.

That is why, in this era of official evasion and posturing, we offer instead a detailed agenda for national renewal, a written commitment with no fine print.

This year's election offers the chance, after four decades of one-party control, to bring to the House a new majority that will transform the way Congress works. That historic change would be the end of government that is too big, too intrusive, and too easy with the public's money. It can be the beginning of a Congress that respects the values and shares the faith of the American family.

Like Lincoln, our first Republican president, we intend to act "with firmness in the right, as God gives us to see the right." To restore accountability to Congress. To end its cycle of scandal and disgrace. To make us all proud again of the way free people govern themselves.

On the first day of the 104th Congress, the new Republican majority will immediately pass the following major reforms, aimed at restoring the faith and trust of the American people in their government:

FIRST, require all laws that apply to the rest of the country also apply equally to the Congress;
SECOND, select a major, independent auditing firm to conduct a comprehensive audit of Congress for waste, fraud or abuse;
THIRD, cut the number of House committees, and cut committee staff by one-third;
FOURTH, limit the terms of all committee chairs;
FIFTH, ban the casting of proxy votes in committee;
SIXTH, require committee meetings to be open to the public;
SEVENTH, require a three-fifths majority vote to pass a tax increase;
EIGHTH, guarantee an honest accounting of our Federal Budget by implementing zero base-line budgeting.

Thereafter, within the first 100 days of the 104th Congress, we shall bring to the House Floor the following bills, each to be given full and open debate, each to be given a clear and fair vote and each to be immediately available this day for public inspection and scrutiny.

1. THE FISCAL RESPONSIBILITY ACT
2. THE TAKING BACK OUR STREETS ACT
3. THE PERSONAL RESPONSIBILITY ACT
4. THE FAMILY REINFORCEMENT ACT
5. THE AMERICAN DREAM RESTORATION ACT
6. THE NATIONAL SECURITY RESTORATION ACT
7. THE SENIOR CITIZENS FAIRNESS ACT
8. THE JOB CREATION AND WAGE ENHANCEMENT ACT
9. THE COMMON SENSE LEGAL REFORM ACT
10. THE CITIZEN LEGISLATURE ACT

Further, we will instruct the House Budget Committee to report to the floor and we will work to enact additional budget savings, beyond the budget cuts specifically included in the legislation described above, to ensure that the Federal budget deficit will be *less* than it would have been without the enactment of these bills.

Respecting the judgment of our fellow citizens as we seek their mandate for reform, we hereby pledge our names to this Contract with America.

Name _____   State/District _____

Source: Republican National Committee

Figure 8-1

hand, are viewed as being somewhat liberal. They push for a strong national government and often support government regulation of the economy and social programs for the poor.

A SPLIT PERSONALITY GOVERNMENT

After the 1994 elections, America had what some observers called a "split personality government," one with both conservative and liberal elements. As had happened so many times before, voters had refused to give one party control. A liberal Democrat, Bill Clinton, was in the White House. Republicans, however, controlled Congress and pledged to push a conservative agenda as shown in their Contract With America (see Figure 8.1).

party platforms official views and goals of a political party

plank single issue in a party platform

The Republicans swept the 1994 elections, winning control of Congress for the first time since the 1954 elections. The gain of 52 House seats and 9 Senate seats encouraged Republican conservatives to push their Contract With America. Republican leaders believed that the American people had voted for the Republican agenda in unprecedented numbers. During the first 100 days of the new Congress, the Republican leadership pushed for a balanced budget amendment, school prayer, and tax cuts.

The 1994 elections also gave Republicans control of a majority of governorships, including Texas and New York where Democratic incumbents were tossed out. Party power in the state legislatures and at the local level, however, remains mixed. No single party dominates. While many mayors of large cities tend to be Democrats, Republicans tend to control executive offices in smaller towns and cities and in rural areas. In city councils and county boards nationwide as well, political power is shared between the parties.

third parties minor parties in a two-party system

In this cartoon, the "shark" swimming toward President Clinton is a Republican elephant—after the Republican sweep in 1994. This illustrates one way in which power is divided in the United States. In what other ways is power divided?

Minor Parties

In addition to the Republican and Democratic parties, minor parties known as **third parties** have competed for political power throughout our history. Although smaller than major parties, they have been successful in getting some officials elected on all levels of government. Some of these parties, and their platforms, are noted in Figure 8-2. Some of the minor parties have been successful, but rarely has that success existed for more than a short period of time. The exception is the Republican party, the only minor party to become a major party. Some parties are active only in one state or for a single election. Others, like the Prohibition party, have been around for decades and continue to compete nationwide.

PERSONALITY PARTIES
Third parties arise for a number of reasons. Some are formed to elect a specific person. The United We Stand movement, for example, arose in 1992 to support H. Ross Perot's independent run for President. The American Independent party was organized in the 1960s to support George Wallace's candidacy for chief executive. Other examples are the Progressive ''Bull Moose'' party of Theodore Roosevelt and the Progressive party of Robert LaFollette. These ''personality parties'' exist only so long as their candidates remain popular with the voters.

IDEA PARTIES
Far more common are minor parties organized to promote an idea rather than a person. These parties are important in American politics because they bring controversial issues before the public. Libertarians, for instance, argue strenuously for a smaller, less active government.

SIGNIFICANT MINOR PARTIES

PARTY*	MAJOR PLATFORM POSITION	FINAL STATUS OF PARTY
Liberty 1840	Opposed slavery	Merged in 1848 to form Free Soil party
Free Soil 1848	Opposed the extension of slavery into newly acquired territories	By 1852, most members had returned to their old parties
Know Nothing 1856	Opposed immigration and the Roman Catholic Church	Ended after 1856
Constitutional Union 1860	Supported preservation of the Union and called for national unity	Ended after election of 1880
Labor Reform 1872	Supported a larger and more elastic money supply; called for 8-hour work day	Ended after election of 1872
Prohibition 1872	Favored elimination of manufacturing and selling of liquor	Still exists
Greenback 1876	Favored the issuance of large amounts of paper money	Ended after election of 1884
Socialist Labor 1892	Supports working class's control of the means of production	Still exists
Populist 1892	Promoted reforms to help farmers and workers; favored free coinage of silver; favored direct election of senators	After 1896, most members joined the Democratic party
Socialist 1900	Promotes collective ownership of the means of production and equal distribution of wealth	Still exists
Progressive "Bull Moose" 1912	Supported Theodore Roosevelt as a presidential candidate; favored women's suffrage	Most members rejoined Republican party in 1916
Communist 1924	Calls for creation of a government ruled by the working class	Still exists
States' Rights "Dixiecrats" 1948	Opposed Democratic party's civil rights plank	After 1948, party broke up and members returned to Democratic party
People's Progressive 1948	Opposed Truman's handling of the cold war	Ended after election of 1952
American Independent 1968	Supported George Wallace as a presidential candidate	In 1976, party split into the American party and the American Independent party
Libertarian 1972	Favors limited government	Still exists

*Date under each political party's name indicates the year the party first chose a presidential candidate.

Figure 8-2

The Populist party is another example of the impact minor parties can have. In 1892 it proclaimed that it had witnessed "the struggle of the two great political parties for power and plunder, while grievous wrongs have been inflicted upon the suffering people." In response, the Democrats adopted many Populist ideas into their 1896 platform and, by 1908, had succeeded in putting the Populist party out of business. Still, it might be said that the Populists were victorious when their ideas caused the Democrats to change their platform.

A number of political changes have come out of issues raised by idea parties. Laws concerning child labor, women's suffrage, income tax, popular election of United States senators, and government regulation of business all were first advocated by idea parties.

Independents voters who choose not to join a political party

In 1994 Governor George Voinovich of Ohio was part of the national Republican landslide. He captured 72 percent of the vote. What are some factors that influence party choice among Americans?

Section Review

1. What was America's first political party?
2. How do the two leading political parties differ?
3. Why do minor political parties exist?
4. **Challenge:** How can third parties influence government in the United States?

3 Party Membership

How do you become a member of a political party in the United States? It is easier than you might think. There are no mandatory dues to pay or tests to pass. You are not required to work for the party or to attend party meetings. You do not even have to vote for the party candidates. All you have to do is simply register as a member of the party you want to join.

Party Members

American citizens may declare themselves Republicans, Democrats, or members of a third party. Or they may consider themselves **Independents.** Some may not even vote, let alone claim membership to a party.

In many states, however, citizens must declare their party preference when they register to vote in certain kinds of elections. Although these voters are "registered" as Democrats or Republicans, they may change their minds whenever they wish. In other states, one's party preference need not be officially registered in order to vote.

What causes people to prefer one party over another in the first place? Party ideology, of course, plays a

TOTAL RESPONDENTS	30%	34%	36%	TYPE OF COMMUNITY			
				Urban	23	39	38
SEX				Suburban	32	34	34
Male	30	29	41	Rural	35	28	37
Female	28	39	33				
				REGION			
RACE				East	24	39	37
White	32	31	37	Midwest	27	30	43
Non-White	12	58	30	South	32	37	31
African American	6	63	31	West	32	32	36
AGE							
18–29	23	30	47				
30–49	29	31	40				
50–64	35	38	27				
65+	33	44	23				

REPUBLICANS   DEMOCRATS   INDEPENDENTS

Source: Gallup Polls, August 1994

Figure 8-3

major role in this decision. And tradition also may be a basis for party preference. Each election is different, and what attracts a person to cast votes for a party in one election may not hold true later.

Even though both parties include citizens of all ages, races, and religions, there are some common traits among party members. Figure 8-3 shows, for instance, that Protestants and those with higher incomes are more likely to be Republican. Ethnic minorities, union members, and those with lower incomes, on the other hand, tend to favor the Democrats. And since Reagan's election in 1980, a new distinction has emerged: women are more likely than men to vote Democrat. But never have all members of any large group or geographic area favored only one party.

What Party Members Do

People who participate in political parties have a greater chance of influencing government than those who do not. Because membership is voluntary, there are no requirements for what party members must do. The most common activity is voting. But in order to survive, a party needs continual support from active volunteers at all levels of government.

During campaigns, workers are needed to answer phones, mail party literature, and rally voters. After elections are over, upcoming races must be planned, candidates must be located, and the other party's weaknesses must be researched. And, of course, money must be raised.

Fund-raisers are the life blood of political parties because millions of dollars are needed to finance election costs. Dedicated party workers trek door to door or use phone banks and direct mail to raise contributions for candidates. Guests pay anywhere from a few dollars to a thousand dollars to attend dinners, parties, concerts, and lectures sponsored by the party. Picnics, bingo games, and rallies are also organized to raise money.

Party leaders decide how to split up party funds among various candidates. In some cases, highly successful politicians may receive more campaign funds than they can use. So they redistribute the excess to other candidates in their party. This redistribution of funds is controlled by campaign finance laws.

Declining Party Membership?

As Figure 8-4 indicates, there are more Democrats than Republicans, 34 percent to 29 percent in 1994. That difference, though, is less than it was in 1980 when Democrats held a 46 percent to 24 percent lead. But, there is a large percentage of Americans who do not want a party label yet are active in politics. Not committed to a single party, these people often shift their votes across party lines depending on the issues and the candidates. There are about as many Independents in the nation as there are Republicans. Consequently, most political campaigns must appeal to the Independent voter to win a majority at election time.

What has caused the growth of Independents? One reason may be the increase in young voters, who often are not party members. In 1971, when the voting age was lowered from 21 to 18, the number of Independents shot up dramatically. Another reason may be that voters just do not believe that any one party has all the answers.

There is one major disadvantage to being an Independent. In most states, the right to pick the Republican and Democratic nominees is usually reserved for party members only. Thus, the Independent voter's only choice is between candidates selected by the parties.

Figure 8-4

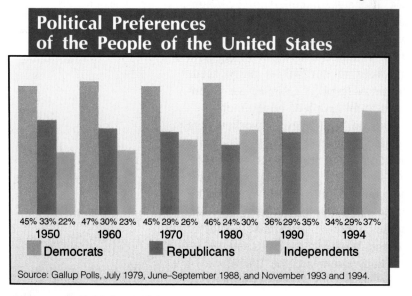

Political Preferences of the People of the United States

	1950	1960	1970	1980	1990	1994
	45% 33% 22%	47% 30% 23%	45% 29% 26%	46% 24% 30%	36% 29% 35%	34% 29% 37%

■ Democrats ■ Republicans ■ Independents

Source: Gallup Polls, July 1979, June–September 1988, and November 1993 and 1994.

Section Review

1. How does a person join a political party?
2. What are some factors that may cause people to prefer one political party over another?
3. What activities are carried out by members of political parties?
4. What is a major disadvantage to being an Independent?
5. **Challenge:** If you registered to vote today and had to list a party preference, which party would you choose? Why?

4 Party Organization

The job of managing a nationwide organization is a huge undertaking. How does a group with millions of members from all areas of the country coordinate its activities? One answer is that power within the party is decentralized. This means that decisions are made at every level, with no single group or individual issuing orders from one place. This decentralized party structure parallels, and is a direct result of, the nation's federal form of government. Because candidates are elected at all levels of government, each major party has its own local, state, and national organizations.

National Party Organization

The President is considered to be the official leader of the party. But both parties have a **national chairperson** whose duties include heading the national party organization, raising funds, and being the party's official spokesperson. For the party not represented in the White House, it is the national chairperson who officially leads it. The national chairperson of either party should be a person of high prestige and ability. In addition, he or she ultimately must be approved by his or her respective **national committee.**

COMMITTEES
Who actually makes up the national committees? Usually it is party members from around the nation, several members from each state committee, and elected officials from all levels of government. In some cases committee members are selected from certain groups, such as the elderly or ethnic minorities, to ensure that the committee will respond to the concerns of all groups within the party.

The national committee directs party business. One of its tasks is to argue policy issues and debate a party platform. Organizing campaigns, teaching candidates how to raise funds, and planning national strategies for elections also are functions of the national committee.

Also included in national party organization are Congressional Campaign Committees. There are four of these committees, one for each party in each house of Congress. Committee members—senators and representatives already in office—are chosen by their congressional colleagues to serve on the committees for two-year terms. The purpose of the committees is to support the election or reelection campaigns of party members running for Congress.

CONVENTIONS
Every four years the national party organization hosts a widely publicized spectacle called the **national convention.** Planning this convention is one of the national committee's most important duties. It is at this gathering that delegates from each state decide their party's nomination for President and Vice President and adopt the platform the candidate will run on. Delegates to this convention are not randomly selected from party members. Instead, they are elected by other party members. Generally, they are the activists, the persons who have demonstrated the highest levels of effort and involvement for a candidate or party. Many elected officials also are delegates. Combined party enthusiasm hits its peak at the national convention. One observer commented on the 1928 convention in this way:

national chairperson individual who directs the work of the national committee

national convention meeting of political party members from all over the country for the purpose of adopting a platform and nominating presidential and vice-presidential candidates

national committee group that directs party business at the national level

PROFILE: HALEY BARBOUR

CHAIRMAN OF THE REPUBLICAN PARTY

On November 8, 1994, the American voters went to the polls. When the ballots were counted, the Republicans had won a landslide victory, winning control of both houses of Congress for the first time since the 1950s. Among the many Republicans celebrating the great electoral victory was the chairperson of the Republican National Committee, Haley Barbour.

Barbour and the Republicans had much to cheer about the day after the election. Less than two years before, the party had seemed divided and even bound for failure. George Bush had been turned out of office, and the Democrats controlled Congress.

Then came Haley Barbour. In January 1993, leading Republicans met in St. Louis to elect a new party leader. Badly divided, the Republicans had several candidates from which to choose. It was the first time since 1977 that there had been such fierce competition for the party's top job.

The voting was tense and closely contested. On the first two ballots, no candidate received the majority needed to win. Finally, on the third ballot, Barbour captured 90 of the 165 votes and became the new chairperson. A longtime Republican from Yazoo City, Mississippi, Barbour had practiced law and was a partner in the law firm of Barbour and Rogers, with offices in Mississippi and Washington, D.C.

Barbour had held other positions in the Republican leadership before he was elected chairperson. In 1985 he had worked in the Reagan White House as Deputy Assistant to the President and Director of the White House Office of Political Affairs. He was also active in George Bush's 1988 presidential campaign.

A seventh generation Mississippian, Barbour attended public schools and received a law degree from the University of Mississippi in 1973. He practiced law in Yazoo City and also served as Executive Director of both the Mississippi Republican party and the Southern Association of Republican State Chairmen.

In addition to heading the Republican party, Barbour chairs the National Policy Forum and is on the board of directors of Mobile Telecommunications Technologies, Inc. and of Deposit Guaranty National Bank, Mississippi's largest bank. He also is active on the board of trustees of the Mississippi Nature Conservancy.

As Republican leader, Barbour assumed the role of coalition builder. He had no small task to perform because the party included moderates, conventional conservatives, and right-wing conservatives whose most important issue appeared to be opposing abortion.

Shortly after he took office, Barbour told the Republicans that he thought the party "came across as shrill, strident, hard-edged" during the 1992 presidential campaign. He stated that he wanted to make it clear to the voters that the Republicans were "diverse and tolerant." Based on the results of the 1994 congressional elections, Barbour successfully executed his plan.

1. What roles had Barbour played in the Republican leadership before he was elected chairperson?
2. What criteria would you use to judge Barbour's success in office? Develop an "effectiveness checklist" for a party chair.

This political convention of 1992 (left) was, in some ways, very similar to the same type of convention 54 years earlier (right). What are the major events at a political convention?

Bands play popular airs; party heroes are greeted with prolonged cheering as they appear on the scene; wire-pullers rush here and there among the delegations, making and extracting promises; all are apparently intoxicated with boisterous party zeal. It is indeed a cool-headed politician who is not swept off his feet by the excitement of the hour.

This spirited description still holds true for conventions today. In fact, due to widespread media coverage, each party's national convention has become a highly staged event, designed by professionals to attract voters' attention.

The first few days of the convention are the most low-key. They are taken up with general party business: adopting the official platform that lists the party's positions on issues and negotiating behind the scenes to settle any disputes and bring unity to the party. Although first in importance, the selection of the nominees for President and Vice President comes last in time.

Even if the party's nomination for President is a foregone conclusion, other names may be brought forward, either as a matter of principle or simply as an honor to the nominees. Nomination speeches often are forums for extolling the virtues of a candidate and for presenting political

Political Parties   189

This building served as a local Democratic headquarters during the 1992 campaign. When do state, local, and national political organizations work most closely together?

takes a majority of delegates to win the nomination. Excitement rises as the 50 percent mark approaches, and states vie with each other for the distinction of providing the final votes needed to push the nominee into the winner's circle. If no one nominee receives a majority vote, balloting goes on until one does. It is interesting to note that, in most cases, each presidential candidate has received enough votes to win on the first ballot.

Next, the convention chooses the vice-presidential candidate, a person usually named by the presidential candidate. The two candidates make their acceptance speeches, which are aimed at prime-time television audiences as well as the delegates in the auditorium. After these speeches are given, the convention is over.

State and Local Organizations

In both major parties, the state and local organizations are separate from the national party organizations. In fact, these groups may work closely only during major elections.

State laws determine party structure at this level, and since the laws vary, so do party organizations. In general, though, most states have a central committee and state chairpersons to lead the state parties. They raise funds for state candidates, help members run for office, and coordinate the many local party organizations. In some states, the parties hold conventions, like their national counterparts, to organize party platforms and nominate candidates for state offices.

As with state organizations, local party structures differ greatly from one another. Each electoral district, county, or city may have its own party committee. At the grassroots level of party organization is the **precinct.**

points of view. Shifts and rifts in the party sometimes show up in these speeches. Finally, each state delegation votes, and the chairperson for each delegation announces his or her state's vote for its chosen candidate. It

precinct smallest voting district in an area

Political parties elect or appoint precinct workers to do the day-to-day work of gaining voter support in their areas. This includes distributing campaign material, registering voters, and volunteering on local, state, and national campaigns. Precinct leaders often elect the higher level officials in the party organization.

It is easier for citizens to take part in local party organizations than in state or national organizations. Many, if not most, party leaders and elected officials started by working at the local levels of their party.

Section Review

1. Why are political party organizations in the United States decentralized?

2. What work is done by a political party's national committee?

3. What does a precinct worker do?

4. **Challenge:** What are the advantages of a decentralized organization for political parties? What might be advantages of a centralized system?

Summary

1. Political parties are formed to help give people a say in government decisions that affect them.

2. There are three types of party systems: one-party, two-party, and multiparty. The United States has a two-party system.

3. Political parties nominate and campaign for candidates, organize government if elected, and monitor the party in power.

4. Party loyalties play a part in organizing government, sometimes through patronage.

5. Political parties are not mentioned in the Constitution and were opposed by many of the Founders of American government.

6. The Republican and Democratic parties evolved over time and have controlled America's two-party system for more than 135 years.

7. The Republican and Democratic parties have different patterns of strength at different levels of government.

8. Minor parties have arisen to support a single personality or to promote certain ideas.

9. To join a political party, one needs only to register as a member of that party.

10. There are some common traits among the members of the two parties, but not all members of any major group belong to the same party.

11. Party members may play a number of voluntary roles to support candidates and issues.

12. Party membership in the two major parties has declined as the number of Independents has risen.

13. Party organization is decentralized among the three levels of government. The national organizations receive the most publicity, especially during their national conventions.

Chapter 8 Review

★ Building Vocabulary

Unscramble the following vocabulary terms so that they are spelled correctly. Then use each word in a sentence about political parties in the United States.

1. eaionmnt
2. klnap
3. acilpotil setapri
4. nicaiolto
5. trinepcc
6. driht tasprei
7. grantaeop
8. tanioaln tnicvooenn
9. yptra strafplom
10. eenIdpndnste

★ Reviewing Facts

1. What are the main purposes of a political party?
2. How does a two-party system differ from a multiparty system?
3. What are the main activities of a political party?
4. When did America's first political groups form? What were they called?
5. When was the Democratic party founded? The Republican party?
6. What are the primary differences between major parties and minor, or third, parties?
7. What are two kinds of minor parties?
8. What factors usually influence a person's political party preference?
9. What do political party members do to help their party?
10. Why has political party membership declined in recent years?
11. What is the typical political party organization in the United States?
12. How do many party leaders and elected officials get started in political activities?

★ Analyzing Facts

1. Why do minor parties have a difficult time succeeding in America's two-party political system?

2. Why do some people choose to consider themselves Independents rather than members of a political party?
3. Do you think the Democratic and Republican parties are similar? Why or why not?
4. In your opinion, is it good or bad that political parties no longer have as many patronage jobs to fill as they once did? Explain?
5. How do you think declining party membership affects election outcomes?
6. What do you think the two major parties could do to increase their membership?
7. Is a "split personality" government good for the country? Defend your answer.
8. In your opinion, in what ways could voting procedures be changed so that more people would choose to vote?

★ Evaluating Ideas

1. How might the nomination and election of candidates be different if there were no political parties?
2. How might working for a political party before becoming a candidate help a politician?
3. If you had the opportunity to join one of the minor parties listed in this chapter, which would you join? Why?

Using Your
Civic Participation Journal

Review the information on volunteer opportunities with political parties that you recorded in your Civic Participation Journal. Prepare a two-minute oral presentation describing these opportunities and encouraging your classmates to volunteer their time.

4. What are three issues you feel should be addressed in a party platform? Explain why you made those choices.

5. If you were an elected official, what types of political jobs would you like to be able to fill?

★ Critical Thinking
Comparing and Contrasting

Comparing and contrasting involves putting things side-by-side to see how they are the same and how they are different. Comparing means looking for similarities in things. Contrasting means looking for the differences.

Explanation   It is useful to examine the similarities and differences among things in order to fully understand and evaluate them. When comparing and contrasting, look for similarities first, and then look for differences. The following guidelines will be helpful:

1. Decide on two items you want to compare and contrast.

2. Find a common area or areas in which you can make comparisons.

3. Look for similarities and differences in these areas.

Practice   Look at the two statements below. Each is a reaction to a pay raise for Congress.

The manner in which the recent congressional pay hike was accomplished tells the story. Working furtively, in the dead of night, the leadership rushed through this outrageous increase, leaving the citizenry to discover their loss in the morning, like the victims of a burglary.
    —LETTER TO THE EDITOR, *WATERVILLE TIMES-HERALD*

Though we do not approve of the manner in which the pay increase was handled, we support the modest increase Congress has awarded itself. It is high time that hardworking members of Congress got a raise. In oreder to attract good people to government, the public must be willing to pay them a decent salary. Any member of Congress—and there are a few—who doesn't deserve this increase wasn't earning the old salary either.
    —EDITORIAL, *TOPSFORD DAILY LEDGER*

Areas in which these two statements might be compared include their subject matter (a congressional pay increase), the source of each statement (one is a letter to the editor, the other an editorial), whether the authors support the pay increase (the first does not, the second does), and whether they support the manner in which it was done (neither does).

Independent Practice   Study the two cartoons below. Write a paragraph comparing and contrasting the two.

SPEAKING OF HOT SEATS....

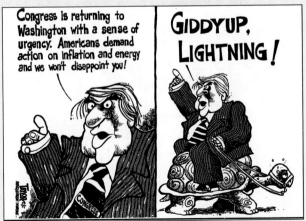

Interest Groups

Throughout our nation's history, Americans have formed interest groups to make their concerns known to public officials. Today, a vast number of these groups tug at the levers of power at all levels of American government.

Chapter Preview

TERMS TO KNOW
interest groups, public policy, lobbying, amicus curiae, political action committees

READ TO DISCOVER
- what interest groups are and what they do.
- what kinds of interest groups exist in the United States.
- who belongs to interest groups and how interest groups are regulated.
- the role of political action committees in the political process.

★ ★ ★ ★ ★

Civic Participation Journal

Choose one of the interest groups described in this chapter or one that you know has an office in your community. Contact the interest group and ask them to describe their position on key issues. Ask the contact person to send you information on the group and record the information in your journal.

1 What Is an Interest Group?

Interest groups, also known as pressure groups, are as old as the history of our nation. "No taxation without representation," for instance, was the opinion of a large interest group in colonial times. Yet James Madison, writing in *The Federalist* in 1787, deplored the possible influence of "factions" on the government. If he were alive today, Madison would probably be amazed at the number of "factions," or interest groups, that have developed. What are interest groups, and how do they influence our government?

Interest groups are groups of people organized to promote the interests or concerns of their members. They try to do this by influencing **public policy**, the laws and regulations established by government that determine who gets what, when, and how.

Interest groups can form around every imaginable issue, from finding dwellings for the homeless to censoring rock-music lyrics. They range from business and labor groups to sporting associations and neighborhood clubs. Often it is hard to identify an interest group since a group may serve several purposes at once. A rule of thumb is that whenever a group takes a position on a public issue, it is acting as an interest group.

Interest groups differ from political parties. Parties have legal status in the election process. They are concerned with nominating candidates, winning elections, and controlling government. Interest groups, on the other hand, have no legal status in the election process, though they do try to influence it. Further, political parties have positions on a wide range of public issues while interest groups, in most cases, focus only on select issues their members feel are vital.

Issues and Concerns

People join interest groups for many reasons. Often they believe they can best enhance their well-being by joining others with similar concerns. Their hope is that by pooling their time, knowledge, and money they can gain greater influence than if they acted alone.

What kinds of issues concern an interest group? Are they single issues that affect the members of the group directly or are they public interests that affect most or all Americans? The answer is "both." Residents living near the highly polluted Rocky Mountain Arsenal, for instance, formed a group called PANIC to work for health safeguards. Thus, they focus on an issue that affects the members of the group directly. In contrast, the 4-million-member Students Against Drunk Driving focuses on an issue clearly in the public interest. Another group, Lead or Leave, focuses on finding ways to lower the national debt as quickly as possible.

The *number* of issues an interest group is concerned with can vary also. A wildlife group, for instance, may be concerned only with whales or with all wildlife or with issues that

interest groups people who work together to promote common political goals or interests

public policy course of action designed by a government to manage its affairs

The Greenpeace organization is an interest group dedicated to preserving our environment. What are some other issues on which an interest group might focus?

combine wildlife, pollution, recreation, and natural resources. Some interest groups, then, promote a single interest, while others promote many. And while groups with many interests tend to last longer, they may not be able to focus their efforts as well as single-issue groups.

Membership

Who may join an interest group? It depends on what the group stands for and whether it has open or closed membership. An open group such as the National Wildlife Federation allows anyone who pays the membership fee to join. A closed group such as the American Bar Association requires applicants to be lawyers.

It is often difficult to tell whether a given interest group truly represents the people it *says* it represents. One reason is that not all eligible persons choose to become members. Not all cattle ranchers, for instance, belong to the American Cattlemen's Association. Then, too, some people who *are* members of interest groups may disagree with the group's position on an issue. Finally, because some individuals belong to more than one interest group, they may find themselves supporting groups with opposing positions. For example, a person who belongs to a religious group that has taken a stand against abortion may also be a member of a group that supports legal abortion.

Sometimes interest groups are formed based on a geographic area, such as a city or a state. A state ballot issue, for instance, may lead to the formation of a state-wide band of supporters or opponents. Usually, though, interest groups are not formed on political borders. The American Medical Association and the United Auto Workers, for instance, have

This button is worn to show support for Mothers Against Drunk Driving. Interest groups like MADD help to shape public policy. Who may join an interest group?

members spanning our country. And members of the environmental group Greenpeace hail from all over the world.

Targets of Influence

An interest group will try to influence whomever it can. Anyone who is in a position to change public policy, from the White House to city hall, is fair game. A group might target members of the different branches of government, too: the legislative branch as it makes policy; the executive as it carries out policy; and the judicial as it interprets policy. Other targets could be political candidates, the media, businesses, the public, or even other interest groups.

Section Review

1. How are interest groups different from political parties?
2. Why do individuals join interest groups?
3. How do interest groups accomplish their goals?
4. **Challenge:** Do you agree with Madison's warning against ''factions''? Why or why not?

2 Kinds of Interest Groups

Interest groups differ in some ways, such as membership and targets of influence. But they do have some common characteristics. Because of these, they can be placed into two categories—work-related groups and personal-interest groups.

Work-Related Groups

Since interest groups are often formed to further the economic well-being of their members, it is not surprising that many groups focus on issues related to salaries, working conditions, and employee benefits. Labor unions and professional organizations are two examples.

This illustration depicts the headquarters of a striking union of the 1890s. Then, as today, labor unions served the interests of their members. What are some important labor unions and professional organizations today?

LABOR AND PROFESSIONAL GROUPS

The largest labor organization is the American Federation of Labor-Congress of Industrial Organizations (AFL-CIO). Consisting of about 125 separate member unions, it represents workers such as teachers, steelworkers, carpenters, meatcutters, and chemists. And there are a number of other large unions affiliated with the AFL-CIO, such as the United Mine Workers and the International Brotherhood of Teamsters.

Like labor unions, professional organizations have been created to promote and protect the interests of *their* members. One of the largest, the National Education Association, was founded in 1857 to represent teachers and other school employees. Other professional groups are the American Medical Association, the National Association of Legal Secretaries, and the National Association of Social Workers.

Because both labor unions and professional organizations offer their members many services, ranging from training to obtaining loans, they exist for purposes beyond just an interest group. Nevertheless, these groups also act as true pressure groups, voicing their members' concerns to those who make or carry out public policy. It is not unusual for unions and professional organizations to take a strong approach when dealing with government, although some jump into a political battle only when important issues are at stake.

BUSINESS GROUPS

Just as labor and professional organizations protect their interests, hundreds of business interest groups form to guard their own concerns. The size of business groups ranges from ones that are local, such as the main street merchant association, to nationwide organizations, such as the United States Chamber of Commerce.

Business interest groups have long influenced public policy. The New York Chamber of Commerce, which was formed in 1768, may have been our nation's first interest group. Since that time, business groups have grown in number and complexity until, today, it seems as though every industry has at least one specialized group to represent it. Among the thousands of business groups that have sprung up are the National Potato Board, the Aerospace Industries Association, and the Southern Coal Producers Association.

Some segments of the business population are represented by more than one group. The interests of farmers, for instance, are promoted by the National Grange, the American Farm Bureau Federation, and the National Farmers Union. But just as other businesses specialize in their products, so does the farming industry. And this leads to specialized interest groups, such as the National Milk Producers Federation, which promotes the interests of only dairy farmers rather than all farmers.

In general, business groups support policies that help business. But as you can imagine, the groups often disagree on specific ways to go about this. Oil companies, for example, want favorable tax rates to encourage their industry. Coal producers and nuclear power companies, on the other hand, argue *against* rates favoring oil companies. Instead, they seek special government assistance that will help them.

Personal-Interest Groups

Not all interest groups are work-related groups. Some, called per-

These older Americans represent one special population group. What are some other influential special population groups?

sonal-interest groups, concern matters other than a person's occupation. They are organized around *causes* ranging from local one-time issues to long-term social movements.

SPECIAL POPULATION GROUPS

One kind of personal-interest group is a special population group. It is formed to promote the concerns of one or more segments of our population. Both the National Association for the Advancement of Colored People (NAACP) and the Urban League are special population groups that struggle to achieve equal opportunity for African Americans. Similarly, Hispanics have formed the League of United Latin American Citizens, and Croatians have organized the Croatian Fraternal Union.

But not all such groups are based on nationality or race. Other slices of our American society have formed special population groups as well. The Eagle Forum expresses the opinions of fundamentalist Christians, while the B'nai B'rith represents special concerns of Jewish Americans.

THE BOSSES OF THE SENATE.

Trusts were interest groups in the nineteenth century. This Thomas Nast cartoon shows that many Americans believed the trusts controlled Congress. What are the targets of interest groups today?

Women formed the National Organization for Women and older Americans have created such groups as the Gray Panthers and the American Association of Retired Persons.

The purpose of each of these special population groups is to help one portion of our population. They do this by focusing on the social, cultural, or religious needs of their members and presenting their aims to government and to the rest of society.

PUBLIC INTEREST GROUPS

Another kind of personal-interest group is a public interest group. Rather than focusing on one segment of society, public interest groups instead zero in on *issues*. An issue may be local in scope, such as saving a historic building. Or the issue may be sweeping, such as passing a constitutional amendment to allow prayer in public schools. But in all cases, public interest groups work to make the government reflect their values and positions on various issues.

A well-known public interest group active at local, state, and national levels is Common Cause, whose goal is better government. At the state level, it has promoted the right of the people to attend all meetings of the state legislature. At the national level, it is working to eliminate the influence that certain special interest groups have on members of Congress. The League of Women Voters and the American Civil Liberties Union are other prominent public interest groups active at national as well as local levels.

When an issue is controversial, public interest groups arise on both sides. The Right to Life group and the National Abortion Rights Action League, for instance, take opposing stands on the issue of abortion. The National Rifle Association (NRA) and Handgun Control, Inc. are other examples. They "face off" on the issue of gun control.

Ballot issues also bring opposing public interest groups to the forefront. Often these groups already exist. But sometimes new groups are formed before or during an election to address a particular issue and are disbanded after the issue has been resolved.

Section Review

1. What are two major categories of interest groups?

2. What is the main reason that many interest groups are formed?

3. For what purpose is a special population group formed?

4. **Challenge:** If you had the opportunity, what special interest groups would you choose to join? Explain your choices.

ISSUE: GUN CONTROL

INTEREST GROUPS AND POLITICAL ACTION

America's founding fathers understood that an armed people are a free people. . . . That's why the individual armed citizen remains one of democracy's strongest symbols.

> From a newspaper ad by the National Rifle Association

I have tried to stick to the facts—the fact that John Hinckley would not have been able to purchase that gun had there been a waiting period or a background check.

> Sarah Brady, Handgun Control, Inc., wife of President Reagan's press secretary James Brady, who was shot by John Hinckley, Jr.

The National Rifle Association (NRA) and Handgun Control, Inc. are two interest groups vitally concerned with the issue of gun control. Although they use some of the same strategies to present their views on the subject, the similarities end there.

Founded in the 1870s, the NRA did not become politically active until the 1960s, when political assassinations spurred calls for gun control. With millions of members, the NRA has a multi-million dollar annual budget that supports a large staff and a wide range of activities.

Through its computer system, the NRA can rally members to flood officeholders with mail and phone calls. It advertises heavily to keep its issues before the public and makes campaign contributions to candidates who support its views. At the polls, the NRA traditionally has been able to rely not only on its own members but also on 70 million gun owners and sympathetic supporters. Candidates who oppose NRA positions have felt its power on election day.

But recent polls indicate that opposition to the NRA may be growing; 54 percent of Americans polled felt the NRA has too much power. A Gallup poll reported that 70 percent of Americans responding to rising murder rates, armed drug dealers, and schoolyard attacks on children, favored stricter gun sale laws. The NRA also has lost the support of some police groups because it opposes bans on armor-piercing bullets and automatic weapons that are popular with drug dealers.

Handgun Control, Inc., established in 1974, has sought to capitalize on these changing attitudes toward the NRA and its positions. With a small membership, staff, and budget, the group cannot mobilize comparable resources. Instead, it has concentrated on building coalitions of law enforcement, unions, teachers, religious groups, the business community, African Americans, and traditional liberals to demonstrate that the NRA can be defeated on specific issues and in elections.

In a 1988 Maryland referendum to curb cheap handguns, for example, the NRA outspent Handgun Control, Inc. by nearly ten-to-one. But the gun control measure passed anyway. In Kansas, gun control advocate Nancy Kassebaum was sent to the Senate by the same voters who earlier elected gun control opponent Senator Robert Dole.

In 1993 Congress created a waiting period for gun purchasers. At the same time, some states have passed constitutional amendments to prevent local communities from enacting their own gun control measures. Thus, the duel between these two interest groups is likely to continue for some time to come.

1. What are some activities that both the NRA and Handgun Control, Inc. undertake?
2. Do you think voting on the basis of a single issue is a good way to choose between candidates? Why or why not?

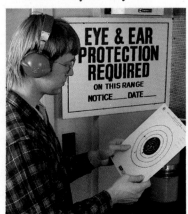

3 Activities of Interest Groups

Interest groups try to affect how government conducts its business. They try to influence what decisions and plans are made and what priority is given to various needs. They especially try to influence the policymakers. How they go about doing this depends on their goals and resources, and on legal restrictions.

Critics of interest groups worry that it is too easy for them to wield influence. Many believe that interest groups are more successful at blocking actions than pushing for solutions. One critic, Senator John Anderson, issued the following warning during his presidential campaign in 1980:

We are close to becoming a stalemated society. . .where each interest group blocks any policy, no matter how wise and how necessary, if its own interests are threatened.

Influencing Elections

One way interest groups can affect public policy is to influence the election of the policymakers. Many inter-est group members join and work within the political parties. In this way, they can influence the parties' platforms and the nomination of candidates. And to guarantee a "friend" in office, some groups may donate to more than one party or candidate. Most importantly, interest groups can urge their members to vote for candidates who support their views.

The influence of interest groups during election campaigns often seems to overshadow that of political parties. While party influence may wane once a candidate is nominated, the influence of interest groups continues long after. Any candidate expecting to win must have the support of or little opposition from powerful interest groups. Yet, no candidate can be popular or acceptable to all. As a result, a candidate must choose carefully which interest groups to court and which to ignore.

At the same time, interest groups use a variety of methods to decide what candidates to back. Some groups ask candidates to answer a set of questions on issues important to the group. Other groups study candidates' voting records and issue "report cards." For instance, one environmental group identifies the 12 members of Congress whose voting record on environmental issues is unacceptable and calls them the "Dirty Dozen." In similar fashion, the Communication Workers of America (CWA) label policymakers who take a position consistent with their own as "Heroes," and those taking the opposite position as "Zeros."

"Report cards" and similar techniques can be used to drum up support for or opposition to lawmakers that goes beyond the district they represent. This means that candidates often receive financial aid from individuals who cannot vote for them. Critics

Interest groups work to publicize issues of importance to them. Here, a billboard advocates raising teachers' salaries. What are some other activities of interest groups?

believe this practice interferes with the rights of local voters to choose their own representatives. Others counter that, since members of Congress vote on matters that affect the nation as a whole, any person who wishes to should have a say in the outcome of any congressional race.

Interest groups play other roles in the election process as well. In some states, they may use a recall petition to try to remove an elected official from office. Citizens in certain states also have the right to petition to take an issue directly to the voters. Because of such efforts, the direct influence of interest groups has increased.

Lobbying

Another way interest groups try to influence government policy is by **lobbying,** a term that comes from the idea that the easiest way to contact legislators is to stop them in the lobby. Lobbying is done by interest group members, volunteers, and paid professional lobbyists. These include former members of the Cabinet or Congress and experts in such technical fields as health care, wildlife, or banking. Some lobbyists can earn million-dollar fees lobbying for wealthy clients.

WHAT LOBBYISTS DO
Lobbyists engage in several types of activities. They often act as the link between an interest group and elected officials, making sure that information passes from one to the other. They also may recommend and set up a strategy to pressure officials. It is not uncommon, for instance, for groups to print postcards or letters that present their view and ask their members to send them to their representatives. Other lobbying tactics include phone calls, petitions, letters to local newspapers, and personal visits to policymakers.

While lobbyists can be very helpful to the groups they represent, they also help lawmakers. In fact, politicians *depend* on lobbyists for a number of reasons. Lobbyists provide information that politicians need to write better and more popular legislation. Sometimes lobbyists even *write* bills, which are then sponsored by legislators. Lobbyists may also testify on a bill. The power of their arguments plus the power of their group carry a lot of weight in legislators' minds. John F. Kennedy, while a U.S. senator, explained how useful lobbyists can be:

Lobbyists are in many cases expert technicians and capable of explaining complex and difficult subjects in a clear, understandable fashion. They engage in personal discussions with Members of Congress in which they can explain in detail the reason for positions they advocate. . .they are necessarily masters of their subject and, in fact, they frequently can provide useful statistics and information not otherwise available.

Lobbyists help to influence legislation by working with interest groups and members of Congress. How is the work of lobbyists beneficial to both groups?

lobbying attempting to influence those who make or carry out public policy

Although lobbyists are most visible in trying to affect the decisions of the legislative branch, interest groups may use the same tactics to lobby the executive branch as well as other levels of government. Lobbyists at the federal level, for instance, may want to impact standards set by the Nuclear Regulatory Commission, while the same interest group at the state level may need to make sure that the State Health Commission agrees with the group's position. And mayors, city council members, and appointed board members may be the targets at the local level.

Lobbying public officials in any branch, and at any level, is an expensive activity. More than $1 billion are spent annually lobbying the federal government alone. That does not include the vast sums spent lobbying at the state and local levels.

REGULATION OF LOBBYING

Because interest groups have so much power, local, state, and federal governments have passed laws to regulate them. The public has a right to know, for example, who is paying or *being* paid to influence their elected representatives. The federal Regulation of Lobbying Act addresses this. It requires paid lobbyists to register with the government, name the organization they work for, list their salary, and report how group funds are received and spent. Under federal law, lobbyists must file a report every three months. The reports are then published in the *Congressional Record*. Failure to follow the federal law can lead to fines of $10,000, a prison term of up to five years, and a three-year suspension of the right to lobby. However, this law and similar state laws are not well-enforced. Nor is the accuracy of the reports checked by any government authority.

The law also states that lobbyists must register only if the *principal* purpose of the group they represent is to influence government legislation. Many interest groups claim they have other primary purposes and, therefore, are not covered by the law. This explains why only about 5000 of the estimated 15,000 lobbyists in Washington are registered. Finally, at the national level, the law applies only to lobbying the legislative branch of government, not to lobbying federal agencies or the executive branch.

Going to Court

Sometimes interest groups try to influence public policy by taking issues to court. In these cases, interest groups and their lobbyists give their lawyers the information needed to bring suit and then ask members to testify on behalf of the issues. But legal proceedings have two distinct drawbacks—they are costly and slow.

Still, some groups believe going to court is a good option when judicial rulings are the easiest way to make changes. Such groups as Common Cause, the American Civil Liberties Union, and the National Association for the Advancement of Colored People have won many victories in the courtroom.

Some groups exist mainly to research legal opportunities and then bring suit. For example, the National Resources Defense Council sued the Environmental Protection Agency (EPA), charging that the EPA was not protecting consumers. The lawsuit asked the courts to require the EPA to keep cancer-causing pesticides out of food under existing federal safe food laws.

Other groups, like the Sierra Club Legal Defense Fund, routinely use the court system either to force certain actions to happen or to *prevent* them from happening. Groups like this usually target the executive branch, which is required to enforce various state and federal laws. In 1989, for instance, the Defense Fund filed suit to block construction of a hotel complex on the North Rim of the Grand Canyon. The group wanted to prevent the National Park Service from allowing irreparable damage to the area.

In a similar case, the National Audubon Society claims that the Army Corps of Engineers is threatening the Arkansas National Wildlife Refuge, the last natural habitat of the whooping crane. The Society threatened to sue the Corps to make them stop dredging within the refuge. The Corps could voluntarily comply with the request or the question could be decided within the courts.

If a group itself does not bring a lawsuit over an issue, it may still join the efforts of another group or person that does. By filing a statement of the group's position, an interest group acts as **amicus curiae.** This allows additional arguments for or against a lawsuit to be considered by the court, without the interest group having to actually bring suit. According to one study, interest groups play a role in 60 percent of the cases brought before the Supreme Court.

Since the judiciary is less open to political influence than the other two branches, interest groups do not lobby the courts. But they can affect court decisions by having a say in who gets to be judge. For example, local and state bar associations endorse candidates running for judge, and the American Bar Association (ABA) rates nominees for federal courts, including the Supreme Court. If the ABA does not approve a nominee, the Justice Department withdraws that

The National Audubon Society threatened legal action in order to safeguard the natural habitat of the whooping crane. What are some legal actions that a group might take to further their cause?

nominee from consideration. The ABA's unusual power was demonstrated in 1987 when it played a major role in the defeat of Robert Bork, President Reagan's nomination for Supreme Court justice.

amicus curiae Latin phrase meaning "friend of the court"

Section Review

1. What is the main goal of any interest group?

2. What are some interest group activities?

3. What does a lobbyist do?

4. What are some restrictions placed on lobbyists?

5. **Challenge:** Do you think the activities of elected officials would change if there were no interest groups? Explain.

4 Members of Interest Groups

The success of any interest group, no matter its goals, concerns, targets, or areas of activity, depends on how it uses its resources. And its most important resource is its membership. By giving time, ideas, and information, members strengthen their organization. They also provide the financial support a group needs to carry out its activities. Without active members or funds, an interest group will not be able to survive.

At times a charismatic individual unifies a large number of people who, then, form an interest group. Reverend Jerry Falwell, for instance, inspired the formation of the Moral Majority, and Robert Welch's views gave rise to the John Birch Society. Similarly, the Public Interest Research Groups found in many states are the brainchild of public advocate Ralph Nader.

This tobacco plant represents a means of livelihood for some American farmers. You might expect these farmers to oppose a ban on smoking in public places. How would such individuals make their opinions known?

Although some interest groups owe their existence to the work of one person, most groups form when people with common interests feel strongly about an issue and unite. Having members with diverse backgrounds can be a plus for an organization because it can argue that it reflects a large segment of public opinion. But a diverse membership is not an advantage for interest groups that represent the views of a certain segment of the population. The Korean Business Committee, for instance, has a limited focus and a limited, though presumably united, membership.

Most interest groups represent, to some extent, many segments of our country's population. Members of a large labor union, for example, come from different ethnic and religious backgrounds, vary in age, live in different regions of the country, and support different political parties. The only thing that brings them together is their occupation.

Just as an interest group represents a variety of the population, so each person may be represented by more than one interest group. Someone may belong to a Japanese-American club, the American Bar Association, and the National Organization for Women all at the same time.

Most interest group members do little more than pay dues and attend annual meetings. The daily activities of interest groups are carried out primarily by small groups of dedicated volunteers or paid professionals. When the need is urgent, however, members are expected to join lobbying efforts. At times like these, their phone calls, letters, and petitions may provide the crucial difference.

These same members must also provide the funds for an interest group to accomplish its goals. Staff salaries

1994 Election Campaign Contributions of Selected Political Action Committees

Committee	Connected Organization	Money to Congressional Candidates	Share given to	
			Democrats	Republicans
Realtors PAC	National Association of Realtors	$1,126,510	56.0%	44.0%
American Medical PAC	American Medical Association	$1,932,699	44.9%	55.1%
Democratic, Republican, Independent, Voter Education Committee	International Brotherhood of Teamsters	$2,403,102	97.3%	2.7%
American Telephone and Telegraph Company PAC	American Telephone and Telegraph Co.	$1,141,699	62.5%	37.5%
National Education Association PAC	National Education Association	$2,223,850	98.7%	1.3%

Figure 9-1   Source: Federal Election Commission

must be paid, and newsletters, telephones, and advertising can be costly. Groups that have high profiles in lobbying, bringing lawsuits, or promoting various candidates have even more expenses. And it is the members who care enough to dig into their own pockets to finance the group's actions.

Section Review

1. What is the most important resource of an interest group?

2. Who carries out the daily work of most interest groups?

3. Who provides the funds needed to operate an interest group?

4. **Challenge:** In addition to the activities mentioned in the text, what can individual members of an interest group do to strengthen their organization?

5 Political Action Committees

By far the most controversial aspect of interest groups is their financial arm, **political action committees** (PACs). There are more than 4800 PACs today. Their growth can be traced to a 1972 Supreme Court ruling stating that any independent group cannot be stopped from giving money to a political candidate as long as the group does not have legal ties to the candidate.

PACs may distribute money into a campaign in two ways. First, each PAC may directly contribute $5000 to a candidate's primary race and an additional $5000 to the candidate's general election. There is no limit, however, on the number of candidates a PAC may support. Second, a PAC may spend an unlimited amount on its own to support a candidate. This

political action committees organizations that collect contributions from members and direct that money to political candidates

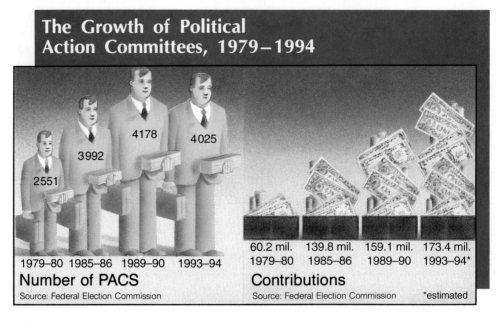

The Growth of Political Action Committees, 1979–1994

Number of PACS

2551 — 1979–80
3992 — 1985–86
4178 — 1989–90
4025 — 1993–94

Source: Federal Election Commission

Contributions

| 60.2 mil. | 139.8 mil. | 159.1 mil. | 173.4 mil. |
| 1979–80 | 1985–86 | 1989–90 | 1993–94* |

Source: Federal Election Commission   *estimated

Figure 9-2

means that the candidate's official campaign has no control over the funds. For instance, a PAC may mail letters to its members urging them to vote for a specific person. Between these two funding methods, PACs spent more than $349 million on federal races alone during the 1988 elections. Because PACs are active in state and local campaigns as well, the total amount spent that year is actually much higher.

Controversy surrounds PAC funding of campaigns. The question is, What does the money buy? According to Senator Robert Dole of Kansas, "When PACs give money, they expect something in return other than good government. It's making it more difficult to legislate." The concern that Dole and others have centers on whether the votes of legislators, who are funded by PACs, reflect the needs of special interest groups rather than the broader public good. For instance, the tobacco industry spent $1 million in the 1994 national campaigns. Is it a coincidence, then, that Congress has lagged far behind the states and local communities in passing laws that restrict smoking?

Two other interesting PAC practices point to the conclusion that PACs try to buy the attention of legislators. One is that many PACs contribute funds to *both* candidates in a race, hoping to have a friend in office regardless of who wins. Second, PACs donate funds even to candidates who run unopposed; that is, they are assured of being elected because no one else is on the ballot. The PACs cannot be attempting, in such cases, to make sure the "right" person is elected. The only explanation for this can be that the PACs presume their causes will be given sympathetic attention.

Finally, PACs generally favor the incumbent over the challenger. In the 1994 congressional races, for instance, 74 percent of all PAC contributions went to those running for reelection. Thus, PACs as a whole seem less interested in politics than in having familiar faces in office.

Few people seem happy with the current campaign financing practices. Many legislators are concerned about the excessive influence interest groups can have due to their financial arm. Yet, because campaigns are so expensive, most candidates depend on PAC donations. And most contend that if an *opponent* takes PAC money, they would be throwing away their own elections if they refused it.

Support for PAC reform is building. Surprisingly, some of it comes from PACs themselves. They have expressed concern that legislators are expecting even more funds and that the PACs are taken for granted as major donors. Some PACs feel that they are in a no-win situation, competing with one another to see which group raises and gives away the most money.

Whether PACs are simply a well-refined mechanism for the public to express its wishes or constitute a destructive perversion of the electoral system is widely debated. There is no doubt that interest groups have a great influence on government at all levels. Whether that influence is necessarily in the best interests of the *public,* however, is not really clear.

Section Review

1. What event led to the growth in the number of political action committees?

2. In what ways may PACs direct money into a campaign?

3. What are some common PAC contribution practices?

4. **Challenge:** Do you support stricter regulation of PAC funding? Why or why not?

Summary

1. Interest groups are made up of people working together for common goals.

2. Interest groups achieve their goals by influencing those who make or carry out public policy.

3. People join interest groups to achieve economic or personal well-being or to support an issue in which they believe.

4. Two major kinds of interest groups are work-related groups and personal-interest groups.

5. Major activities of interest groups include influencing elections and legislation, lobbying public officials, and taking issues to court.

6. An interest group's success depends on how well it manages its resources.

7. Local, state, and federal governments have passed laws to regulate the power and influence of interest groups.

8. PACs are the financial arm of interest groups, using members' donations to support political candidates.

9. To get the attention of elected officials, PACs may donate to all candidates, to candidates facing no opposition, and to current officeholders.

Chapter 9 Review

★ Building Vocabulary

Listed below are the vocabulary words from this chapter. Using these words, write a paragraph explaining the role of interest groups in the United States.

1. interest groups
2. public policy
3. lobbying
4. amicus curiae
5. political action committees

★ Reviewing Facts

1. What do interest groups seek to influence through their activities?
2. What are some of the reasons that people join interest groups?
3. Into what categories are interest groups commonly placed?
4. What branches of government do interest groups attempt to influence?
5. How do interest groups try to influence elections? Legislators and other public officials? The courts?
6. Where did the term *lobby* originate?
7. How can lobbyists help public officials make sound public policy decisions?
8. In what ways do interest groups use their resources?
9. What are arguments in favor of PAC political contributions? Against PAC contributions?
10. What major problems are encountered in attempts to regulate interest groups?
11. How may PACs contribute to a political campaign?
12. How much money may a political action committee contribute to a political candidate?
13. Why and how have national, state, and local governments tried to control interest groups?
14. Why are many people concerned about the power of interest groups?

★ Analyzing Facts

1. How do interest groups and political parties differ? Should these differences continue to exist? Why or why not?
2. Interest groups influence elections, legislation, and the courts, yet they are not mentioned in the Constitution. Do you think interest groups should be allowed to exist? Why or why not?
3. The President, governors, mayors, and legislators are elected by, and must answer to, the people. Lobbyists answer only to their interest group. Do you see any conflict in this situation? Explain.
4. The First Amendment to the Constitution guarantees the right of interest groups to freedom of expression. Have interest groups grown so powerful that they abuse this right? Explain.
5. Do you think candidates should agree to take tests given to them by interest groups? What would be the likely result if a candidate refused?

★ Evaluating Ideas

1. In your opinion, how might the nomination and election of political party candidates be different if there were no interest groups?

Using Your
Civic Participation Journal

Review the information you recorded in your Civic Participation Journal. Working with two of your classmates, create a collage that displays the information you received. Your collage should illustrate the major needs and services the interest groups meet. Collages should also provide details of the ways that citizens can work for the interest groups.

2. Do you think someone can be active in an interest group and a political party at the same time? Explain.

3. What additional restrictions, if any, do you think should be placed on the activities of interest groups?

4. A single person may belong to several interest groups. In your opinion, how might such membership come into conflict? How can an individual resolve the issue of membership in groups with conflicting interests?

★ Critical Thinking
Identifying Assumptions

An assumption is a fact, belief, idea, or opinion that is taken for granted. People often base their actions on assumptions. Sometimes assumptions are stated, but frequently they are not. If people assume that you share their beliefs, they may not think it is necessary to explain their words or actions. Such beliefs are called unstated assumptions. Yet, you must be able to recognize both stated and unstated assumptions to fully understand and evaluate what people say, write, or do.

Explanation One way of recognizing unstated assumptions is to ask questions. In other words, always seek explanations. In understanding written material, there are three steps you can follow to help you recognize unstated assumptions. First, as you read the material, examine point by point the information the writer is presenting. Second, for each point, ask yourself what terms or statements you do not understand because the writer has not explained them. Third, ask yourself what unstated beliefs, ideas, facts, or opinions you must know to understand or evaluate the writer's point of view.

Practice Read the following excerpt from a community interest group's statement. The unstated assumptions are identified for you.

The city's parks are in trouble. The streets are overcrowded, noisy, littered, and congested with traffic. Due to overuse, the grass and flowers are being damaged. [It is assumed the reader agrees that crowded parks are undesirable.] *Another problem is that the taxes of city residents pay for the parks. Yet suburban residents use the parks at no charge, contributing to overuse.* [It is assumed the reader agrees that people should pay for the enjoyment.] *The mayor and city council members agree that there is a problem but have done nothing to resolve it.* [It is assumed that the problem can be solved.]

A recent survey showed that 74 percent of city residents want park conditions improved. Shouldn't you be concerned too? [It is assumed that if most people want something, everyone should.] *Jerry Jackson of the Hawks and Paule LeMonde of the Superstreaks support the Improve Our Parks program.* [It is assumed that if important people support something, it is worthwhile.] *You should also become active in building a better city to live in.* [It is assumed that parks are important to the quality of a city.] *Join CUNL!* [It is assumed that group action can solve problems.]

Independent Practice Examine the cartoon below. What assumptions about your knowledge of political affairs does the artist make?

Chapter 10

The Electoral Process

In our country, important public officials serve at the pleasure of the citizens. That is, we elect those public officials who will govern. If we are unhappy with our government, we may change those who hold public office. This entire process of political campaigning, nominating party candidates, and electing public officials is complex. In this chapter, you will learn how the electoral process in the United States works and why it is important for us to take part in electing public officials.

Chapter Preview

TERMS TO KNOW
partisan elections, nonpartisan elections, general elections, primary elections, plurality, run-off primary, closed primary, open primary, special election, initiative, recall, referendum, caucus, write-in, polling place

READ TO DISCOVER
- the kinds of elections held in the United States.
- how candidates are nominated for political office.
- how political campaigns are conducted.
- how elections are conducted.

★ ★ ★ ★ ★

Civic Participation Journal

Most local party organizations have specific procedures for nominating candidates for office. Contact the local Republican or Democratic headquarters to learn how the party organization selects candidates in your community. Record your findings in your journal.

1 Kinds of Elections

In elections, voters select their leaders and decide on a vast array of different issues. At both the state and national levels, most public offices are filled through **partisan elections.** The President, senators, representatives, governors, and state legislators, for instance, are elected this way. Some local officials, such as mayors and city council members, are also elected in partisan elections.

At the local level, however, many city and county officials are chosen in **nonpartisan elections.** There are no party labels on the ballot next to the names of these candidates. Sometimes the mayor, city council members, county officials, and school board members are so selected, depending on the state. In more than one-third of the states, local and state court judges also run in nonpartisan races.

Both partisan and nonpartisan elections have advantages and disadvantages. Many people favor nonpartisan elections because candidates stand for election on their own merit, not on those of a party. Supporters believe more candidates will run for office if it is a nonpartisan race. On the other hand, nonpartisan candidates do not get the support and financial aid that party candidates receive. And, since the most important political offices are partisan, voter interest and turnout is far greater in partisan elections. Clearly, there are benefits to both systems, which is why both kinds of elections continue to be used.

General Elections

Of the hundreds of elections held in the United States every year, general elections are probably the most familiar to you and attract the greatest interest. In **general elections,** voters select their government leaders from candidates nominated by political parties or who run independently. A general election decides which political party will control the various branches and levels of government.

partisan elections elections in which candidates represent political parties

nonpartisan elections elections in which candidates for office are not identified by party membership

general elections regularly scheduled elections to select local, state, or national officials

Signs such as these are commonly seen during political campaigns. At the local level, nonpartisan elections often are held to select city and county officials. What are some advantages to a nonpartisan election?

Under the Constitution, Congress has the power to set the "times, places, and manner of holding elections" for Congress and the presidency. Today general elections for these federal offices are held in even-numbered years on the first Tuesday following the first Monday in November. To make it easier for voters and to reduce costs, state and local elections are often held on the same date. However, other general elections may be regularly scheduled for other state and local races.

In general elections, citizens may also be asked to vote on proposed laws or special issues, such as tax increases or an amendment to the state constitution. So, in a single general election, citizens could possibly make their choices for President, Vice President, members of Congress, a governor, state officials, local officials, and several issues or proposals.

Campaign buttons, bumper stickers, and posters, like those shown here, are often used in attempts to influence voters at election time. When do elections take place?

Primary Elections

How are candidates chosen to run in general elections? One way is through regularly scheduled **primary elections** in which party candidates for a particular office compete against one another. The winner then faces the other parties' primary winners in the general elections.

There are three kinds of primary elections: closed, open, and run-off. State law determines which kind each political party will use. By far the most common is the **closed primary;** three-fourths of the states use it. In closed primaries only voters who have identified themselves as party members may vote. Voters declare their party preference either when they register or at the time of the election itself, depending on the state. In this kind of election, voters receive only the ballot of their own party and select

among competing candidates who will be the party nominee for the general election. In most states that use the closed primary, the winner is the candidate with a **plurality** of the votes. In nine states, however, a **run-off primary** is held between the two top vote-getters if no candidate receives a majority of the votes.

In a closed primary, Independent voters, those who do not declare a party preference, cannot vote for party nominees. Independents may, however, vote on any issues on the ballot.

Independents may also vote in open primary elections. In an **open primary,** all qualified voters, regardless of party affiliation, may take part. Each voter receives a single ballot listing all the candidates from every party. The voter must select one party and then choose from that party's

When Richard Cheney was appointed as secretary of defense, his seat in the House of Representatives was left vacant. A special election was held so that the people of Wyoming could elect a representative to take his place. What are some other reasons to hold a special election?

candidates. In most cases, only a plurality is needed to win.

Open primaries follow a somewhat different procedure in some states. In Alaska and Washington, for instance, each voter receives a ballot listing all the candidates and may choose one for each office from any party. For instance, a voter may choose a Democrat for senator and a Republican for representative.

Opinions vary on the merits of open versus closed primary systems. Supporters of the closed primary believe it makes the candidates more responsible to their party and its members. Other citizens, however, favor the open primary. Such elections, they say, protect voters' privacy because no public disclosure of party preference is required. In addition, the open primary allows Independents to take part in the important process of nominating candidates. This argument has become more important, and controversial, with the rising number of Independent voters.

Special Elections

General and primary elections take place on a regular schedule. A **special election**, on the other hand, is called whenever an issue must be decided *before* a regular election is due. Special elections are called, for instance, to fill an office that becomes vacant when an official dies or takes another job. Although state laws differ, special elections usually must be held within 30 to 120 days after an office becomes vacant. At the local level, special elections are held to allow the people to decide certain tax or bond issues or approve spending money for such special projects as a new sports stadium or convention complex. In general, fewer voters take part in special elections than in primary or general elections. There usually is a high turnout, though, when a controversial item is on the ballot.

Ballot Issues

Often, certain issues appear on ballots during general, primary, or special elections for voter approval or disapproval. Three kinds of ballot issues are the initiative, referendum, and recall. States have widely varying laws on ballot issues.

INITIATIVE
In nearly one-half the states, local and state laws allow citizens to propose new laws through a process called the **initiative.** To put an initiative on the ballot, supporters must gather a required number of voter signatures on a petition asking that a certain matter be put to public vote. The number of required signatures varies from state to state. North Dakota, for instance, requires at least 2 percent of the state's population. Arizona, on the other hand, asks that at least 10 percent of the number who

voted in the most recent governor's race sign before a proposal can be acted upon. Initiatives are popular in those states where the signature numbers are not too high. It may be easier to get a law passed by initiative than to get the same idea adopted by the normal legislative route. Interest groups nationwide are paying increased attention to this option.

Sixteen states allow a direct initiative, in which a proposal is placed on the ballot of the next general election after enough signatures are gathered. If approved, it becomes law without the legislature's involvement. Eight other states allow an indirect initiative, in which a proposed law first goes to the state legislature. If the legislature fails to pass it, the public is allowed to vote on it.

REFERENDUM

Like the initiative, the **referendum** allows citizens to play a direct role in making laws. The exact role varies according to state law. About one-half of the states allow a popular referendum, in which citizens may petition to have a law already passed by the legislature referred back to the voters, who may then accept or reject the law in the next election.

State law often requires the legislature to refer certain decisions back to the voters. These mandatory referendum issues usually deal with changes in the state constitution or other items of major importance. State legislatures also use the optional referendum, in which proposed legislation is put on the ballot. Often, this happens with controversial issues that the legislators do not want to decide on their own.

RECALL

In 15 states and in many local communities, citizens may also take part in another kind of electoral pro-

cess known as the **recall** election. A recall may be held when a large group of citizens believes a public official is incompetent, dishonest, or in some way not carrying out the duties of office. Though laws differ from state to state, the recall may be used for both executive and legislative officials as well as for judges.

To force a recall election, a certain number of citizens must sign a petition. The number of signatures is set by state law and usually is rather high. In Wisconsin and Michigan, for instance, forcing a recall election of the governor requires the signatures of 25 percent of the number of people who voted for governor in the most recent election. If enough signatures are gathered and no other election is soon due, the recall is scheduled as a special election. A successful recall means voters must choose someone to fill the vacancy, either through a general election or another special election. Though often threatened,

Here, Michigan's Governor John Engler holds a news conference. What requirement must be met before a recall election of the governor is called in Michigan?

recall direct action allowing voters to remove an official from state or local office before the end of his or her term

referendum method by which voters may approve or reject legislation referred on by their local or state government

recall elections are not held often. Most people prefer to allow an elected official to finish a term in office, especially when they consider the expense of a special election.

Section Review

1. Why do some favor partisan elections? nonpartisan elections?

2. What is the difference between primary elections and general elections?

3. What are three kinds of primary elections?

4. **Challenge:** If you could choose the primary system for your state, would you prefer an open or closed primary? Explain your answer.

2 Nominating Candidates

Before citizens can choose their officials in a general election, a nomination, or naming of candidates, must take place. Various methods of nominating candidates have been used at different times and different places. Today, no single method is used exclusively.

Self-Nomination

One traditional method of candidate nomination is self-nomination. This is simply announcing publicly one's candidacy for a particular office. The next step for the self-announced Democrat or Republican is to work through the party system to become the party's nominee for the general election. That process might

Early in the 1992 campaign, Democratic presidential candidates met to debate the issues among themselves. After announcing his or her candidacy, what is the next step for a Republican or Democratic office seeker?

In 1992, Senator J. Danforth Quayle received the Republican party's nomination for Vice President. What are some of the ways by which a candidate is nominated for office?

include primaries, caucuses or party conventions. In some instances, a self-nominated candidate who fails to gain the support of party leaders may challenge their choice in a primary election.

For the self-announced Independent or minor party candidate, on the other hand, the next step is to gather enough signatures on a nominating petition to run in the general election. All hopefuls must meet numerous state or local requirements, such as filing certain notices, as they formalize their intention.

Not all self-nominated candidates finish the race for office. Lack of funds may cause a candidate to drop out early. Usually, most self-nominated candidates first "test the water" to see what support their announcements will bring. If there is little support, they take the hint and never start a full-scale campaign. If a self-nominated candidate fails to gather enough signatures to win a place on the ballot or fails to get a party's nomination, he or she may still run as a **write-in.** For these write-in votes to

be counted, most states require the candiate to register with the local Board of Elections before election day. Write-ins, however, rarely are elected.

Party Caucus

The **caucus** method of nomination was widely used in the country's early years. Originally, the caucus was a secret meeting of wealthy and influential members of a community who picked the candidates. With the growth of political parties, the caucus became a closed meeting of party leaders, but most party members had no say in choosing who would run. Neither the caucus nor its nominees represented the average party member or voter. By the presidential race of 1824, the caucus had become a heated issue. Andrew Jackson and his followers felt it was undemocratic and dubbed it "King Caucus."

Faced with mounting opposition to the caucus system, party leaders turned to other ways to nominate. The decline of the closed caucus was part

caucus conference of party members to select leaders

write-in vote cast by writing in the name of a candidate that does not appear on the ballot

The Electoral Process 219

The Republican National Convention of 1992 brought together people from all over the country. How has our current convention system developed?

of a movement toward greater public participation in government. Today, about 20 states use a different, much more open form of the caucus. There all the party members may attend neighborhood meetings to vote on party candidates. The modern caucus system is usually combined with party conventions, which actually do the nominating.

Party Conventions

As the closed King Caucus system died, the convention system was born. By 1840, the convention system had become the most common way to nominate candidates for public office. Party members met to vote on candidates first at a local convention, then at county and state conventions, and finally at the national convention. At each level, members chose delegates to attend the next level of convention, where they were supposed to cast their votes for candidates selected at the previous level. Delegates at the national convention made the party's final choice for the nomination of national candidates.

Because it permitted more people to take part, the party convention was supposed to be more democratic than the caucus system. Yet, the new system, too, was subject to abuse. Historian Charles Beard described how corrupt party leaders during the late 1800s destroyed the integrity of conventions:

They packed [conventions] with their henchmen, who drove out or overwhelmed dangerous opponents. They padded the rolls of party members with the names of dead men. . . . They stuffed the ballot boxes, and they prepared the slates which were forced through the nominating convention in the face of opposition.

Such widespread abuses soon became public knowledge, and, as criticism mounted, state legislatures took steps to restrict how parties conducted their business. Some states did away with conventions, opting instead for direct public primaries. Other states set formal convention rules that eliminated the sources of corruption. By the early 1900s, party mechanisms were largely cleaned up.

Today, the national convention is still used by the two major political parties to select presidential candidates. Delegates are chosen according to party rules and state law. Each party allows each of the 50 states a number of delegate votes equal to the number of that state's members in Congress. Each state may also receive bonus delegates based on its past support of party candidates. To encourage wider participation, both major parties try to select delegates from all segments of the population. Parties try, for instance, to include a wide spectrum of ethnic and racial minorities and age groups as well as delegates from both sexes.

Presidential Candidates

The race for the presidency is perceived by many of us as the pinnacle of the American election process. But the route across 50 states that a candidate must travel, beginning with the nominating process, is a maze of confusing and constantly changing rules. Not only does each state handle presidential nominations in its own way, but the two major parties have slightly different sys-

tems, even within the same state. Figure 10-1 summarizes the options open to states for conducting these nominations.

Presidential nominations combine elements from all the nominating methods: self-nominations supported by petition, caucuses and conventions, and direct primaries. Together they serve to allow each state to make two decisions. The first is the election of delegates to the parties' national conventions. The second is the selection of candidates those delegates will support.

PRESIDENTIAL PRIMARIES

In presidential primaries, rivals for a party's nomination compete directly against one another in those states that have presidential primaries. In most states, votes are cast directly for a candidate. In a few states, however, voters choose delegates who represent one of the candidates. In still other states, voters select both the delegates and their presidential preference.

Today, 37 states hold presidential primaries every four years, but not

Three Methods of Nominating a Candidate for Public Office

Self-Nomination   Party Caucus   Party Convention

Figure 10-1

Senator Robert Dole of Kansas ran for the 1996 presidential nomination. He heavily campaigned in New Hampshire, site of the first primary election. Why, do you think, is the New Hampshire primary important to candidates?

necessarily on the same day. Each state sets the dates for the different primaries as well as its own rules concerning campaigning, finances, and ballot counting. The traditional opening of the primary season is the New Hampshire primary in February of the election year. Since it is the first primary, most candidates focus attention on winning. A good showing in New Hampshire means plenty of media attention and momentum for the primaries that follow. By June preceding the November general election, all 37 primaries will be finished.

Not surprisingly, candidates spend more time in primary states with large numbers of delegates, such as California and New York, than they do in smaller states. Some states have moved up the dates of their primaries to attract greater attention from both the candidates and the media. In 1988, for instance, in an attempt to increase their influence, 14 southern states held their primaries on the same day and called it "Super Tuesday." Ironically, the vote was split among several candidates, and no candidate emerged as the leader.

When an incumbent President is running for a second term, there is usually little or no opposition from within the party. No President in recent history seeking reelection has failed to get the party's nomination. But for the party out of power, it is a different story. Typically, several candidates joust for the nomination, and the lead often shifts back and forth depending on the latest primary results. Candidates face a tremendously wearisome task in primaries. They must become well-known and well-liked in a very short time from coast to coast. Those who are already famous have an easier time.

Some candidates have enough money and large enough staffs of volunteers and paid professionals to put together a full-fledged campaign in every state. Those who lack the money and staff for a nationwide campaign, try to build from a regional base. Occasionally, such a candidate may challenge the frontrunners. In 1976, for instance, Governor Jimmy Carter of Georgia did just that by winning the Democratic nomination and then the presidency.

At one time, a candidate who won a primary garnered all of that state's convention votes, but this is no longer the case. Now, almost every state awards delegates on a proportional basis. A candidate, for instance, that receives 40 percent of Louisiana's primary votes gets 40 percent of the state's delegates.

As the primary season winds down, the number of presidential hopefuls decreases. For those who finish worse than expected in a primary, funds begin to dry up, their campaigns lose momentum, and it is only a matter of time before they drop out of the race. In most cases, the party's nominee has been decided by convention time, but sometimes no candidate has won enough primary delegates to clinch the nomination. When there is no clear nominee, the national convention becomes far more exciting.

CAUCUSES AND CONVENTIONS

Instead of presidential primaries, a few states use a nominating system that combines local caucuses and conventions. The system used in Colorado is typical. On caucus night, neighbors gather at designated Republican or Democratic precinct locations, often at someone's home. Anyone may attend, but only party members may vote. Those at the caucus may air their feelings about the candidates before the party members vote for their preferred candidates.

Each caucus is allowed to elect a certain number of delegates to the county convention. These delegates are divided among the candidates based on the number of votes each received at the caucus. If, for instance, a caucus has 10 delegates, then a candidate who receives 40 percent of the votes gets 4 delegates. Backers of each candidate then choose their delegates.

Although on a larger scale, the county convention uses the same general system used by the local caucuses. Delegates from the local caucuses vote, the votes are tallied, and the number of delegates per candidate is determined. Then, each candidate's delegates select a few representatives to go to the Colorado state convention. There, delegates from the state's 63 counties vote and select the delegates to the national convention. The process from caucus to national convention takes several months.

NATIONAL CONVENTIONS

Whether elected by primaries or by caucuses and conventions, each state's delegates finally reach the national convention. Although the convention may resemble a big party complete with noise, music, and silly hats, its task is a serious one. This is when delegates from each state adopt the official party platform and decide who will be the party's presidential candidate and vice-presidential candidate.

OTHER OPTIONS

The presidential nominating process is complex, even chaotic. The rules change from state to state and often from year to year. A serious candidate must begin campaigning for the office years before the convention. Some candidates never stop campaigning. If the candidate already holds a public office, then it is difficult to do that job well and campaign at the same time.

Those who support the current nominating system argue that, while the process is complicated, it allows many different candidates to compete. Supporters argue that the competition weeds out weaker candidates and allows those with greater appeal to gradually broaden their support.

Jesse Jackson sought the Democratic presidential nomination in 1988. He took part in primary elections in many states. Why are there several different kinds of primaries across the country?

Critics contend, on the other hand, that the system leads to nominations based on superficial appearances, like how well candidates appear on television, rather than on how they stand on issues and ideas.

There are many suggestions about how to reform the nominating process. One is to hold a single, nationwide presidential primary. Supporters argue that a national primary would result in an executive who would feel more responsible to the people than to politicians. On the other hand, detractors point out that a national primary would give candidates only one opportunity every four years to become known. The advantage clearly would lie with those who already had national reputations or large "war chests" to buy TV advertisements. In addition, candidates more than ever would focus on states with a large number of delegates, further reducing the influence of the smaller states. Despite these drawbacks, the idea of a national primary remains popular. A 1988 Gallup poll showed that 65 percent of those surveyed were in favor.

But most politicians show little desire for a national primary. So, a compromise between the current system and a national primary is the idea of regional primaries. Under this system, the nation would be divided into four or five regions, with each holding a primary on a different date. Another idea is to have the smaller states hold their primaries first, then medium-sized states, and finally the largest states. Supporters contend that such a system would keep small states from being ignored and, at the same time, allow darkhorse candidates to emerge without having to spend the huge sums of money needed to campaign in the large state primaries.

Although each of these nominating systems has its advantages and drawbacks, and the current system does not please everyone, there is no full-fledged movement to change it. Representative Al Swift, chairperson of the House election subcommittee, noted:

A lot of people would like to have a nice, orderly process, but I am not sure it would change the result. They may argue that [the current system] is too expensive; they may argue that it is too long; but I don't think they can argue that it doesn't get the job done—however messy the process may be.

Richard Nixon and John F. Kennedy participated in the first televised debate between presidential candidates. Some critics feel that television has hurt the political process. Why is this so?

Section Review

1. In what ways may a candidate be nominated?

2. Why do many states use primaries instead of caucuses or conventions to choose candidates?

3. What are some criticisms of presidential primaries? What are some alternatives?

4. **Challenge:** Presidential primaries differ from state to state. Do you think all states should choose presidential candidates the same way? Why or why not?

3 Political Campaigns

How candidates campaign is both a science and an art. Their methods depend on the office they are seeking, the competition for that office, and the available resources. Running for local office may merely require that a candidate gather signatures on a petition and talk to voters door-to-door. But campaigns for higher-level offices are more complicated, expensive, and time-consuming. A candidate for the U.S. Senate, for instance, visits several cities every day to deliver speeches, make television appearances, and attend fund-raisers. Such a campaign requires millions of dollars and hundreds of volunteers.

Levels of Typical Campaign Organization

CANDIDATE

Campaign Manager

Fund–Raiser
Treasurer
Press Secretary
Media Director
Political Advisers

Volunteer Workers and Campaign Committees

Figure 10-2

Organization

Early in a major campaign, a candidate sets up an organization similar to the one shown in Figure 10-2. Good organization is crucial. For that reason, finding a good manager and campaign workers who are knowledgeable and hardworking is essential. This, however, is not always easy because much of the work is specialized and the pay is usually low. Most campaign workers are volunteers. They are the foot-soldiers in the campaign battle for votes.

Despite this, many people serve in campaign after campaign. They work for a number of reasons. Some join because they believe in the party or the candidate. Others have their own political ambitions. Still others simply enjoy the excitement. Campaign workers' tasks include taking opinion polls, soliciting funds, typing mailing lists, delivering campaign literature door-to-door, answering the phone at headquarters, and organizing rallies.

Funding

More individuals would run for office if they could afford the staggering costs of a campaign. The professional staff must be paid, banks of phones be made available, and tons of literature copied and mailed. Then there is the high cost of advertising, especially if television is used. U.S. Senate races usually cost several million dollars, and a House of Representative race can cost perhaps a million dollars.

The cost of a campaign is usually more manageable in a local contest. But each candidate, no matter what the office, faces the same problem—who pays for the campaign? Most candidates are funded by donations from supporters. A few wealthy candidates dig into their own pockets, some spending as much as several million dollars of their own funds. Political parties and political action committees also provide funds. In 1994, PACs gave over $175 million to candidates for federal offices.

H. Ross Perot ran for President in 1992 as an independent. Why do minor party and Independent candidates have a difficult time winning elections?

Presidential campaigns have the advantage of partial government funding. After years of debate over the issue, federal funds were made available in the 1976 election for all qualified presidential candidates and their parties. The purposes of this funding are to ease the money worries for candidates and to allow persons who do not have personal fortunes to run for President. The program is funded through a tax donation set up by the Revenue Act of 1971. Taxpayers are given the option of earmarking $1 of their federal income taxes to the Presidential Election Campaign Fund. By law, this campaign fund may be spent for three purposes: for the primary race, for the party's national convention, and for the general election in the fall.

To receive funds for primary elections, candidates must meet certain qualifications. They must raise a certain amount of money on their own, which the federal government matches. In the general election, on the other hand, the nominees of the two major parties automatically qualify for the funds. The federal funds are all the funds that the official campaigns may receive. However, other money may be spent for the campaign by state and local organizations or by PACs. So the federal funds limit on the amount of money to be spent on a campaign is more theory than practice.

Third-party or Independent candidates may receive federal funds only if they garnered 5 percent of the popular vote in either the previous presidential election or the current one. Of course, in the latter case, they cannot receive the federal money until the election is over.

The way the Presidential Election Campaign Fund is set up obviously favors candidates from the two major parties. Federal funds have climbed since 1976. In that year, Jimmy Carter and Gerald Ford each received $21.8 million for the general election. In 1988, George Bush and Michael Dukakis each got $46.1 million from the Fund during the presidential election of 1988. In 1980 John Anderson was the first Independent candidate to qualify for funds from the Fund. In the election of 1992, H. Ross Perot captured enough popular votes to qualify for federal funds. He refused to accept the funds, however.

Regulation

Americans have long been concerned about the rising cost of election campaigns, especially when candidates depend on wealthy donors.

Congress passed the first campaign finance laws in 1907. State and local laws regulate state and local campaign financing. In 1971, Congress passed the Federal Election Act, and three years later, an independent agency, the Federal Election Commission (FEC), was set up to carry it out. The FEC verifies which presidential candidates qualify for federal funds and enforces contribution and spending limits for those presidential candidates who accept federal funds.

The agency also keeps track of all money raised or spent by candidates for any federal office. For example, a congressional candidate must report to the FEC the names, addresses, and occupations of all persons or groups who contribute more than $200. Each candidate must also report all campaign expenses more than $200, including who got the money and for what purpose. This information is open to the public.

CONTRIBUTIONS

Federal law regulates campaign contributions in all federal elections. Individual contributions to a candidate, political party, or PAC cannot exceed $25,000 in any year. In addition, an individual may not give more than $1000 to any one candidate for federal office per election. Primaries and general elections count separately. Businesses and labor unions are not permitted to contribute directly to political campaigns, but they can and do make great use of political action committees.

SPENDING

The only federal limits on spending are on those presidential candidates who accept federal funds. During the 1992 presidential primaries, the limit for each candidate was $27.7 million, half of which were federal funds. In addition, each party could spend a maximum of $11 million on its na-

In 1989, L. Douglas Wilder was elected governor of Virginia. Wilder is shown here attending a fund-raiser during his campaign. What is the maximum amount of money an individual can contribute to a candidate's campaign?

"Stumping," a painting by George Caleb Bingham, illustrates an early technique of campaigning. What are some other ways in which candidates campaign for office?

tional convention, all of which were federal funds. And for the general election race, Republican nominee George Bush and Democratic nominee Bill Clinton each had $55.2 million of federal funds to spend.

Attempts to set limits on spending for congressional campaigns have failed. Since candidates for Congress receive no federal funds, the Supreme Court has ruled that spending limits are unconstitutional.

Campaigning

By early September, campaigning for the November general election reaches full pitch. Candidates focus their time and efforts where they can win the most votes. An area that appears to be solidly for or against the candidate usually receives fewer visits than places where gains can be made.

In the early days, candidates traveled by horseback, carriage, stagecoach, or riverboat to the place they wanted to speak. When they got there, they stood on a tree stump or some other raised area, and the audience gathered around. As a result, campaigning in one place after another became known as "stumping."

CAMPAIGNING METHODS

Beginning with the election of 1896, another way of campaigning became popular. Democrat William Jennings Bryan was the first politician to campaign throughout the country. He spoke from the platform of a special train as it paused in hundreds of towns, or "whistle-stops." Whistle-stopping soon became an important way of campaigning. Whistle-stopping today is carried on by plane or auto, as candidates race from town to town to be seen in person.

A priority of every candidate is to get public attention. Two major ways to get attention are speaking opportunities and mass media coverage. Candidates are especially lucky when they can do both, such as having evening TV news show them speaking

In 1989, David Dinkins became New York City's first African American mayor. Although many criticize the campaign process, our system offers an opportunity for candidates to discuss important issues and to communicate with voters. What are some things that candidates do to make their views known?

to an enthusiastic crowd. On a local level, there is no substitute for a candidate to become a familiar face. The simple acts of shaking hands and asking for a person's vote win many votes.

Some candidates discuss issues at candidates' meetings in cities and towns. There, rival candidates speak on the same issue and answer questions from the audience. Often candidates debate one another. A well-run debate can be the best opportunity that citizens have to judge how the candidates feel about vital issues.

ROLE OF CAMPAIGNING

At times it might seem to you as though political campaigning never stops. What's more, you might consider campaigns a nuisance. But consider how political scientists Donald Herzberg and J.W. Peltason describe the role of campaigns in a democracy:

This system. . .offends some. They find it distasteful to see candidates courting voters. . . .They complain about the appeal to emotions and dislike the baby kissing and over-simplified speechmaking. But they forget that this system is the most effective method ever devised . . . for reconciling differences. . . . In many countries the only avenue open to those dissatisfied with their governments is to appeal to violence. In the United States, peaceable two-party competition is the traditional method of reconciling differences, of determining who shall get what, where, when, and how.

Section Review

1. What activities do campaign workers often carry out?

2. How are campaigns financed?

3. What does the Federal Election Commission do?

4. **Challenge:** Do you think a limit should be set on the amount of money an individual may give to a political campaign? Explain.

4 The Election

On election day, the long process of nominating and campaigning is over, and the voters make their decisions. No other event more clearly shows the nature of democracy than the election itself.

Polling Place

Every voter lives in a precinct. Within each, voters cast their ballots at one **polling place,** sometimes simply called "polls." There are about 150,000 precincts in the United States today, with an average of 500 to 600 voters living in each.

Election officials set polling places and ensure that state laws are followed. They also provide ballots or voting machines, and in most states they provide the official list of registered voters. When the polls close, these officials count the votes and report the results. In addition, each party may have a representative at each polling place to make sure the election is run fairly. These representatives are called "poll watchers."

Ballots

In colonial times, most voting was done publicly by voice vote. Voters risked being cheered or mocked as they stated their preferences. Since this method allowed voters to be influenced by fear, many people wanted to change the system. A switch was made to paper ballots. By the mid-1800s, political parties printed and passed out their own ballots. But because each party's ballot was a different color and the ballot box was in public view, any watcher could tell who voted for whom. As a result, voters were open to vote-buying and political pressure, and many local and state governments came under the control of political machines.

Reform came in 1888 with the introduction of the Australian ballot. The ballot, printed by election officials at public expense, lists all candidates for each office on a single ballot instead of on different ballots for each party. In addition, it is passed out only at the polling places to qualified voters who then cast their votes in secret. The Australian ballot is also used on voting machines.

polling place location where voters cast their ballots

The paper ballot is still used in many areas on election day. What types of changes have helped to make our system easier to work with and more fair to voters and candidates?

Voting machines like this one are common in polling places today. Due to such machines, votes are more quickly counted, and results can be made public much sooner than in earlier times. Some people feel this can be unfair to voters. What is the basis for this argument?

Today, two variations of the Australian ballot are used in the United States. On the office-group ballot, sometimes called the "Massachusetts ballot," all candidates for a particular office are listed together, and each is identified by party. On the party-column ballot, or "Indiana ballot," each party's candidates are listed in one column under the party label. Frequently, there is a place at the top of the ballot where a voter, with one mark, can vote for all the party's candidates.

In addition to voting for public officials, voters may also be asked to approve or reject various issues and proposals. As a result, ballots often become very long. Critics feel that such ballots are so tedious as to make it almost impossible for voters to make intelligent decisions on so many items. Supporters of long ballots, on the other hand, uphold the public's right to get as involved in government decision-making as they want.

Today, the use of voting machines, instead of paper ballots, has made voting and the job of counting the votes much easier. Some election districts have even begun to use computerized voting machines.

Election Results

After the polls close, election officials scurry to add up all the votes from the various polling places. The returns from each precinct are then sent to city and county election boards or commissions. The results, however, are not official until state election officials certify the winners of the election.

In a close race, state or local laws may call for an automatic recount to verify the results. Or there may be a recount if there are charges of fraud or error in the original count. Recounts sometimes do change the outcome of a race. Disputed elections are sometimes settled in court. In a congressional race, Congress itself may make the final decision. This happened in 1984 in a close race for one of Indiana's seats in the House of Representatives. A winner was not declared until almost six months after the election.

One controversy over election results, particularly in the case of presidential races, concerns the trend for television networks to project winners even before the polls close. It is argued that voters on the West Coast, in Alaska, and in Hawaii, where polls are open for a few hours later than on the East Coast, may not bother to vote if forecasts and early returns indicate that one candidate has already won. To prevent this from happening, Congress may set standard polling hours throughout the United States. Another option is not permitting East Coast results to be announced until all voters have had an opportunity to go to the polls.

Section Review

1. What role do election officials play at the polls?
2. What are some advantages and disadvantages of the Australian ballot?
3. What happens to votes after the polls close?
4. **Challenge:** In your opinion, how could voting procedures be changed so more people would vote?

Summary

1. In partisan elections, candidates are identified by the political party they represent.
2. In nonpartisan elections, candidates are not identified by political party.
3. In a general election, voters select government leaders from candidates who are either nominated by political parties or running independently.
4. Special elections are held to decide an issue or fill a vacant office before a regularly scheduled primary or general election.
5. Three kinds of ballot issues are initiative, referendum, and recall.
6. The methods by which candidates are nominated are self-nomination (including petition), party caucus, party convention, and primary election.
7. The presidential nominating process ends with the selection of candidates for President and Vice President at the parties' national conventions.
8. Alternatives to the current presidential nominating system include a nationwide primary, a series of regional primaries, and primaries based on state size.
9. Candidates rely on contributions from individuals, groups, political parties, PACs, and other political organizations.
10. Campaign financing is regulated by federal law for national office and by state and local laws for state and local offices.
11. Elections are conducted by election officials at official polling places in local precincts.

Chapter 10 Review

★ Building Vocabulary

Several of the new terms introduced in this chapter appear below. Use each word correctly in a sentence. Try to use two or more words in the same sentence. For example:

1. Two kinds of *primary elections* are *open primaries* and *closed primaries*.

1. paritisan elections
2. general elections
3. closed primary
4. open primary
5. initiative
6. recall
7. write-in
8. polling place
9. nonpartisan elections
10. primary elections
11. plurality
12. special election
13. referendum
14. caucus
15. run-off primary

★ Reviewing Facts

1. How do partisan elections differ from nonpartisan elections?
2. Why are primary elections and general elections held?
3. What is the difference between open and closed primaries?
4. What is a special election?
5. What do initiatives, referendums, and recalls have in common?
6. In what ways may a person be nominated as a candidate for public office?
7. What is the role of the national conventions of the two major parties?
8. What functions does a campaign organization perform?
9. In what two ways are campaigns regulated by federal law?
10. How is the Australian ballot different from earlier methods of voting?
11. What innovations have made voting and counting votes easier than in the past?
12. How are election winners determined?

★ Analyzing Facts

1. Which public offices do you think should be filled through partisan elections? Through nonpartisan elections? Explain.
2. Do you think the process of nominating presidential candidates should be made easier or more difficult? Explain.
3. In your opinion, does the nomination process encourage or discourage good people from running for public office? Why?
4. Theodore Roosevelt once said, "The Federal Government should finance basic election campaign needs as an essential cost of democratic government." Do you agee or disagree with Roosevelt's statement? Why or why not?
5. Do you think the increase in categories of citizens eligible to vote has influenced elections? Explain.

Using Your
Civic Participation Journal

Review your Civic Participation Journal entries on selecting political candidates in your community. Work with two of your classmates to prepare a flow chart describing all the steps in the nomination process. Display your chart on the bulletin board.

★ Evaluating Ideas

1. If you could make one change in the electoral process, what would that change be? Support your idea.
2. Which nomination process—caucus, convention, primary—do you think is the most democratic? Why?
3. Do you favor the present method of nominating presidential candidates? If so, why? If not, what alternative method of nomination would you favor? Why?
4. If you were to plan a campaign strategy for a class president election, what would be your strategy? Explain.

★ Critical Thinking
Fact vs. Opinion

An opinion is a belief held without absolute knowledge or proof, while a fact is supported by evidence. No other evidence can be found to disprove it. Facts and opinions are closely related because the value of an opinion often depends on whether or not facts support it.

Explanation When you read written material, or when you listen to a person speak, you should always try to distinguish between factual statements and the opinions of the author or speaker. This is not always easy to do because people sometimes present their opinions as fact. The key is to be ready and willing to challenge information you are given, either in your own mind or by questioning the person who provides it. Is there evidence to prove the statement beyond a doubt? Or might another person have a different way of looking at it, a different point of view? If the statement is the only possible conclusion that can be drawn from the evidence, then the statement is fact. All other statements are opinions.

Practice The statement below is taken from debate over whether Congress should continue to spend tax money to support the arts through the National Endowment for the Humanities (NEH) and the National Endowment for the Arts (NEA).

> *The NEH has proved a worthy guardian and sponsor of our nation's history.*
> —REP. E. THOMAS COLEMAN

Can this statement be proven? It might seem that data about the number of projects the NEH has aided would help prove this statement, but that would not really be evidence that the NEH has been "a worthy guardian." A critic might agree that the NEH has backed many projects but claim they were not worthy projects. The worthiness of a project is based on values and beliefs. This statement is an opinion.

> *In the 25-year history of the NEA, fewer than 25 grants out of some 85,000 have even caused a stir.*
> —REP. CLAUDINE SCHNEIDER

This is a statement of fact. By examining NEA records, one could determine how many of its grants have been controversial. The controversy may have been over questions of opinion, such as whether the projects were ugly or offensive or a waste of money, but whether or not there was a controversy is a fact.

Independent Practice Study the cartoon below. What elements of the cartoon are factual? What elements are opinions?

TWO REVIEW

REVIEW QUESTIONS

1. How have changes in voting qualifications and methods affected the process of political socialization?

2. What might the decline in party membership and the increase in the Independent vote reveal about the current political attitudes of Americans?

3. In what ways have minor parties contributed to the reform of our political system?

4. What role do interest groups play in partisan elections? in nonpartisan elections?

5. How do the rights and responsibilities of citizenship balance each other? Explain.

6. In your opinion, why do Americans vote in such relatively low numbers?

7. To what extent should public officials' decisions be influenced by public opinion? To what extent should public officials be public opinion leaders? Justify your answer.

8. What factors have had the greatest influence on your own political socialization?

9. Do you think that the political philosophies of the two major political parties differ substantially? Why or why not?

10. Do you think interest groups are a positive or a negative influence on the American political process? Explain.

11. What are the most common ways people in the United States participate in the political process?

12. In what ways do you think political attitudes of a registered Democrat or Republican would differ from those of an Independent voter?

13. What are the major types of elections held in the United States?

14. How is it possible for people to know the results of a presidential election before the electoral votes are counted?

15. How do political parties get funds for political campaigns?

SUGGESTED READINGS

1. Drury, Allen. *Preserve and Protect*. Garden City, New York: Doubleday & Co., 1968. What happens in the heat of a campaign when violence is dedicated to the cause of a presidential candidate?

2. Hoffer, Eric. *The True Believer*. New York: Harper & Row, 1951. Analysis of why people join interest groups and support causes.

3. Kennedy, John F. *A Nation of Immigrants*. New York: Harper & Row, 1964. The story of immigrants who have come to America and enriched the country by their coming.

4. Kessner, Thomas, and Betty Boyd Caroli. *Today's Immigrants, Their Stories*. New York: Oxford University Press, 1981. From Indochina to Peru, Korea to Russia, Greece and Italy to China and Honduras—immigrants to America—these are their stories.

5. McCarthy, Eugene, et. al. *A Political Bestiary*. New York: McGraw Hill, 1978. Cartoons and commentary satirize politics in the United States.

6. Piven, Frances Fox, and Richard A. Cloward. *Why Americans Don't Vote*. New York: Pantheon Books, 1988. Analyzes the sources and significance of nonvoting.

7. White, Theodore. *The Making of the President, Nineteen Sixty: A Narrative History of American Politics in Action*. New York: Macmillan Publishing Co., Inc., 1988. A prize-winning reporter chronicles the inside machinations of a presidential campaign.

COOPERATING

The ability to cooperate with others, both those who are like us and those who are not, to achieve group goals lies at the heart of citizenship in a democratic society. This competency is especially important today as the population in the United States is becoming increasingly diverse.

As a concerned citizen in a complex and highly organized society, you may often find it impossible to bring about many changes by acting alone. You must be able to cooperate with other citizens in order to achieve personal and social goals. Such cooperation requires the ability to express your ideas clearly and to assume various tasks within a group. By working together toward a common goal, your group can advance its own concerns. At the same time, you can learn to accept the differences in others and to treat different opinions with respect.

The activity below will give you an opportunity to practice the skill of cooperation by working with your classmates and several adults to gain a greater understanding of a problem and to accomplish a common task.

1. Conduct a class discussion to identify what your class believes are the three or four most important problems or concerns of high school students in your community.

2. Choose several students to contact community resource people to invite to your class. These could include a police officer; mental health worker; mayor; guidance counselor; local legislative representative; caseworker; or judge, prosecutor, or defense attorney from juvenile court.

3. Inform the community resource people of what your class believes are the main problems and concerns of high school students in your community.

4. Have the resource people react to your ideas and concerns. Discuss their reactions.

5. Select and focus on one problem or concern. Ask the resource people what the class could do to begin to deal with the problem.

6. Outline a strategy for achieving your project. Suppose your class decided to collect money for a charity that assists homeless people in your community. You first would find out the needs of the organization and where you could best make your contribution. Second, you might decide how you would contact people for funds—by phone, mail, or door-to-door appeals. Then, you would divide among class members the various responsibilities, such as collecting, counting, and recording donations.

7. Whatever project your class decides to carry out, when you have finished the activity, review what you have done. How did your class make decisions? Was cooperation a factor? What would have happened if each class member had refused to cooperate? Could your class have reached any decision if each member had refused to listen to the others? By evaluating your class's performance, you can easily see the importance of cooperation when solving society's problems.

Unit 3

THE LEGISLATIVE BRANCH

Every nation has its most cherished ideals as well as symbols that represent those ideals. In the United States, our most cherished ideal is liberty, and its symbol is the Statue of Liberty in New York City harbor. The photo on the facing page shows the Statue of Liberty during the spectacular celebrations of its 100th anniversary on July 4, 1986.

Over the years, Americans have linked the ideal of liberty to the concept of law. In many other countries, the two have not gotten along well together. For example, some governments have deliberately passed laws to deprive citizens of their individual or group liberties. In the United States our government, despite shortcomings, has tried to enact laws that guarantee the freedoms of citizens.

Our nation's lawmaking body on the national level is Congress. The picture on this page shows the Capitol, where Congress meets in Washington, D.C. Like the Statue of Liberty, the Capitol with its magnificent dome and porch also serves as a symbol of the nation's liberty. Both the Statue of Liberty and the Capitol are stunning embodiments of the phrase "Liberty under Law" that has guided Congress for more than 200 years.

Chapter 11

The Congress

Whether the actions of the Senate and House of Representatives go unnoticed or grab headlines, the ultimate reason your legislators are in Washington, D.C., is to voice the concerns of the people they represent. For three centuries, since the Virginia House of Burgesses first met in 1619, the idea of citizens' opinions guiding elected officials has been a cornerstone of our political thought. For this reason, the legislative branch appears first in the Constitution and is often called "the first branch of government."

★ ★ ★ ★ ★

Chapter Preview

TERMS TO KNOW
constituents, ombudsman, bureaucracy, regular sessions, adjourn, incumbents, recesses, censure, expel, president pro tempore, majority leader, census, apportion, reapportionment, reprimand

READ TO DISCOVER
- the duties of Congress and its members.
- the way the Senate and the House of Representatives are organized.
- the benefits and privileges held by members of Congress.
- who helps legislators carry out their duties.

Civic Participation Journal

Write a letter to your representative in Congress asking him or her to support a specific project that you think would be good for your community. Keep a copy of your letter for your journal. You will undoubtedly receive a reply. Keep a copy of the reply in your journal as well.

1 What Is Congress?

On both our national and state levels, government is divided into three branches—legislative, executive, and judicial. Congress is the national legislature of the United States and is made up of two houses—the Senate and the House of Representatives.

What Congress Does

Recall that under the Articles of Confederation, the national legislature had only one house. But the Great Compromise changed this. At the Constitutional Convention, the Framers set up a bicameral Congress. What do these two houses do?

MAKE LAWS

The main function of Congress is to make the laws that govern our nation. Thousands of proposals for legislation are submitted to Congress each year, and hundreds of these are passed as laws. The issues that members of Congress must decide may concern only a few individuals or may encompass our entire American population. How much money to set aside for antipoverty programs, what changes should be made in our immigration policy, and how much you will pay in taxes are only a few examples of issues Congress wrestles with.

SERVE CONSTITUENTS

Lawmaking is not the only responsibility senators and representatives have. Members of Congress serve the needs of their **constituents,** the people who live in the state or district they represent. In this role of **ombudsman,** congressional members act as a link between their constituents at home and the federal government in Washington, D.C. In fact, Americans often turn to their senators or representatives for help in dealing with the

constituents people in a legislator's district or state

ombudsman government official who serves as a link between constituents and the government to investigate and resolve complaints by citizens about the government's actions

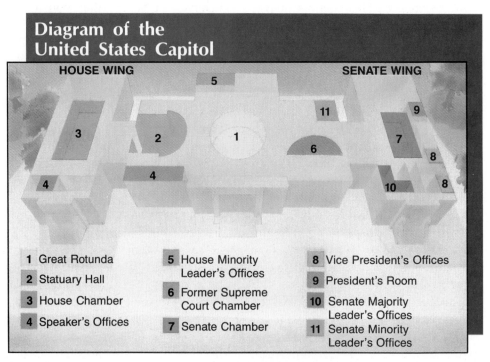

Diagram of the United States Capitol

HOUSE WING   SENATE WING

1 Great Rotunda
2 Statuary Hall
3 House Chamber
4 Speaker's Offices
5 House Minority Leader's Offices
6 Former Supreme Court Chamber
7 Senate Chamber
8 Vice President's Offices
9 President's Room
10 Senate Majority Leader's Offices
11 Senate Minority Leader's Offices

Figure 11-1

bureaucracy. And many members of Congress believe that helping their constituents is their most important job; after all, these are the people who elect and *reelect* them to office.

PRACTICE OVERSIGHT

The legislature also monitors or "oversees" the executive branch. This oversight function allows Congress to keep an eye on the executive branch and its agencies to make sure their work is being carried out as Congress intended. One way Congress does this is through congressional investigations. These allow Congress to gather information and hear testimony from key witnesses to determine if government programs have been administered properly and to see that laws are being upheld. In the last 30 years, many important congressional investigations, such as the Iran/Contra hearings, have been televised, giving us an opportunity to witness some of the most dramatic moments of Congress.

Congress can also conduct investigations to expose government programs that waste or misuse the taxpayer's money. This not only gives Congress more control over public policy but affords individual legislators political clout at reelection time as well. Voters are more likely to remember a representative or senator who was actively involved in a congressional investigation.

VOTE IN CONGRESS

Senators and representatives have differing opinions on their fourth role as legislators for their state or district. In that role, they use their votes in Congress to voice the views of the people back home. Some members believe they should reflect those views as faithfully as possible. This means finding out what their constit-

bureaucracy agencies and departments of the executive branch that carry out policy on a day-to-day basis

This 350-foot-long petition was signed by 10,000 people from this senator's home state. In what ways do members of Congress try to communicate with their constituents?

uents think about an issue and voting accordingly, even if they do not agree with their constituents' view. Others believe, however, that constituents want members of Congress to use their own judgment in making decisions. So they form an opinion based on available information and their own experience and then let constituents know the reasons for their decision. Still other legislators base their votes strictly on the views of their political party. These members feel a special loyalty to their party and believe it is their responsibility to uphold party positions.

Many factors influence the voting behavior of legislators. The amount of public attention an issue receives is an important factor. If a particular issue, such as raising taxes, causes strong protests or generates bags of mail, members of Congress are much more likely to pay close attention to their constituents' opinions. But if an issue

A DAY IN THE LIFE OF A MEMBER OF CONGRESS

9:35 A.M.	Arrive Washington, D.C., from home district
10:00 A.M.	Committee hearing—Banking Subcommittee on Consumer Affairs and Coinage
11:30 A.M.	Meet with lobbyists
12:00 NOON	House convenes; presence on floor requested by party whip
1:00 P.M.	Give speech to Electronic Funds Transfer Association
1:15 P.M.	Meet with Republican Party Policy Committee
2:30 P.M.	Meet with representatives of the American Medical Oxygen Sales Corporation
3:00 P.M.	Meet with representative of the Coin Dealers Association
4:00 P.M.	Meet with state delegation of the International Council of Shopping Centers
4:30 P.M.	Record public service announcement in House recording studio for the Osteoporosis Society
5:00 P.M.	Meet with fellow party members for strategy session
6:00 P.M.	Attend reception given by the Mississippi Bankers Association
7:00 P.M.	Attend reception for National Restaurant Association.
8:30 P.M.	Return home—See the kids—Review committee reports—catch up on reading
11:30 P.M.	Go to bed

Based on the article, "The Unbearable Lightness of Being A Congressman," by Fred Barnes, from *The New Republic*, February 15, 1988, pp 18–22.

Figure 11-2

attracts little interest in the home district, members are more likely to follow their own or their party's convictions.

Whom Congress Represents

Although equal in power with the executive and judicial branches, the legislative branch is sometimes said to be the "closest" to the American people. Members of Congress are elected directly by the voters, while the President and Vice President are chosen indirectly through the electoral college, and members of the federal judiciary are appointed by the President with approval of the Senate. Members of Congress, then, are the national leaders most directly responsible to you and other Americans. Because of this responsibility, Congress has often been called the "people's voice in government."

In order to make sure they accurately represent the people, members of Congress use a variety of ways to communicate with their constituents. One method is through newsletters and questionnaires. Newsletters inform constituents of their representative's stand on certain issues, while periodic questionnaires are an easy way for members of Congress to poll their constituents.

Legislators also keep in touch by returning to their home state or district to make speeches and meet with voters and community leaders. The average member of Congress usually spends two weekends a month in his or her home state or district. A "congressional weekend," however, is different from the average person's weekend. The House of Representatives meets on Tuesday through Thursday, giving representatives a four-day weekend to conduct business at home. In 1988, the Senate began a new schedule of three five-day weeks followed by one week off to travel home. Members of Congress also return home during holidays and elections and other times when Congress is not in session. All this travel can lead to a very hectic lifestyle. Figure 11-2 shows what the typical day of a representative can be like.

Many members of Congress use radio and television to stay in touch with their constituents. For example, both the Senate and the House have television studios that are equipped with satellite dishes. Senators and representatives can beam interviews, commentaries, speeches, or two-way teleconferences to television stations in their home state or district to be used in local newscasts. Another television outlet, the Cable Satellite Public Affairs Network (C-SPAN), broadcasts congressional proceedings daily to more than 21 million households across the United States.

When Congress Meets

The Constitution specifies that Congress must meet at least once a year for as long as necessary at the same time and place. Each term of Congress lasts two years. Before 1933, Congress began its term in December of every odd-numbered year. But since elections were held in November of every *even*-numbered year, newly elected members did not attend sessions until 13 months later. At the same time, members who were *not* reelected, known as "lame ducks," were required to attend the session after their defeat. Such lame duck sessions were criticized because they failed to reflect the true will of the voters.

In 1933, the Twentieth Amendment changed congressional terms to begin on January 3 of every odd-numbered year. Today, a lame duck Congress will only meet between the November elections and the beginning of a new term on January 3.

Congressional terms have been numbered since the first Congress met in 1789. The Congress elected in November 1994, which met for the first time on January 3, 1995, became the 104th Congress.

In this cartoon, a member of Congress looks in the gallery to see if a constituent is watching him vote. As a representative of the people, how do members of Congress serve their constituents?

DUNAGIN'S PEOPLE

10-18

"BEFORE I STAND UP TO BE COUNTED ON THIS ISSUE, I WANT TO SEE WHO'S COUNTING."

CASE STUDY: THE MEDIA

TELEVISION AND ELECTION POLITICS

A drastic change has occurred in where Americans get their news and information. In 1961, 57 percent reported they used newspapers, 52 percent said television, 34 percent radio, and 9 percent magazines. Clearly, most Americans relied on more than one source.

By the 1990s more than two-thirds of Americans relied on television. Fewer people used more than one source; more than 50 percent depended on television alone.

The growing role of television as a source of news and information has aroused a great deal of controversy and concern. Television's advocates claim that it benefits society because it disseminates information so widely. Critics respond that the information television presents is incomplete and shallow. They note that newspapers devote much more space and time to in-depth analysis of issues than do half-hour nightly news programs on television. They observe that televi-

sion's attempts to provide more thorough and thoughtful coverage on news specials and regular programs, such as *Meet the Press,* attract fewer viewers.

One topic that increasingly has attracted attention is the influence of television on election politics. Campaign managers divide candidates' use of television into paid and unpaid media. Paid media is commercial time purchased by the candidate. Although television advertising has made political campaigns increasingly expensive, many campaign strategists think unpaid media—getting the candidate onto the nightly news—is even more important. They theorize that voters are more likely to believe what they see on a news program than on a paid commercial. So campaigners have become skilled at getting their messages into the unpaid media. In the 1992 presidential election, for example, the major candidates appeared on *Larry King, Live,* a national television program, for late-night interviews. Many viewers supported

one candidate over another because of the television image he presented during these interviews.

Campaign managers also plan "media events" and "photo opportunities" designed to get extensive television coverage for their candidates. In the 1970s, for example, a number of Democratic candidates set off to walk across their states, supposedly to talk to the people, but also to gain nightly television exposure.

Experts disagree on whether use of media really shapes how people vote. Social critic Neil Postman claims that television changes political judgments from thoughtful consideration of issues to emotional responses based on images. But analyst Don Fry thinks citizens deserve more credit: "Part of the folklore born in [the 1984] election is that Mr. Reagan won only because of television. His smile, charm, and generalities were supposed to play well. Indeed, they did play well, but it is patronizing to the people who voted for Mr. Reagan to say they did so only because they were beguiled. It supposes that Americans perceive . . . politics the same way they do *Dallas.*"

1. In the past few years, which news source has gained most among Americans? Which has lost most? How might you explain this change?
2. Do you agree that voters are less influenced by paid media than by unpaid media? Why?

BEGINNING OF A TERM

The weeks before each new term of Congress are usually very hectic. Senators and representatives may try to get assigned to powerful committees or important leadership posts. New members must set up offices and master the rules that govern the day-to-day operations of Congress. With all this activity, political parties help make the beginning of a new term easier for everyone.

CAUCUSES

Even though no single group is very powerful, political parties are often the most powerful groups in Congress. The party with more members in the House or Senate is called the majority party for that house; the other party is the minority. Before a new term begins, Democratic and Republican members of Congress meet in separate party conferences called caucuses. The purpose of these caucuses is to plan legislative strategy for the new term and help party members act as a unified force when voting on legislation. Today there are more than 100 special interest caucuses in Congress, including the Congressional Black Caucus, the Congressional Women's Caucus, and the Congressional Sunbelt Caucus.

OPENING DAY

Only one-third of the Senate faces reelection every two years. So on opening day, the Senate usually just swears in new members and fills committee vacancies. It then informs the House that it is ready for the President's annual message to Congress.

Because *all* the members of the House of Representatives are elected every two years, the House meets as a newly elected body each new term. Thus, many decisions about organization must be made on opening day. After roll call, the members officially approve a Speaker of the House, the presiding officer chosen by the majority party caucus. The Speaker is sworn in, and he or she, in turn, swears in the remaining representatives. House members then adopt rules that will direct their proceedings throughout the term. Next, committee chairpersons, also determined by the majority party caucus, are selected.

Committee assignments, both in the House and Senate, are not taken lightly. As you will learn later, most of Congress's work is hammered out in committees and subcommittees. Being assigned to chair or even simply to belong to certain committees can lead to extremely prestigious and

The President's State of the Union speech is delivered each year to Congress and the nation. What does the President include in the State of the Union Address?

Characteristics of the 101st and 104th Congresses

	101st Congress 1989–1991			104th Congress 1995–1997		
	Senate	**House**	**Total**	**Senate**	**House**	**Total**
Average Age	55.6	52.1	52.8*	58.4	50.9	52.2*
Women	2	26	28	8	49	57
Minorities						
African Americans	0	24	24	1	39	40
Hispanic Americans	0	12	12	0	18	18
Asian Americans	2	5	7	2	6	8
Native Americans	0	0	0	1	0	1
Religion						
Protestant	54	191	245	65	278	343
Roman Catholic	19	120	139	20	125	145
Jewish	8	31	39	9	24	33
Other	19	93	112	6	8	14
Occupation**						
Aeronautics	2	3	5	1	1	2
Agriculture	4	19	23	9	19	28
Business/Banking	28	138	166	24	163	187
Clergy	1	2	3	0	2	2
Education	11	42	53	10	76	86
Engineering	0	4	4	0	6	6
Journalism	8	17	25	8	15	23
Labor Officials	0	2	2	0	2	2
Law	63	184	247	54	170	224
Law Enforcement	0	8	8	0	11	11
Medicine	0	4	4	1	10	11
Professional Sports	1	4	5	1	2	3
Public Service/ Politics	20	94	114	12	102	114
Party Preference						
Democrats	55	261	316	47	204	251
Republicans	45	174	219	53	230	283
Independent	0	0	0	0	1	1

* The average age of a member of Congress
** Some members have worked in more than one occupation
*** Includes vacancies and independents

Source: *Congressional Quarterly Almanac,* 1975, and *Congressional Quarterly Weekly Report,* November 12, 1994

Figure 11-3

powerful positions for legislators. Finally, opening day for the representatives ends when the Speaker informs the Senate that the House, too, is ready for the President's message.

STATE OF THE UNION

After both houses have organized, a joint committee of the House and Senate notifies the President that Congress is ready to begin work. Later, usually within a few weeks, the President delivers a State of the Union Address to a joint session of Congress. This momentous and well-published speech outlines the President's goals for the year and sets the agenda for Congress.

REGULAR SESSIONS

Each term of Congress is divided into two **regular sessions** with one session held each year of the term. Although

regular sessions periods of time during which Congress assembles and carries out its business

adjourn end a session of a legislative body

incumbents members already in office

recesses periods in which Congress is not in session

the Constitution states that regular sessions begin on January 3, Congress itself can decide when to **adjourn** a session. In 1946, Congress decided by law to adjourn no later than July 31, except in times of national emergency. Because of the heavy workload, however, it seldom adjourns by this date. Neither house may adjourn for more than three days without the consent of the other, but both houses have brief **recesses,** usually around national holidays or during elections.

SPECIAL SESSIONS

Congress as a whole, or either house, may be called into special session by the President, usually to handle emergency business. The House of Representatives by itself has never been called into special session, but the Senate has been, to act upon presidential appointments and treaties. Because regular sessions are so long, special sessions are rarely needed.

Who Congress Is

Even though members of Congress represent Americans from all walks of life, they are not a cross section of American society. Congress generally is made up of white males, who are well-educated, middle-aged, and come from professional backgrounds. While African Americans constitute about 12 percent of our population, only 7.5 percent of the 104th Congress was African American. Women held only 10.6 percent of the seats, and only 18 Hispanics, 8 Asians and Pacific Islanders, and one Native American occupied seats. The characteristics of that Congress and the 101st Congress are compared in Figure 11-3 on page 247. As it was nearly 15 years ago, lawyers and businesspersons make up the majority of legislators. In addition, the average age of legislators has changed little.

A significant characteristic of Congress in general is that many of its members are not new to Capitol Hill. The tendency to return **incumbents** to office, however, has lessened in recent elections. When the 101st Congress began its first term in January 1989, for example, only 43 members were newly elected. When the 104th Congress met in 1995, however, it included 98 members who had never served in Congress. Nevertheless, voters return most incumbents to office. How do incumbents become so entrenched?

Incumbents succeed for many reasons. First, most voters recognize the name of someone who has already been in Congress over that of a challenger who might be new to national politics. Second, a member of Congress is in a better position to raise the necessary campaign funds, a task that discourages many challengers. Finally, an incumbent can use his or her resources to handle constituents' problems. The hope is that voters will remember the attention they received and will show their gratitude at election time.

Section Review

1. What is the main duty of Congress?

2. Why has Congress been called the "people's voice in government"?

3. What are three ways members of Congress stay in touch with their constituents?

4. **Challenge:** In your opinion, should incumbent legislators be permitted to use the resources of their office to campaign for reelection? Why or why not?

2 The Senate

The Senate, the upper house of Congress, has 100 members. Two senators are elected from each state, regardless of that state's population. Article V of the Constitution specifies that ''no state without its consent shall be deprived of its equal suffrage in the Senate.'' This provision further guarantees that the states' equal representation in the Senate cannot be changed by any amendment.

Election

Members of the Senate are elected by the citizens of each state in the November general elections that are held in even-numbered years. The two senators from each state never run for election in the same year unless a vacancy occurs because of death, retirement, resignation, or expulsion. In these cases, the governor of the state may call a special election to choose a replacement. Sometimes, a state legislature will allow the governor to *appoint* a replacement until an election is held.

Terms and Qualifications

Senators serve six-year terms. The terms of all 100 senators are arranged so that one-third of the Senate seats are up for election every two years. Because of these overlapping terms, the Senate is considered to be a continuous body.

This method of election was established in 1789 by the first Congress to give stability to the legislative branch. Having a six-year term gives senators time to gain an understanding of public issues without worrying about an election campaign every two years. It also gives senators more opportunity to act without regard for public opinion.

The Constitution requires a senator to be an American citizen for at least nine years before taking office. In addition, he or she must be at least 30 years old and a resident of the state he or she represents.

The Constitution also allows the Senate to judge the qualifications of its own members and to enforce standards of behavior. By a simple majority vote, senators can **censure** another member. With a two-thirds vote, they may **expel** a member. Taking either of these actions has been rare in the Senate's history. Unless there is a gross violation of the rules, most senators tend to protect their colleagues.

censure expression of disapproval of improper conduct

expel force from office

Robert Dole became Senate majority leader in the 104th Congress. In this role he guides the activities of the Republican party in the Senate. What are some of the duties of the Senate majority leader?

Richard Gephardt,
House minority leader

president pro tempore
member of the Senate who
temporarily presides over the
Senate when the Vice President is absent

majority leader member
of a legislative house elected
by members to lead the majority party

minority leader member
of a legislative house elected
by members to lead the minority party

Senate Leadership

The official leader of the upper house is the president of the Senate, a position held by the Vice President of the United States. This role includes such routine powers as calling on members to speak and putting questions to a vote. In practice, however, the Vice President has little real influence in the Senate. As an elected member of the *executive,* rather than legislative, branch, the Vice President cannot debate issues on the Senate floor or vote, unless there is a tie.

Because the Vice President is rarely available to preside over the Senate, a **president pro tempore** is elected to perform those duties. Chosen by the whole Senate after being endorsed by the majority party caucus, the president "pro tem" usually the majority party member who has served the longest.

Other leadership positions are organized around political parties, too. The **majority leader** heads the party in power and holds the most powerful office in the Senate. The leader plans the Senate's daily agenda and has considerable influence over the party's committee assignments. Working closely with individual senators, key committee leaders, and various congressional groups, the majority leader also organizes other party members to support legislation favored by their party.

On the Senate floor, it is the majority leader's duty to see that business flows smoothly. The most powerful part of the job is scheduling which bills will be debated and *when* they will be debated. The success or failure of a bill often hinges on where it falls on the schedule.

The other leader elected by the political parties is the **minority leader,** who heads the opposition party. Although not as powerful as the majority leader, he or she has similar duties. The minority leader is always present on the floor during consideration of bills and has a strong voice in committee assignments for minority party members. His or her primary duty, however, is to lead fellow party members in their struggle to change or defeat the policies and programs of the majority party. It is the minority leader who persuades influential minority party members and committee leaders to follow the party's position. In addition, if the minority leader belongs to the same political party as the President, he or she usually acts as the President's spokesperson on the floor.

The two floor leaders are aided by party whips, or assistant leaders, who are chosen by party caucuses. Whips keep track of their party's support on various issues and try to "whip up" more backing by persuading members to vote for or against a particular piece of legislation. They provide information on bills for members, advise floor leaders on how much support their party has for certain bills, and ensure that their members are in full attendance during important floor votes.

Section Review

1. How are senators chosen today?

2. Why is the Senate known as a continuous body?

3. What qualifications must a person meet to be a senator?

4. **Challenge:** In your opinion, should the Vice President have less power or more power in the Senate? Why?

3 The House of Representatives

Although the House of Representatives is the lower house of Congress, it is just as important as the Senate. The 435 House seats are filled according to state populations. The more people a state has, the more representatives it sends to the House. Our nation's territories and possessions are also represented in the House. The District of Columbia, American Samoa, Guam, Puerto Rico, and the American Virgin Islands each send one nonvoting delegate to the House.

Regardless of population, each state is guaranteed at least one House seat, which benefits less-populous states. For example, North Dakota and Delaware, two of the least populated states, have one representative each in the House. To determine the exact number of people in each state, the Constitution calls for a **census** to

census official count of the people of the United States taken every 10 years since 1790

Representation to the House of Representatives is based on the population of each state. Because of this, larger states control more House seats than do smaller states. How is the population of each state determined?

apportion distribute and assign legislative seats

be taken every ten years. The results are used to **apportion** the 435 seats among the 50 states.

Distribution of Seats

From 1789 to 1793, the House of Representatives had only 65 members. With each new census after 1790, Congress increased the number of seats to keep up with our country's growing population. By 1910, the House had reached its present size of 435 members.

As the census of 1920 approached, House leaders were alarmed at the prospect of an even larger membership. Once the official census figures were issued in 1921, the House stalled for many years before taking any action to increase its membership. In 1929, President Herbert Hoover called a special session of Congress to provide apportionment guidelines for the upcoming 1930 census. As a result, Congress passed a new law establishing a permanent system of **reapportionment** following each census.

reapportionment redistribution of legislative seats based on a new law or formula

According to this system, states with significant drops in population would lose representatives, while growing states would gain representatives. The total number of representatives, however, would remain at 435.

After each census, the Bureau of the Census decides the number of seats that each state should receive according to the latest population figures. The Bureau then presents a plan to the President that shows the new distribution of seats. The President submits this information to Congress, and in 60 days, if Congress does not object, the plan goes into effect.

As Figure 11-4 illustrates, population varies by region. And *shifts* in population can greatly affect the distribution of seats. When, for instance, many factories in the North and East were shut down and workers laid off in the 1960s and 1970s, many people went to the ''sun belt'' states of the South and the West. There, such high technology industries as computer manufacturing were flourishing. As a

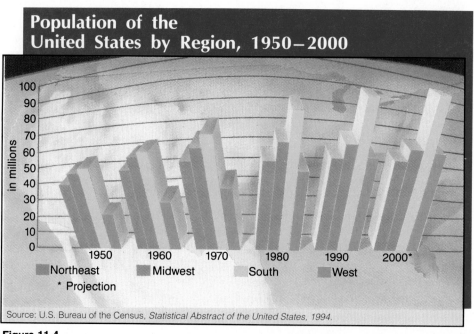

Figure 11-4

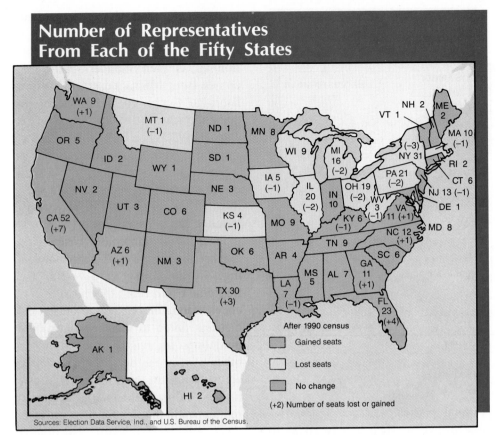

Number of Representatives From Each of the Fifty States

WA 9 (+1)
OR 5
MT 1 (−1)
ND 1
MN 8
ID 2
WY 1
SD 1
WI 9
MI 16 (−2)
NV 2
UT 3
CO 6
NE 3
IA 5 (−1)
IL 20 (−2)
IN 10
OH 19 (−2)
CA 52 (+7)
KS 4 (−1)
MO 9
KY 6 (−1)
WV 3 (−1)
AZ 6 (+1)
NM 3
OK 6
AR 4
TN 9
VA 11 (+1)
NC 12 (+1)
TX 30 (+3)
LA 7 (−1)
MS 5
AL 7
GA 11 (+1)
SC 6
FL 23 (+4)
NH 2
VT 1
ME 2
MA 10 (−1)
NY 31 (−3)
RI 2
PA 21 (−2)
CT 6
NJ 13 (−1)
DE 1
MD 8

AK 1
HI 2

After 1990 census

Gained seats

Lost seats

No change

(+2) Number of seats lost or gained

Sources: Election Data Service, Ind., and U.S. Bureau of the Census.

Figure 11-5

result, some northeastern and midwestern states have lost seats in the House, while states in the West and the South have gained them.

Representation

Unlike senators, who are elected on a state-wide vote, representatives are elected from areas known as congressional districts. One representative is elected from each district. If a state's population allows it to have only one representative, as in the case of Vermont, the entire state is the congressional district.

This form of representation for the House was not always used. In the early 1800s, each state had the right to decide whether or not to have districts. In states without them, voters chose all the representatives by a single ballot. But over the years, many people became dissatisfied with this. It was unfair, they claimed, because the political party that had the most members in the state, and thus more votes for its candidates, could capture all of the House seats for the state.

In 1842, Congress passed a law requiring all states to elect representatives from districts. And each state legislature was given the responsibility for drawing up its own district boundaries. The districts were to have adjoining boundaries and contain about the same number of people so that each House member would have a nearly equal number of constituents.

In the years that followed, however, the 1842 act was largely ignored. Many state legislators continued to seek advantages for their own

Qualifications for Members of Congress

A Senator must:	A Representative must:
have been a United States citizen for at least nine years	have been a United States citizen for at least seven years
be at least 30 years of age	be at least 25 years of age
be a resident of the state they represent	be a resident of the state they represent

Figure 11-6

political parties. District boundaries were drawn in such a way so as to place many of the opposition party's supporters in as few districts as possible. That way, most districts would be controlled by the ruling party. Other times, legislators created many districts in which the opposition would have the support of only a minority of voters.

While such districts were purposely created in some states, more often states simply failed to reapportion districts as their populations changed. And as more Americans moved to the cities, the problem of unequal apportionment grew. Traditionally, many state legislatures were controlled by rural areas. By intentionally creating districts that were not equal in population, rural leaders hoped to block the transfer of seats to growing urban areas. So rural areas maintained more seats and greater influence in Congress than their population deserved, while urban areas had fewer seats and

votes, even though they contained more people.

The term used for this unfair apportioning is gerrymandering, which comes from Massachusetts Governor Elbridge Gerry. In 1812, Gerry redrew the state's districts to favor his own party. When a famous painter, visiting a local Massachusetts newspaper office, commented that a map of the new districts resembled a salamander, a news editor remarked, "Better say a Gerrymander!"

In 1964 a landmark case ruled against the practice of gerrymandering. In *Westberry v. Sanders,* the Supreme Court ruled that large differences among Georgia's congressional districts failed to meet constitutional guidelines for fair representation. In other words, one person's vote has to count as much as another's. Following the ruling, legislatures began to redraw their district lines in order to meet the new standard. No longer could a state have population differences among its districts, unless it had proof that it had tried to achieve equality in redistricting. After the 1970 census, new districts were formed. Although many of them are not of equal geographic size, they are equal in population.

According to recent population figures, each congressional district is currently made up of about 536,000 people. This means that a member of the House represents more than 500,000 people. A senator, though, may represent millions of people living in an entire state, so many representatives tend to stress local concerns rather than national or state issues.

Terms and Qualifications

Each representative serves a two-year term. The Framers of the Constitution believed that such a short term

A representation of the Gerrymander

THE GERRY-MANDER!

of office would make the House of Representatives more responsive to public opinion.

All representatives are elected in November of even-numbered years and begin their terms the following January. Thus, the House of Representatives is not a continuous body; it begins anew following each election. If, for any reason, a member cannot finish his or her term, the governor of the representatives's state must call a special election to fill the vacant seat.

The Constitution requires a House member to be at least 25 years old, to have been a citizen of the United States for seven years, and to be a resident of the state from which he or she is elected. Most representatives live in the district they represent so they can be familiar with that area's needs.

Like the Senate, the House has the power to judge the qualifications and punish the misconduct of its members. It too may vote to censure or expel members. Also like the Senate, the House has been faced with cases of misconduct by members it did not want to punish by expulsion or censure. In those instances, it uses a less severe form of censure called a **reprimand.** After it votes to reprimand a member, no additional action is taken against him or her.

Congress also has power to refuse to seat an elected member, but that power is limited. In the 1969 case of *Powell v. McCormack,* the Supreme Court ruled that Congress can exclude only those members who do not meet the three requirements for office stated in the Constitution.

House Leadership

The most powerful leader in the House of Representatives is the Speaker, a post that the Constitution requires to be filled by a majority vote at the beginning of each term. The candidate for Speaker is selected by the majority party caucus and the entire House simply approves the selection.

The powers of the Speaker cannot be understated. According to the Presidential Succession Act of 1947, the

reprimand
mildest form of censure voted by a house of Congress

Newt Gingrich, Speaker of the House, is a powerful influence in the House of Representatives. What is the main duty of the Speaker of the House?

The Congress   255

MAJORITY PARTIES IN CONGRESS AND PARTY OF THE PRESIDENT, 1867–1997*

YEARS	HOUSE	SENATE	PRESIDENT	YEARS	HOUSE	SENATE	PRESIDENT
1867–1869	R	R	R	1931–1933	D	R	R
1869–1871	R	R	R	1933–1935	D	D	D
1871–1873	R	R	R	1935–1937	D	D	D
1873–1875	R	R	R	1937–1939	D	D	D
1875–1877	D	R	R	1939–1941	D	D	D
1877–1879	D	R	R	1941–1943	D	D	D
1879–1881	D	D	R	1943–1945	D	D	D
1881–1883	R	R	R	1945–1947	D	D	D
1883–1885	D	R	R	1947–1949	R	R	D
1885–1887	D	R	D	1949–1951	D	D	D
1887–1889	D	R	D	1951–1953	D	D	D
1889–1891	R	R	R	1953–1955	R	R	R
1891–1893	D	R	R	1955–1957	D	D	R
1893–1895	D	D	D	1957–1959	D	D	R
1895–1897	R	R	D	1959–1961	D	D	R
1897–1899	R	R	R	1961–1963	D	D	D
1899–1901	R	R	R	1963–1965	D	D	D
1901–1903	R	R	R	1965–1967	D	D	D
1903–1905	R	R	R	1967–1969	D	D	D
1905–1907	R	R	R	1969–1971	D	D	R
1907–1909	R	R	R	1971–1973	D	D	R
1909–1911	R	R	R	1973–1975	D	D	R
1911–1913	D	R	R	1975–1977	D	D	R
1913–1915	D	D	D	1977–1979	D	D	D
1915–1917	D	D	D	1979–1981	D	D	D
1917–1919	D	D	D	1981–1983	D	R	R
1919–1921	R	R	D	1983–1985	D	R	R
1921–1923	R	R	R	1985–1987	D	R	R
1923–1925	R	R	R	1987–1989	D	D	R
1925–1927	R	R	R	1989–1991	D	D	R
1927–1929	R	R	R	1991–1993	D	D	R
1929–1931	R	R	R	1993–1995	D	D	D
R REPUBLICAN		D DEMOCRAT		1995–1997*	R	R	D

*to January 1997

Figure 11-7

Speaker of the House becomes *President* if the President and the Vice President cannot serve.

The main duty of the Speaker is to preside over the sessions of the House of Representatives. He or she decides who may speak and when, announces the order of business, interprets parliamentary rules, sees that correct procedures are followed, calls for votes, and decides the results of voice votes. The Speaker can literally decide the fate of laws by referring bills to certain committees and by placing members of his or her own party into committees.

Unlike the president of the Senate, the Speaker is an elected member of Congress who represents a district from his or her home state and may debate and vote on any measures. According to the rules of the House, the Speaker *must* vote in case of a tie.

As the leader of the majority party in the House, the Speaker helps to develop that party's legislative course of action. If the Speaker belongs to the President's political party, he or she often acts as the administration's spokesperson in the House. If the Speaker belongs to the "loyal opposition," his or her skills in negotiation and compromise become even more important.

In the early years of the House, Speakers acted only as presiding officers and avoided taking sides on issues. But gradually, they began using the powers of their office to promote their party's political agenda. Two examples are Thomas B. Reed, who served in the late 1800s, and Joseph G. Cannon, who served in the early 1900s. Both used the powers of their post to give the majority party complete control of the lawmaking process. Both often refused to recognize members who would interfere with their party's plans for a particular bill. Finally, in 1911 the members of the House curtailed the Speaker's powers over recognition and procedures.

A more recent Speaker of the House who used his strong personality effectively was Thomas P. "Tip" O'Neill, a Democratic representative from Massachusetts. He served as Speaker from 1977 to 1987. Friend and foe alike described O'Neill as a tireless worker whose ability to persuade made him an effective leader.

The Speaker of the House is assisted by the majority leader. As in the Senate, each party in the House elects majority and minority leaders and whips. But even though the House majority leader's duties are similar to those in the Senate, his or her influence is somewhat limited by the overshadowing position of the Speaker. Many Speakers, though, gained needed experience by serving first as majority leader of their parties in the House.

Thomas P. "Tip" O'Neill was an important figure in congressional history. He served as Speaker of the House for ten years, influencing many of the actions there. The Speaker's role has changed significantly over the years. What are some of the changes that have taken place?

Section Review

1. What determines how many representatives a state will have in the House?

2. How are representatives elected?

3. What qualifications must a person meet to serve in the House of Representatives?

4. **Challenge:** Why do you think the Speaker of the House is considered to be the second most powerful leader in the country?

4 Compensation

Members of Congress receive more than just an annual salary for their efforts. Along with the job comes certain benefits and privileges as well.

Benefits

Members of Congress receive a number of fringe benefits, including free office space, a pension, and various insurance programs. They also receive free mail service known as the franking privilege to keep constituents informed about current issues and their voting record. Instead of postage, they may use their printed signatures, called franks, on official correspondence.

Most members of Congress have an office and home in Washington, D.C., as well as in their home state or district. They receive travel allowances for trips between the two locations and a tax deduction is allowed for one of their homes. Legislators who have served five or more years receive generous retirement benefits.

Privileges

Article I, Section 6 of the Constitution grants other special privileges to members of Congress. Under the Privilege-from-Arrest clause, members cannot be arrested while performing their duties as legislators. Protection from arrest applies in civil cases, such as nonpayment of debts, but it does *not* protect members from criminal arrests, including serious traffic violations. Such protection came about before the colonies became independent. Because British officials would often harass colonial legislators to keep them from carrying out their duties, early American lead-ers wanted to make sure this could never happen in the new republic. Our Presidents, however, have never posed such a threat to Congress.

CONGRESSIONAL PAY

YEAR	SALARY
1789–1795	$6 per day
1795–1796	$6 per day (House) $7 per day (Senate)
1796–1815	$6 per day
1815–1817	$1500 per year
1817–1855	$8 per day
1855–1865	$3000 per year
1865–1871	$5000 per year
1871–1873	$7500 per year
1873–1907	$5000 per year
1907–1925	$7500 per year
1925–1932	$10,000 per year
1932–1933	$9000 per year
1933–1935	$8500 per year
1935–1947	$10,000 per year
1947–1955	$12,500 per year
1955–1965	$22,500 per year
1965–1969	$30,000 per year
1969–1977	$42,500 per year
1977–1978	$44,600 per year
1978–1981	$57,500 per year
1981–1983	$60,662 per year
1983–1984	$69,800 per year
1984–1985	$72,200 per year
1985–1987	$75,100 per year
1987–1989	$89,500 per year
1990	$96,600 per year (House)
1990	$98,400 per year (Senate)
1991	$125,100 per year (House)
1991	$101,900 per year (Senate)
1992	$129,500 per year
1993–1997	$133,600

Source: Congressional Quarterly

Figure 11-8

ISSUE: CONGRESSIONAL PAY

SHOULD CONGRESS EARN MORE?

Nearly every working person in the United States gets a raise at least once a year. Yet, in the more than 200 years that it has met, Congress has received few pay raises. This situation can be explained by the way congressional pay is determined.

Article 1, Section 6 of the Constitution declares that "The Senators and Representatives shall receive a compensation for their services, to be ascertained by law." Thus, since legislation is required, only Congress can give itself a raise. Traditionally, members have been reluctant to increase their pay, fearing that the people back home will object and that the voters will retaliate on election day.

Supporters of congressional pay raises say that although members make what appears to be a lot of money, $133,600 in 1990, it often isn't enough to meet their living expenses. The cost of living in Washington, D.C., is one of the highest in the country. Everything from rent and food to clothes and utilities costs more there than in nearly every other city in the nation.

Pay raise advocates also point to other expenses that are unique to being a member of Congress. Most senators and representatives must maintain a residence in their home state or district in addition to their residence in Washington, D.C. To remain in touch with the people they represent, they travel between Washington, D.C., and their homes frequently throughout the year. Many also reach their constituents through regular newsletters.

Pay raise opponents object that members of Congress enjoy many benefits and privileges not available to the public — such as expense accounts, special tax deductions for second homes, and office space and staff paid for by the taxpayers. Pay raise advocates counter that even these "perks" are inadequate. They note that some members' expenses exceed their allowances.

Although, historically, congressional pay hikes have been few and far between, Congress increased its pay five times in the 1980s and kept the issue at the forefront of public attention. In

1989, Congress responded with complicated legislation that raised salaries in the executive and judicial branches and made major changes in its own pay structure. The law created "cost of living" increases in both houses in 1990 and 1991, and granted House members an additional 25 percent raise in 1991. In return, representatives were prohibited from keeping speaking fees or honoraria, which in the past brought them as much as $26,850 per year in additional income. Although the ethics of such outside earnings has aroused much controversy, the Senate voted to pass up the raise and keep the outside income.

Critics of the 1989 legislation were angered not only by the size of the increases, but also by what they regarded as a transparent attempt to disguise it as ethics reform. These critics helped add momentum to the drive to ratify the Twenty-seventh Amendment. Originally proposed in 1789, the amendment was resurrected. The states ratified it, and it became a part of the Constitution in 1992. The amendment prohibits any congressional pay raises from taking effect until the next session of Congress.

1. Do you think members of Congress deserve to earn more? Why or why not?
2. Should the way that congressional pay is determined be changed?

The Freedom of Information Act does not require Congress to open its files to the public. Why is Congress exempt from this law?

Under the Speech-or-Debate clause, members of Congress are guaranteed freedom of speech while conducting congressional business. This means they can address their colleagues in open debate without fear of court suits for making "harmful" or "false" statements. Called congressional immunity, this protection applies only during official sessions and includes floor debates, committee meetings, reports, and resolutions. It does not cover speeches, articles, or conversations made in public apart from legislative business.

Congress has also made itself and its members exempt from many laws. For example, laws against discrimination in employment based on age, race, color, religion, sex, or national origin do not protect congressional employees. In addition, Congress is exempt from the Occupational Safety and Health Act, which requires employers to maintain certain health and safety standards for their employees.

Finally, Congress has failed to apply to itself several regulations passed expressly for the executive branch. One of these is the Freedom of Information Act, which forced the executive branch to open its files to the public, while congressional files remain closed. Congress is exempt from these and similar laws because they are enforced by executive agencies. And, traditionally, Congress has rejected any attempt by the executive branch to regulate its affairs.

Section Review

1. Besides salaries, what other benefits do senators and representatives enjoy?

2. What special privileges does the Constitution grant members of Congress?

3. **Challenge:** Do you think Congress should be exempt from laws enforced by executive agencies? Explain.

5 Congressional Support

When the first Congress met, the population of the United States was about 4 million people. Today Congress is the lawmaking body for over 250 million of us. With this dramatic change in population came a change in public needs. With more older Americans, for instance, a shift in the type of social services is needed. As population shifts from rural areas to cities, new demands are heard for public housing, mass transportation, and jobs. And new laws are needed for pollution control, energy shortages, and skyrocketing crime rates.

All this means that Congress must handle a overwhelming volume of government business, much of which deals with highly technical issues. Since few members have the specialized background and skills to understand every aspect of all the issues, most must rely on help from a staff and legislative agencies.

Staff

Until the 1900s, the only help Congress had came from a very small clerical staff. In 1946 the Legislative Reorganization Act recognized professional assistance for members of Congress as a basic and growing need.

PERSONAL STAFF

Today each member of Congress staffs an office in Washington, D.C., as well as one or more offices in his or her state or district. The typical congressional staff consists of one administrative assistant (AA), several legislative assistants (LAs), teams of caseworkers for the Washington and home-state offices, a press aide, and general clerical help. The most

These congressional staff members assist members of Congress with legislative duties. How has the role of congressional staff members changed over the years?

KEY LEGISLATIVE AGENCIES

Congressional Budget Office:
provides expert technical and computer service to Congress; analyzes the budget proposal of the Office of Management and Budget; determines the economic consequences of legislation.

General Accounting Office:
checks to see that government spending is proper and reasonable; headed by the comptroller general who is appointed by the President, with the Senate's approval, for a 15-year term.

Government Printing Office:
prints the *Congressional Record;* does all the national government's printing; distributes government publications and reprints documents for public purchase.

Library of Congress:
serves national, state, and local governments and the public; contains over 20 million books.

Offices of Legislative Counsel:
provide legal assistance to congressional committees in drafting bills.

Office of Technology Assessment:
studies new scientific developments and the likely effects of technological change on society.

Figure 11-9

influential staff member is the administrative assistant in each Washington office. He or she supervises the legislator's staff. In most cases, the AA is the member's principal political adviser and often acts as campaign manager during election years.

Legislative assistants help with all aspects of a member's lawmaking responsibilities. Most are highly trained in legal matters or have professional experience in a particular field. Having such backgrounds enables them to research issues and draft bills and amendments.

Caseworkers serve their senator or representative by directly serving his or her constituents. They help constituents who are having trouble with the bureaucracy. In recent years, more members began locating the majority of their casework staff in their home-state offices. This shift in emphasis from Washington brings the work of the legislators closer to the community.

Press aides, meanwhile, promote news coverage of the member's legislative activities. They prepare press releases that often contain excerpts from the member's speeches or report on his or her involvement with pending legislation.

COMMITTEE STAFF

In addition to each legislator's personal staff, there are over 3700 congressional staff members who serve the needs of the congressional committees and subcommittees.

Committe staff collect and analyze information on issues, identify and research problems, suggest policies, schedule committee hearings, and prepare committee reports. The rules of the House of Representatives permit each committee to hire 30 staff members, plus an additional number of investigative staff. The investigative staff varies annually with the specific goals set by each committee for that year. For example, in 1987 the chairpersons of the special committees investigating the Iran/Contra affair requested more funds for additional lawyers and support staff to sift through the thousands of documents presented as evidence.

Due to the Senate's smaller size, senators have more flexibility in determining the number of committee staff. Each committee chairperson presents the committee's budget for salaries and office expenses to the Senate Rules and Administration Committee each year. Each chairperson hires staff according to the committee's work load and budget limitations.

Legislative Agencies

Because of the essential and exhaustive work performed by congressional staff and members of Congress, six offices or agencies have been added to the legislative branch since 1789.

Legislative agencies provide support for Congress in such areas as committee work, casework, and the development of new policies. These agencies are listed and their house duties are described in Figure 11-9. The General Accounting Office (GAO), for instance, examines the expenditures of government agencies to assure that federal funds are being spent for the purposes and programs that Congress intended. Thus, the GAO acts as the "watchdog of the treasury." The GAO also assures that sound accounting practices are used by the executive branch to account for federal government expenditures. In this capacity, the GAO is one of the world's largest accounting firms.

Section Review

1. Why does a member of Congress today need a large support staff?
2. Who makes up the typical staff of a United States senator or representative?
3. **Challenge:** If you were to seek employment as a congressional staff member, for which position would you apply? Why?

Summary

1. The Congress of the United States, made up of the Senate and the House of Representatives, is the nation's lawmaking body.
2. The responsibilities of Congress include lawmaking, helping constituents, monitoring the executive branch, and representing the views of constituents.
3. Senators and representatives maintain close contact with their constituents through newsletters, questionnaires, personal visits, radio, and television.
4. A congressional session is the period during which Congress meets.
5. The Senate is made up of two members from each state.
6. Membership in the House of Representatives is based on each state's population.
7. Senators must be at least 30 years old, residents of the state from which they are elected, and American citizens for nine years. Representatives must be at least 25 years old, residents of the state from which they are elected, and American citizens for seven years.
8. The number of congressional districts in each state depends upon the state's population and may change every ten years based on the United States census.
9. In addition to an annual salary, members of Congress receive certain benefits and privileges as compensation for their work.
10. As the task of governing has become more complex, members of Congress and congressional committees have had to rely on staffs of experts to help them with their work.

Chapter 11 Review

★ Building Vocabulary

Use the terms you learned in this chapter to complete the following statements.

1. The member of a legislative house elected by members to lead the minority party is the _____ _____.

2. The _____ is the official count of the people of the United States.

3. The period of time during which Congress assembles and carries out its business is called a _____ _____.

4. _____ is the redistribution of legislative seats based on a new law or formula.

5. The temporary presiding officer of the Senate when the Vice President is absent is the _____ _____ _____.

6. To end a session of a legislative body is to _____.

7. The _____ _____ is the member of a legislative house elected by members to lead the majority party.

8. Having to _____ a member is an extreme action that has been rare in the history of the Senate.

★ Reviewing Facts

1. What are the duties of Congress?
2. According to the Constitution, how often must Congress meet?
3. What is the purpose of caucuses at the beginning of a congressional term?
4. What is the number of the present congressional term?
5. What advantages do incumbent legislators have in elections?
6. Describe the system used to elect senators that ensures that the Senate is a continuous body?
7. What three methods of disciplining members of Congress for misconduct are used in the House and Senate?

8. How are representative seats apportioned? When does reapportionment occur?
9. From what type of arrests are members of Congress protected while they are performing their legislative duties?
10. Why have congressional staffs grown in recent years?

★ Analyzing Facts

1. The Constitution contains only a few requirements for a person to be a U.S. representative or senator. What additional requirements would you add?
2. The success rate of incumbents in Congress at election time is very high. Based on what you learned in this chapter, what do you think would be required to unseat an incumbent member of Congress?
3. Congressional staffs have grown considerably during recent years. Some people say that these staffs actually run the government. Do you agree with this view? Why or why not?
4. Traditionally, senators deal more with national and state concerns, and representatives focus more on local or district problems. Do you think this helps or hinders the lawmaking process? Explain.

Using Your
Civic Participation Journal

Review the letters in your Civic Participation Journal. Mount both your letter and your representative's response on poster board and describe each to your classmates.

★ Evaluating Ideas

1. Why do your think the Framers of the Constitution discussed the legislative branch instead of the executive branch in the first article of the Constitution?

2. Congress depends on party caucuses to help select its leaders. Can you think of another way Congress might organize itself to assure that members would be responsible for party policies?

3. The Constitution says nothing about the selection of Congressional leaders according to party membership. Why do you think this has become important in the organization of Congress? Explain.

★ Critical Thinking
Identifying Trends and Making Forecasts

Forecasts are predictions that are based on trends. A trend is the general direction something is taking.

Explanation Trends can be identified by studying historical statistics or by examining past events to see if they show a pattern or direction. If the pattern is fairly consistent over time, it likely is a trend. Based on this trend, you can make a forecast.

Use the following to identify trends and make forecasts.

1. Gather data on a topic.
2. Use historical information.
3. Group information by characteristics.
4. Look for directions, or other relationships, over time. These directions are possible trends.
5. Make your forecast based on the direction of the trend you have identified.

Practice The following headlines from newspapers identify a trend. They help predict potential changes in this state's number of seats in Congress.

1. **HOUSING STARTS HIT NEW HIGH**
   Building Permits Also Up
2. **ACME INDUSTRIES TO OPEN PLANT**
   14,000 Jobs Created
3. **UNEMPLOYMENT AT 6 PERCENT**
   Down From 9 Percent Last Year
4. **SURGING SCHOOL ENROLLMENT**
   40,000 More Students This Year

Based on these headlines, you should be able to conclude the following:
Trend—The state's population is growing.
Forecast—Based on the current trend, this state will gain seats in Congress after the next census.

Independent Practice Study the graph below. What trends can you identify? What forecast can you make about the Northeast in 2010?

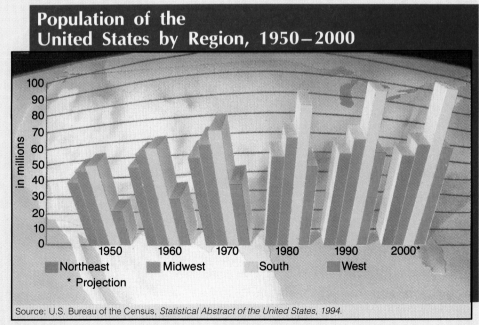

Population of the United States by Region, 1950–2000

Northeast   Midwest   South   West
* Projection

Source: U.S. Bureau of the Census, *Statistical Abstract of the United States, 1994.*

Figure 11-4

265

Chapter 12

Congressional Powers

Although the powers of Congress are great, it is important that you keep in mind that they are not unlimited. Congress has only those powers that are expressly granted to it by the Constitution.

The Framers reserved certain authority to the states and gave other powers to the executive and judicial branches of the government. In addition, the Framers limited Congress as well as the other branches when they stipulated that some powers be shared among them.

In this chapter you will learn how the legislative and nonlegislative powers of Congress affect your daily life. You will also learn how congressional power has evolved.

Chapter Preview

TERMS TO KNOW
expressed powers, tariffs, revenues, appropriations, federal budget, imports, currency, legal tender, interstate commerce, national debt, copyrights, patents, infringement, exports, trademarks, bankruptcy, legislative veto, implied powers, strict construction, loose construction, impeach, executive agreements

READ TO DISCOVER
- the legislative powers of Congress.
- the nonlegislative powers of Congress.
- the evolution of congressional power.

★ ★ ★ ★ ★

Civic Participation Journal

Members of Congress often sponsor students to work as pages in Congress. Call or write one of your senators or your representative to learn the requirements for pages and the type of work they do. Record your findings in your journal.

1 Legislative Powers

Like the other two branches of the federal government, Congress receives its authority from the Constitution. Article I, Section 8 lists most of the powers of the legislative branch. Because they are directly stated, they are called the **expressed powers** of Congress.

Power of the Purse

Three important monetary powers are given to Congress—power to tax, to spend, and to borrow. Together they are known as the power of the purse, shown in Figure 12-1. No other constitutional power gives Congress as much influence in shaping public policy.

TAXING POWER

Every government, regardless of its structure, needs **revenues** to carry out its programs. In the United States, the federal government raises money mainly through its power to tax. This power was written into the Constitution to prevent the government from running short of money, as it had under the Articles of Confederation. Under the Articles, the government could not collect funds from the states but had to rely solely on their voluntary contributions. As a result, the government never had enough money to function well.

The Constitution tried to remedy this problem by permitting Congress to levy taxes. Originally, however, this power was limited by states' rights, and the government had to rely on **tariffs** as the primary source of its revenues. As the nation expanded, tariffs did not keep pace with the amount of funds needed. As a result, Congress proposed the Sixteenth Amendment, providing for the collection of personal income taxes. Ratified in 1913, this amendment gave Congress the power to: "lay and

expressed powers powers listed in the Constitution

tariffs taxes charged on imported items

revenues monies raised by a government to pay for its activities

Three Important Legislative Powers Known as the Power of the Purse

TAXING   SPENDING   BORROWING

Figure 12-1

Representative John Kasich, a Republican from Westerville, Ohio, became Chairman of the House Budget Committee in the Republican-controlled 104th Congress. The Budget Committee works with important issues such as tax bills. Why are tax issues of such importance?

collect taxes on income, from whatever source derived, without apportionment, among the several states, and without regard to any census or enumeration.''

Since the passage of this amendment, income taxes have become the major source of federal tax revenues. Smaller sources of revenue include payroll taxes for social insurance and taxes on such items as gasoline, liquor, and telephone service. All these revenues help pay for such varied government services as highway construction, the maintenance of national parks, and a strong national defense. They also are used to set up and maintain health and safety standards and to conduct welfare programs to help the disadvantaged.

Congress may also levy taxes to contribute to the growth and strength of our economy. For example, tariffs on **imports** raise their prices and may help protect American companies from overseas competitors. Likewise, to encourage economic growth, Congress may increase or decrease tax rates at home. In 1981, for instance, Congress lowered personal income taxes by 25 percent over a three-year period. This tax cut was favored by President Reagan in the hope of boosting the nation's economy.

SPENDING POWER

After taxes are levied and money raised, Congress's role does not stop. It has the power to decide how that money should be spent. Article I, Section 9 states that ''No money shall be drawn from the treasury, but in consequence of appropriations made by law.'' This means that Congress can spend federal funds only by passing a law authorizing that a certain amount of money be spent on a particular program. Such **appropriations** originate in the House of Representatives and provide government departments and agencies with the funds they need to carry out their work.

This power to control spending is directly related to the **federal budget,** which details how much money the government plans to spend over the next year, how much needs to be raised, and how it will be distributed. Because the budget is vital in setting national spending priorities, congressional members spend most of their time during a session dealing either directly or indirectly with the federal budget.

Since 1921, Congress has permitted the executive branch to prepare the budget proposal each year. The President submits this proposal to

appropriations government expenditures

federal budget yearly blueprint for the raising and spending of federal funds

imports goods shipped into a country

This early poster encourages Americans to buy bonds. How does the sale of bonds affect the finances of the federal government?

Help Uncle Sam Stamp Out The Kaiser!

3rd LIBERTY LOAN

BUY U.S. GOV'T BONDS

currency money

legal tender money that is legally valid and must be accepted in payment of a debt

interstate commerce trade between the states

national debt total amount of money that the federal government owes as a result of borrowing

Congress in January, after which House and Senate budget committees study it and make changes. The final budget is usually a compromise between the presidential and congressional versions.

BORROWING MONEY

The actual amount of money needed to finance the operation of the national government is staggering. In 1989, for instance, President George Bush estimated that more than $1.16 trillion would be needed in 1990 alone! And while this amount is incredible, the government often spends more than it collects in taxes and other forms of revenue. When this happens, money must be borrowed. This borrowed money makes up the **national debt,** which currently exceeds $4.6 trillion.

The Constitution grants Congress the authority to ''borrow money on the credit of the United States.'' It does this by selling bonds or certificates to investors who, in return, receive interest as well as the original

amount at a later date. Meanwhile, the government uses the money to help finance current expenditures or pay off interest on the national debt. While there is no constitutional limit on the power of the national government to borrow money, Congress can limit the level of the national debt.

Coining Money

Besides the powers of raising, spending, and borrowing money, the Constitution also gives the legislative branch the power to issue **currency.** This power was granted to Congress to prevent the confusion and weakened economy that resulted from each state issuing its own currency under the Articles of Confederation. Congress also may decide what is **legal tender.** Years ago, a controversy developed over whether Congress could issue paper money along with metal coins. In 1884 the Supreme Court ruled that the constitutional right to coin money also gave Congress the authority to issue paper money as legal tender. For this reason, the sentence ''This note is legal tender for all debt, public and private'' is now printed on paper money.

Commerce Powers

Under the Articles of Confederation, Congress was permitted to handle foreign commerce, or trade, but could not regulate **interstate commerce.** This lack of control led to economic wars between the states, with each taxing the other's goods and restricting the products that could pass beyond their own state borders. The nation's economy was in shambles.

The Framers of the Constitution wanted to avoid another such calamity and provide the nation with a stable economy. So, in the Commerce

Clause, the Constitution states that Congress has the power to "regulate commerce with foreign nations, and among the several states."

According to the Supreme Court's interpretation of the Commerce Clause, interstate commerce includes the manufacturing, buying, selling, and carrying of all goods, persons, or information across state boundaries. In this century, Congress has expanded its application of the clause to include a wide range of laws that affect interstate commerce, such as child labor laws, minimum wage laws, and the rights of workers to organize in unions.

But there are limits on how Congress can use its commerce power. According to the Constitution, Congress cannot levy taxes on **exports,** for instance. Nor can it tax goods moving from state to state. In addition, it may not favor any port in the United States over another.

Other Regulatory Powers

With constitutional authority, Congress has other regulatory powers covering a wide range of activities. For example, Congress may set quo-tas for the number of immigrants and refugees who can legally cross the nation's borders, as well as set up the procedures for them to become naturalized citizens. It also has the power to establish and maintain a postal service.

The Constitution allows Congress to protect the creative work of writers, inventors, musicians, scientists, artists, and even computer programmers. This protection comes about through the granting of **copyrights** and **patents.** A copyright may be obtained by registering with the Copyright Office in the Library of Congress, and it extends for the life of the copyright owner plus 50 years. If **infringement** occurs, the owner may sue for damages in civil court. Similarly, the Patent and Trademark Office in the Department of Commerce issues patents varying from 14 to 17 years, depending on the invention. This office also issues **trademarks,** which are registered for 20 years.

Congress also has the power to standardize all weights and measures in the United States. In 1836 the English system (pound, foot, gallon) was established as the legal standard in the country. Thirty years later,

copyrights exclusive legal rights to reproduce, publish, or sell one's works

patents exclusive legal rights that protect inventions

infringement violation of the rights of copyright owners

exports goods shipped out of a country

trademarks distinctive words or symbols that identify a company or its products

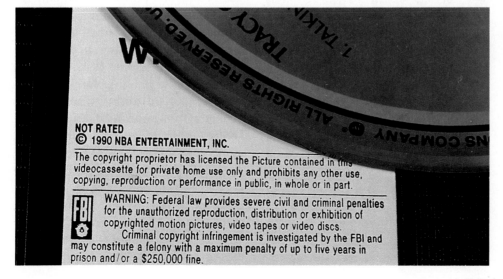

NOT RATED
© 1990 NBA ENTERTAINMENT, INC.
The copyright proprietor has licensed the Picture contained in this videocassette for private home use only and prohibits any other use, copying, reproduction or performance in public, in whole or in part.
WARNING: Federal law provides severe civil and criminal penalties for the unauthorized reproduction, distribution or exhibition of copyrighted motion pictures, video tapes or video discs.
Criminal copyright infringement is investigated by the FBI and may constitute a felony with a maximum penalty of up to five years in prison and/or a $250,000 fine.

By issuing copyrights like the one cited here, Congress protects original works. What is the penalty for infringement of a copyright?

Congress also legalized the metric system (gram, meter, liter), but the American public and industry were not asked to voluntarily change to this system until 1975. And to ensure that all instruments measuring time, distance, and weight are accurate and uniform, Congress established the National Bureau of Standards in 1901. It maintains the national clocks, scales, and other measuring devices against which all other instruments in the nation are checked and corrected.

Finally, Congress has the power to pass laws dealing with **bankruptcy.** Using these laws, an individual or business may begin bankruptcy proceedings in court. If a court decides a debtor is bankrupt, the debtor's property may be sold, with the proceeds then divided among creditors. In many cases the courts free debtors from any remaining debts, giving them a chance for a new start.

bankruptcy the condition of being legally unable to pay one's debts

The Vietnam Veterans' Memorial stands in Washington, D.C. Due largely to the conflict in Vietnam, the War Powers Act of 1973 was passed. What is the purpose of this Act?

Judicial Powers

Congress has several judicial powers granted by the Constitution. The most important of these is the right to organize and set up federal courts below the Supreme Court. Another is to decide punishments for federal crimes, such as counterfeiting money or committing treason. Still another of its powers is the discretionary authority to accuse, try, and remove from office leaders of the other two branches of government.

War Powers

The Constitution grants war powers to both the legislative and executive branches, with Congress having the power to declare war and the President to direct the armed forces. The Framers of the Constitution gave Congress these powers because they believed it would not rush into war as quickly as the President. In actuality, however, Presidents often have sent American forces into military action without a formal congressional declaration of war. The Vietnam War (1962-1973) is a prime example.

As a result of such presidential actions, Congress passed the War Powers Act of 1973, which limited the President's power to send American troops overseas without congressional approval. According to this act, the President must report to Congress, in writing and within 48 hours, after committing troops to a foreign country. Troop involvement is then limited to 60 days unless Congress approves a longer commitment. If Congress opposes involvement, the President may be forced to withdraw the troops.

The War Powers Act was passed during President Richard Nixon's administration. Nixon opposed it, as has every President since. The reason for this opposition stems from the fact

Pamela Harriman served as United States ambassador to France during President Clinton's administration. Congress must approve an individual's appointment before he or she may become an ambassador. What are some other congressional powers that deal with foreign relations?

that the act contains a **legislative veto,** which Congress uses to make sure that the executive branch carries out the law as the legislature intended. But in 1983 the Supreme Court declared the use of legislative vetoes unconstitutional, arguing that to be legal and enforceable, all acts of Congress must include the participation of the President, either through his approval or veto. By denying the President the opportunity to respond to congressional actions, such as the forced withdrawal of troops in the War Powers Act, Congress would be withholding the President's right of participation.

Foreign Relations

Although the President is primarily responsible for foreign policy, Congress does have some powers in this area. It can approve treaties, declare war, regulate foreign commerce, and approve presidential appointments of diplomatic officers. And through its power of the purse, it controls funding for national defense, foreign aid, and the State Department.

Implied Powers

In addition to its expressed powers, Congress has **implied powers.** These powers are not stated word for word in the Constitution. Instead, they are based on the Necessary and Proper Clause in Article I. In it, Congress is granted the power to make any laws ''necessary and proper'' in carrying out its duties. But the idea that Congress held powers not *expressed* in the Constitution caused a heated debate from the very beginning.

The debate began after Secretary of the Treasury Alexander Hamilton called upon Congress to establish a national banking system in 1790. Secretary of State Thomas Jefferson opposed the idea, arguing that the functions of the federal government should be limited by a **strict construction** of the words of the Constitution. In explaining his position to President Washington, Jefferson said:

To take a single step beyond the boundaries thus specially drawn around the powers of Congress is to take possession of a boundless field of power.

legislative veto provision allowing one or both houses of Congress to block executive actions

implied powers powers not specifically mentioned in the Constitution

strict construction narrow interpretation of the Constitution

Congressional Powers 273

Alexander Hamilton took a view of "loose construction" regarding the Constitution. What is meant by the phrase, "loose construction"?

loose construction broad interpretation of the Constitution

Hamilton, on the other hand, took a position of **loose construction** and believed that the Necessary and Proper Clause gave Congress any additional powers it needed to carry out its expressed powers. He argued:

The whole turn of the clause indicates that it was the intent of the Convention by that clause to give a liberal latitude to the exercise of the specified powers. . . . If the end be clearly comprehended within any of the specified powers, and if the measure have an obvious relation to that end, and is not forbidden by a particular provision of the Constitution, it may safely be deemed to come within the compass of the national authority.

President Washington was persuaded by Hamilton's argument and signed the national bank into law. The Supreme Court upheld Washington's view when, in 1819, it ruled in *McCulloch v. Maryland* that the Framers may have meant no more by the words "necessary and proper" than that the laws passed by Congress must be "convenient or useful" in carrying out its duties.

Over the years, however, the Supreme Court has required that the Necessary and Proper Clause be linked with one or more of its expressed powers before Congress takes action. Because this clause has expanded congressional powers, it often is referred to as the Elastic Clause.

Denied Powers

Because limited government was so important to Americans, an entire section of the Constitution—Article I, Section 9—lists the powers Congress may not exercise. These prohibit Congress, for instance, from suspending writs of habeas corpus or from passing bills of attainder or ex post facto laws. The Bill of Rights further restricts the powers of Congress with the Tenth Amendment, which reserves to the states or to the people all powers not granted to the national government nor denied to the states. This means, for example, that Congress cannot set penalties for state crimes, nor can it establish a national system of education.

Section Review

1. How does Congress exercise the power of the purse?
2. What does interstate commerce include?
3. According to the Constitution, who may declare war?
4. What is the difference between expressed and implied powers of Congress?
5. **Challenge:** Do you think Congress should have both the power to raise money and to decide how it will be spent? Explain.

2 Nonlegislative Powers

Although the most important duty of Congress is to make laws, it also has powers outside the legislative process. Some are specified by the Constitution, some stem from the nature of Congress's responsibilities, and many pertain to the operations of the other two branches of government. Figure 12-2 summarizes these nonlegislative as well as the legislative powers of Congress.

Conducting Investigations

One nonlegislative power, that of conducting investigations, is not granted to Congress by the Constitu-tion. Instead, it is an implied power. Why would Congress want to conduct an investigation? One reason is to look into charges against public offi-cials. Another is to obtain information on proposed laws. Congress might also conduct investigations to deter-mine the effectiveness of laws and to educate the public about the issues and problems facing the nation.

The first congressional investiga-tion occurred in 1792 to find out why 600 American soldiers were killed by Native Americans on the Ohio fron-tier. Since then, Congress has used its investigative powers extensively to keep itself—and the American people—informed.

Usually the most dramatic and far-reaching investigations are those

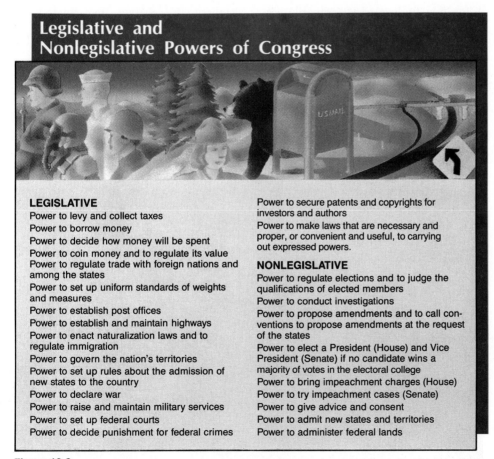

Legislative and Nonlegislative Powers of Congress

LEGISLATIVE
Power to levy and collect taxes
Power to borrow money
Power to decide how money will be spent
Power to coin money and to regulate its value
Power to regulate trade with foreign nations and among the states
Power to set up uniform standards of weights and measures
Power to establish post offices
Power to establish and maintain highways
Power to enact naturalization laws and to regulate immigration
Power to govern the nation's territories
Power to set up rules about the admission of new states to the country
Power to declare war
Power to raise and maintain military services
Power to set up federal courts
Power to decide punishment for federal crimes

Power to secure patents and copyrights for investors and authors
Power to make laws that are necessary and proper, or convenient and useful, to carrying out expressed powers.

NONLEGISLATIVE
Power to regulate elections and to judge the qualifications of elected members
Power to conduct investigations
Power to propose amendments and to call con-ventions to propose amendments at the request of the states
Power to elect a President (House) and Vice President (Senate) if no candidate wins a majority of votes in the electoral college
Power to bring impeachment charges (House)
Power to try impeachment cases (Senate)
Power to give advice and consent
Power to admit new states and territories
Power to administer federal lands

Figure 12-2

looking into alleged wrongdoing by government officials. The Senate's investigation of the Watergate affair, for instance, probed the actions of the President. In 1972 officials working for the reelection of President Richard Nixon broke into the Democratic national headquarters to plant listening devices in order to spy on that party's strategy in the upcoming election. The Senate's investigation ultimately led to Nixon's resignation in 1974.

Most congressional investigations, however, are conducted to obtain information on proposed laws. Since legislators cannot be expected to know everything about the hundreds of pieces of legislation appearing before them each year, they call on expert witnesses to testify on the details of a particular bill. In some cases, these investigations may involve fact-finding trips to enable legislators to get firsthand information. For example, several members of Congress visited the Soviet Union in 1988 to examine radar installations that appeared to conflict with arms control treaties. Such trips often are controversial. Supporters view them as necessary in order for legislators to understand world problems. Critics argue that the trips—at the taxpayers' expense—are nothing more than costly vacations.

As part of its oversight or "watchdog" responsibility, Congress also investigates how well existing laws are administered by the executive branch. One such investigation helped Harry Truman become President. As senator, Truman headed a committee that uncovered wasteful practices in war preparations during World War II. His success brought him to the attention of President Franklin D. Roosevelt, who chose Truman as his running mate in 1944. When Roosevelt died in April 1945, Truman succeeded him.

Finally, Congress conducts investigations to inform the public about important matters. In 1933, for instance, the Senate investigated the stock market collapse of 1929 to determine what went wrong and to discuss what could be done to prevent such an event from happening again. In 1979 the House held investigative hearings to examine the accident at the Three Mile Island nuclear power plant in Pennsylvania.

One of the best-known congressional investigations centered around the Watergate affair in the early 1970s. What is the purpose of most congressional investigations?

Amending the Constitution

Congress may propose an amendment to the Constitution by a two-thirds vote in each house. And, although it has never done so, it may also call a convention to propose amendments at the request of two-thirds of the state legislatures. Congress also determines how an amendment is to be ratified—by the legislatures of three-fourths of the states or by conventions called for that purpose in three-fourths of the states.

Admitting New States

Article IV, Section 3 gives Congress the power to admit new states to the Union, with certain limits. No state may be created out of an existing state. Nor may any state be formed by combining two or more states without their consent and that of Congress.

Recently both Puerto Rico and the District of Columbia have considered statehood. In 1967 the citizens of Puerto Rico rejected such plans. But President Bush, in his first message to Congress in 1989, called for new efforts to make Puerto Rico the fifty-first state. Residents of the District of Columbia, on the other hand, voted in support of statehood in 1980. They even drew up a state constitution and selected New Columbia as its name. But Congress has yet to pass an act of admission.

Governing Federal Territories

Congress also has the authority to govern various areas under United States control, including military and naval bases; federal prisons, parks, court houses, and post offices; and American territories, such as the Virgin Islands, Guam, and American

On August 21, 1959, Hawaii became the 50th state to join the Union. What are some restrictions concerning the formation of new states?

Samoa. In addition, Congress has special jurisdiction over Washington, D.C., the nation's capital. The District of Columbia is made up almost entirely of federal lands and is therefore a territory, not a state. Its citizens, likewise, are citizens of the United States but not of any particular state.

For many years, Congress acted as the government of the District, deciding on everything from the annual budget to building codes. Residents had no say in their government and were prevented from voting for city administrators or even in national elections. By the late 1950s, however, residents were demanding change. Partly as a result of their outcries, the Twenty-third Amendment was adopted in 1961, giving residents the right to vote in national elections.

Further changes were made in 1971, when Congress allowed the District to have a nonvoting delegate in the House of Representatives, and in 1973, when the District achieved limited home rule. The District would have achieved full representation in Congress—one representative and two senators—had a 1978 constitutional amendment been ratified. But by the deadline for ratification in 1985, only 16 of the required 38 states had approved the amendment. Since this attempt failed, the District has not made any major efforts to achieve statehood.

Choosing Executive Officials

Under unusual circumstances, the House of Representatives has an important role in the selection of a President. For example, if no presidential candidate receives a majority of electoral votes, House members, casting only one vote per state, select a winner from among the three leading candidates. The House has done this only twice in its history—in the 1801 election of Thomas Jefferson and in the 1825 election of John Quincy Adams. Likewise, the Senate chooses a Vice President if no candidate gets a majority of electoral votes. This has happened only once, when the Senate chose Richard M. Johnson as Vice President in 1837.

The Twenty-fifth Amendment involves both houses of Congress in the vice-presidential selection process whenever that post is vacant due to illness, death, or resignation. According to the amendment, if this happens, the President chooses a Vice President who then must be confirmed by Congress. This has happened twice—once in 1973 with the confirmation of Gerald Ford and again in 1974 for the confirmation of Nelson Rockefeller.

In 1973, President Richard Nixon appointed Gerald Ford as Vice President. This appointment was then confirmed by Congress. How many times has the office of Vice President been filled in this way?

Removing Officials

Article II, Section 4 of the Constitution states that the "President, Vice President, and all civil officers of the United States shall be removed from office on impeachment for and conviction of treason, bribery, or other high crimes and misdemeanors." This removal process is divided between the two houses of Congress. The House, by a majority vote, has the power to **impeach** an official; the Senate then sits as a court to determine that person's guilt or innocence. A two-thirds vote of the senators present is needed for conviction. The official is then removed from office and, in some cases, barred from holding any public office in the future. The Constitution also states that the official also may be tried in a regular court of law.

Only rarely has the impeachment process been used. As of 1994, the House has impeached 15 officials, including one President, one Cabinet officer, one senator, and 12 federal judges. And only seven, all judges, were convicted and removed from office. The most famous case concerned President Andrew Johnson, who was impeached in 1868 for removing an appointed official in violation of a federal law. He was later found not guilty by the margin of a single vote in the Senate.

More recently, in 1974, the House Judiciary Committee recommended to the House that President Richard Nixon be impeached on three charges — obstruction of justice, abuse of power, and contempt of Congress — based on his involvement in the Watergate affair. Nixon resigned just 10 days before the House was scheduled to begin debate on the impeachment charges, and they were subsequently dropped.

Giving Advice and Consent

According to the Constitution, the Senate has the right to give its "advice and consent" concerning many appointments made by the President. Accordingly, each nomination by the President is reviewed by a Senate committee, which then sends its recommendations to the entire Senate. There, a decision is made by a majority vote to approve or reject the nominee.

This nonlegislative power of the Senate was relatively obscure for many years because the Senate quickly approved most presidential choices for Cabinet offices, ambassadorships, and other top executive offices. But in the last 20 years, senators have probed deeper into the backgrounds of the appointees and now tend to raise many questions. A recent example concerned President Clinton's nomination of Lani Guinier, an African American law professor, to head the civil-rights division of the Justice Department. Many senators expressed concern that Guinier's scholarly writings on race relations were extremist. Amid mounting criticism from conservative members of Congress, President Clinton withdrew the nomination before Guinier went through the Senate's confirmation proceedings.

Presidential choices of federal officials who serve in the states — judges, United States attorneys, or regional directors of federal agencies — also are open to debate. By a long-standing practice of "senatorial courtesy," the Senate usually rejects a nominee if the senators from that state oppose the nomination.

Besides presidential appointments, the Senate also gives its "advice and consent" to treaties made by the

Lani Guinier

impeach formally bring charges against an official

Characteristics of a Treaty vs. an Executive Agreement

A TREATY

is a formal agreement by two or more countries.
is negotiated under the direction of the President.
requires approval by two-thirds of the Senate.

AN EXECUTIVE AGREEMENT

is an agreement between the President and the heads of foreign governments.
does not require Senate approval.

Figure 12-3

executive agreements
agreements made by the President with leaders of other countries that do not require Senate approval

President. For many years after the Constitution was adopted, the Senate as a whole advised the President before a treaty was signed. Today, however, the President usually consults with the Senate Foreign Relations Committee while the treaty is still under consideration. When the treaty comes up for a vote, the Senate can follow any one of three courses. It may consent, reject, or amend it by a two-thirds vote of the members present. If one is rejected, the President may present the international agreement to *both* houses, where it may pass by a simple majority vote in each.

While the House of Representatives does not have the constitutional right to ratify treaties, it does control the funding needed to put them into effect. For this reason, the President often finds it politically wise to consult with leading House members from both parties on most matters concerning treaties.

In recent years, Presidents have been able to bypass Congress completely by entering into **executive agreements.** Figure 12-3 explains the main differences between treaties and executive agreements. While most such agreements are used for routine matters, such as trade, others may deal with important military questions or foreign aid.

The potential for presidential misuse of executive agreements led Congress to adopt the Case Act in 1972, which requires the President to submit to Congress for review the actual texts of all agreements within 60 days of signing. In 1984, for instance, President Ronald Reagan signed an executive agreement with the People's Republic of China on industrial and technological cooperation between the two nations. When Congress objected to several promises made by the administration in this agreement, the President amended it.

Section Review

1. What are four reasons that Congress conducts investigations?

2. What are some nonlegislative powers given to Congress?

3. What two steps are required before an official can be removed from office?

4. In what types of appointments is the practice of senatorial courtesy used?

5. **Challenge:** What are the advantages and disadvantages of executive agreements?

3 Evolution of Congressional Power

From the very beginning of our nation's history, the executive and legislative branches have struggled over who should lead the nation. By its nature, the judiciary is isolated from political confrontations. But since the courts determine the constitutionality of the laws passed by Congress and the actions of Presidents, the judicial branch often acts as the final decision maker in their struggle.

Congress Versus the President

Congress and the President often have opposed each other in forming public policy. One reason for this conflict is that the system of checks and balances has given the legislative and executive branches powers that are closely related. Congress, for instance, can pass laws, the President can veto them, and Congress can override a presidential veto.

Another reason is that the two branches represent different constituencies and interests, and the needs of a district or a state do not always coincide with the needs of the nation. For example, a representative may work hard to get a bill passed that proposes dam construction in his district, thus ensuring local farmers a plentiful water supply. But the President may veto the bill on the grounds that the money for dam construction can better be spent on national water conservation programs.

Still another source of conflict stems from the fact that sometimes the President and the majority of congressional members belong to different political parties. Thus, the leaders of the majority party may defeat presidential programs and adopt their own.

Whatever the reason for their opposition to each other, power has shifted back and forth between the executive and legislative branches for most of American history. Which branch holds the most power at any given time may depend on several factors, including the makeup of Congress, who is President, the mood of the public, and the issues at hand.

Early Congress

By its own choice, initially Congress did not exercise many of its powers. With George Washington establishing the executive branch as the major force in government, Congress assumed the role of "caretaker," overseeing day-to-day operations for its first 50 years. Most senators and representatives considered their government positions part-time services, attending Congress for only a brief period of the year. In fact, legislators did not have to meet much of the time because their work load was so small. For example, the first session of the 11th Congress was only 38 days long—from May 22 to June 28, 1809—whereas the first session of the 100th Congress lasted 351 days—from January 6 to December 22, 1987.

There was a high turnover of members in the early days of Congress because many people did not consider a legislative career important or profitable. In addition, Washington, D.C., in its early history, was not a pleasant city in which to live and work. Many streets were unpaved, its hot and humid summers often were unbearable, and it boasted few social activities, such as theaters or music halls. Senators and representatives

Here, President Harry Truman holds his first press conference (1945). How did the development of radio and television affect the power of the President?

often served their terms and left—never to return. With few senior legislators around to exert any influence, the President remained dominant in government.

Over time, however, Congress became more stable. Political parties grew in strength to ensure the reelection of their members. And, not surprisingly, congressional work loads increased as the nation—and the needs of its citizens—grew, and legislators began to focus on national issues rather than on day-to-day operations of government. By the time of the Civil War in the 1860s, Congress had become a formidable force.

Even before the Civil War, Congress tried to avert the conflict by passing a series of compromises designed to equalize the number of slave and free states. And after the war, Congress proved its strength through its impeachment of President Andrew Johnson and its passage of reconstruction policies to reunite the nation. By the 1880s, Congress as we know it today had emerged.

Presidential Resurgence

As Congress began exerting more power, Presidents began to fight back. This struggle continued for most of the early 1900s until, with the advent of radio and television, Presidents gained a tremendous advantage over Congress. With these tools of mass media, Presidents could quickly make their views known to millions of Americans. Congress, on the other hand, remained an almost invisible, unknown institution. Many people viewed Congress as 535 separate voices who could not agree on anything. But the President spoke with one voice, and soon people began to look to the President as the person who could best deal with the nation's problems.

Congress's Rebirth

From the early 1930s to the mid-1970s, Congress passed nearly 500 federal laws that, as a group, gave extraordinary powers to the President.

PROFILE: PAT SCHROEDER

A WOMAN FOR PRESIDENT?

"Run, Pat, run! Run, Pat, run!" Crowds often repeat this chant when Representative Patricia Schroeder of Colorado appears. Although Schroeder has considered running for President, she has decided that the effort would place too much strain on her family. Despite her decision not to seek the presidential nomination, a Gallup poll has ranked Schroeder as one of the six most respected women in America.

Pat Schroeder was born in Portland, Oregon, in 1940. She attended the University of Minnesota and Harvard Law School, where she received her law degree in 1964.

A Democrat from Denver, Colorado, Schroeder was elected to Congress in 1972. It was her first political office, and she has been returned ever since. In 1994 she polled 60 percent of the vote.

Representative Schroeder is the most senior of the 49 women in the House. She is the first woman ever to serve on the House Armed Services Committee and is a member of the House Judiciary Committee, the House Committee on Post Office and Civil Service, and the House Select Committee on Children, Youth, and Families. She also is active in the Congressional Caucus for Women's Issues, a bipartisan group of representatives devoted to advancing women's legislation in Congress. When the proposed Equal Rights Amendment died in 1982, Schroeder was one of the first to reintroduce it.

Representative Schroeder is more than an outspoken leader on women's issues. She has led efforts against wasteful defense spending, championed arms control, and supported nuclear weapons test bans. If her views on defense are not supported in committee, she is not afraid to carry her fight to the House floor. "We have all become afraid of being called a wimp," says Schroeder. "Our constituents are going to think we are the weak ones if we cannot possibly stand on our own two legs and talk back."

Throughout her activities, Schroeder has earned a reputation for her intelligence, her keen and irreverent wit, and her sense of humor. It was Pat Schroeder who first labeled Ronald Reagan the

"Teflon President." While many of her colleagues find Schroeder refreshing, some consider her behavior inappropriate. During an Armed Services trip to China during Easter, she dressed up in a bunny suit and handed out jellybeans and candy eggs to the shocked Chinese.

In Congress, Schroeder has been a leading advocate on family issues, including affordable, quality day care for children of working mothers, unpaid leave for new parents, and special programs for latchkey children. When her proposals are blocked in the House, she is willing to take her issues directly to the public. Consequently, Schroeder is one of the most sought-after speakers in Congress.

And what about the Presidency? If she ran, Schroeder was asked, would her candidacy be largely symbolic? "It's bloody work," she said, "Why do it just for the symbol?" And, in her usual style, she added that she felt America was "man enough to elect a woman President." The next time the crowds chant "Run, Pat, run!" may be when Pat Schroeder has the chance to see if she is right.

1. What issue has Pat Schroeder been most concerned about in Congress?
2. Do you think voters in the United States will ever elect a female President? Why or why not?

impeach formally bring charges against an official

For example, one law stated that once a state of emergency was declared in the United States, a President could seize property, control the means of production, and assign military forces to maintain control. Then in the 1960s and 1970s, two major events—the Vietnam War and the Watergate affair—led to the return of power and influence to Congress.

Many government leaders and citizens felt that the undeclared war in Vietnam was an abuse of the President's war powers. As a result, Congress tried to reestablish itself as an equally strong policy-making force. Through the passage of the War Powers Act of 1973, Congress narrowed the war powers emanating from the White House. And through other measures, Congress tried to regain more control over foreign policy. Beginning in 1972, it began to review all executive agreements, and in 1974 it refused to allow the administration of President Gerald Ford to give special trading privileges to the Soviet Union. It also revoked many of the powers it had given the President in times of emergency.

After the Watergate affair and the resignation of President Nixon, Congress reasserted itself even more. In 1975 it created permanent committees to oversee the government's domestic and foreign intelligence operations. The Senate took a tougher stand on approving presidential appointments, and Congress developed a new budgeting process that increased its control over the power of the purse.

Who's in Charge?

In the 1980s and 1990s, opinions differed about the effects of the struggle between Capitol Hill and the White House. Some people believed that Congress overreacted to the Vietnam War and Watergate and was damaging the President's effectiveness. Others claimed that Congress's actions had restored the proper working order of checks and balances and had not endangered the presidency.

Recently, the pendulum of power has swung between Congress and the President. In 1980, Republican Ronald Reagan won the presidential election with a platform that called for a

Governor and Mrs. Ronald Reagan greet delegates at the 1980 Republican National Convention. From here, Reagan went on to win the Presidency. How did presidential power change during the early Reagan years?

stronger presidency. Congress was forced to take a back seat as Reagan, during his first term in office, was able to get many of his programs approved, including decreased social spending, tax cuts, and increased defense spending.

Despite winning a landslide reelection in 1984, however, Reagan saw power returning to Congress. The Iran/Contra affair revealed wrongdoing in the White House and severely weakened Reagan's credibility as an effective and informed leader. In addition, in 1986 the Democrats took control of the Senate. With a majority in both houses of Congress, the Democrats were in a position to stop any Reagan proposals during his last two years in office.

Section Review

1. What are some factors that may determine which branch holds the most power at any given time?

2. Why could the early Congress be called a ''caretaker government''?

3. What factors contributed to the early Congress not exercising many of its powers?

4. What two major events in the 1960s and 1970s led to a resurgence of congressional power?

5. **Challenge:** Do you think the struggle for power between the legislative and executive branches strengthens or weakens the effectiveness of the national government? Explain.

Summary

1. The Constitution lists many of the powers of Congress. They are known as expressed powers.

2. Among the expressed powers of Congress are the power of the purse, the power to coin money, the right to regulate commerce, and the power to declare war. Congress also has certain judicial, military, and regulatory powers.

3. The power of the purse gives Congress the ability to raise money through taxes and other means, to spend money through the budget-making process, and to borrow money through the sale of government bonds.

4. Congress also has certain implied powers that allow it to make any laws ''necessary and proper'' to carry out its duties.

5. In addition to its legislative powers, Congress has many nonlegislative powers, such as the power to conduct investigations, propose amendments to the Constitution, admit new states, and govern United States territories.

6. The House of Representatives may impeach officials for various acts of wrongdoing. The Senate then sits as a court to judge the case.

7. The Senate approves most executive appointments and treaties made by the President. Recently, however, the President has bypassed the Senate by entering into executive agreements.

8. Political power in national government shifts between the legislative and executive branches. The ability of Congress to use its power to shape public policy depends largely on the makeup of Congress, who is President, the mood of the public, and the issues at hand.

Chapter 12 Review

★ Building Vocabulary

Divide your paper into three columns titled "Monetary Powers," "Commerce Powers," and "Other Regulatory Powers." Now look at the following vocabulary terms. All of these terms relate to congressional powers. Put each term in the appropriate column, and tell why it belongs there.

1. copyrights
2. patents
3. bankruptcy
4. legal tender
5. trademarks
6. appropriations
7. legislative veto
8. tariffs
9. interstate commerce
10. exports
11. national debt
12. currency
13. federal budget
14. infringement

★ Reviewing Facts

1. What is the source of congressional power?
2. What are three expressed powers of Congress?
3. What power was granted to Congress in the Sixteenth Amendment?
4. What is the constitutional foundation for the implied powers of Congress?
5. How can Congress amend the Constitution?
6. What constitutional limits are placed on Congress for admitting new states to the Union?
7. Under what circumstances might the House of Representatives choose a President?
8. What powers does the Senate have in regard to treaties and nominations submitted by the President?

★ Analyzing Facts

1. Read Article I, Section 8 of the Constitution. Are there any powers listed there that you think Congress should not have? Why? Are there any powers not listed there that you think should be given to Congress? Why?

2. The War Powers Act of 1973 limits the President's power to send American troops overseas without a declaration of war. Some observers say that this act severely limits the President in carrying out United States foreign policy goals and prevents the President from responding quickly in a crisis. Others say that the act is necessary to prevent Presidents from committing America's military resources to lengthy wars without congressional approval. They say that armed combat is too costly, in both material resources and human lives, to leave the decision to only the President and his advisors. With which argument do you agree? Why?

3. Senators and representatives travel thousands of miles every year, at the taxpayers' expense, as part of Congress's power to investigate. Do you think it is necessary to get information this way? Explain.

4. Why do you think the authors of the Constitution believed it was necessary to specify the powers of Congress in the Constitution?

★ Evaluating Ideas

1. Do you think a presidential appointee should be questioned about his or her personal life by the

Using Your
Civic Participation Journal

Review the information about qualifications for congressional pages that you recorded in your Civic Participation Journal. Do further research to learn how many pages your representative or senators have sponsored. Write a letter to one of these pages asking for his or her impressions of life as a congressional page. Share your findings with the class.

Senate? What characteristics and qualifications do you think the Senate should look for in presidential appointees?

2. In your opinion, why did the Framers of the Constitution believe there should not be a national system of education?

3. Do you think that there should be limits on the lawmaking powers of Congress? Explain.

★ Critical Thinking Summarizing

A summary is a list of major points or themes of something. To summarize is to present those points or themes briefly and without details.

Explanation You see and hear summaries almost every day. For example, most television newscasts actually are summaries of the day's events. In a typical 30-minute program there is only enough time to show the highlights or major points of important news stories or events. Each news event is summarized.

The following guidelines will help you make good summaries.

1. Read, listen, or observe carefully and identify the main points.

2. List the main points of the writer, speaker, or event in your own words.

3. Do not use examples except to clarify main ideas or concepts that may be new to you or to your audience.

4. Leave out minor or less important details.

5. Do not repeat information or add your opinion to the summary. Your goal is only to list the main point.

6. Remember, a summary is only a brief "snapshot" of what you read, heard, or saw.

Practice Read the following excerpt from President Franklin Roosevelt's State of the Union Address to Congress in 1941. Summarize what Roosevelt believed to be the four essential freedoms.

In the future days, which we seek to make secure, we look forward to a world founded upon four essential human freedoms. The first is freedom of speech and expression, everywhere in the world. The second is freedom of every person to worshop God in his own way, everywhere in the world. The third is freedom from want—which, translated into world terms, means economic understandings which will secure to every nation a healthy peacetime life for its inhabitants—everywhere in the world. The fourth is freedom from fear—which, translated into world terms, means a world-wide reduction of armaments to such a point and in such a thorough fashion that no nation will be in a position to commit an act of physical aggression against any neighbor—anywhere in the world.

Summary: Roosevelt believed there were four essential freedoms that should be enjoyed by everyone. These are: freedom of speech, freedom to practice any religion, freedom from want, by which he meant economic security, and freedom from the fear of war. (Note that the summary uses one example to clarify the meaning of "freedom from want.")

Independent Practice You can summarize visual material as well. Study the cartoon below, which appeared after the Republican landslide of 1994. Then summarize the material being printed.

THIS COULD BE THE FIRST DOCUMENTED CASE OF ELEPHANTINE AMNESIA!!

TERM LIMITS... TERM LIMITS... WHAT TERM LIMITS??

287

Chapter 13

Congressional Decision Making

The incredibly complex process of turning an idea into a law was established by our Constitution and has been shaped by more than 200 years of tradition. Even so, critics charge that our lawmaking procedure is a cumbersome and time-consuming maze. Supporters, on the other hand, claim that it accurately translates the ideas, wants, and needs of Americans into the "law of the land."

How Congress handles its primary responsibility, that of making our national laws, is the story of this chapter.

Chapter Preview

TERMS TO KNOW
standing committees, bills, select committees, subcommittees, joint committees, discharge petition, seniority system, public bills, private bills, joint resolutions, simple resolutions, concurrent resolutions, hopper, pigeonholed, markup session, report, junkets, quorum, quorum call, riders, unanimous consent agreements, filibuster, engrossed, cloture rule, conference committee, pocket veto

READ TO DISCOVER
- the role of congressional committees.
- the process by which a bill becomes federal law.

Civic Participation Journal

Members of Congress often welcome student volunteers to work in their offices or on their election campaigns. Call or write your representative or one of your senators to learn what volunteer opportunities exist. Because members have local offices, these opportunities would be in your community. Record your findings in your journal.

1 The Committee System

Congress is bombarded with thousands of proposed laws each year. Because it would be impossible for every legislator to become an expert on each of these proposals, the work load is divided among committees.

The committee system was not created by the Constitution but developed gradually in response to the needs of Congress. In the 1790s, new bills were immediately considered on the Senate or House floor. After agreement was reached on general principles, members formed temporary committees to pound out the details. When the work on the bill was finished, the committee was dissolved. Eventually, these temporary committees became permanent.

Standing Committees

Each house of Congress has a number of **standing committees.** These powerful, permanent committees are responsible for a particular subject area, such as agriculture or the budget. The main job of standing committees is to study **bills** before they are debated in the Senate or House. When studying bills, the committees can defeat the proposals, set them aside for weeks, amend them, or speed them on their way.

Although standing committees are considered permanent, their number is not fixed and can be changed by Congress. For example, in 1913 there were 61 standing committees in the House and 74 in the Senate. Belonging to so many committees, however, left members with little time to spend on each of their committee assignments. Congress realized that it had to develop a more efficient way of doing business. In 1946, Congress passed the Legislative Reorganization Act, which reduced the number of committees. The Senate again reorganized its committee system in 1977, further reducing the number of committees as well as limiting the committee assignments a member can accept. Today, there are 16 standing committees in the Senate and 22 in the House. These are listed in Figure 13-1.

COMMITTEE ASSIGNMENTS

Each committee varies in the number of members it has. In the Senate, committee membership ranges from 6 to 29 while in the House as few as 11 to as many as 57 representatives may sit on one committee. As you learned

standing committees permanent committees that deal with certain subject areas

bills proposed laws or drafts of laws to be considered by Congress

Senator Nancy Kassebaum chairs the Labor and Human Resources Committee. What factors help to determine who will serve on a particular committee?

in Chapter 11, party leaders assign members to committees at the beginning of each congressional term. And while a member's education, background, and skills are considered, it is seniority and political influence that primarily determine which committee a member will serve on.

Typically, a representative serves on two standing committees and senators on four. A member's rank, or standing, on a committee is based on how long that member has been in office. Thus, all new members must start at the bottom. Most legislators keep their original committee assignments, then, slowly rise through the ranks to more powerful positions within the committee.

Party membership on each committee is proportional to its strength in the House as a whole. This means that if the Senate were composed of 60 Democrats and 40 Republicans, the membership of a 20-person committee would be in the same 60-40 ratio: 12 Democrats and 8 Republicans.

SUBCOMMITTEES

Because standing committees handle so much proposed legislation, most are further divided into **subcommittees.** A subcommittee studies one aspect of a proposed bill. For example, some of the subcommittees under the House Education and Labor Committee are Elementary, Secondary, and Vocational Education; Employment Opportunities; and Post-secondary Education.

Since the 1970s, the number of subcommittees has increased dramatically. Today, the House has more than 150 subcommittees, and the Senate has 80 such panels. This growth is due in part to the increased complexity of the issues facing Congress and to the increased demands of special interest groups and citizens.

Select Committees

In addition to the standing committees in both houses, Congress also sets up **select committees.** These groups make recommendations to their house of Congress, but do not formally report on proposed bills. Select committees may be created by either house or may include members from both houses.

Some select committees carry on extensive investigations. For example, the Select Committee to Study Government Operations with Respect to Intelligence Activities met in 1975 and 1976 to review the Central Intelligence Agency (CIA) and various federal law enforcement agencies.

select committees legislative committees that meet for a limited time and for a special purpose not covered by standing committees.

subcommittees small groups into which committees are divided to carry out some special duty

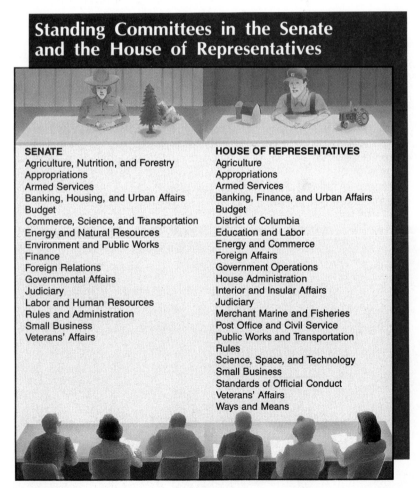

Standing Committees in the Senate and the House of Representatives

SENATE	HOUSE OF REPRESENTATIVES
Agriculture, Nutrition, and Forestry	Agriculture
Appropriations	Appropriations
Armed Services	Armed Services
Banking, Housing, and Urban Affairs	Banking, Finance, and Urban Affairs
Budget	Budget
Commerce, Science, and Transportation	District of Columbia
Energy and Natural Resources	Education and Labor
Environment and Public Works	Energy and Commerce
Finance	Foreign Affairs
Foreign Relations	Government Operations
Governmental Affairs	House Administration
Judiciary	Interior and Insular Affairs
Labor and Human Resources	Judiciary
Rules and Administration	Merchant Marine and Fisheries
Small Business	Post Office and Civil Service
Veterans' Affairs	Public Works and Transportation
	Rules
	Science, Space, and Technology
	Small Business
	Standards of Official Conduct
	Veterans' Affairs
	Ways and Means

Figure 13-1

Other select committees have investigated communism in the United States, the Watergate coverup, and the Iran/Contra affair.

Joint Committees

Congress also has **joint committees** made up of legislators from both houses. Joint committee membership is usually divided equally between the two houses with the position of committee chairperson alternating every two years between a representative and a senator. Most joint committees are permanent groups dealing with special issues that concern both houses. Examples include the Joint Economic Committee and the Joint Committee on Taxation.

Chairpersons

Each committee and subcommittee is headed by a chairperson. Chairpersons decide when the committee will meet, preside over the meetings, and choose what legislation to send to the floor. When committee bills *are* debated on the floor, chairpersons guide the measures through to final passage or defeat.

Senator Edward Kennedy sits on the Labor and Human Resources Committee in the Senate and served as committee chair when the Democrats controlled the Senate. What are some of the responsibilities of a committee chairperson?

A chairperson can use his or her power to influence committee members to support or oppose a measure. By not scheduling a bill for debate, a chairperson can stop it from reaching the floor. This is called "killing" a bill. But committee members who want to bring it back to "life" can oppose the chairperson by issuing a **discharge petition** to the entire house. If a majority of legislators approve, the bill is forced onto the floor for action. Committee members of the majority party, however, seldom overrule the chairperson.

Chairpersons were formerly chosen by the majority party caucus, using the **seniority system.** During the 1970s, attempts were made to stop this system. Critics claimed that it ignored the talents and contributions of younger committee members. Supporters, on the other hand, said that this method ensured that committees would have experienced leaders who knew the "ins and outs" of the legislative process.

By 1975, the majority parties of both houses agreed that chairpersons should be elected by party caucuses using a secret ballot rather than by seniority appointment. Subcommittee chairpersons would also be elected, and no member could chair more than one subcommittee. These changes have opened more leadership positions to junior senators and representatives.

Power Centers

With 38 standing committees, more than 200 subcommittees, and several select and joint committees, power in Congress is widely dispersed. Yet members of Congress may seek "power centers" where they can exert considerable influence over national policy decisions.

RULES COMMITTEE

An example of a power center in the House of Representatives is the Rules Committee. Although the standing committees in both houses can control legislation that pertains to them, the House Rules Committee controls *all* legislation in the House. It examines the bills from other committees before they reach the floor. A "ruling" granted by this committee explains the guidelines under which a bill will be debated. By the committee's decisions, any bill can be acted on quickly, delayed, or withheld from floor action. In this way, the Rules Committee plays "traffic cop," regulating the flow of legislation onto the floor.

MAJOR COMMITTEES

Any committee dealing with money matters is also considered a power center. Members of Congress who serve on these major committees can have a huge impact on the nation's taxing and spending priorities. For example, the House Ways and Means Committee and the Senate Finance Committee write the nation's tax bills. Other major committees in the House include Agriculture, Energy and Commerce, and Foreign Affairs. In the Senate, major committees include Armed Services, Budget, and Foreign Relations.

SUBCOMMITTEES

Subcommittees are another source of power and influence in Congress. Today, most of the work done by Congress takes place in subcommittees, with the full standing committee often simply approving the recommendations of its subcommittees. Subcommittees also hold hearings, draft bills, and handle legislation on the floor—activities formerly performed only by the full standing

committees. Thus, a member who chairs a subcommittee can have a great deal of power.

With so many members of Congress wanting powerful posts, congressional leaders are often forced to find "volunteers" who are willing to sit on "lesser" panels. But the power and prestige of a committee can fluctuate. For example, whenever a Supreme Court nominee needs to be confirmed, the Senate Judiciary Committee is in the spotlight.

Senator Strom Thurmond chairs the Senate Armed Services Committee. What are some of the other major Senate standing committees?

Section Review

1. What is the main job of standing committees?

2. Why has the role of subcommittees grown?

3. For what general purpose do joint committees meet?

4. Why can the Rules Committee be considered the most powerful committee in the House?

5. **Challenge:** If you were a member of Congress, on which House or Senate committee would you most like to serve? Why?

2 How a Bill Becomes a Law

Congress considers thousands of proposals each term, but very few become law. In the 103rd Congress, for example, more than 11,000 bills and resolutions were introduced, but less than 700 were passed into law. Proposals must wind their way through the complex legislative process as shown in Figure 13-2. This process contains numerous opportunities for a proposal to be changed or defeated before it reaches the House or Senate floor. Those proposals that *do* survive become part of the law of the land and usually will affect you in some way. Thus, the legislative process, or how a bill becomes a law, is an important function of Congress.

Kinds of Legislation

Congress deals with several kinds of legislation. Most are in the form of bills, of which there are two types, public and private. Examples of **public bills** are tax measures and laws setting health care guidelines. **Private bills** are introduced to deal with the problems of constituents at home or other individuals and small groups.

About 2.5 percent of the bills passed by Congress today are private

public bills bills that deal with matters of general interest and affect everyone

private bills bills that deal with specific matters and affect only a few people

How a Federal Bill Becomes a Law

INTRODUCTION
Introduced in House

INTRODUCTION
Introduced in Senate

COMMITTEE ACTION
Referred to House Committee and Subcommittee*
Reported by Full Committee

COMMITTEE ACTION
Referred to Senate Committee and Subcommittee*
Reported by Full Committee

FLOOR ACTION
House Debate, Vote on Passage

FLOOR ACTION
Senate Debate, Vote on Passage

CONFERENCE ACTION
Compromise Bill Sent Back to Both Houses

FINAL APPROVAL
House and Senate Vote on Final Passage, Approved Bill Sent to President

ENACTMENT
President Signs Bill into Law**

* Committee may accept, reject, amend, or pigeonhole the bill.

** President may sign bill into law or veto it. Congress may override veto by two-thirds majority vote.

Figure 13-2

Both houses of Congress may join to pass a concurrent resolution marking a special event such as the first moon landing, pictured here. What are some other purposes that a concurrent resolution might serve?

bills. Critics claim that these take up time that should be spent on public bills. Supporters, on the other hand, claim that legislative bodies in a democracy must have the right to act on behalf of individuals.

JOINT RESOLUTIONS

Joint resolutions are similar to bills in that they must be approved by both houses and the President. But joint resolutions usually deal with temporary matters, such as approving the President's actions in foreign affairs or authorizing funds for a special military action overseas. Members of Congress might also use a joint resolution when they want to propose amendments to the Constitution.

CONCURRENT RESOLUTIONS

Like other measures, **concurrent resolutions** must be passed by both houses of Congress, but the Presi-

dent's signature is *not* required because these resolutions do not have the force of law. Concurrent resolutions may, for example, commemorate the anniversary of a successful spaceflight or welcome an important foreign visitor. They may make or amend joint rules that affect both houses, such as the time for adjournment of Congress. They may also voice disapproval of presidential actions or the actions of foreign nations.

SIMPLE RESOLUTIONS

Since **simple resolutions** deal with matters that only apply to one house of Congress, they are not sent for approval to the other house nor to the President. They only express an opinion of one house and may be used to advise the President in foreign policy or other areas. Like concurrent resolutions, they do not have the force of law.

joint resolutions legislative proposals with the force of law that must be passed by both houses and approved by the President

simple resolutions measures that deal with matters in only one house

concurrent resolutions measures intended to express an opinion or an official policy

103D CONGRESS
2D SESSION

H. R. 3222

To contain health care costs and improve access to health care through accountable health plans and managed competition, and for other purposes.

IN THE HOUSE OF REPRESENTATIVES

OCTOBER 6, 1993

Mr. COOPER (for himself, Mr. ANDREWS of Texas, Mr. GRANDY, Mr. KLUG, Mr. STENHOLM, Mrs. JOHNSON of Connecticut, Mr. PAYNE of Virginia, Mr. GUNDERSON, Mr. PETERSON of Florida, Mr. HOBSON, Mr. CARR of Michigan, Mr. HOUGHTON, Mr. McCURDY, Mr. QUILLEN, Mr. BARCIA of Michigan, Mr. BOEHLERT, Mr. BROWDER, Mr. CLEMENT, Mr. CLINGER, Mr. DOOLEY, Mr. EDWARDS of Texas, Mr. EMERSON, Mrs. FOWLER, Mr. GILCHREST, Mr. GORDON, Mr. GOSS, Mr. HAYES, Mr. HORN, Mr. HUGHES, Mr. HUTTO, Mr. LAUGHLIN, Mrs. LLOYD, Ms. LONG, Mr. McHALE, Mr. McMILLAN, Mr. MACHTLEY, Mr. MILLER of Florida, Mr. MONTGOMERY, Mr. MORAN, Mr. NEAL of North Carolina, Mr. NUSSLE, Mr. ORTON, Mr. PARKER, Mr. PETRI, Mr. PORTER, Mr. SHAYS, Ms. SNOWE, Mr. TANNER, and Mr. TAUZIN) introduced the following bill; which was referred jointly to the Committees on Energy and Commerce, Ways and Means, Education and Labor, and the Judiciary

OCTOBER 27, 1993
Additional sponsor: Mr. SABO

JANUARY 27, 1994
Additional sponsors: Mr. SYNAR, Mr. KOLBE, Mr. MINGE, Mr. REGULA, Ms. ENGLISH of Arizona, Mr. CAMP, and Mr. WALSH

A BILL

To contain health care costs and improve access to health care through accountable health plans and managed competition, and for other purposes.

This bill (left) is one of many written each session. In the documents room (right) the bills are assembled and filed. How are bills introduced in the House and Senate?

Introducing Legislation

Where do the ideas for new laws come from? Most new proposals originate in the executive branch—the White House and its executive agencies. Special interest groups, such as agricultural organizations, business groups, or trade associations, may also propose new laws. Even you can play a role in the legislative process by suggesting new laws to your senators or representative.

Although almost anyone can *propose* legislation, only members of Congress can formally introduce a bill. There is no limit to the number of bills a legislator can introduce in a session. Although the Constitution states that all *revenue* bills must be introduced in the House of Representatives, all other types of legislation may begin in either house. Representatives introduce bills by dropping the written proposal into the **hopper.** Senators introduce bills either by presenting them to the clerk at the presiding officer's desk or by making a formal announcement from the floor.

Bills introduced during a term of Congress must be passed into law by the end of that term. Otherwise, they "die" and can no longer be considered. Backers of dead bills, however, may reintroduce them during the next term and begin the process again.

hopper box into which representatives drop bills to introduce them into the House

Often, more than one member of the Senate or the House will sponsor, or introduce, the same bill. The sponsors must then work to convince a *majority* of the House and the Senate, or 269 individuals, that their bill is worthy of passage.

In every stage of the legislative process, the sponsors of a bill must rally support for their legislation if it is to move on to the next step. They will use many tactics to gain this support, including lobbying, agreeing to amendments, or deleting offending parts of the bill. One of the main methods of gathering support for a bill is called "logrolling." Logrolling can best be described as "you scratch my back, I'll scratch yours." For example, Senator A agrees to vote for Senator B's bill only if Senator B will vote for Senator A's bill.

IDENTIFICATION

Bills are numbered for identification in the order in which they are introduced in each house. The first bill introduced in the House of Representatives during the new term is called H.R.1. The second is H.R.2 and so on. In the Senate, bills are numbered S.1, S.2, and so on.

READINGS

For a bill to become law, it must have three readings during its progress through either house. The first reading takes place when a bill is introduced. Neither house actually reads the text of a bill on the day it is introduced. Instead, it is printed in the *Congressional Record,* a written account of the proceedings in both the Senate and the House. The second reading usually comes when the floor action begins. The third takes place after any amendments are added to the bill and the house is ready to take a final vote.

Studying Legislation

In the House of Representatives, the Speaker assigns a bill to an appropriate standing committee for study. For example, a bill concerning rapid transit systems would go to the Public Works and Transportation Committee. In the Senate, a bill is assigned to a committee by the presiding officer.

Each committee sorts through the bills it receives and considers only those it feels are important. In most cases, a bill will be **pigeonholed** by the chairperson. The term relates to the old desks in committee rooms that had open "pigeonholes" or small compartments for papers.

Pigeonholing usually kills a bill. Out of the more than 11,000 bills introduced in the 103rd Congress, less than 5 percent came out of committee.

If a bill is not pigeonholed, it is placed on a committee's agenda to be

pigeonholed a bill put aside in a committee and not referred to the House or Senate for action

The federally funded Amtrak system provides daily transportation for many Americans. What congressional committee would study a bill concerning a new transportation system?

Here, the House Administration Committee meets for a hearing on proposed legislation. What is the purpose of such a hearing?

markup session
subcommittee meeting in Congress to make changes in a proposed bill

report action of sending a bill to the full house by a legislative committee

junkets trips by members of Congress to gather information

considered and usually assigned to a subcommittee. At this time, committee *staff* members go into action. They research all aspects of the bill and ask government agencies and special interest groups for their views on the proposal. To gather more information, the subcommittee holds hearings, where supporters and critics of the bill testify as witnesses. The public and the press may attend open hearings, but they are barred from closed meetings known as "executive hearings." Hearings on national security, for example, are often executive hearings.

Sometimes, committee or subcommittee members may make **junkets** to gather information on the bill. For instance, if the proposal concerns the construction of new veterans' hospitals, members of the House Veterans' Affairs Committee may visit existing hospitals to see if the need for new facilities is warranted. Since junkets are funded at the public's expense, they are often criticized as expensive and wasteful. But, most members of Congress claim that junkets are the only way they can get firsthand information.

When both the legislators and their staffs have fully studied a bill, the subcommittee makes any recommended changes during a **markup session.** The subcommittee may choose to make slight changes in the bill, combine several bills on the same subject into one comprehensive measure, or even substitute a new bill, called a "clean bill," for the original.

The *full* committee then meets for its own markup session. It may choose to hold hearings of its own and amend the subcommittee's version of the bill. Or it may simply approve the subcommittee's recommendations.

Finally, the committee will **report** the bill back to the full house. The committee can report the bill favorably, report the bill with amendments, or report a clean bill. It may also report a bill unfavorably, but will usually prefer to pigeonhole it instead. At this time, copies of the reported bill are made available to all members of the house.

Scheduling Legislation

Next, the bill is placed on a calendar and scheduled for floor debate.

PROFILE: DAVID EVANS

CONGRESSIONAL STAFF MEMBER

What is it like to be a part of the legislative process? According to David Evans, staff director of the Subcommittee on Education, Arts, and the Humanities in the U.S. Senate, "It's one crisis after another and never the same thing twice." Looking at the jurisdiction of Evans's subcommittee, it is easy to see why his life on Capitol Hill is so hectic. The subcommittee's responsibilities include higher education and student aid, elementary and secondary education, vocational education, aid to private schools, construction of school facilities, and Native American education programs.

As staff director, Evans's own responsibilities are just as wide-ranging. He directs the subcommittee's professional staff, develops and analyzes legislation, plans congressional hearings, provides information to the Senate staff on issues related to federal education policy, acts as a liaison to national education associations, and is responsible for congressional oversight of the Department of Education.

Originally from Nebraska, Evans received his bachelor's degree in American studies from Grinnell College in Iowa in 1964 and a master's degree in political science from Rutgers University in 1965. He was a special assistant to the governor of Nebraska, an administrative assistant to the governor of Rhode Island, and an independent political consultant before joining the congressional staff in 1978.

Evans believes that although staff members in powerful positions like his can have a considerable impact on the legislative process, there are limits to what they can do. "Anyone can have an influence, but aides are only as effective as senators allow them to be," observes Evans. In that relationship, he says, aides must always remember who is the elected one. Staff members are expected to be a "mirror reflection" of their bosses and to always represent their bosses' points of view.

Because he is so close to the legislative process, Evans has unique insights into how a bill becomes a law. He says that "the most challenging part of my job is building a consensus on any piece of legislation. You may have to give up some points, but you never sacrifice what is important to your member of Congress. That's why compromise is so important."

Evans admits that he is part of a huge lawmaking machine that is sometimes slow and cumbersome. But he claims this characteristic is actually very good. Because Congress sometimes takes so long to solve problems, many different groups have a chance to examine all aspects of a bill before it is voted upon. Yet, while he realizes this pace protects the rights of all people, Evans says he gets frustrated by the amount of influence special interest groups have on the legislative process. He notes that it is often very difficult to develop clear public policy when everyone wants an exception to the rule.

Thus David Evans, in his role as staff director for the Senate Subcommittee on Education, Arts, and Humanities works for many constituencies—his senator, his subcommittee, the Senate as a whole, and, in the end, the American people.

1. According to Evans, how much power do committee staff members have in the legislative process?

2. Explain what you think Evans means when he says "compromise is so important" in the legislative process.

The Senate has two calendars, the *calendar of business* for legislative proposals and the *executive calendar* for action on nominations and treaties coming from the President. Bills usually reach the Senate floor according to their order on the calendar. Because of the incredible number of bills introduced in the House, it has five calendars for different kinds of bills. These House calendars are listed in Figure 13-3.

The House has established an elaborate system in which bills placed on the calendars are considered on certain days each month. But even if the calendar schedules were closely followed, many proposals would never reach the House floor. So instead, a House member is more likely to get his or her legislation on the floor through the Rules Committee.

The powerful Rules Committee determines the actual order in which the House considers legislation. It sets up special rules for a bill such as limiting the time for debate or the number of amendments that can be suggested.

The committee can effectively kill a bill before it reaches the House floor by refusing to set the rules for debate.

There are ways, however, for House members to work around the Rules Committee. If a bill is blocked by the Rules Committee, the chairperson of the standing committee that reported the bill can call it to the floor on special days known as Calendar Wednesdays. In addition, by a two-thirds vote, the House can suspend all rules on certain days. This allows a bill to go through all the stages for passage in a single day. Finally, some bills are privileged bills. These include general appropriations, reports of conference committees, and special rules.

The Constitution requires in Article I, Section 5 that ''a majority of each (house) shall constitute a **quorum** to do business.'' Once a bill reaches the floor, 218 members of the House or 51 senators must be present before any action on the bill can take place.

In practice, both House and Senate often work with less than a quorum present unless a member makes a **quorum call.** When this happens, the members on the floor must be counted. If a quorum does not exist, the chamber must adjourn or send party whips and the Sergeant at Arms to round up more members.

Action in the House

Many bills that reach the House floor are minor pieces of legislation that require little or no debate. But major items, such as appropriations bills, tax reform, or legislation calling for new programs, attract greater attention and controversy. The House has developed a method to conduct such business and avoid the quorum requirement.

quorum minimum number of legislators who must be present before a legislative body can act

quorum call request of a legislator that members on the House and Senate floor be counted to determine if a quorum exists

If three members object to a bill that comes up on the Consent Calendar, it is sent to the House or Union Calendar.

Calendars in Use in the House of Representatives

Union Calendar	for bills dealing with finance, revenues, and government property
House Calendar	for all other public bills
Private Calendar	for private bills
Consent Calendar	for all bills from the Union or House Calendars which are debated out of regular order
Discharge Calendar	For petitions to discharge bills out of committee and onto the floor

Figure 13-3

COMMITTEE OF THE WHOLE

To speed action on a bill, the House may decide to go out of session and sit as a Committee of the Whole. Only 100 members need to be present. A temporary chairperson is appointed by the Speaker and the usual formal House rules do not apply. The bill is debated and given a second reading—and amendments may be added. When the Committee of the Whole finishes its work, it adjourns and the House returns to normal session. Because it is so much simpler, much House business is conducted in this manner.

HOUSE DEBATE

Due to so many members in the House, the time for debate must be limited. This is a major consideration of the Rules Committee. During debate, the chairperson of the standing committee reporting the bill takes charge of the session. Under the Speaker's direction, he or she recognizes those who may speak, yields to questions, and considers amendments. After the allotted time has ended, a floor vote must be taken on the measure.

Action in the Senate

Unlike the House, the Senate is small enough to allow more informal proceedings and almost unlimited debate.

SENATE DEBATE

Senators may speak on any subject for as long as they want. Senate rules do not even require them to speak about the bill under consideration and do not allow routine motions to call for a vote. Senate debates on most major bills are ended by **unanimous consent agreements.** These are proposals made by the majority leader, joined by other senators, to speed up debate

Although the two houses of Congress are similar in many ways, differences do exist. What are some differences in legislative procedures between the Senate and the House of Representatives?

and call for a final vote. Each unanimous consent proposal is voted on by the full Senate and can be rejected by a single vote. If a unanimous consent motion fails, debate continues.

As in the House, Senate members may propose amendments while the bill is debated on the floor. Some of these amendments, known as **riders,** are often attached to important bills, such as tax or appropriations measures, in order to get proposals approved that would not pass on their own merits. For example, in 1987 Congress passed a huge appropriation bill just before its Christmas recess that provided funds for the continuing operation of the federal government. Attached to this important bill were countless riders benefiting special interest groups and constituents. President Reagan was nevertheless forced to sign the bill into law. If he did not, the federal government faced the possibility of shutting down because of a lack of funds.

Unlimited debate is a prized characteristic of the Senate. Most senators believe that by freeing debate from time limits, legislation can be studied—and discussed—from every possible angle. However, this freedom can lead to abuse.

riders   provisions added to a bill that are not related to it

unanimous consent agreements   vote by the Senate with no dissenting votes to end debate on a bill

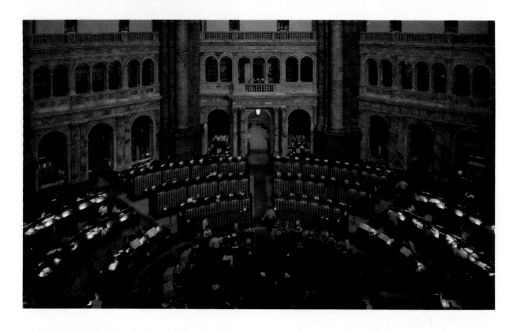

Legislative staffs use the Library of Congress, shown here, to gather information that is needed to write legislation. What other methods do legislators use to gather information for a bill?

FILIBUSTER

In very important legislative battles, Senate members may use their unlimited freedom of debate to **filibuster.** Senators can gain control of the Senate floor by refusing to stop talking. They lose that control only if they sit down or walk off the floor. In a filibuster, senators may at first make long speeches on the bill under consideration. Later, they may grow hoarse speaking on any topic they wish. Why would a senator do such a thing?

A filibustering senator is usually a member of the minority party who hopes to stall long enough to defeat a bill. As a result of this tactic, Senate business comes to a screeching halt and pressure is placed on the majority party to change or withdraw its bill. Over the years, many important bills have been killed on the floor by filibusters or the threat of them. Senator Strom Thurmond of South Carolina holds the record for the longest individual filibuster. In 1957 he spoke for 24 hours and 18 minutes against civil rights legislation!

The Senate can end filibusters by using the **cloture rule.** This procedure allows a minimum of 16 senators to move that debate be limited. If three-fifths of the entire Senate (60 senators) approves, no senator may speak for more than one hour on the bill being considered. At the end of that time, the bill must be brought to a vote.

Even the *threat* of a filibuster usually brings calls for a cloture vote, or a compromise is reached before a filibuster can get rolling. Today, other delaying tactics such as continual quorum calls, roll call votes, and parliamentary rulings have taken the place of the filibuster.

Voting on Bills

After the House or Senate bill has been fully debated and amended, it is **engrossed.** The bill then has a third reading, and a vote on the entire bill is taken on the floor. Bells ring throughout the Capitol, calling members who might be in committee hearings, in their offices, or even at lunch in one of the congressional dining rooms to come to the floor for a vote. Congress has four procedures for taking votes — voice votes, standing votes,

filibuster   tactic used by a senator to delay or block action on a bill by speaking continuously

engrossed   printed with the agreed-upon changes

cloture rule   procedure by which members of Senate can end a filibuster and limit debate

302   Congressional Decision Making

teller votes, and roll call votes. These are shown in Figure 13-4.

A voice vote is the most common method of taking a floor vote. The presiding officer asks those members in favor to say ''yea'' and those opposed to say ''nay.'' If the vote is close, or if the results are questioned, members may ask for a standing vote, a teller vote, or a roll call vote.

To take a standing vote, the presiding officer asks all members in favor of the measure to stand and be counted. After those in favor sit down, members opposed stand. This kind of vote is also called a division vote.

The teller vote is used only in the House of Representatives, specifically at the request of one-fifth of a quorum. The Speaker appoints one member from each party to stand in the aisles and act as tellers. The Speaker then instructs those in favor of the bill to pass between the tellers and be counted. Another count of those opposed to the bill is taken. No record of how members voted is kept.

A roll call vote, sometimes called a record vote, is the most accurate type of floor vote. As each member's name is called, the legislator responds by saying ''yea,'' ''nay,'' or ''present.'' Because of the time involved in reading the roll of its 435 members, the House has used an electronic system for recording roll call votes since 1973. When a roll call vote is called, each member has 15 minutes to reach one of 40 voting stations on the House floor. Here, they insert a personalized plastic card and press a button to record their vote. The results are displayed on electronic boards throughout the House chamber and on consoles on the leadership tables.

Four Methods of Voting in Congress

VOICE VOTE

TELLER VOTE

STANDING VOTE

ROLL CALL VOTE

Figure 13-4

Here, President Bush signs a bill into law. The President is required to act on every bill that passes the House and Senate. What four actions may the President take?

The ''present'' vote is used by those members who want it known that they are in attendance but are not voting for or against a measure. If the vote concerns an override of a President's veto, however, this privilege is withdrawn, and only ''yea'' or ''nay'' votes are accepted.

Conference Committee

Bills passed by one house are then sent to the other. There, the legislative process begins *all over again,* and the bill's sponsors in the new house must work to build support for their legislation. Usually, the final House and Senate versions of a bill are different. Does this matter? Yes, because they must be in identical form before they can be sent to the President.

At this point, a **conference committee** meets. This temporary joint

conference committee temporary committee made up of members from both houses of a legislature that tries to settle differences in a bill

committee is responsible for working out the differences in the House and Senate versions to produce a compromise bill acceptable to both houses. The conference committee is made up of members of the standing committees that handled the bill in both houses. Also present are other important members who had a part in guiding the bill through Congress.

The conference committee can consider only those aspects of the bill about which the houses disagree. In theory, new proposals are not allowed to be added. But in reality, the conference committee often changes the bill. This is the last chance special interest groups, lobbyists from the executive branch, and individual legislators have to get their viewpoints into the bill. Under this kind of pressure, most bills are rewritten by the conference committee.

After the compromise bill is completed, it is presented to both houses. Here the measure must be accepted or rejected as rewritten; no further amendments may be added. If the bill is approved by both houses, it is finally ready to be sent to the White House.

Role of the President

The Constitution requires every bill that passes the House and Senate to be sent to the President for approval. The President has four choices in handling a bill. First, the President may approve the legislation by signing the bill into law. Second, if the President is not *strongly* in favor of a bill, he or she can refuse to act on it for ten days, excluding Sundays. After this time, it automatically becomes law.

Third, the President can veto the bill. To do this, the President returns the bill unsigned to the house where it originated, along with a statement of objections. Congress may then amend the bill to suit the President or try to override the President's veto. A two-thirds vote of both houses will override a veto and enact a bill into law.

Finally, if Congress adjourns within ten days of placing the bill on the President's desk, and the President has not signed it, the bill is automatically killed. This is called a **pocket veto.**

When a bill becomes law, it is registered with the National Archives and Records Service. There, it is given a new number that reveals the Congress in which the bill passed, the number of the law for that term, and whether it is a public or private law. For example, Public Law 302 under the 99th Congress is written as PL 99-302. Then, it is printed in the United States Code, a collection of federal laws currently in force. The next step involves enforcing the law, a responsibility that rests with the executive branch of the federal government.

Section Review

1. What is the difference between a public and a private bill?

2. What happens to a bill once it is sent to a standing committee?

3. What are four ways of taking votes in Congress?

4. What is the purpose of a conference committee?

5. **Challenge:** Do you think the President's signature should be necessary for a bill to become a law? Explain.

pocket veto special power of the President whereby bills not signed die after a specified time

Summary

1. Most of Congress's work is done in committees. Each house of Congress has permanent, or standing, committees that deal with a particular subject area.

2. A member of Congress is appointed to a committee by party leaders. Committee membership reflects the same party ratio as is in the House as a whole.

3. Subcommittees are taking on more responsibilities in the legislative process.

4. Chairpersons of standing committees are elected by party caucuses and can greatly influence legislation.

5. The Rules Committee of the House of Representatives controls all legislation in the House.

6. The power and influence of a committee can rise and fall, depending on the issues currently facing the nation.

7. When considering legislation, Congress deals with public and private bills.

8. Although almost anyone can propose legislation, only members of Congress can introduce a bill in Congress.

9. A proposed law must go through a number of steps before it is sent to the President. It must be introduced, studied, scheduled, and debated before a vote is taken.

10. The President has several choices when he or she receives a bill from Congress. For example, the President may sign the bill into law or veto it.

Chapter 13 Review

★ Building Vocabulary

Using the vocabulary words listed below, make up a vocabulary quiz. The quiz should include four true-false questions, four fill-in-the-blank questions, and four matching questions. Then, on a separate piece of paper, write the answers to your quiz questions.

hopper	riders
bills	pigeonholed
discharge petition	cloture rule
seniority system	engrossed
joint resolutions	pocket veto
subcommittees	quorum

★ Reviewing Facts

1. What are three types of committees found in Congress?
2. Which committee in the House decides the guidelines under which a bill is debated?
3. Who may propose legislation for Congress to consider?
4. What is the *Congressional Record?*
5. How many members present constitute a quorum in both houses of Congress?
6. How do members of Congress sometimes get proposals approved that might otherwise not pass Congress?
7. How does a member of Congress get assigned to a committee?
8. How does the Senate end a filibuster?
9. What four actions can a President take when he or she receives a bill from Congress?
10. How are standing committees different from select committees?
11. What are the five kinds of proposals that Congress deals with?
12. How is floor action in the House of Representatives different from the Senate?
13. Where must money bills be introduced?
14. What effect does pigeonholing a bill have on its passage?
15. What are the main steps in passing a bill through Congress?

★ Analyzing Facts

1. From what you learned about the seniority system in Congress, do you think seniority should still be a factor in determining who chairs congressional committees?
2. The filibuster and other delaying tactics can hold up legislation in the Senate. Do you think the Senate should limit the time for debate on legislation? Why or why not?
3. Woodrow Wilson once wrote, "Congress in its committee rooms is Congress at work." What do you think he meant?

★ Evaluating Ideas

1. Some people say that the large number of subcommittees in Congress slows down the legislative process by forcing bills to go through several reviews. Others, however, claim that subcommittees allow members to examine closely all the details of a particular piece of legislation. With which argument do you agree? Why?
2. Why, do you think, might a committee chairperson pigeonhole a bill rather than report it unfavorably to the full House?

Using Your
Civic Participation Journal

Review the entries you made in your Civic Participation Journal about volunteer opportunities with your representative or one of your senators. Write a newspaper editorial based on this information. Your editorial should try to convince others to volunteer.

3. Do you think logrolling and other similar tactics a member of Congess will use to gain support for legislation are justifiable? Why or why not?

4. Appropriations bills can be introduced only in the House of Representatives. Why do you think this is so? Do you think the Senate should have the power also? Why or why not?

5. The seniority system for selecting chairpersons of congressional standing committees often is criticized. What alternative could you suggest to assure continuity and experienced leadership?

★ Critical Thinking Analyzing Information

To analyze is to break something complicated into smaller parts that you can examine more easily. When confronted with complex information, analyzing it first makes understanding it easier.

Explanation These guidelines will help you analyze information.

1. Identify and gather the information you wish to analyze.

2. Break the information into smaller parts. Look at each specific part of the information and its characteristics.

3. Put the information into your own words.

Practice You can apply the above steps for analyzing information to many situations. Suppose you are researching the 1994 elections. You came across the following quotation.

It was a revolution without the bullets.

First, the statement is probably only a minor part of the information you have compiled. But what does it mean? To analyze this information, you need to know that it was made by a political observer. You also need to understand that a revolution is a sudden change in government. Because he points out that there were no bullets, you know that he is talking about a peaceful revolution. You might put the statement in your own words by stating:

The 1994 election changed so much in American politics that it literally transformed the government.

Independent Practice You can also use the steps to analyze information when you examine political cartoons. Study the cartoon below and put the information the artist is relaying into your own words.

THREE REVIEW

REVIEW QUESTIONS

1. Why, do you think, might a member of Congress pay closer attention to the needs of his or her constituents than to the many national issues facing Congress?

2. Which role that a member of Congress plays do you think is the most important? Why?

3. From what you learned in this unit, consider the impact that congressional staffs may have on the legislative process. Should there be more control over what staffs may and may not do? Why or why not?

4. In your opinion, does Congress have the powers necessary to effectively govern the nation? Why or why not?

5. Some people have argued that the lawmaking process is too tedious and time-consuming. Describe what you think are the advantages and disadvantages of this drawn-out lawmaking process.

6. Draft an idea for a piece of legislation that you will present to your representative to introduce in Congress. What arguments in support of your legislation might you suggest?

7. If you were a member of Congress, on which committees might you wish to sit? Why?

SUGGESTED READINGS

1. Barone, Michael, Grant Ujifusa, and Douglas Matthews. *Almanac of American Politics: The Senators, the Representatives, the Governors—Their Records, States, and Districts*. New York: Dutton, odd-numbered years. Includes political histories of states and districts.

2. Chancy, Paul, and Shirley Elder. *TIP: A Biography of Thomas P. O'Neill, Speaker of the House*. New York: Macmillan, 1980. Highlights O'Neill's congressional career.

3. Coffey, Wayne R. *How We Choose the Congress*. New York: St. Martins, 1980. The long struggle of a man or woman to win election to Congress.

4. *Congress A to Z*. Washington, D.C.: Congressional Quarterly, Inc., 1988. A lively, anecdotal examination of nearly every term, concept, and process associated with Congress.

5. *Congressional Quarterly's Guide to Current American Government*. Washington, D.C.: Congressional Quarterly, Inc., annual. Chiefly for reference.

6. Drury, Allen. *Advise and Consent*. New York: Doubleday and Co., Inc., 1959. A timeless novel about the Senate's obligation to "advise and consent," in relation to presidential appointments.

7. Fox, Harrison W., Jr., and Susan Webb Hammond. *Congressional Staffs: The Invisible Force in American Lawmaking*. New York: Free Press, 1977. Explains how personal and committee staffs actually operate in Congress.

8. Green, Mark. *Who Runs Congress?* New York: Bantam, 1979. A behind-the-scenes look at Congress, produced in conjunction with the Nader Congress Project.

9. *How Congress Works*. Washington, D.C.: Congressional Quarterly, Inc., 1983. Offers a clear overview of the structure and workings of Congress.

10. *The Presidential-Congressional Political Dictionary*. Santa Barbara, CA: ABC-Clio Information Services, 1984. Explanations of 300 terms pertaining to the President and to Congress.

11. Ripley, Richard B. *Congress: Process and Policy*. New York: W. W. Norton and Company, 1983. A detailed analysis of the way Congress decides public policy.

COMMUNICATING

Being able to communicate your ideas to others—friends, family, peers, and public officials—is an essential part of citizenship in a democracy. There are many ways to do this. One way of communicating is by passing along or transmitting information to others either in written or oral form.

For your message to be effective, the information you pass on must be correct and must deal directly with the issue you are addressing. You also must develop any arguments carefully and have good reasons supporting your point of view. This includes learning to disagree respectfully with opposing positions and understanding other people's reasons for their positions. Finally, you must decide with whom you want to communicate and what form your message should take.

Do you want to discuss your reasoning only with friends, or do you think a letter to the editor of your local newspaper would be most effective? Perhaps it makes sense to write to a public official. If so, who should that official be—the mayor of your town, the governor, your representative in Congress?

The following activity will help you to develop your skill in communicating ideas.

1. Use newspapers, news magazines, television newscasts, or radio news programs to find out about current issues being decided in the Congress. Then, select one of these issues to focus on.

2. What alternatives are the various members of Congress discussing? Consider each of these alternatives and decide which one you think is the most defensible. (You may wish to study the questions outlined in the Citizenship Competency Skill in Unit 7 to help you in this task.)

3. Develop arguments supporting your position or point of view.

4. Which groups in your community do you think would support your arguments? Why? Which groups in your community probably would oppose them? Why?

5. After you have gone through these steps, you are ready to communicate your opinion. You can let people who agree with you know of your position and how you plan to try to change the minds of those who oppose your argument.

6. Draft a letter either to the editor of your local newspaper or to your representative stating your position and explaining your reasons for believing as you do.

7. Exchange drafts with a student partner for critique. Ask your partner to write down how he or she feels about the issue you presented and to identify the point(s) in your letter by which he or she was most influenced. These responses will help you to determine how well you communicated your views.

8. To make your communication even more effective, be sure to use correct letter form and avoid any spelling or punctuation errors.

9. Rewrite the letter, taking into account your partner's criticisms.

THE
EXECUTIVE BRANCH

When you hear the term *federal government,* what image first pops into your mind? At first, you might pull a blank, since the term is so difficult to imagine. But, if you are like many people, you might think of thousands of busy workers trying to get a gigantic machine to function properly. Whatever image first strikes you, you'll probably in the end focus on the President of the United States. For many Americans, thinking about the President seems to bring the operations of a large, impersonal government down to their level.

In spite of being the most powerful official in our national government, the President can present an appealing human side that helps ordinary people easily identify with him or her. The picture on the facing page shows President Clinton and his wife.

Although the President is a human being, he or she has a seemingly superhuman job—getting the vast and complex machinery of government moving to achieve the goals set by the American people.

Chapter 14

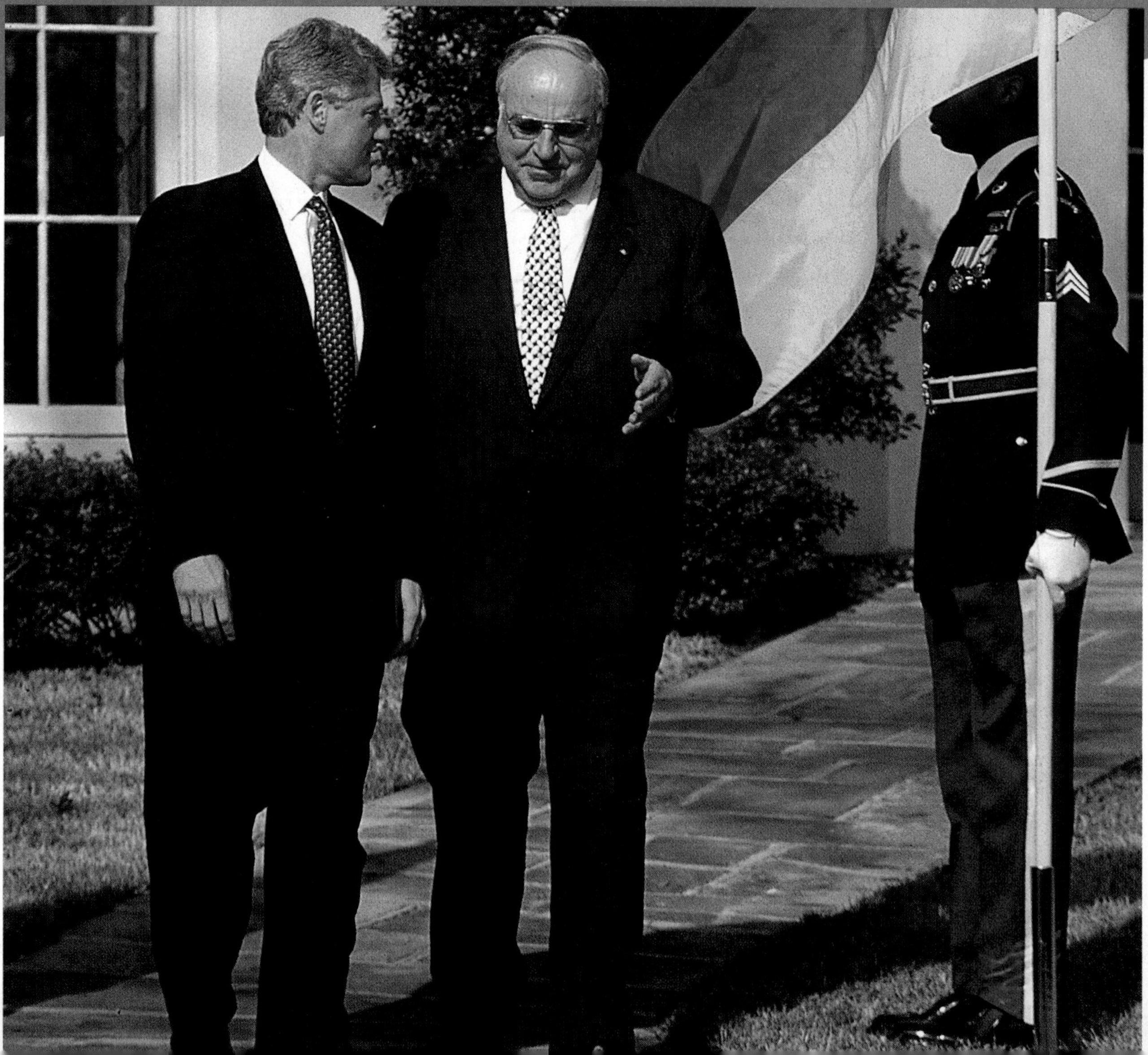

The Presidency

If our nation's government were a stage play or a movie, the individual with the starring role would undoubtedly be the President of the United States. The President's power and influence touch the lives of all American citizens and the lives of citizens in other countries as well. In this chapter, you will learn why the Framers of the Constitution organized the office of the President as they did and the many ways the office has changed over time in response to new circumstances.

Chapter Preview

TERMS TO KNOW
electoral college, slate of electors, electoral vote, popular vote, President-elect, inauguration, federal bureaucracy, executive orders, executive privilege, recognition, armistice, State of the Union Address, pardons, reprieves, amnesty, order of succession

READ TO DISCOVER
- what the constitutional qualifications of the President are.
- how we choose our President and Vice President.
- what the powers of the President are.
- what the functions of the Vice President are.
- the order of presidential succession.

★ ★ ★ ★ ★

Civic Participation Journal

Keep track of all the news coverage that the President receives during a one-week period. Record at the end of each day how the media reports on presidential activities. Keep a tally of the daily stories and classify the coverage as positive, neutral, or negative.

1 The Office of President

The Constitution sets only three qualifications for the nation's chief executive as Figure 14.1 shows. However, there are also many "unwritten" qualifications that have been common characteristics of most of the nation's past 41 Presidents.

A majority of chief executives have come from large, heavily populated states. Most were born and raised in small towns or rural communities, and all have been Protestants, except John Kennedy who was a Roman Catholic. Most Presidents have come from middle-class backgrounds, and more than half of them were lawyers. All had some political or military experience before entering the White House. And in this century, all of the Presidents, with the exception of Harry Truman, have had university or college educations. Although no woman or member of an ethnic or racial minority has ever been President, many people feel this will eventually change.

Terms

After a heated debate on the length of the presidential term, the Framers of the Constitution finally agreed on four years. Most delegates felt this was enough time for the President to gain experience, exhibit leadership, and implement policies. The Constitution was silent, however, on the number of terms a President could serve.

George Washington served two terms as President but declined to seek a third one, establishing a tradition followed by all Presidents until well into the twentieth century. Then Franklin Roosevelt was elected in 1932 and again in 1936. In 1940, with a war raging in Europe and the effects of the Great Depression lingering at home, Roosevelt felt he had work to complete and ran again. He was elected to a third term in 1940 and to a fourth in 1944. This unprecedented action led Congress to propose a constitutional amendment limiting presidential terms. The Twenty-second Amendment, ratified in 1951, made law what has been called the "two-term tradition."

Salary and Benefits

The President receives a salary that is set by Congress. Originally, the President's salary was $25,000 a year. Currently, the salary is $200,000 a year and is taxed just as other Americans' incomes are. But

Qualifications for Becoming President

A President must—

Be a natural-born citizen of the United States.

Be at least 35 years old.

Have lived in this country for at least 14 years before taking office.

Figure 14-1

unlike most Americans, the President receives some other financial benefits and privileges for being the nation's chief executive, including a $50,000-a-year taxable expense account and a $100,000-a-year nontaxable allowance for travel and entertainment.

Two residences, the White House and Camp David in Maryland, are available to the President. In addition, the office carries with it the use of numerous helicopters, automobiles, and the private presidential jet, *Air Force One*. The finest medical and dental care and Secret Service protection round out the Chief Executive's benefits.

Some of these compensations continue when a President retires or is defeated for reelection. Former Presidents receive a lifetime pension of $99,500 a year, financial support for staff, free office space, and continued Secret Service protection.

Section Review

1. What three qualifications does the Constitution set for being President?

2. What are some common characteristics that United States Presidents have shared?

3. How many terms may a President serve?

4. Describe three presidential benefits besides salary.

5. **Challenge:** Why have some unwritten rules about presidential characteristics changed in recent years?

Use of the presidential jet, *Air Force One,* is numbered among the benefits that the President enjoys. What are some other benefits associated with holding the office of President?

electoral college winning slates of presidential electors from each state

2 Choosing the President

If you vote in the next presidential election, you will indicate your preference for President and Vice President. But did you know that you will not actually be casting your vote *directly* for the President and Vice President at all, even though the candidates' names appear on the ballot? Instead, you will be choosing a **slate of electors** from your state that represent a party's ticket for President and Vice President.

A slate of electors is chosen before the general election by state committees or conventions of each political party with a presidential candidate on the ballot. The number of electors on each party's slate equals that state's number of members in both houses of Congress. New Mexico, for instance, has 5 electors vote because it has 2 senators and 3 representatives. Each elector from a state casts an **electoral vote** for President and another one for Vice President. With rare exception, the candidates who win the **popular vote** in the state get all of that state's electoral votes.

These signs show the national totals for the popular vote in the 1992 presidential election. What role does the popular vote play in presidential races?

Electoral College

Together, the winning slates of electors from each state are known as the **electoral college.** The Constitution gives the electoral college, instead of the voting public, the responsibility of choosing the President and the Vice President.

The electoral college never actually meets as a national body in one place. Instead, the slate of electors supporting the winning presidential ticket in each state gather in their state capital the December following the election to cast their ballots for President and Vice President. In most states, the electors are pledged to vote for their party's candidates. However, the Constitution does not hold them to their pledges. In fact, in a number of elections, individual electors or groups of electors have *not* voted for the candidates in whose names they were chosen.

Once the votes are cast, the ballots are then sent to Washington, D.C., where they are opened and counted in early January by the current Vice President before a joint session of Congress. The candidates on the ticket who receive a majority of electoral votes—at least 270 of the 538 votes cast—are declared the elected President and Vice President.

But what happens if no candidate receives a majority of the electoral votes? Then, it is the duty of the House of Representatives, voting by state, to select the President from among the top three candidates. Each state has one vote in such an election, and a majority is necessary for a candidate to win. The House has chosen the President twice—in the elections of 1800 and 1824.

If no person receives a majority of the electoral votes for Vice President, a different procedure is used. The

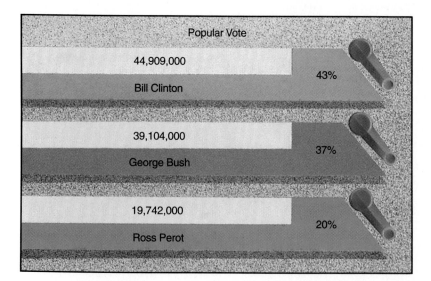

Popular Vote

44,909,000
Bill Clinton
43%

39,104,000
George Bush
37%

19,742,000
Ross Perot
20%

Senate picks the Vice President from between the two candidates with the most votes. Each Senator has one vote, and a majority is required.

Why did the Framers feel it was necessary to set up this system for electing the President and Vice President? One reason is that the Framers tended to distrust the average voter who they felt might not make wise political decisions for such an important office. So they planned for the President and Vice President to be chosen by electors. These were well-known citizens, thought to be free from influence, who would use sound judgment in making the election decision.

However, the development of political parties has limited the independence of the electors. Political parties select the electors who are pledged to that party's candidates. The electors act as party representatives who, by and large, have become "rubber stamps," voting almost unfailingly for their party's candidates. In most cases, then, the people of the United States know who has been elected as President and Vice President before the electors cast their ballots. As a result, the voting of the electoral college is now only a routine ceremony.

CRITICISMS

There are a number of criticisms of the present method of electing the President. One is that it does not accurately express the will of the people and blocks the democratic process. Critics point out that in some states electors are not legally bound to the decisions of the voters. This happened in the 1988 election. The Democratic presidential candidate, Michael Dukakis, won the popular vote in West Virginia. But for President, one of the state's electors voted for Senator Lloyd Bentsen, who was

In 1974, the Watergate hearings, shown here, led to the resignation of President Richard Nixon. Vice-President Gerald Ford succeeded him as chief executive. How does a person usually become President?

listed on the ballot as the Democratic vice-presidential candidate. As a result, the state's electoral votes did not completely reflect the will of the people. Although this has happened eight times previously, it has never affected the outcome of a presidential election. However, the possibility exists that electors who change their votes *could* elect a candidate who actually lost the general election.

Another criticism is that a candidate's electoral votes may not accurately reflect his or her share of the popular votes. In 1960, for instance, John F. Kennedy defeated Richard M. Nixon by 303 electoral votes to 219. Yet, the difference in the popular vote was less than 120,000 of the nearly 70 million votes cast—only one-tenth of 1 percent.

The winner-take-all system is the basis of another criticism. Since the candidate winning *most* of a state's popular votes wins *all* of that state's electoral votes, millions of people who supported the losing candidate are not represented in the electoral college.

A related criticism—and perhaps the most telling—is that the electoral college system can result in the election of a President who has fewer popular votes than an opponent.

In the election of 1888, for instance, the Democratic candidate, Grover Cleveland, received nearly 100,000 more popular votes than his opponent, Benjamin Harrison. Yet, Harrison was elected because he won several of the larger states, notably New York, by narrow margins while Cleveland won a number of the smaller states by large margins. Two other Presidents—John Quincy Adams in 1824 and Rutherford B. Hayes in 1876—were also elected despite losing the popular vote.

Another criticism has to do with the fact that some states have many more electoral votes than others. Because of this, critics claim that candidates concentrate their campaign efforts in states with large numbers of electoral votes, such as California with 54, and overlook the distinctive needs and problems of other "less important" states.

PROPOSED REFORMS

Opponents of the electoral college have proposed several reforms. One that is often raised is to do away with the electoral college entirely and replace it with a direct election of the President by the people. Supporters of direct election claim that it is more democratic since it gives everyone's vote equal weight.

Although public opinion polls show strong support for direct election, the chances for adopting it are slim. First, it involves the long and complicated process of amending the Constitution. Second, it would reduce the impor-

tance of the states in selecting the President. Small states, especially, fear that their votes would be overpowered by the urban votes of large states. In addition, many Republican and Democratic party leaders fear that getting rid of the electoral college would give third parties more influence.

Other proposals support the reform of the electoral college, not its elimination. One proposal, known as the direct plan, calls for the selection of electors in each state in the same way that members of Congress are chosen. That is, two electors would be chosen to represent the entire state. Other electors would be selected from each of the state's congressional districts.

Another proposal, the proportional plan, favors eliminating electors but keeping electoral votes. Each presidential candidate would receive the same share of a state's electoral vote as he or she received of that state's popular vote. Suppose, for example, that a candidate won 48 percent of the popular vote. He or she would then automatically receive 48 percent of the electoral votes from that state.

A third proposal is known as the plurality plan. It also supports an end to electors, but it keeps a state basis for voting. Under it, a candidate would have to win a plurality in a majority of states to win the election.

In spite of the reservations and criticisms of the present system, there are many people who support the electoral college as it is. Supporters argue that critics overstate the problems of this system. They note that the system has worked well in the past and has yet to break down. Many also fear that changing the system could add to the expense and length of the campaign process. Thus, none of the proposals appear likely to be approved in the near future.

The presidential and vice presidential inaugural ceremonies take place on Capitol Hill. What is the most dramatic moment of the inauguration?

After the Election

The candidate selected to be the new President is called the **President-elect.** Between the election in November and the twentieth of January, the President-elect organizes the new administration, selecting a Cabinet and other top appointees. Meetings take place with the outgoing President to smooth the transfer of the government. In addition, the President-elect receives information on specific problems, especially in foreign affairs.

The **inauguration** is held on January 20 following a presidential election. Generally held on the steps of the Capitol, the ceremony centers on swearing into office the new President and Vice President.

The most dramatic moment comes when the President takes the oath ''to preserve, protect, and defend the Constitution of the United States.'' At this time, the transition from old to new administration legally takes place. Following the custom set by George Washington, the new President then gives an inaugural address, presenting the visions and goals of the new administration.

President-elect person who has been elected President, but has not yet taken office

Section Review

1. What is the role of the electoral college in electing the President and Vice President?

2. Who chooses the President and Vice President if no candidate receives a majority of electoral votes?

3. What are three of the criticisms of the electoral college system?

4. **Challenge:** Do you favor keeping, eliminating, or reforming the current system of electing the President? Explain.

inauguration ceremony of installing the President into office

3 Powers of the President

Presidential powers are outlined by the Constitution and are described in Figure 14-2. Other powers have become a part of the presidency over time, due to custom and tradition. Compared to the powers granted to the legislative branch, the chief executive's powers seem limited and unclear. There is a reason for this. After fighting a bloody revolution for independence, many delegates at the Constitutional Convention feared that granting the President too many powers would make the office more like an elected king than a representative of the people. Others, however, wanted a strong chief executive with discretionary powers that could be used in times of crisis. A compromise was eventually reached, leaving the President's powers broadly defined but limited by the checks and balances of the other branches.

Executive Powers

The Constitution authorizes that "the executive power shall be vested in a President of the United States." Over the years, this "executive power" has evolved, giving the President considerable control over the national government.

Article II, Section 3 states that the President "shall take care that the laws be faithfully executed." This means that Presidents must carry out

Powers of the President of the United States

Executive Powers include:
enforcing laws, treaties, and court decisions.
issuing executive orders in carrying out policies.
appointing and removing officials.
presiding over the Cabinet.

Legislative Powers include:
giving annual State of the Union Address.
issuing annual budget and economic reports.
signing and vetoing bills.
proposing legislation
calling special sessions of Congress

Diplomatic Powers include:
appointing ambassadors and other diplomats.
making treaties and executive agreements.
according diplomatic recognition to other governments.

Military Powers include:
acting as commander in chief of the armed forces.
providing for domestic order.

Judicial Powers include:
appointing members of the federal judiciary.
granting reprieves, pardons, and amnesty.

Figure 14-2

all federal laws, treaties, and court decisions, whether or not they agree with them. But Presidents can, and do, interpret these laws as they see fit, thus carrying them out according to their own interpretations. What allows Presidents to do this? Typically, Congress writes laws in fairly broad terms, leaving the details and implementation to the President and the executive branch. In 1989, for example, Congress passed a bill designed to rescue the debt-ridden savings and loan industry. The bill established new agencies to bail out some of these institutions and close others. The executive branch was then charged with deciding which institutions to close and how to distribute the refinancing funds among those kept open.

FEDERAL BUREAUCRACY

The President, however, cannot get personally involved in every one of the nation's problems. In fact, about 3 million employees help the executive branch do its work. As the "boss" of this **federal bureaucracy,** the President acts like the head of a large corporation, deciding policy and issuing orders for departments and agencies to carry out.

EXECUTIVE ORDERS

Presidents also have the power to issue **executive orders,** an implied power that allows them to carry out the law or change government regulations. All executive orders must be constitutional and agree with current federal laws. And while most of these orders only pertain to establishing the government agencies needed to carry out the law, some have far-reaching effects. President Truman, for example, used an executive order in the late 1940s to end racial segregation in the armed forces. And, in 1986 President Reagan issued a secret executive order, later made public, authorizing the

In this cartoon, President Truman is unhappy with the "size" of his authority and is asking for more. What modern factors work to keep the presidency one of the most powerful offices in the world?

sale of missiles to Iran in the hope of securing the release of American hostages held in Lebanon.

APPOINTMENT POWERS

Unlike executive orders, the power of appointment is expressed in Article II, Section 2 of the Constitution. It is interesting to note that the President and Vice President are the only elected offices in the executive branch. All other officials are either hired through the civil service system or appointed by the President. Specifically, the President may "appoint ambassadors, other public ministers and consuls, judges of the Supreme Court, and all other officers of the United States whose appointments are not otherwise herein provided for." Presidents use this important power to place trusted and like-minded people in influential positions to shape and direct public policy. The Senate, however, acts as a check through its power to approve most presidential appointments. A few appointments, most of which are in the White House office, do not require the Senate's approval.

federal bureaucracy government employees who do the work of the executive branch

executive orders presidential rules that have the force of law

The Presidency 321

As the nation's leading diplomat, the President is host to foreign officials when they come to Washington, D.C. Here, President Bush is discussing world issues with a visiting African leader. What is the President's most important power in foreign affairs?

REMOVAL POWERS

The President also has the authority to remove some officials from office. As a general rule, the President has the power to remove those who were appointed. The Constitution, however, does not state these removal powers clearly, giving no guidelines as to how or why an official may be removed. The Supreme Court has tried to remedy this gray area by placing limits on this power, forcing the President to seek Senate approval on the removal of officials from independent regulatory agencies.

EXECUTIVE PRIVILEGE

The Supreme Court also stepped into the executive arena when it placed limits on the presidential claim to **executive privilege.** Although Presidents have used executive privilege for many reasons, most often they claim it when there is a need for secrecy in foreign affairs or in matters of national security. This privilege was first invoked by George Washington, when he refused to supply the House of Representatives with papers concerning the Jay Treaty negotiations. In most recent times, too,

Presidents have used executive privilege, usually with little challenge. But the practice was seriously criticized during the Watergate affair, when President Nixon tried to declare executive privilege absolute in all matters.

During the congressional hearings on this affair, the prosecutor sought access to tape recordings of the President's conversations with White House staff members in the Oval Office. President Nixon refused to hand over the tapes, claiming that they contained sensitive information vital to national security. In *United States v. Nixon*, the Supreme Court did not accept the President's claim of executive privilege and forced him to release the tapes.

Diplomatic Powers

Although Congress plays an important role in foreign affairs, its size and slower procedures prevent it from acting quickly. Therefore, Congress has delegated wide powers in conducting foreign policy to the executive branch.

The most important presidential power in foreign affairs is making

executive privilege right of the President to withhold information from Congress, the courts, or the public

treaties with other nations. This power is checked by the Senate, however, which must approve treaties by a two-thirds vote. The Senate has approved about 70 percent of all treaties submitted to it by past Presidents. One notable exception occurred in 1919, when President Woodrow Wilson failed to get approval of the Treaty of Versailles that ended World War I. And, in some cases, the Senate may attach amendments or other provisions to a treaty, requiring the President to renegotiate the agreement.

The President, however, can bypass Senate approval of treaties through the use of executive agreements. As you learned earlier, these agreements have the same legal status as treaties but do not require Senate approval. And while many deal with routine matters, such as trade or fishing rights, some have vital importance. In 1940, for example, President Franklin Roosevelt made an executive agreement with Prime Minister Winston Churchill to lend American destroyers to Great Britain during World War II. By the late 1960s, the extensive use of these agreements led Congress to pass the Case Act in 1972. This Act requires the President to inform Congress within 60 days of making any executive agreement.

Another diplomatic power of the President is the power of **recognition.** Even if the United States does not wholeheartedly approve of a foreign government, recognition occurs to maintain friendly relations with that country. Sometimes, however, another government's actions are completely opposed by the President, and recognition is withheld. This is the case today with the nations of Cuba, North Korea, and Vietnam. And recognition can be removed from a country that has already been recognized to express disapproval of its actions or policies.

recognition acceptance of the legal existence of another country's government

In 1994, President Clinton witnessed the signing of a friendship treaty between Israel's Prime Minister Yitzhak Rabin (left) and Jordan's King Hussein (right). What are a President's diplomatic activities?

Military Powers

The Constitution names the President, a civilian elected by the people, as commander in chief of the armed forces. The Framers did this because they distrusted military commanders, who could use their power to impose a dictatorship. Also, in naming the President for this role, the Framers chose to put the supreme command of military affairs in the hands of one person. They believed, as Alexander Hamilton wrote in *Federalist No. 74*, that "the direction of war most peculiarly demands those qualities which distinguish the exercise of power by a single hand."

At the same time, however, the Framers made some aspects of military control a shared power between the executive and the legislative branches. Congress has the power to declare war, to maintain and regulate the armed forces, and to supply funds for defense. But the President has the ultimate authority to make military decisions. In 1945, for example, President Truman made the decision to drop atomic bombs on Hiroshima and Nagasaki, Japan, ending World War II. And in 1986 President Reagan ordered American warplanes to bomb the Libyan capital of Tripoli in response to the belief that Libya was involved in terrorist attacks against Americans.

WAR POWERS

As head of the military, Presidents have made extensive use of their war powers. On some occasions, they have taken active roles in the command of federal forces. George Washington led federal troops in putting down the Whisky Rebellion in 1794. During the Civil War, Abraham Lincoln visited battlefields to consult with generals. Today, however, most Presidents delegate military authority to others. The President, with the consent of the Senate, appoints all high-ranking military officials and also can dismiss them. In 1951 President Truman fired General Douglas MacArthur from his command in the Far East after he publicly disapproved of Truman's war policy in Korea.

Several Presidents have extended their war powers to send armed forces into conflict without a formal declaration of war. President James Polk sent American troops into territory disputed with Mexico, an action that led to the Mexican War (1846-1848). President Lyndon Johnson sent soldiers to Vietnam during the 1960s. And President Reagan used the armed forces without congressional approval in several combat situations in the 1980s, including an invasion of the island of Grenada.

Even in wars declared by Congress, Presidents exercise considerable pow-

In 1994, President Clinton ordered American troops to Haiti to oversee the transition from a military dictatorship to a democratic government. From what source does this presidential power come?

In 1989, an earthquake severely damaged parts of the San Francisco area in the state of California. Presidents often send troops to help in emergencies such as this. What are some examples of such federal action?

ers. They may spend money for weapons, set up military governments in conquered lands, and end hostilities by calling an **armistice.** And, affairs at home may not be immune to presidential control during wartime. During World War II, for instance, President Roosevelt set up emergency government agencies; rationed food, gasoline, and other materials; and regulated wages and prices. Although such seemingly unlimited war powers have been rare, it has caused concern and eventually led to legislative restraints. The War Powers Act was passed by Congress in 1973, limiting the President's powers in cases where war has not been declared.

ENFORCEMENT POWERS

Besides their war powers, Presidents also can use the military to enforce federal laws and restore order at home. In 1954 President Dwight Eisenhower sent troops to Little Rock, Arkansas, to enforce desegregation of the public schools there. President Johnson ordered federal troops to quell riots in Detroit in 1967. Federal troops also can be called out in the event of a natural disaster to help with relief operations.

Legislative Powers

The Constitution gives the President certain legislative powers, allowing the chief executive to influence and direct Congress's agenda. Although Congress makes the laws, the President is involved in the legislative process from beginning to end.

LEGISLATIVE PROGRAMS

Article II, Section 3 states that the President "shall from time to time give to Congress information of the state of the Union. . . ." Originally, the **State of the Union Address** was a long, often boring, review of department and agency goals and activities. Thomas Jefferson set the precedent of submitting the speech in writing, claiming that speaking before Congress was too much like the English monarch's practice of opening a session of Parliament.

Jefferson's precedent was broken in 1913 by Woodrow Wilson, who personally delivered his first State of the Union Address before Congress. He also began the practice of using the speech as a chance to outline the administration's legislative programs and to urge the passage of these

armistice   end to fighting

State of the Union Address   speech laying out the President's legislative goals for the coming year

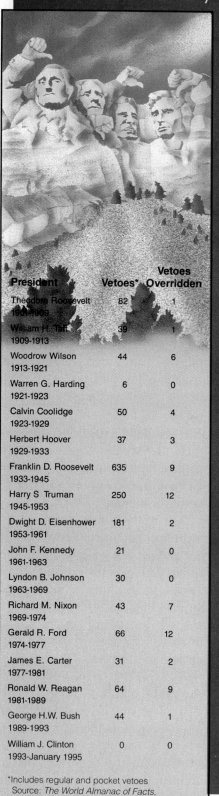

Presidential Vetoes of the Twentieth Century

President	Vetoes*	Vetoes Overridden
Theodore Roosevelt 1901-1909	82	1
William H. Taft 1909-1913	39	1
Woodrow Wilson 1913-1921	44	6
Warren G. Harding 1921-1923	6	0
Calvin Coolidge 1923-1929	50	4
Herbert Hoover 1929-1933	37	3
Franklin D. Roosevelt 1933-1945	635	9
Harry S Truman 1945-1953	250	12
Dwight D. Eisenhower 1953-1961	181	2
John F. Kennedy 1961-1963	21	0
Lyndon B. Johnson 1963-1969	30	0
Richard M. Nixon 1969-1974	43	7
Gerald R. Ford 1974-1977	66	12
James E. Carter 1977-1981	31	2
Ronald W. Reagan 1981-1989	64	9
George H.W. Bush 1989-1993	44	1
William J. Clinton 1993-January 1995	0	0

*Includes regular and pocket vetoes
Source: *The World Almanac of Facts,* 1989, and *Congressional Quarterly,* 1994.

Figure 14-3

programs by Congress. Radio and television added to the importance of the speech until, today, the State of the Union Address is a huge ceremonial affair, given every January before a joint session of Congress.

Also in January, the President sends to Congress two written messages, a budget and a yearly Economic Report. The budget estimates the amount of money the government will need to spend and raise in the coming year. The Economic Report discusses the economy and recommends ways to improve or maintain the nation's economic health.

The President is not limited to these formal avenues for suggesting legislation, however. He or she also works closely with individual legislators, contacting them to discuss bills or sending aides to lobby on Capitol Hill. In addition, the President uses news conferences, televised addresses to the nation, and other public appearances to persuade Congress and the people to support administration policies.

VETO POWER

The President ends the legislative process by either signing or vetoing bills passed by Congress. As you learned earlier, a President can handle a bill in one of four ways: sign the bill, making it law; veto it and return it to Congress; take no action, permitting the bill to become law without signing it; or, if Congress is due to adjourn within 10 working days, kill the bill by simply not acting on it.

In the early days of the nation, Presidents vetoed only those bills they thought were unconstitutional or poorly written. Recently, however, Presidents have used the veto to show disapproval of congressional actions. Figure 14-3 shows how often this power has been used in this century.

Judicial Powers

Presidential powers related to the judicial branch of government are stated outright in the Constitution. These include the powers to grant **pardons** for federal offenses, except in cases of impeachment, and **reprieves.** One of the most controversial presidential pardons in American history was given by President Gerald Ford to Richard Nixon in 1974. Ford pardoned Nixon for any crimes the former President may have committed in office. The President also has the power to grant **amnesty.** For instance, in 1977 President Jimmy Carter granted limited amnesties to young people who evaded the draft during the Vietnam War.

Through the power of appointment, the President affects the judiciary in another way. All judges to federal courts are appointed by the President. And although the Senate must approve these appointments, this power gives Presidents an opportunity to fill openings with persons who share their political and legal views. Since these appointments are for life, a President may influence judicial decisions long after leaving office. Nowhere is this influence more evident than in the Supreme Court, even though justices are not bound to follow the President who appointed them. The Court is an independent body, and the justices are free to follow their consciences in interpreting the law.

The Supreme Court and the federal courts as a whole depend on the executive branch to carry out their decisions. Usually Presidents do this without question, but conflicts between the chief executive and the Court sometimes do arise. In 1989, for instance, the Court ruled that burning the American flag was within the First Amendment right of free

At a Washington, D.C., patriotic rally in 1989, President George Bush (right) announced his support for a constitutional amendment making the burning of the American flag illegal. What position has the Supreme Court taken on this issue?

speech. President George Bush strongly disagreed with the Court's ruling and asked Congress to consider a new amendment making the burning of the flag illegal.

Section Review

1. What five kinds of powers may be exercised by the President?
2. What is the difference between a treaty and an executive agreement?
3. Why did the Framers of the Constitution make the President, a civilian, commander in chief of the nation's armed forces?
4. **Challenge:** Why are the powers of appointment and removal important to the President?

pardons   acts that free persons from responsibility and punishment for crimes

reprieves   acts that postpone criminals' sentences for a certain period of time

amnesty   a special pardon given to a group of people

4 The Vice President

During much of the nation's history, the office of Vice President has been viewed as an insignificant position, one to be avoided by ambitious politicians. In declining the Whig party's nomination as their vice-presidential candidate in 1848, Daniel Webster said, "I do not propose to be buried until I am dead."

Even in the 1900s, the vice-presidency has been the subject of jokes. Alben Barkley, who held the post during the Truman administration, often gave his opinion of the vice-presidency in a story. A woman had two sons. One of them, he said, joined the navy and went to sea. The other son became Vice President "and neither of them was ever heard of again."

Why was the office of Vice President so often viewed with such ridicule—even by some of the individuals who held the office? One explanation for this attitude can be found in the job description.

Vice-presidential candidate Gore greets representatives to the 1992 Democratic National Convention. What are some of the responsibilities of the Vice President?

Duties and Benefits

According to the Constitution, the main job of the Vice President is to preside over the Senate. But aside from casting tie-breaking votes, this job is mainly ceremonial. Other than performing this one task, the Vice President is assigned duties by the President and must be ready to assume that office if the President dies, becomes disabled, resigns, or is removed from office. Thus, the qualifications for Vice President are the same as those for the President. Unlike the President, however, the Vice President can serve any number of four-year terms.

The Vice President also may be assigned other specific duties by the President. A Vice President may perform such ceremonial tasks as attending a state funeral in another country in the President's place. Often, too, the Vice President is asked to serve on special commissions that study national problems and present recommendations to the President and Congress. However, it is only recently that Vice Presidents have taken part in such tasks. For the most part, most Presidents did not make their Vice Presidents true "second in commands." Some Presidents may have even purposely limited the duties of their Vice Presidents for fear of being upstaged.

Despite the sometimes limited duties of the office, the Vice President still enjoys many benefits. The salary is $171,500 per year, plus a yearly taxable expense allowance of $10,000. The Vice President has a staff and the use of *Air Force Two*, the official vice-presidential plane. In addition, a mansion on the grounds of the Washington Naval Observatory is provided as the official residence of the Vice President.

Selection

Many observers point out that the manner in which Vice Presidents are selected also lessens the importance of the office. Presidential candidates usually pick their own running mates, often choosing someone to "balance the ticket." That is, Vice Presidents often are chosen not for their leadership potential but to improve the presidential candidate's prospects of winning the election. Thus, the vice-presidential candidate often comes from an area of the country or wing of the party different from that of the presidential candidate. In 1976, for instance, the Democratic candidate for President, Jimmy Carter of Georgia, chose Walter Mondale of Minnesota as his running mate.

Another consideration in choosing a running mate is age. A presidential candidate, for instance, may choose a younger running mate in an attempt to appeal to younger voters. Many political observers say this is one reason 64-year-old George Bush placed 41-year-old Dan Quayle on the Republican ticket in 1988.

RECENT CHANGES

The assassination of President John F. Kennedy and the attempts on the lives of Presidents Ford and Reagan have underlined the importance of the Vice President in recent years. As a result, greater consideration is given to the qualifications of the person who is "only a heartbeat away" from assuming the responsibilities and pressures of the highest office in the land. And recent chief executives have given their Vice Presidents more than just ceremonial responsibilities. A Vice President may take part in Cabinet meetings, serve on the National Security Council, act as a representative in goodwill missions to other countries,

Democrat Walter Mondale selected Geraldine Ferraro as his running mate in the 1984 presidential election. Many observers felt that this choice represented an attempt to attract women voters. What factors are considered when selecting a running mate?

and provide a link between the White House and Congress. With a more influential role, Vice Presidents have become more capable of taking over the presidency if necessary.

Section Review

1. What are the constitutional qualifications for Vice President?

2. What two duties are assigned to the Vice President by the Constitution?

3. What kinds of changes have taken place recently in the role of the Vice President?

4. **Challenge:** Do you think the importance of the role and responsibilities of Vice President should be increased or decreased? Explain.

5 Presidential Succession

The presidency is sometimes called the toughest job in the world. Presidents have described it in various ways. Thomas Jefferson called the presidency "a splendid misery." Harry Truman wrote that being President is "like riding a tiger." John F. Kennedy noted that "the problems are more difficult than I had imagined them to be."

In carrying out the duties of the office, the President is exposed to many dangers, as well as mental and physical pressures. If something should happen to the President, a quick and effective transfer of power is necessary to begin a new administration.

Order of Succession

Article II, Section 1 of the Constitution states that:

In the case of the removal of the President from office, or his death, resignation, or inability to discharge the powers and duties of the said office, the same shall devolve to the Vice President. . . .

The Framers thus established who would be in charge if the President were unable to serve, but they left unanswered many other questions. For example, how was the transfer of power to occur? Would the Vice President automatically become President or simply assume the power and duties of the office until a new President was chosen? And who would fill the office of Vice President? These and many other questions took the nation almost 200 years of precedents, laws, and constitutional amendments to resolve.

One of the first times succession came into question was in 1841 when President William Henry Harrison died, and Vice President John Tyler succeeded him. Many leaders believed that Tyler should serve only as acting President until a new one was elected. Tyler, however, insisted on serving as President with all the benefits and powers of the office. Tyler's view prevailed, and that precedent was established.

But what would happen if the Vice President were unable to succeed? It became apparent that an **order of succession** was needed. Congress was given the responsibility of deciding

order of succession legal order in which government officials may succeed to the presidency

Succession to the Presidency

- Vice President
- Speaker of the House
- President Pro-Tempore of the Senate
- Secretary of State
- Secretary of the Treasury
- Secretary of Defense
- Attorney General
- Secretary of the Interior
- Secretary of Agriculture
- Secretary of Commerce
- Secretary of Labor
- Secretary of Health and Human Services
- Secretary of Housing and Urban Development
- Secretary of Transportation
- Secretary of Energy
- Secretary of Education
- Secretary of Veterans' Affairs

Figure 14-4

COMPARISON: THE PRESIDENCY

THE UNITED STATES AND FRANCE

The President of the United States is not the only "President" in the world. Other nations as diverse as El Salvador, India, and Portugal have governments containing the office of president. How do the powers, duties, and responsibilities of the President of the United States compare with similar presidents in other countries? Because of its many similarities as well as its differences with American government, France offers a good comparison.

The government of France is a democratic republic led by a president. Like the President of the United States, the French president heads the executive branch and also exercises limited legislative and judicial powers. Both the American and French presidents serve as commander in chief of their nation's armed forces and also as their country's top diplomat. Yet each country's constitution differs on how the president is elected and in the restrictions it places on presidential powers.

In the United States, the President is chosen indirectly by voters through the electoral college. But in France, the president is chosen by direct popular vote. Once elected, American Presidents serve a four-year term and may be reelected only once. French presidents, however, can serve an unlimited number of seven-year terms.

Major differences exist in the authority granted to each chief executive. Unlike the United States, France is a parliamentary democracy. Daily operation of the government is carried out by a prime minister, who is appointed by the president from the party that controls Parliament. The smooth running of France's government depends on close cooperation between the president and the prime minister, even when they happen to belong to opposing political parties. Thus, unlike the President of the United States, the French president is forced to share executive power.

In addition, the system of checks and balances in the French constitution is not the same as the system in the Constitution of the United States. The French president has more power over the Parliament than an American President has over Congress. In France, for example, the president may dissolve the lower house of Parliament and call for new elec-

tions. Furthermore, the French president can bypass the Parliament altogether and submit new legislation directly to the voters in a national referendum. However, the President of the United States has one legislative advantage that the French president does not have—American Presidents can veto legislation. The president of France cannot.

One power of the French president not shared by the President of the United States is the ability, with parliamentary approval, to assume emergency powers and rule by decree. However, the French president must have approval of a Constitutional Council before proposing any major changes in the government.

As can be seen from this brief examination, although France and the United States both have presidents, they differ greatly in the powers they have in their respective countries. A similar comparison between the President of the United States and the president of another country would result in the same conclusion—that is, although there are many presidents in the world today, no two are exactly alike.

1. How is the power of the French presidency limited?
2. Based on their powers, which do you think is a more effective leader—the president of France or the President of the United States? Explain.

The final word on presidential succession came in 1967 when the Twenty-fifth Amendment to the Constitution was adopted. This amendment made formal the precedent started by John Tyler, stating that if the President is removed from office, "the Vice President shall become President."

The Twenty-fifth Amendment also provides for the new President to name a new Vice President, subject to the approval of Congress. In 1974, Richard Nixon nominated Gerald Ford for Vice President after Spiro Agnew resigned. Later that year, when Ford succeeded Nixon to the presidency, he nominated Nelson Rockefeller as Vice President.

Presidential Disability

In the past, the nation has faced critical moments when a President was disabled while in office. In 1881 President James Garfield lived for 80 days after being shot, but he was unable to govern. Woodrow Wilson suffered a severe stroke in 1919 and could not serve during part of his second term. Dwight D. Eisenhower suffered three serious illnesses while serving two terms, including a major heart attack. These and other serious situations left many people wondering what to do in a case where a President is disabled while in office. Again, the Twenty-fifth Amendment makes clear how to deal with such emergencies.

According to the amendment, the President must inform Congress of his or her inability to perform in writing. Or, the Vice President and a majority of the Cabinet members can do so if the President is totally disabled. The Vice President then takes over as acting President until the President can resume the duties of office. If the President wants to resume office, but

From his hospital window, President Reagan greets well-wishers after his recovery from surgery. Should the President become unable to govern while in office, what actions would be taken?

the proper order. According to the Presidential Succession Act passed by Congress in 1947, the Vice President is succeeded by the Speaker of the House of Representatives and then by the president pro tempore of the Senate. These officials are followed by the secretary of state and each of the other Cabinet heads in order of the year in which the department was founded. Figure 14-4 lists the entire order of succession.

the Vice President and most Cabinet members are opposed, Congress settles the dispute. If, by a two-thirds vote, both houses of Congress decide that the President is unable to serve, the Vice President continues to act as President.

As of 1994, the only Vice President to serve as acting President was George Bush. President Reagan underwent cancer surgery in 1988 and Vice President Bush was made acting President for the eight hours that Reagan was under anesthetics and in the recovery room.

Section Review

1. What precedent did John Tyler set in 1841?
2. What are the main provisions of the Twenty-fifth Amendment?
3. As of 1994, who was the only person to serve as acting President?
4. **Challenge:** In your opinion, what impact on world politics might result from a temporary vacancy in the presidency of the United States?

Summary

1. The President of the United States holds one of the most powerful elective offices in the world.
2. To become President, one must be a natural-born citizen of the United States, be at least 35 years old, and have lived in the country for at least 14 years before taking office.
3. The President is elected for a term of four years and may serve two terms.
4. The Constitution uses broad, vague terms to describe the President's powers. In addition to these duties and responsibilities, the President has others that are based on custom and usage.
5. The President's executive powers include executing the laws, heading the federal bureaucracy, issuing executive orders, appointing and removing federal officials, and using executive privilege.
6. The President's diplomatic powers include making treaties and executive agreements and recognizing other governments.
7. Military powers include commanding the nation's armed forces, making military decisions, and enforcing domestic order.
8. Legislative powers of the President include setting a legislative agenda and signing or vetoing bills passed by Congress.
9. The President can grant pardons and reprieves to convicted criminals and amnesty to large groups of offenders. By appointing justices to the Supreme Court, the President can influence judicial decisions.
10. The qualifications for Vice President are the same as those for President, while vice-presidential duties include presiding over the Senate and assuming the presidency if it becomes vacant.
11. The Twenty-fifth Amendment outlines the order and procedures to be followed if the President is unable to carry out the duties of office.

Chapter 14 Review

★ Building Vocabulary

Study the following vocabulary terms and write two paragraphs about the office of the President of the United States. At least seven of the ten terms must appear in your paragraphs.

1. federal bureaucracy
2. executive orders
3. executive privilege
4. recognition
5. armistice
6. State of the Union Address
7. pardons
8. reprieves
9. amnesty
10. order of succession

★ Reviewing Facts

1. Why did the Framers agree to a four-year presidential term?
2. What is the purpose of the Twenty-second Amendment?
3. Does the President pay income tax?
4. Why were some delegates at the Constitutional Convention afraid of giving the President too much power?
5. Why are executive orders useful for Presidents?
6. What are two posts the President can fill without Senate approval?
7. What was the outcome of the Supreme Court case *United States v. Nixon?*
8. How might the Senate change a treaty negotiated by the President?
9. How might Presidents use their military powers domestically?
10. What are two benefits given the Vice President?
11. Which Cabinet department head would be the last in line to become President?

★ Analyzing Facts

1. Of the characteristics common among the nation's Presidents, which do you think are the most important for a person to be an effective leader? Which do you think are least important?
2. Presidents have used executive privilege and secret executive agreements to keep information from Congress. Do you think Presidents should be allowed such secrecy? Why or why not?
3. Do you agree with President Carter's decision in 1977 to grant limited amnesty to young people who evaded the draft during the Vietnam War? Why or why not?
4. As you learned, the Presidential Succession Act defines the order of presidential succession. Many object to its provisions. They point out that the Speaker and the president pro tempore are elected by the people of the states they represent while Cabinet officers are not elected at all. Given your understanding of our political system and the federal structure, what problems do you see with the order of succession as set out in the Act?

★ Evaluating Ideas

1. In your opinion, does the President have too few or too many war powers? Explain.
2. If you had the job of Vice President, what would you do to promote the image of the office?

Using Your Civic Participation Journal

Review the tally of presidential news coverage that you kept in your Civic Participation Journal. Work with four classmates to compare notes and construct a mock newspaper page showing the major stories.

3. Do you think the office of the President has turned into an "elected monarch," as some of the Framers feared? Why or why not?

4. Vice-presidential candidates often are chosen to balance the ticket of a political party. Do you agree or disagree with this method? Why?

★ Critical Thinking Detecting Bias

Since everyone has opinions about certain topics, what they say or write about those topics is not always free from the influences of their personal views, even if they try to be fair. When a speaker or writer shows a set opinion about someone or something, this is known as bias.

Explanation Detecting bias is important because people often accept what they read or hear as fact, without considering how the personal opinions of the author or speaker influence what they write or say. Bias can be detected almost everywhere, including newspaper articles, television newscasts, and political speeches. Knowing a writer's or speaker's purpose, or where he or she is "coming from," will help you determine if the information being presented to you is accurate and objective. The following guidelines will help you detect bias.

1. Be aware of words or statements that transmit either positive or negative feelings.

2. In written materials, note the use of punctuation—for example, exclamation points—and the use of italics, underlining, and boldface terms to emphasize certain views.

3. Look out for rhetorical questions, questions that imply only one correct answer, or for which no answer is expected.

4. Try to use an author's or speaker's background to provide clues about how he or she arrived at a specific point of view.

Practice Read the following paragraphs and determine which one is biased.

A. *When the President visited a seaside resort in Italy, he brought about 100 aides and associates to the important meetings taking place here. The President was obviously tired from the long flight, saying at one point that he was "happy to be here in France." Although he later apologized for the mistake, it was an embarrassing moment.*

B. *The President arrived today for important meetings at this seaside resort in Italy. He was accompanied by his typical collection of about 100 fans and followers. The President, looking tired and confused as usual, said upon arrival that he was "happy to be here in <u>France</u>." Could there have possibly been a more embarrassing moment in the President's trip?*

Obviously, paragraph B is biased against the President. Use of words like "typical collection," "fans and followers," and "confused as usual" convey an unfavorable impression. Underlining helps to emphasize a negative point, as does the use of a rhetorical question.

Independent Practice Study the cartoon below. It appeared shortly after the 1994 election. What examples of bias can you detect?

Chapter 15

Presidential Leadership

The source of the President's authority is the Constitution, which says: "The executive power shall be vested in a President of the United States of America." This executive authority includes many powers used by Presidents to carry out the duties of the office. The way in which these powers are used often spells the difference between an effective President and a poor one.

Chapter Preview

TERMS TO KNOW
presidential government

READ TO DISCOVER
- the roles of the President.
- how the office of the President has developed and grown.

★ ★ ★ ★ ★

Civic Participation Journal

The President is the most visible American official. Almost all citizens have an opinion about what kind of job he or she is doing. Interview 10 adults in your community to learn whether they approve of the current President's leadership. Record the results in your journal.

1 The President in Action

The position of President of the United States is held by one person. Yet that person must fill many and varied roles. Often, these roles overlap and may even conflict with one another.

Presidential Roles

As *chief executive,* the President sees that the laws of the nation are carried out. To accomplish this feat the President directs employees of the federal bureaucracy, who implement the laws and programs of Congress and enforce the rulings of the Supreme Court.

As *chief of state,* the President is the ceremonial head of the nation. In this role the President is a symbol of American ideals and a personal representative of you and other Americans. Duties as chief of state include welcoming important visitors and extending honors to dignitaries from other countries. Other ceremonial duties are not as important to the nation, but receive much attention. Lighting the national Christmas tree, giving awards and medals to American citizens, making public service statements, and meeting public figures are all considered a part of the President's job.

Although the roles of chief executive and chief of state are combined in the United States, these two roles are distinct in most other countries. In Great Britain, for example, the king or queen serves as chief of state, but the prime minister heads the government and carries out its policies.

In the role of *commander in chief,* the President heads our nation's armed forces. The President also has control over our military weapons. The role of commander in chief corresponds with that of chief of state. The President as military leader represents the people in times of peace and war.

Closely linked to the role of military leader is that of *chief diplomat.* In this role the President directs United States relations with other countries and represents our nation in meetings with other leaders. At times, some of these duties are given over to the secretary of state or to other officials. But it is the President who makes the final decisions and takes responsibility for the nation's actions.

By working with Congress, the President also serves as *chief legislator,* or chief designer, of American public policy. In this role the President proposes and supports legislative action from Congress. Usually the President reveals a legislative program in the annual State of the Union message to Congress. The President then follows up with details presented to Congress throughout the year.

Finally, Presidents are *party leaders,* or heads of the political parties that nominated them for office. In most of their official duties, Presidents work toward the best interests of our nation as a whole. But as party leaders, they tend to favor the views of their own party. For example, Presidents have the power of patronage and supply thousands of jobs to party workers and supporters. They also support the campaigns of other party members and appear at fundraising events. From the White House, the President influences the nature and direction of party policy, providing leadership to the party's representatives in Congress and seeking their support for administration programs.

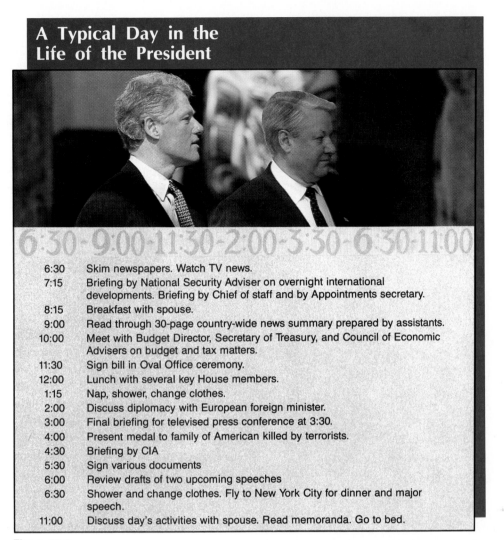

A Typical Day in the Life of the President

6:30-9:00-11:30-2:00-3:30-6:30-11:00

6:30	Skim newspapers. Watch TV news.
7:15	Briefing by National Security Adviser on overnight international developments. Briefing by Chief of staff and by Appointments secretary.
8:15	Breakfast with spouse.
9:00	Read through 30-page country-wide news summary prepared by assistants.
10:00	Meet with Budget Director, Secretary of Treasury, and Council of Economic Advisers on budget and tax matters.
11:30	Sign bill in Oval Office ceremony.
12:00	Lunch with several key House members.
1:15	Nap, shower, change clothes.
2:00	Discuss diplomacy with European foreign minister.
3:00	Final briefing for televised press conference at 3:30.
4:00	Present medal to family of American killed by terrorists.
4:30	Briefing by CIA
5:30	Sign various documents
6:00	Review drafts of two upcoming speeches
6:30	Shower and change clothes. Fly to New York City for dinner and major speech.
11:00	Discuss day's activities with spouse. Read memoranda. Go to bed.

Figure 15-1

Here, President Clinton, acting as chief diplomat, meets with President Boris Yeltsin of Russia. What other roles does the President assume?

Carrying Out the Roles

How Presidents carry out their roles depends on many factors, including their personalities, their views of the job, the issues they are dealing with, and public pressure. Each role influences the other; none can be isolated. And this overlapping nature of presidential roles can cause conflicts. As chief of state, for instance, the President often addresses the nation about important issues. But in an election year, the President, as party leader, may use such an address to ask for support of party programs. Is this fair? Only a skillful chief executive is able to blend these conflicting roles successfully, so that the overall position of the presidency is still seen as fair and open.

Section Review

1. What various roles are filled by the President?

2. Who helps the President carry out the role of chief diplomat?

3. **Challenge:** In your opinion, how does the President's role as leader of a political party influence his or her other presidential roles?

2 The Changing Presidency

A total of 41 men have held the office of President of the United States. Their beliefs, leadership styles, and personalities have affected how we view the presidency and what we expect from our national leader.

The office of President has changed considerably since George Washington took office in 1789. What factors have influenced the power held by the President?

Historical Development

Many powers that a President exercises are not directly stated in the Constitution. Instead, they have developed over the years to meet changing needs and circumstances. The Founders probably had no idea that the presidency would change so, but as government and society became more complex, presidential power grew. Today, the President is recognized as the center of authority in our government and one of the truly influential leaders in the world.

THE CONSTITUTION

One of the most important tasks that faced the delegates to the Constitutional Convention was creating an executive branch for the federal government. The delegates wanted the source of political power to rest with the people, not in the hands of a monarch. But, the nation still needed a leader, an individual who could unite the people behind the new government.

For weeks, delegates quarreled over how much power the executive branch should have and what the branch's relation to Congress should be. Some delegates, like Alexander Hamilton of New York, favored a strong executive, independent of the legislature. Others agreed with Roger Sherman of Connecticut that a weak executive, appointed by Congress and subject to its will, was best. Still others wanted to place executive duties in the hands of two or three persons who would have equal powers.

Finally, the delegates compromised and created the office of President, with powers that were only vaguely defined. It would be up to the individuals who held the post to better define and shape these powers.

EARLY PRESIDENTS

The Framers of the Constitution expected George Washington to be the first President, and they created the office with him in mind. Washington possessed many of the qualities they thought a chief executive should have: dignity, fairness, wisdom, and, above all, the ability to balance executive authority with the rights of citizens.

Washington was the first in a line of chief executives who more clearly defined the duties of the President. He set precedents that future Presidents would follow, including establishing a Cabinet, holding regular Cabinet meetings, and limiting the number of presidential terms to two. Washington also set precedents for protocol and etiquette for official state functions. During his two terms in office, Washington displayed the integrity and ability necessary to launch a new government and showed that a strong chief executive could function well within the system.

The Presidents who succeeded Washington continued to define and change the office. Some early Presidents, most notably Andrew Jackson and Abraham Lincoln, greatly strengthened the presidency. Jackson believed that the President was a direct representative of the people, and the times and circumstances made Jackson the leader of a rising democratic movement in the 1820s. A number of states rewrote their election laws to say that members of the electoral college would be chosen by popular vote, rather than by state legislatures. The people thus would share a more direct voice in electing the President. Since this change was in place in 1828, many historians consider Andrew Jackson the first popularly elected President.

Jackson once stated that the "executive must. . .be guided by his own

Andrew Jackson helped to expand the power of the presidency. What was Jackson's philosophy concerning the office that he held?

opinions of the Constitution," and, once in office, Jackson took that philosophy to heart. Unlike previous Presidents who used the veto sparingly and only when they considered a bill unconstitutional, Jackson vetoed bills for other reasons as well. For example, his veto of the 1832 bill to recharter the National Bank was based in part on disagreements with Congress. Jackson's use of the veto extended the President's powers and changed forever the relationship between the executive and legislative branches.

Just as Jackson had extended presidential power over the legislative process, Lincoln greatly strengthened presidential war powers. During the Civil War, Lincoln enlarged the army and navy beyond congressional limits

PRESIDENTS OF THE UNITED STATES

NAME	STATE*	AGE ON TAKING OFFICE	POLITICAL PARTY	YEARS IN OFFICE
George Washington	Virginia	57	Federalist	1789–1797
John Adams	Massachusetts	61	Federalist	1797–1801
Thomas Jefferson	Virginia	57	Democratic-Republican	1801–1809
James Madison	Virginia	57	Democratic-Republican	1809–1817
James Monroe	Virginia	58	Democratic-Republican	1817–1825
John Quincy Adams	Massachusetts	57	Democratic-Republican	1825–1829
Andrew Jackson	Tennessee	61	Democratic	1829–1837
Martin Van Buren	New York	54	Democratic	1837–1841
William Henry Harrison	Ohio	68	Whig	1841
John Tyler	Virginia	51	Whig	1841–1845
James K. Polk	Tennessee	49	Democratic	1845–1849
Zachary Taylor	Louisiana	64	Whig	1849–1850
Millard Fillmore	New York	50	Whig	1850–1853
Franklin Pierce	New Hampshire	48	Democratic	1853–1857
James Buchanan	Pennsylvania	65	Democratic	1857–1861
Abraham Lincoln	Illinois	52	Republican	1861–1865
Andrew Johnson	Tennessee	56	Democratic	1865–1869
Ulysses S. Grant	Illinois	46	Republican	1869–1877
Rutherford B. Hayes	Ohio	54	Republican	1877–1881
James A. Garfield	Ohio	49	Republican	1881
Chester A. Arthur	New York	50	Republican	1881–1885
Grover Cleveland	New York	47	Democratic	1885–1889
Benjamin Harrison	Indiana	55	Republican	1889–1893
Grover Cleveland	New York	55	Democratic	1893–1897
William McKinley	Ohio	54	Republican	1897–1901
Theodore Roosevelt	New York	42	Republican	1901–1909
William Howard Taft	Ohio	51	Republican	1909–1913
Woodrow Wilson	New Jersey	56	Democratic	1913–1921
Warren G. Harding	Ohio	55	Republican	1921–1923
Calvin Coolidge	Massachusetts	51	Republican	1923–1929
Herbert Hoover	California	54	Republican	1929–1933
Franklin D. Roosevelt	New York	51	Democratic	1933–1945
Harry S Truman	Missouri	60	Democratic	1945–1953
Dwight D. Eisenhower	New York	62	Republican	1953–1961
John F. Kennedy	Massachusetts	43	Democratic	1961–1963
Lyndon B. Johnson	Texas	55	Democratic	1963–1969
Richard M. Nixon	New York	55	Republican	1969–1974
Gerald R. Ford	Michigan	61	Republican	1974–1977
James E. Carter	Georgia	52	Democratic	1977–1981
Ronald W. Reagan	California	69	Republican	1981–1989
George Bush	Texas	64	Republican	1989–1993
William J. Clinton	Arkansas	46	Democratic	1993–

*State of residence when elected

Figure 15-2

and spent millions of dollars without consulting Congress. In addition, Lincoln was sharply criticized for going beyond his powers when he suppressed activities of Northerners sympathetic to the Confederate cause. In 1862 he announced that individuals "guilty of any disloyal practices, affording aid and comfort to rebels" should be tried by court-martial and denied the protection of habeas corpus. By the end of the war, more than 13,000 persons had been arrested and imprisoned by military authority. This action was condemned by critics as an infringement of civil liberties, but Lincoln contended that anyone who opposed a war fought in defense of constitutional government was not protected by the Constitution.

It is wrong to assume, however, that the powers of the President increased with every new administration. Periods of presidential growth alternated with periods of declining power. Between the administrations of Jefferson and Jackson, and again between Jackson and Lincoln, mostly "weak" Presidents were in the White House. Later in the 1800s, powerful members of Congress, judges, and business interests chipped away at the power of the President.

MODERN PRESIDENTS

Presidential power shot up dramatically during the 1900s. Long periods of national emergency during war and economic depression *forced* Presidents to take a more active role. At these times, the chief executive often instituted social reforms, increased government regulations, and supplied leadership for our nation that Congress and the courts could not provide.

Theodore Roosevelt is considered the first "activist" President of the 1900s. Upon succeeding to the presidency after the assassination of President William McKinley in 1901, Roosevelt showed he favored a broad view of presidential powers, following what became known as the stewardship model. Roosevelt explained this idea in his autobiography:

. . .every executive officer in high position was a steward of the people, bound actively and affirmatively to do all he could for the people. . . . My belief was that it was not [the President's] right but his duty to do anything that the needs of the nation demanded, unless such action was forbidden by the Constitution or by the laws.

President Theodore Roosevelt (center) appears with a group of coal miners in the early 1900s. How did Roosevelt view his presidential power?

343

Roosevelt believed that the President should play a dominant role in the American system, and he worked to expand the power and influence of his administration both at home and abroad. Roosevelt changed the presidency in another way, too. More than any President before him, he understood the role the media could play in getting the President's views on issues across to the people.

Roosevelt's view of the presidency was shared by Woodrow Wilson, whose policies further added to the authority of the office. Wilson was the first President to introduce social reform legislation, and, during World War I, he regulated the economy to carry out the war.

After a lessening of presidential influence in the 1920s, Franklin D. Roosevelt took presidential power to its highest level. During the Great Depression of the 1930s, he persuaded Congress to support many social and economic programs to restore the failing economy. During World War II, Roosevelt used his executive authority to manage the war effort, placing government controls on industry and regulating trade. In addition, he placed restrictions on civil liberties in order to control strikes, and he authorized the relocation of more than 100,000 Japanese-Americans to wartime camps in isolated areas.

After 1945 the United States emerged as a leading world power and became involved in a complicated web of relations with other countries. At the same time, the federal government continued to be involved in promoting the general welfare of its citizens through economic and social programs. Both developments kept the presidency at the center of government, and presidential power continued to expand. Harry Truman used the powers of the office to oppose the spread of communism in Europe and Asia, and he became recognized as the leader of the anti-Communist nations around the world. Although Truman's successor, Dwight D. Eisenhower, preferred a reduced role, the federal government had already expanded to the point that Eisenhower could not completely reverse the trend toward a strong presidency.

This trend continued in the 1960s. Without a declaration of war by Congress, Presidents John F. Kennedy and Lyndon B. Johnson committed American advisors and troops to fight in Vietnam. Both Presidents also strongly supported federal laws to protect civil rights and bring about social reforms.

By the 1970s, however, there was a strong reaction among Americans against the growth of presidential authority, resulting mainly from our nation's involvement in the Vietnam War and Richard Nixon's alleged abuse of power in the Watergate scandal. Many people claimed that an

President Lyndon B. Johnson signed the Civil Rights Bill into law in 1964. What type of presidential support characterized Johnson's administration?

imperial, or kingly, presidency had developed since the 1930s. Critics contended that the role of commander in chief had overwhelmed the President's other roles, turning the office into more of a military post than that of a leader of the people. Others criticized the practice of Presidents resorting to secrecy or withholding information from the public and Congress. Some warned that presidential power had grown so much that Presidents felt they could govern without regard to constitutional restraints.

By the mid-1970s, many people believed that limits *had* to be placed on the powers of the President. At the same time, Congress asserted its authority by taking back some of the war and emergency powers it had given to the President. Presidents Gerald Ford and Jimmy Carter took seriously the public's reaction against the "imperial presidency." Both men tried to develop a more informal style of governing that stressed the President's role as a moral leader. Each promoted the idea of an open administration and did away with much of the ceremony surrounding White House activities. But, Ford's ability to govern effectively was hampered because he was an "appointed," rather than an elected, President. And Carter's inability to persuade Congress to adopt many of his programs was seen as a weakness. As the decade came to a close, some suggested that the "imperial presidency" had been replaced by the "imperiled" presidency.

By the 1980s, the memories of Vietnam and Watergate were fading. The nation was facing difficult economic and international issues, and opinion polls indicated that Americans wanted stronger presidential leadership. Many saw the election of Ronald Reagan in 1980 as a move toward a stronger presidency.

To emphasize their informal style, President and Mrs. Jimmy Carter walked to the White House on inauguration day. In what other ways did Carter work to abolish the image of the "imperial presidency"?

Modern Influences

Although Presidents in the past used the office to expand their powers, and in some cases used their powers to handle emergencies without regard to the Constitution, such actions were more the exception than the rule. Today, the world is a much different place than it was when George Washington took the oath of office. The role the chief executive must fill has changed as well. Now, Presidents must deal on a daily basis with many complex problems. Among these are regional conflicts that spring up in many parts of the world, the existence of huge stockpiles of nuclear weapons throughout the world, and pressing social and economic concerns. Responding to problems of such magnitude requires a strong central authority.

These two characters are discussing the relationship between Congress and the President. How might a President's style help to determine his or her relationship with Congress?

THE PRESIDENT BLAMES CONGRESS AND CONGRESS BLAMES THE PRESIDENT! WHAT'S GOING ON HERE?

NO-FAULT GOVERNMENT—

Washington Star Syndicate. Inc

3-19

BRICKMAN

Because the presidency consists of one person, it can respond more quickly to these emergencies than can the other two branches. For instance, although Congress tries to set guidelines for foreign policy, it allows the President a large share of power to work out relations with other countries. The Supreme Court also recognizes the need for "one voice" to speak for the country and tends to avoid placing many limitations on presidential actions.

The growth of the federal bureaucracy, headed by the President in the role of chief executive, has also contributed to the expansion of presidential power. In addition, daily media exposure has made the President the most visible figure in American politics. For all these reasons, many of us now look first to the President, rather than to Congress and the courts, to solve our nation's problems.

Power, Management, and Politics

Each of our Presidents has had an effect on presidential authority. Some have greatly expanded the powers of the office, others have limited it. In large part, this is due to their attitudes toward power, their management styles, and the influence of politics on their leadership.

POWER
Presidents have had differing ideas about the powers of the office, depending on their interpretation of the Constitution. James Madison and William Howard Taft were among those who held a "strict construction" view. Thus, they limited the use of their powers to enforcing and administering the laws. Those who adhered to this view are sometimes labeled "weak" Presidents.

"Strong" Presidents hold a "loose construction" view of the presidency. Such Presidents as Jackson and Lincoln viewed the powers of the office broadly and thereby expanded presidential authority. But in spite of the differences between "weak" and "strong" Presidents, there has been an overall movement toward **presidential government.**

MANAGEMENT
How Presidents manage the people around them and how much trust they place in their own instincts can also affect presidential authority. Some Presidents tend to make all the decisions and, consequently, believe that to be effective they must know every aspect of every issue. Critics claim, however, that those Presidents who try to master every detail of our nation's complex problems may eventually lose sight of the *broad* themes

presidential government
a government in which the President exercises stronger leadership than does Congress and the courts

that define their administrations and serve as rallying points for the people. Such detail-oriented leaders may have trouble seeing the "big picture" and find it difficult to make important decisions quickly. Thus, their ability to lead the nation effectively may be hampered.

On the other hand, some Presidents prefer to act as "chairpersons." They establish general policies and principles and then delegate authority to others. These Presidents believe they are "staying above politics" by not getting caught up in the day-to-day operation of the government. A danger here is that Presidents who delegate power to others may lose control of the reins of government, often not knowing what is being done or said in their name. This lack of knowledge may hurt a President's ability to lead the nation. President Reagan, for instance, suffered a loss of prestige when he said he knew nothing about the illegal activities carried out by certain advisers during the Iran/contra affair.

Although some Presidents have been primarily detail-oriented and others have been "chairpersons," most chief executives have taken a middle road. They master some details and leave others to their aides. Most observers believe that a President's energy, skills, and intellect are best used in this way.

POLITICS

As you have learned, the person who occupies the presidency must fill a number of demanding roles. But a President who hopes to serve a second term also must follow the campaign trail. This means, critics claim, that the last two years of the President's first term are directed largely toward winning reelection—at the expense

Oliver North was a key figure in the Iran/contra affair. His actions led some to question President Reagan's involvement in national affairs. Why did this concern affect Reagan's prestige as President?

CASE STUDY: PRESIDENTIAL LEADERSHIP

RATING THE PRESIDENTS

Americans seem to rate nearly everything that touches their lives. From the top 10 movies, the top 20 football teams, the top 40 songs, to best seller book lists, Americans want to know what is number one and what is at the bottom. So it should come as no surprise that the nation's Presidents also have been rated.

In 1948 historian Arthur M. Schlesinger asked 55 historians to rate the nation's past Presidents as great, near great, average, below average, or failure and to rank them within each category. The results of his poll were as follows.

Great: Lincoln, Washington, F. D. Roosevelt, Wilson, Jefferson, Jackson

Near Great: T. Roosevelt, Cleveland, J. Adams, Polk

Average: J.Q. Adams, Monroe, Hayes, Madison, Van Buren, Taft, Arthur, McKinley, A. Johnson, Hoover, B. Harrison

Below Average: Tyler, Coolidge, Fillmore, Taylor, Buchanan, Pierce

Failure: Grant, Harding

Schlesinger repeated his poll in 1962 with new participants and got similar results. Two Presidents were added—Truman was ranked "near great" while Eisenhower was placed in the "average" category.

The Schlesinger polls were very popular and soon others began to appear, expanding the number of participants and including current Presidents. Although those at the top of Schlesinger's polls stayed the same in later polls, Presidents in the middle changed as new scholarship revealed new insights. For example, ranked at the bottom of the "average" category in 1962, Eisenhower moved up to "near great" in a 1981 poll. Interestingly, the results of later polls were often very hard on recent occupants of the Oval Office. For example, the 1981 poll rated Jimmy Carter and Richard Nixon as failures.

Not to be outdone by scholars, the Gallup and Harris polling organizations have asked average Americans for their ratings. These polls reveal some surprising differences between the public view and historians' views of past Presidents. John Kennedy, rated near "average" by the scholars, usually ends up the greatest U.S. President in the public's eyes. A 1987 Harris poll, for example, ranked Kennedy first, followed by

Franklin Roosevelt and Ronald Reagan.

Although many people find presidential ratings interesting, the practice also has its critics. Some say it is impossible to judge all Presidents by the same criteria. Each had to face his own set of problems, in his own times, with the resources he had on hand. Some were able to meet great challenges and do great things, while others were not so fortunate. Critics of presidential ratings note that most "great" and "near great" Presidents served at a time of national crisis, when strong leadership was required. In contrast, those ranked "average" or below served, for the most part, when strong presidential power was neither needed nor desired by Congress or the people. But who is to say, these critics ask, that under a different set of circumstances, Presidents currently rated "average" or below would not have achieved a higher rating?

Shakespeare said "Some are born great, some achieve greatness, and some have greatness thrust upon [th]em." Your "rating" of presidential ratings may depend on whether you think this is true.

1. Using Schlesinger's categories, rate the last five Presidents. On what criteria did you base your judgment?

2. In your opinion, are great Presidents made by their times, or is their greatness due to personal qualities? Explain.

of other more important duties. One proposed solution to this problem is to amend the Constitution, limiting the President to a single six-year term in office.

Those who favor such a change believe it would result in more responsible leadership. A President not worried about reelection, for instance, could devote the time and energy needed to lead the nation. A President not concerned with political ''favors'' could appoint more qualified officials. And, a President freed from campaigning could exercise greater independence in making decisions.

Yet the amendment has never received full support. One reason is that many people fear that such a change would result in Presidents who are *less* responsible to the people. A President removed from campaigning, they claim, has six long years to ignore the wishes of the people. Only by the frequent elections called for in the Constitution will the President be held accountable. Historian Clinton Rossiter offers another view:

It troubles many. . .to watch their chief of state dabbling in politics, smiling on political hacks. . . .Yet if he is to persuade Congress [and] achieve a loyal and cohesive administration, if he is to be elected in the first place (and reelected in the second), he must put his hands firmly to the plow of politics.

Presidents and the People

Over the years, Americans have developed a love/hate relationship with their Presidents. On the one hand, we respect the power and authority of the office and rally around the President in times of national crisis. And the sorrow of the people when a President dies in office shows

how deeply Americans identify with the individual.

At the same time, no other government official faces as much criticism and ridicule. We expect a lot from our Presidents and are not against expressing our disapproval when we believe a President has failed.

Some political observers point out that people's expectations of the President often are contradictory. Most Americans, for example, want a President who shows compassion. Yet, at the same time, we are unyielding when the President is confronted with a tough decision.

Similarly, Americans want a President who sets high goals and inspires them with great dreams. But we also believe a leader should not promise what cannot be delivered. Then, too, Americans expect a President to be bold and decisive, but those who are too bold are viewed as ''dictators.'' Such conflicting expectations place

Here, President John F. Kennedy talks with runner Wilma Rudolph at the White House. Many people regard Kennedy as one of our most ''positive'' Presidents. How can the President's power be affected by his or her interpretation of the Constitution?

Presidential Leadership   349

Here, President George Bush takes the oath of office. As Americans, we expect a great deal from our President. Why do some believe that our expectations are too high?

Presidents in a no-win situation. No matter what action they take, a large number of Americans will criticize it.

A New Perspective

Ever since the foundations of our government were laid, Americans traditionally have turned to the President for leadership in times of crisis or uncertainty. In 1789 George Washington received word at his home in Virginia that he had been elected the first President. He then set off on horseback for New York City, the temporary capital, to take the oath of office and begin his duties. For two weeks, along the 240-mile route, Washington was greeted everywhere by adoring crowds. They displayed flags, shot off fireworks, and held parades in his honor. Undoubtedly, it was the longest inauguration parade in American history. But it was also a collective sigh of relief from the nation. Finally, someone was in charge.

The public's perception of the President has changed little since Washington's time. In fact, expectations that the President will solve our nation's problems have increased. According to American novelist John Steinbeck, these expectations put too much pressure on the President:.

We give the President more work than a man can do, more responsibility than a man should take, more pressure than a man can bear. We abuse him often and rarely praise him. We wear him out, use him up, eat him up. . . .he is ours and we exercise the right to destroy him.

Some observers say that conflicting expectations and the complexity of today's issues make it impossible for the chief executive to be an effective leader. We elect Presidents to do a superhuman job and then are disappointed when they fail. To avoid *appearing* as failures, Presidents sometimes shift the blame to Congress or the courts. In recent years, some Presidents have even avoided dealing directly with issues and have presented the people with more "style" than substance. According to some observers, Americans, by demanding so much from their Presidents, have helped create an institution that is isolated from, and less responsive to, their needs.

To remove some of the pressure from the presidency, some suggest that other institutions take a stronger lead in governing the nation. Congress, the courts, and political parties need to assert their power and become more responsive and capable parts of government. They also need to rebuild their prestige in the public eye.

Others say that the Constitution should be changed to limit Presidents to a single six-year term in office, claiming that this would remove the pressure of running for reelection. It would also give the President the opportunity to establish long-term programs, rather than short-term solutions designed to win votes.

Still other observers claim that Americans must stop thinking of the President as the only individual in government with the power to solve their problems. Instead, we should look to other levels of government, such as governors, mayors, city councils, and other local officials, for creative solutions and effective leadership.

Finally, some claim that it is time for Americans to lower their expectations of what the President can do. Over the past 200 years, the office of President has changed to fit new circumstances and political realities. Expectations must also change if Presidents are to be effective leaders. Despite these concerns, it is likely that we will continue to expect much from our Presidents.

Section Review

1. What are two precedents established by George Washington as the nation's first President?

2. How did Andrew Jackson's use of the veto affect the role of the President?

3. What is the main difference between Presidents who are labeled strict constructionists and those who are labeled loose constructionists?

4. How may the public's expectations affect a President's ability to lead?

5. **Challenge:** Are you for or against the proposed amendment to limit the President's term? Explain?

Summary

1. The President has many different roles, including chief executive, chief of state, commander in chief, chief diplomat, chief legislator, and political party leader.

2. How a President carries out the roles of office depends on many factors, including the President's attitude toward power, management style, and politics.

3. Since the Constitution does not clearly define the powers of the President, it has been left to the nation's chief executives to define and develop the office.

4. Presidential power and authority has grown over the last 200 years.

5. George Washington established many precedents for future Presidents, including establishing a cabinet and determining White House protocol.

6. Since the beginning of the 1900s, presidential power has grown due to national emergencies, such as wars and economic depressions.

7. Strict constructionist Presidents believe that the Constitution limits their powers to enforce and administer the laws.

8. Loose constructionist Presidents believe that their powers go beyond what is expressly stated in the Constitution.

9. The way a President manages can affect the amount of power that a President exerts.

10. During the first term of office, some Presidents devote much time and energy to campaigning for reelection.

11. Americans have conflicting expectations of the President.

Chapter 15 Review

★ Building Vocabulary

Based on the roles of the President discussed in this chapter, write two paragraphs describing the development of presidential government in the United States.

★ Reviewing Facts

1. What are six roles typically carried out by the President of the United States?
2. Give one example of the President filling the role of chief of state.
3. What were two proposals given at the Constitutional Convention on the creation of the office of President?
4. What belief of Andrew Jackson helped make him the leader of a rising democratic movement in the 1820s?
5. Why did presidential power grow in the twentieth century?
6. What factors after 1945 resulted in continued expansion of presidential power?
7. In what ways did John Kennedy and Lyndon Johnson continue the trend toward strong presidential government in the 1960s?
8. What are some of the complex problems modern Presidents must deal with on a daily basis?
9. Describe one "conflicting expectation" Americans may have for the President.
10. Explain how a single six-year term might relieve some leadership pressure from the President.
11. What factors have influenced either the growth or limitation of the powers of the President?

★ Analyzing Facts

1. Imagine that you are asked to redefine the job of President of the United States. As part of your responsibilities, you must eliminate two roles the President traditionally has filled. What two roles would you remove from the presidential job description? Why?

2. From what you have learned in this chapter about the growth and development of presidential power over the last 200 years, do you think the President has too much power today? Explain.
3. Several suggestions to make Presidents more effective leaders are outlined in this chapter. Which suggestion do you think is best? Why?
4. Some people believe that the President has too much power in foreign affairs. Do you agree or disagree? Explain.

★ Evaluating Ideas

1. Some Presidents have freely used the veto power over legislation. Others have hardly used it at all. How do you account for this difference between Presidents? Explain your answer.
2. Theodore Roosevelt once said, "Oh, if I could only be President and Congress too for just ten minutes." What do you think President Roosevelt meant when he made that statement?
3. Do you agree with some experts who claim that the job of being President is too much for one person to handle? Why or why not?
4. In a time of peace, which of the President's roles do you think are the most important? in wartimes? in an economic depression? Explain.

Using Your
Civic Participation Journal

Review the tally of opinions of presidential job performance you kept in your Civic Participation Journal. Work with the entire class to compile the results of your polls and construct a circle graph showing the results of the survey.

★ Critical Thinking
Making Generalizations

A generalization is a broad statement, without any details or evidence, about a certain topic. Generalizations serve many purposes. They can be used to summarize several pieces of information about the same topic, or they can help in making evaluations and predictions. However, despite their purpose, to be useful generalizations must be supported by evidence.

Explanation For example, if you know the generalization that management style, personality, and attitude about power all affect a President's ability to lead, you can use this generalization to evaluate and determine the effectiveness of the current President. Although they can be handy, there are two limitations to be aware of when using generalizations.

First, while generalizations are usually true, they are not always true. For example, if you were to examine one presidential election and find that the majority of Americans did not vote, and then examined several other elections, always reaching the same conclusion, you would be safe to generalize that the majority of Americans do not vote in presidential elections. However, if you found a presidential election or two where the majority of Americans *did* vote, your generalization would still be true. So generalizations are not absolutely accurate. They are only "generally" true.

Second, generalizations should be supported with as much evidence as possible. Be aware of the "hasty generalization," the broad statement made without careful consideration of all the facts. Generalizations are best when they are tested over time and under differing circumstances. Hasty generalizations are often based on opinions or emotions rather than on factual evidence.

The following guidelines will help you make good generalizations.

1. To make generalizations, summarize several pieces of information into one broad conclusion.

2. Have ample evidence available to make and support your generalizations; avoid hasty generalizations.

3. Remember that since they are broad statements, generalizations need not *always* be true. They only need to *usually* be true.

Practice Read the following statements and then make a generalization about presidential power.

1. The Constitution provides only vague explanations of presidential power.

2. Since the time of Abraham Lincoln, Presidents have expanded their war powers.

3. Beginning with Theodore Roosevelt, most twentieth-century Presidents can be described as activist Presidents.

4. The President is considered the most powerful figure in American government today.

From this information you should be able to generalize that presidential power has greatly expanded since the Constitution was written.

Independent Practice Study the photograph below of President Harry S Truman. What generalization about his attitude toward presidential authority can you make based on the sign?

Chapter 16

The Federal Bureaucracy

Every President relies on the federal bureaucracy for the day-to-day operation of the government. This bureaucracy is divided into three areas—the Cabinet departments, the Executive Office of the President, and the independent agencies. Because the 3 million people that work in these areas are responsible—either directly or indirectly—to the President, they are part of the executive branch.

Chapter Preview

TERMS TO KNOW
Cabinet, secretaries, executive departments, staff agencies, line agencies, classified employees, unclassified employees, iron triangles

READ TO DISCOVER
- what role the Cabinet plays in presidential decision making.
- who makes up the Executive Office of the President.
- how the civil service developed.
- what the functions of federal agencies are.
- how the three types of independent government agencies function.

★ ★ ★ ★ ★

Civic Participation Journal

The federal bureaucracy has grown so large that it affects almost everyone's daily life. Contact the local office of one of the agencies described in this chapter. Ask them to describe the role the agency plays in your community. Write your findings in your journal.

1 The Cabinet

Not mentioned in the Constitution, the **Cabinet** arose out of practical necessity. When George Washington created the first Cabinet in 1789, he held regular meetings on policy matters with the secretaries of state, treasury, and war and the attorney general. Today, the Cabinet is made up of the Vice President, the **secretaries** of the **executive departments,** and other officials chosen by the President. These have included the ambassador to the United Nations, the budget director, the United States trade representative, and one or two of the President's top aides in the Executive Branch.

The Cabinet has always been an informal group of advisers with no set number of members. But because of their high visibility, the secretaries of the executive departments often are viewed exclusively as "the Cabinet." Each secretary specializes in a specific government activity and heads a large number of agencies that help administer the duties of his or her department.

Over time, executive departments have come and gone or changed their functions. Thus, as the number of executive departments changes, so has the number of Cabinet secretaries. And while a President can reorganize the Cabinet, Congress must approve.

Selection

The President appoints the heads of the executive departments with the approval of the Senate. Rejections are rare. Out of 500 such nominations in American history, about a dozen have been turned down. Sometimes, however, nominees face difficult times in confirmation hearings before Senate committees. This may be due to events in the nominees' backgrounds or because members of Congress do not share their political views. Former Senator John Tower, for example, was President Bush's first choice to be secretary of defense. But after Senate investigations raised questions about Tower's personal affairs, his nomination was rejected.

In appointing members of the Cabinet, Presidents consider many factors. First, they try to choose individuals who are outstanding leaders and have broad experience in a given area, such as labor relations or foreign policy. Since each secretary heads a department that has thousands of employees, he or she also must be a good business manager. In addition, most Cabinet members belong to the President's political party.

Presidents also take into account the desires of special interest groups

Figure 16-1

THE PRESIDENT'S CABINET

Attorney General
Secretary of Agriculture
Secretary of Commerce
Secretary of Defense
Secretary of Education
Secretary of Energy
Secretary of Health
and Human Services
Secretary of Housing
and Urban Development
Secretary of the Interior
Secretary of Labor
Secretary of State
Secretary of Transportation
Secretary of the Treasury
Secretary of Veterans Affairs
Vice President
Other key advisers selected
by the President

that are directly affected by the actions of an executive department. The President, for instance, usually chooses someone who is liked by labor union leaders to be secretary of labor, or a well-known banker is named secretary of the treasury.

Geography, too, plays a role in Cabinet selection. The secretary of the interior, for example, usually is a person from a western state because of the West's vast amounts of federal lands. The secretary of agriculture often comes from one of the farming states of the Great Plains or the Midwest. If the President is from the West, people from the East and South may be appointed to the Cabinet in order to bring a balance of regions to the White House.

Another factor Presidents consider in filling Cabinet posts is the number of women and minorities being appointed. In recent years, public pressure has forced Presidents to seek a Cabinet that reflects the racial, ethnic, and religious composition of the country.

Franklin Roosevelt appointed the first woman to serve in the Cabinet when he named Frances T. Perkins to be his secretary of labor in 1933. Robert C. Weaver became the first black appointed to the Cabinet when Lyndon Johnson named him to head the newly created Department of Housing and Urban Development in 1966. And Ronald Reagan named the first Hispanic to the Cabinet when Lauro Cavazos become the secretary of education in 1988. Although most Presidents try to fill Cabinet posts with people they know, attempts to balance geographical, racial, and other factors sometimes can lead to a "government of strangers."

F.D.R.'s Secretary of Labor, Frances Perkins, shown here with workers in 1936, was the first woman to hold a Cabinet post. What factors influence Presidents in their Cabinet selections?

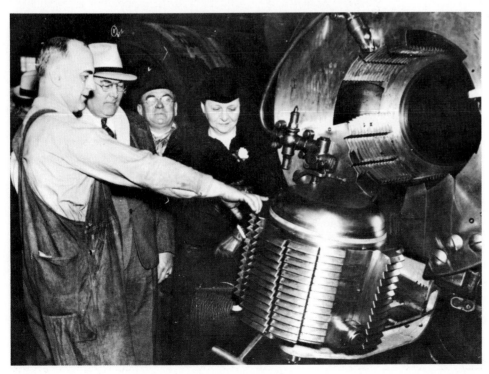

Conflicting Loyalties

As both department heads and advisers to the President, Cabinet members often are confronted with conflicting loyalties. The first loyalty of Cabinet members is supposed to be to the President because they were chosen to represent presidential policies to the rest of the executive branch and to members of Congress. Secretaries, then, are expected to fit the concerns of their departments into the President's programs. In addition, Cabinet members maintain close contacts with key legislators in order to help prepare and pass laws that support the President's policy goals. To do this, they often appear at congressional hearings to present information on issues concerning their departments.

At the same time, Cabinet members are the heads of their individual departments, and they push for their department's programs. Cabinet members listen to the needs of interest groups affected by their department's activities and often become spokespersons for these groups, sometimes to the point of undermining a President's policies.

When this happens, life may become difficult for a Cabinet member. Richard Nixon, for instance, appointed his long-time friend Robert Finch to head the Department of Health, Education, and Welfare (HEW) in 1969. Shortly after being confirmed, Finch was ordered by Nixon to cut HEW funds. But Finch believed the programs at HEW were vital to the public welfare and argued with the President to preserve the funds and jobs in HEW. Eventually, Finch was forced to resign.

Thus, Cabinet members may be caught in a dilemma of either supporting the President or their own individual departments. Because of these potential tugs-of-war, Cabinet members, on the whole, tend to move cautiously and shy away from bold actions that might upset established norms or the President's programs.

Hazel O'Leary (left), Secretary of Energy, and Federico Pēna (right), Secretary of Transportation, were appointed to the Clinton Cabinet in 1993. What are the functions of the Cabinet?

Seated next to George Washington (left) are members of the first Cabinet—Henry Knox, Alexander Hamilton, Thomas Jefferson, and Edmund Randolph. What effect do Cabinet members have on presidential decisions today?

Influence

The President determines the extent of the Cabinet's power and influence. In fact, the President is not required by law to form a Cabinet at all or to hold regular meetings. Nor are Presidents bound to follow the advice of their Cabinets. Abraham Lincoln is reported to have rejected a unanimous vote of his Cabinet, saying "Seven nays, one aye—the ayes have it." Lincoln's vote, of course, was the aye.

Some Presidents, such as George Washington, James Buchanan, and Warren Harding, relied heavily on their Cabinets for advice and assistance. Others, such as Woodrow Wilson, Theodore Roosevelt, and John Kennedy attached less importance to their Cabinets and rarely brought members together. In fact, Kennedy once referred to Cabinet meetings as "a waste of time."

Some Presidents have ignored their Cabinets altogether, preferring to get advice and ideas from others. Andrew Jackson, for instance, relied on a small group of friends and minor government officials for advice. When he called this group together, they often arrived at the rear doors of the White House and thus were referred to as the "Kitchen Cabinet." Franklin Roosevelt had a group of friends and advisers known as the "Brain Trust," who helped him construct many of the New Deal programs of the 1930s.

Traditionally, some department heads play a greater role in decision making than others. An "inner" and "outer" Cabinet usually develops in most administrations. By its very name, the inner Cabinet is closer to the President and has a greater role in making the important decisions. Including the secretaries of state, treasury, defense, and the attorney general, the inner Cabinet deals with broad, national issues such as the economy, national security, and foreign policy. On the other hand, the outer Cabinet includes the secretaries of agriculture, commerce, education,

President Clinton and his Cabinet meet in the White House. What role might future Cabinets have in the executive branch?

energy, health and human services, housing and urban development, interior, labor, transportation, and veterans' affairs. Note that these Cabinet secretaries push for very specific concerns and issues and tend to work less closely with the chief executive. Consequently, they are more active in the ranks of their departments than in national decisions.

Future of the Cabinet

Although most Presidents rely on advice from their inner Cabinets, the Cabinet as a whole has little effect on presidential decisions today. Since most members represent specific rather than national interests, the Cabinet often is not a cohesive group that advises the President with one voice. Consequently, most Presidents view Cabinet meetings as a chance to exchange information, not as formal policy planning sessions.

Some observers question the effectiveness of the Cabinet and wonder if it has lost its viability as an advisory body to the President. Many people believe that the responsibilities of members should be more clearly defined and that Cabinet meetings be used more effectively as open forums for the free exchange of views on the issues. Others, however, say the Cabinet in its present form works well because the concerns of particular groups are heard. These individual interests may lose a valuable voice in the White House if all Cabinet members concentrate on broad, national issues while ignoring the specifics.

Section Review

1. What were the three original Cabinet departments?

2. What factors does a President take into account when choosing Cabinet officers?

3. What was Andrew Jackson's "Kitchen Cabinet"?

4. Which four Cabinet members make up the "inner" Cabinet?

5. **Challenge:** What changes would you make to the Cabinet to improve its effectiveness as an advisory body to the President?

2 Executive Office of the President

Besides the Cabinet, the President is aided by the people who staff the Executive Office of the President (EOP). Although not really an "office," this vitally important part of the executive branch is made up of several agencies, advisory councils, and assorted assistants who work directly with the President.

President Franklin Roosevelt set up the Executive Office under the Reorganization Act of 1939. At that time, he needed assistance coping with the increased responsibilities brought on by the Great Depression. Since then, the EOP has become the most influential voice in presidential government, even surpassing the Cabinet.

The many divisions of the EOP perform countless functions, from advising the President on foreign and domestic policy to monitoring the economy. Other EOP agencies do more routine—but still extremely important—jobs such as outlining the President's daily schedule. Presidents, themselves, can change the structure of the EOP to suit their own particular management style. Thus, with each new administration, the EOP is likely to be altered in some way. Figure 16-2 shows the structure of the Executive Office.

White House Office

Of all the EOP divisions, the White House Office is the most important and has the closest contact with the President. It serves as a "command center," filtering information to the President or to an appropriate executive branch agency. Made up of the President's most trusted advisers, White House Office members, known as the White House staff, include presidential assistants; diplomatic, military, and economic specialists; and other aides. Most members are chosen by the President and do not need to be confirmed by Congress.

SIZE OF STAFF

Each President may have as large, or as small, a staff as desired. President James Buchanan hired the first government-paid White House secretary in 1857 to help him with his duties. By 1900 several dozen people served at a cost of less than a few hundred thousand dollars a year.

Today, the White House staff includes about 400 people and operates at a cost of several million dollars a year. Most of these officials work in the two crowded wings that adjoin the White House, shown in Figure 16-3. Because the White House is a relatively small office building, only the most powerful advisers have offices in the West Wing, where the President's Oval Office is located. Lower ranking officials must make do with offices in buildings near the White House.

ORGANIZATION

Who are these people who have such close connections to the President? Traditionally, the White House staff is organized into three levels. First, a tightly knit group of top aides reports

---

EXECUTIVE OFFICE OF THE PRESIDENT

White House Office
Office of Management and Budget
Council of Economic Advisers
National Security Council
Office of Policy Development
Office of the United States Trade Representative
Council on Environmental Quality
Office of Science and Technology Policy
Office of Administration

Figure 16-2

to the chief executive through a chief of staff, who is usually a close friend of the President. Middle-level White House staff members help to smooth the flow of presidential business but are not typically involved in decision making. The press secretary, for example, makes public statements for the President. He or she also relays information from the Oval Office to the reporters assigned to the White House. Finally, lower-level staffers include the President's personal physician, social secretaries who arrange state dinners and receptions, and the director of the staff for the First Lady. Although many of these officials have little daily contact with the President, they all work directly for him or her.

Four hundred people may seem like too many for a President to manage directly. Consequently, the Presidents have generally used different styles when managing their White House staffs. How Presidents do this often is dictated by how much information they wish to receive before making important decisions.

The traditional presidential management system has the heads of various offices reporting to one top aide—usually the chief of staff—who then reports directly to the President. Under this system, the chief of staff wields great power because all the information that the President reads or hears is "filtered" through this one person. In addition, the chief of staff acts as a "gate-keeper," controlling who can, and cannot, see the President. Recent Presidents, such as Nixon and Ford, worked according to the traditional White House system. Jimmy Carter, on the other hand, disliked putting too much power in the hands of one person. In his first two years as President, he worked without a chief of staff. Instead, Carter had several different aides reporting to him. This method became too cumbersome, however, and Carter eventually re-

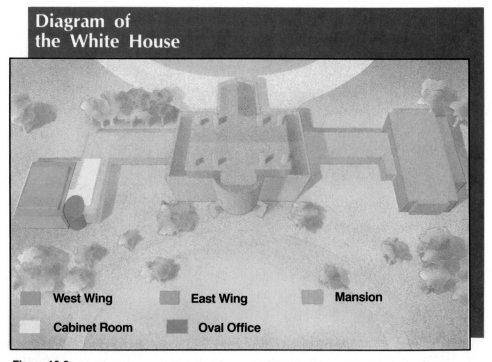

Diagram of the White House

West Wing   East Wing   Mansion

Cabinet Room   Oval Office

Figure 16-3

turned to the traditional system for the remainder of his term.

Ronald Reagan, in his first year as President, developed yet another system of White House management. He placed control of the White House Office in the hands of three aides—Presidential Counselor Edwin Meese, Chief of Staff James Baker, and Deputy Chief of Staff Michael Deaver.

George Bush brought back the traditional management system to the White House by having all aides report to his Chief of Staff John Sununu. When making important policy decisions, however, Bush preferred to personally hear opposing viewpoints from his top advisers before choosing an option.

President Clinton tried to maintain contact with all levels of his staff. For important decisions, he deferred to his top advisors such as Chief of Staff Leon E. Panetta.

BUDGET DIRECTOR

Although still part of the White House Office, several key advisers merit a separate category because of the help they give the President in vital areas of concern. Collectively, these staffers form an ''inner circle'' of friends, advisers, and confidants of the President. They provide the chief executive with information and advice needed to make decisions and also ensure that, once made, the decisions are carried out.

The Office of Management and Budget (OMB) helps the President prepare and administer the annual federal budget. As a result, the OMB is the largest agency in the EOP, making its director a powerful and influential White House staff member. Yet until recently, most budget directors were more concerned with accounting techniques than making

President Clinton relied on White House Chief of Staff Leon E. Panetta to perform many functions. How has the management style of the White House Office changed from one President to another in recent years?

public policy. But in the early 1980s, the position of budget director rose to new heights.

During the first year of the Reagan administration, Budget Director David Stockman changed the image of the office. He consistently presented controversial budgets aimed at checking the growth of, or eliminating, government spending in certain key areas, such as social welfare programs. Since Stockman's stormy tenure, budget directors have taken a more active role in dictating the nation's spending levels.

NATIONAL SECURITY ADVISER

Another key presidential aide is the national security adviser, who serves as the President's chief adviser on foreign policy. This person also directs the staff of the National Security

Council (NSC), a group of senior aides who helps the President conduct United States foreign policy.

The President can appoint the national security adviser without congressional confirmation. As such, he or she does not come under legislative scrutiny very often. Until recently, in fact, much of the work of the national security adviser and the NSC staff went unchecked by Congress.

As someone who consults with the President on foreign policy, the national security adviser often comes into conflict (sometimes publicly) with the secretary of state, the President's other main foreign policy adviser. During President Nixon's first term, National Security Adviser Henry Kissinger and Secretary of State William Rogers often did not see eye-to-eye on foreign policy matters. After several public battles, Rogers eventually resigned. Jimmy Carter experienced the same problems with his National Security Adviser Zbigniew Brzezinski and Secretary of State Cyrus Vance. And during the Reagan administration, the "free reign" of the national security adviser to conduct foreign policy without congressional consent was questioned when investigations revealed a secret plan by the NSC staff to secure the release of American hostages.

In the mid-1980s, National Security Adviser Robert McFarlane and his successor Vice Admiral John Poindexter oversaw a secret operation to sell arms to Iran in exchange for the release of United States hostages held in Lebanon by pro-Iranian forces. In addition, the profits from the arms sale were to be diverted to rebels, called Contras, who were fighting the pro-Communist government in Nicaragua. Although the plan did succeed in freeing some of the hostages, the result of congressional hearings and government investigations into the matter decreased the power of the NSC staff—and the national security adviser—to freely conduct the nation's foreign policy.

SPECIAL COUNSEL

A third adviser, the special counsel, serves as the administration's private lawyer. Although the attorney general, head of the Department of Justice, can give the President legal advice, he or she serves as the nation's lawyer. The special counsel, on the other hand, is the President's own personal attorney and gives advice on a vast number of legal concerns. The special counsel, for example, checks the legality of any proposed legislation, reviews treaties, oversees the selection of federal judges, and helps the Federal Bureau of Investigation (FBI) conduct security checks for presidential appointees. But most importantly, the special counsel often is asked to judge the potential actions of the President and White House staffers. As such, he or she has the power to veto executive decisions on the grounds that they may be considered illegal.

STAFF POWERS

Top members of the White House staff are close friends and loyal supporters of the President. They hold the same views as the President and try to promote them. Because of this loyalty, Presidents today tend to rely more heavily on their staffs than on the Cabinet, members of Congress, or party leaders for advice. Thus, the White House staff exerts considerable influence and control over executive branch decision making. They summarize issues and possible policy choices for the President and develop legislative and political strategies.

As Director of the FBI, Louis Freeh heads the federal government's chief investigative agency, which is an agency located within the Department of Justice. How does the FBI assist the White House Office?

White House staffers work out agreements among Cabinet members, legislators, and special interest groups. In addition, they work to project a positive image of the President to the media and the nation.

In recent years, the President's chief advisers have been given even more power and responsibility in making decisions. Ronald Reagan, more than most Presidents, depended on his aides to present policy choices that he would then accept, change, or refuse. His aides generally had a large role in carrying out White House affairs.

In contrast, Bush appointed many close friends to Cabinet posts, not to White House staff positions, as is usually the case. Of the 14 Cabinet secretaries, Bush had known 10 for at least a decade or more and tended to consult with them—either individually or in small groups—when wrestling with big decisions. As one White House aide put it, "The Cabinet has played a very important role in all major decisions. [Bush] wants them to be running things—not the White House staff. He wants the staff to serve as staff." But even in an administration such as Bush's, where the Cabinet took an assertive role in the decision-making process, most observers say that power inevitably drifts to the White House staff. A Cabinet secretary's tendency to protect his or her department's interests often forces the President to seek more "neutral" advice from the White House staff.

This growth of power of the staff is controversial. Many people claim that the present system makes Presidents too dependent on their staffs. And, as unelected officials, staff members have too much influence on presidential decision making and often isolate the chief executive from Congress, the people, and outside opinions. In addition, White House staffers may give the President only the advice they think he or she wants to hear.

Those who defend the system claim that in spite of drawbacks, it is a good working arrangement. They believe it is a natural consequence of the growth of the presidency. As the power of the President's office has increased, so has the need for a staff to help carry out its many duties.

Staff Agencies

Besides the White House Office, the EOP is made up of several **staff agencies** that provide advice and information on a variety of issues. The Office of Management and Budget, headed by the budget director discussed earlier, helps the President prepare and administer the annual federal budget and is the largest agency in the EOP. The National Security Council, another agency mentioned earlier, helps the President conduct American foreign policy and directs many of the operations of the Central Intelligence Agency (CIA). The Office of Policy Development, the Council of Economic Advisers, the Council on Environmental Quality, the Office of Science and Technology Policy, and the Office of Administration are other staff agencies and are presented in more detail in the Federal Bureaucracy Handbook that appears after this chapter.

The President appoints the heads of staff agencies. The President tries to appoint people who are loyal to the administration's goals and policies, but often is bombarded with requests for staff agency jobs by members of Congress and special interest groups. And, sometimes the President chooses to appoint people to these positions in return for political favors.

staff agencies agencies that support the President and the White House Office

The size of individual staff agencies and the number of these agencies as a whole can vary from administration to administration, depending upon the issues a President wishes to concentrate on while in office. For example, President Lyndon Johnson established the Office of Economic Opportunity (OEO) to help implement his Great Society job programs. But President Richard Nixon eliminated this agency in 1975. The newest staff agency in the EOP is the Small Business Administration, which was added to the EOP as a Cabinet level position in 1994. This office is charged with protecting the interests of small businesses that are so important to the smooth functioning of the free enterprise system in the United States today.

Office of the Vice President

The Vice President has certain functions in the federal bureaucracy. He or she takes part in all Cabinet meetings and, by law, is a member of the National Security Council.

Generally, Vice Presidents in the modern era also have focused on two or three issues during their terms. As Vice President during the Reagan administration, for example, George Bush headed the White House Special Situation Group, a crisis management team, and was the administration's spokesperson for national drug policies. Bush's Vice President, former Indiana Senator Dan Quayle, headed the National Space Council, a group working to design United States space policy for the future. He also chaired the Council on Competitiveness, a group that evaluated the preparedness of American industries in the face of increasing competition from foreign manufacturing companies.

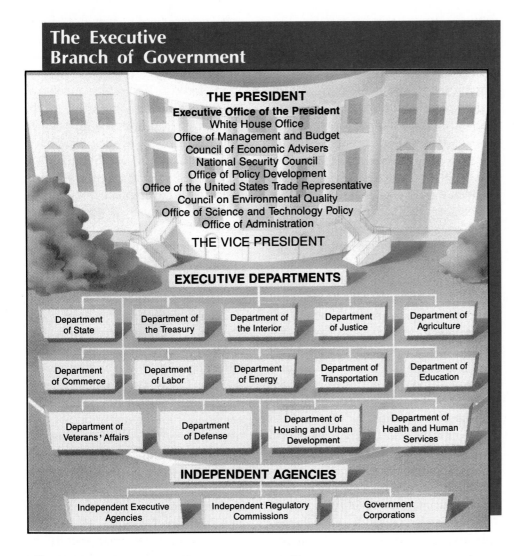

The Executive Branch of Government

THE PRESIDENT
Executive Office of the President
White House Office
Office of Management and Budget
Council of Economic Advisers
National Security Council
Office of Policy Development
Office of the United States Trade Representative
Council on Environmental Quality
Office of Science and Technology Policy
Office of Administration
THE VICE PRESIDENT

EXECUTIVE DEPARTMENTS

| Department of State | Department of the Treasury | Department of the Interior | Department of Justice | Department of Agriculture |

| Department of Commerce | Department of Labor | Department of Energy | Department of Transportation | Department of Education |

| Department of Veterans' Affairs | Department of Defense | Department of Housing and Urban Development | Department of Health and Human Services |

INDEPENDENT AGENCIES

| Independent Executive Agencies | Independent Regulatory Commissions | Government Corporations |

Figure 16-4

Section Review

1. What are the duties of the White House chief of staff?

2. What is the traditional presidential management system for the White House staff?

3. What are the duties of the national security adviser?

4. What is the newest staff agency in the Executive Office?

5. **Challenge:** Do you think the size and power of the Executive Office of the President should be reduced, stay the same, or be increased? Explain.

3 Federal Agencies

Federal agencies are those that support the 14 executive departments discussed earlier. They are sometimes called **line agencies** and can be thought of as being on the "front lines" of the federal government's work. These agencies are directly involved in the daily affairs of the national government. All types of government services, including health care for the poor and elderly, safeguards for the environment, transportation systems, and protection of civil liberties, are provided by these federal agencies and their employees.

line agencies agencies directly involved in the daily affairs of the national government

Government Employees

The number of people employed by the federal government has grown significantly since the founding of the nation. President George Washington had only a few hundred people to help him carry out the nation's laws. By the time Andrew Jackson took office in 1829, thousands of men and women were working in the executive branch. In 1992, the number of employees totaled more than 3 million.

Who hires all these people? In the early years, filling government jobs was largely handled by the President alone. George Washington hired only qualified people to serve in the federal government, regardless of party affiliation. Other early Presidents hired workers based on objective job qualifications, too, but preferred members of their own party. It was not until the presidency of Andrew Jackson in 1829 that political appointments to federal jobs were based primarily on party membership.

When Jackson took office, he fired a significant number of government workers and replaced them with people loyal to the Democratic Party. He believed that "to the victor belong the spoils." In this case, the spoils were government jobs. Jackson paid little attention to a person's qualifications; he felt that most government jobs were easy and that anyone with a minimal education and a little experience could perform well. This "spoils system," which was based on political patronage, came into full bloom under Jackson.

In time, however, opposition to the spoils system began to grow. Critics charged that the federal government had become inefficient and that dishonest workers were using their positions to make money for themselves and their friends. Reform of the federal government's way of hiring workers was demanded.

Finally, in 1883 Congress passed the Civil Service Act, often called the Pendleton Act. Though amended over the years, the main provisions of this act still control how the government can hire people. The act established the United States Civil Service Commission, which carries out regulations concerning government workers. The Pendleton Act also set up two different types of workers—classified employees and unclassified employees.

Most government workers are **classified employees** who are chosen on the basis of merit, or ability. This is determined when they take a civil service exam. If a person passes, his or her name is placed on a list with other applicants for a job that matches their qualifications. When an opening occurs, a federal agency can only hire someone from the top of one of these lists. On the other hand, **unclassified employees** do not have to pass tests to be chosen for a position. The members of the President's Cabinet, for instance, are unclassified employees. This two-level system of selection assures that most bureaucrats are hired because of their abilities, not because of their loyalty to a political party, cause, or individual.

At first, only 10 percent of federal employees were placed in the Civil Service System. But President Theodore Roosevelt, a former director of the Civil Service Commission, greatly expanded the number of classified employees. When he left office, two-thirds of all federal employees were classified. Presidents after Roosevelt increased the number even more. Today about 9 of every 10 federal workers are hired through the Civil Service System.

With so many people to hire and fire (and the job-related problems that

classified employees
federal workers chosen on the basis of merit

unclassified employees
federal workers appointed to office

go with these practices), the Civil Service Commission became bogged down under its own weight. In 1979 two agencies were formed to take its place. The Office of Personnel Management (OPM) recruits, tests, and promotes classified employees. The Merit System Protection Board (MSPB), a three-member panel appointed by the President with approval of the Senate, hears federal employee complaints about a particular agency's hiring or firing practices.

Once hired, where do all these employees work? Washington, D.C., has the largest number of federal government employees of any American city—about 345,000. But the remaining number of federal workers are found in offices spread throughout the 50 states. Some cities, such as Boston, Denver, and San Francisco, are regional headquarters for the national government. The Department of the Treasury, for example, has a regional office in Kansas City to administer its programs—such as collecting federal income taxes—in Kansas, Missouri, Nebraska, and Iowa.

Legislative Functions

Most bureaucrats in the line agencies are experts in their fields. Thus, they have a direct role in proposing, writing, and testifying about many laws that come before Congress each year. Legislators, in fact, rely on federal bureaucrats to supply them with information on a variety of topics, ranging from space exploration to crop rotation. Although unknown by the public, bureaucrats can greatly influence public policy and, thus, can affect the lives of all of us.

As part of their legislative functions, federal agencies often develop **iron triangles** with members of Congress and interest groups. Sometimes known as subgovernments, iron triangles work in a particular way. For example, suppose an environmental group wants to change federal law to make it easier for the government to acquire land for national parks. The environmental interest group goes to the National Park Service (a federal agency within the Department of the Interior) and proposes the idea for the law. The National Park Service likes the plan—it sees an opportunity to widen its authority and increase its funding through the acquisition of more park land. The Park Service and the interest group then go to Congress with the proposal. Members of the committee responsible for such a law agree to it because they see an

iron triangles close relationships between federal agencies, interest groups, and members of Congress

Components of the Iron Triangle

GOVERNMENT AGENCY

INTEREST GROUP

MEMBERS OF CONGRESS

Figure 16-5

The nation's national parks, such as North Cascades in the state of Washington, rely on an iron triangle for funding. How does an iron triangle work?

opportunity to attract tourists to their districts and boost the local economy, thus increasing their chances for getting more votes in the next election. In return for congressional support, the interest group makes a contribution to the committee members' re-election campaigns. Once the law passes, all sides of the triangle get what they want—the interest group gets more national parks, the National Park Service gets more funding, and members of Congress get more campaign contributions.

Hundreds of iron triangles exist in the federal government. Although they are a fact of life in American politics, they have many critics who believe that iron triangles allow interest groups too much of a role in setting public policy. These subgovernments, according to critics, operate almost exclusively outside the realm of the President or the White House staff and are difficult to break or control. Some critics feel that regulations are needed to curb the actions of interest groups and to

prevent further iron triangles from forming.

Executive Functions

Although line agencies do play a part in the drafting of laws, as evident in the iron triangle scenario, their main function is to carry out the laws already passed by Congress. For instance, the Internal Revenue Service (IRS) administers federal income tax laws. It establishes federal income tax regulations, provides information to taxpayers, collects tax money, and makes tax refunds. Similarly, the Department of Agriculture carries out laws that deal with many different kinds of programs. These include providing low-cost food for school lunches, promoting the sale of American farm products overseas, and providing financial and technical assistance to farmers. In carrying out these federal laws, line agencies have two major responsibilities: to establish government regulations and to apply them on a daily basis.

Line agencies develop and adopt the rules or regulations necessary for carrying out a particular law. Congress, for example, may pass a law that calls for safer air travel. To achieve part of this safety goal, the Federal Aviation Administration (FAA) is given the power to make sure that only qualified pilots are allowed to fly planes in American air space. The FAA establishes rules that dictate how much training and testing is required to license pilots to fly different kinds of aircraft.

It should not be assumed, however, that federal agencies have unlimited powers to set regulations. Congress serves as a "watchdog" over the federal bureaucracy, ensuring that all federal regulations pass three tests: they must be in accord with the law and the intent of Congress, they must be reasonable in what they require of the public, and they must be effective in achieving the goals of the law.

Establishing regulations to carry out the law is very similar to the lawmaking function of Congress. Here, the lines between the powers of the separate branches become hazy. Laws written by Congress only lay out the general goals and objectives of a bill. The details needed to actually implement the law and make it work are left to one or more of the federal agencies to fill in. Thus, bureaucrats working in federal agencies have the power to determine how the nation's laws will operate in real life. Some people believe that unelected bureaucrats have taken over the duties of elected representatives. They charge that Congress allows federal agencies to actually make laws through regulations rather than having Congress pass more detailed legislation.

One of the leading line agencies is the Federal Aviation Administration (FAA). FAA officials investigate plane crashes by checking wreckage and analyzing the black box (inset), which contains recorded messages between pilots and ground control. What are the functions of a line agency?

The federal agency that carries out the nation's space program is the National Aeronautics and Space Administration (NASA). Here, the space shuttle is launched from Cape Canaveral in Florida. Why are line agencies often controversial?

On the other hand, those who support the present system argue that Congress has neither the time, the staff, nor the expertise to work out all the details of each and every law that moves through the legislative calendar every year. Supporters believe that the present system is practical—Congress writes the laws and practices oversight while federal agencies write the detailed rules for enforcing the laws.

This enforcement power, in turn, gives line agencies judicial-like powers. This means that these agencies are able to punish people, businesses, and state or local governments that fail to follow federal rules. In the 1970s, for instance, Congress passed laws concerning the quality of air and water in the United States. The Environmental Protection Agency (EPA) was instructed to set up rules to make sure that the country's air and water supplies did not harm people and to establish punishments for states not following the rules. In the late 1970s, the EPA determined that certain states had not followed the clean air regulations and withheld federal funds needed by local and state governments to build sewer systems or repair and build highways. Once the guilty states established plans to meet clean air standards, their federal funds were restored.

Section Review

1. What was the spoils system?
2. What are the three "sides" in an iron triangle arrangement?
3. What three tests must all federal agency regulations pass to meet congressional approval?
4. **Challenge:** In your opinion, should all federal employees be classified? Why or why not?

4 Independent Agencies

Besides the executive departments with their supporting line agencies and the Executive Office of the President, the third part of the executive branch is made up of more than 200 independent agencies. The term "independent" means that these agencies conduct their work outside of the Cabinet departments. They are not, however, "independent" of the rules of Congress, the President, or the rest of the executive branch.

Until the late 1800s, the Cabinet departments carried out most federal business, and there was no need for additional agencies. Since then, however, the amount of work done by the federal government has increased substantially. Congress has been forced to set up scores of agencies to handle the increased work load. These agencies perform many tasks, from regulating air and ground transportation to delivering the mail.

There are several reasons why Congress sets up independent agencies. Congress organizes some agencies so that they are protected from interest group pressures and from political influence. In some cases, Congress may establish one in response to public pressure. Responding to complaints about the safety of products, Congress responded by creating the Consumer Product Safety Commission in 1972 to set safety standards for consumer goods. Congress also may establish agencies to handle specific programs that do not clearly belong to a Cabinet department. For instance, the highly specialized area of space exploration has been placed under the control of the National Aeronautics and Space Administration (NASA).

Still other agencies are created to exercise very broad responsibilities that, in turn, affect many other agencies and departments. The General Services Administration (GSA) is an example of such an agency. It is the federal government's service organization that is responsible for managing buildings, purchasing office furniture and supplies, and allocating government vehicles. Its activities, then, affect the entire executive branch.

With more than 200 agencies working at various tasks and employing millions of people, it may be confusing to determine what agency has which responsibility. To better understand how the government's independent agencies operate, it is best to examine them as three broad categories: independent regulatory commissions, independent executive agencies, and government corporations.

Along with other consumer goods, fruits and vegetables come under the safety standards set by the Consumer Product Safety Commission, an independent agency of the federal government. Why has Congress set up independent agencies?

SELECTED INDEPENDENT REGULATORY COMMISSIONS

AGENCY	YEAR ESTABLISHED	MAIN DUTIES
Interstate Commerce Commission (ICC)	1887	Regulates all transportation that crosses state lines.
Federal Communications Commission (FCC)	1934	Regulates foreign and interstate communications by radio, television, cable, and wire.
Securities and Exchange Commission (SEC)	1934	Regulates the sale of listed and unlisted securities and brokers, dealers, and bankers who sell them.
Nuclear Regulatory Commission	1975	Licenses, inspects, and regulates commercial uses of nuclear energy.

Figure 16-6

Independent Regulatory Commissions

Independent regulatory commissions are established to regulate various parts of the nation's economy. Each commission is usually headed by a board of commissioners. Board members are appointed by the President with the consent of the Senate. Unlike Cabinet members, commissioners generally cannot be removed from office at the wish of the President. They can be removed only for causes set by Congress, such as corruption or mental incompetence.

REPRESENTATION

To have a variety of views among commissioners, members must, by law, represent the two major political parties. This is done by balancing the number of Republicans and Democrats on each board. As another means of assuring their freedom from outside pressure, commissioners are appointed for relatively long terms, ranging from 5 to 14 years. This way, members can carry out their duties without the fear that they will be replaced by a President who may disagree with their policies.

POWERS

Under authority from Congress, regulatory commissions have powers that are executive, legislative, and judicial in nature. They set rules and regulations that have the force of law. While Congress, for example, has made it unlawful for businesses to practice false advertising, it is the Federal Trade Commission (FTC), by its rules and regulations, that defines what is false advertising.

Using judicial powers, commissions may hold hearings to settle disputes in areas under their authority. If a public utility company wants to build a nuclear power plant, for instance, it may be opposed by environmental groups. The Nuclear Regulatory Commission (NRC) would hold hearings, take testimony from all sides, and decide whether or not to issue a permit for the plant to be built. Independent regulatory commissions are further described in the Federal Bureaucracy Handbook on page 398.

Independent Executive Agencies

Independent executive agencies deal with specific government policy areas. Each is headed by a person appointed by the President with Senate approval. Unlike the regulatory commissions, executive agencies are under more direct presidential control.

Many independent executive agencies are large enough to rival Cabinet departments when comparing the sizes of their staffs, budgets, and political influence with Congress. The Small Business Administration (SBA) and the Federal Election Commission (FEC) are two examples. But there are scores of executive agencies with small staffs and budgets that also are important in implementing government programs. Examples of these include the Susquehanna River Basin Commission, the Indian Arts and Crafts Board, and the East-West Foreign Trade Board. Descriptions of selected independent executive agencies are found in the Federal Bureaucracy Handbook on page 397.

Government Corporations

Congress has set up more than 50 government corporations to carry out a variety of business activities. Government corporations are managed much like private corporations. A board of directors, appointed by the President with Senate approval, sets general policy. A general manager

SELECTED INDEPENDENT EXECUTIVE AGENCIES

AGENCY	YEAR ESTABLISHED	MAIN DUTIES
General Services Administration (GSA)	1949	Manages federal government property and records.
Commission on Civil Rights	1957	Evaluates programs and laws regarding discrimination practices.
National Aeronautics and Space Administration (NASA)	1958	Conducts research into the problems of space flight.
Office of Personnel Management	1978	Develops examination and evaluation procedures for Civil Service personnel; administers retirement and insurance programs for federal workers.

Figure 16-7

SELECTED GOVERNMENT CORPORATIONS

CORPORATION	YEAR ESTABLISHED	MAIN DUTIES
Federal Deposit Insurance Corporation (FDIC)	1933	Insures deposits in banks that are members of the Federal Reserve System.
Tennessee Valley Authority (TVA)	1933	Generates and sells electricity; controls flooding.
National Railroad Passenger Corporation (Amtrak)	1970	Operates intercity passenger trains throughout the nation.
United States Postal Service	1970	Delivers and processes the nation's mail.

Figure 16-8

CASE STUDY: THE FEDERAL BUREAUCRACY

IT'S BIG. . .BUT IS IT BETTER?

If there was ever a part of the national government that needed an image change, it is the federal bureaucracy. The hundreds of agencies that carry out government programs are generally viewed unkindly by politicians and citizens alike, and, when something goes wrong, the bureaucracy usually gets the blame.

During election campaigns, most politicians like to "run against the government," accusing the bureaucracy of being wasteful, inefficient, and the reason for the problems facing the nation. Candidates promise that, once elected, they will reduce bureaucratic regulations to make life easier for most Americans. For example, Ronald Reagan had few kind words for the bureaucracy when he was running for President. Reagan said that he would "get the bureaucracy off of our backs and out of our pocketbooks," and that "government is not the solution to our problems, government *is* the problem." Such campaign talk does little to improve the image of the bureaucracy.

The bureaucracy's negative image is also perpetuated by the American public, which associates it with long lines, confusing paperwork, and lazy, uncaring civil servants. Most people have been frustrated at some point in their lives with a bureaucratic ordeal—such as obtaining a driver's license or paying taxes—and

assume that all agencies operate in the same way.

One of the biggest complaints about the bureaucracy is that it wastes money. Critics say that the federal government is involved in too many programs and that spending often goes unchecked. News stories in the late 1980s about the Pentagon paying more than $400 for a $7 hammer and over $30 for a $1 machine screw did not help to dispel the image of a bureaucracy freely spending the taxpayers' money with little concern about costs.

Despite the criticism, however, the federal bureaucracy does have its supporters. They point out that compared to the bureaucratic structures of foreign governments, the American bureaucracy is a model of efficiency. For example, the U.S. Postal Service, always a target of criticism, is in fact one of the best run and least expensive mail delivery systems in the world.

Also, contrary to popular belief, a recent study by the University of Michigan shows that nearly two-thirds of the people who dealt directly with a bureaucrat said that they found him or her to be responsive to their problems and very helpful. So, why the negative image? The authors of the study claim that old stereotypes die hard, and the negative view most people have of the bureaucracy survives despite its overall good work.

Are the millions of employees who work for the federal government destined to be forever saddled with this negative image? No one denies that the federal bureaucracy is big, often slow moving, and has its fair share of inefficiency and mismanagement. At the same time, most people agree that the country would be at a great loss if the bureaucracy were to suddenly cease operations. Political scientists believe that greater efforts should be made to increase bureaucratic productivity. They also recommend that until such measures can be implemented, Americans should take a more understanding view of this vital part of the national government.

1. Why do most Americans have a negative view of the federal bureaucracy?
2. How can the image of the federal bureaucracy be improved?

takes care of the day-to-day operations. And, just like private businesses, government corporations sometimes lose rather than make money. When this happens, the federal government must make up the loss or raise the price of the service. The United States Postal Service, a government corporation, loses money almost every year. In this case, the government usually makes up for the loss by raising the fee charged for the Post Office's service—that is, the price of stamps goes up.

Section Review

1. Why does Congress establish independent agencies?
2. What are three categories of governmental independent agencies?
3. How are government corporations similar to those of private businesses?
4. **Challenge:** Why, do you think, is it important that regulatory commissions be free from political pressure?

Summary

1. The President relies on the three major parts of the executive branch—Cabinet departments, the Executive Office of the President, and independent agencies—to help manage the national government.
2. The federal bureaucracy consists of the agencies and departments of the executive branch that carry out public policy on a daily basis.
3. The Cabinet serves as an advisory body to the President and consists of the heads of the 14 executive departments, the Vice President, and other advisers chosen by the President.
4. Recent Presidents have relied less on the Cabinet as a whole and more on individual department heads and staff members.
5. The Executive Office of the President is made up of the top advisers who help the President carry out major duties.
6. The White House Office consists of the President's closest and most trusted advisers. It is traditionally a tightly knit group that smooths the flow of presidential business.
7. The number of government employees in the federal bureaucracy has grown considerably over the years. Today, most government employees are hired through the Civil Service System.
8. Federal bureaucrats often propose and help to write new laws by working with Congress and interest groups in what are known as iron triangles.
9. The three categories of independent agencies in the executive branch are independent regulatory commissions, independent executive agencies, and government corporations.
10. Independent regulatory commissions affect the economy by regulating various kinds of businesses in the United States.

Chapter 16 Review

★ Building Vocabulary

Match each of the numbered definitions with the correct lettered vocabulary term.

1. federal workers appointed to office
2. group of advisers chosen by the President
3. close relationships between federal agencies, interest groups, and members of Congress
4. agencies that support the President and the White House Office
5. employees of the bureaucracy
6. federal workers chosen on the basis of merit
7. major administrative divisions of the executive branch, such as the Department of State
8. agencies directly involved in the daily affairs of the national government

A. bureaucrats
B. Cabinet
C. executive departments
D. staff agencies
E. line agencies
F. classified employees
G. iron triangles
H. unclassified employees

★ Reviewing Facts

1. What groups make up the Cabinet?
2. How much influence does the Cabinet have today in presidential decision making?
3. Who makes up the White House Office?
4. What are the responsibilities of the Office of Management and Budget?
5. How much influence does the White House staff have in presidential decision making?
6. Why was the Civil Service System adopted?
7. What is the major difference between classified and unclassified government employees?
8. How might bureaucrats influence the making of public policy?
9. What is another name for an iron triangle?

10. Are independent agencies truly "independent" of the government?

★ Analyzing Facts

1. Why do you think Presidents generally listen more to the advice of their White House staff than to the Cabinet? Explain.
2. The President's closest advisers in the White House are appointed without congressional approval. Do you agree with this practice? Why or why not?
3. Some observers say that the federal bureaucracy has become overgrown, that there are too many departments and agencies with too many overlapping duties. If you were a member of Congress on a budget committee that decided which Cabinet departments to fund or not, for which ones would you increase funds? Which ones would lose funds? Which ones should be phased out? Which ones should be consolidated? Give reasons for your decisions.

★ Evaluating Ideas

1. Some experts say that the federal bureaucracy actually is a "fourth branch" of government. Do you agree with this assessment? Why or why not?

Using Your
Civic Participation Journal

Review the information on a federal agency that you compiled for your Civic Participation Journal. Work with five of your classmates who chose different agencies to compare results. Construct a collage showing your group's agencies major functions.

2. How would you strengthen the role of the Cabinet in presidential decision making? What do you think would be the results of these changes?

3. A report by the National League of Women Voters says: "The Civil Service System has its pros and cons. On one hand, there is a good deal to be said for a system based on merit. . . . But experience has shown that when employees are 'set for life' their efficiency and zeal may decline with the years. . . ." Do you agree or disagree? Explain.

★ Critical Thinking Interpreting Point of View

A point of view is the reason a person feels the way he or she does about a topic. Many factors help shape a person's point of view, including experiences, knowledge, biases and prejudices, and values. Emotions, such as fear or anger, sometimes also contribute to a person's point of view.

Explanation Being able to interpret or understand points of view is a valuable skill in almost every area of life. If you know why people feel the way they do about a topic, you can better evaluate their opinions.

The following guidelines will help you interpret points of view.

1. Determine the main topic of the speaker or writer and his or her opinion on that topic.

2. Identify factors from his or her background that may have shaped the opinion. Remember that everyone brings a point of view to any discussion.

3. Recognize that his or her point of view may cause the speaker or writer to focus on narrow aspects of a topic.

4. Reserve your judgment of the speaker's or writer's opinion until you have determined his or her point of view.

Practice The following statement was made by a picketer in front of the Department of Education in Washington, D.C. Use the above guidelines to determine her point of view.

I come from a long line of protesters and political organizers. My father marched against the war in the 1960s, and my grandfather was a union leader in the 1920s. I believe that we have to protest government policies we don't like because the government—especially the bureaucracy—has no idea what the American people really want. I was supposed to receive a government grant to study overseas last year, but due to bureaucratic red tape, my application was late, and I will not be able to go now.

This point of view resulted from a background of protest as an acceptable behavior, and from an unhappy personal experience with the bureaucracy. Her point of view caused her to judge the entire government by focusing only on the Department of Education.

Independent Practice Study the cartoon below, which has President Clinton acting as a firefighter after the Republican landslide in 1994. What is the artist's point of view about how the President's role has changed now that Republicans control Congress?

A Problem

Federal Bureaucracy Handbook

Introduction

To perform the many duties of office, each President relies on the help and advice of a well-organized executive branch. Three administrative groups are central to this branch—the Executive Office of the President, the Cabinet, and a large number of independent agencies. Although each of these groups is designed to fulfill different needs, some agencies and departments serve overlapping functions.

The first group, the Executive Office of the President, is a group of advisers and assistants who help the President carry out such major duties as providing information on foreign and domestic policy, preparing and implementing the federal budget, and monitoring the national economy. It also performs routine jobs, such as arranging the President's daily schedule and writing his speeches. The duties and responsibilities of the Executive Office are divided among several staff agencies.

The second group, the Cabinet, is a group of advisers appointed by the President. Even though the Constitution did not mention a Cabinet, it did not take long before the need for a select group of presidential advisers became apparent. It was George Washington who created the first Cabinet in 1789, when he regularly held meetings with the Vice President, the Attorney General, and the Secretaries of State, Treasury, and War. Today the Cabinet is made up of the secretaries of the 14 executive departments, the Vice President, and other key leaders chosen by the President. The executive departments are set up by Congress to deal with specific areas of government, and with the approval of the Senate, the President appoints a secretary for each. Each of the executive departments is divided into agencies and bureaus that carry out its policies and programs.

The third group, the independent agencies, vary widely in number of employees, size of budget, and amount of political influence. Currently there are about 200 such agencies performing many different tasks. Congress may establish independent agencies for three reasons. One is to oversee government services that do not fall under a Cabinet department. Another is to protect government programs from the influence of special interest groups. And the third is because public pressure has convinced Congress that there is a need for a new independent agency. The agencies themselves can be divided into three

The center of our federal bureaucracy is in the nation's capital, Washington, D.C. One of the capital's famous landmarks is the Washington Monument. What administrative groups of the executive branch are in Washington, D.C.?

groups—independent executive agencies, independent regulatory commissions, and government corporations. Independent executive agencies are under the direct control of the President, while Congress intended independent regulatory commissions to be beyond the President's direct control. Government corporations, on the other hand, are set up to operate a variety of businesses and are managed much like private businesses. And even though they receive public money, they are intended to make a profit from the services they provide.

Executive Office of the President

Established in 1939 by Franklin D. Roosevelt, the Executive Office of the President includes many staff agencies that are modified as the needs of the executive branch change.

The **White House Office** helps the President with day-to-day activities. Led by a chief of staff, its members include a deputy chief who manages the President's time schedule and daily appointments, speechwriters, a correspondence secretary who handles the President's mail, a press secretary who issues public statements for the President, and advisers who inform the President on current issues, suggest policy changes, and develop political strategies.

The **Office of Management and Budget** (OMB) was created in 1970 and is the largest group in the Executive Office. Although its main duty is helping the President prepare and execute the federal budget, it also administers the budget, ensures that federal agencies use their funds

The White House is the official residence of the President of the United States. How does the White House Office assist the President in his or her tasks?

efficiently, and evaluates the effectiveness of budget allocations. The Director of the OMB, who is appointed by the President with the Senate's approval, is also a Cabinet member.

The **National Security Council** (NSC) was set up in 1947 to advise the President on matters of national security both at home and abroad. Headed by the President, its other members include the Vice President, the Secretary of State, and the Secretary of Defense. Occasionally other advisers attend meetings, particularly the Director of the Central Intelligence Agency and the chairperson of the Joint Chiefs of Staff. Although its role varies with each President, most Presidents call it into session when a serious crisis arises.

The **Central Intelligence Agency** (CIA) is the main intelligence organization of the federal government. Technically an independent agency, it was established in 1947 under the National Security Council. The CIA works closely with the President and the NSC in all of the government's intelligence activities and collects foreign intelligence information other departments and agencies cannot get. Although the CIA has political influence, it has no law enforcement powers.

The **Office of Policy Development**, formerly the Domestic Policy Staff, helps the President devise and administer long-range domestic policies on such matters as farming, interstate trade, and energy.

The **Council of Economic Advisers**, established in 1946, analyzes the national economy, conducts economic studies, advises the President of economic developments, and recommends strategies for economic growth and stability.

The **Council on Environmental Quality** was created in 1969 to help the President protect the nation's land, air, and waterways. It studies the environmental impact of government programs, recommends policy changes, and helps the President prepare the annual environmental quality report to the Congress.

The **Office of Science and Technology Policy** analyzes current scientific information that can be used by various government departments and agencies, provides technological advice to other agencies, and reviews the scientific contributions of the federal government.

The **Office of the United States Trade Representative** establishes United States trade policy, represents the United States government at international trade meetings, and helps negotiate trade agreements with foreign governments.

Department of State

The oldest executive department, the Department of State was founded in 1789 to advise the President on foreign policy. The overall goal of the Department is to ensure the security and well-being of the United States. To achieve this goal, it consults Congress, other federal departments and agencies, and foreign governments. Its major functions are to establish, formulate, and carry out United States foreign policy. In addition to speaking for the United States in the United Nations and other international organizations, the Secretary of State may represent the President in meetings with foreign leaders.

The **Undersecretary for Economic and Agricultural Affairs** helps establish and conduct foreign economic policy, specifically in the areas of international trade, agriculture, energy, transportation, and relations with developing nations.

Regional Bureaus, one for each of the five major geographic regions of the world, advise the Secretary on foreign policy matters within their jurisdiction. They include the Bureaus of African Affairs, East Asian and Pacific Affairs, Near Eastern and South Asian Affairs, European and Canadian Affairs, and Inter-American Affairs.

The **Foreign Service** conducts most of the United States' relations with other countries. Its responsibilities include maintaining embassies, consulates, and other U.S. offices in other countries; negotiating agreements with foreign governments; and maintaining cordial relations with the government and people of these countries. Ambassadors, who represent the President, are responsible for implementing and explaining the official foreign policies of the United States within the country of their assignment.

The **Bureau of Human Rights and Humanitarian Affairs** develops and implements U.S. policy on human rights matters throughout the world. The Bureau functions as liaison with nongovernmental human rights organizations, prepares the annual State Department report on human rights practices in countries that receive U.S. assistance or are members of the United Nations, and advises the Immigration and Naturalization Service on applications for political asylum.

The **Bureau of Public Affairs** coordinates communication between the Department of State and the public, monitors public opinion of foreign

President George Bush is shown here with South Korean leaders during his visit to Seoul, South Korea's capital, in 1989. How does the Department of State help the President in conducting the nation's foreign policy?

policy, and produces educational materials on U.S. foreign policy for the public.

The **Bureau of Consular Affairs** issues passports and visas. It also protects the welfare of U.S. citizens and interests abroad.

The **Bureau of Intelligence and Research** directs and coordinates intelligence and research programs for the Department and other federal agencies.

The **Bureau of Politico-Military Affairs** establishes Department policy in areas of U.S. security, nuclear policy, military assistance, and arms control. It also advises other federal agencies on military and political affairs.

The **Office of the Chief of Protocol** advises the federal government and the President on diplomatic procedure, international laws, and foreign customs. It also determines eligibility for diplomatic immunity and resolves legal problems arising from diplomatic or consular immunity. In addition, the Office coordinates visits of foreign officials and dignitaries, maintains the President's guest house, and conducts official ceremonies and public events.

Department of the Treasury

Established in 1789, the Department of the Treasury is the federal government's primary financial agency. It advises the President on both domestic and international economic policy, including tax policy; collects tax revenues; manages the public debt; enforces criminal law in the areas of counterfeiting, smuggling, and tax evasion; manufactures coins and currency; and supervises national banks.

The **Internal Revenue Service** (IRS) administers and enforces federal tax laws, provides information to taxpayers, and collects nearly all federal taxes, including personal and corporate income taxes, social security, and excise, estate, and gift taxes.

The **United States Customs Service** collects duties on imported goods, inspects goods entering and leaving the United States, enforces customs and smuggling laws, and confiscates contraband, including illegal drugs.

The **Bureau of the Public Debt** supervises most federal borrowing, including the payment of interest, manages the public debt, and performs the bookkeeping for most federal borrowing.

The **Bureau of Engraving and Printing** designs, engraves, and prints all U.S. paper currency, postage stamps, food coupons, Treasury bonds and notes, and other U.S. securities. It also helps other federal agencies design and produce any government documents that require protection from counterfeiting.

The **United States Mint** manufactures all U.S. coins; produces national medals, some foreign coins, and commemorative coins; and oversees the federal government's reserves of gold and silver.

The **Office of the Comptroller of the Currency** supervises the operation of national banks, administers federal banking laws and regulations, approves charters for new national banks, and supervises the operations of approximately 4800 national and District of Columbia banks.

The **United States Secret Service,** originally established to prevent counterfeiting, protects the President and Vice President, members of their immediate families, former presidents and their spouses, presidential and vice presidential candidates, and visiting heads of foreign states.

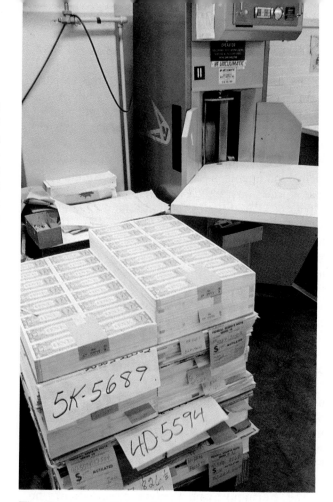

The Bureau of Engraving and Printing designs, engraves, and prints all U.S. paper currency. Here, newly-printed bills are ready for distribution. What are the Bureau's other functions?

The **Federal Law Enforcement Training Center** conducts training programs for federal law enforcement agencies and state and local law enforcement personnel.

The **Financial Management Service** is the federal government's primary bookkeeper and financial reporting agency and oversees the payment of federal salaries, income tax refunds, and social security and veterans' benefits.

The **United States Savings Bonds Division** sells United States savings bonds and promotes public awareness of the savings bonds program.

The **Bureau of Alcohol, Tobacco, and Firearms** administers and enforces federal laws regulating the production and distribution of firearms, explosives, alcohol, and tobacco products and collects excise taxes from the tobacco and alcohol industries.

Department of the Interior

Established in 1849, the Department of the Interior is the chief conservation agency of the federal government. It is responsible for fostering the wisest use of natural resources, which includes protecting and managing public lands, including national parks and historic sites; establishing guidelines for the best use of water resources; supervising the federal government's hydroelectric power facilities; assessing the country's mineral resources; protecting fish and wildlife; and managing Native American Indian reservations and U.S. island territories.

The **Fish and Wildlife Service** works to conserve the nation's fish, wildlife, and endangered species by protecting the natural habitats of fish and wildlife; helping develop environmental policy guidelines based on ecological principles, scientific knowledge, and a sense of moral responsibility; maintaining 442 National Wildlife Refuges, 150 Waterfowl Production Areas, 36 university-based research units, 70 National Fish Hatcheries; and a staff that enforces federal wildlife and conservation laws across the nation.

The **National Park Service** protects and preserves the natural environment and historic sites; manages more than 340 national parks, historic monuments, recreation areas, and scenic waterways; and controls the Urban Park and Recreation Recovery Program, which provides recreation services in the nation's cities.

The **Bureau of Mines** manages the nation's mineral resources; conducts research and provides information on methods of extracting, refining, and processing minerals and on safe recycling techniques; and establishes guidelines for the health and safety of mine workers.

The **United States Geological Survey** (USGS) identifies and locates land, mineral, and energy resources; prepares maps; classifies federal lands according to their resource potential; conducts geographical and geological experiments; and investigates such natural disasters and hazards as earthquakes, volcanoes, and landslides.

The **Office of Surface Mining Reclamation and Enforcement** protects the people and environment from any harmful effects resulting from mining by administering and enforcing federal laws regulating coal and strip mining and helping states establish regulatory programs; and works to reclaim abandoned mines and mined land.

The **Bureau of Indian Affairs** provides educational programs and community assistance to the country's Native American Indian and Native Alaskan population, particularly the estimated 600,000 Native American Indians who now live on or near the nation's more than 260 reservations.

The **Minerals Management Service** assesses the nature, value, and recoverability of offshore minerals, specifically those on the Outer Continental Shelf.

The **Bureau of Land Management** oversees 270 million acres of public lands, located mainly in the west and Alaska.

The **Bureau of Reclamation** manages water projects for the nation's arid and semiarid states, including irrigation projects, drinking water supplies, and flood control efforts.

The federal government regulates mining operations, such as this open pit gold mine in the Black Hills of South Dakota. What agency is responsible for enforcing federal mining laws?

Department of Justice

Created in 1870 and headed by the Attorney General, the Department of Justice is the largest law firm in the nation. It represents the United States government in legal matters, handles all Supreme Court cases involving the United States, enforces the law in the public interest, protects the public from crime, ensures healthy business competition, safeguards the consumer, and enforces immigration and naturalization laws.

The Attorney General provides legal advice for the President and the heads of the other executive departments, may appear before the Supreme Court in extremely important cases, and supervises the activities of the U.S. attorneys and U.S. marshals in the nation's judicial districts. A Solicitor General, however, usually represents the United States before the Supreme Court and decides which lower court decisions the government should ask the Court to review.

The **Federal Bureau of Investigation** (FBI) investigates violations of federal criminal laws, pursues and arrests most persons suspected of or charged with federal crimes, and locates witnesses for federal cases.

INTERPOL, an acronym for **International Criminal Police Organization**, is an international organization of 136 countries that promotes cooperation and mutual assistance among law enforcement authorities and helps prevent international crime by investigating international offenses and locating and arresting international fugitives.

The **Immigration and Naturalization Service** administers and enforces the nation's immigration laws, facilitates the entry of qualified aliens, oversees the naturalization of qualified resident aliens, and apprehends aliens who are in the country illegally.

The **Drug Enforcement Administration** administers and enforces federal laws and regulations concerning narcotics and other controlled substances and tries to prevent major drug trafficking by investigating major violations, coordinating law enforcement efforts at all government levels, and maintaining a national narcotics intelligence system.

The **Antitrust Division** helps promote and maintain competition among businesses by enforcing federal antitrust laws that prohibit monopolies, price-fixing conspiracies, and other illegal business practices.

The **Civil Rights Division** enforces federal laws prohibiting discrimination based on race, national origin, religion, sex, or handicap; protects citizens from discrimination in the areas of voting, education, housing, and employment; and seeks to eliminate discrimination in programs receiving federal financial assistance.

The **Criminal Division** devises criminal law enforcement policies in many areas, including organized crime, fraud, espionage, and narcotics and drug trafficking.

The **Land and Natural Resources Division** represents the United States in suits involving public lands, Indian lands and claims, and wildlife and natural resources, including cases involving federal environmental protection laws.

The **Tax Division** represents the United States in cases involving the internal revenue laws. Although its primary client is the Internal Revenue Service, it may represent other federal departments, agencies, and officials in suits arising from tax laws.

The **Bureau of Prisons** supervises and operates all federal penal institutions.

Dr. Martin Luther King, Jr., the noted civil rights leader, addressed this large crowd at the 1963 civil rights march in Washington, D.C. What division of the Department of Justice enforces federal civil rights laws?

Department of Agriculture

Created in 1862, the Department of Agriculture assists the nation's farmers and helps ensure the quality of food and other agricultural goods. In addition to helping farmers with a wide range of their concerns, including improving and maintaining their incomes, expanding foreign markets for U.S. crops, and maintaining the quality of the nation's soil and water, it also inspects crops and growing practices, enforces food quality standards, and recommends and administers federal nutrition programs.

The **Farmers Home Administration** provides low-interest, long-term loans to rural farm families who cannot obtain credit from private lenders. Most of the loans are used to cover farm operating costs, purchase or improve farmlands, or provide relief from natural disasters.

The **Rural Electrification Administration** makes low-interest, long-term loans to nonprofit groups for the construction and installation of electric power and telephone utilities in rural areas.

The **Agricultural Cooperative Service** helps farmers organize and operate cooperatives to market their crops and purchase farm tools and supplies.

The **Agricultural Marketing Service** helps farmers market their products by issuing daily reports on crop conditions, demands, prices, and other national market data; enforcing laws that prohibit deceptive agricultural marketing practices; and developing standard grades of quality for agricultural products ranging from livestock and eggs to nuts and wool.

The **Foreign Agricultural Service** promotes the exportation of U.S. agricultural products by developing and expanding foreign markets, eliminating trade barriers, and providing loans to countries that import U.S. farm goods. It also donates food for famine relief and school lunch programs.

The **Agricultural Stabilization and Conservation Service** bolsters farm incomes by trying to stabilize the prices and production of wheat, corn, cotton, milk, and other agricultural commodities through loans and subsidy payments to qualified farmers. It also coordinates food production during national defense crises.

Here, a farmer in the Midwest is fertilizing a large field of tomatoes. What services does the Department of Agriculture provide for the nation's farmers?

The **Commodity Credit Corporation** helps protect farm income by purchasing surplus farm products and donating, selling, or storing them.

The **Federal Crop Insurance Corporation** sells insurance to farmers to cover crops destroyed by unavoidable causes, including weather conditions, insects, and fires.

The **Food and Nutrition Service** administers the Food Stamp Program and provides funding and donates food to such federal food programs as the National School Lunch Program.

The **Food Safety and Inspection Service** inspects the meat and poultry industries to ensure the quality and accurate labeling of meat and poultry.

The **Forest Service** supervises 191 million acres of national forests and grasslands and provides research grants in forestry.

The **Animal and Plant Health Inspection Service** prevents, controls, and eradicates animal and plant pests and diseases through inspection, quarantines, and regulation.

The **Soil Conservation Service** helps conserve soil and water by providing farmers with technical and financial assistance and directs anti-pollution programs.

387

Department of Commerce

Founded in 1903 as the Department of Commerce and Labor, the Department of Commerce is concerned with all aspects of the nation's international trade, economic growth, and technological advancement. Its programs, which cover a wide range of areas, strive to promote the nation's economic interests while maintaining a competitive free enterprise system.

The **National Bureau of Standards** develops and maintains uniform standards for all weights and measures used in the nation, including physical and chemical measurements; organizes conversion standards from U.S. to foreign measurement systems; performs scientific and engineering tests and experiments; and provides research to government agencies and private industry.

The **Bureau of the Census** takes a census of the U.S. population every 10 years, particularly to determine the apportionment of seats in the House of Representatives, and tabulates and publishes a variety of statistical data about the nation's economy and people.

The **Patent and Trademark Office** issues patents of invention and design to more than 75,000 applicants each year and registers the trademarks businesses use to distinguish their products.

The **National Oceanic and Atmospheric Administration** (NOAA) runs the National Weather Service, which produces weather reports and issues early warnings for floods, tidal waves, hurricanes, and tornadoes; uses a national satellite system to forecast the nation's weather; conducts worldwide oceanic research and maps the oceans; and conducts seismological and general environmental research.

The **Bureau of Economic Analysis** prepares and publishes reports and accounts of the gross domestic product (GDP, the total dollar value of final goods and services produced in a year); provides an accurate picture of the nation's economy; analyzes the nation's commercial structure; forecasts economic developments; and studies trends in the areas of personal income and foreign trade.

The **National Technical Information Service** is the central source for information on government-sponsored research and scientific and tech-

Newscasters routinely cover national disasters. What subdivision of the Department of Commerce handles weather-related concerns?

nical information gathered by both foreign and U.S. sources, which it provides to both government agencies and private industry.

The **United States Travel and Tourism Administration** helps the travel industry, both at home and abroad, to encourage people to visit the United States for a variety of purposes, including business, education, and vacation.

The **Minority Business Development Agency** helps minority-owned businesses succeed in commercial industry and develops and coordinates a variety of federal, state, and local programs designed to help organize and strengthen minority-owned businesses.

The **International Trade Administration** promotes U.S. foreign trade by reporting and analyzing business conditions and opportunities overseas and conducts trade fairs and runs trade centers abroad.

Department of Labor

Created in 1913, the Department of Labor promotes the welfare of the nation's wage earners by enforcing laws ensuring safe working conditions, fair wages, and freedom from job discrimination; overseeing the activities of labor unions, the workers' compensation program, and the unemployment insurance system; and advising the President on federal labor and employment policies.

The **Employment and Training Administration** operates the unemployment insurance program, which provides financial support for the unemployed; provides job placement and job training services; coordinates state and local unemployment efforts; and supervises public service employment programs; and, through the Work Incentive Program, helps welfare recipients become self-supporting.

The **Employment Standards Administration** administers and enforces laws regulating wages, including minimum wages, overtime wages, and wages paid under government contracts; oversees affirmative action programs; enforces laws that provide injury and accident payments to federal employees; and enforces federal laws regulating maximum work hours.

The **Occupational Safety and Health Administration** (OSHA) administers and enforces federal laws that set minimum safety and health standards in almost all industries, investigating businesses to make sure working conditions are as safe as possible and imposing penalties on employers who fail to comply with standards.

The **Mine Safety and Health Administration** enforces federal laws that establish minimum safety and health standards for the nation's mining industry.

The **Pension Welfare Benefits Administration** enforces laws that regulate the administration of private pension and welfare plans.

The **Office of Labor-Management Standards** regulates the internal procedures of labor unions, including the election of officials and the handling of union funds, and supervises the labor organizations of post office workers and other federal employees.

The **Bureau of Labor-Management Relations and Cooperative Programs** coordinates efforts to improve relations and collective bargaining procedures between labor and management.

The **Veteran's Employment and Training Service** devises and implements government programs to facilitate the reemployment and other work benefit rights of veterans.

The **Bureau of Labor Statistics** gathers, analyzes, and publishes statistical and general data on employment, unemployment, work hours, and wages, including the Consumer Price Index, which tabulates the average costs of the nation's families.

What services does the Department of Labor provide to the nation's workers, such as these power line workers?

Department of Defense

The Department of Defense was formed in 1949 from the Department of War, the Department of the Navy, and the U.S. Air Force. The Air Force, Army, and Navy now occupy separate departments, each with its own secretary, within the Department of Defense. The largest executive department, the Department of Defense is headquartered in the Pentagon and employs about 1.1 million civilians.

The Department maintains the nation's military forces, which are made up of approximately 2.2 million people on active duty and an additional 1.7 million people in reserve forces. The Secretary of Defense, who must be a civilian, serves as the President's chief adviser on matters of national defense.

The **National Security Agency** protects the federal government's communications systems, including computer systems, by establishing security procedures. In addition, the agency conducts surveillance and gathers information about foreign governments.

The **Joint Chiefs of Staff** serve as key military advisers to the President, the National Security Council, and the Secretary of Defense. The Joint Chiefs are also responsible for handing down the President's orders to the nation's military units, preparing strategic plans, and recommending military actions.

The **Department of the Air Force** maintains services for the nation's air defense, operates air reconnaissance, and provides air transportation for all U.S. military cargo and personnel.

The **Department of the Navy** includes both the U.S. Navy and the U.S. Marine Corps. It is responsible for protecting the nation by patrolling the oceans and carrying out military actions at sea. The Navy's forces are composed of ships, submarines, and aircraft. The Marine Corps defends naval bases and provides forces for the land-based operations necessary in many Navy campaigns.

The **Department of the Army** trains, organizes, and outfits the nation's land forces. The department strives to keep Army forces prepared for immediate response for any land operation. In emergencies, the Army also helps state and local governments.

The **Strategic Defense Initiative Organization** conducts research and recommends strategies for reducing the threat posed by nuclear ballistic missiles.

The **Defense Nuclear Agency** is primarily concerned with nuclear weapons research and testing. The agency advises the Joint Chiefs of Staff on all nuclear matters.

The **Defense Advanced Research Projects Agency** performs both basic and advanced research for prototype projects, particularly those involving technologies which may be used in other defense programs.

The **National Defense University** educates selected military officers and civilian officials, conducts strategy research, and coordinates military education. The university also performs policy analysis for the Secretary of Defense and the Joint Chiefs of Staff.

Specialized **Service Academies** are operated by the Department of Defense to provide both college education and military training. These academies include the U.S. Military Academy in West Point, New York; the U.S. Naval Academy in Annapolis, Maryland; and the U.S. Air Force Academy in Colorado Springs, Colorado.

The Department of the Army trains, organizes, and outfits the nation's land forces. Here, the Army's 25th Infantry carries out a program of basic training for recruits. What are the responsibilities of the Department of the Army?

Department of Housing and Urban Development

Created in 1965, the Department of Housing and Urban Development (HUD) is responsible for the housing needs of the people, including the development and renovation of both urban and rural communities. It also ensures fair access to housing, sets safety standards for housing construction, and offers loans and subsidies for housing repairs. In addition, HUD offers mortgage insurance programs and rental assistance programs for lower income families.

Unlike most of the executive departments, which administer programs through bureaus or agencies, almost all of HUD's programs are controlled directly by several assistant secretaries. Each assistant secretary supervises one or more of the Department's programs.

HUD's Office of Block Grant Assistance has helped renovate urban neighborhoods, such as this one in Cincinnati, Ohio. What kind of official heads this and other HUD offices?

The **Office of Block Grant Assistance** provides grants to renovate urban neighborhoods. Its primary focus is in the areas of housing, economic development, and community services. The purpose of the grants is to improve the quality of life for city communities of low and moderate income persons. The office also provides qualified communities with loan guarantees to purchase property and improve publicly-owned property.

The **Emergency Shelter Grants Program** provides money to improve, build, and operate emergency shelters for the homeless. These grants may also be used to provide the homeless with support services and other essential social services.

The **Office of Urban Development Action Grants** promotes private investment in cities that are experiencing severe economic problems. Action grant funds are used by local governments to generate economic activity, which creates permanent jobs and increases local tax revenues.

The **Urban Homesteading Program** encourages urban renovation by transferring the titles of certain federally-owned, unoccupied family residences to qualified homesteaders. Homesteaders must agree to repair the property and to live in the residence for a minimum of five years.

The **Assistant Secretary for Fair Housing and Equal Opportunity** develops and implements policies involving civil rights and equal opportunity in housing and community development. The assistant secretary works to prevent housing dis-

crimination based on race, national origin, sex, handicap, or age.

The **Assistant Secretary for Housing**, or **Federal Housing Commissioner**, conducts such HUD programs as mortgage insurance; the rent supplement program, which helps low-income families with rental costs; the housing development grant program; and the housing loan program for the elderly and handicapped. The assistant secretary also administers and enforces regulations designed to protect the consumer.

The **Assistant Secretary for Public and Indian Housing** assists in all public and Native American Indian housing programs, including the planning and operation of public housing programs. The assistant secretary also supervises programs that modernize the nation's low-income housing projects.

The **Government National Mortgage Association** provides financing and mortgage assistance for veterans and certain other qualified applicants.

The **Office of Environment and Energy** establishes policies for communities to protect and enhance the environment and conserve energy. The office sets minimum distances between housing and sources of noise pollution and establishes guidelines for home weatherization.

391

Department of Transportation

Created in 1966, the Department of Transportation oversees the transportation policies of the nation. The Department supervises both recreational and commercial transportation of goods and people via land, air, and water. It is also responsible for planning and constructing highways, ensuring the safety of lives and property on the nation's highways and waterways, and advising the President on federal laws and policies related to transportation. Other Department responsibilities are enforcing federal and international laws on the high seas, regulating the safety standards of bridges and ports, and ensuring the safety of recreational boats.

The **United States Coast Guard** enforces both federal and international water transportation laws, notably smuggling laws, and ensures the safety of the nation's navigable waters. One of its main duties is conducting search and rescue missions to save both lives and property on the high seas. The Coast Guard also enforces safety standards for commercial and recreational vessels; breaks ice and operates lighthouses to facilitate safe navigation; and enforces pollution and cargo spillage laws. During times of war, or by presidential order, the Coast Guard operates as a division of the Navy.

The **Federal Aviation Administration** (FAA) regulates all air navigation and commerce, including licensing pilots, enforcing aircraft and airport safety laws, and controlling air traffic. In addition, the FAA regulates air navigation by the nation's military forces.

The **Federal Highway Administration** is involved with all aspects of the nation's highway system, including some rural roads and urban streets. The administration oversees the design, construction, maintenance, and beautification of highways; enforces highway safety laws; and provides for safety signs and signals to eliminate safety hazards. It also designs and builds roads in national parks and on Native American Indian reservations. Other administration programs are conducting research on motor vehicle and road safety; providing grants for highway improvement; and maintaining the nation's 42,500-mile interstate freeway system.

In recent years, air travel has increased tremendously. Here, a plane at the Phoenix Airport is getting ready for a flight. What are the responsibilities of the Federal Aviation Administration?

The **Federal Railroad Administration** promotes railroad safety, primarily through enforcing federal rail safety laws. It also provides advice and financial assistance to certain railroads, particularly those in economic difficulties, and conducts research on rail safety and new railroad technology.

The **National Highway Traffic Safety Administration** ensures the safety of all citizens on the nation's highways. The administration enforces federal motor vehicle safety laws, operates various programs designed to reduce highway accidents, and determines the nation's speed limit laws. It also sets fuel economy standards and conducts research on ways to lessen the severity of motor vehicle accidents.

The **Urban Mass Transportation Administration** offers grants and loans for the development and maintenance of mass transit systems in urban areas. These funds are available to private businesses as well as state and local governments. The administration also conducts research to improve the safety and efficiency of mass transit systems.

The **Maritime Administration** promotes all aspects of the nation's merchant marine. Administration activities include conducting merchant marine research and operating the U.S. Merchant Marine Academy at Kings Point, New York.

Department of Energy

Formed in 1977, the Department of Energy is charged with fostering the wisest development, use, and conservation of the nation's energy resources. Its main goal is to foster a cohesive national energy plan. The Department oversees a number of federal energy programs previously carried out by several of the other executive departments. It is responsible for the research, development, and incorporation of all areas of energy technology, including nuclear, fossil, geothermal, and solar energy.

The **Office of Fossil Energy** handles research and development programs involving the fossil fuels: coal, natural gas, and petroleum. The office provides the fossil fuel industry with information on mining, drilling, and other extraction methods. It also manages various petroleum storage projects.

The **Office of Nuclear Energy** develops programs and conducts research on the use and production of nuclear fission energy. The office evaluates proposed nuclear technologies, oversees the development of nuclear reactors, and researches possible uses of nuclear energy in space.

The **Office of Defense Programs** coordinates research on the development, testing, and production of nuclear weapons in the United States. The office also collects information on the development and testing of nuclear weapons by foreign countries.

The **Office of Conservation and Renewable Energy** directs various programs to increase the production and use of renewable energy sources, particularly solar, wind, and geothermal technologies. The office researches these technologies and provides financial assistance to the states to promote energy planning and conservation.

The **Office of Civilian Radioactive Waste Management** directs various programs that foster the safe storage and disposal of highly radioactive waste generated by nuclear reactors.

The **Office of Energy Research** coordinates the basic physics and fusion research projects of the Department. The office provides funds for university research and other research projects outside the Department. It also evaluates the environmental and health safety of the government's energy projects.

The **Energy Information Administration** gathers, analyzes, and publishes statistical data in the energy area, including information on energy resources, energy production, and energy consumption.

The **Office of International Affairs and Energy Emergencies** recommends and develops the federal government's international energy policies and programs. The office assists both foreign governments and international organizations in developing energy programs and monitors and analyzes energy prices and trends throughout the world.

The **Federal Energy Regulatory Commission** is an independent commission within the Department of Energy. The five-member commission sets rates for transporting natural gas, electricity, and oil and licenses hydroelectric power projects.

The **Economic Regulatory Administration** enforces federal laws regulating some aspects of the production, sale, and uses of energy.

The energy needs of the United States have greatly expanded since the time when this old gas light was installed in Philadelphia. What are the responsibilities of the Department of Energy in regard to the nation's future use of energy?

Department of Health and Human Services

Originally established in 1953 as part of the Department of Health, Education, and Welfare, the Department of Health and Human Services began to operate on its own in 1979. Headed by the Secretary of Health and Human Services, and concerned primarily with the health and social needs of the nation's people, it administers a variety of social welfare, public assistance, and public health programs; funds and operates public health care facilities; regulates safety standards in the food and drug industries; and provides health insurance for the elderly and disabled.

The **Social Security Administration** administers several national social insurance programs. These programs provide direct financial assistance to needy elderly, blind, and disabled persons, as well as giving cash payments to retired or disabled workers and their families. Most of the funds used by the administration come from compulsory payroll taxes paid by employers and wage earners.

Many medical experts claim that cigarette smoking is a major cause of lung cancer and other diseases. What agency researches disease prevention and treatment?

Quit smoking now. Before you have to quit.

The **Family Support Administration** provides financial assistance to low-income families. In addition, it makes sure that states carry out federal laws requiring the enforcement of the child support payment obligations of absent parents.

Aid to Families with Dependent Children, a program operated by the Department's Family Support Administration, provides states with federal grants to aid children of low-income families.

The **Food and Drug Administration** (FDA) tests foods, drugs, cosmetics, and medical devices to ensure their purity and protect the consumer from unsafe products. The FDA establishes and enforces standards for the purity, quality, and labeling of food and drugs.

The **Centers for Disease Control and Prevention** (CDC) conducts research and education programs for the prevention, treatment, and control of diseases. Since the CDC is concerned with communicable and preventable diseases, it also researches the effects of avoidable health hazards, such as smoking.

The **Health Care Financing Administration** administers Medicare, a health insurance program for the elderly, and Medicaid, a federal grant program which helps pay health care bills of low-income families and needy disabled persons.

The **Health Resources and Services Administration** provides grants to nonprofit hospitals and other health care facilities to strengthen the quality of their health care services.

The **National Institutes of Health** conducts research on the causes, prevention, and cure of major diseases, including arthritis, cancer, diabetes, and allergies.

The **Office of Human Development Services** oversees several programs, primarily those concerned with providing support services to older persons, Native American Indians, Native Alaskans, and handicapped citizens.

The **Substance Abuse and Mental Health Services Administration** performs research and provides information on the causes, treatment, and prevention of alcoholism, drug abuse, and mental illness.

The **Administration for Children and Families** seeks to promote child welfare on many levels. The administration coordinates a variety of programs for the benefit of runaway, abused, and neglected children, oversees the adoption opportunities program, and administers the Head Start Program.

Department of Education

Originally part of the combined Department of Health, Education, and Welfare, the Department of Education became a separate executive department in 1979. The Department develops and administers policies and programs concerned with education, and also coordinates state public education efforts. Its policies and activities affect the Americans who attend school—nearly one-fourth of the total population.

The **Office of Special Education and Rehabilitative Services** offers grants for programs that meet the special educational needs of children with disabilities. Funds are provided for training teachers, conducting research, and performing special media services, such as captioning educational films for the deaf.

The **Office of Elementary and Secondary Education** provides grants and administers programs that support the preschool, elementary, and secondary education efforts of state and local governments. Special efforts are made to fund local school districts and public agencies to educate Native American Indians, migrant children, delinquent students, and students who might suffer educationally because of racial segregation and discrimination.

The **Office of Postsecondary Education** administers grant programs designed to maintain and expand the instructional services in colleges and universities. The office also provides several different types of grant and loan programs for students, including the Guaranteed Student Loan and Basic Educational Opportunity Grants programs.

The **Office of Vocational and Adult Education** provides grants to state and local governments to support vocational training, professional education, and adult education. In addition to assisting urban community colleges, the office helps coordinate adult education efforts in rural areas.

The **Office of Civil Rights** ensures that civil rights laws in the area of education are carried out. The office also makes sure that any education programs receiving federal funding meet civil rights requirements.

The education of the nation's students is assisted by grants from the Department of Education. What offices make up the Department of Education?

The **Office of Bilingual Education and Minority Languages Affairs** promotes the educational rights of students with limited English skills. The office supports the development and implementation of programs designed to educate such children in public schools.

The **Office of Educational Research and Improvement** conducts research and provides grants to support a wide range of state and local education efforts. These areas include basic reading and math skills, awareness of alcohol and drug abuse, health education, laboratory resources, and library skills.

Various **Federally Aided Corporations** within the Department provide educational opportunities for specialized groups. These institutions include: the American Printing House for the Blind, Louisville, Kentucky; Gallaudet College, Washington, D.C., which provides postsecondary education for the hearing-impaired; and the National Technical Institute for the Deaf, a part of the Institute of Technology in Rochester, New York.

Department of Veterans Affairs

Created in 1989, the Department of Veterans Affairs is the newest executive department. It is responsible for all of the duties of the Veterans Administration, founded in 1930, which was the nation's largest independent agency. With more than 260,000 employees, the Department of Veterans Affairs is the second largest executive department. For its first year, the Department budget provided $28.1 billion of which more than 95 percent was used for direct payments and services to veterans.

Department services and benefits include hospitals and medical services, insurance, pensions, disability allowances, loans, education financing, and housing benefits. The Department establishes and administers veterans programs and advises the President on all government policies affecting veterans. Since there are more than 27 million veterans and 53 million dependents and survivors of veterans, about one of every three American citizens is eligible for benefits and services.

The Department retains the structure of the Veterans Administration, organizing its activities under three major program areas: health care, benefits, and memorial affairs.

The **Health Care Services** of the Department provide emergency and outpatient medical services. The Department operates the largest medical system in the country, consisting of 172 hospitals, 231 outpatient clinics, 119 nursing homes, and 27 domiciliaries.

The **Benefit Programs** offered by the Department consist, for the most part, of direct monetary payments to veterans. These payments include compensation to veterans disabled in service, educational assistance, and vocational rehabilitation. The Department also guarantees home loans and operates the nation's fifth largest life insurance program.

The **Memorial Affairs** branch of the Department includes the operation and maintenance of 112 national cemeteries.

Medical Training is offered by the Department in facilities throughout the nation. The Department is affiliated with over 160 medical and dental schools, and over half of all practicing American physicians have trained in Department facilities.

Here, West Point cadets are in line for inspection. When these future officers eventually retire from the military, they will rely on the Department of Veterans Affairs for benefits. How many Americans today depend on the Department of Veterans Affairs?

Independent Executive Agencies

The largest number of independent agencies in the executive branch are commonly classified as independent executive agencies. Each of these agencies is headed by a person appointed by the President, but they are not members of the Cabinet. Yet, many independent executive agencies rival executive departments in terms of size, budget, and political influence with Congress.

ACTION administers federal volunteer programs. ACTION volunteers are mainly involved in helping low-income individuals and communities overcome poverty. ACTION develops and supervises a wide range of volunteer service organizations and actively encourages private businesses and citizens of all ages and ethnic backgrounds to become involved in its programs.

The **Commission on Civil Rights** evaluates federal laws related to discrimination or denials of equal protection of the law because of race, color, religion, sex, age, handicap, or national origin. Specific efforts are made in the areas of voting rights, enforcement of federal civil rights laws, and equality of opportunity in education, employment, and housing. Although the commission reports its findings and has political influence, it has no enforcement functions.

The **Environmental Protection Agency** (EPA) coordinates, evaluates, and enforces federal programs to fight air, water, and environmental pollution by toxic substances, solid wastes, pesticides, and radiation.

The **Federal Election Commission** administers and enforces the Federal Election Campaign Act, which regulates campaign contributions and disclosures. The commission also supervises the public funding of political campaigns.

The **General Services Administration** (GSA) affects every department and agency in the executive branch. The GSA manages government property, purchases furniture and supplies, stores forms and records, and allocates vehicles for other federal agencies and departments.

National Aeronautics and Space Administration (NASA) was established in 1958 to direct the nation's space exploration program. NASA also formulates, researches, and directs non-military uses of space. In addition, it distributes any new

The *Gemini XII* spacecraft orbits Earth in this photo. This and other space voyages have brought many scientific advances. What agency directs the nation's space program?

technological or scientific knowledge discovered through space-program research to private businesses for use in commercial projects.

The **National Science Foundation** initiates and supports fundamental, long-term research, primarily in the areas of science, engineering, and computer technology.

The **Office of Personnel Management** (OPM) supervises the civil service merit system for federal employees. The OPM establishes criteria for testing, hiring, and promoting people based on their knowledge, skills, and other merits, thus preventing political affiliations from affecting the government's hiring procedures.

The **Peace Corps** promotes world peace by sending specially-trained American volunteers to other nations. Peace Corps volunteers serve for two years and help the people of developing nations combat such problems as drought, disease, and overcrowding.

The **Small Business Administration** promotes and protects the interests of the nation's small businesses through a variety of grant and assistance programs.

Independent Regulatory Commissions

Independent regulatory commissions are established by Congress to regulate various parts of the nation's economy. Regulatory commissions enact, carry out, and enforce guidelines controlling certain industries. Although they are part of the executive branch, independent regulatory commissions are intended to be beyond the direct control of the President.

Commissions are carefully structured to ensure that they remain free from any political pressures. Each commission must consist of a balance of members of the two major political parties. Each commission is headed by a board of 5 to 11 members, chosen by the President with the approval of the Senate. Unlike the heads of executive departments and agencies, commissioners are appointed for long terms. As a result, usually no more than one seat on each commission becomes vacant each year. This ensures that the President cannot "pack" a commission.

The **Interstate Commerce Commission** (ICC) was established in 1887 to regulate all ground transportation across state lines.

The **Federal Reserve System** was set up in 1913 as the central bank of the United States. The Federal Reserve System regulates the monetary and credit policies of member banks.

The **Federal Communications Commission** (FCC) directs all mass communication activities in the nation. Established in 1934, the FCC establishes guidelines and standards that ensure orderly communication via television, radio, telegraph, and satellite. The FCC assigns tuning frequencies and call letters to radio and television stations, regulates signal strengths, and monitors the government's emergency broadcast system. It also issues licenses to public broadcasters and ensures the technical quality of their broadcasts.

The **Securities and Exchange Commission** (SEC) was established in 1934 to regulate the sale of both listed and unlisted securities. It also monitors the brokers, dealers, and bankers who sell securities.

Established in 1914, the **Federal Trade Commission** (FTC) ensures fair economic competition among American businesses. The commission's activities are focused in two areas: enforcing the federal antitrust laws, which guard against mo-

The prices of the nation's major grain and meat products are set at the Chicago Board of Trade. What independent regulatory commission works to ensure fair competition among businesses?

nopolies and unfair trade restrictions, and preventing deceptive trade practices. Consumers may ask the commission to investigate unfair business practices they encounter, including deceptive advertising and misleading product labeling. Violators of the commission's rules are punished by the courts.

The **National Labor Relations Board**, established in 1935, prevents unfair labor practices, settles labor disputes, and administers federal labor-management laws.

Established in 1964, the **Equal Employment Opportunity Commission** (EEOC) is responsible for investigating discrimination charges against employers and labor unions.

The **Consumer Product Safety Commission**, formed in 1972, establishes and enforces safety standards and conducts safety tests on consumer products. The commission also initiates recalls of defective products and prohibits the sale of unsafe products.

Established in 1974, the **Nuclear Regulatory Commission** (NRC) issues permits for the construction of the nation's nuclear power plants and regulates the operation of these plants. Other commission duties include licensing companies that use, process, and own nuclear materials; inspecting these companies to ensure compliance with commission safety rules; and investigating nuclear accidents.

Government Corporations

Government corporations are set apart from the other independent agencies because they are intended to make a profit by providing necessary services to the public. Government corporations are operated much like private corporations. A board of directors is appointed by the President with Senate approval. This board establishes general policy, and a general manager supervises the corporation's day-to-day operations. Government corporations receive public money and their profits go to the government.

Government corporations vary widely in size, services, and profits. Some, such as the Tennessee Valley Authority, affect only the people of one geographic area; while others, such as the United States Postal Service and the Federal Deposit Insurance Corporation, provide services almost everyone uses.

The **Federal Deposit Insurance Corporation** (FDIC) was set up in 1933 to insure deposits made in banks that belong to the FDIC system. In part, the FDIC was set up to prevent a repeat of the bank failures that took place during the Great Depression. If an FDIC bank fails, each account is insured for up to $100,000.

The **Tennessee Valley Authority** (TVA) is a government-owned corporation dating from 1933 that supplies electricity in the Tennessee Valley region. The TVA generates and sells power at wholesale rates to 160 communities in seven states. It also maintains flood control systems in the Tennessee Valley region.

The **National Railroad Passenger Corporation**, also known as Amtrak, operates almost all passenger trains in the nation. Established in 1970, Amtrak operates about 210 trains a day, serving more than 500 station locations in both rural and urban areas. Because Amtrak often loses money or makes very small profits, the corporation sometimes needs federal assistance to keep the trains running.

Until 1970, the postal service operated as a department of the executive branch of government. Today, mail is handled by the **United States Postal Service** (USPS), an independent agency. The USPS handles more than 153 billion pieces of mail each year and employs more than 790,000 people. To reach its goal of fast, reliable delivery, the USPS has a number of research, development, and technical departments under it. Other USPS groups protect the mail from loss or theft and protect consumers from mail fraud.

Established in 1972, the **Pennsylvania Avenue Development Corporation** directs a comprehensive plan for the revitalization of more than 21 blocks in Washington, D.C., focusing its efforts on the stretch of Pennsylvania Avenue between the White House and the Capitol. Much of the PADC's efforts are devoted to two kinds of projects. One involves public improvements and includes repaving, landscaping, developing public parks, facilitating traffic, and preserving historic landmarks along Pennsylvania Avenue. The second is to encourage private businesses to develop projects that further the goals of the Pennsylvania Avenue Plan.

The **Pension Benefit Guaranty Corporation** (PBGC) guarantees the payment of pension benefits for certain private businesses. The PBGC administers benefit insurance programs for more than 112,000 pension plans. The PBGC ensures that pension benefits will be paid even if a pension plan terminates without sufficient funds. The corporation covers the pensions of about 40 million workers.

One of the leading government corporations is the United States Postal Service. Why are government corporations set apart from other independent agencies?

FOUR REVIEW

REVIEW QUESTIONS

1. What powers are given to the President by the Constitution?

2. Of all the presidential powers, which do you think is the most important? Why?

3. What factors have influenced the growth of presidential power?

4. What advantages in the exercise of power and influence do today's Presidents have over their predecessors?

5. How is personality a factor in the exercise of presidential power?

6. Political scientists often refer to a President's "judicial legacy." What do you think is meant by this term?

7. Do you think Americans expect too much from their Presidents? Why or why not?

8. In what ways have the actions of Congress and the actions of the Supreme Court influenced the development of the presidency?

9. Congress acts as a "watchdog" over the bureaucracy. Explain how you think Congress does this and if you think this control and supervision effectively safeguards the democratic process.

SUGGESTED READINGS

1. Armbruster, Maxim. *The Presidents of the United States and their Administrations from Washington to the Present*. New York: Horizon Press Pubs., 1981. Discusses the personalities and characters of those who have led the nation.

2. Barber, James David. *The Presidential Character: Predicting Performance in the White House*. Englewood Cliffs, New Jersey: Prentice-Hall, 1977. Well-known treatment and categorization of presidential personalities.

3. Bernstein, Carl and Bob Woodward. *All the President's Men*. New York: Simon & Schuster, 1974. This true story of the Nixon White House is a gripping account of the Watergate scandal.

4. *Congressional Quarterly's Guide to the Presidency*. Michael Nelson, editor. Washington, D.C.: Congressional Quarterly, Inc., 1989. A comprehensive guide to presidential powers and history.

5. Gray, Lee Lerner. *How We Choose a President*. New York: St. Martins, every four years. Discusses the selection process from the search for candidates through election.

6. Jordan, Hamilton. *Crisis: The Last Year of the Carter Presidency*. New York: G.P. Putnam's Sons, 1982. Jimmy Carter's chief adviser gives a firsthand account of the inner workings of the White House.

7. Lyons, Thomas. *The President: Preacher, Teacher, Salesman: Selected Presidential Speeches, 1933-1983*. Wellesley, MA: World Eagle, Inc., 1985. Highlights the leadership role of the President.

8. Neustadt, Richard. *Presidential Power: The Politics of Leadership from FDR to Carter*. New York: John Wiley & Sons, 1980. A classic analysis of the modern presidency, recently updated and revised.

9. *The Presidency and the Political System*. Michael Nelson, editor. Washington, D.C.: Congressional Quarterly Press, 1984. An examination of how Presidents rely on interest groups, Congress, political parties, and the people for support and survival.

10. *The Winning of the White House 1988*. Time Magazine. New York: Time Incorporated, 1988. The inside story of the 1988 presidential campaign.

ASSESSING INVOLVEMENT

Assessing your own and others' involvement in political situations often means making some political decisions. How might certain political events and policies affect you? Maybe you never get involved because you do not understand that government decisions may change the very conditions under which you live. Decisions, for example, regarding food and drug laws may affect your health. Policies regarding taxation may affect your wealth. A decision to abolish a civilian review board for the police force could affect your safety, rights, and liberty. Efforts of local merchants to control shoplifting may result in your packages being searched before you leave a store.

The impact of decisions such as these are reasonably easy to see. However, there are some political decisions that might have serious consequences that are not quite so clear-cut. For example, does a governmental decision to build a superhighway through a town affect only those whose homes may be torn down, or does it also have an impact on merchants, schools, hospitals, trucking companies, and paving contractors? Will parks be lost? If some people are made homeless, what might be the effect on taxpayers? The more groups that are affected, the more likely there will be an impact on you as an individual.

The following exercise will help you to identify and assess a wide range of implications that might result from a governmental decision.

Federal law requires that all persons and baggage be searched by airport officials before passengers can board airplanes. To help prevent airplane hijackings, weapons such as guns, knives, and bombs can be confiscated. Persons who even jokingly say they are carrying a weapon or bomb can be detained, fined, and imprisoned.

The Constitution gives the national government power over interstate commerce. Thus, the government has been able to act to ensure passenger safety because air travel involves the carrying of goods and people across state boundaries.

On the other hand, the Fourth Amendment affirms "the right of people to be secure in their persons, houses, papers, and effects, against unreasonable searches and seizures." This amendment also says that there can be no searches without probable cause and without a search warrant.

1. What, if any, is the difference between airport searches and store searches?

2. Do you think your rights as a citizen are violated by the federal law requiring airline passengers to submit to searches without probable cause and without a search warrant?

3. Do you as an individual citizen have an obligation to give up part of your rights in order to secure greater safety for all airline passengers?

4. As a concerned citizen, you can become involved in government decisions. One way is by making known your views on existing laws or on pending legislation by writing to your congresspersons and to the editor of your local newspaper.

Unit 5

THE FEDERAL GOVERNMENT AT WORK

The federal government functions not only in Washington, D.C., but its operations extend throughout the country and even reach into your local community. Many of the services that you and your family rely on—for example, schools and highways—are provided at least in part by the federal government.

This widespread influence of the federal government is relatively new. Many of your grandparents can recall a time when the federal government was not as active as it is today. However, as problems have grown more complex, the federal government with its enormous resources has intervened.

Today, the federal government carries out a variety of tasks. The photo on the facing page shows federal officials leaving by plane for a raid on illegal drug smugglers. The federal government also carries out less dramatic, but equally important, pursuits, such as protecting the environment. It is important to remember that these and other services are not available free of charge. The federal government has to rely on money provided by taxpayers, such as your parents or maybe you.

Chapter 17

Public Policy

Our federal government makes countless policy decisions concerning Americans. There are policies providing health care for the poor and elderly; policies to stabilize our national economy; policies to set standards for clean air and water; and policies to maintain a strong national defense. The list could go on and on, but by now you can see that your government is involved in many aspects of your life. All the rules, laws, and standards that have an impact on what you can and cannot do are collectively known as public policy.

★ ★ ★ ★ ★

Chapter Preview

TERMS TO KNOW

fiscal policy, monetary policy, recession, inflation, discount rate, reserve requirement, margin requirements, quotas, free trade, welfare, public services, trust, subsidies, collective bargaining, injunctions, mortgage, conservation, public land, price supports, foreign policy, diplomacy, isolationism, containment, detente, diplomatic recognition

READ TO DISCOVER

- how public policy is made.
- how government regulates the economy.
- how the general welfare of citizens is promoted by government.
- the government's role in addressing the needs of business, labor, and consumers.
- how our natural resources are managed and used.
- the goals, methods, and history of American foreign policy.

Civic Participation Journal

Contact four banks or savings and loans in your community. Ask each institution how much they pay on savings accounts and on one-year certificates of deposit. Also ask them how they determine how much interest they pay. Record your findings in your journal.

1 Making Public Policy

Public policy is the course of action the government takes in response to some problem or issue. Our government establishes public policy usually with a certain goal in mind, such as ensuring a quality education for all Americans, maintaining a clean environment, or building a strong defense.

Decisions about public policy involve choices. Regardless of the issues, policymakers must first answer two basic questions:

1. *Should the government be involved at all?* Some issues are too politically charged for the federal government to make a decision. Other issues are best left to state or local governments to solve. In these cases, federal policymakers may simply decide not to act at all.

2. *If government involvement is necessary, what action should it take?* In other words, if our government does decide to tackle the issue, our elected leaders must hammer out a policy for it. There are at least two (and usually more) alternatives to every issue facing the government.

Tradeoffs

How do our officials answer these two basic questions? Deciding whether or not the government should solve an issue or what course of action to take is no easy matter. Public policy decisions involve tradeoffs. A tradeoff means that some sacrifice must be made to achieve a desired outcome. We may ask our government, for example, to make coal-burning power plants install special devices on their smokestacks to reduce the amount of chemicals released into the air we breathe. The power companies, in turn, may pass on the cost of installing the devices to us, the consumers. The tradeoff is higher utility costs for a cleaner and safer environment.

When making public policy, decision makers must carefully gauge the people's willingness to accept such tradeoffs. Is the public willing to accept the loss of lives to ensure American freedom? Are the people willing to accept fewer government regulations to achieve greater competition in the airline industry? Will the people accept higher prices for safer products? These are the types of questions our national decision makers must answer every day.

To promote clean air, coal-burning power plants, such as this one in Louisiana, have installed devices on their smokestacks to reduce air pollution. What trade-off is often involved in public-policy decisions about air pollution?

Defense spending is an important issue in the making of public policy. Here, naval aircraft are about to engage in maneuvers over the Pacific Ocean. In what areas other than defense does our government enact public policy?

Who Makes Public Policy?

Public policy is made in a number of different ways. Our President, for instance, may establish a national antidrug policy, or Congress may pass legislation designed to combat water pollution. The bureaucracy also makes public policy. A federal agency may enact regulations that make all trucking companies charge fixed rates for their services. In most cases, however, the President, members of Congress, and members of the bureaucracy make public policy in *response* to the needs and desires of the American people.

You, in fact, play a vital role in deciding the public policy agenda. If enough Americans demand that the government solve a problem, answer a question, or face up to an issue, our nation's leaders will likely respond. You can bring issues to the attention of the government in many ways—by voting for or supporting the political party and candidates who share your views; by pressuring your elected officials through letters, petitions, or protests; and by joining or supporting special interest groups. Conversely, when the government is pressured to

do something, its resulting policy choices will reflect back on you in some way. Citizens may be directly affected in the form of higher or lower taxes, increased or decreased government spending, or new laws and regulations.

Our government enacts public policy in five main areas or arenas—the economy, human services, public services, natural resources, and foreign and defense policies. Although not every issue fits neatly into one of these categories, these five public policy arenas are the focus of much of the federal government's work.

Section Review

1. What are the two basic questions to be answered in all public policy decisions?

2. Who makes public policy?

3. What role do the American people play in the process of making public policy?

4. **Challenge:** In your opinion, why are public policies sometimes changed?

2 The Economy

Economic systems differ greatly from one country to another. The United States is a leading example of the free enterprise economic system known as capitalism. "Free enterprise" means that businesses make most of their decisions independent of the government. But our government *is* involved in the overall economy.

In fact, its influence on the economy is substantial. Among the "tools" most widely used by the government to promote and regulate the economy are fiscal policy, monetary policy, and trade policy.

Fiscal Policy

The most direct way the government affects our economy is through **fiscal policy,** found in the budget prepared each year by the President and Congress. By changing spending and taxing levels, the government decides the nation's priorities—that is, which problems to tackle and how much money will be spent on each.

The main purpose of government spending is to provide the public with services, such as transportation, health care, or defense. *How much* money the government decides to spend each year affects the economy. If the government decides to build a new national highway system, for example, industries involved in road construction will need to hire more workers to do the job. These workers, in turn, will stimulate further economic growth when they buy houses, cars, food, and clothes. On the other hand, if the government decides to cut back on road construction, some companies may have to lay off workers. High unemployment in one industry affects others, as people out of work do not have the income to buy as many goods and services.

fiscal policy government's plan for collecting and spending money

The government has the power to issue as well as to spend money. Here, a government worker proofs sheets of five dollar bills. How does the government's spending of money affect the national economy?

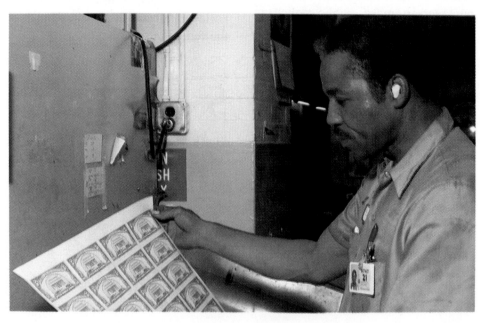

To pay for federal services, the government raises money through borrowing or taxing. The level of taxes a person, business, or large corporation pays has an impact on the economy. If the government increases taxes, for example, consumers have less money to spend. Industries may have to cut back on production as demand for consumer goods decreases. Conversely, if the government decreases taxes, consumers have more money to spend, and the demand for goods and services increases. With increased demand, production levels rise and more jobs are created.

Monetary Policy

Money is the accepted payment for goods and services and is essential to the economy of any nation. The basis for our national money system is found in Article I of the Constitution, which gives Congress the power to "coin money" and to regulate its value. In other words, Congress has the power to set up a national system of currency.

At the same time, the amount of money in circulation (money supply) affects how much consumers will have to spend and businesses can borrow. The government's regulation of the money supply is known as **monetary policy** and is controlled by the Federal Reserve System.

FEDERAL RESERVE SYSTEM

The Federal Reserve System was founded by Congress in 1913. Besides regulating the money supply, it also supervises commercial banks in the United States and provides a means of transferring checks from one bank to another. In this way, the "Fed," as it is sometimes called, serves as a "banker's bank." The Fed also invests the government's money

and handles government bonds, payments, and exchanges of money with other countries.

All banks chartered, or licensed, by the federal government must belong to the Federal Reserve System. State banks have the option of joining the system but must meet certain requirements to do so. Banks in the Federal Reserve System deposit a certain amount of money in one of 12 Federal Reserve banks. The Fed holds this money in reserve and banks can then borrow money from the Fed when their funds run low. Figure 17-1 shows how the Federal Reserve System is divided into 12 regions across the country.

The Fed is supervised in Washington, D.C., by a seven-member Board of Governors who are appointed by the President and approved by the Senate. They serve 14-year terms, with vacancies occurring every two years. One member of the Board of Governors is chosen by the President as chairperson.

MONEY SUPPLY

How does the Federal Reserve System control our nation's money supply? If the economy is in a **recession**, or downward trend, more money is needed to finance business expansion. The Fed may follow an "easy money" policy, one that makes more money available to make the economy grow. If, on the other hand, there is danger of **inflation**, a "tight money" policy is used to restrict the supply of money. The Board of Governors has several ways in which it can make monetary policy, as outlined in Figure 17-2.

First, the Fed can buy and sell government securities in the bond market. This activity is known as open market operations and works as follows. If there is not enough money

monetary policy manipulation of the money supply to affect the economy in a desired way

recession decline in economic activity

inflation increase in the general level of prices and a decrease in the value of money

discount rate interest rate the Federal Reserve System charges member banks to loan them money

reserve requirement amount of money member banks must deposit in the Federal Reserve System

margin requirements percentage of money people can legally borrow to buy stock

in circulation, the Fed starts buying government securities from member banks. This increases the money supply and makes it easier for people to borrow money. On the other hand, if there is too much money in circulation, the Fed sells government securities to member banks and decreases the money supply, making it more difficult to borrow money and slowing the economy.

The second way the Fed controls the money supply is through the **discount rate.** If the Fed wants to expand the country's money supply, it lowers the discount rate to encourage member banks to borrow. Generally, banks will put the borrowed funds in their reserve accounts and, thus, have more money to loan to individuals. But increasing the discount rate discourages banks from borrowing money. Banks will have less money

to loan to individuals, so less money will be in circulation.

A third monetary policy tool available to the Fed concerns the **reserve requirement.** The money supply decreases when the Fed raises the reserve requirement. Banks are required to deposit more money in the Federal Reserve System and so, have less money to loan. When the Fed lowers the reserve requirement, the money supply increases because banks deposit less in the Federal Reserve System.

A fourth and final way the Fed controls the money supply is by setting the **margin requirements** for the purchase of stock. A margin requirement of 75 percent means that 75 percent of the price of stock must be paid for in cash and 25 percent may be borrowed. Raising the margin requirement makes stock purchases

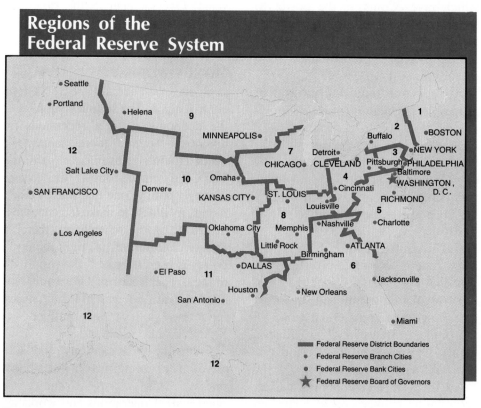

Figure 17-1

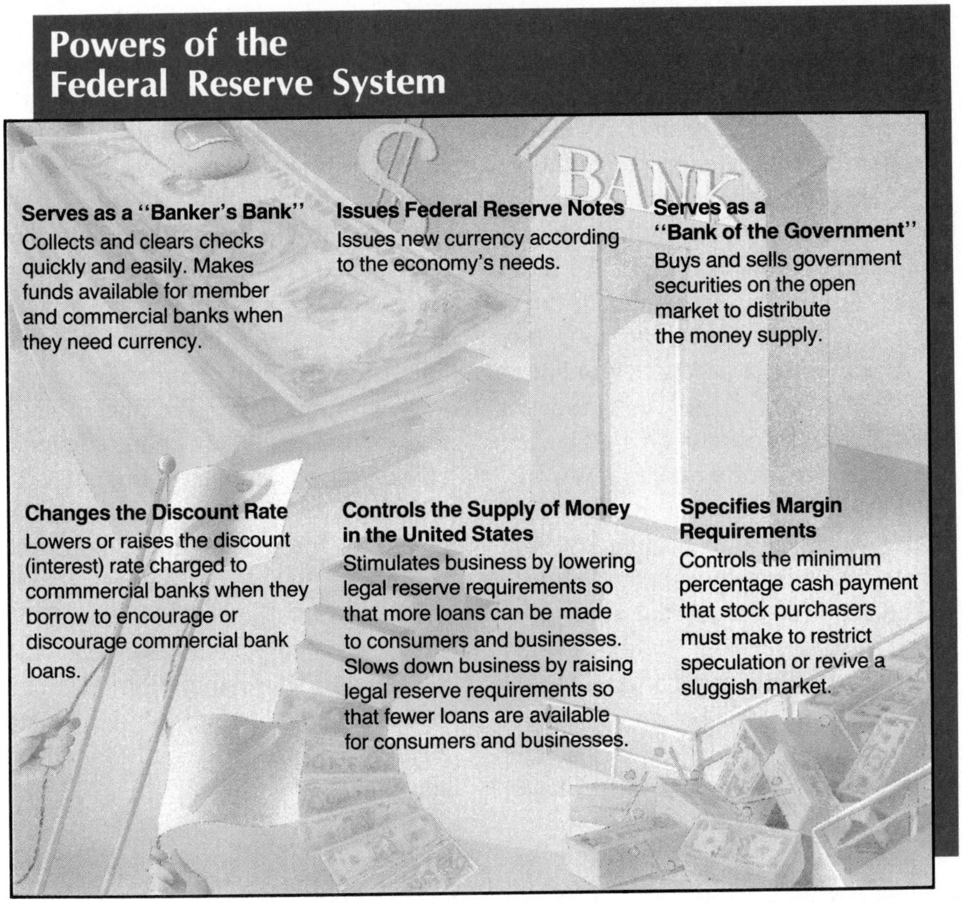

Powers of the Federal Reserve System

Serves as a "Banker's Bank"
Collects and clears checks quickly and easily. Makes funds available for member and commercial banks when they need currency.

Issues Federal Reserve Notes
Issues new currency according to the economy's needs.

Serves as a "Bank of the Government"
Buys and sells government securities on the open market to distribute the money supply.

Changes the Discount Rate
Lowers or raises the discount (interest) rate charged to commmercial banks when they borrow to encourage or discourage commercial bank loans.

Controls the Supply of Money in the United States
Stimulates business by lowering legal reserve requirements so that more loans can be made to consumers and businesses. Slows down business by raising legal reserve requirements so that fewer loans are available for consumers and businesses.

Specifies Margin Requirements
Controls the minimum percentage cash payment that stock purchasers must make to restrict speculation or revive a sluggish market.

Figure 17-2

more difficult. Thus, less money is circulated. But lowering the requirement makes stock purchases easier for most people and, thus, more money is pumped into the economy.

Trade Policy

America's trade policy toward the rest of the world also has a major impact on the *national* economy. Many businesses want our federal government to provide them with opportunities to sell their goods overseas. With this in mind, national decision makers seek to establish a trade policy that stimulates economic growth at home, encourages free competition in the world economy, and protects American jobs. The gov-

ernment's main "tools" in constructing a trade policy are trade barriers, trade loans, and trade agreements.

BARRIERS

Many American industries face stiff competition from overseas. The automobile, steel, and electronics industries must compete with foreign manufacturers that often have lower labor costs and can produce products less expensively than their American counterparts. As a result, American industries lose business and must lay off workers. Such action severely affects our national economy. How can our government help American businesses that are facing overseas competition?

The government can set up trade barriers by restricting imports. This can be done in two ways. First, it can impose tariffs. Tariffs on imported goods raise the price of foreign products and may help protect American companies from foreign competitors.

Second, our government can restrict imports through **quotas**. Quotas can be more powerful and have more of an impact on international trade than tariffs. A quota can be set as low as zero to keep a product from entering our country at all. Sometimes a specific quota does not have to be set; the mere *threat* of a quota may work. In 1981, for example, our government, in response to complaints from American automobile manufacturers, asked Japan to reduce the number of cars it was sending to the United States. Fearing that Washington might set a specific quota, Japan voluntarily limited the number of cars it was exporting to the United States.

quotas limits on the amount of foreign goods that can be imported

LOANS

In addition to trade barriers, our government can help American industries compete with foreign manufacturers in other ways. One way is to provide low-cost loans. Another way is by providing research grants and loans to U.S. industries engaged in developing new technologies, such as superconductivity and high definition television (HDTV). In another type of loan program, the government may loan a foreign nation money to purchase American-made products. In 1988 it gave $705 million in special loans to foreign nations under the condition that a percentage of the money would be used to buy U.S. steel, machinery, and other products. Some loans also require that a certain percentage of the goods the nation buys be shipped on U.S. merchant ships.

Tariffs placed on imported goods, such as these cars, increase their selling price on the market. This may encourage shoppers to buy American-made goods. What is another result of trade barriers?

The 1989 free trade agreement between the United States and Canada created a single economic market in North America. Here is one of the major border crossings between the two countries. What international organization has worked to reduce world trade barriers?

AGREEMENTS

When it is to a nation's advantage, its government works to promote **free trade.** Oftentimes the United States and another nation enter into an agreement to reduce trade barriers. For example, in 1989 a free trade agreement between the United States and Canada took effect. The agreement is designed to eliminate all tariffs between the two nations. The North American Free Trade Agreement (NAFTA), ratified by Congress in 1993, extended the U.S.-Canadian agreement to include Mexico. In addition, several international trade organizations, such as the General Agreement on Tariffs and Trade GATT), have been formed to resolve world trade problems

EFFECTS

Nearly every nation's economy is tied to the rest of the world, and our nation is no exception. Whatever trade policy our government makes affects not only our national economy, but may have a rippling effect across the globe. If the U.S. government, for example, restricts imports by issuing high tariffs, other nations may impose their own tariffs. Foreign consumers would not buy the more expensive American goods, which would result in lower profits for our companies. If our government, however, chooses not to implement tariffs, some U.S. industries may be forced to reduce production in the face of less expensive foreign goods. Thus, our government's trade policy can have far-reaching consequences for the American economy.

free trade   trade that places no legal barriers on import or export of goods between countries

Section Review

1. What "tools" are most widely used by government to promote and regulate the economy?

2. How does fiscal policy affect the economy?

3. What are four ways the Fed can affect the nation's money supply?

4. What three methods does the government use to establish trade policy?

5. **Challenge:** Do you think the federal government should have more or less control over the nation's economy? Explain.

During the Great Depression, one out of every four American workers was unemployed. Many people who were desperate for work had to sell apples on street corners. How did the federal government's role change during the Great Depression?

3 Human Services

Our national government plays a large role in looking out for the health, education, and welfare of its citizens. But this has not always been the case.

History

Since the time of the pioneers, Americans have clung to the ideal of "rugged individualism." That is, if you worked hard you could earn a decent living and would not have to rely on the help of others. For those who did experience hard times, friends, families, private groups, and perhaps local and state governments would provide relief and support—but not the federal government. The Great Depression, however, changed this way of thinking forever. Banks failed, life savings were wiped out, and millions of people had no jobs. For the first time, there was a widespread belief that the federal government was the only institution with the resources to meet the challenge of putting the nation back together again.

President Franklin D. Roosevelt was elected in 1932 on the promise of a "New Deal" for all Americans. Roosevelt set up programs to provide temporary relief for the needy and to put the unemployed back to work. Social insurance programs and agricultural assistance programs were also instituted.

RECENT EVENTS
After World War II, various Presidents and Congresses developed other long-range social programs to meet the changing needs of Americans. By the time Ronald Reagan became President in 1981, social programs in the United States made up more than one-third of the federal budget. Reagan felt federal spending for social programs was "out of control." He worked to convince the public and Congress that reducing expenditures for social programs was necessary. At the same time, he proposed to leave a "safety net" for the "truly needy." Some programs were eliminated, others had their budgets cut, and several cut the number of people eligible for the service.

SOCIAL PROGRAMS TODAY
Despite the cuts made in the 1980s, our government is still involved in many programs designed to promote your health and welfare. There are two basic kinds of human service programs that exist in the United States—social insurance and public assistance. Figure 17-3 explains some of these programs.

Social Insurance

Social insurance pays benefits to anyone, whether rich or poor, who has worked and paid taxes in the past. Social insurance programs pay out hundreds of billions of dollars every year in pensions, benefits, and direct payments. Two major social insurance programs, Social Security and Medicare, will be examined here.

SOCIAL SECURITY
The Social Security program, sometimes called the Old Age, Survivors, and Disability program (OASDI) was approved by Congress in 1935. It is the largest social program in the United States, providing funds to retired or disabled workers and their dependents. Here's how it operates: During working years, employees, their employers, and the self-employed make contributions to the

Social Security fund through a payroll tax called the Federal Insurance Contributions Act tax (FICA). These contributions are placed in special government trust funds. The funds provide monthly cash payments to those who qualify for them; that is, retired or disabled workers.

The amount of benefits a person receives may vary. Benefits are determined by the number of years a person worked as well as the amount of money he or she earned per month while employed. In 1993 the largest benefit a person could receive at the age of 65 was $1128 per month.

From its beginnings, the Social Security program experienced steady growth. However, starting in the 1970s, economic recessions and rising inflation made Social Security more costly. In addition, Americans were living longer than ever before due to advances in medicine and health care. When Social Security began, the average life expectancy of most Americans was 61 years; today it is 74 years. By 1981 Social Security faced a severe cash shortage. Outgoing payments were higher than incoming payroll taxes, forcing the government to rely on reserve funds to make up the difference.

In 1983 a $164.3 billion bill aimed at saving the Social Security program was passed by Congress. The bill proposed to refinance the Social Security program by increasing the payroll taxes paid by employers, by requiring federal workers who were hired after January 1, 1984, to join the program, and by taxing the pensions of some recipients. In addition, the bill boosted the retirement age gradually from 65 years to 67 years by the year 2027.

MAJOR SOCIAL PROGRAMS IN THE UNITED STATES

SOCIAL INSURANCE PROGRAMS	Provide benefits to workers who have paid into programs.
Social Security	Pays benefits to retired workers, those unable to work, and survivors of workers who have died.
Unemployment Insurance	Pays workers who have lost their jobs.
Workers' Compensation	Provides cash and medical care payments to those workers who have been hurt on the job.
Medicare	Provides free hospital and low-cost medical insurance for the elderly and the disabled.
PUBLIC ASSISTANCE PROGRAMS	Provide benefits based on need rather than prior employment or contributions.
Aid to Families With Dependent Children	Provides benefits to single parents in financial need.
Supplemental Security Insurance	Provides benefits to people who are blind, elderly, or physically disabled and who are not covered by Social Security.
Medicaid	Provides payments to low-income persons in need of medical care.
Food Stamps	Provide food for persons and families in need.

Figure 17-3

MEDICARE

Medicare started in 1965 as a program to provide health care for the elderly. It presently covers those people over 65 years of age who receive Social Security benefits or who are disabled.

The program has two plans. The first is a hospital insurance plan that pays for the major costs of hospital and nursing care. This plan is backed by a portion of the Social Security taxes.

The second plan is a voluntary medical insurance plan. This plan helps pay medical expenses, such as doctor's bills, drugs, treatments, and areas not covered by hospital insurance. Insured members pay a monthly fee and then the government contributes to this amount. Payments are made to members to cover approximately 80 percent of their yearly medical costs.

Like Social Security, Medicare has had its share of financial problems. The combined factors of inflation, rising medical costs, and a rise in the number of elderly Americans have forced the Medicare program to pay out more than $128 billion in benefits

to 35 million people in 1992 alone. Legislators and other public officials are challenged with searching for ways to keep Medicare costs down while still providing adequate health care for America's senior citizens.

Welfare Programs

Unlike social insurance, **welfare** programs provide benefits based on a person's *need*. These programs pay out about $80 billion per year. Two major welfare programs are Aid to Families with Dependent Children (AFDC) and Medicaid.

AFDC

AFDC provides financial aid to low-income families with children where one of the parents is either absent or dead, and the other parent is unable to support the family. This program was created by Congress in 1935 as a joint federal-state operation.

Although the federal government provides the majority of funding, the states run their own AFDC programs. Each state estimates the minimum income needed to support families of different sizes. If a family's income falls below this level and if the family has no other means of support, then it qualifies for AFDC payments in the state.

MEDICAID

Medicaid is another federal-state program that provides health care to many people who cannot afford it. Medicaid pays for hospital stays, doctor's fees, and laboratory tests. The federal government takes care of a percentage of state Medicaid costs. This percentage varies from 50 to 83 percent, depending on the average income of the people in a state. All states currently participate in the Medicaid program.

welfare government programs that provide food, money, and other necessities to people who are legally entitled to assistance

Older Americans are living longer and contributing more to American society. What impact has the rise in the number of elderly Americans had on the Medicare program?

Other Human Service Programs

The federal government provides many other programs that meet people's needs. These programs are enacted because most Americans believe the government should provide for the general welfare of its citizens.

PUBLIC HEALTH

Public health refers to the health of everyone in a community. Here, too, the federal government plays an important role.

Congress established the Public Health Service (PHS) in 1912 to promote the protection and advancement of physical and mental health for all Americans and to cooperate in health projects with other nations. The PHS fulfills these goals by conducting medical research, controlling disease, providing health education, and performing many other services.

A leading PHS agency is the Centers for Disease Control and Prevention (CDC). Created by Congress in 1946, this agency investigates and attempts to find cures for contagious diseases, especially epidemics, or the rapid spread of one particular disease. Currently the CDC is involved in finding a cure for Acquired Immune Deficiency Syndrome (AIDS).

Since the early 1980s when the disease was first identified, AIDS has been a major focus of the research conducted at the CDC. AIDS attacks a person's immune system, leaving the body with no defense against infectious disease. AIDS is nearly 100 percent fatal; more than 200,000 people in the United States have died of AIDS in the last decade. Although there is no current cure for AIDS, scientists and medical researchers at the CDC say that making the public aware that the disease is spread through the exchange of bodily fluids is the best prevention until a vaccine can be found.

EDUCATION

Control of public education belongs to the states. The federal government contributes funds, but not nearly as much as the amount spent by state and local governments.

The federal government's role in education is twofold: 1) to try to ensure that all children receive equal educational opportunities, and 2) to provide funds for certain types of education that will benefit the nation as a whole. If the states meet these goals, the government provides financial support for elementary, high school, and college education; vocational education; bilingual education; education for persons with physical and mental handicaps; and education for the gifted and the disadvantaged. In addition, our government acts as the nation's chief research institution for education, collecting and publishing data about new teaching methods and educational programs.

Section Review

1. What event changed the government's role in providing relief and support for America's people in need?

2. What are two basic kinds of welfare programs in the United States today?

3. What is the difference between social insurance and welfare programs?

4. What role does the federal government play in education?

5. **Challenge:** Do you support or oppose federal involvement in human services? Explain.

The aircraft industry is one of the industries regulated by the Federal Trade Commission. Why was the FTC established?

public services government services for the general benefit of the people by aiding certain groups within society

trust combination of companies to control the production and price of a product and to reduce competition

4 Public Services

The national government provides a number of **public services** that benefit business, labor, and consumers. Thus, they affect the quality of life for all Americans. Examples are laws regulating business transactions, safety standards for the workplace, and nutritional requirements for many different kinds of food. Without the help of the federal government, most of these services would be too costly for local or state governments and too unprofitable for business.

Business

President Calvin Coolidge once said, ''The business of America is business.'' He was referring to the fact that the growth of business and industry in the United States had given the nation one of the world's highest standards of living. But how is our government tied to the business community? You have already read that it helps maintain a stable economy in which business can prosper. Further, under powers granted it by the Constitution, Congress regulates commerce among the states and other nations, fixes standards for weights and measures, imposes tariffs, makes laws for bankruptcies, and coins money. All of these powers are directly related to the operation of business in America.

But besides these constitutional powers, the government works to maintain competition in the business community, gives businesses loans and tax breaks to promote growth, and provides up-to-date information for business leaders.

COMPETITION

Under the American free enterprise system, businesses are allowed to compete for profit with a minimum of government interference. From time to time, however, the government has stepped in to monitor business activities. Federal regulations often work to promote competition among the companies within an industry. This competition ensures that fair prices are maintained for consumers.

Our government also regulates the *size* of businesses to make sure that they do not become so large or powerful that they unduly eliminate competitors. One of the earliest laws to tackle this problem was the Sherman Antitrust Act, passed in 1890. It declared illegal any business combinations in the form of a **trust**. Another law set up the Federal Trade Commission (FTC), which received the power to investigate business practices that might violate antitrust laws.

The federal government has not eliminated all trusts, however. Public service companies, such as the utilities and certain other industries, may have some features of trusts. The government allows them to exist because they serve the public interest and because they operate under strict controls.

Today, our government is faced with newer, more complex problems surrounding competition. Corporate mergers (two companies combining), takeovers (one company buying another), and hostile takeovers (one company buying another against its wishes) are tactics that have been used to increase profits in many industries, including airlines, automobile manufacturing, and entertainment.

The government must approve most mergers and takeovers, but it is often hard to judge if such actions will hurt or help the economy. Some mergers and takeovers can actually help to maintain competition, create jobs, and promote a healthy economy when weaker companies are moved in with stronger ones. But sometimes, a company created by a merger may force its competition out of business, allowing one company to completely dominate an entire industry.

SUBSIDIES

The government provides **subsidies** to businesses to help defray costs when they are expanding and to help new businesses form. The government may subsidize research into new manufacturing technologies, which could help reduce costs for companies and lead to reduced prices for consumers. The government also operates the Small Business Administration (SBA), which provides technical information, loans and training programs for people struggling to go into business for themselves.

To give businesses a chance to make profits, our government provides the business community with many tax breaks. Businesses can save these profits, distribute them to shareholders or officers, or reinvest them. Companies and entrepreneurs can deduct, or "write off," on their taxes their costs of expansion, investments, and many charitable contributions.

Finally, the government can give outright loans to businesses and large corporations if they are threatened with collapse. The government grants these loans because if large businesses fail, the resulting unemployment could have a profound effect on our nation's economic system. Recent examples of businesses and corporations that received these loans, or "bailouts," include Penn Central Railroad and the savings and loan industry.

INFORMATION

American business runs on information. Who buys what products and when? What are the latest population trends? How will inflation affect sales this year? The government supplies business with answers to these and other questions and with up-to-date information, most of it for free. The Bureau of the Census, for example, supplies a variety of population data concerning the age, sex, income, marital status, and race of people living in the United States. Much of the census data is published in the *Statistical Abstract of the United States*. This book, published since 1878, is the standard summary on the economic, social, and political life of the United States.

Labor

More than 65 million people make up America's work force. Many believe that the federal government should monitor the needs and problems of our nation's working men and women. However, the federal government has not always followed such a course.

subsidies grants of money

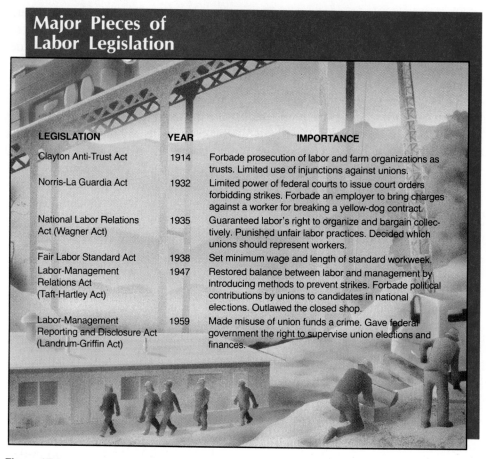

Major Pieces of Labor Legislation

LEGISLATION	YEAR	IMPORTANCE
Clayton Anti-Trust Act	1914	Forbade prosecution of labor and farm organizations as trusts. Limited use of injunctions against unions.
Norris-La Guardia Act	1932	Limited power of federal courts to issue court orders forbidding strikes. Forbade an employer to bring charges against a worker for breaking a yellow-dog contract.
National Labor Relations Act (Wagner Act)	1935	Guaranteed labor's right to organize and bargain collectively. Punished unfair labor practices. Decided which unions should represent workers.
Fair Labor Standard Act	1938	Set minimum wage and length of standard workweek.
Labor-Management Relations Act (Taft-Hartley Act)	1947	Restored balance between labor and management by introducing methods to prevent strikes. Forbade political contributions by unions to candidates in national elections. Outlawed the closed shop.
Labor-Management Reporting and Disclosure Act (Landrum-Griffin Act)	1959	Made misuse of union funds a crime. Gave federal government the right to supervise union elections and finances.

Figure 17-4

For a long time, labor was on its own. Children and adults in our country worked long hours for low pay, often under unsafe and filthy conditions.

To help their plight, workers in many different trades formed unions. By the late 1880s, unions were using strikes and **collective bargaining** to seek better pay and working conditions. But because of several violent strikes, public attitude and the courts often sided with management, and several states passed laws restricting union activity.

It was not until the Great Depression that many Americans began to change their attitudes toward labor. The climate shifted from one favoring management to one favoring labor and labor unions, and government followed suit. Many laws were passed in the 1930s that guaranteed basic rights to labor unions. These laws guaranteed workers the right to organize unions and bargain collectively, limited the power of the federal courts to issue **injunctions** forbidding strikes, and set a minimum wage.

Although labor has experienced some gains and some setbacks since then, government has continued to address its concerns. One area of concern is worker protection on the job. The Occupational Safety and Health Act established safety and health standards for work places, and set up the Occupational Safety and Health Administration (OSHA) to make sure these standards were met.

collective bargaining negotiation of workers, represented by a union, with employers

injunctions court orders

420 **Public Policy**

The federal government is also involved in helping individuals find work. Under the Department of Labor, several agencies have been set up to promote employment of the work force. The United States Employment Service, for instance, matches jobseekers with available positions. Another program, the Job Corps, provides job training for disadvantaged youths.

The primary job program of the federal government was set up by the Job Training Partnership Act of 1982. Under it, state and local governments receive federal funds to provide job training for youths and adults. The job training is supplied by private business.

Consumers

As part of its responsibility to protect the general welfare of all Americans, our federal government works to prevent businesses from engaging in unfair or unsafe practices. The government also has established programs to help American consumers make one of their most expensive purchases—a home.

PROTECTION

In the past, if you found a product to be unsafe or shoddy, you had little recourse against the manufacturer. But recently ''consumer rights'' has became a major movement in the United States. Consumer rights advocates seek to protect you from false advertising claims, defective products, and unsafe materials. The rise of this movement has forced the government to pass legislation setting safety and health standards for many industries.

One of the first industries to be singled out by consumers was the automobile industry. In 1965 con-

sumer advocate Ralph Nader, in his book *Unsafe At Any Speed*, examined the safety record of the Corvair, a rear-engine car built by General Motors. Nader claimed the car was too dangerous to drive. As a result, Congress investigated the automobile industry and in 1966 passed the Motor Vehicle Safety Act. This law requires automobile manufacturers to meet certain safety standards for their cars and to notify buyers of any defects discovered in the cars after they are purchased.

In response to growing consumer complaints in other areas, Congress established the Consumer Product Safety Commission (CPSC) in 1972 to determine the safety of many products and to establish safety standards. The CPSC examines hundreds of products every year and develops safety standards on items like infant furniture and toys, power tools, and appliances.

FOOD AND DRUGS

The government's involvement in regulating the food and drug industries goes back to the turn of the century. In the late 1800s, mass

Car manufacturers now conduct experiments using crash dummies to test air bags and other safety features. Why was the Motor Vehicle Safety Act passed?

production techniques were incorporated for the first time in many food industries, such as meat-packing and canning. Although production increased, many health problems occurred. Some foods were contaminated and working conditions were unsanitary. At the same time, drug companies were flourishing in the United States, and many advertised their "drugs" using false statements and misleading claims. Public outcry over unhealthy foods and worthless drugs forced the government to take action.

In 1906 Congress passed the Pure Food and Drug Act. This law set standards for the quality, purity, and safety of food, drugs, and cosmetics sold in the United States. The Pure Food and Drug Act also created the Food and Drug Administration (FDA).

Today, FDA agents regularly inspect food processing plants, chemical laboratories, and drugstores to prevent unsafe and unsanitary conditions and practices. The FDA makes sure that products purchased by consumers are properly labeled. It also tests and approves new drugs before they are released on the market.

HOUSING

Perhaps the most expensive product you will ever buy is a home. Owning a home has always been a central part of the "American Dream." The federal government is involved in making this part of the American Dream attainable for Americans by backing the loans people obtain to buy a home.

When purchasing a home, most people make a down payment on part of the total price and borrow the remainder. The buyer signs a **mortgage** with a money-lending institution. Our government, through the

Federal Housing Administration (FHA), provides a mortgage-insurance program that helps qualifying home buyers get loans—that is, the insurance program promises to pay the balance of the loan to the lender if the buyer fails to do so. Another FHA program makes loans available at lower interest rates to persons who qualify.

But what about those who cannot afford a mortgage or even rent payments? The government has set up programs that provide housing assistance for low-income families. Public housing for low-income families is usually controlled by local housing authorities. These organizations, with members appointed by a local government, determine the need for public housing and then plan, develop, and manage the projects.

Local housing authorities receive funds from the federal government to build and to operate public housing. The government pays the difference between the cost of the housing and the amount that low-income families can pay in rent. Today, a family on this plan pays no more than one-fourth of its income for rent.

Section Review

1. Why does the federal government regulate the formation of trusts?

2. What were the main goals of labor legislation of the 1930s?

3. What are the major duties of the Food and Drug Administration?

4. How does the federal government help low-income families afford housing?

5. **Challenge:** Do you think the federal government should be involved in helping individuals find employment? Why or why not?

mortgage claim on property given to a lender in the event that the loan is not paid on time

5 Natural Resources

You live in a country that is rich in land, forests, wildlife, minerals, and water. Over the years, we have used these natural resources to build a powerful agricultural and industrial nation. At one time, it was believed that America was an inexhaustible storehouse of resources. As a result, little consideration was given for future generations.

About the turn of the century, influential Americans, such as President Theodore Roosevelt, recognized that our natural resources could one day be gone. The government was urged to practice **conservation.**

Since then, the conservation movement has grown in many different, and sometimes opposing, ways. Some groups view America's unused resources as productive assets that could be used to advance our nation's economic growth. Others claim that the more natural resources used up for industry and other development, the more the delicate balance of nature is upset. This group wants to maintain areas of natural beauty by halting the spread of development into them.

The federal government manages and supervises the use of America's natural resources. It owns vast tracts of land, setting aside some of these holdings for preservation as special scenic areas. It also maintains standards for the care of the natural environment—the air, land, and water. In addition, it provides assistance to the nation's farmers in farm management and food production.

The Land

The federal government owns more than one-third of the land in the United States. This **public land** is mostly located in the West and is used for a variety of purposes.

LAND USE

The government sets aside a portion of public land for national parks. The national park system began more than 100 years ago when concerned citizens in the West persuaded the government that certain areas should be declared public because of their natural beauty. In 1872, President Ulysses S. Grant signed a bill declaring a section of Wyoming known as Yellowstone as America's first national park. Since then, more than 300 other areas have been added to the national park system. Parklands include not only parks, but historic sites, buildings, and monuments.

Other public lands are designated as national forests. The government leases portions of national forest land for commercial lumbering and mining and for grazing livestock. However, it tries to ensure that the forests remain plentiful and that development does not deplete this valuable resource.

conservation   careful management and use of natural resources

public land   land owned by the federal government

Yellowstone National Park is known for its variety of scenery and wildlife. Here, two moose browse along the Yellowstone River. Why was the National Park system established?

The red fox is among the many animal species found in wildlife preserves created by the federal government. What is the purpose of wildlife preserves?

The government also seeks to protect America's abundant fish and wildlife by designating parts of public land as wildlife preserves. Migrating birds, endangered animal species, and many species of fish are protected in national wildlife preserves and waterways. The federal government does allow hunting and fishing in some of these areas, but only under strict regulations.

Public land is also used for military purposes. Weapons testing sites, nuclear weapon facilities, and military bases and ports are all on land owned by the federal government.

CONTROVERSY

As can be seen, the government owns a huge amount of land and property in the United States. How it uses this land is often controversial.

The government tries to conserve the resources of public lands while, at the same time, encouraging their economic development. It seeks to balance the competing interests of developers and conservationists—both of whom believe they have a stake in the future of public lands. These efforts have won both enemies and friends.

The government's use of 174 million acres of public land in the western United States illustrates this controversy. These lands contain a great deal of wealth—50 percent of the West's coal reserves; 80 percent of the nation's oil shale reserves; more than 1 billion board feet of timber; and more than 170 million acres of rangeland that provide grazing for about 9 million head of livestock. For many years, the federal government paid little attention to these lands. Ranchers, miners, and loggers used the land as they desired.

In 1976, Congress passed the Federal Land Policy and Management Act. This law, and others following it, signaled a more active role for the federal government in managing public lands and their resources. The most far-reaching policy of this act is known as multiple use/sustained yield.

Multiple use calls for managing public lands and their resources in such a way that will best meet the present and future needs of the nation. Sustained yield requires that resources such as timber be harvested at an annual rate that can be maintained for successive years. In other words, the use of natural resources cannot be so high in the short run that future use is limited or jeopardized. Neglect of this principle had led to serious damage on thousands of acres of public land.

This policy raises conflicting demands from the public about land use. Some ranchers charge that the policy restricts livestock grazing in areas that have long been used for this purpose. Miners and developers say it blocks the use of mineral wealth needed for our nation's economy. Environmentalists claim that the government permits the cattle and sheep owned by ranchers to chase wildlife out of their natural surroundings. These and other criticisms over the public land use policy makes this one of the federal government's most controversial public policy issues.

The Environment

In addition to land use, the federal government sets policies for other segments of the natural environment, such as the air we breathe and the water we drink. But government regulation of the environment has been slow in coming.

As America industrialized in the 1800s, little thought was given to protecting the air and water. Factories belching smoke into the sky or dumping wastes into rivers and lakes were signs of success and prosperity. Only slowly did this view begin to change.

By the 1960s, concern over the environment reached national levels. In 1962, Rachel Carson's book *Silent Spring* captured the public's attention with its frightening tale of the dangers of the widespread use of pesticides.

Increasing interest in ecology, which is the study of the relationship between living creatures and their environment, led to a nationwide movement that demanded the government do something to clean up the nation's air and water.

The federal government began to set standards for the environment in 1970, when President Richard Nixon signed the National Environmental Policy Act. This law stated that it was the nation's goal to create and maintain "conditions under which man and nature can exist in productive harmony." This statement has been the guiding principle behind most of the federal government's antipollution legislation.

Under the provisions of the National Environmental Policy Act, all federal agencies must develop studies on the impact their future activities will have on the environment. Later in 1970, President Nixon asked Congress to create the Environmental Protection Agency (EPA), which would coordinate all of the government's antipollution activities.

That same year, Congress passed the Clean Air Act, which required the EPA to determine air quality standards for the nation and to set deadlines for meeting these standards. A similar law dealing with water pollution, the Safe Drinking Water Act, was passed by Congress in 1974.

As a result of these and many other laws, our air, lakes, rivers, and streams are cleaner and clearer. But the costs have been high. Many industries—such as automobile manufacturers, public utilities, and chemical producers—have passed on to consumers the cost of installing antipollution devices on their products and in their factories. At the same time, still more work needs to be done. Many cities have not met clean air standards mandated by the EPA. And new threats to the environment, such as the greenhouse effect, toxic wastes, and ocean pollution, are challenging our leaders to expand America's environmental policy.

Agriculture

For many years, the federal government was only minimally involved in agriculture. It was not until the 1930s that the federal government became *actively* involved in attempts to stabilize farm income and manage the supply of farm products. A new idea, raising farm prices by encouraging farmers to limit production, was introduced in the 1930s. Those farmers who agreed to reduce the amount they produced were promised a subsidy from the government, paid for from appropriations by Congress.

In addition to limiting production, the government helped control farmers' income through **price supports**. Under this plan, farmers were guaranteed a minimum price for certain

crops. When market prices fell below the support levels, the government either bought the crops or made a cash payment for the difference.

Over the years, the federal government has continued these basic policies. However, it has modified these programs to keep pace with changes in agriculture.

In 1985 Congress passed a comprehensive farm bill to help the nation's farmers. The bill called for lower price support for crops, but increased the number of low-cost loans available to farmers. With the help of this new bill, many farmers enjoyed their first profitable growing season in several years. But severe floods in 1993 made the good times short. Congress responded with a special $2.5 billion flood relief bill that helped farmers with further income and price supports. These bills are evidence of the farm industry's reliance on government help.

The question of whether government should play a role in farming is controversial. Critics point out that no

price supports programs in which the federal government purchases surplus production of certain crops

As a result of governmental action beginning in the 1970s, vast areas of wilderness, such as this coastal area in the state of Washington, have been protected from industrial pollution. What federal agency coordinates all of the government's antipollution efforts?

CASE STUDY: THE GREEN-HOUSE EFFECT

THE HEAT IS ON

Good morning for December 12, 2050. It looks like another hot day with temperatures reaching about 95 degrees. Meanwhile, Hurricane Lou is dumping up to 12 inches of rain on parts of the South and Southwest. And it looks like no part of the nation will have a white Christmas this year—our long-range forecast says the temperature will be in the 90s right up through New Year's Day.

This weather forecast of the future may not be as far-fetched as it seems. Scientists believe that the world's temperature is slowly rising so that by the year 2050 global temperatures could be three to nine degrees higher than they are now. This could possibly cause big changes in world climate. This global warming is attributed to the greenhouse effect.

The greenhouse effect is a natural process that keeps heat from escaping the atmosphere. Gases produced in nature by plants and animals, mainly carbon dioxide, trap the heat and keep Earth warm. Without the process, temperatures would be below zero most of the time. The problem is that the greenhouse effect currently may be out of control.

Since the industrial revolution of the 1800s, the world has added billions of tons of carbon dioxide to the atmosphere by burning gas, oil, coal, and other fossil fuels to provide energy for factories, power plants, and cars. Scientists believe the atmosphere now contains 25 percent more carbon dioxide than just 100 years ago, causing Earth to hold more heat and the planet's temperature to rise.

Many scientists are becoming alarmed that if current trends continue, the world's weather patterns could change, turning winters into summers and producing frequent and violent storms. The polar ice caps could partially melt, raising ocean levels more than six feet in some areas and covering low-lying islands and shorelines. Dry regions of the world—such as northern Africa—could have monsoonlike conditions.

Some scientists say we are already experiencing the affects of a warmer planet. They point to recent severe droughts and the problems meteorologists are having in accurately predicting the weather as signs that the greenhouse effect is beginning to change Earth's climate. Others, less sure, say that the greenhouse effect is overblown. Instead they claim there is evidence that Earth's climate moves in long heating and cooling cycles that can last up to ten thousand years. These scientists say that while we should be careful about the amount of carbon dioxide we are releasing in the air, it is not time to panic.

So what should be done about the greenhouse effect? Among the proposals is one to replace fossil-fuel energy sources with nuclear, solar, wind, and geothermal power. But the costs for such a huge project may be too steep. Halting destruction of the world's rain forests is another answer, since trees use carbon dioxide in photosynthesis. However, nations with large rain forests—such as Brazil—object to any plan they think would hinder their economic development.

At this time, it is difficult to judge what there is to be gained or lost from an accelerated greenhouse effect. But most scientists do agree on one thing—the warming of Earth over the next 100 years, whatever its effects, may be irreversible unless something is done soon.

1. What is the greenhouse effect?
2. What solution to the greenhouse effect do you think is the best? Why?

industry is subsidized to the extent that agriculture is. During the 1980s, the government spent between 2 and 3 percent of its annual budget on farming. Some critics think that farmers should be less dependent on government for income and more dependent on the workings of the open market. The answer to overproducing, they note, should be based on farmers finding more buyers, lowering prices, or reducing production, not relying on government to bail them out.

On the other hand, proponents of government aid point out that most agricultural products do not get federal support. Support is concentrated on such basic crops as grains, cotton, rice, soybeans, and dairy products. Fruits, vegetables, livestock, and specialty crops are not subsidized. They also point out that most farmers do not receive federal funds. In the 1990s, less than one-fourth of American farms were part of a subsidy program. Those who support government aid also note that pitting American farmers, operating via the open market, against subsidized foreign farmers would be ruinous.

Oil barge

Energy

Energy is vital to the United States. Without enormous amounts of energy to power cars, light and heat homes, and run factories, we as a nation could not function. For the past 25 years, Americans have been increasingly concerned about declining energy sources. During this period, our population increased 28 percent, but energy use increased 75 percent!

Today, the United States does not produce enough oil or natural gas to meet its needs and must import these and other products from overseas. Because of limited energy supplies and expected increases in their costs,

we have been trying to increase our own supplies and to make more efficient use of energy sources currently available. New forms of energy are also being researched. At the same time, the federal government has been encouraging Americans to use less energy.

What can be done to keep from depleting our energy sources? Some leading energy experts and economists feel that the best way is to let private enterprise have free rein. They argue that the higher market prices will provide the incentive for private enterprise to find and develop sufficient energy supplies. Others, however, warn that only if the federal government has an active role can we produce the energy supplies we need at affordable prices. Producing synthetic fuels, they note, is too costly and risky an endeavor for private enterprise, and such fuels would be essential during a long-term shortage. Thus, government help is needed to make sure we have these alternative energy sources.

Section Review

1. What are two ways the government uses public lands?

2. What law is the basis for the government's environmental policy?

3. How did Congress help farmers during the flood of 1993?

4. Why have Americans been increasingly concerned in recent years about declining energy sources?

5. **Challenge:** In your opinion, who should have control of public lands and their economic benefits?

6 Foreign Policy

During the twentieth century, the United States has played a major role in world affairs. One reason is our nation's industrial power and its close ties to other countries. As a leading trading nation, the United States needs foreign supply sources, producers, and markets to make and sell its products. To maintain its economic strength, the United States tries to keep foreign markets stable. Thus, it either works with or against other governments to protect American economic interests. The United States is also a politically influential world power. It becomes involved in world affairs to promote and defend certain political values. These include democracy, international justice, and human rights. The federal government makes and carries out **foreign policy** based on these economic and political concerns.

Goals

Our nation's foreign policy goals are usually broadly stated. They include protecting the national security and prosperity of the United States, self-government for all nations, freedom of the seas, and international peace and stability.

Specific foreign policy goals tend to change rapidly. Foreign policy experts in the federal government analyze world issues and decide how they affect American political and economic interests. A specific policy for each issue is then developed. Because the world situation is constantly changing, making and carrying out foreign policy is a continuous process.

All Americans are affected by foreign policy decisions. Foreign policy affects the stability of our nation's economy, the ability to buy and sell goods in other countries, the amount of taxes Americans pay, the ability of American businesses to operate abroad, and access to information and travel. For example, for many years the United States did not officially recognize the Communist government of the People's Republic of China (P.R.C.). There was little trade or travel between the two countries. In 1979, China and the United States established diplomatic relations. This renewed contact reawakened American interest in Chinese history, art, and culture. Imports of such items as Chinese silk, embroidery, tea, and artwork became popular, and many Americans began to travel to China. But recent events in the People's Republic of China have threatened the relationship between the nations. The Chinese government's violent crackdown on student protesters in June 1989 forced the U.S. government to issue economic sanctions against the People's Republic of China. These sanctions, however, were later lifted and relations between the two nations returned to normal.

Methods

The United States government uses many different methods to achieve foreign policy goals. Most of these come under the general heading of **diplomacy.** Diplomatic representatives often use negotiation in resolving differences. After 18 months of on-again, off-again negotiations, for example, North Korea and the United States signed an agreement about nuclear weapons on October 21, 1994. This agreement outlined the procedure by which North Korea would stop its nuclear weapons program.

President Nixon in China

foreign policy   set of goals that define a nation's relations with other nations

diplomacy   management of relations between nations

The Middle East's Persian Gulf is one of the most important oil transport routes in the world. What action did the United States take in the 1980s to keep the Gulf open for shipping?

isolationism policy of avoiding political and military alliance with other countries

Other means of achieving foreign policy goals include persuasion and propaganda. In 1994, for example, the United States helped to persuade Arabs and Israelis to reach a peace accord. Voice of America radio broadcasts to other countries are often called propaganda. The broadcasts are usually made in the language of the country receiving the transmission. It is hoped that by providing news and information to citizens of other countries, their political beliefs will change.

The United States government also uses foreign aid, or economic assistance, to carry out foreign policy. After World War II the Marshall Plan, named for Secretary of State George Marshall, promoted economic recovery in Europe. Many other foreign aid programs have followed.

Another foreign policy tool is trade. Cutting or increasing imports can be used to put economic pressure on another country to change its policy. In the 1990s President George Bush ordered a ban on all imports of oil from Iraq. President Bush's goal was to influence Iraq to stop menacing Kuwait by cutting off sales of Iraq's chief export.

Often, the threat or actual use of armed forces is used to try to bring about foreign policy goals. For exam-

ple, in 1994 the United States sent troops to Haiti, a nation in the Caribbean. The action was taken to restore the democratically elected president to power.

Even in peacetime, the nation's military strength supports foreign policy. During the Iran-Iraq war in the 1980s, U.S. warships were sent to the Persian Gulf to protect tankers transporting oil from the Middle East. This action was a show of force by the United States against forces threatening the stability of the Middle East.

History

Many factors directly or indirectly shape foreign policy. A government's power to carry out a policy is based on, among other things, its nation's economic and military strength, its ability to win support from the governments of other nations, actions it takes in response to events in other parts of the world, and public opinion. All of these factors have influenced U.S. policy.

During its early years, the United States was weak economically and militarily and had little influence in world affairs. Americans favored isolationism, a policy the U.S. government would follow in the 1870s to 1880s and after World War I.

In 1823, President James Monroe gave broader meaning to the nation's policy of isolationism. In what became known as the Monroe Doctrine, European nations were told not to interfere with any of the independent nations of the Western Hemisphere. President Monroe believed that any attempt by European nations to regain control of their colonies would threaten American security. This doctrine also stressed that the United States would stay out of European affairs.

In the early 1900s, President Theodore Roosevelt, acting under the African proverb to "speak softly and carry a big stick," adopted a policy that changed the emphasis of the Monroe Doctrine. Instead of opposing intervention by European nations in the Western Hemisphere, Roosevelt said that the United States would intervene when necessary to guarantee political and economic stability around the world. This idea has been a cornerstone of American foreign policy throughout much of the twentieth century. To combat the rise and influence of the Soviet Union after World War II, the U.S. government adopted **containment** as its central policy. The United States gathered allies in Western Europe and elsewhere to prevent Communist governments from gaining power. The Soviet Union responded by establishing Communist governments in Eastern Europe and seeking more allies around the world. This resulted in a "cold war," a war fought not with bullets, but with propaganda, arms build-ups, and attempts to gain allies through providing economic and military assistance.

At times, the cold war turned "hot," when the United States came to the aid of nations threatened by Communist military invasions. Several times, however, there were "thaws" in the cold war. President Richard Nixon's policy of **detente** is one example of such a thaw. During detente, the United States and the Soviet Union signed nearly a dozen agreements to foster communication and cooperation between the two nations. And in the 1980s, the United States and the Soviet Union came to terms on several agreements designed to reduce nuclear weapons, encourage cultural exchanges, and increase trade.

Foreign Policy Issues

Recently, other nations besides the Soviet Union have gained the attention of U.S. foreign policymakers. The economic power of Japan, South Korea, and other nations of the Pacific Region is now a formidable force for U.S. leaders to consider. Political unrest and religious fanaticism in the Middle East continues to threaten U.S. oil supplies. Civil war, political violence, and economic instability in many Central and South American nations threaten the security of the United States and the entire Western Hemisphere.

For many years, the relationship with the Soviet Union and its allies dominated American foreign policy. That emphasis began to change in 1985 when Mikhail Gorbachev came to power in the Soviet Union. He immediately began to seek a more open dialogue with U.S. leaders. Under his policy of *glasnost,* or "openness," Gorbachev also instituted many internal reforms in the Soviet Union. He began to allow greater Jewish immigration; the release of previously banned books, films, and works of art; and the establishment of more liberal economic measures, such as private ownership and profit-making.

Gorbachev's initiatives soon led to even more radical reforms. By the early 1990s, the Soviet Union had collapsed. Throughout the former Soviet Bloc, national governments proclaimed their independence and their intention to create entirely new governments. The largest of these new countries was Russia, where for the first time since 1917, citizens went to the polls and freely elected their leaders. The United States welcomed the new reforms and pledged economic support. By the mid-1990s the

containment   policy to try to prevent the spread of communism

detente   reduction of tensions

Mikhail Gorbachev

formerly Communist nations were working toward a democratic political system and a free market economy.

Makers of Foreign Policy

According to the United States Constitution, the federal government is responsible for foreign policy. States may *not* conduct diplomacy with foreign governments or declare war against them.

LEGISLATIVE BRANCH

The Framers of the Constitution intended for Congress and the President to share responsibility for foreign policy. Congress has the power to declare war, approve treaties and the appointment of ambassadors, provide funds to carry out American foreign policy, and maintain the armed forces. With these powers, Congress influences what the President can do in foreign relations. After a budget for foreign aid is prepared, for example, the President must convince Congress to approve it.

Several congressional committees are directly concerned with foreign and defense affairs. The most important are the Armed Services and International Relations committees in the House and the Armed Services and Foreign Relations committees in the Senate. Members on these committees specialize in foreign policy matters. There are other committees that are indirectly concerned with foreign affairs. Agricultural committees, for instance, are involved in foreign policy because large amounts of American farm products are sold overseas, and foreign products impact U.S. agricultural markets.

EXECUTIVE BRANCH

The Constitution names the President to serve as commander in chief of the armed forces and entrusts the President with the power to negotiate treaties. The chief executive also receives representatives from and sends representatives to foreign governments. In carrying out such actions, the President grants or refuses **diplomatic recognition** between the United States and a foreign nation.

Because of these powers, the President takes the lead in making foreign policy. The Office of the White House has a strong, centralized administration that enables the chief executive to act quickly and decisively in an emergency. The foreign policy responsibilities of the President are especially important because the President has ultimate control over the use of nuclear weapons.

Defense Policy

Along with foreign policy, the United States has a defense policy. Both policies support each other and operate together. They are similar in that they both define our nation's interaction with other countries and are used to promote and protect American interests.

United States defense policy is designed to ensure national security as well as preserve the political independence of the country. National security also includes protecting our nation's supplies of natural resources from overseas, preserving the independence and national security of our allies, and helping to resolve regional conflicts that threaten world peace.

To carry out defense policy, the federal government maintains armed forces—the Army, Navy, Air Force, and Marines—which come under the direction of the Department of Defense. It is hoped that the existence of these armed forces will prevent war. Current American policy is to use military force only when all peaceful

diplomatic recognition official knowledge of the government in power

means of protecting the nation's interests have failed.

The Framers placed the leadership of the armed forces under the control of civilian, or nonmilitary, officials. This was done because they viewed military power as a direct threat to a democratic form of government. Thus, the Constitution makes the President commander in chief of the armed forces and gives war powers to Congress. The President also appoints the leaders who make and carry out defense policy, including the Joint Chiefs of Staff who are the highest ranking military officers in the armed forces.

Section Review

1. What are the basic goals of United States foreign policy?

2. What are three methods used by the United States government to achieve foreign policy goals?

3. What were the main points of the Monroe Doctrine?

4. According to the Constitution, who has responsibility for foreign policy?

5. **Challenge:** Which United States foreign policy goal do you feel is most important? Why?

Summary

1. The federal government makes public policy to solve problems facing the nation.

2. Public policy decisions usually involve tradeoffs, or sacrifices, to achieve a particular goal.

3. The government can influence the national economy through fiscal, monetary, and trade policies.

4. The government provides two basic types of human service programs in the United States—social insurance and welfare programs.

5. Social insurance programs provide benefits to persons (and their dependents) who have worked and paid taxes in the past.

6. Welfare programs provide benefits to all individuals in need who meet certain requirements.

7. The federal government provides public services for the benefit of business, labor, and consumers.

8. America's natural resources are protected by the federal government.

9. Public policy concerning the environment must be balanced between conservationists, who wish to protect the nation's natural resources, and developers, who wish to use the nation's natural resources to promote economic growth.

10. Government aid programs to agriculture include price and income supports, subsidies, and drought relief.

11. The United States conducts relations with other nations to protect American economic interests and to promote and defend certain political values, such as democracy and human rights.

12. U.S. defense policy is designed to ensure our national security and the national security of our allies.

Chapter 17 Review

★ Building Vocabulary

Several of the new terms introduced in this chapter appear below. Use each word correctly in a sentence. Try to use two or more words in the same sentence. For example:

1. The government can regulate imports through *quotas* and *free trade*.

1. fiscal policy
2. monetary policy
3. recession
4. inflation
5. quotas
6. free trade
7. welfare
8. collective bargaining
9. public services
10. subsidies
11. injunctions
12. mortgage
13. conservation
14. public land
15. foreign policy
16. detente
17. diplomacy
18. trust
19. isolationism
20. containment

★ Reviewing Facts

1. What are two ways public policy might directly affect individual citizens?
2. In terms of fiscal policy, what is the main purpose of government spending?
3. How does the Federal Reserve System serve as a "banker's bank"?
4. What are two ways the government might use loans to increase United States' exports?
5. What was President Reagan's policy toward social programs?
6. How does the Social Security system work?
7. How does the federal government protect the health of American citizens?
8. How might a merger of two companies help the economy?
9. What caused antiunion sentiment in the national government during the late 1800s?
10. How did the federal government become involved in agriculture in the 1930s?
11. Why has the United States played a major role in world affairs during the twentieth century?
12. How are United States foreign policy and defense policy similar?

★ Analyzing Facts

1. In the past, the federal government has given loans to large businesses and corporations on the verge of bankruptcy to keep them operating and to save thousands of jobs. Do you agree with this policy? Why or why not?
2. Do you think the United States should have an energy policy designed to prepare the nation for a energy crisis? Why or why not?

★ Evaluating Ideas

1. Since the 1930s the federal government has operated programs to support the nation's farmers. Do you think it is important to do so? Explain.
2. The government's policy on land use can be controversial. Some conversationists believe that public lands should be left alone for the people to enjoy. Developers, on the other hand, point out that public lands contain valuable resources the nation could use to fulfill its energy needs and to promote economic growth. If you were President, whom would you favor—the conservationists or the developers? Why?

Using Your
Civic Participation Journal

Review the information that you collected for your Civic Participation Journal about the current interest rates financial institutions are paying. Work with five of your classmates to construct a chart comparing the interest that various institutions would pay on a $1,000 deposit at the end of one year.

3. Under what circumstances do you think America's use of military force is justified? Explain.

★ Critical Thinking
Forming an Opinion

An opinion is a belief based on what seems to be true or probable. Because opinions are not absolute, how we form them is very important.

Explanation Good opinions are reasoned judgments. A reasoned judgment involves examining all the available evidence about a subject carefully exploring your feelings about that subject, and forming an opinion based on those facts and feelings. Sometimes we form opinions based on feelings only, or before we have examined all the facts. Such opinions can be described as "snap judgments."

A good opinion is formed only after all perspectives of the issue are examined. If you were a judge hearing a case, you probably would not form an opinion about the guilt or innocence of the accused based only on the prosecutor's side of the story. To form a good opinion, you must hear the case from the perspectives of both the prosecution and the defense.

The following guidelines will help you form good opinions.

1. Before forming an opinion, be sure you have examined all the evidence. Avoid snap judgments. Remember, a quick judgment may change after you examine things from different perspectives and gain additional understanding.

2. Do not reject the opinion or views of others simply because they disagree with you. After you understand the reasons why they hold that opinion, you may find their perspective has some value.

3. Be sure you use facts to back up your opinion. A good opinion is a reasoned judgment supported by evidence that can be proven.

Practice Reread the material on Social Security in Section 3. You can use this information and the above guidelines to form an opinion about whether the government should reduce benefits for retired or disabled workers.

A "snap judgment" based on emotion, or from the incomplete perspective of a Social Security recipient, might be that old or disabled people who worked throughout their productive years and contributed to the program deserve a generous pension. Others, such as a currently employed worker, might have different perspectives and opinions. The worker might look at the large FICA deduction from his or her paycheck and want Social Security benefits reduced. Someone with a relative depending on a monthly Social Security check as his or her only form of income might oppose such cuts. Facts to be considered in forming an opinion on this issue include the lengthening life expectancy of Americans (increasing the time they receive benefits and the total amounts they receive), the financial condition of the Social Security system, the size of the FICA tax, and alternative solutions. A reasoned opinion might favor benefit reductions.

Independent Practice Study the photograph below of police arresting a suspect. How would you form an opinion about the police actions?

Chapter 18

Federal Finance and Issues

Our federal government spends staggering amounts of money—about $1.5 trillion in 1994 alone. Where does the government get such an amount of money? In this chapter, you will look at how government raises these funds, how it decides to spend them, and some of the issues surrounding these decisions.

Chapter Preview

TERMS TO KNOW
progressive tax, tax returns, deductions, regressive tax, user fees, fiscal year, gross domestic product, first budget resolution, second budget resolution, continuing resolutions, budget deficit, debt ceiling, line-item veto, earmarked, entitlement programs, cost-of-living adjustment

READ TO DISCOVER
- how the federal budget process works.
- what issues face the federal government

★ ★ ★ ★ ★

Civic Participation Journal

For one week, keep track of economic news as reported in your local newspaper. Write a brief summary of the news in your journal each day. Use the chart on page 443 to classify each day's news as a particular kind of leading economic indicator.

1 Federal Finance

The countless services provided to Americans today by the federal government cost money—billions and billions of dollars every year. How does the government raise the money to cover its expenses? Just like regular businesses, the government must raise revenues, or income, in order to function.

Federal Revenues

The federal government collects revenues, or income, from a number of sources. Most of these revenues are in the form of taxes paid by individuals.

The largest source of federal government revenue is individual income taxes. In 1994 our government collected more than $550 billion in income tax. As its name implies, this tax is levied on the income of anyone who earns a wage or salary, interest, or profits from investments. And, because it is based on one's ability to pay, the income tax is considered a **progressive tax.**

Although the Constitution gives Congress the power to tax, the federal income tax has been a major source of government revenue only for about the last 75 years. Except for a brief time during the Civil War, there was no federal income tax during the nation's early years. Back then, the government's chief source of revenue was the tariff, a tax paid by foreign manufacturers who shipped goods to the United States. But as the nation grew, and the need for more government services expanded, the need for more revenues also began to grow. Congress passed an income tax, but the Supreme Court declared it uncon-

stitutional. Finally, in 1913 the Sixteenth Amendment was ratified, giving Congress the right ''to lay and collect taxes on incomes.''

Today most employers automatically withhold income tax from their workers' paychecks and send the money to the Internal Revenue Service (IRS), the agency in the Treasury Department charged with collecting taxes.

Each paycheck lists the exact dollar figure that has gone to the federal government. And by April 15 of every year, Americans double check this amount when they personally file their **tax returns** with the IRS. If it turns out that an employer has withheld more than the amount of taxes owed for that year, the IRS issues a refund. But if the amount withheld is *less* than the taxes owed, the taxpayer must make up the difference.

Most Americans reduce the amount of taxes they pay through the use of **deductions.** Recently, though, the widespread use of deductions, tax credits, and numerous other ''loopholes'' led some lawmakers to declare the nation's tax system unfair. In 1986 Congress passed the Tax Reform Act, a sweeping rewrite of the nation's tax code. The legislation simplified the tax system, closed a number of loopholes, and eliminated many deductions. Wealthy individuals and corporations (some of which previously received tax refunds) now must pay a minimum tax and can no longer avoid all taxes. The legislation also helped many low-income people, who now do not have to pay any income tax.

A tax that *is* paid by every wage earner at the same rate, regardless of the amount he or she earns, is the social insurance tax. This tax makes up the second largest source of federal revenues. In 1994 the government collected more than $461 billion in these taxes, which are divided among such programs as Social Security, unemployment benefits, and workers' compensation. Since the tax rate is not adjusted to a person's earnings, the social insurance tax is a **regressive tax.** As such, people with low-paying jobs pay a higher portion of their income toward social insurance than higher income people.

Also contributing to government revenues is the corporate income tax, levied on the income of businesses and corporations. This tax brought more than $130 billion to the federal government in 1994. Exempt from this tax, however, are nonprofit corporations such as universities, churches, and labor unions.

A fourth form of revenue is the excise tax, which is placed on the manufacture, sale, or consumption of certain goods and services. Currently, federal excise taxes are imposed on such goods as liquor, tobacco, gasoline, and airline tickets. Because they are included in the price of the goods, excise taxes commonly are called "hidden taxes."

Various other taxes, such as customs duties and estate and gift taxes, account for a limited amount of federal revenues. The government, however, raises money in ways other than taxes. It has instituted **user fees** for many of the services it provides. As the name implies, consumers pay to use something the government supplies or controls. A user fee may be paid when one enters a national park, for example, or to receive some government data such as weather maps from the National Oceanic and Atmospheric Administration.

But what happens when the total of all these taxes and fees falls short of what the government spends? Just as individuals borrow money in an emergency to "make ends meet," the federal government can borrow when it spends more than it collects. The Constitution, in Article I, Section 8, gives Congress the power to "borrow

regressive tax tax that everyone pays at the same rate, regardless of income

user fees fee paid for the use of a government product or service

Excise taxes on such items as gasoline and tobacco are important sources of revenue for the federal government. What are other sources of government revenue?

money on the credit of the United States.'' This is done by selling government securities—savings bonds, Treasury certificates, or Treasury notes called T-bills—to citizens, banks, savings and loans, and even foreign governments. Such sales are really loans taken out by the government from the individual or institution buying the security. Why would people lend their money to the United States government? They know that, after a certain period of time, the government will pay back the original amount, plus a bonus amount, called interest.

Federal Expenditures

All the revenues raised by government are used to cover federal expenditures. These reached the sum of over $1.4 trillion in 1993. How much, really, is a trillion dollars? Figure 18-2 illustrates this almost incomprehensible amount. On what does the federal government spend $1.4 trillion annually?

GOVERNMENT SPENDING

About 31 cents of every tax dollar goes to two programs—Social Security and Medicare. The Social Security program provides benefits to retired or disabled American workers and their families. Currently, one in 6 Americans receives Social Security benefits. Medicare provides funds for the medical and health care expenses of the elderly. Medicare serves nearly 33 million people annually.

The Department of Defense takes about 21 cents of every tax dollar.

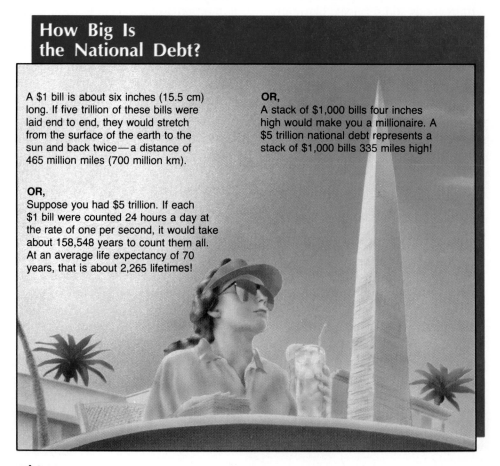

How Big Is the National Debt?

A $1 bill is about six inches (15.5 cm) long. If five trillion of these bills were laid end to end, they would stretch from the surface of the earth to the sun and back twice—a distance of 465 million miles (700 million km).

OR,
Suppose you had $5 trillion. If each $1 bill were counted 24 hours a day at the rate of one per second, it would take about 158,548 years to count them all. At an average life expectancy of 70 years, that is about 2,265 lifetimes!

OR,
A stack of $1,000 bills four inches high would make you a millionaire. A $5 trillion national debt represents a stack of $1,000 bills 335 miles high!

Figure 18-2

In 1994, President Clinton ordered troops to the Persian Gulf to protect vital Kuwaiti oilfields from a possible Iraqi invasion. How much of every tax dollar is spent on defense?

This money goes to buy equipment for the armed forces, to pay for the training and salaries of all military personnel, and to fund the development, testing, and production of new weapon systems.

A little more than 14 cents of every tax dollar pays for the interest on loans the government takes out to help meet its expenses. Another 14 cents goes to provide income security payments, such as housing and food stamp programs.

The government spends seven cents of every tax dollar on health programs, including Medicaid, a joint state-federal program providing health care for low-income families. Three cents go to education and other social services, and less than two cents goes toward developing new energy sources and maintaining America's natural resources.

With about 10 cents remaining, the government must pay for a large variety of programs and services.

Some of these include farm subsidy payments, funds to maintain American embassies around the world, and money to finance the space program.

THE FEDERAL BUDGET

How is this breakdown of the federal tax dollar determined? The answer to this question is found in the federal budget, the nation's annual taxing and spending plan. By giving dollars to one program and not another, the President and Congress set public policy, determining which social, economic, and military problems they will attempt to solve. In a sense, the federal budget is a national shopping list, detailing what we as a nation want and what we can afford. As one can imagine, determining what should go on the list—and in what amount—often leads to disagreements among decision makers.

Congress and the President share the major responsibility for making the budget. Figure 18-3 outlines the

Spring 1995
Office of Management and Budget (OMB) begins to collect agency budget requests for fiscal year 1997 (FY97).

Summer 1995
Department and agency representatives meet with OMB staff to justify and explain spending levels. OMB finalizes budget.

January 1996
The President submits budget to Congress.

March 15, 1996
All congressional committees submit estimates of program costs and needs revenues to House and Senate Budget Committees.

April 15, 1996
House and Senate Budget Committees report first budget resolution, setting non-binding spending limits in 13 budget categories.

May-August, 1996
Congress completes action on all appropriation, or spending, bills.

September 15, 1996
Congress adopts second budget resolution, setting mandatory spending limits. Work begins on bringing appropriation bills and new spending targets in line.

September 25, 1996
Congress completes action on budget, sending 13 appropriation bills to the President.

October 1, 1996
Fiscal year 1997 begins.

Figure 18-3

fiscal year financial year

many steps the government takes in deciding how to spend more than $1 trillion a year. About 18 months before the government's **fiscal year** October 1 to September 30 begins, the Office of Management and Budget (OMB) in the executive branch goes to work on the nation's spending and taxing blueprint. The director of the OMB, appointed by the President, has the sole power to draw up the federal budget based on the administration's policies and goals. The budget director's first step in this massive undertaking is to ask representatives from all federal agencies to submit estimates on their financial needs for the next fiscal year. Everything from new desks to new battleships is included in

these estimates. The OMB staff then holds hearings, during which the heads of the agencies and departments explain and defend their estimates.

In addition to input from these specific federal agencies, when preparing the budget, OMB personnel also rely on general information concerning the economy. The current economic health of the nation must be looked at before any new taxing and spending levels are implemented. Such factors as the unemployment rate or current price levels give budget makers a starting point. And, by carefully studying the leading economic indicators shown in Figure 18-4, the OMB staff makes predictions on the future direction of the economy. One indicator in particular, the **gross domestic product** (GDP) tells the OMB what goods and services currently are being produced and allows the staff to gauge the future health of the economy.

After compiling all this information, the director of the OMB presents a budget to the President for his approval. If the President approves, the budget is handed over to the Government Printing Office, where it is printed. It is then presented to Congress.

The President is required to submit a budget to Congress by the first Monday in January that Congress is in session. During the nine months between the time the budget is submitted to Congress until the new fiscal year starts, the President's proposal is scrutinized, probed, and usually changed. Congress can change the President's budget by increasing or decreasing the funding for certain programs, eliminating others, or passing legislation to raise or lower taxes.

When the budget reaches the legislative branch, committees in both the House and the Senate review only those parts that pertain to them. Department secretaries and agency chiefs testify again, this time seeking *congressional* support for their spending levels. At the same time, representatives of interest groups or special constituencies lobby members of Congress to present their views on the budget and to prevent any cuts on the programs they favor. Citizens also can influence budget decisions by writing to their representatives and senators, participating in demonstrations, or contributing to organized interest groups in an effort to bring their issues to the attention of members of Congress.

By March 15, after being bombarded with funding requests, the committees reviewing their portions of the budget must report their recommended changes in the President's plan to the House and Senate Budget Committees. The Budget Committees then have one month to examine these recommendations before presenting the **first budget resolution** to Congress on April 15. The resolution breaks down government spending into 13 broad categories, such as defense, agriculture, or income security. Both houses must agree on the first budget resolution by May 15.

During the summer, action on the budget continues, with congressional committees working within the 13

gross domestic product
total dollar value of all final goods and services produced annually in a country

first budget resolution
nonbinding joint resolution of Congress that sets targets for government spending and taxing and the amount of the surplus or deficit that can be anticipated within these targets

Leading Economic Indicators

REPORT	CONTENT	
Gross Domestic Product (GDP)	Total dollar value of the final goods and services produced in a year.	
Personal Income	Before tax income received in wages and salaries, interest and dividends, or other payments.	
Retail Sales	Estimate of total sales at retail level.	
Housing Starts	Number of new houses under construction as well as number of new building permits.	
Leading Indicators	Movement of several indicators that tend to predict change in the GNP.	
Consumer Prices	Changes in prices for a fixed market basket of about 360 goods and services.	
Producer Prices	Changes in prices of goods at various levels of production from crude materials to finished product.	
Unemployment Rate	Percentage of workforce that is involuntarily out of work.	
Industrial Production	Changes in output of nation's factories, mines, and electric and gas utilities.	

Commerce Department   Labor Department   Federal Reserve Board

Figure 18-4

second budget resolution
resolution that adjusts the targets set in the first budget resolution

continuing resolutions
large bills with several, or all, appropriations bills combined

As part of the budget process, employees in the General Accounting Office examine the financial records of government departments and agencies. Why do they carry out this type of examination?

budget categories and the targets established by the first budget resolution. Through the usual legislative process, the House and the Senate consider 13 separate appropriations bills, each of which provides the legal authority for a federal department or agency to spend the government's money. All action on these bills must be completed by mid-September, when Congress adopts a **second budget resolution.** The new spending and taxing limits are binding, meaning that no new appropriations exceeding these limits can be made. If the totals in the second budget resolution and the 13 appropriations bills do not add up, those committees affected must go back and draft legislation making any required changes. After this is done, both houses of Congress must agree on the 13 separate bills. Finally, when passed by Congress, the President must sign all 13 bills for the budget to be complete.

All of this work must be done by October 1, the start of the new fiscal year. If Congress does not pass the appropriations bills or the President does not sign them, the government cannot legally spend any money. If this happens, Congress must pass emergency spending bills to keep the government operating until it hammers out a budget.

Once the budget is approved and in place, the General Accounting Office (GAO) takes over. The GAO audits, or examines, the financial records of government departments and agencies to certify that all monies are spent in accordance with the law. A final audit is presented to Congress on November 15. With this final audit, the budget process for one fiscal year is complete. Meanwhile, Congress is already in the process of debating *next year's* budget, and the President is busy preparing a budget for two years in the future.

BUDGET PROCESS PROBLEMS

Although this budget process was designed to help the federal government manage its money, the process rarely works as planned. Deadlines often are missed, and the process gets bogged down by disagreements between opposing factions in Congress, between the houses themselves, and between Congress as a whole and the President. The budget process is slowed even further by the fact that decisions must be based on the needs and wants of so many competing interests. Thus, most budget decisions are compromises, which are often difficult and time-consuming to reach.

In recent years, Congress has resorted to passing **continuing resolutions** to avoid starting a new fiscal year without a budget in place. These must be passed or federal agencies would have no money to operate. But because a continuing resolution is such a huge bill (sometimes numbering in the thousands of pages) and because it usually occurs when Congress is in a hurry to adjourn, riders, or amendments, can easily be attached to these bills.

Riders often are added by members of Congress to provide federal funds for projects or interests in their districts. Such bills are known as pork-barrel legislation and, while they may be beneficial to a member's district, the motivation behind them often is questioned by a member's opponents and even by the general public.

It is a simple fact of political life that most members of Congress (all of the House of Representatives and one-third of the Senate) are up for reelection every two years. No member wants to face the voters with nothing to show for his or her past years in office. Thus, pork-barrel legislation is a way of getting votes. Members of Congress who bring millions of federal dollars into their districts are more likely to succeed at the polls.

There is no law against pork-barrel legislation, and most members of Congress see it as part of their legitimate duties. Since many members take advantage of such legislation, fellow members are likely to pass these bills without considering their merit. After all, if one votes against such bills, his or her own sponsored legislation may suffer the same fate in the future.

During the 1980s, Congress worked to trim federal spending, leaving it with less money to spend on pork-barrel projects. The competition among current legislators to distribute this shrinking amount of money is intense and further slows the budget process.

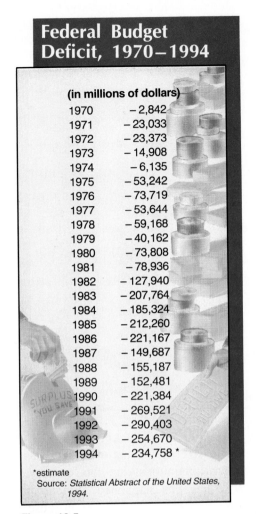

Federal Budget Deficit, 1970–1994

(in millions of dollars)	
1970	– 2,842
1971	– 23,033
1972	– 23,373
1973	– 14,908
1974	– 6,135
1975	– 53,242
1976	– 73,719
1977	– 53,644
1978	– 59,168
1979	– 40,162
1980	– 73,808
1981	– 78,936
1982	– 127,940
1983	– 207,764
1984	– 185,324
1985	– 212,260
1986	– 221,167
1987	– 149,687
1988	– 155,187
1989	– 152,481
1990	– 221,384
1991	– 269,521
1992	– 290,403
1993	– 254,670
1994	– 234,758 *

*estimate
Source: *Statistical Abstract of the United States, 1994.*

Figure 18-5

Deficits and Debts

Each year, more and more money is needed to run the federal government. Revenues, however, have not kept pace with spending. In 1993 the government collected just over $1 trillion. But in that same year the government had to borrow $254 billion to help meet its expenses. This borrowing usually occurs because the government is running a **budget deficit,** a not uncommon occurrence. Figure 18-5 shows the growth of the budget deficit over the last twenty years. The total of all budget deficits incurred by the federal government is known as the national debt.

budget deficit situation in which more money is spent than is collected

The National Debt, 1960–1994

1960	290,525
1970	380,921
1980	908,503
1990	3,206,207
1994*	4,676,029

Millions of Dollars

Source: *Statistical Abstract of the United States, 1994.*

*estimated

Figure 18-6

debt ceiling limit beyond which the debt may not legally go

The size of the national debt has grown continuously in this century. Why has this happened? Financing war has been the most common cause. In fact, the first national debt resulted after the federal government assumed the debts that the states had incurred during the Revolutionary War. The cost of fighting World War I set the debt soaring—from $1 billion to $25 billion by war's end. Between 1940 and the end of World War II in 1945, the national debt grew from $43 billion to more than $250 billion. Then the conflicts in Korea in the early 1950s and in Vietnam in the next two decades caused other large increases. However, war is not the only reason for the rising debt. In the 1980s, for instance, reductions in taxes and increases in defense spending led to another sharp rise in the debt. Today the debt is decreasing slowly.

How can the government keep spending money it does not have? There is no constitutional limit to the amount of debt the federal government can carry. In this regard it is different from state governments, whose constitutions often set a **debt ceiling.** Congress, too, has adopted a debt ceiling each year since 1917, when the limit was fixed at $11.5 billion. But whenever the debt threatened to rise above the ceiling, Congress simply changed the ceiling, allowing the government to keep borrowing money and to go deeper into debt.

What effect does a staggering national debt have on the average taxpayer? One immediate effect is that a larger share of federal expenditures must go to pay off the interest on the borrowed money. In 1945 the American government paid just over $3 billion in interest. By 1994 the interest payment had climbed to $200 billion. This means that today's taxpayers are paying off the debts of previous generations, while tomorrow's taxpayers (meaning you) will be paying for today's debts.

Can anything be done to decrease the national debt and balance the budget? These and other issues facing the federal government will be explored in the next section.

Section Review

1. How does the federal government raise money?

2. When does the federal fiscal year begin and end?

3. What are the main functions of the General Accounting Office?

4. **Challenge:** Do you agree with the practice of pork-barrel legislation? Why or why not?

CASE STUDY: GOVERNMENT REPORTS

NUMBERS NEVER LIE—OR DO THEY?

And now the news. It was reported today that the nation's trade deficit rose again last month to over $1.5 billion, sending shock waves through Wall Street and pushing the Dow Jones average down 59 points. The new figures were also a concern to the President who has promised to reduce the trade deficit. A poll conducted today shows that 56 percent of Americans think the President is not doing a good job.

Could one statistic trigger such a response among stock traders, elected officials, and the general public? Not always, but it was that very announcement—a trade deficit figure of $1.5 billion—that helped cause a stock market crash in October 1987.

The power of numbers in the United States today is greater than ever before. Government uses numbers to make major decisions. Population figures, for example, control representation in state legislatures and Congress. Standardized test scores are used to evaluate educational reforms. Law enforcement officials cite rising crime statistics as a reason to increase budgets. The number of low-income people in a city determines how much federal money it will receive for housing and job training programs. The government uses statistics in countless ways. But where do these numbers come from?

Most of the statistics the government uses to determine public

policy come from the government itself. The chief agency for collecting data is the Census Bureau, which tracks the nation's population and economy, compiling information on everything from birth and death rates to foreign trade. The Bureau of Labor Statistics keeps track of unemployment levels, wages and prices, and living conditions. The Bureau of Justice Statistics follows the arrest records of local police departments to determine national crime rates. In all, more than 70 state and federal agencies collect statistics for the federal government.

Because numbers are so important, critics say America has become a nation of statistics watchers. But some people question the government's reliance on statistics

and are beginning to ask: Can we count on the numbers the government uses to always be accurate?

Many problems are associated with statistics. Some areas the government measures—such as the economy or trade—are constantly changing. So data to support an accurate figure often can be incomplete or unavailable. To compensate for this, government statisticians make an educated guess as to what the final figure will be when all the data is collected. Even so, when preliminary statistics are released, they can be weeks or months old. Then, after all the data is in, the figure is readjusted but important decisions may have been made based on the original figure.

Finally, some say that the biggest problem with government statistics is the public's willingness to accept them as fact. If a number originates from a government agency, the immediate reaction of most Americans is to accept it as objective and absolute. But statistics can be manipulated to show what someone wants them to show. According to critics, the old saying "numbers never lie" is taken far too much for granted in America.

1. How might statistics be manipulated to get the desired results?
2. Why do you think people take as fact statistics released by the federal government?

2 Federal Issues

The American people have high expectations of their government. It is expected to deal with the hundreds of problems facing the nation. These problems are diverse in scope but similar in one respect— most of them are expensive to solve. For every problem the American people ask the government to address, policymakers must consider one fundamental question: Can we afford a solution?

Budget Issues

The government addresses most issues facing the nation through the federal budget. The budget determines which problems are most crucial and how much solving them will cost. Thus, taxing and spending issues surrounding the budget affect other decisions made by policymakers.

Here, President Clinton greets children at the White House. One of the most pressing concerns today is to control government spending so that a heavy financial burden will not be passed on to younger generations. What ways have been proposed to balance the budget?

BALANCING THE BUDGET

For many policymakers, balancing the federal budget is one of the most important issues facing the country today. The deficits of the 1980s have mushroomed into a huge national debt that drains billions of dollars from the government every year. The interest payment on this debt alone accounts for the third highest component of the budget.

Those who advocate a balanced budget say that these interest payments could be paying for new and existing programs that might help millions of Americans. The federal government, they say, should set an example of sound fiscal management for the 50 states and the rest of the world.

While many agree with these arguments, there is much debate over how to balance the federal budget. Some advocate a Constitutional amendment requiring the government to produce a balanced budget every year. For example, in the Republican Contract with America in 1994, congressional candidates pledged to introduce a balanced budget amendment in the 104th Congress. When Republicans swept the elections, they made good on their promise. But, amending the Constitution is no simple task, and some consider it unnecessary or inappropriate.

Another recommendation is to enact federal legislation that limits government spending. In 1985 Congress passed the Balanced Budget and Emergency Deficit Control Act, also known as Gramm-Rudman-Hollings (GRH) for the bill's chief sponsors. This law was an attempt to bring government spending under control by forcing the President and Congress to meet certain spending targets. If the targets were not met, automatic spending cuts would be instituted by the GAO. The bill failed to produce the desired results and was abandoned.

Some people believe that changing the way the budget is made would help balance it. Among the proposals they recommend is a **line-item veto** for the President. Currently, if Presidents disagree with a particular program within a department's budget, they must eliminate the *entire* budget for that department, not just the funding for the program they dislike. This policy forces the President to make difficult choices about budgets.

A line-item veto would permit Presidents to go through the budget—literally line by line—and delete any spending they felt was unnecessary or too costly. Many legislators, however, strongly oppose giving this power to the President, claiming that it would reduce Congress's traditional "power of the purse." So, despite presidential efforts, the line-item veto has not been incorporated into the Constitution. The first time that it was seriously considered was after the Republicans won control of the 104th Congress.

Another group of people say that all efforts to balance the budget are doomed to fail until the President and Congress admit that Washington cannot cure all the nation's ills. The President and Congress must be willing to say "no" to federal agencies, interest groups, state and local governments, and constituents asking for more federal dollars. In addition, legislators must learn to control their own spending habits by eliminating pork-barrel legislation.

With this many options facing the President and Congress, it is unlikely they will agree on how—or if—the budget should be balanced. This same indecision is evident in another budget issue—taxes.

Unlike the President, certain state governors have the right to use a line-item veto. George Bush, Jr., of Texas, shown here, is one governor who has this power. Why do some oppose a line-item veto for the President?

line-item veto power that allows the executive branch to veto individual items in a bill

TAX ISSUES

A central question surrounding federal tax policy is whether the government should raise taxes. To some people, raising taxes seems a logical way to help pay for increased expenditures. Yet many Americans are extremely vocal in their opposition to this option, forgetting that taxes pay for services they want. As economist Milton Friedman once said:

The voting public ask their Congressmen to enact goodies in the form of spending, but they are unhappy about having taxes raised to pay for those goodies.

Most elected officials in Washington are reluctant to raise taxes for any reason because they fear being rejected at the polls. Recent presidential

Taxes were a major issue in the 1994 congressional election. How has the tax issue played a role in the 1988 and 1992 presidential elections?

earmarked   designated

But many people believe that raising taxes can have positive effects. The government could reduce the deficit. New programs that address the nation's problems could be financed. And, to make sure that the new revenues go where the public wants them, tax increases can be **earmarked** for specific purposes.

Faced with the growing budget deficit, the federal government has tried various tactics to raise revenue in recent years. As you learned earlier, the 1986 Tax Reform Act raised corporate taxes and closed tax loopholes—ways in which businesses and individuals could avoid paying all or part of their taxes. However, these changes were not intended primarily to raise additional revenue, but rather to make sure all corporations and individuals pay their fair share of taxes. Even the growing number of user fees affects only those who use specific government services.

Other options to raise revenues remain open. Some decision makers propose changing the entire nature of the American tax system. They want to change the income tax to a flat rate and institute a value added tax on all goods produced. But, interest groups that would be affected by these tax increases oppose them.

campaigns illustrated how the issue of taxes can help affect election outcomes. In 1988 Republican candidate George Bush based most of his campaign around the line, "Read my lips—no new taxes." Bush easily defeated his opponent, Massachusetts Governor Michael Dukakis, who made no such pledge. During his term in office, however, Bush agreed to support a tax hike. Democratic candidate Bill Clinton made the hike an issue in the 1992 presidential election, and Bush was voted out of office.

Besides political suicide, lawmakers do not like raising taxes for another reason. Higher taxes take money out of consumers' pockets, leaving them with less money to support businesses and industries. If these fail, the economy could slow down, causing a recession.

SPENDING ISSUES

The federal budget is the administration's statement on where it plans to lead the nation. The government uses the budget to set priorities by allocating money for the programs it wishes to support. Faced with the priorities of legislators, interest groups, and individual citizens, however, "dividing up the budget pie" has become more difficult than ever.

During the mid-1990s, the budget process was marked by disagreement over priorities between Democratic

President Bill Clinton and the Republican controlled Congress. Congress wanted to cut expenditures in many social areas such as welfare, education, and job programs. At the same time, it proposed increasing the defense budget. The President, disagreed with the congressional proposals.

The budget battles of the 1990s illustrate a major government spending issue—how to spread out limited resources to as many people as possible. This problem is complicated by the fact that huge chunks of the budget are considered off-limits to spending cuts or redistribution. One such area is entitlement programs.

Entitlement programs, such as Social Security, student loans, and Medicare, affect nearly 40 million households—about 47 percent of the population. Most politicians do not want to anger this many voters and, therefore, do not touch these programs. Thus, entitlement programs, which make up about 46 percent of the budget, are automatically funded every year.

Another area of the budget considered off-limits to cuts is the 14 percent used to pay off the interest on the national debt. Since this money is committed by the government and is really a loan payback, it cannot be cut.

A final area where spending cuts are difficult to make is defense. The amount of money spent in this area is tremendous—about $280 billion, or 19 percent of the federal budget. Although Congress recently did cut some defense spending, the budget deficit will not be impacted for many years. The reason for this is that much of the defense budget goes toward paying off long-term contracts for the development and construction of aircraft, tanks, and weapons.

These three areas added together account for about 79 percent of the budget. This leaves only about 21 percent—about $311 billion—for the President and legislators to divide up among hundreds of programs. Since few groups are willing to sacrifice their priorities or their share of the budget, the competition for these dollars is intense.

Policy Issues

Many issues today are too big for local or state governments to handle. The federal government often is called upon to make decisions on policies that affect all Americans.

DEFENSE ISSUES
The United States defense policy is designed to protect American interests at home and abroad. The United States also is committed to protecting its allies, especially those in Europe. For these reasons, the federal government spends billions of dollars every year to cover the equipment and operating expenses of the Defense Department. As a result, defense spending has accounted for a large share of the federal budget. And during wartime, defense requires even larger expenditures.

entitlement programs programs that provide benefits to all individuals who qualify for them

Public spending for education has been a concern since colonial times. Harvard University, shown here, is America's oldest educational institution. How has education fared in recent budget battles?

Many Americans disagree as to how strong the nation's military capability needs to be. Heated debates often take place over defense goals and the amount of money needed to reach them. Some people argue that defense spending should be cut to allow more funds for social programs or to reduce the budget deficit. Others call for increased spending to make sure our defense remains strong. This "guns versus butter" debate intensified when Ronald Reagan became President in 1981.

President Reagan believed that the military was weak and inefficient due to funding cuts after the Vietnam War. He claimed that if the United States wanted to deal with the Soviet Union on equal terms, the nation must rebuild its armed forces. During Reagan's first six years in office, more than $2 trillion were allocated for defense. This amount included expenditures for new nuclear weapons, such

as the MX missile, and for development of a controversial space-based defense system known as the Strategic Defense Initiative (SDI). The result was the largest peacetime military buildup in the nation's history.

But by the mid-1980s, many members of Congress began to resist Reagan's requests for further increases in defense spending. They argued that all spending areas, including defense, had to be cut to control the budget deficit. In addition, public sentiment turned against large defense budgets in light of the scandals uncovered by congressional investigations. Congressional committees, for example, discovered that some large defense contractors had billed the government for costs unrelated to defense. These included country club memberships, entertainment, political donations, and public relations campaigns. In other instances, these companies charged outrageous prices for products available more cheaply—and better made—on the open market.

As a result of its investigations, Congress began to more closely scrutinize all defense spending requests. And after the collapse of Communist governments, many legislators called for more reductions in United States defense spending. Although everyone agreed that the United States must maintain strong military forces, defense budgets were decreased from about $300 billion in 1990 to about $280 billion in 1994. Americans who believed that defense had been cut too much were reassured during the Persian Gulf War when the American high-tech forces soundly defeated Iraq.

The MX missile is an important part of the nation's nuclear arsenal. Here, a single MX missile is shown in its underground silo. What effect did the Reagan Administration have on spending for the MX and other defense projects during the 1980s?

ENVIRONMENTAL ISSUES
Since the 1970s much progress has been made in cleaning up the nation's air and waterways. Today, however,

newer and potentially more dangerous environmental issues threaten the country. One of the most serious problems is toxic waste.

Toxic wastes are the poisonous by-products of chemical, steel, and plastics manufacturing. This waste often is carcinogenic, or cancer-causing, and, therefore, it is difficult to find ways to dispose of it. If dumped into rivers and lakes, it contaminates the water. If buried in drums, it may eat through the containers and seep into ground-water.

Before the dangers of toxic waste were completely understood, companies dumped their waste byproducts into open pits, ponds, and landfills. In the 1970s the government began regulating toxic waste disposal by licensing dump sites and mandating numerous safety controls. And in 1980 Congress created the Superfund program to help companies get started with the cleanup of waste sites. But because the problem was ignored for so long, questions have arisen over whether the companies responsible for the waste or the government should pay for the cleanup.

It is estimated that more than 20,000 illegal or old toxic waste sites exist in the United States. Many are more than 20 years old. In many cases, the companies that dumped the waste no longer exist. Furthermore, tracing illegally dumped waste to the companies responsible is almost impossible, meaning that they cannot compensate the individuals whose homes are contaminated by the wastes. Should the government pay for the cleanup? Many people think it should, but such a solution would be very expensive to the taxpayer. And while this debate is going on, United States industries continue to produce more than 260 million tons of toxic waste every year.

This toxic waste site in Idaho is among the 20,000 such sites found in the United States. What steps has the federal government taken to deal with dangers of toxic wastes?

The problem with toxic waste disposal illustrates a central environmental issue facing the government. Some people believe the government should ease environmental regulations because they interfere with economic development. They say that the strict regulations forced on chemical companies raise costs for both consumers and businesses. Others believe that no cost is too great if we want a clean and safe environment. Ultimately, the question surrounding most environmental issues is: What price is the nation willing to pay for a healthy environment?

SOCIAL SECURITY ISSUES

Social Security is the largest government social program, paying out more than $320 billion to over 35 million retired or disabled workers and their families. Nearly bankrupt in 1983, Social Security was saved through a

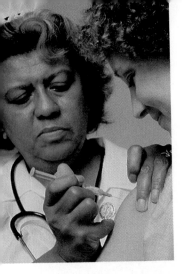

Health care costs have increased dramatically in the last few years and are expected to increase further during the 1990s. What proposals have been made to stem these increases?

cost-of-living adjustments increases in the amount of benefits recipients receive based on the rate of inflation

refinancing plan by Congress. Part of this plan led to a Social Security surplus that is expected to reach about $12 trillion in the year 2030. At about this same time, the number of Social Security recipients will exceed the number of workers paying into the system. The surpluses will be needed to make up the difference.

Some policymakers believe that it is unfair for one program to collect such a huge surplus when the nation is experiencing budget deficits and is deeply in debt. They say that the current Social Security system is safe and that the program should be scaled back. One such plan to do this calls for freezing or delaying annual **cost-of-living adjustments,** or COLAs. A COLA freeze for just one year would save the government about $6 billion, and a three-year freeze would result in a $27 billion savings. Those who oppose a freeze, however, point out that it would push nearly 500,000 elderly recipients into poverty, forcing them to seek government help. A freeze, then, may actually cost the government more than it saves.

Another issue concerning Social Security is that many of today's young workers object to paying high payroll taxes that benefit current retirees when their own future benefits are in doubt. When the number of people collecting Social Security outweighs the number of workers supporting the program, the surplus reserves will have to be tapped. By 2048, the system will be drained dry. This means that those who enter the workforce in the 1990s, and pay into the Social Security system their entire lives, will receive nothing in return when they retire. Many of today's workers are demanding that Social Security payments be cut so that benefits can be spread out more equitably among future generations.

HEALTH CARE ISSUES

The average American's health care bill is almost $3000 a year. Although many people have medical insurance, more than 30 million Americans are uninsured and must pay for medical expenses out of their own pockets. And by the year 2000, these costs will rise more. Some experts predict that insurance companies will not be able to handle these soaring costs. Many will go out of business, adding to the number of uninsured. Many people believe that these rising costs and lack of proper insurance have put the United States' health care in a crisis.

Although Medicare and Medicaid help millions of elderly and lower-income Americans pay their medical bills, some say the government should adopt a national health plan that would cover *all* citizens, regardless of age or income. They point out that the United States and South Africa are the only two industrialized nations that do not offer medical insurance to all their citizens. Supporters of national health insurance believe that such coverage would keep health care costs down by regulating what doctors and hospitals could charge for their services.

The first major push for a complete overhaul of America's health-care system came during the Clinton administration. After months of study, a special commission issued recommendations for a nationally funded health-care system that would cover all Americans. Congressional leaders, however, believed that the program was far too expensive. They pointed out that the plan would plunge the nation ever deeper into debt. They also believed that the President's plan would severely limit people's freedom to choose their own physicians. These critics pointed to the British system where patients often must wait for months for certain surgical procedures. They believed that the same situation would develop in the United States if the government became involved in health care.

Supporters of national health care point to the rapidly rising costs of medical care. Medical experts, however, blame rising health care costs on the patients themselves. They point out that 97 cents of every health care dollar go to the treatment of disease, while only 2.5 cents go for preventive care, such as annual checkups. If people took better care of themselves *before* they got sick, they say, health care costs would drop dramatically.

Section Review

1. What are the provisions of the Gramm-Rudman-Hollings law?

2. Why were there disagreements over budget spending priorities in the 1980s?

3. Why did Congress cut defense spending in the 1990s?

4. What are two reasons that health care costs are rising?

5. **Challenge:** If the Gramm-Rudman-Hollings Act had not been passed, how would you go about reducing the federal deficit and balancing the federal budget?

Summary

1. The main source of federal revenue is individual income tax.

2. The nation's taxing and spending plan is found in the federal budget.

3. The President submits an annual budget to Congress. Congress can change the budget by increasing or decreasing funds for certain programs, eliminating others, and raising or lowering taxes.

4. The national government has spent more than it took in for most of the last 45 years. The result is a national debt of almost $5 trillion.

5. The Gramm-Rudman-Hollings Act of 1986 set spending targets for the President and Congress to meet every year. The law, however, failed.

6. Federal tax issues center around whether or not the government should raise taxes to increase revenues.

7. Setting spending priorities is difficult because the government has less money to distribute to an increasing number of programs.

8. During the 1980s, defense spending was increased as American military forces went through their largest peacetime buildup in history. However, after the cold war, defense budgets were cut.

9. Solutions to environmental issues must take into account the monetary costs American taxpayers are willing to pay for a clean and healthy environment.

10. Although Social Security funds are currently running at a surplus, the surplus could be used up by the middle of the next century.

11. Adequate medical insurance for all Americans and soaring medical costs are two major health care problems facing the United States today.

Chapter 18 Review

★ Building Vocabulary

Use at least ten of the following vocabulary terms to write a paragraph about federal finance and issues in the United States.

1. progressive tax
2. tax returns
3. deductions
4. regressive tax
5. user fees
6. fiscal year
7. gross domestic product
8. first budget resolution
9. second budget resolution
10. continuing resolutions
11. budget deficit
12. debt ceiling
13. line-item veto
14. earmarked
15. entitlement programs
16. cost-of-living adjustments

★ Reviewing Facts

1. Which amendment to the Constitution gave Congress the power to enact a federal income tax?
2. What was the federal government's chief source of revenue before a federal income tax was enacted?
3. What are two ways that the 1986 tax reform law changed the nation's tax system?
4. What are hidden "taxes"?
5. How does the federal government borrow money?
6. What is the main function of the Office of Management and Budget?
7. What are two ways Congress can change the President's budget?
8. When is the budget process for one fiscal year complete?
9. What is one effect the national debt has on the average taxpayer?
10. What are the top three spending categories of the national government?
11. Describe two ways to balance the budget.
12. Why did Ronald Reagan want to build up America's defense in the 1980s?
13. Why will Social Security have to draw on its $12 trillion surplus in the future to make payments to retirees?
14. Explain the difference between a progressive tax and a regressive tax.

★ Analyzing Facts

1. The President and Congress have not passed a balanced budget for many years. Do you think this is a problem? Why or why not?
2. In your opinion, should Social Security benefits be cut now so that funds can be distributed to future generations? Why or why not?
3. In a democracy, how do you think voters can influence national spending policies?

★ Evaluating Ideas

1. Imagine that you are asked by the President to set national spending priorities for next year's budget. What five areas (such as defense, education, and social services) would you consider to be the most important and would require the most funds? Explain your answer.
2. Do you think there should be national health insurance for all Americans? Why or why not?
3. As you learned in this chapter, huge chunks of the federal budget are considered off-limits to spending cuts or redistribution. These chunks include entitlement programs, interest on the national debt, and spending for national defense. In your opinion, should these spending areas continue to be protected from spending cuts? Why or why not?
4. Refer to the quotation by economist Milton Friedman on page 449. What do you think Friedman meant by his statement?

Using Your
Civic Participation Journal

Review the economics articles that you noted in your Civic Participation Journal. Based on the information in these articles, write a one-paragraph forecast for the economy for the coming year.

★ Critical Thinking
Supporting an Opinion

Supporting an opinion means to have facts, data, and other pieces of information that will strengthen your viewpoint and perhaps persuade others to your way of thinking.

Explanation   There are many ways to support opinions. You can use facts or other pieces of information to strengthen a point you are making. Statistics, written materials, or other types of data from reputable authorities can be useful as well. Evidence such as eyewitness accounts of events or illustrative examples that support your opinion are also helpful. However, it is best not to use the opinions of others to support your own. Another person's opinion may be based on faulty evidence, unsound reasoning, or personal bias rather than on facts. If you agree with another person's opinion, check out the information on which they base their opinion and make sure their facts are sound.

Whenever you are gathering information to support an opinion, keep in mind that facts, statistics, and even eyewitness accounts can be disputed by someone who does not want to agree with you. Therefore, have as many sources as possible as back-up evidence. In other words, try to find at least two sources for any statistics or facts you might use to support an opinion. Usually, the more sources you have, the more likely people will accept a piece of information.

The following guidelines will help you support your opinions.

1. Never state an opinion without first knowing why you think that way.

2. Use facts, statistics, and other types of information to support opinions.

3. Avoid using the opinions of others to support your own views.

4. Look for several sources when gathering information to support your opinion.

Practice   Read the following passage and determine if the opinion stated is well supported.

I think the budget deficit is the biggest problem facing the nation today. According to a poll done by the Gallup Organization, the majority of people said that the deficit was the nation's chief problem—surpassing homelessness, inflation, and even drugs. Similar polls by three major newspapers across the country agree with the Gallup findings. The deficit must be controlled because the government spends more money than it takes in every year. I agree with those people—such as my representative—who say that the government must reduce the deficit now if we are to continue to prosper as a nation.

This opinion is well supported because many of the viewpoints are backed by facts.

Independent Practice   Study the photo below that you studied when you were learning about forming opinions in chapter 17. Suppose that someone has formed an opinion, based on the photo, that the police have used excessive force. How would you determine whether the opinion is valid?

FIVE REVIEW

REVIEW QUESTIONS

1. Why has the federal bureaucracy been criticized? What steps have been taken to counter this criticism?

2. It has been said that the Great Depression of the 1930s dramatically changed the relationship between the federal government and the American people. What do you think this statement means?

3. Federal government budget decisions ultimately affect all Americans. Choose one budget category discussed in this unit and describe how it might affect you if Congress decided to severely cut funds in this category.

4. Do you think taxes should be raised to pay for the programs and services the government offers? Why or why not?

5. In what ways do executive departments "promote the general welfare"?

6. What executive departments, other than State or Defense, have an influence on foreign and defense policies?

SUGGESTED READINGS

1. *Budget in Brief*. Washington, D.C.: United States Government Printing Office. Published yearly. Gives an overview of spending by each federal agency.

2. Carson, Rachel. *Silent Spring*. Boston, MA: Houghton Mifflin Company, 1987 (25th Anniversary Edition). The ground-breaking book that helped to start the ecology movement in the United States.

3. *Economic Report of the President*. Washington, D.C.: United States Government Printing Office. Published yearly. Information on the nation's economic policy, the federal budget and income, employment, and production. Also contains the annual report of the Council of Economic Advisers.

4. Goldstein, Eleanor C., ed. *Habitat*. Boca Raton, FL: Social Issues Resources Series, Inc., 1985. Series of articles reprinted from a variety of newspapers, magazines, government documents, and journals dealing with urban, suburban, and farm housing with its impact on the environment and on the economy.

5. McMahan, Jeff. *Reagan and the World: Imperial Policy in the New Cold War*. New York: Monthly Review Press, 1985. Examines the principal tenets of United States foreign policy in the postwar period.

6. Murray, Charles. *Losing Ground: American Social Policy 1950-1980*. New York: Basic Books, Inc., a subsidiary of Harper & Row Publishers, Inc., 1986. In this examination of the welfare system, Murray suggests that government programs to help the poor actually create a permanent underclass of citizens dependent on public assistance.

7. Peters, Charles. *How Washington Really Works*. Reading, MA: Addison-Wesley, 1983. Unique assessment of lobbies, the press, the bureaucracy, the foreign service, the military, courts, and regulators.

8. Sinclair, Upton. *The Jungle*. Champaign, IL: University of Illinois Press, 1988. Discusses the abuses of unbridled capitalism in the meat-packing industry in Chicago at the turn of the century; relates its effects on workers and their attempts to organize.

9. Yost, Charles. *History and Memory: A Statesman's Perceptions of the 20th Century*. New York: W. W. Norton & Co., 1980. Review of the course of history through the eyes of a Foreign Service Officer who witnessed significant developments and associated with individuals whose actions affected the course of events.

Promoting interests

The First Amendment to the Constitution acknowledges your rights as a citizen to freely approach government for "redress of grievances." This right includes your being able to promote and protect your own interests and values with government. As government has expanded, however, your ability to exercise this right has grown increasingly difficult. There are thousands of bureaus, agencies, and departments at all three levels of government that have been established to deal with the needs and interests of individual citizens. Some agencies, for example, provide welfare payments and food stamps. Others finance low-interest mortgages, operate school buses, inspect the foods we eat and the medicines we use, run hospitals, maintain our highways, and protect wilderness areas. Still others were established in order to protect the interests and values of citizens. The Bureau of Indian Affairs deals with issues relating to Native Americans; the Environmental Protection Agency is set up to preserve the environment; and the Office of Economic Opportunity provides assistance to persons who historically have been discriminated against in one way or another.

Unfortunately, not all the names of governmental agencies so clearly reflect the issues they handle. Many are hard to identify and locate. The problem is made more difficult by the fact that governmental units that have similar purposes and functions exist at the local, state, and national levels. In order to protect your interests, you have to become familiar with locating these institutions and determining which level of government will best respond to your needs.

The following exercise will help you develop your skill in promoting your interests. Read the following paragraph and answer the questions that follow. If you need help, refer to the "Federal Bureaucracy Handbook" in this textbook.

Mary Jones is a member of a group of working mothers with children ranging in age from six months to ten years. The goal of Mary's group is to get funding from the government to establish a system of well-staffed day-care centers in communities throughout the United States. The group's basis for the funding is that the mothers need to work; and good day-care centers, conveniently located, would enable them to do so.

1. What level of government should Mary's group work with to achieve its purpose?

2. What public, or social service, agencies in Mary's community could she contact for information and help to support her group's lobbying efforts?

3. What departments and agencies in Washington should the group lobby? Explain how each of these departments and agencies would be able to help Mary's cause.

4. What arguments and data could Mary's group use to support its cause?

5. How might Mary's state and federal legislative representatives be useful in helping the group succeed in achieving its goal?

6. What ways could Mary use to draw attention and support from others with the same goal?

Unit 6

THE JUDICIAL BRANCH

After federal laws have been enacted and carried out, it remains the task of the judicial branch of the federal government to interpret and enforce the laws. This aspect of government may seem very complex and even remote to you. But it has an important impact on our daily lives and on the protection of our rights. In many ways, federal court decisions have a more immediate impact on your life than do Congress and the President.

All of you at one time or another have watched dramatic scenes of courtroom trials in the movies or on television. In all cases, the legal system attempts to treat people—rich or poor, young or old—equally. It has been said that "justice is blind." In fact, many courts in the United States have figures of blind justice similar to the one on the facing page, outside the court building.

Chapter 19

The Federal Judiciary

This chapter introduces you to our nation's federal courts. Notice that the word "courts" used here is plural. Most of you are aware of the Supreme Court. But the Supreme Court stands at the top of an entire system that includes other federal courts.

★ ★ ★ ★ ★

Civic Participation Journal

Contact a local lawyer's office to learn more about the judicial system. Ask the lawyer to describe what kind of cases they work on and how much of a caseload they have. If you have time, you might visit the office and find out what type of training you would need to become a lawyer in your community. Record your findings in your journal.

1 Features of the Judicial Branch

The third branch of government in our federal system, the judiciary, is responsible for interpreting and applying the national law. It also has the responsibility for making sure that the laws passed by Congress and the states and the actions of those in an executive role are constitutional.

Under the Articles of Confederation, the United States did not have a national judiciary. The state courts interpreted and applied both national and state laws. This resulted in considerable confusion, since court decisions in one state were often ignored or rejected by other states.

Both the Federalists and the Anti-Federalists considered the absence of a national court a grave weakness. Alexander Hamilton said that the ''crowning defect'' of the government under the Articles was that there was no national judiciary. But while most people felt that a national judiciary was needed, there was little agreement about the form it should take. The Federalists wanted a system that included a Supreme Court and **inferior courts.** The Anti-Federalists, on the other hand, feared that lower federal courts would weaken the powers of the states.

Constitutional Basis

The Framers of the Constitution decided the matter. The power of the federal judiciary comes from Article III of the Constitution. Section 1 of this article states in part:

The judicial power of the United States shall be vested in one Supreme Court, and in such inferior courts as the Congress may from time to time ordain and establish.

This seemingly straightforward statement is interesting as much for what it does *not* say as for what it does say. The only court that is absolutely required by Article III is the Supreme Court. There is no mention of the number of inferior courts to be set up. Neither is there a specific total given for the number of justices who are to serve on the Supreme Court. As a check on the power of the judiciary, Congress is given the power to determine the number of inferior courts and the number of justices. At the same time, however, the Framers wanted the federal judiciary to be independent of the other two branches, and they provided that its powers, like theirs, should come directly from the Constitution.

When the first Congress met, it passed the Judiciary Act of 1789, which established a judicial system made up of a Supreme Court, three circuit courts, and thirteen district courts.

Jurisdiction

The Constitution established the **jurisdiction** of the federal courts by defining the kinds of cases these courts may hear. Recognizing the dual nature of the American court systems, it gave state courts jurisdiction in cases that involve state law. In fact, 80 percent of the cases that come to trial in our country are heard by state courts.

Federal courts were given jurisdiction over cases because of either their subject matter or the parties involved. Article III, Section 2 lists the kinds of cases in which the federal courts have jurisdiction. These are:

1. cases that involve an interpretation or application of the Constitution (subject matter).

inferior courts   lower courts

jurisdiction   legal authority of the courts

2. cases that involve an interpretation or application of federal laws (subject matter).

3. cases that involve a treaty made by the federal government (subject matter).

4. cases that involve admiralty or maritime law (subject matter).

5. cases in which the federal government is a party (parties involved).

6. cases that involve ambassadors, ministers, and consuls (parties involved).

7. cases that involve disputes between state governments or between citizens from different states, providing the amount in question is over $10,000 (parties involved).

8. cases in which a foreign government, or its citizens, brings suit against a state, or its citizens (parties involved).

The federal courts have **exclusive jurisdiction** in most of the kinds of cases listed above. These cases as well as those involving patents, copyrights, bankruptcy, and federal crimes can be tried only in federal courts.

Congress also allows some cases to be tried in *either* federal or state courts. In such instances, federal and state courts have **concurrent jurisdiction.** For example, cases between citizens of different states where the amount of controversy exceeds $10,000 may be heard in either a federal or a state court.

The jurisdiction of federal courts is also divided according to the *level* at which a case is heard. The lowest level in the federal court system, the district courts, have **original jurisdiction.** Federal courts of appeals, the next level, have only **appellate jurisdiction.** The Supreme Court has both appellate and original jurisdiction, although most of its cases are heard on appeal.

Limits on Judicial Power

Not all disputes are considered to be within the scope of judicial power. Federal courts must often decide if a case is **justiciable.** The Constitution itself places limits on the kinds of cases the courts may hear. Article III, Section 2 states that judicial power shall extend only to cases and controversies that involve certain parties and subject matters. This means that there must be two disputing sides, or adversaries, before the courts can act. In such an **adversary system,** the court's role is one of impartial and neutral arbiter between two opponents.

The adversary system requires our nation's courts and judges to be passive. That is, they cannot act until people whose rights are being denied bring their grievances to the courts.

In addition, federal courts cannot give even an advisory opinion about a point of law to members of the other

justiciable appropriate for review by the courts

adversary system judicial system in the United States in which two parties in conflict bring the matter to court

exclusive jurisdiction authority of a court to try only certain kinds of cases

concurrent jurisdiction authority of two or more courts to hear the same kind of case

original jurisdiction authority of a court to try a case the first time it is heard

appellate jurisdiction authority of a court to review a decision of a lower court

BICENTENNIAL
U.S. SUPREME COURT
USA
25

Chief Justice John Marshall

© UNITED STATES POSTAL SERVICE 1989

This postage stamp, issued in 1989, commemorates the 200th anniversary of the founding of the Supreme Court. It also shows John Marshall, who served as Chief Justice from 1801 to 1835. What does the adversary system require of the Supreme Court?

Supreme Court proceedings are held in this courtroom of the Supreme Court Building in Washington, D.C. At the front of the room is the bench, where the nine Supreme Court justices sit. What are the limits on federal judicial power?

standing condition of having a personal interest that has been, or is in danger of being, denied by an action or a law

two branches. The Supreme Court established this basic precedent during George Washington's presidency, ruling that an advisory opinion does not have the characteristics of a case or controversy.

A second limit on federal judicial action allows courts to rule only on legal questions, not political matters. The Supreme Court has ruled that political questions should be directed to one of the other branches of the federal government, to state governments, or to other court systems.

A third restriction on justiciability is that all parties to a federal lawsuit must have **standing** before they can bring a case. It is not enough merely to be interested in a subject, or to believe that a law may be unconstitutional. The parties must prove they have a substantial personal interest that has been—or is in danger of being—denied by a law or executive action.

A fourth limit on federal judicial action is the tradition that the federal courts will not hear a case until all other remedies have been exhausted. A federal judge may, for example, refuse to hear a case that could be better handled by another government agency. This also means that even when cases seem significant, they must begin at the lowest level of the federal courts and work their way up through the system.

Another limit on federal court powers is that in federal cases the burden of proof is on the person or group bringing the case. This means that laws are presumed to be legal until proven otherwise by evidence.

A sixth restriction on justiciability is that federal court cases must be based on a specific portion of the Constitution. One cannot challenge a law merely because it "violates the spirit of the Constitution."

Finally, a person may not challenge a law from which he or she has benefited. For example, someone receiving welfare payments may not bring suit questioning the constitutionality of the welfare system.

Section Review

1. What does the Constitution state about the establishment of a Supreme Court and inferior courts?

2. Identify the eight kinds of cases in which the federal courts have jurisdiction.

3. What are the limits on the justiciability of cases brought to the Supreme Court?

4. **Challenge:** In your opinion, what would be the effects on national politics if the Supreme Court were allowed to rule on political matters?

2 Evolution of the Judicial Branch

Because of its power to interpret the law and the Constitution, the Supreme Court has played a major role throughout American history. Figure 19-1 outlines some of the important decisions of the Supreme Court that have had an impact on the quality of life in the United States.

But the Supreme Court was not always considered powerful. For the first three years of its existence, almost no business at all came before the Court. Justices who had received Supreme Court appointments were even required by the Judiciary Act of 1789 to travel twice a year to remote parts of our country to preside over circuit courts.

Judicial Review

After a period of being largely ignored, the Court became more active when President John Adams nominated his secretary of state, John Marshall, as chief justice. Marshall asserted the principle of judicial review. As you learned earlier, judicial review is today one of the basic principles of the American constitutional system. It means that the federal courts have the power to decide on the constitutionality of legislative and executive actions at the local, state, and federal levels. Because the Court is the ultimate interpreter of the Constitution, it has the final say in deciding what the document's provisions mean.

As basic as this principle is, though, it is not mentioned in the Constitution. It was not until 1803 in the case of *Marbury v. Madison* that the Court, under John Marshall, claimed the power. The story about how the Court was able to do this

begins in 1800 when Thomas Jefferson was elected President, defeating Federalist John Adams. Jefferson's party, the Democratic-Republicans, also won control of Congress. Before leaving office, President Adams and the defeated Federalist Congress quickly created several new federal judgeships. The night before Jefferson took over, President Adams signed a number of commissions to fill these offices with Federalist judges. He then gave the commissions to his Secretary of State John Marshall to deliver. Among them was Marshall's own commission as chief justice of the Supreme Court.

When Jefferson discovered this "court-packing" scheme, he ordered several undelivered commissions to be held by his new Secretary of State James Madison. Among them was one for William Marbury, who had been appointed a justice of the peace for the District of Columbia. Marbury immediately asked the Supreme Court for a **writ of mandamus,** ordering Madison to deliver the commission.

writ of mandamus court order requiring a public official to carry out a specific act or lawful duty

Built during the 1930s, the Supreme Court Building is a prominent landmark in Washington, D.C. In what case did the Supreme Court first claim the power of judicial review?

SIGNIFICANT SUPREME COURT CASES

CASE	THE DECISION AND ITS IMPORTANCE
Marbury v. Madison (1803)	A section of the Judiciary Act of 1789 was declared unconstitutional. This set a precedent for judicial review.
Fletcher v. Peck (1810)	Georgia violated the Constitution by not honoring a contract. This was the first time a state law was declared unconstitutional.
McCulloch v. Maryland (1819)	This case determined that the national government could establish a Bank of the United States and that Maryland could not tax this bank. Here the principle of national supremacy and the doctrine of implied powers were established.
Gibbons v. Ogden (1824)	New York State could not grant exclusive navigation rights. Interstate commerce was interpreted to include navigation. Congress was to regulate interstate commerce.
Dred Scott v. Sanford (1857)	It was decided that blacks were not citizens of the United States and the Congress could not ban slavery in the territories. This strengthened the abolitionist cause and made the Civil War almost inevitable.
Plessy v. Ferguson (1896)	A state could require racial segregation in public transportation if the facilities were equal. This strengthened segregation.
Schenck v. United States (1919)	This case established that freedom of speech may be restricted if a "clear and present danger" exists, as in times of war.
Brown v. Board of Education of Topeka, Kansas (1954)	Forced racial segregation in public schools was judged to be in violation of the equal protection clause of the Fourteenth Amendment. This gave impetus to the civil rights movement.
Miranda v. Arizona (1966)	It was decided that criminal suspects must be warned of the right to remain silent before questioning begins.
In re Gault (1967)	It was found that the state of Arizona had denied due process of law to 15-year-old Gerald Gault. Juveniles are entitled to the same legal process as adults.
Roe v. Wade (1973)	Privacy was ruled a "fundamental right" guaranteed by the 9th and 14th amendments. The case legalized a woman's private right to an abortion under certain circumstances.
Regents of the University of California v. Allan Bakke (1978)	Allan Bakke was admitted to medical school based on his academic performance and test results. This set some limitations on the implementation of affirmative action programs.
United States v. Leon (1984)	This case determined that evidence seized by the police under an invalid search warrant could be used in court if the officers had believed the warrant to be valid.
Wisconsin v. Mitchell (1993)	This case allowed states to impose longer prison terms on people convicted of "hate crimes" without violating their freedom of speech.

Figure 19-1

Congress, you see, had given the Court the power to issue writs to federal officials in the Judiciary Act of 1789.

Chief Justice Marshall, however, was afraid that if the Court issued the writ, it would be ignored by the Democratic-Republicans, who held the Court in low regard. But *not* issuing it would show that the Supreme Court lacked the power to take action regarding the other two branches. Marshall's final opinion was a masterpiece of judicial strategy.

The Court decided that Marbury was entitled to his commission, but refused to issue a writ of mandamus. Why? In the decision, Marshall also found that the section of the Judiciary Act of 1789, which granted the Court the power to issue writs of mandamus, conflicted with the court's jurisdiction as outlined by the Constitution. Congress, Marshall said, did not have the power to enlarge upon the original jurisdiction of the Court. By declaring only one section of an act of Congress unconstitutional, Marshall had set the precedent for judicial review. Thus, the Court lost some authority, that of issuing writs of mandamus, in return for the recognition that it was an equal branch of government.

You may be surprised to know that this power of reviewing the acts of Congress has been used sparingly. It was not until 1857, in the *Dred Scott* case, that another law was declared void.

On the other hand, the Court has acted more vigorously in challenging state and local laws. This happened first in the 1810 case of *Fletcher v. Peck*. In this case, Chief Justice Marshall wanted to assert that the Court could review state actions. He also wanted it clearly understood that where state laws were in conflict with

Here, Supreme Court Chief Justice William Rehnquist administers the oath of office to President Clinton. Relations between the Court and the presidency have not always been friendly. What controversy divided the Court and F.D.R. during the 1930s?

the Constitution or national laws and treaties, the state laws must give way.

Today, judicial review remains a vital part of our constitutional system. More than 1000 state or local laws and approximately 100 federal laws have been overturned by the Supreme Court.

The Court-Packing Scheme

Not all the decisions the Supreme Court makes have been popular. Some meet with strong disapproval.

When the stock market collapsed in 1929, it looked as if the American economy was heading for ruin. Following the election of Franklin D. Roosevelt as President, Congress began to pass legislation dealing with the emergency. By June 1933, 15

The front of the Supreme Court Building shows symbols and inscriptions representing the ideals of the nation's judicial system. How has the Court's understanding of "Equal Justice Under Law" changed during the twentieth century?

major "New Deal" laws had been passed. But in 1935 the Supreme Court declared Roosevelt's National Recovery Administration unconstitutional and struck down several more reform laws. Over the next two years, federal district courts issued more than 1600 injunctions to keep acts of Congress from being enforced.

In November of 1936, Roosevelt was reelected by a margin of 10 million votes, leading him to believe that his recovery programs had the support of the people, if not the Court. So in 1937 he sent a recommendation for court reform to Congress. Emphasizing the "limited vision of older men," Roosevelt asked Congress for the power to name an additional justice whenever a sitting justice aged 70 did not retire. Since six justices were already 70 or older, Roosevelt's plan would have increased the Court to 15 members. Recognizing that this "court-packing" scheme might upset the balance between the three branches of government, public opinion turned against Roosevelt. Even members of Congress, who were Democrats like

Roosevelt, joined the opposition, thus assuring defeat for the plan.

But even before Roosevelt's plan was rejected, the Court had upheld a Washington State minimum wage law and ruled favorably on other state and congressional legislation. So the Supreme Court had, in a sense, preserved its independence by beginning to interpret the Constitution in ways that would better meet the needs of an industrialized society.

Section Review

1. Why is it important for the federal courts to have the power of judicial review?

2. Explain why *Marbury v. Madison* is considered an important case.

3. In which case did the Supreme Court claim the power to declare state actions unconstitutional?

4. **Challenge:** Do you agree with Franklin Roosevelt's plan to appoint additional justices to the Supreme Court? Why or why not?

3 Structure of the Courts

The Supreme Court is the only federal court specifically named in the Constitution. Congress has the responsibility to establish all of the lower federal courts. Those that Congress has set up are of two basic types.

Constitutional federal courts are those that carry out the duties specified in Article III. The Supreme Court is a constitutional court as are federal district courts, courts of appeals, the Court of Appeals for the Federal Circuit, and the Court of International Trade.

Congress, under the authority of Article I, created *legislative* federal courts to hear cases that are directly related to the exercise of the legislative powers of Congress. These courts include the Court of Military Appeals, the United States Claims Court, the United States Tax Court, the territorial courts, and the courts of the District of Columbia.

District Courts

Most cases having to do with federal laws are first tried in federal district courts, and it is here that most cases are settled. Because they handle about 300,000 cases a year, the district courts have been called the "workhorses of the federal judiciary."

JURISDICTION

District courts are trial courts, so they have original jurisdiction in most civil and criminal cases. About 87 percent of the district court caseload is civil in nature and involves such issues as bankruptcy, property damage, contract disputes, civil rights, or postal laws. These cases are mostly heard by a judge without a jury.

Criminal cases tried in federal district courts involve such crimes as forgery, counterfeiting, fraud, narcotics, and interstate automobile theft—any crimes that break federal laws. Criminal cases are usually tried before both a judge and jury.

ORGANIZATION

The federal district court system is organized into areas known as judicial districts. Each state has at least one judicial district and, therefore, one district court. States with large populations, such as California, New York, and Texas, have as many as four judicial districts. The Judiciary Act of 1789 provided for 13 district courts. As shown in Figure 19-2, there are 91 district courts today, including one in Washington, D.C., and one in Puerto Rico.

JUDGES

Each district court has from 2 to 27 judges, depending on the caseload of the court. There are more than 550 permanent judgeships in the 50 states, 11 in the District of Columbia, and seven in Puerto Rico. Although district court cases are usually heard by

Here, the official seal of the Supreme Court shows the national emblem with the motto (in Latin), "From Many, One." What two basic types of federal courts exist under the Supreme Court?

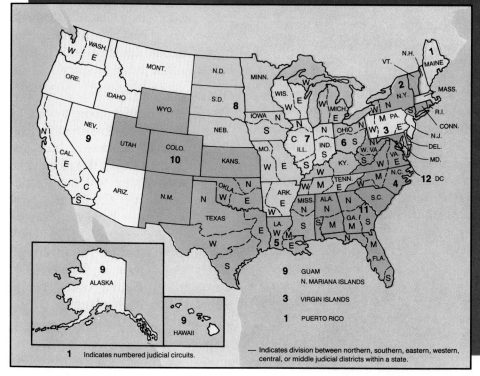

United States Judicial Districts and Circuits

9 GUAM
N. MARIANA ISLANDS

3 VIRGIN ISLANDS

1 PUERTO RICO

1 Indicates numbered judicial circuits.

---- Indicates division between northern, southern, eastern, western, central, or middle judicial districts within a state.

Figure 19-2

one judge, a panel of three judges often hears major cases, such as those involving congressional redistricting, civil rights, or antitrust actions.

Courts of Appeals

In the years immediately following ratification of the Constitution, the Court heard all federal appeals cases. By 1887, however, the Supreme Court had fallen almost four years behind in its work! The United States Courts of Appeals were established by Congress in 1891 to relieve the Supreme Court of some of its work load.

JURISDICTION

Appeals courts have the power to review all final decisions of federal district courts, except in those few cases where the law allows for direct review by the Supreme Court. Ap-

peals courts also review decisions of certain administrative agencies of the federal government such as the Securities and Exchange Commission and the National Labor Relations Board.

The function of courts of appeals is to determine whether federal law has been correctly applied by the district courts or regulatory agencies. In these courts, no witnesses are heard, no new evidence is presented, and there are no juries. A panel of judges hears arguments from attorneys for both sides before announcing its decision. The panel may uphold, reverse, or change a decision of the lower court. The judges may also **remand** the case, or send it back to the lower court for a new trial.

ORGANIZATION

The courts of appeals are organized by geographic areas called **circuits.** As shown in Figure 19-2, the United

remand send back to the lower court

circuits geographic regions in which a federal district court of appeals is located

States is divided into 12 circuits. Each circuit has only regional jurisdiction, which means it can hear cases only within its own particular geographical area.

JUDGES

Each court of appeals has from 6 to 28 permanent circuit judgeships, totaling 168 in all. The number of judges assigned to each court of appeals varies, depending on the work load of the court and the size of the circuit. In addition to appeals court judges, a justice of the Supreme Court is also assigned to each circuit.

Other Federal Courts

A number of other constitutional courts have been established by Congress. These courts, which are shown in Figure 19-3, have jurisdiction only in specific cases.

The Court of Appeals for the Federal Circuit was created in 1982 to handle appeals in certain kinds of civil cases. It is the successor to the United States Court of Customs and Patent Appeals and has nationwide jurisdiction. The court hears some appeals from district courts, including cases having to do with patents, copyrights,

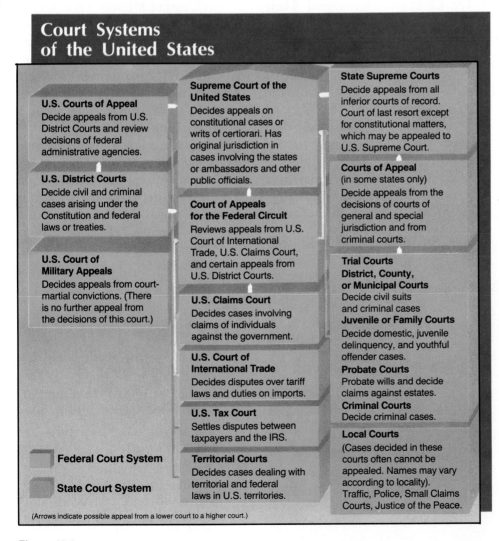

Court Systems of the United States

U.S. Courts of Appeal
Decide appeals from U.S. District Courts and review decisions of federal administrative agencies.

U.S. District Courts
Decide civil and criminal cases arising under the Constitution and federal laws or treaties.

U.S. Court of Military Appeals
Decides appeals from court-martial convictions. (There is no further appeal from the decisions of this court.)

Supreme Court of the United States
Decides appeals on constitutional cases or writs of certiorari. Has original jurisdiction in cases involving the states or ambassadors and other public officials.

Court of Appeals for the Federal Circuit
Reviews appeals from U.S. Court of International Trade, U.S. Claims Court, and certain appeals from U.S. District Courts.

U.S. Claims Court
Decides cases involving claims of individuals against the government.

U.S. Court of International Trade
Decides disputes over tariff laws and duties on imports.

U.S. Tax Court
Settles disputes between taxpayers and the IRS.

Territorial Courts
Decides cases dealing with territorial and federal laws in U.S. territories.

State Supreme Courts
Decide appeals from all inferior courts of record. Court of last resort except for constitutional matters, which may be appealed to U.S. Supreme Court.

Courts of Appeal
(in some states only)
Decide appeals from the decisions of courts of general and special jurisdiction and from criminal courts.

Trial Courts
District, County, or Municipal Courts
Decide civil suits and criminal cases
Juvenile or Family Courts
Decide domestic, juvenile delinquency, and youthful offender cases.
Probate Courts
Probate wills and decide claims against estates.
Criminal Courts
Decide criminal cases.

Local Courts
(Cases decided in these courts often cannot be appealed. Names may vary according to locality).
Traffic, Police, Small Claims Courts, Justice of the Peace.

☐ **Federal Court System**

☐ **State Court System**

(Arrows indicate possible appeal from a lower court to a higher court.)

Figure 19-3

and trademarks. It also hears cases on appeal from the United States Claims Court and the Court of International Trade. In addition, the Court of Appeals for the Federal Circuit hears appeals that arise from some administrative rulings.

The United States Claims Court was established in 1855 to hear cases in which Congress allows citizens to bring suit against the federal government. Having nationwide jurisdiction, its 16 judges travel throughout the country to hold trials. Decisions of the claims court are final but may be reviewed by the Court of Appeals for the Federal Circuit.

The Court of International Trade hears civil cases that deal with tariffs, import taxes, and other trade-related laws. Panels of three judges hear cases at major ports of entry, such as New York and San Francisco. The court is composed of a chief judge and eight associate judges, not more than five of whom may belong to one political party.

The United States Tax Court is a special court established by Congress under Article I of the Constitution. It decides cases dealing with the application of tax laws, usually involving disputes between taxpayers and the Internal Revenue Service. The court is composed of 19 regular judges as well as a number of special trial judges who serve at the pleasure of the court.

Territorial courts were created by Congress to handle cases in the American territories of Guam, the Virgin Islands, and the Northern Mariana Islands. Territorial courts are similar to state courts in that they handle matters dealing with the laws of that territory, but they can also rule on questions involving federal laws.

The Court of Military Appeals is an appellate criminal court that deals only with military law. It is composed of three civilian judges who are appointed for 15-year terms. They hear appeals having to do with court-martials, or trials of persons accused of breaking military law.

Article I, Section 8 gives Congress the power to develop a judicial system for the nation's capital. In addition to a federal district court and a court of appeals, which are located in the District, Congress has set up various local courts to handle both civil and criminal cases.

The U.S. Virgin Islands are among the American territories that are under the jurisdiction of a territorial court. What cases are handled in territorial courts?

Section Review

1. What are the two basic kinds of federal courts?
2. What is the role of the district courts in the federal system?
3. How are territorial courts similar to state courts?
4. **Challenge:** Why, do you think, does the Court of Appeals for the Federal Circuit have nationwide, rather than just geographical, jurisdiction?

4 How Courts Are Administered

Although the federal courts carry out their business independently of one another, they are all a part of one federal court system. Efficient administration of the entire system is necessary in order to meet the needs of the people.

Federal Judges

Federal judges are the most visible persons in the daily operation of the federal court system. They are expected to have a high level of legal expertise and a basic understanding of the principles undergirding the Constitution of our country.

SELECTION

The Constitution states in Article II, Section 2 that the President "by and with the advice and consent of the Senate, shall appoint. . .judges of the Supreme Court." Congress has applied this to the selection of *all* federal judges serving in constitutional courts.

The President makes judicial nominations only after consultation with many individuals and groups, including the attorney general, the White House staff, advisers, and influential senators. Candidates for federal judgeships are then evaluated by a committee of the American Bar Association and by the Senate Judiciary Committee.

Presidents usually consider at least five factors in determining who will be nominated to a federal judgeship. First, the political party to which a judge belongs is usually an important consideration. As a rule, Presidents favor judges from their own party.

Second, Presidents tend to prefer candidates who have judicial philoso-phies similar to their own. As a result, they typically choose persons who agree with their views on current issues.

A third factor is the experience of the individual being considered. Almost all federal judges are, or have been, practicing attorneys who have served as judges at the state or local level. A few have been professors of law.

Considerable time and energy is also spent in examining the background of potential nominees. Every effort is made to find persons who are respected by their peers and who have personal integrity and high ethical standards.

In naming judges, Presidents may also follow a practice known as senatorial courtesy. When a state has a judicial opening, the President gives the senator or senators of that state the opportunity to approve or veto a potential candidate before his or her name is submitted to the entire Senate.

TERMS

Judges are appointed for life terms, which tend to insulate them from political pressures. Having to stand for election can make people more concerned about the good will of voters than about the constitutionality of laws. Similarly, Congress is forbidden to lower the salaries of jurists so that salary reduction cannot be used as a threat against them. Thus, the judicial branch is the least political of the three branches of government, and judges are generally not as swayed by public opinion as are those in the other two branches.

SALARIES

Although Congress cannot lower the salaries of individual judges, it can decide how much judges, as a group, should be paid. Today, the salaries range from $133,600 a year for judges in some of the lower courts to $171,500 a year for the chief justice of the Supreme Court.

Support Personnel

While federal judges hear and decide cases, the daily administrative tasks of the courts are handled by other officials. Each district court has a United States marshal, who makes arrests in federal cases, serves official papers, guards prisoners, and maintains order in the courtroom.

Each district court also has a United States attorney who brings legal proceedings against persons charged with federal crimes within the district. United States attorneys also represent the government in federal cases.

A federal magistrate is empowered to issue warrants for arrests and to hold hearings to decide if an accused person will be released on bail or held for trial. He or she also tries cases involving minor federal offenses if the accused gives up his or her right to a district court trial.

Each district court also has a clerk who records court proceedings, maintains the court calendar, and validates official documents. The clerk is assisted by several deputy clerks, secretaries, and others who work to keep the court running smoothly.

Administrative Structures

To help the federal courts keep up with increasing demands, Congress has established a group of organizations to handle certain tasks. The Judicial Conference of the United States, established in 1922, is responsible for setting policy in several areas, such as transferring judges, recommending new judges, and developing court budgets. Recommendations from the Conference are made in the form of proposed legislation for congressional consideration.

The Administrative Office of the United States Courts manages the daily affairs of the federal courts. This includes collecting data on cases heard by the courts, lengths of trials, and selection procedures and uses of jurors. The Administrative Office also serves as an advocate for the judiciary in its dealings with Congress, the executive branch, professional groups, and the public.

The duties of the Federal Judicial Center fall generally into three categories: to analyze research on the federal courts, make suggestions to improve the administration of the federal courts, and develop training programs for personnel of the judicial branch. The center conducts seminars on how to manage difficult civil cases, cope with unruly defendants, and adjust to new roles.

Finally, each circuit has at least one judicial conference and judicial council. These groups meet at least once a year to provide an opportunity for judges to exchange ideas and propose solutions to common problems.

Section Review

1. Name four factors a President may consider in appointing a federal judge.

2. How is the judicial branch the least political of the three branches of government?

3. How do United States marshals assist the district court judges?

4. Who manages the day-to-day affairs of the federal courts?

5. **Challenge:** What advantages and disadvantages do you see in federal judges being appointed for life?

5 The Supreme Court

The Supreme Court of the United States is the final authority in all questions arising under the Constitution, federal laws, and national treaties. It is the legal center of American life, and its decisions have a strong impact on social, economic, and political forces in our society.

Setting

Since 1935, the Supreme Court has met in a five-story marble building across the street from the Capitol. Inscribed above the entrance of the building are the words "Equal Justice Under Law." While not as well known as the White House or the Capitol, the Supreme Court building was designed to be an edifice ". . .of dignity and importance suitable. . . for the permanent home of the Supreme Court of the United States."

Jurisdiction

As you learned earlier, the Constitution gives the Supreme Court both original and appellate jurisdiction. The Supreme Court has original jurisdiction when a *state* is a party to a case and in cases that involve United States ambassadors, ministers, or consuls. But these cases make up only a fraction of the Court's work load, about one to five cases per term.

The vast majority of Supreme Court cases fall under its appellate jurisdiction, or its authority to confirm or reverse the decisions of lower courts. Cases reviewed by the Supreme Court usually come from the federal courts of appeals and the specialized appeals courts in the federal court system. The Supreme Court may also hear cases brought directly from the district courts in instances where an act of Congress was held unconstitutional by that court.

In addition, cases can come from state supreme courts, but only if they involve claims under federal law or the Constitution. In such instances, the Supreme Court can rule only on the federal issue involved in the case.

Term

The Supreme Court begins its term, or time during which it carries out business each year, on the first Monday of October. A term runs until the justices have handled all the business coming before the Court, usually not until well into July of the following year.

Anthony Kennedy, known for his conservative views on constitutional issues, was appointed a Supreme Court associate justice in 1987. When do Kennedy and the other justices begin their term each year?

SITTINGS

Terms are divided into two-week sittings, or periods in which the Court is formally in session. During each sitting, public courtroom sessions are held from Monday through Thursday.

On some days, the Court may listen to oral arguments by the lawyers from each side in the case being heard. On other days, the Court may announce cases that have been accepted for review, discuss and vote on current cases, or read from written opinions.

RECESSES

Each sitting is followed by a two-week recess, or break in the judicial term. These are not really "breaks," though. During recesses, justices decide which cases to hear, research cases that are pending, study briefs, and issue written statements announcing their decisions on cases.

Justices of the Supreme Court

The present Supreme Court consists of nine judges who are known as justices, one of whom serves as chief justice. The remaining justices are known as associate justices.

NUMBER

As mentioned earlier, Congress has the authority to determine the number of justices on the Court. The first Court had six justices. Over the years, this number has varied from five to ten. Changes in the total number were made for several reasons, one of which was to help the justices in their workload. Partisan politics was another factor, with members of Congress using the changes to "punish" the Court or its individual members. Since 1869, however, the number has been set at nine.

President Clinton appointed Ruth Bader Ginzburg, a judge on the United States Court of Appeals, to the Supreme Court in 1993. She is the second woman to serve on the Court. How are Court sittings conducted?

QUALIFICATIONS

Although the Constitution sets no specific qualifications for Supreme Court justices, all who have served share certain characteristics. First, all members have had legal training.

Second, all justices have been white males, with four exceptions. In 1967, Thurgood Marshall, a lawyer active in civil rights cases, became the first African American member of the Court. When Marshall retired, he was replaced by Clarence Thomas, another African American. Sandra Day O'Connor, a judge from the Arizona State Court of Appeals, became the first female member of the bench in 1981. The second female was Ruth Bader Ginzburg, appointed by President Clinton in 1993.

TERMS AND SALARIES

Supreme Court justices are appointed for life terms. While they can be removed from office by impeachment, none has ever been so removed. Today, associate justices receive a salary of $164,100 a year and the chief justice is paid $171,500.

DUTIES

The duties of the justices include selecting which cases to hear, deciding these cases, and writing legal opinions about their decisions. Each justice is also assigned to at least one of the 12 federal circuits. The justices are expected to take special actions regarding their circuits. Justices may also occasionally consult on a nonofficial basis with members of Congress or the President.

SELECTION

The same factors that influence the President in choosing lower court judges are at work in the President's choice of a nominee to the Supreme Court. These factors, remember, include a candidate's political party,

personal background, and experience. Presidents also choose candidates whose political philosophies are similar to their own. That is, conservative Presidents seek out conservatives and liberal Presidents try to place liberals on the bench.

After the President nominates someone to fill a vacancy on the Supreme Court, the nomination is sent to the Senate for confirmation. The Senate Judiciary Committee holds hearings and then votes on whether or not to recommend the candidate. After committee action, the nomination is referred to the Senate floor, where it is debated and then voted upon.

Most presidential appointments have been confirmed by the Senate, although a few faced stiff opposition. In the 1900s, only four of the nominees considered by the Senate have failed to get confirmation. Recent

William Rehnquist is the current chief justice of the Supreme Court. Appointed to the post in 1986, Rehnquist had earlier served as an associate justice for 14 years. What factors are involved in the selection of Supreme Court justices?

examples include Judge Robert Bork, an outspoken conservative, who failed to be confirmed by the Senate in 1987. And Judge Douglas Ginsburg withdrew after it was revealed he had smoked marijuana as a youth.

In addition to the President and the Senate, several individuals and groups play a part in selecting a judicial candidate. For example, those who are already members of the Court may become involved in the selection process by writing letters of recommendation or identifying people with whom they could or could not cooperate. The American Bar Association (ABA) also plays an important role in the selection of Supreme Court jus-

discuss list a list of petitions the Supreme Court will consider

tices. The ABA's Committee on the Federal Judiciary rates the candidates whom the President nominates as ''qualified'' or ''unqualified.'' It would be unlikely for the Senate to approve a President's nomination if the ABA gave the candidate an ''unqualified'' rating.

Besides the ABA, many other interest groups in the United States have been active in the judicial selection process in recent years. Some of these groups are labor organizations, the National Association for the Advancement of Colored People (NAACP), the American Civil Liberties Union (ACLU), and the National Organization for Women (NOW).

CHIEF JUSTICE

Chief justices wield great power. They preside over the Court during oral arguments and in conferences, directing discussion and helping to shape decisions. The chief justice has several other important responsibilities. One is the job of creating the **discuss list**. This responsibility gives the chief justice a significant role in determining which cases are set aside without requiring the entire Court to participate in the decision.

The chief justice also assigns the justices to circuits, approves regulations for the protection of the court building and grounds, and is responsible for the administrative leadership of the entire judicial system. In addition, the chief justice presides at the swearing in of a President and over any impeachment trial.

The Supreme Court is generally referred to by the name of its chief justice. Thus, in 1969, when Warren E. Burger became chief justice, the Supreme Court became known as the Burger Court. Figure 19-4 lists some information about the former chief justices of the Supreme Court.

Chief Justices of the Supreme Court

Name	Appointed by President	Dates of Service
John Jay	Washington	1789–1795
John Rutledge	Washington	1795
Oliver Ellsworth	Washington	1796–1800
John Marshall	John Adams	1801–1835
Roger B. Taney	Jackson	1836–1864
Salmon P. Chase	Lincoln	1864–1873
Morrison R. Waite	Grant	1874–1888
Melville W. Fuller	Cleveland	1888–1910
Edward D. White	Taft	1910–1921
William H. Taft	Harding	1921–1930
Charles E. Hughes	Hoover	1930–1941
Harlan F. Stone	F. Roosevelt	1941–1946
Frederick M. Vinson	Truman	1946–1953
Earl Warren	Eisenhower	1953–1969
Warren E. Burger	Nixon	1969–1986
William H. Rehnquist	Reagan	1986–

Figure 19-4

PROFILE: SANDRA DAY O'CONNOR

THE FIRST WOMAN ON THE SUPREME COURT

"She is truly a person for all seasons, possessing those unique qualities of temperament, fairness, intellectual capacity, and devotion to the public good which had characterized the 101 brethren who had preceded her." With these words, President Reagan announced the appointment of the first female Supreme Court justice, Sandra Day O'Connor.

Born in El Paso, Texas, in 1930, O'Connor grew up on her family's ranch in Arizona. Attending Stanford University, she received a bachelor's degree in economics. In 1952, she graduated from Stanford University Law School, ranking third in her class. By coincidence, William H. Rehnquist, the current chief justice of the Supreme Court, ranked first. Her husband, John J. O'Connor III, was also in that class.

After practicing law for several years in Phoenix and raising three sons, O'Connor became an assistant attorney general in Arizona. In 1969, she was appointed to a vacant state senate seat. In 1970 she was elected to a full term, then reelected in 1972. During her second term, she was chosen by Republican legislators as majority leader. Thus, O'Connor became the first woman to be majority leader of a state legislature.

In 1974 O'Connor was elected to the Superior Court of Maricopa County as trial judge. Five years later, Governor Bruce Babbitt, a Democrat, appointed her to the Arizona Court of Appeals. She was serving in this capacity when the President appointed her to the nation's highest court. In September 1981 the Senate unanimously confirmed Sandra Day O'Connor's appointment as the 102nd justice of the United States Supreme Court.

In Washington, D.C., O'Connor has easily blended into the local social scene, where she has earned a reputation as an enthusiastic partygoer and avid tennis player and golfer. Barbara Bush is a frequent tennis partner.

On the bench, Associate Justice O'Connor is known as a careful

legal thinker with a respect for legal precedent. She has generally supported judicial restraint. Those holding this view tend to be reluctant for the Supreme Court to interfere with laws passed by Congress or state powers. However, O'Connor has not favored judicial restraint in every case, nor has she voted exclusively with the majority. During her early years on the Court, O'Connor generally sided with the more conservative justices. In recent years, however, she has taken an increasingly independent role on the bench, sometimes even supporting liberal positions. In a 1989 case, for example, O'Connor sided with her more liberal colleagues in support of affirmative action employment policies that favor women and minorities over men in hiring and promotions.

Increasingly, Justice O'Connor is coming to be seen as the "swing" vote on the Court. The 34 opinions she wrote during her first term reflect her tendency toward judicial independence. Of these, 12 were majority opinions, 13 were concurring opinions, and 9 were dissenting opinions.

1. What positions did O'Connor hold in the legislative branch of state government? the judicial branch?
2. How would you describe Justice O'Connor's judicial philosophy?

The Work of the Court

The most important work of the Court involves the justices in three major tasks. These are selecting which cases to hear from among the thousands that come before them, deciding the cases, and explaining the reasoning behind the decisions.

SELECTING CASES

The majority of cases handled by the Supreme Court have to do with its appellate jurisdiction. These reach the Court either on appeal or by **writ of certiorari**.

The Court is required by law to hear all cases involving the constitutionality of laws passed by Congress. These cases are called cases on appeal, and most are eventually dismissed because they do not involve important constitutional questions. If they are dismissed without full consideration of the Supreme Court, the decisions of the lower courts are accepted as final.

Most appeals, however, do not involve the constitutionality of a federal law, and so the Court can choose the cases it will hear. If a person who loses in a lower court wishes to have the case heard by the Supreme Court, he or she must petition it to issue a writ of certiorari. In requesting the writ, the party submits a written claim that the lower court has erred in handling the case and asks the Supreme Court to review the ruling. Out of the more than 5000 cases appealed each year, only a few hundred are accepted for a hearing.

When petitions come to the Court, they are screened by the chief justice and several law clerks. The cases that the chief justice believes should be considered are put on the discuss list. All other cases are denied hearings automatically unless another justice asks that they be added to the list.

Later, all of the justices decide which cases on the discuss list they wish to issue writs for. If at least four of the justices vote to issue a writ, the case will be given the full consideration of the Court. This is known as the "rule of four."

Because the number of cases that the Court can carefully review is limited, each one that *is* considered must be of great consequence to the smooth functioning of our democracy. The case must have national significance and not merely be important to the person or group bringing the case.

The justices will also consider some cases to bring clarity and uniformity to case law. This can happen when decisions from two or more of the federal courts of appeals appear to be in conflict.

Occasionally, the Court may select and decide a case without hearing oral arguments. On such occasions, it will issue only a brief opinion that is labeled *per curiam,* or "by the Court," rather than issue an opinion signed by a justice.

writ of certiorari an order from the Supreme Court requiring a lower court to send a record of a case to the Supreme Court

David Souter became an associate justice of the Supreme Court in 1990. On Supreme Court cases, Souter has taken moderate positions. What are the three major tasks of justices in carrying out the work of the Court?

DECIDING CASES

Justices of the Supreme Court hear oral arguments concerning all cases in a courtroom open to the public. However, much of their work is accomplished in judicial conference rooms and in their private offices. Before a case is argued, lawyers on both sides present written briefs, or arguments summarizing their side of the case, to the justices. This is done so that the justices can study the case before it comes to the Court.

The Court also takes into consideration *amicus curiae,* or "friend of the court" briefs. These are submitted by interested parties who are not directly involved in the case but who want to provide information they feel would be of value to the Court in making its decision. Briefs of this kind are often submitted by interest groups, private individuals, or even government agencies.

Following the filing of briefs, the lawyers for each side in a case present oral arguments before the Court. Usually, each side has only one-half hour to summarize the position it represents. During those oral presentations, the justices interrupt the lawyers, often more than 100 times an hour, to raise questions or challenge the points being made in the argument.

Each Friday during the term is a private conference day when the justices meet to discuss petitions and cases they have heard and vote on final decisions. Only the justices are present, and no records are kept of the discussion within the conference.

At least six of the nine justices must be present to decide a case. The chief justice begins discussion with a summary of the facts and an analysis of the law in each case. Next, the associate justices, in order of seniority, all present their views.

Antonin Scalia is an associate justice of the Supreme Court. He was named to the post in 1986. How do Supreme Court justices come to a decision about a case?

The decision of the Court is determined by a majority vote. If a tie occurs because a member is absent, the decision of a lower court is upheld.

Although many cases are decided unanimously, or by a solid majority, justices sometimes disagree sharply about how to interpret the law. In these instances, cases may be decided by a five to four, or split, vote. In recent years, the Court has split on a number of crucial issues such as the death penalty and abortion.

The justices announce and give the reasons for their decisions in written statements called **opinions.** If all the justices vote the same way, the chief justice selects one justice to draft a **unanimous opinion.** If more than

opinions written statements by a judge or judges of the reasons for the decision of the court

unanimous opinion single written explanation of a court decision representing the view of the entire court

majority opinion written explanation of a court decision expressing the view of more than half the court

concurring opinion judgment by one or more judges that supports the majority opinion but offers different reasoning

dissenting opinion judgment of one or more judges that disagrees with the majority opinion

half the justices agree, then they issue a **majority opinion**. If the chief justice voted with the majority, he or she selects a justice in the majority to write the decision. But if the chief did *not* vote with the majority, the senior justice among the majority chooses who will write the opinion.

A justice may agree with the majority position but not with the reasoning behind it. He or she may prepare what is known as a **concurring opinion.** There may be more than one in a single case.

Any justice who disagrees with the majority's decision may write a **dissenting opinion.** In some cases, dissenting opinions have become the majority opinion in a similar case at a later date.

After an initial version of a majority or unanimous opinion is written by a justice and his or her law clerks, it must be read and commented upon by the other justices. At this point, changes may have to be made to please other justices. The document must win the support of at least four justices, who may have voted the same way but perhaps for different reasons. Occasionally, a justice's view on a case may change, either by writing an opinion or by reading another justice's opinion. Justices often take several weeks to discuss, change, and rewrite opinions.

When all the opinions are written and all justices have determined which opinion they will join, the decision is announced in open court,

Stephen Breyer became an associate justice of the Supreme Court in 1994. Before serving on the Supreme Court, Breyer had served as an appellate court judge. What kinds of court opinions are given by Supreme Court justices?

usually on a Monday. Decisions are then published in a series of volumes called the *United States Reports*.

The majority opinion in a Supreme Court case is important. First, it explains the Court's decision. Also, it expresses the principles that a lower court should follow in rehearing a case. Finally, the majority opinion lays down general principles of law that may apply to other cases.

How Justices Decide

Many things guide justices as they decide cases and interpret the law and the meaning of the Constitution. People have sometimes been confounded when justices decide a case differently than their past behavior might have indicated.

Members of the Court are intentionally insulated from public and political pressure so that their decisions will be as rational as humanly possible. The job of a justice is not to make law but rather to interpret and apply laws that others have made.

Some justices are reputed to be aggressive in their decision making, an approach called judicial activism. But many tend to rule as narrowly as possible, unwilling to move the Court suddenly beyond its precedents. A basic doctrine of the American legal system, in fact, is the idea of **stare decisis,** or "let the decision stand." This principle holds that a case should be decided by following precedents set in other cases. This gives the law predictability and accountability, and lower courts can get their directions from the decisions of higher courts.

Another influence on some justices is the persuasiveness of other members of the Court. One reason the opportunity to assign the writing of opinions to particular justices is highly prized is because some justices

Associate Justice John Paul Stevens (top photo) is known for his moderate decisions. Associate Justice Clarence Thomas (bottom photo) has moderate to conservative viewpoints. Why is the majority opinion of the Court important?

are so skilled in crafting these documents they can often change the minds of other members of the Court.

stare decisis rule whereby a decision applies in similar cases

The Supreme Court as Policymaker

Through its interpretation of the law and the Constitution, the Supreme Court has played a part in making public policy throughout our history.

LEGISLATIVE REVIEW

One way the Supreme Court affects policy in the United States is through legislative review. In the past, the Court has reviewed legislation covering a range of public policies, from labor relations, social welfare, and economic practices to environmental protection.

When the Court practices legislative review, it often spends time interpreting the wording of a law rather than reviewing its constitutionality. This involves the Court in trying to analyze the literal meaning of certain words. At other times, the Court tries to figure out the meaning of obscure phrases such as "due process of law."

The Court sometimes interprets a law by determining the intentions of those who wrote it. Researching a law's historical record is one way the Court makes this determination. This might include reviewing discussions held about the law in congressional committees or before a vote is taken in either house of Congress.

Sometimes, the Court must apply an old law to new technology. For example, when the Fourth Amendment requirements for searches and seizures were written, wiretapping was not technologically possible. Justices of modern times have been forced to speculate what the intentions of those who approved the amendment would have been toward wiretapping.

The Court's interpretations of laws and the Constitution have a profound effect on public policy. For example, by 1954 many Americans were opposed to racial segregation. The Court ruled, in *Brown v. Board of Education of Topeka,* that segregation in public schools was inherently unequal and, thus, unconstitutional. Only after the *Brown* decision was rendered did Congress and the executive branch begin to move toward establishing racial equality in other areas of American life.

EXECUTIVE REVIEW

In addition to legislation, the Supreme Court also rules on the legality of executive orders. Presidential decisions and actions can be challenged on the grounds that they conflict with federal laws, with the Constitution, or with both. The Court can overturn presidential actions just as it can overturn legislation, although this power is used much less frequently in the case of the executive.

One striking example of the power of the Supreme Court over executive privilege occurred during investigations of the Watergate episode of 1973. President Nixon attempted to invoke executive privilege when he withheld recordings of conversations with White House staff members in the Oval Office. The Supreme Court refused to accept the President's claim of executive privilege and ordered him to release the recordings.

Section Review

1. In what kinds of cases does the Supreme Court have original jurisdiction? appellate jurisdiction?

2. How are Supreme Court cases selected?

3. What four kinds of opinions may be issued by the Supreme Court?

4. How does the Supreme Court use its power of executive review?

5. **Challenge:** Why, do you think, must the Supreme Court be careful in choosing the cases it will hear?

1. The judiciary is the third branch of government in the American federal system.

2. The judicial branch interprets and applies the nation's laws.

3. Article III of the Constitution deals with the powers of the judiciary. The Constitution gives Congress the power to establish inferior federal courts.

4. The jurisdiction of federal courts is set down in the Constitution. Among the cases in which federal courts have jurisdiction are cases involving an interpretation of federal law, cases where the federal government is a party, and disputes between state governments.

5. The federal court system of the United States consists of the federal district courts, the courts of appeals, other special courts, and the Supreme Court, which is the highest court in the federal judicial system.

6. Congress has established two basic types of lower federal courts to handle a growing number of cases. These are constitutional federal courts and legislative federal courts.

7. Federal district courts are organized into judicial districts. The district courts are trial courts, and most of the cases that are heard are civil cases.

8. Federal appeals courts were established to ease the caseload of the Supreme Court. Their function is to determine if federal law has been correctly applied by district courts or regulatory agencies.

9. Courts have support personnel to help them carry out their duties. Among these are federal marshals, U.S. attorneys, federal magistrates, and court clerks.

10. The Supreme Court has both appellate and original jurisdiction. Most cases, however, are appellate.

11. The Constitution states no qualifications for Supreme Court justices. However, all have had considerable legal training and experience.

12. Justices have three major tasks. These are to select cases, to decide cases, and to explain decisions.

13. In addition to cases heard under its original jurisdiction, there are two ways that cases reach the Supreme Court—by appeal and by writ of certiorari.

14. In deciding cases, justices read written briefs, hear oral arguments, hold judicial conferences, and then, vote on a decision. One justice is designated to write the majority opinion, and others may write concurring or dissenting opinions.

15. A majority opinion explains the Court's decision and establishes guidelines for a lower court to follow if it rehears the case. It may also lay down general law principles that apply to other cases.

16. Because it interprets the law and the Constitution, the Supreme Court has helped to make policy throughout American history.

Chapter 19 Review

★ Building Vocabulary

Unscramble the following vocabulary terms so that they are spelled correctly. Then use the word in each sentence about the United States federal judiciary.

1. idrujiscitno
2. usiijtcelba
3. nnaitdsg
4. stricciu
5. noiinops
6. tears scediis
7. otjiarmy nonpiio
8. oriefrni struoc
9. tlepaplae nicdiujrsito
10. srevdaary tyssme

★ Reviewing Facts

1. What is the function of the federal judiciary?
2. Who has the power to establish inferior federal courts?
3. Which federal courts have original jurisdiction? Which have appellate jurisdiction? Which, if any, have both?
4. How is national judicial power limited?
5. Why was the case *Marbury v. Madison* important for the future of the Supreme Court?
6. What is the difference between constitutional federal courts and legislative federal courts?
7. What is the function of the courts of appeals?
8. Why does the Constitution prohibit lowering the salaries of certain federal judges during their terms in office?
9. How do most cases get to the Supreme Court?
10. Why is a majority opinion important for future Supreme Court decisions?
11. Why has the Supreme Court been important in making policy throughout United States history?
12. In what ways have Supreme Court decisions changed public policy in regard to issues such as civil rights, rights of the accused, and First Amendment freedoms?

★ Analyzing Facts

1. Some people believe it is important that federal judges have the same political philosophy and belong to the same political party as the President. Do you agree? Explain.
2. For several years, the idea of a National Court of Appeals has been discussed. Such a court, its supporters say, could reduce the caseload of the Supreme Court. In your opinion, should there be a National Court of Appeals? Explain.
3. Most cases that come before the Supreme Court are not granted writs of certiorari. Do you think the selection system is fair? Why or why not?

★ Evaluating Ideas

1. Some analysts have criticized the Supreme Court's policy-making role. They claim that it often makes law instead of interpreting the law. Do you agree or disagree? Explain.
2. Judges in many state and municipal courts are elected. However, all federal judges are appointed. Do you think federal judges should be elected or appointed? Why?

Using Your
Civic Participation Journal

Review your entries in your Civic Participation Journal about the requirements to become a lawyer. Work with three of your classmates to create a flow chart showing the steps necessary to become a practicing attorney in your community.

3. The Supreme Court has original jurisdiction in only two types of cases. What are these types of cases? Why do you think the Constitution specifies that such cases can be heard only by the Supreme Court?

4. Charles Evans Hughes, chief justice of the Supreme Court from 1930 to 1941, once said, "We are under a constitution, but the Constitution is what the judges say it is." What do you think he meant? Do you agree or disagree? Explain.

★ Critical Thinking
Identifying Arguments

An argument is a viewpoint and a series of reasons that support that viewpoint. People use three kinds of reasons to support their views—facts, rules, and generalizations.

Explanation Identifying the other person's argument when you are in a dispute is a step in finding a way to resolve the disagreement. It also can help you take a side when you witness a disagreement. Asking yourself these questions will help you identify arguments.

1. What viewpoint is the person stating?
2. What reasons does the person give to support that viewpoint?
3. What kinds of reasons are they—facts, rules, or generalizations?

Practice You can use the above questions to identify the argument in the following excerpt about the Supreme Court under Chief Justice John Marshall. For this exercise each sentence is numbered.

(1) *During Marshall's tenure the Supreme Court declared unconstitutional acts of more than half of the states. (2) In practically every case the state involved naturally objected in some form to the Court's decision, and often the state received sympathetic support from other states with sim-*ilar statutes or interests. (3) *Frequently, however, other states supported the Court. (4) In nearly every instance the state was motivated primarily by concern for its immediate interests rather than by a broad political theory or constitutional concept. . . . (5) The Court's repeated invalidation of state statutes demonstrated that the states' rights [supporters] had largely failed in their efforts to make the states rather than the Court the final arbiter in disputes between the states and the central government.*

Alfred H. Kelly and Winfred A. Harbison, *The American Constitution: Its Origins and Development*

The authors' viewpoint is stated in sentence (5). The reasons used to support that viewpoint are given in sentences (1) through (4). The reason used in (1) is a fact that can be proven by surveying the cases decided. The reasons used in (2), (3), and (4) are generalizations.

Independent Practice Political cartoonists often have specific viewpoints. Study the cartoon below. It appeared after the 1994 election and shows President Clinton being served by a Republican elephant. (Remember, Newt Gingrich became Speaker of the House.) On what is the artist basing his viewpoint?

Chapter 20

The American Legal System

The American system of justice is based on law. In one sense, justice can mean the enactment and administration of the law. It also means the fair and impartial application of the law. This carries with it the idea that nothing or no one, including the government, is above the law. In this chapter, you will learn what the nature of law is, what kinds of laws there are, the sources of today's laws, and the characteristics that most good laws share.

Chapter Preview

TERMS TO KNOW

law, law codes, common law, habeas corpus, administrative law, statutes, complaint, plaintiff, defendant, pleadings, subpoenas, interrogatories, verdict, equity suit, enjoin, deposition, arraignment, prosecutor, indictment, information, plea bargain, acquittal, probation

READ TO DISCOVER

- the nature and purposes of law and the legal system.
- the origins and sources of American law.
- what procedures are followed in civil and criminal cases.

★ ★ ★ ★ ★

Civic Participation Journal

Arrange to visit the courthouse in your community. You should telephone first to find out when court is in session. Then visit when you can sit in on a trial. Record your impressions of the court procedures in your journal.

1 The Nature of Law

Everyone has a general idea about what law is because everyone's life is affected by it in some way. The law is in effect 24 hours a day. And yet, when asked to describe the effect of law on their lives, most of us think of it only in terms of the restrictions it imposes—restrictions against speeding, against murder, against stealing, and so on. In a free society, however, law promotes as well as restricts.

Law defines the individual's rights and obligations and specifies the ways citizens and government relate to each other. Also, law provides a way for the government to set goals for society and to distribute resources. The law *does* establish penalties for people who violate the rules, and it states how the government should enforce those rules, but this is done for the protection of society as a whole.

The Functions of Law in America

Law serves several functions in our society. What are the social goals that are achieved through law?

RESOLVE CONFLICT
One reason for having a government is to help people live together with a minimum of conflict. Law establishes socially acceptable ways for people to settle disputes without having to resort to violence. The American legal system provides courts of law where disagreements and conflicts can be settled. In these formal, government-sanctioned settings, judges and juries apply specific laws to cases and hand down decisions that take into account the interests of both sides. The alternative to this could be John Locke's and Thomas Hobbes's state of nature, where the strongest and most powerful always wins when there is a conflict.

PROTECT RIGHTS
Citizens of the United States have numerous rights, many of which are outlined in the Constitution and the Bill of Rights. Literally thousands of laws have been enacted to protect these rights, as well as to put the principles of the Constitution into effect. Laws also have been enacted to make sure that one person's rights do not interfere unduly with the rights of others.

LIMIT GOVERNMENT
One of the main purposes of the Constitution is to limit government. The laws supporting the Constitution in this regard are intended to prevent

law set of rules and standards by which a society governs itself

This antismoking poster reflects the view that life can be beautiful without cigarettes. Many communities now have laws banning smoking in certain public places. What is the relationship between social behavior and law?

the government from taking away our rights and privileges without good reason. Examples of these limitations are the Fourth Amendment, which prohibits unreasonable searches and seizures, and the Eighth Amendment, which keeps the government from setting excessive bail and sentences and from inflicting cruel and unusual punishments.

PROMOTE GENERAL WELFARE

The quality of living in the United States is higher than in most parts of the world. Thousands of laws are written each year to promote our general welfare and to maintain or improve the quality of our lives. These include laws that assure safe drinking water and food and laws that provide attractive recreational areas. Laws also help determine what services we should receive, how those services should be distributed, and how they should be regulated.

SET SOCIAL GOALS

One of the functions of government is to develop public policies to achieve social goals. In 1932, for example, when the United States was in the depths of the Great Depression, Franklin Roosevelt promised to work with Congress to pass laws that would improve the economy. Such policy-making occurs at all levels of government and can be successful only when there are laws to support the desired goals.

CONTROL CRIME

Even though most people obey laws and are concerned about the rights of others, there are those who do commit crimes. Laws define criminal acts and provide guidelines for dealing with persons who engage in them. Further, there are laws that specify appropriate punishments for different levels of criminal activity. In the case of murder, for instance, the punishment might range from a long prison term

With the aim of promoting the general welfare, laws have been written to ensure safe drinking water. Here, inspectors from the Environmental Protection Agency are checking the pollution level of a stream. What are the functions of law in America?

to the death penalty. Less serious crimes, such as traffic offenses, could result in only a fine.

Elements of Good Laws

In a democracy, the people, either directly or through their representatives, determine whether a law should be passed, changed, or even dropped. Making judgments about whether a law is good or poor, however, requires balancing it against a set of standards. In American society there are certain basic characteristics found in all good laws that can be used as standards against which other laws can be measured.

JUST LAWS
The idea that laws should be just or fair has always been prominent in American thought. In colonial times, the colonists revolted against Great Britain because they believed they were being treated unjustly. The Preamble to the Constitution establishes justice as one of the basic goals of American government. Today, we still believe that people should be treated fairly. For example, it would be unjust if two people who committed identical crimes under identical circumstances received different punishments. In reality, however, applying this general standard of justice to specific laws is not always easy or possible.

REASONABLE LAWS
In some cases, it might be more just to apply the principle of ''reasonableness'' to laws, even if people are treated differently because of it. For example, most of us believe it is reasonable to treat juvenile offenders less harshly than adults, even if they commit the same crimes. The reasoning behind this view is that adults are expected to be more mature and responsible. The entire American system of juvenile law is based on this idea. Of course, in a society as diverse and complex as ours, not everyone will agree on what is reasonable. But those who do find a law unreasonable can work through their representatives or the courts to change it. Some people have argued, for instance, that laws should be changed to enable juvenile drug dealers to be treated like adults.

An entire society also can change its ideas about what is reasonable. For over 150 years, segregating black people from white people was considered reasonable and lawful. Blacks were forced to attend different schools, ride at the backs of buses, and live in separate neighborhoods. Over time, this sort of differential treatment was no longer considered reasonable by the majority of Americans, and they made it unlawful.

Figure 20-1

Elements of a Good Law

just · reasonable · enforceable · understandable

1 + 2 = 3

ENFORCEABLE LAWS

A law that is not enforceable is almost the same as having no law at all. Suppose there was a law against earthquakes and floods. How would such a law be enforced? Laws cannot prevent natural disasters from occurring, of course, but they can help a society deal with such disasters. Building codes, for instance, can help assure the stability of structures, and laws damming rivers may prevent flooding from occurring.

There also are laws that cannot be enforced because they violate our norms, or unwritten standards that guide our behavior. If a law was passed requiring everyone to stop watching television, most of us would simply ignore it because we do not believe that watching television is wrong.

Several laws, in fact, have been repealed because so many people have ignored or broken them. In 1919 the Eighteenth Amendment, which made it illegal to make, transport, or sell alcoholic beverages, was ratified. But because so many people did not view alcohol as bad and made or bought their own alcoholic beverages illegally, the police were unable to effectively enforce the law. Since it was virtually useless, the Eighteenth Amendment was repealed by the Twenty-first Amendment in 1933.

UNDERSTANDABLE LAWS

Citizens are absolutely required and expected to obey the law. But what if we cannot understand a law because it is so complex? For years, considerable pressure has been applied by interest groups and individual citizens encouraging city councils, state legislatures, and Congress to draft their legislation in simple, straightforward language. While these efforts have not been entirely successful, more and

Building codes require construction companies to meet certain standards of quality in erecting structures, such as the homes in this housing development. What characteristic makes a law enforceable?

more representatives have become aware that, if they expect the people to obey the law, the people need to understand it.

Section Review

1. What are six functions of law in American society?

2. What are four elements of good laws?

3. Why must a good law be an enforceable law?

4. **Challenge:** Do you think young people and adults should be treated equally before the law? Explain.

2 Law in America

Today's American legal system was established by the Constitution. Yet many of the ideas on which our legal system is based were developed long before the Constitutional Convention was held. These ideas, some dating back thousands of years, were borrowed from different societies and cultures.

History of American Law

The earliest laws actually were unwritten traditions and customs. With the advent of writing some 5000 years ago, people began classifying their unwritten rules into **law codes.** Of these early codes, one of the best known was the Code of Hammurabi, written about 4000 years ago. Other early laws came from religious sources, such as the Torah or the Bible.

Americans also owe a special debt to the Romans, who developed the most highly organized legal system in the ancient world. As early as 450 BC, the Romans were assembling their laws into codes, the most well-known being the Justinian Code. It regulated every aspect of human life. The Roman legal system also made provisions for an efficient body of law-enforcement officers and numerous courts. Roman law was so highly refined and sophisticated that law began to be considered a science. In fact, the word *jurisprudence,* which means the science of law, comes directly from Latin, the language of the Romans.

By far the greatest influence on our laws and courts, however, has come from the British, who gave us the system of **common law.** Common law originated when judges began using earlier court decisions as precedents on which to base their decisions in similar cases. In time, these decisions became "common throughout the realm." Today, common law is used on the national level in the United States, as well as by 49 state governments. Only one state, Louisiana, partially bases its law on a written system called the Napoleonic Code, which originated in France.

Other events in England also have influenced our legal system. In 1215 English nobles forced King John to sign the Magna Carta, which established the idea that even the king and queen must obey the law. Also from the Magna Carta came two other rights we now enjoy through the Constitution—the right to trial by jury and the right of **habeas corpus.**

As might be expected, the English settlers who came to America firmly believed and understood British principles of law. In fact, the colonial claim of independence was based on common law principles. When the United States was established, however, the people of the new nation went one step further. They incorporated their ideas about law in a written document —the Constitution.

law codes written lists of laws

common law law based on court decisions rather than on a legal code

habeas corpus order from a court to police or other law enforcement agencies to "produce the body" of a person held in jail so that the court can determine whether that person is being held legally

In 1215, King John was forced to sign the Magna Carta, which limited the English monarch's powers. What other benefits came from the Magna Carta?

Sources of Law

In our present legal system, laws stem from several sources. The ultimate source of laws is the Constitution, which outranks all other laws. It states:

This Constitution, and the laws of the United States which shall be made in pursuance therefore . . . under the authority of the United States, shall be the supreme law of the land.

Within a state, a state constitution is the supreme law, but it too is superseded by the Constitution.

Constitutional law is intended to give stability to government so that rules and forms of government may not be changed quickly during brief political, social, or economic upheaval. For this reason, constitutional provisions can be amended only through a time-consuming process that requires the consent of a large number of people.

STATUTORY LAW

Today's laws also come from all three levels of lawmaking bodies. Using powers granted to them by constitutions, Congress, state legislatures, and local lawmaking bodies pass **statutes** that often translate constitutional provisions into action. And while statutory law can be changed much more easily than constitutional law, both bodies of law are interpreted and applied by the courts.

CASE LAW

The judicial branch is a third source of present laws. Very often, common-law legal systems, such as those of the United States, Canada, and Great Britain, are required to settle cases in which no written statutes apply. In these instances, judges rely heavily on **case law,** which is based on decisions in real cases. These decisions provide the precedents on which new decisions are based.

The courts also have used case law as a basis for interpreting constitutional provisions and statutes. Judges search out precedents and apply their principles in deciding new and similar cases. It is important to remember, however, that few cases that come before the courts are *exactly* the same as earlier cases. Furthermore, times and values change. Over time, old case law is dated and *new* case law will reflect current social needs.

ADMINISTRATIVE LAW

A fourth source of laws today is the executive branch. Administrative agencies established by national, state, and local governments must handle the details related to their scope of operation. The Federal Communications Commission, for instance, must deal with any problems arising from mass communication activities. **Administrative law,** then, is the body of rules and regulations that agencies establish to carry out their responsibilities. But since these agencies are set up by statutes, the agencies must not exceed the powers they have been given by the legislatures.

Section Review

1. What is one of the earliest known written law codes?

2. How was our legal system influenced by the Romans? the British?

3. What is the foundation of the American legal system?

4. What are four kinds of law in the United States?

5. **Challenge:** What would your life in America be like today if there were no laws?

administrative law rules and regulations developed by executive agencies to carry out their duties

statutes laws enacted by legislatures

case law body of law containing decisions of judges

3 Law and the Courts

Courts apply law and administer justice. Thousands of cases involving all kinds of problems and issues are taken to court in the United States each year. These can be classified as either civil or criminal cases.

Court Procedures in Civil Cases

Civil cases most often involve a dispute over a contract or some sort of damage to an individual or group. The government's primary role in civil actions is to provide the laws, courts, and judges needed to settle the disputes.

By far, the vast majority of civil cases are tried in state courts. Civil cases are tried in federal courts only if federal laws, such as tax proceedings, bankruptcies, or copyright infringements, are involved. In addition, federal courts are involved if one of the parties to a civil suit is the national government. This could happen, for instance, if a postal truck hits a private vehicle and the vehicle's owner sues for damages.

The majority of civil cases are suits at law, or lawsuits. A person or group who believes a wrong has been committed by another begins a lawsuit by filing a **complaint.** The party who files the complaint is the **plaintiff,** and the party accused of wrongdoing is the **defendant,** who must respond by filing a written statement.

After the filing of these **pleadings,** a case moves into the pretrial stage. During this time, a trial date is set and the parties and their attorneys gather evidence and prepare for the trial. One method of gathering information is by using **subpoenas.** Attorneys also may issue **interrogatories.** The next procedure is the trial itself.

THE TRIAL

During the trial, the parties and their witnesses are given the opportunity to present their side of the case in a courtroom. A typical courtroom is diagrammed in Figure 20-2. Civil cases may be heard by a judge alone or by a judge and jury, depending on the preferences of the parties involved.

In jury trials the potential jurors are chosen at random from voter registration lists or tax rolls. Each state establishes its own qualifications for jurors, which may include literacy, length of residence, education, citizenship, or eligibility to vote. Although trial juries, especially for criminal cases, often consist of 12 persons, many states require only six jurors to sit in civil cases.

The persons selected are summoned by mail and given directions as to when and where to report. They are carefully questioned by each side's attorneys, who seek to identify fair and impartial jurors. An ideal jury is composed of people who have no opinions or prior knowledge of the case; do not know either the plaintiff or defendant; and have not been influenced by media reports of the dispute. Finding such a jury that is acceptable to both sides in the case is often difficult. As a result, the process of jury selection can be lengthy.

As the trial begins, opening statements are made by the attorney for the plaintiff and then by the defense attorney. Witnesses are called and evidence introduced to support the attorneys' arguments. Those same witnesses may be cross-examined by the opposing side. Following the testimony, the attorneys make their closing statements in which they try to

complaint statement that tells the court the facts about the dispute

plaintiff party who brings suit against another

defendant party accused of wrongdoing

pleadings papers filed with a court

subpoenas court orders to produce a witness or a document

interrogatories sets of questions that the opposing side must answer

show how and why they have proved their case and where their opponent has failed.

THE VERDICT

When the closing statements are completed, the jury retires to a private room to arrive at a **verdict.** Under common law, juries had to reach a unanimous verdict. But today this usually is required only in a trial for serious crimes. For lesser offenses and in civil cases, a majority decision is the norm. And if there is no jury, the judge will render the verdict.

The harshness of the verdict depends on the nature of the suit and the issues involved. In a suit for damages, for instance, the jury or the judge determines who is liable and sets the amount of damages to be paid. Other kinds of civil cases may involve decisions relating to custody of children or division of property.

Although a civil suit ends when the verdict is announced, the case may not end there. Legal motions may extend the proceedings, or the loser may appeal to a higher court.

EQUITY

Some civil cases require a special kind of action. One example is an **equity suit.** Those involved in an

verdict decision

equity suit suit that allows a person or group to seek "fair treatment" in court when there is no law to remedy a situation

Diagram of a Typical Courtroom

Observers' Gallery
Jury
Witness
Court Reporter
Plaintiff (in civil cases)
Prosecuting Attorney
Judge
Defendant
Defense Attorney
Clerk-Bailiff

Figure 20-2

equity suit seek to prevent harmful actions before they occur. Two people who claim to own the same building, for example, might disagree about its use and become involved in an equity suit. If one wants to preserve the building as a historic monument and the other wants to tear it down, the first person can petition the court under equity to halt the building's destruction until ownership is established by the courts.

The person filing a petition is the plaintiff, who requests the court to **enjoin** the defendant from acting in a detrimental way. The defendant then can answer, the issues are determined, and arguments are prepared. Although testimony may be heard by a judge, more often it is gathered by **deposition.** After these procedures have been followed, the judge considers the issues and comes to a decision.

If the judge decides in favor of the plaintiff, an injunction may be issued, which requires the defendant to stop a certain action. In other cases, the judge may issue a writ of mandamus, an order requiring the defendant to *take* a certain action. Anyone failing to comply with either of these orders risks a fine or a jail term.

Court Procedures in Criminal Cases

Criminal cases involve acts committed against public safety and order. The process by which accused persons are brought before criminal courts is different from that followed in civil cases. While minor offenses usually can be settled quickly, more serious misdemeanors and felonies involve a longer procedure that begins when the government brings action. Why does the government get involved in criminal cases? Any crimes committed against people are consid-

ered to have been committed against the government, since it is the legal representative of society.

ARREST
Criminal proceedings begin when a suspect is arrested and charged with a crime. According to the 1966 Supreme Court ruling in *Miranda v. Arizona,* all suspects must be read a list of their constitutional rights before they are asked for information; otherwise, their information cannot be used as evidence in court. Once at the police station, the accused is booked, photographed, and fingerprinted. The suspect also has the opportunity to contact a lawyer or to have one appointed to the case by the state.

PRELIMINARY HEARING
After being booked, the accused will be taken before a judge for a preliminary hearing. This is where the judge decides whether the accused should be released from jail before the case comes to trial. Some people may be released on their own recognizance, which means they are freed until the case is called. Others may be released on bail. The amount of bail varies according to the severity of the crime, but it may not be excessive, as guaranteed by the Eighth Amendment.

ARRAIGNMENT
Accused persons are formally charged with a crime at a hearing known as an **arraignment.** In some states, charges may be brought by the **prosecutor** before a grand jury made up of 16 to 23 citizens. If the grand jury feels there is enough evidence to bring the defendant to trial, it issues an **indictment.** In many states, though, an indictment may be substituted by an **information.** In fact, almost all misdemeanor cases and most felonies are filed through an information rather than heard by a grand jury.

enjoin prohibit

deposition testimony put in writing before a trial begins

arraignment hearing at which a formal charge is made against a suspect

prosecutor government's representative in criminal cases

indictment formal written accusation

information accusation made under oath by the prosecutor

At the arraignment, the accused is told of the charges and asked to plead "guilty" or "not guilty." If a defendant pleads guilty, the judge will set a date for sentencing. If the plea is not guilty, a trial will be scheduled. But in 90 percent of all criminal cases, a trial never takes place because a **plea bargain** is reached. Often, the defendant agrees to plead guilty to a lesser charge in return for a lighter sentence. Plea bargaining is a subject of great debate. Some jurisdictions have banned the practice altogether.

THE TRIAL

For those cases that do go to trial, the pretrial period is similar to that of civil cases. Attorneys for both sides gather information, subpoena witnesses, and select jurors, although the accused may waive the right to a trial by jury. During the trial itself, the attorneys offer opening statements, present their side of the case, cross-examine witnesses, and present closing remarks. One difference between civil and criminal court procedures, however, is that in a criminal case the government must prove the defendant "guilty beyond a reasonable doubt." In a civil case, a party may win simply because there is a "preponderance of evidence" supporting his or her position.

THE VERDICT

After the closing statements, the jury retires to decide on a verdict, which must be unanimous. A decision of not guilty is called an **acquittal** and results in the immediate release of the defendant. If a guilty verdict is returned, either the judge determines the sentence or may ask the jury to recommend a penalty. Sentencing usually takes place at a later date. However, what happens if the jury cannot reach a unanimous decision? In this instance, a mistrial must be declared. The defendant can be given a new trial with a new jury, or the charges might be dropped.

Appeals

In both civil and criminal cases, there is a chance to appeal the court's decision. The procedures at the appellate level are quite different than those at the trial level. Appellate courts assume that the evidence and the facts that were presented to the trial court are correct. Thus, no new evidence is introduced nor are there juries. Appellate courts are only responsible for assuring that the law has been applied properly. The appellant, or loser in a lower court, files a transcript of the trial and provides briefs that give the reasons why he or she believes errors were made in the lower court. The opposing side is required to present arguments against the appeal.

Cases on appeal usually are heard by state courts of appeals or, if federal laws are involved, by the United States Courts of Appeals. A party that is unhappy with the decision of the state appeals court may try to take the case to the state supreme court. If constitutional questions are involved, the case may be taken to the ultimate appeals court, the United States Supreme Court.

Scales of Justice

plea bargain agreement between the prosecutor and the defendant

Section Review

1. What two kinds of court cases are common in the American legal system?

2. How is a jury selected?

3. How is an equity suit different from other lawsuits?

4. **Challenge:** Do you agree with the practice of plea bargaining? Why or why not?

acquittal declaration of not guilty

CASE STUDY: UNCLOGGING THE COURTS

ALTERNATIVE DISPUTE RESOLUTION

Americans have long been inclined to take their grievances to court. The number of cases in the nation's court systems has increased tenfold since the end of World War II, as our eagerness to sue one another has led to a litigation explosion. Despite a significant increase in the number of judges, federal and state courts are clogged with huge backlogs.

While an increase in criminal cases has added to the problem, it is the volume of private civil cases that has truly overburdened the legal system. In the Chicago area alone, for example, over 70,000 civil cases await trial. "Sometimes I've thought there is some form of mass neurosis developing in the country that leads people to think courts were created to solve all the problems of society," says former Chief Justice Warren Burger.

Some law professionals also blame the backlog of cases on the legal system itself. They note the time consumed when each party must argue his or her case in court. Also, the process focuses on the differences between the parties, rather than emphasizing points of agreement. One party wins and the other loses, with little room for compromise. Everyone agrees that traditional methods prevent speedy resolution of conflicts, increase legal costs, and heighten tensions for the parties involved. Since the mid-1980s some courts have ad-

dressed these concerns with an innovative approach called alternative dispute resolution (ADR).

ADR can take several forms. Two of the most common are mediation and arbitration. In mediation, a neutral third person explores the interests of each party in a case, helps them identify areas of agreement, and works with them to reach a solution they both will accept. In arbitration, the neutral person actually makes the decision, which can be binding if both parties agree beforehand. Some courts require an attempt at mediation or nonbinding arbitration before they will hear certain kinds of cases. Such approaches are more informal and faster than going to court, lower legal costs significantly, and allow courts to concentrate on complex civil disputes and criminal cases.

Other ADR programs involve minitrials in which lawyers for the

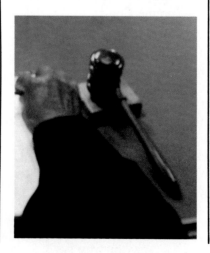

parties present short versions of their cases to a neutral adviser or to a mock jury. Although the "verdict" is not binding, this indication of how their case might actually be decided in court often encourages the parties to settle.

Private judging is the least traditional and most controversial ADR method. Used mainly in California, it permits parties to hire a retired judge to hear and decide their case outside the legal system. Although private judging provides quick and high-quality justice, it is blamed for allowing the wealthy to leave the public courts to the poor and to those accused of crimes.

Despite some criticisms, ADR has become increasingly popular as a way to unclog the courts. The success of the first programs in Philadelphia, New York, and Columbus, Ohio, has encouraged additional programs throughout the country. Former Supreme Court Justice Byron White sees ADR as an idea whose time has come. Growing demands on the courts "have made it necessary for us to explore and use other dispute resolution mechanisms," he says. "It is hoped that they will co-exist throughout the country with established forums within the judicial system."

1. What problems are there in the legal system today?
2. Would you be willing to settle a case by binding arbitration? Explain.

4 Juveniles and the Legal System

Reform movements begun in the late 1800s resulted in the development of a juvenile court system and an array of procedures for dealing with juveniles accused of committing crimes. Prior to 1899, when Illinois established the first juvenile court, juveniles were processed through the adult criminal justice system. Children could be given long prison terms, corporal punishment, and even the death penalty. With the reform movement, however, it was decided that juveniles needed treatment rather than punishment. And to protect young people from the stigma of criminal proceedings, a different court environment was thought to be necessary.

Juvenile Courts Today

All 50 states and the District of Columbia maintain a separate court system for juveniles. While most ju-venile courts still focus on treatment, they also believe that juveniles must bear a certain degree of personal responsibility for their actions. Thus, the courts also are equipped to provide for punishment and incarceration. Today, juvenile courts deal mostly with two different groups of offenders, status offenders and juvenile offenders.

STATUS OFFENDERS

In 1992, 16 percent of all young people referred to juvenile courts committed status offenses, such as running away, truancy and curfew violations, and liquor violations. Because these actions would not be considered crimes if committed by adults, they pose special problems for the courts.

In recent years, a number of programs have been established to assist such offenders. These include counseling centers, shelter homes, and a nationwide toll-free number for runaways. In cases where parents have filed a Person-in-Need-of-Supervision

Juvenile offenders often spend short periods of time at a detention facility, where the emphasis is on rehabilitation rather than on punishment. How has the treatment of juveniles accused of crimes changed over the years?

against their child, the youth is entitled to an attorney. Occasionally, parents may be found at fault, and the court may file a negligence petition. Typically, juveniles in this position are made wards of the court.

JUVENILE OFFENDERS

Juvenile offenders are young people who have actually committed crimes. States differ on the maximum age at which someone may still be considered a juvenile. But all states allow juveniles to be tried as adults under certain conditions, depending on the seriousness of the crime and the criminal record of the juvenile. In fact, because of a get-tough attitude toward juvenile crime, many states are making it easier to transfer juveniles into the adult court system.

Protecting Juveniles

Juveniles who are allowed to stay in the juvenile court system are protected from some parts of the legal process. They usually are not photographed or fingerprinted when arrested. In court, cases often are handled at informal hearings with only a judge, a social worker, the accused, and his or her parents present. And each juvenile's records are kept confidential. This means that when the young person reaches adulthood, his or her criminal record is wiped clean.

Although juvenile courts have been in operation in most states since the early 1900s, not all have always acted in the best interest of juveniles. Some did not even provide young people with many of the rights guaranteed to adults. In 1967 the Supreme Court acted to remedy this situation. The case that led to guidelines for juvenile procedures was *In re Gault*. Gerald Gault, a 15-year-old boy from Ari-

probation time period during which a guilty offender is given the chance to show he or she can reform

zona, was arrested for making indecent phone calls to a neighbor. His parents were not home at the time of his arrest. Gerald had no lawyer present at his hearing, nor did his neighbor come to testify against him. He was sentenced to spend six years in the state reformatory for a crime which, if committed by an adult, would have resulted in no more than a small fine and two months in prison.

Gault's parents appealed the case, claiming that their son was not given the same rights of due process as an adult. The Supreme Court agreed, and four important changes came about as a result of the ruling. Juveniles now have the right to know the charges against them. They have the right to a lawyer. They must be protected against self-incrimination. And they have a right to face and cross-examine the witnesses who testify against them. Juveniles, however, were not given *all* legal rights of adults. They do not, for example, necessarily have the right to a jury trial, which may be withheld to protect the young person from publicity.

Punishing Juveniles

Although the juvenile court system has been more aggressive on young offenders, it still operates on the belief that juveniles can be rehabilitated. For this reason, punishment is designed to improve behavior.

Many judges and social workers feel that confinement in prison is not the best punishment. One of the most common penalties given to young offenders is **probation.** While on probation, the young person must follow certain rules, including following curfews and meeting frequently with a probation officer. Sometimes a stern warning from the judge can be enough to keep the young offender out of further trouble. And where punishment *is* applied, judges try to make it fit the crime. For example, the court may order a young person found guilty of robbing a store to work for the store owner, or a juvenile charged with vandalism may be required to complete community service projects. More serious or repeat offenses, of course, result in more severe penalties for offenders.

After other attempts to help the young person have failed, a juvenile can be sent to a correctional facility. Institutions for most lawbreakers under age 18 are called training schools, and most inmates are held in these for six to nine months. Institutions at which shorter times are served are called detention centers. The emphasis in both types of facilities is on rehabilitation rather than punishment.

Section Review

1. Where and when was the first juvenile court established in the United States?

2. What two kinds of cases are handled by juvenile courts?

3. How do juvenile courts differ from adult courts?

4. **Challenge:** Explain the significance of the decision rendered in *In re Gault*.

Summary

1. One basic purpose of law is to provide rules and standards to serve as a basis of conduct.

2. The functions of law are to resolve conflict, protect individual rights, limit government, promote the general welfare, set social goals, and control crime.

3. Good laws are just, reasonable, enforceable, and understandable.

4. The American legal system is based on ideas from different societies. Two early law codes are the Code of Hammurabi and the Justinian Code.

5. Our system of common law, the right to trial by jury, and habeas corpus are derived from British principles of law.

6. Present-day sources of law are the Constitution and the legislative, judicial, and executive branches.

7. Two kinds of legal cases are civil cases and criminal cases.

8. A civil case usually involves a dispute or a damage claim. Lawsuits make up the majority of civil cases.

9. A special type of civil case is the equity suit, which provides remedies when there are no laws to help decide a case.

10. Criminal law deals with acts committed against public safety and order.

11. Juveniles who commit crimes are usually treated more leniently than adults. A separate court system has been established for juveniles.

Chapter 20 Review

★ Building Vocabulary

Listed below are the definitions of several vocabulary terms from this chapter. Number your paper from one to ten. Beside each number, write the term that correctly fits the definition.

1. laws enacted by legislatures
2. party who brings suit against another
3. decision
4. formal written accusation
5. prohibit
6. declaration of not guilty
7. rules and standards by which a society governs itself
8. hearing at which a formal charge is made against a suspect
9. papers filed with a court
10. party accused of wrongdoing

★ Reviewing Facts

1. What is the basic purpose of law?
2. In what ways do laws meet society's needs?
3. How may laws be judged to be good or bad?
4. How did English common law develop? Why is its development important to the American legal system?
5. What are the sources of today's American law?
6. What role does the Constitution have within the American legal system?
7. What is the difference between civil cases and criminal cases?
8. What kinds of verdicts might be issued in a civil case?
9. What are the main differences between a writ of mandamus and an injunction?
10. What actions must law enforcement officers take as a result of *Miranda v. Arizona*?
11. How are criminal trials different from civil trials?
12. Why is the juvenile system different from the adult legal system?

★ Analyzing Facts

1. Do you think a society could function without laws? Explain.
2. Many different kinds of laws make up the American legal system. Why are so many kinds necessary? Do you think it is effective to have so many different kinds of laws? Explain.
3. What are the advantages of having 50 state court systems as well as a separate federal system? the disadvantages?

★ Evaluating Ideas

1. A British prime minister, Benjamin Disraeli, said, "Justice is truth in action." Do you agree or disagree with this statement? Explain.
2. What do you think are the strengths and weaknesses of the jury system?
3. Why is it important in the American legal system for people to willingly serve on juries?
4. In your opinion, what are the advantages of a case being tried by a judge and a jury? What are the advantages of a case being tried by a judge alone?
5. In other countries, judges are professionals trained for their position. In the United States, federal judges do not go through a special train-

Using Your
Civic Participation Journal

Review the entries you made in your Civic Participation Journal after you visited the local courthouse. Use your entries to write a two-paragraph essay explaining your impressions of the legal procedures you witnessed.

ing process. Instead, they usually are appointed through political patronage. What do you think are the advantages and disadvantages of the American system?

★ Critical Thinking Case Study Analysis

Case study analysis is a reasoning process that involves asking questions; defining elements important to a situation; analyzing, synthesizing, comparing, and contrasting the elements; and finally making judgments.

Explanation   The steps that follow will help you apply the case study analysis technique to almost any situation.

1. Determine the facts.
2. Develop the issues by asking additional questions to get a clear understanding about the practicality, legal and ethical concerns, personal rights, and public policy matters involved with the situation.
3. Develop arguments that support your answers and also arguments that refute your answers.
4. After studying the supporting and refuting arguments, reach a decision by identifying your most persuasive answers to the questions.
5. Evaluate your decision by comparing your solution and reasoning about a situation with the decision already reached.

Practice   You can apply the above steps to solving the following complex legal situation:

Ben Gitlow was arrested in New York for distributing pamphlets similar to Karl Marx's Communist Manifesto. Some people who read the pamphlet felt Gitlow was hoping for strikes and other mass disturbances, so he was charged under the state's Criminal Anarchy Act. The law permitted speaking and discussing radical ideas but outlawed language advocating or advising the unlawful overthrow of organized gov-

ernment. Gitlow's defense was that he was protected by his free speech rights under the first Amendment.

The facts are straightforward in this case, although more information about the content of the pamphlet would have been helpful. Gitlow distributed a pamphlet; people read the pamphlet and thought it was illegal; Gitlow was arrested.

The issues are equally clear. On the legal issue, Gitlow's action was unlawful. But in arguing the rights issue, he raised a second legal issue about whether the law was constitutional. There are no significant ethics here. You might think you want to consider whether the Criminal Anarchy Act was a good law. But such arguments would not be relevant to the situation being decided. Gitlow was convicted. In 1925 the Supreme Court upheld both the law and the conviction.

Independent Practice   Interpreting photographs is also useful when you analyze a specific case. Study the photo below. It shows riot police in Moscow attacking demonstrators. How would you use the photo to analyze what is going on? What other information will you need?

SIX REVIEW

REVIEW QUESTIONS

1. Why is a national judiciary an important and necessary part of a constitutional system?

2. As you have learned, the Supreme Court has ruled many more state and local actions unconstitutional than it has federal laws. Why do you think this has been necessary?

3. Why is such care taken in the identification and selection of federal court judges, particularly those at the appellate court levels?

4. For what reasons do you think the federal courts have refused to deal with "political questions"?

5. Senator Joseph Biden, as chief counsel of the Senate Judiciary Committee, pointed out that the role of the chief justice of the Supreme Court is particularly critical in our federal system. What do you think he meant?

6. Why is it important that Supreme Court opinions be clearly written and understandable?

7. If you were chosen for jury duty, would you rather serve for a civil or a criminal case? Why?

8. In your opinion, is justice better served in society if all criminals do not receive the same treatment?

9. In the United States, laws are made by elected representatives. Do you think it would be better to have laws made by legal experts chosen for life? Explain.

10. There are many in the United States who believe that juvenile courts should operate according to the same rules as adult courts. Do you think this would be effective in decreasing juvenile crime? Explain.

11. Why do you think the judicial branch is the most active branch of government in the protection of citizens' rights?

SUGGESTED READINGS

1. Arbetman, Lee, and Richard Roe. *Great Trials in American History: From the Civil War to the Present*. St. Paul, MN: West Publishing Co., 1985. Describes famous and not-so-famous trials that have added an important dimension to American case law.

2. Baum, Lawrence. *The Supreme Court*. Washington, D.C.: Congressional Quarterly Press, 1981. Goes behind the scenes to elaborate on the workings of the Supreme Court and its justices, with a discussion of the Court's history and several landmark cases.

3. Gustafson, Anita. *Guilty or Innocent?* New York: Holt, Rinehart, and Winston, 1985. Enables students to act as jurors in sensational real-life cases.

4. Lee, Harper. *To Kill a Mockingbird*. New York: Warner Books, Inc., 1982. This Pulitzer Prize winning novel describes a lawyer's attempt to get justice for an accused person.

5. Price, Janet R., Alan R. Levine, and Eve Cary. *The Rights of Students*. Carbondale, IL: Southern Illinois University Press, 1987. Describes student rights under present law and offers suggestions for how to protect these rights.

6. Rehnquist, William H. *The Supreme Court: How It Was, How It Is*. New York: William Morrow and Company, Inc., 1987. Discusses the history of the Court and the justices who have played prominent roles.

7. Turner, Mary Jane, and Lynn Parisi. *Law in the Classroom*. Boulder, CO: Social Science Education Consortium, Inc., 1984. Offers innovative strategies for teaching about the American legal system.

8. Wishman, Seymour. *Anatomy of a Jury: The System on Trial*. New York: Penguin Books, Inc., 1987. Step-by-step examination of the American judicial system.

ACQUIRING AND USING INFORMATION

You already have learned that finding information and then organizing and analyzing it are skills you need in order to be an effective citizen. You also know that locating information often is much easier than understanding and using it.

Many judges and attorneys use a structured process for analyzing the information that comes before them in the form of cases. The process is based on following a series of actions, or steps.

These steps are:
1. determine the facts.
2. develop the issues.
3. develop the arguments.
4. reach a decision.
5. evaluate the decision.

This process may help you to improve your ability to analyze information you have acquired.

Read the Supreme Court case *Abington School District v. Schempp* (1963) below. Then, using the information in that case and what you have learned about the First Amendment, follow the analyzing process described above to determine how you would decide the case.

In 1958, the Pennsylvania legislature passed a law directing that at least ten verses from the Bible "be read to every class at the beginning of each school day." The following year, the law was amended to allow students to be excused from the readings upon the written request of a parent or guardian. At Abington High School, the verses were read each morning over the school's intercom without any accompanying statements. Students were also requested to stand and repeat in unison the Lord's Prayer and to salute the flag. Students were told they could leave the room or remain and not participate.

The law was challenged by the members of the Schempp family. They claimed that the law was unconstitutional support of religion and of particular denominations.

1. To determine the facts, answer the following questions: What occurred in the case? Who are the persons or parties involved? Why did the persons act as they did? What facts are important? unimportant? missing?

2. To develop the issues, ask yourself questions such as: Was Pennsylvania's law constitutional? Were the actions of the school district legal? Does the First Amendment mean that states cannot require readings from the Bible? Should a state ever force religious exercises to enforce morality? Can states legislate morality? Are there other questions you have?

3. To develop the arguments, you need to answer your questions and then develop reasons both supporting and rejecting your answers. Which arguments are most persuasive in terms of constitutionality, legality, and rights?

4. To reach a decision, you need to analyze your answers to the previous questions and determine the most reasonable overall response.

5. To evaluate the decision, compare your final answer with the Supreme Court's decision explained in Chapter 4.

Unit 7

STATE AND LOCAL GOVERNMENTS

In addition to the federal government, the political structure of the United States also includes state and local governments. These two levels of government are closer to your needs and the needs of other individual citizens than is the federal government. Because of this fact, there has been a shift of some powers from the federal government to state and local authorities in recent years. People now demand and expect more services from state and local governments. As a result, the financial burden placed on these governmental bodies has considerably increased.

Like the federal government, state and local governments depend on a network of officials to plan and carry out policies. The photo on the facing page shows the skyline of the city of Atlanta, the capital of Georgia and one of the growing centers of state government in the Southeast.

As you study this unit, you will see that all levels of government must cooperate and share resources if they are to effectively meet the needs of your nation, state, and community.

Chapter 21

American Federal Government

Under our federal system, important government roles are played by state governments, not just the federal government. In this chapter, you will learn which powers have been granted to the federal government and which powers have been reserved to the states. You will also see how the relationship between the various levels of government has changed

TERMS TO KNOW
delegated powers, enumerated powers, inherent powers, reserved powers, exclusive powers, concurrent powers, National Supremacy Clause, full faith and credit, privileges and immunities, cooperative federalism, grants-in-aid, categorical grant, block grant, nationalists, urbanization

READ TO DISCOVER
- why the United States adopted a federal form of government.
- high powers are divided between the federal government and the states.
- what are the characteristics of inter-governmental relations in the United States.
- how relations among the various levels of government have changed.

★ ★ ★ ★ ★

Civic Participation Journal

Under the federal system, each state government must honor the rules of other states, including rules for licensing drivers. Choose one of the other 49 states. Write a letter to the department of motor vehicles in that state to learn their qualifications for granting driver's licenses. Record your findings in your journal.

1 A Federal Government

Delegates at the Constitutional Convention faced a difficult task when they met in Philadelphia in 1787. What should be the role of the national government, and what powers should it have? What about the rights of the states?

Delegates had different answers to these questions. Many wanted to limit the powers of any new government and to guarantee the rights of the people. Therefore, a unitary form of government would not do.

Yet, delegates desired a strong national government to meet the many challenges facing the new nation. This was very important to them, since the earlier confederate form of government had ended in disillusionment. Many delegates, however, needed assurance that the powers of the states would not be swept away.

To the convention delegates, the solution to their dilemma was found in the idea of federalism, a system of government in which powers are shared between a national government and the various state governments. Under a federal form of government, the central government would have enough power to stabilize and unify the country and to act in such matters of widespread national concern as defense, foreign relations, and the general welfare. At the same time, the states would act in matters of more local concern.

Federalism also fit well with the delegates' desire to restrict governmental powers. Each level would have a specific realm of authority and power; its own public officials, government agencies, and duly enacted laws; and legal authority within its own geographic boundaries. Both levels of government would exercise their authority at the same time and over the same people, yet neither could act outside the powers granted to it by the Constitution. By creating a federal system, the delegates ensured that the government would have the strength to endure and the flexibility to succeed.

Here, Pete Wilson acknowledges the cheers of supporters after his 1994 reelection to the governorship of California. Federalism distributes power between the national government and state governments. What responsibility did the Framers of the Constitution give to state governments?

Section Review

1. What forms of government were rejected by the Constitutional delegates?

2. Why did the Framers of the Constitution want to divide power between the national and state governments?

3. How was federalism a solution to the problem of unifying the states?

4. **Challenge:** If you had been a delegate at the Constitutional Convention, which form of government would you have favored? Why?

2 Powers Divided

An underlying value of our system of government is that the people are the source of all power. We give away to our government only enough of that power to accomplish certain common purposes. These purposes were set forth in the Preamble to the Constitution and provided a general framework for the delegates to design a new federal form of government.

The delegates were also influenced by a knowledge of political theory and history, as well as their own practical experience. Those writing the Constitution fully realized that the national government would need more power than the states, at least in certain areas, to achieve such goals as providing for the common defense and building a more perfect union. They also knew that strong state governments, close to the people, could more readily deal with pressing local issues.

Powers Granted to the National Government

Once the delegates decided what powers were necessary to achieve the general purposes of the government, these powers were delegated, or given, to the national government through the Constitution. There are three kinds of **delegated powers**—enumerated, implied, and inherent.

ENUMERATED POWERS

The **enumerated powers,** also known as expressed powers, are perhaps the easiest to understand because each is stated clearly in the Constitution. Many of these powers are spelled out in Article I, Section 8. For example, the first clause states:

The Congress shall have power:
1. To lay and collect taxes, duties, imposts, and excises, to pay the debts and provide for the common defense and general welfare of the United States; but all duties, imposts, and excises shall be uniform throughout the United States.

Additional powers delegated to Congress in Section 8 include the powers to borrow money on the credit of the nation, to coin money, to fix standard weights and measures, to set up post offices, and to establish a court system below the Supreme Court. Congress may also regulate foreign trade and trade between the states, raise and support the armed forces, and declare war against other nations.

The executive and judicial branches of government are also expressly granted powers by the Constitution. For example, in Article II, Section 2 the President is given the power to act as commander in chief of the nation's armed forces. Other executive powers include the ability to make treaties with other nations and to appoint such federal officials as ambassadors, federal judges, and other important leaders with the "advice and consent" of the Senate. Article III of the Constitution enumerates the powers granted to the Supreme Court and the other federal courts.

Several of the enumerated powers had been given to the national government under the Articles of Confederation. Powers added in the Constitution, especially those enumerated in Articles I, II, and III, made the national government even stronger. This government was made still stronger by certain amendments to the Constitution. For instance, the Sixteenth Amendment, adopted in 1913, granted Congress the power to impose an income tax.

delegated powers
powers—enumerated, implied, or inherent—given the national government by the Constitution

enumerated powers
powers of the national government expressly named in the Constitution

Post Office Worker

IMPLIED POWERS

The implied powers of the national government are those powers indirectly expressed, or implied from powers that are expressly delegated. Their constitutional basis is found in Article I, Section 8 in a clause frequently referred to as the Necessary and Proper Clause:

The Congress shall have power: To make all laws which shall be necessary and proper for carrying into execution the foregoing powers, and all other powers vested by this Constitution in the government of the United States, or in any department or officer thereof.

inherent powers powers that belong to all national governments simply because they govern nation-states

Although war was not declared, the U.S. sent a peacekeeping force to Somalia in 1992. What are examples of inherent powers?

The authors of the Constitution clearly felt that Congress should have the powers necessary to make the government work. At the same time, they knew that they could not list all such powers. Therefore, they inserted this clause to enable Congress to stretch its powers as necessary. For this reason, this clause is sometimes called the Elastic Clause.

Historically, both Congress and the federal courts have interpreted "necessary and proper" to effectively mean "convenient and useful." For example, Congress does not have the expressed power to print paper money. However, because it has the authority to coin money and to regulate commerce, Congress found it convenient and useful to issue paper money.

INHERENT POWERS

The third kind of powers that are delegated to the national government are **inherent powers**. These include such powers as the right of a nation-state to gain territory by discovery and occupation, to protect itself against invasion or rebellion, and to regulate immigration. Because these powers seemed obvious, delegates probably felt it unnecessary to state them directly in the Constitution.

Many inherent powers are implied by enumerated powers. For example, the power to protect against invasion is clearly suggested by the enumerated power to raise and support armies. Some inherent powers are actually enumerated, such as the inherent power of a nation-state to declare war, a power expressly delegated to Congress. However, inherent powers do not have to be expressed or implied. These powers exist, and can be exercised by the national government, simply because the government exists.

Powers Denied to the National Government

The national government has only those powers delegated to it by the Constitution. Powers not specifically covered by enumerated, implied, or inherent powers are denied to the national government.

To clarify any doubts, some powers are expressly denied. The first eight amendments are clear denials of power to the national government. A further denial of powers is included in Article I, Section 9, which prevents Congress from taking away the privilege of habeas corpus, except in cases of rebellion or invasion, and from passing bills of attainder or ex post facto laws. Finally, there are some powers that, if used, would harm the federal system of government. For example, Congress cannot tax the official activities of the states, because in an extreme case, the national government might be able to tax the states out of existence.

Powers Reserved to the States

The Constitution lists the powers of the national government, but it does not identify the powers of the states. Instead, the Tenth Amendment describes the **reserved powers** set aside for state governments:

The powers not delegated to the United States by the Constitution, nor prohibited by it to the states, are reserved to the states respectively, or to the people.

One of these reserved powers is control over the local governments within each state. The powers and organization of these local governments are derived from each state's constitution. Therefore, local govern-

The Constitution gives states the right to control public education. What other powers are reserved to the states by the Constitution?

ments exist to serve the purposes of the state.

A second power reserved for the states is control over state and local elections. For example, each state sets certain qualifications for voting, which may include residency and registration. States also decide when to hold state and local elections, how to nominate candidates, and what items should be on the ballot.

States also have the power to control public education and to set minimum standards for private education. For example, states specify the number of days students must attend classes, determine which courses students must pass to graduate from high school, and set teacher qualifications. State officials usually help local boards supervise the public schools through a state board of education.

A general police power is also reserved to the states. This power allows states to promote and maintain the public health, safety, morals, and welfare. Traffic speed limits, laws setting the drinking age, and laws against crimes are all part of a state's police power.

reserved powers powers given to the states that have not been granted to the national government or denied to the states

Finally, states have many regulatory powers, including regulating how banks do business, how corporations and industries must act within that state, and how much utilities, such as electric companies, may charge the public.

Powers Denied to the States

Although there is much that states can do, there are some powers they are denied. These are found in Article I, Section 10 as well as in several amendments. For example, states cannot coin or print money, enter into treaties or alliances, or grant titles of nobility. They are also denied the power to take away a person's life, liberty, or property without due process of law or to tax federal agencies or activities.

Without the consent of Congress, states may not tax imports or exports, tax foreign ships, keep troops or warships in times of peace, or sign agreements with other states or foreign powers. Although some of these prohibitions may sound strange today, at the time they were adopted there were real concerns about just how independent each state could be.

Several amendments that have been added to the Constitution through the years have further limited state powers. For example, states may not deny the right to vote because of race, color, previous condition of servitude, or sex. Also, citizens who are at least 18 years old may not be prevented from voting.

Congress also can indirectly limit state powers. For example, by partially funding some state roads, Congress can ensure that the roads are engineered to federal standards. The federal government has also passed laws threatening to withhold federal funds if states do not comply with certain requirements. For example, Congress convinced all states to raise the drinking age to 21 by threatening to cut off federal highway funds for states that did not comply.

State governments also may not change the structure of the federal system. This system may be changed only through a constitutional amendment. In addition, local units of government, such as a city or county government, are created by their states and exercise powers delegated to them by their states. Since there is a unitary relationship between the states and their local governments, those powers which the states are denied are also constitutionally denied to local governments.

Exclusive Powers

Another way to think about the division of powers in our federal system is to consider which powers belong only to the national government and which belong only to the states. These are called the **exclusive powers.** An example of an exclusive national power is that over foreign affairs. An exclusive state power is control over local government.

In some instances, the exclusive powers are determined by how the powers are used. For example, the states are not denied the power to regulate commerce within their state borders. However, if intrastate (in-state) regulations place a burden on commerce between the states, these regulations are not allowed.

Suppose that each state set regulations on the width of railway tracks. If these widths differed from state to state, trains could not move freely across the nation. In this case, the national government could require states to establish uniform regulations

exclusive powers powers that belong only to the national government or only to the state

Division of Power Between State and Federal Governments

POWERS OF THE NATIONAL GOVERNMENT

To regulate foreign trade and commerce between states

To borrow and coin money

To conduct foreign relations with other nations

To establish post offices and roads

To raise and support armed forces

To declare war and make peace

To govern territories and admit new states

To pass naturalization laws and regulate immigration

To make all laws "necessary and proper" to carry out its powers

CONCURRENT POWERS

To collect taxes

To borrow money

To establish and maintain courts

To make and enforce laws

To provide for the health and welfare of the people

POWERS RESERVED TO STATE GOVERNMENTS

To regulate trade within the state

To establish local governments

To determine voter qualifications

To conduct elections

To establish and support public schools

To incorporate business firms

To license professional workers

To ratify amendments

To keep all the "reserved powers" not granted to the national government or prohibited to the states

POWERS DENIED TO THE NATIONAL GOVERNMENT

To tax exports

To suspend writ of habeas corpus

To change state boundaries without consent of states involved

To abridge the Bill of Rights

POWERS DENIED TO BOTH NATIONAL AND STATE GOVERNMENTS

To pass ex post facto laws

To pass bills of attainder

To deny due process of law

To grant titles of nobility

POWERS DENIED TO STATE GOVERNMENTS

To coin money

To enter into treaties

To tax agencies of the federal government

To tax imports or exports

Figure 21-1

based on its exclusive power to regulate interstate commerce.

laws against certain crimes and sets the punishment for illegal acts.

Concurrent Powers

Concurrent powers are those that both the national and state governments have the right to exercise. Examples include the power to tax, to set up court systems, and to charter banks. Note that the two levels of government do not jointly hold and exercise these powers. Rather, each level of government holds and exercises these powers independently. For example, there is a federal *and* a state tax on income. Similarly, each level of government establishes its own

Section Review

1. What is the source of all powers in the United States' system of government?

2. What are three kinds of delegated powers?

3. What are concurrent powers?

4. **Challenge:** If the Necessary and Proper Clause were not included in the Constitution, how would the powers of Congress be changed?

concurrent powers powers that both national and state governments may exercise

3 Government Relations

The heart of American federalism is a two-level system of government. But such a system is complex and difficult to administer because both levels govern the same people, in the same area, at the same time.

National Supremacy

The relationship between the national government and state governments is clearly defined by Article VI, Section 2 of the Constitution:

The Constitution, and the laws of the United States which shall be made in pursuance thereof; and all treaties made, or which shall be made, under the authority of the United States, shall be the supreme law of the land; and the judges in every state shall be bound thereby, anything in the constitution or laws of any state to the contrary notwithstanding.

Here is the front of the Supreme Court Building in Washington, D.C. The Supreme Court plays an important role in resolving disputes between the federal government and state governments. What principle did the Court establish in the case *McCulloch v. Maryland*?

EQUAL JUSTICE UNDER LAW

This **National Supremacy Clause** means that no state or local laws may conflict with the Constitution, treaties, or national laws. The states have extensive authority, but in a head-on clash between national laws and state or local laws, the Constitution clearly supports the national laws. As early as 1819, in *McCulloch v. Maryland,* the Supreme Court ruled that federal law prevails over state law. In almost every similar case since, the Supreme Court has reached a similar decision.

Thus, state and local laws that conflict with national law are unconstitutional. However, an official must first decide that a conflict exists. This responsibility is placed first on state judges, and finally on the Supreme Court, if the state judges cannot resolve the conflict.

The founders of the American system of government fully expected such conflicts to arise. They felt that the overall power of government would be limited if two government levels had to compete for that power. Yet they also knew that too much conflict would weaken the nation and affect all governments' ability to rule. Thus, the delegates wanted to include a way to deal with these conflicts in the Constitution.

As noted, the Supreme Court plays an important role in resolving conflicts between the national and state levels of government. In deciding such disputes, the Court has a difficult responsibility. It must consider the seriousness of the conflict and make a decision in terms of the welfare of all the people.

Occasionally, the Supreme Court has found that Congress exceeded its constitutional authority by taking away powers that belonged to the states. For instance, the Voting Rights Act of 1970 set 18 as the minimum age for voting in all national, state, and local elections. In that same year, the Supreme Court ruled this provision unconstitutional, because setting voting ages for state and local elections is a state power.

In response to the Court's decision, Congress proposed the Twenty-sixth Amendment, which set 18 as the minimum voting age for all public elections in the United States. The states quickly ratified the amendment.

Many believe that the Supreme Court has made it possible for the American federal system of government to survive by settling conflicts in a precise and orderly way. A 30-year veteran of the Court, Justice Oliver Wendell Holmes, Jr., once said of the Supreme Court:

I do not think the United States would come to an end if we lost our power to declare an act of Congress void [using the power of judicial review]. I do think the Union would be imperiled if we could not make that declaration as to the laws of the several states.

National Government Duties to the States

For the benefit of the states, the Constitution places various duties on the national government. These are found in Article IV, Section 4:

The United States shall guarantee to every state in this Union a republican form of government, and shall protect each of them against invasion; and on application of the legislature, or of the executive (when the legislature cannot be convened), against domestic violence.

According to this provision, the national government will guarantee to every state a republican form of government.

This state capitol building at Montpelier, Vermont, is one of 50 state capitols throughout the nation. What form of government does the Constitution guarantee to each state?

As generally interpreted, this means the national government will assure that state governments are formed according to the will of the majority of the people within each state. In other words, state governments should be representative.

The national government must also protect the states against the threat of foreign invasion. This provision may strike you as strange. Today, most of us would consider a foreign attack on any state to be an attack on the entire nation. In 1787, however, every state demanded a mutual pledge of protection before giving up its own war powers to a central government.

Protection against domestic violence, such as riots, is yet another duty of the national government toward the states. Such protection is closely related to the constitutional purpose of insuring domestic tranquility. An individual state is responsible

Under the Constitution, the federal government has certain obligations to the states. For example, it provides aid to states following natural disasters. What duties do states perform for the federal government?

for keeping peace within its own territory, but if it cannot, the national government may provide aid. This happened in 1968 when President Lyndon Johnson sent federal troops into Baltimore, Maryland, and Chicago, Illinois, to help state and local police forces deal with the violence that followed the assassination of Dr. Martin Luther King, Jr. Federal assistance is also called upon in the face of natural disasters, such as fires, floods, and hurricanes.

Normally, the President acts in response to a request for assistance from state officials. But the President need not wait for a call for help if national property is threatened or national laws are being ignored. Presidents Eisenhower and Kennedy both used federal troops to preserve public order, which was being threatened by people attempting to prevent court-ordered school integration.

The Constitution requires the national government to provide yet other protections to the states. Article IV, Section 3 forbids the national government from altering state boundaries or creating new states out of existing states. Such an act would first require the consent both of Congress and the state or states involved. Congress is also prohibited from denying any state equal representation in the Senate without the state's consent.

Not only does the federal government have certain obligations to the states, but the states also perform some duties for the national government. National elections for Congress and the Presidency are conducted under state and local election laws. Similarly, aliens become United States citizens through state courts. Moreover, national laws and government regulations are often carried out on a day-to-day basis by state and local officials and agencies.

Relations Among the States

The Constitution outlines the powers of both the national and state governments. It further defines the responsibilities of the national government to the states and spells out how the states must deal with one another. Most of these responsibilities are found in Article IV.

The authors of the Constitution assumed that each state has a unique existence, separate from all other states. Each state has full power to exercise its reserved powers within the state but, at the same time, cannot exert its powers outside the state boundaries. This kind of legal separation was included to prevent rivalry among the newly formed states.

FULL FAITH AND CREDIT

While each state has its own powers, it also shares responsibilities with the other states. Article IV, Section 1 says:

Full faith and credit shall be given in each state to public acts, records, and judicial proceedings of every other state. And the Congress may by general laws prescribe the manner in which such acts, records, and proceedings shall be proved, and the effect thereof.

Giving **full faith and credit** really means accepting the validity, or correctness, or another state's laws or actions. For example, each state must recognize as valid such things as a judge's ruling, a contract, a marriage license, and a deed of ownership from another state. Criminal laws passed in other states, however, do not have to be accepted.

The full faith and credit concept certainly does not extend to other states' public problems. For instance, a hazardous-waste landfill in Emelle, Alabama, does not have to accept PCB-contaminated dirt from Texas.

PRIVILEGES AND IMMUNITIES

The responsibilities states share with one another also concern **privileges and immunities.** Article IV, Section 2 states:

The citizens of each state shall be entitled to all privileges and immu-

nities of citizens in the several states.

A complete listing of these privileges and immunities does not exist. Still, it is assumed that people can do certain things, such as travel from state to state, live or work in any state they wish, buy and sell property in other states, and take legal action in any state court. In general, one state cannot discriminate against residents from other states unreasonably.

However, certain kinds of discrimination are not considered unreasonable. For example, a state may charge higher tuition at its state colleges and universities to out-of-state students. This is not unreasonable because parents of in-state students pay state taxes to support those schools.

Furthermore, states may protect their natural resources by charging a higher fee to out-of-state users. For instance, a state might charge a higher fee for a hunting license to nonresidents. Also, states may require state workers to live within the state. Similarly, residents of one state cannot vote in another state's elections. Finally, it is not considered unreasonable to require nonresidents to obey the laws of the state they are in.

full faith and credit obligation of each state to accept the validity of acts, records, and proceedings of other states

Section Review

1. What is meant by "national supremacy"?

2. What duties does the national government have to the states?

3. What are the duties of the states to one another?

4. **Challenge:** What, do you think, would happen if the states did not give "full faith and credit" to one another?

privileges and immunities certain rights to which non-residents are entitled when within a state

4 Changing State Relations

The federal system of government today is not what it was in the late 1700s. In its early days, the government resembled a two-layer cake, with the national government comprising the top layer and the state governments comprising the bottom layer. Each level responded to issues and performed its duties independently of the other.

Today, the system more closely resembles a marble cake. Many current problems cut across the divisions of authority between national and state government. For example, state and federal officials may both become involved in dealing with toxic waste at a nuclear facility. Recently state and federal health officials began to closely monitor the Rocky Flats nuclear plant near Denver, Colorado, investigating possible violations of state and federal laws and regulations concerning the safe handling of nuclear materials. As one might expect, such a situation may result in confusion and disagreement, as the two levels of government wrestle with their divided powers.

Cooperative Federalism

To solve public problems, the different levels of government often work together. This governmental cooperation is called **cooperative federalism.** For example, the sprawling interstate highway system that crosses the country was made possible through combined funding and efforts of the national and state governments.

GRANTS-IN-AID

The federal government uses a variety of arrangements to deal with public policy issues and to keep up with the public's demands for services. One such arrangement is the **grants-in-aid** program. State and local governments spend these federal funds on various public programs—highways, airports, agriculture, education, housing, health, and welfare.

The **categorical grant** is the most common federal grant-in-aid to the states. Here the national government provides funds for specific purposes or programs and specifies how state or local governments must spend the funds. For example, under the federally mandated Aid to Families with Dependent Children (AFDC) program, states must match federal funds. Also, state and local governments are frequently required to set up special government units to administer the federal grants. Thus, the AFDC program is commonly administered by state and local departments of social services. Finally, if states fail to follow federal guidelines, they may lose their grant.

cooperative federalism different levels of government working together to solve problems

grants-in-aid direct grants of money from the national government to state and local governments

categorical grant direct grant of money from the national government to state and local governments for a specific purpose

The federal government cooperates with state and local governments in funding many public services, such as airport facilities. What is the most common form of federal aid to the states?

Critics of the categorical grant program believe that the national government has gained too much control over state and local matters. They argue that although this program offers needed funds, it also provides unwanted federal intrusion into state concerns.

The **block grant** program is one answer to the states' demands for fewer federal restrictions. With this type of grant, the federal government provides funds for a group of related programs or projects and allows state and local governments to decide which programs within the group are most useful or needed. Thus, one state may spend its block funds primarily on combating air pollution, whereas another state may divide these funds among air, water, and noise pollution control projects. At times, numerous categorical grants have been combined to form a large block grant. Thus, 19 health grants were recently combined into four block grants dealing with alcohol and drug abuse, maternal and child care, mental health care, and services for preventative health care.

The block grant process allows the national government to maintain some control over how the states spend the federal funds they receive. Yet, the states have greater freedom to pick and choose programs that meet their needs. This is an example of cooperative federalism in action.

REVENUE SHARING
In 1972 Congress began a revenue-sharing program whereby part of the revenue from federal income taxes was distributed among state and local governments. The idea behind this plan was to spread the tax burden for government programs more fairly by using federal funds instead of only state taxes. Compared to grants-in-aid, revenue sharing had few federal restrictions and did not require state matching funds. Thus, those who favored state power over state and local programs favored the revenue sharing idea, whereas those who felt that the national government should maintain control over its tax funds opposed it.

During the 1970s the states received about one-third of the funds with the remainder going to local governments. As part of President Reagan's policy, however, the states were removed from the revenue-sharing program in 1983. By 1987 the entire program was cut because of federal budget difficulties.

OTHER SERVICES
In addition to dispensing funds, the national government also provides a variety of services to states that they might not readily be able to obtain elsewhere. The Census Bureau, for example, provides population figures that help in city and regional planning. The Department of Labor provides labor and employment projections that help states plan for economic development or work to lessen the impact of downturns in the economy. Similarly, the FBI and the Drug Enforcement Administration provide assistance to state and local law enforcement officers.

Changing National Power

The growth in cooperation does not mean that the power of the two levels of government has remained the same. On the contrary, the national government has increased its power over the decades. **Nationalists** believe that the national government best represents all the people. They also believe that the people intended to give the national government, not

block grant funds granted or allotted by the federal government for a group or block of activities

nationalists persons who favor centralization of power

COMPARISON: FEDERAL SYSTEMS

NORTH AMERICAN FEDERALISM

The United States and Canada have often been described as "best friends." Like all best friends, these North American neighbors have both differences and similarities. A good example of each is found in their federal forms of government.

Federalism in each country divides power between national and regional governments. In the United States, the government in Washington, D.C., handles national affairs, and 50 state governments make regional decisions. In Canada, the government in Ottawa decides national policy. The ten provinces deal with regional issues.

Even though they are similar, the two systems developed differently. The Framers of the United States Constitution, reacting to the abuses they felt under the British, wanted a national government with limited authority. However, events over the past 200 years have increased the powers of the national government, often at the expense of the states. In the 1860s, the Civil War finally established the supremacy of the nation over the states. In the twentieth century the growth of industrial society has presented problems too complex for the states to handle.

Still, the states have not withered away. In the past 25 years, many states have adopted new constitutions or made significant changes in their old ones as their leaders work to modernize state government. In addition, recent Presidents, notably Nixon and Reagan, have attempted to shift some power back to the states.

Canada's federalism grew from different needs and has developed differently. When Britain granted Canada self-government in 1867, Canadian leaders wanted a federal system that would preserve the cultural uniqueness of its regions but avoid the divisiveness that led to civil war in the United States. But they also wanted a central government strong enough to resist any efforts of the United States to expand into Canada. As a result, the provinces received only a few powers, such as control of education, transportation, and welfare. Since 1945, however, urban growth has created a greater need for those services and has shifted much of Canada's government to the provinces.

Dissatisfaction with the cultural policies of the national government also has contributed to the growth of provincial power. In the 1970s, for example, the Parti Quebecois argued that Quebec should have a status separate from Canada in order to preserve the heritage and the rights of French-Canadians. Although the citizens of Quebec defeated this proposal in 1980, the controversy caused the national government to pay greater attention to provincial concerns. However, when Canada adopted a new constitution in 1982, it did not significantly change the distribution of power between the levels of government, despite years of debate on the issue.

Although the two federal systems are different, each national government has used its fiscal power to influence state policy in areas where it has no authority. For example, in the 1960s the Canadian government promised to pay half the cost of some social programs if the provinces would enact them. The U.S. government has threatened to withhold federal highway funds if states do not comply with speed limit guidelines.

1. Why did federalism develop differently in Canada and the United States?
2. Are the Canadian and U.S. systems of federalism more alike than they are different? Explain your answer.

the states, the powers to accomplish the purposes set out in the Preamble to the Constitution. Throughout American history, many leaders, including Alexander Hamilton, Andrew Jackson, Abraham Lincoln, Theodore Roosevelt, Woodrow Wilson, and Franklin Roosevelt, have supported these ideas. And, as noted earlier, the Supreme Court has often supported the centralization of powers. When powers conflict, federal powers are the stronger. In support of the Court's interpretations, Chief Justice John Marshall wrote that the American people "did not design to make their government dependent on the states."

The concentration of national power resulted largely from changing economic conditions in the country. As the nation changed from a predominately agricultural society to a highly developed industrial one, the demand for government goods and services grew rapidly. State and local governments were unable to cope with these rapidly changing demands. As a result, what had been state concerns became matters of national concern. At one time, for example, each state had its own food and drug laws. Today, federal laws set health and safety standards for food and drugs nationwide.

Social conditions in the country have also changed. Only 5 percent of the nation's population lived in urban areas in 1790, compared to over 80 percent today. **Urbanization** has both changed and increased the burdens of state and local governments, which have grown in response to citizens' demands for services. In many cases, the money needed for these services—better crime and fire protection, improved schools and transportation systems, and larger parks and recreation facilities—exceeded available resources, so the national

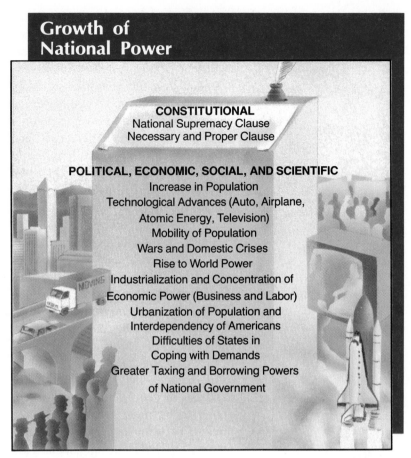

Growth of National Power

CONSTITUTIONAL
National Supremacy Clause
Necessary and Proper Clause

POLITICAL, ECONOMIC, SOCIAL, AND SCIENTIFIC
Increase in Population
Technological Advances (Auto, Airplane, Atomic Energy, Television)
Mobility of Population
Wars and Domestic Crises
Rise to World Power
Industrialization and Concentration of Economic Power (Business and Labor)
Urbanization of Population and Interdependency of Americans
Difficulties of States in Coping with Demands
Greater Taxing and Borrowing Powers of National Government

Figure 21-2

government was asked to help. This, in turn, led to further growth of the national government. The historical reasons for this growth are summarized in Figure 21-2.

It should not be thought that the flow of power is a one-way street. Some powers at the national level have been returned to the states. For example, following a long, emotional battle over abortion rights, a 1989 Supreme Court decision gave the states greater powers to deal with this explosive issue.

Resistance by the States

The states' rights position differs greatly from the nationalist position described above. States' rights advocates oppose any increase in the

urbanization shift of population from rural to urban areas

national government's power at the expense of the states. Although they believe that the enumerated powers rightfully belong to the national government, they feel that the Necessary and Proper Clause should give the national government power to do only what is "absolutely" necessary and proper for carrying out its duties. In the views of Thomas Jefferson, John C. Calhoun, and Ronald Reagan, the clause should not be interpreted to read "convenient and useful."

States' rights advocates feel that even national problems can be better dealt with by state and local governments, which are "closer" to the people and their problems. In short, national solutions and regulations cannot be expected to meet the needs of every locality. States' rights advocates believe that the thinking of hundreds of people in many places is bound to be more creative than the thinking of a few lawmakers in Washington, D.C. If state and local governments are allowed to experiment, solutions that work will be adopted by governments elsewhere. Many states

are acting vigorously today to solve their problems. As former Virginia Governor Gerald Baliles observed, "States are not waiting on Washington. They're developing and implementing programs on their own."

Finally, states' rights supporters favor decentralization, or spreading power among numerous government groups. Centralization, they believe, all too frequently leads to abuses of power. At the local level, they argue, people can immediately see what actions are taken on their behalf and are aware of who is responsible for those actions. They feel that this is more difficult at the national level.

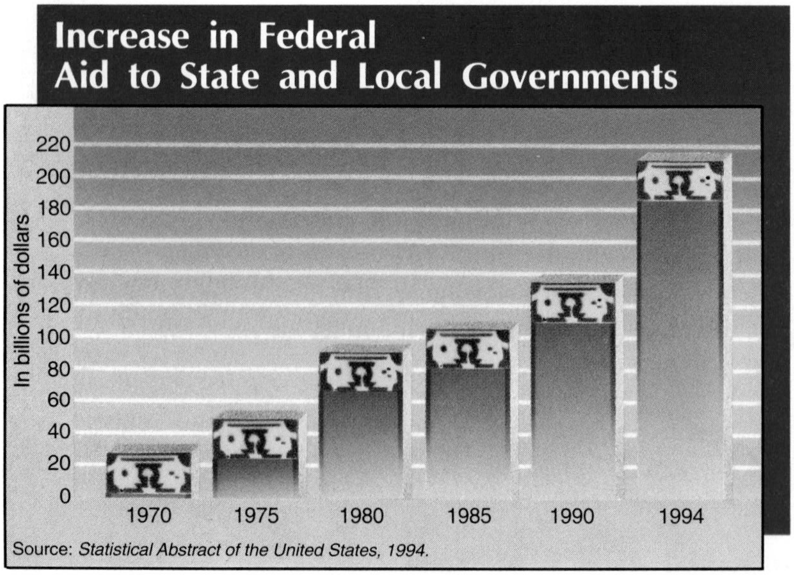

The Future of Federalism

The delegates to the Constitutional Convention chose a federal form of government as a compromise between those who favored a strong, central form of government and those who favored a confederate form of government with strong states. Today, the debate continues between nationalists and states' rights supporters. The arguments used on both sides differ little from those put forth by delegates over two centuries ago: Are the people best represented by the national government or state governments? Which level is more responsive to their needs? Which level is less likely to abuse its powers at the expense of the people? Which level is best equipped to solve the nation's complex problems? And, which level should have the stronger voice over how American tax monies are spent?

The United States will continue to have a federal form of government. But whether the power of the national government will keep growing or the states will reclaim the power remains an issue. In the 1980s President Reagan voiced the view that:

Increase in Federal Aid to State and Local Governments

Source: *Statistical Abstract of the United States, 1994.*

Figure 21-3

The federal government has taken on functions it was never intended to perform and which it does not perform well. There should be a planned, orderly transfer of such functions to states and localities.

As a result, the Reagan administration began to return responsibility for some government programs to the states and their localities. As shown in Figure 21-3, federal aid to state and local governments slowed after a period of high growth. Only time will tell whether this trend will continue.

Section Review

1. What is cooperative federalism?
2. How is the block grant program an example of cooperative federalism in action?
3. Besides dispensing funds, what other services does the national government provide to the states?
4. **Challenge:** In your opinion, will the power of the national government continue to grow, or will the states assume more power? Explain.

Summary

1. Federalism is a system of government that divides power between the national and state governments.
2. The choice of federalism was a compromise made by the delegates to the Constitutional Convention.
3. Powers delegated to the national government consist of enumerated, implied, and inherent powers.
4. Certain powers are denied to the national government either because they are expressly denied or because they are not mentioned in the Constitution.
5. The states retain all powers that have not been granted to the national government or denied to the states.
6. Some powers belong exclusively to the national government, and some belong exclusively to the states.
7. Powers that both the national and state governments have the right to exercise are known as concurrent powers.
8. State and local laws may not conflict with the Constitution or with national treaties and laws. When there is conflict, the Supreme Court must settle the dispute.
9. The national government has several duties to the states. It must guarantee them a republican form of government and protect them from invasion and domestic violence.
10. States must recognize as valid the public records and judicial decisions of other states. They also may not discriminate against residents from other states in an unreasonable manner.
11. Because of changing economic and social conditions, federalism is very different today from what it was in 1787.
12. Over time, the national government's power grew at the expense of states' powers. Currently, however, power appears to be flowing back to the states.

Chapter 21 Review

★ Building Vocabulary

Using the words below, make up 12 questions for a vocabulary quiz. Your quiz should include four fill-in-the-blank questions, four true-or-false questions, and four multiple-choice questions.

1. enumerated powers
2. inherent powers
3. exclusive powers
4. full faith and credit
5. cooperative federalism
6. block grant
7. delegated powers
8. reserved powers
9. concurrent powers
10. National Supremacy Clause
11. privileges and immunities
12. urbanization

★ Reviewing Facts

1. Why did the constitutional delegates prefer federalism to other forms of government?
2. What kinds of powers does the national government have?
3. What kinds of powers do states have?
4. What powers are expressly denied to both national and state governments?
5. How do exclusive powers differ from concurrent powers?
6. In what ways do states use their "police power"?
7. What is the importance of Article VI, Section 2 of the Constitution?
8. What guides the United States Supreme Court in settling conflicts between the national and the state governments?
9. What duties does the Constitution place on the national government for the benefit of the states?
10. What article of the Constitution defines the duties of states to one another? What are these duties?

11. How is federalism today different from the federalism of 1787?
12. What caused much of the growth in the power of the national government in the United States?
13. What questions still are being debated in the United States regarding the federal form of government?

★ Analyzing Facts

1. How can conflict develop when the national government and the state governments are exercising their powers?
2. Do you favor a nationalist or a states' rights position on federalism? Why?
3. In your opinion, why is it important that states have some control over programs that are federally funded?
4. What do you think James Madison meant when he said that the American government would control itself?

★ Evaluating Ideas

1. Do you think the Founders of the American system of government pictures a different role for the states than is theirs today? Explain.

Using Your
Civic Participation Journal

Review the findings about state driver's license requirements that you entered in your Civic Participation Journal. Work with six of your classmates who chose different states. Create a chart showing the requirements in the seven states your group researched.

2. What, do you think, are the benefits and dangers of the expansion of the powers of the national government at the expense of state governments?

3. In what ways does federalism protect differences between the states? unity among states? Which do you think is the most important? Explain.

4. What, do you think, would happen to the federal system of government if the Supreme Court lost its power to declare a state law unconstitutional?

5. In your opinion, what might happen if the principles of separation of powers and checks and balances were not part of our government?

★ Critical Thinking Drawing Conclusions

During the afternoon before a history exam, your teacher tells you to "concentrate on understanding the big ideas, not memorizing names and dates." You probably draw the conclusion that the exam will not be made up of questions about details. To draw conclusions, you need to examine the evidence you have about a topic and use your reasoning to gain further insight.

Explanation To draw conclusions, follow these steps:
• Closely examine the data you have.
• State two or three things that seem important about the information.
• Decide what inferences you can reasonably make from the data you have to draw a conclusion that goes beyond the facts.

Practice Consider the following table, which shows population broken down into age groups from 1960 to 1990. Then answer the questions that follow.

Population by Age Groups				
	1960	1970	1980	1990
65 and over	9.2%	9.8%	11.3%	12.4%
50–64	14.0	14.5	14.7	13.3
35–49	19.4	17.1	16.3	19.7
20–34	18.9	20.8	26.0	25.7
5–19	27.2	29.3	24.6	21.4
under 5	11.3	8.4	7.2	7.5

Source: Statistical Abstract of the United States, 1994

1. Which age group increased steadily as a percentage of the population between 1960 and 1990? *(65 and over)*

2. In what year did all people under the age of 20 first make up less than 30 percent of the population? *(1990)*

3. Based on the table, what conclusions an you draw about the population of the United States? *(It is aging)*

Independent Practice Study the cartoon below. What conclusion about building new roads can you draw? Why?

STATE ROAD-BUILDING FUNDS PIPE-LINE

©1994 THE COLUMBUS DISPATCH

Chapter 22

State Government

It was common, even after the Union was formed, for our ancestors to consider themselves "Virginians" or "Carolinians" rather than "Americans." For many years, it was the *states* that held the primary power to govern.

Eventually, power shifted to the federal government. But today the direction is swinging back again. Our states, once more, are vying for more power to control important issues.

★ ★ ★ ★ ★

Chapter Preview

TERMS TO KNOW

act of admission, constitutional initiative, legislative oversight, interim committees, lieutenant governor, local trial courts, justice of the peace, general trial court, state supreme court, intermediate appellate courts

READ TO DISCOVER

- how states are set up constitutionally.
- how state legislatures are organized and how they fulfill their roles.
- the legislative process in state government.
- the organization and function of state executive branches
- how state judicial branches are organized and how they function.

Civic Participation Journal

Every state has its own constitution. Go to your school or public library to learn more about your own state's constitution. You should record when the constitution was written, how long it is, and how citizens who wish to change it can do so. Record your findings in y our journal.

1 Foundations of State Government

It is astonishing that our nation is made up of 50 separate states, especially when you consider that many of our states are larger in size and population than entire countries in other parts of the world. No other nation has had such a clear-cut policy for growth as the United States. From the first days of the 13 colonies just thinking about banding together, to our powerful nation today, the United States has proved to be truly a union.

Becoming a State

Over the years the original 13 states have been joined by another 37 to make the present Union of 50 states. But this process of joining together is not necessarily complete. The Constitution puts no limit on the number of states that may be admitted to the Union. Both the District of Columbia and Puerto Rico, for instance, have long been considered as possible candidates for statehood.

act of admission bill that formally allows an area to become a state

Alaska and Hawaii both joined the Union as states in 1959. Anchorage (shown here) is Alaska's largest city. How is statehood achieved?

The land included within United States boundaries today did not always belong to the nation. Territory has been added to the United States through negotiation, purchase, and even brute force. Some states in the East and South were formed from territory once claimed by the original colonies. Maine, for example, was carved out of land that once was part of Massachusetts.

Other lands were acquired through treaties or conquests. All or part of seven western states were formed out of territory won in the Mexican War in 1848. Our federal government also bought land claimed by other countries. In 1803 the United States made the Louisiana Purchase, a deal with France to buy a huge tract of land stretching west of the Mississippi River from the Gulf of Mexico all the way to Canada. This vast heartland became all or part of 13 states in the century following the purchase.

It took time for the territories to become states. Figure 22-1 shows the year that each of the 50 states entered the Union. How, exactly, is statehood achieved? In order to become a state, the people of an area must agree to petition the United States Congress for admission. If Congress approves the request, delegates are elected to draft a proposed state constitution. This document must be approved by a vote of both the residents of the potential state and by Congress. Next, Congress votes on an **act of admission,** which, if passed, adds another star to the flag and a new state to the Union.

State Constitutions

Each of the 50 states has its own unique constitution, which outlines how its state and local governments will work. The constitutions give authority to the three branches of government and to various elected officials. The documents also spell out certain things that state and local governments may *not* do. While state constitutions differ widely in many respects, they are the same in many fundamental regards.

POLITICAL PRINCIPLES

The charters of the original colonies served as models for many early state constitutions. In turn, these became examples for the Constitution of the United States. It is not surprising, then, that basic political principles are found at both the national and state levels.

The separation of powers and checks and balances are inherent in every state's constitution. All state governments have three branches, each with specific powers granted to them by the state constitution. Two other political principles, popular sovereignty and limited government, also are at the core of all state constitutions. Public officials, then, can exercise only those powers given to them by the people.

Although the federal Constitution is the supreme law of the land, the state constitution is the supreme law of the state, so long as it does not conflict with national law. Laws made by the state legislature or by local governments, then, must not conflict with the state constitution. Any legal cases arising from such conflicts are heard in the state court system.

Because state constitutions differ, some laws that are constitutional in one state might not be so in another. For instance, some states are constitutionally barred from borrowing money. Thus, a law allowing a state to go into debt would be forbidden in these states, but not in others.

STATES ADMITTED TO THE UNION

Alabama	1819
Alaska	1959
Arizona	1912
Arkansas	1836
California	1850
Colorado	1876
Connecticut	1788
Delaware	1787
Florida	1845
Georgia	1788
Hawaii	1959
Idaho	1890
Illinois	1818
Indiana	1816
Iowa	1846
Kansas	1861
Kentucky	1792
Louisiana	1812
Maine	1820
Maryland	1788
Massachusetts	1788
Michigan	1837
Minnesota	1858
Mississippi	1817
Missouri	1821
Montana	1889
Nebraska	1867
Nevada	1864
New Hampshire	1788
New Jersey	1787
New Mexico	1912
New York	1788
North Carolina	1789
North Dakota	1889
Ohio	1803
Oklahoma	1907
Oregon	1859
Pennsylvania	1787
Rhode Island	1790
South Carolina	1788
South Dakota	1889
Tennessee	1796
Texas	1845
Utah	1896
Vermont	1791
Virginia	1788
Washington	1889
West Virginia	1863
Wisconsin	1848
Wyoming	1890

Figure 22-1

CONTENTS

All state constitutions share certain features. First, they contain a bill of rights listing the fundamental human rights of the people in that state. State bills of rights are generally longer and more detailed than the Bill of Rights in the federal Constitution, although many of the rights are the same.

Second, all state constitutions provide a framework for the three branches of state government. For the executive branch, constitutions typically establish the office of governor, set the length of the governor's term, and describe the powers and duties of the office. Constitutions set up the legislative branch in the same way, specifying legislators' terms of office, some of their duties, and the lawmaking powers of the legislature. All state constitutions, except for Nebraska's, provide for a two-house legislature. For the judicial branch, state constitutions generally establish a state supreme court and a system of lower courts. They indicate the way in which judges are chosen and the powers and jurisdiction of each level of courts in the judicial system.

Third, systems of local governments are established by state constitutions. These may include cities, towns, counties, and special districts. Some state constitutions describe in great detail the structure, powers, duties, and limitations of local governments. Others are brief and leave the details for the state legislature to work out.

Fourth, state constitutions set up state boards, agencies, and institutions that have power in various areas. These include such groups as state boards of education, public utilities commissions, and licensing boards.

In addition, all constitutions regulate the way money is raised and spent by the state. For example, the kinds of taxes that state and local governments may impose might be specified. Most states also have sections in their constitutions dealing with issues that are of particular interest in their states. Western states may have sections concerning water and mineral rights because these matters are of great consequence in the West.

CHANGES

In order to adapt to changing times, state constitutions, like the federal Constitution, include an amendment process. As Figure 22-3 shows, the constitutions in over half the states were written before 1900. Voters have found it necessary to adopt amendments to all of these state constitutions. In many cases this happens because the documents are simply outdated. For instance, the Oklahoma Constitution was recently amended to remove a provision that prohibited women from working in underground mines.

Basic Elements of a State Constitution

A STATE CONSTITUTION CONTAINS

A Bill of Rights
The Framework for the Three Branches of State Government
Regulations Indicating Local Systems of Government
Guidelines Establishing State Agencies, Boards, and Institutions
Regulations Designating State and Local Taxes

Figure 22-2

STATE CONSTITUTIONS

State	Number of constitutions	Current constitution adopted	State	Number of constitutions	Current constitution adopted
Alabama	6	1901	Montana	2	1972
Alaska	1	1956	Nebraska	2	1875
Arizona	1	1911	Nevada	1	1864
Arkansas	5	1874	New Hampshire	2	1784
California	2	1879	New Jersey	3	1947
Colorado	1	1876	New Mexico	1	1911
Connecticut	4	1965	New York	4	1894
Delaware	4	1897	North Carolina	3	1970
Florida	6	1968	North Dakota	1	1889
Georgia	10	1982	Ohio	2	1851
Hawaii	1*	1950	Oklahoma	1	1907
Idaho	1	1889	Oregon	1	1857
Illinois	4	1970	Pennsylvania	5	1968**
Indiana	2	1851	Rhode Island	2	1842
Iowa	2	1857	South Carolina	7	1895
Kansas	1	1859	South Dakota	1	1889
Kentucky	4	1891	Tennessee	3	1870
Louisiana	11	1974	Texas	7	1876
Maine	1	1819	Utah	1	1895
Maryland	4	1867	Vermont	3	1793
Massachusetts	1	1780	Virginia	6	1970
Michigan	4	1963	Washington	1	1889
Minnesota	1	1857	West Virginia	2	1872
Mississippi	4	1890	Wisconsin	1	1848
Missouri	4	1945	Wyoming	1	1889

*Hawaii had five constitutions prior to becoming a state.
**Various sections of the constitution were revised by the limited constitutional convention of 1967–68.
Source: *The Book of the States.*

Another reason for changing state constitutions is to simplify them and make them more flexible in a changing world. Many state constitutions are long, averaging some 30,000 words. In contrast, the federal Constitution has only about 10,000 words. The 174,000-word Alabama Constitution is the longest in the nation. Other detailed constitutions are found in New York with more than 80,000 words, Oklahoma with almost 69,000, and Texas with 62,000.

Because trivial matters sometimes are incorporated into a long constitution, minor changes must occasionally go through a full-blown amendment process. Oklahoma voters, for instance, had to go to the polls to allow railroads to charge more than 2 cents per mile for passengers, a rate that had been written earlier into the state constitution.

These and other minor provisions probably should have been enacted as state statutes rather than being included in the state constitution. The Delaware Constitution, for example, makes the vague statement that public officials may continue to hold their office as long as "they behave themselves well."

The methods for changing state constitutions differ from state to state. But there are two general steps to the amending process, proposal and ratification. Two ways to propose a state constitutional amendment are frequently used. The most common method begins when a member of the state legislature proposes the amendment. If the full legislature adopts the idea by the required margin, usually two-thirds of each house, the amendment is considered officially proposed. About 90 percent of all amendments are proposed in this way.

For the remaining 10 percent, citizens themselves in 17 states may propose amendments through a **constitutional initiative.** In this method, a petition describing the change must be signed by a certain number of the state's voters. These voter-initiated amendments are in many ways the ultimate evidence of popular power.

How often are constitutional amendments proposed across the states? In 1992–93, a typical two-year period, voters across 49 states faced 211 proposed amendments and approved 139 of them. Eighteen of these amendments were proposed by constitutional initiative.

No matter which method of proposal is used, all states except Delaware require an amendment to be ratified by a majority of voters in a general election. In Delaware, an amendment must receive a two-thirds vote by the legislature during two consecutive sessions for ratification. Where voter approval *is* required, those proposals coming from the legislature are adopted far more often than proposals from citizen initiatives, with a 70 percent approval rate versus about 25 percent.

States differ markedly in the number of amendments they have adopted to their current constitutions. In Illinois, voters have adopted only 8 of 14 proposed amendments to their 1970 constitution. On the other hand, California, South Carolina, and Texas have frequently amended their constitutions. California voters have approved 485 of the 814 proposed amendments. South Carolina has made 463 changes and Texas 353.

State constitutions that need major changes may be completely rewritten. In every state the legislature may call a constitutional convention to rewrite part or all of the state constitution. In most states, the people also must vote to approve such a meeting. Since the country was founded, over 230 state conventions have met. Any changes made by the convention must then be submitted to the voters for ratification before the new constitution becomes official. As Figure 22-3 shows, most states have had more than one constitution, with Louisiana's 11 being the record.

Instead of calling a constitutional convention, some states form revision commissions to make suggestions to the legislature. The legislature may take some or all of the commission's ideas and propose them as amendments. Florida, Virginia, California, and Louisiana have used revision commissions.

Powers of the State

The federal Constitution lists the powers of the national government but does not specify the powers of the states. All powers that the people have neither granted to the national government nor denied to the state governments are reserved for the states. But there are limits on state powers. The Constitution and its amendments specifically deny some powers to the states. Other state

constitutional initiative
method of proposing amendments in which a petition describing the change must be signed by a certain number of the state's voters

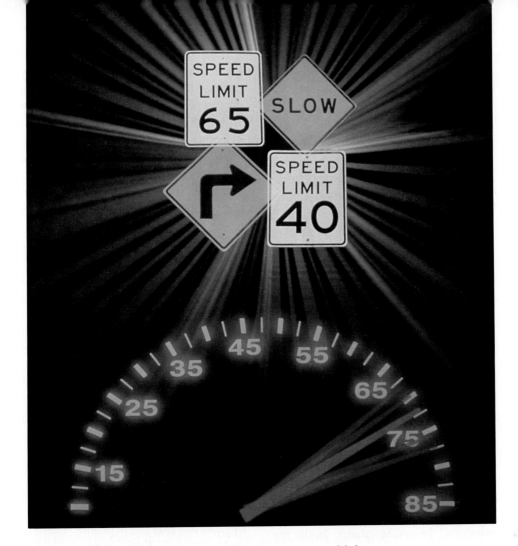

States have the power to set speed limits on many highways, roads, and streets within their borders. However, their authority in this area can be limited by federal regulations. What other factors limit state powers?

activities are restricted because they require congressional approval. Congress also can indirectly limit state powers, even reserved powers, by withholding funds from states that do not comply with congressional wishes. Finally, each state's constitution puts very specific limits on the powers of its own state and local governments.

While not unlimited, the states do wield vast powers. In using their powers, the states certainly affect the daily lives of their residents in a visible way.

Section Review

1. What are some ways that today's state lands were acquired?

2. What political principles are included in state constitutions?

3. What five major elements do state constitutions contain?

4. What powers are reserved to the states?

5. **Challenge:** Do you think every state needs its own constitution? Why or why not?

2 State Legislative Branch

Each state constitution provides for a legislative branch, which in most states is called the state legislature. Other names for this branch include the general assembly, the legislative assembly, or somewhat confusingly, the general court. Whatever name is used, the legislature is organized along similar lines across the states.

Legislative Structure

One main feature of state legislatures is that they are bicameral. Nebraska, with only a senate, is the sole exception. The lower house of the state legislature is usually called the house of representatives, and its members are known as representatives. In a few states the lower house is called the assembly, general assembly, or house of delegates.

The upper house is called the senate in all states, and the members are senators. In most states both the senators and representatives are simply called legislators. The legislature convenes in the State Capitol, known in some states as the State House.

SIZE

Each state's constitution limits the size of the state legislature, except in Montana where the size is set by state law. Some constitutions specify a fixed number of legislators; others set a minimum or a maximum number and let the legislature determine the exact figure.

REPRESENTATION

Each state is divided into legislative districts, with senate districts having larger boundaries than representative districts. One senator per senate district is elected to the state senate.

The same holds true for representatives' districts. Therefore, in every state except Nebraska, each citizen is represented by two state legislators—one senator and one representative.

Each state constitution describes the apportionment, or district boundary lines, for the legislative seats in that state. District lines for both houses are drawn according to population, so that each district has nearly the same number of people. But it was not always this way. For years rural areas were able to dominate state legislatures because geographic area was used more often than population in setting districts. This meant that an area with few residents had the same representation as a heavily populated district of the same land size.

In 1962 the Supreme Court ruled against this practice in *Baker v. Carr* and several subsequent decisions. Writing for the Court, Chief Justice Earl Warren said:

Legislators represent people, not trees or acres. Legislators are elected by voters, not farms or cities or economic interests. . .the Equal Protection Clause requires that the seats in both houses of a bicameral state legislature must be apportioned on a population basis.

As a result of this ruling, all citizens in a state should have equal representation in the legislature. This means "one person—one vote."

Since these court rulings, states have had to redraw their district boundaries. State legislatures today represent the true breakdown of population according to urban, suburban, and rural, so that all interests have a fair voice in lawmaking. As populations continue to shift, lines often are redrawn. Most state constitutions require that legislatures be reapportioned every ten years, after the United States census has been taken.

SESSIONS

State legislatures meet at regular times. The number and length of their sessions are specified in the state constitution. As the business of state government has become more complex, state legislatures are meeting more frequently and for longer periods of time. In 1940 only four state legislatures held regular annual sessions. Now all but seven states hold regular yearly sessions.

Yet 38 states also place a legal limit on how long the session may last. This may be 30, 60, or 120 days, for instance. Usually these limits are found in the state constitution and are designed to keep the legislature focused on business. Regular sessions usually begin in January and continue until the work is completed or the time limit is reached.

Besides regular sessions, legislatures may be called together for special sessions by the governor or the legislature itself. Special sessions usually deal with emergencies, such as a prison riot or extra funding needs for a state program. Sometimes the special session may be called just to clean up issues or vetoes left from the regular session.

MEMBERSHIP

Qualifications for membership in a state legislature are established by state constitution or law. All states require that candidates be a minimum age to run for office, ranging from 18 to 30 years according to the state. Usually a legislator must be a citizen of the United States, a legal resident of that state and district, and a qualified voter.

Legislatures have never fully reflected the wide diversity of the American population. A typical legislator 20 years ago was a white male farmer or lawyer. Today there is a notable rise in the number of minorities and women elected to state legislatures, but full representation still has not occurred.

Candidates generally are nominated in party primaries and elected in the November general elections of even-numbered years. The length of a legislator's term in office varies among the states. Senators serve 4-year terms in 37 states, and 2-year terms in the remaining 13. Members of the lower houses serve 2 years in all states except Alabama, Louisiana, Maryland, and Mississippi, where they have 4-year terms.

Salaries for state legislators also differ from state to state. For example, legislators in New Hampshire receive only $100 per year for working a 45-day session. In New York, legislators are paid $57,500 annually for a year-long session. Legislators also may receive allowances for postage, staff, travel, lodging, or daily expenses.

Here, the Ohio legislature is in session at the Statehouse in Columbus, Ohio. Why have state legislatures been meeting more frequently in recent years?

STATE LEGISLATURES, 1993

STATE	UPPER HOUSE #Members	Term	LOWER HOUSE #Members	Term	Annual Salary
ALABAMA	35	4 yrs.	105	4 yrs.	$50/day
ALASKA	20	4	40	2	24,012
ARIZONA	30	2	60	2	15,000
ARKANSAS	35	4	100	2	12,500
CALIFORNIA	40	4	80	2	52,500
COLORADO	35	4	65	2	17,500
CONNECTICUT	36	2	151	2	16,760
DELAWARE	21	4	41	2	24,900
FLORIDA	40	4	120	2	21,684
GEORGIA	56	2	180	2	10,641
HAWAII	25	4	51	2	27,000
IDAHO	35	2	70	2	12,000
ILLINOIS	59	4*	118	2	38,496
INDIANA	50	4	100	2	11,600
IOWA	50	4	100	2	18,100
KANSAS	40	4	125	2	120/day
KENTUCKY	38	4	100	2	100/day
LOUISIANA	39	4	105	4	16,800
MAINE	35	2	151	2	10,500
MARYLAND	47	4	141	4	28,000
MASSACHUSETTS	40	2	160	2	30,000
MICHIGAN	38	4	110	2	47,722
MINNESOTA	67	4	134	2	27,979
MISSISSIPPI	52	4	122	4	10,000
MISSOURI	34	4	163	2	22,862
MONTANA	50	4*	100	2	55.40/day
NEBRASKA	49	4	—	—	12,000
NEVADA	21	4	42	2	3,900
NEW HAMPSHIRE	24	2	400	2	100
NEW JERSEY	40	4*	80	2	35,000
NEW MEXICO	42	4	70	2	75/day
NEW YORK	61	2	150	2	57,500
NORTH CAROLINA	50	2	120	2	13,026
NORTH DAKOTA	49	4	98	2	90/day
OHIO	33	4	99	2	43,834
OKLAHOMA	48	4	101	2	32,000
OREGON	30	4	60	2	989/month
PENNSYLVANIA	50	4	203	2	47,000
RHODE ISLAND	50	2	100	2	5/day
SOUTH CAROLINA	46	4	124	2	10,400
SOUTH DAKOTA	35	2	70	2	4,000
TENNESSEE	33	4	99	2	16,500
TEXAS	31	4	150	2	7,200
UTAH	29	4	75	2	85/day
VERMONT	30	2	150	2	510/wk
VIRGINIA	40	4	100	2	17,640
WASHINGTON	49	4	98	2	25,900
WEST VIRGINIA	34	4	100	2	6,500
WISCONSIN	33	4	99	2	35,070
WYOMING	30	4	64	2	60/day

*These states combine terms of two years and four years.

Source: *The Information Please Almanac*, 1994.

Figure 22-4

Compared to other professions, legislative salaries remain low. For this reason, legislators in some states continue working at their regular jobs, taking time off to attend sessions. As legislative sessions run longer, though, being a state legislator has essentially become a full-time job. But for such low pay, not everyone can afford the position. Therefore, many states are increasing their legislators' pay, hoping more than just the wealthy can become lawmakers.

Roles of State Legislators

State legislators make decisions that affect almost every aspect of the lives of the people in their state. They must fill many roles in the performance of their duties.

MAKING POLICY

Legislatures make public policy by passing and changing laws, thus shaping a plan of action for state government. The laws and public policies created by state legislatures touch on every area of life. Some laws provide public help to those in need, such as persons who are unemployed, visually impaired, or poor. Other laws support policies regarding education, environment, health, and safety. The state legislature has broad powers with which to act, including the power to tax, to appropriate money, to regulate business, to set up courts, and to define crimes and punishments.

Appropriating funds for the operation of the state government is one of the legislature's major powers. In most states the governor suggests a budget, but final decisions on how to spend tax dollars are the legislature's. Through their power of the purse, then, legislatures actually decide which policies are put into practice, since virtually every government function requires funds.

EXECUTIVE POWERS

Legislatures also use certain important executive powers to carry out their duties. One of these is the power of **legislative oversight.** In performing the oversight function, state legislators review the activities of state executive agencies and their programs, regulations, and policies. Some legislatures require regular reports from various state agencies; others investigate and write the reports themselves. For example, the legislature may set out to see how efficiently the highway department is spending its money. Are the worst roads given the highest priority? Are costs held to a reasonable level? Are plans for future highway needs under consideration? Depending on their findings, legislators may decide to adopt new legislation or revise the legislation that already exists.

Oversight is the source of many changes in state regulations, policy, or programs. But too much detailed oversight by legislators may cross over the line into the executive branch's power and responsibility to operate state programs and fulfill the requirements of the law. As a result, the oversight function is always a source of friction, and even occasional lawsuits, between the two branches of government.

Another executive-type job of the legislature is to make or confirm various appointments. In most states, governors appoint high-level executive officials and the state senate must confirm or vote to approve those appointments. In some states, however, the legislature itself appoints certain officials. For instance, in Tennessee the legislature elects the state treasurer, whereas in Virginia the treasurer is appointed by the governor and confirmed by both legislative houses.

legislative oversight   executive power of reviewing public policy

JUDICIAL POWERS

State legislatures also may have some judicial-type powers, such as the power of impeachment. In all states except Oregon, legislatures have the right to impeach state officials. Those officials that are subject to potential impeachment, however, vary by state and may be limited to just the top elected officials or may extend to all executive and judicial officials. The lower house votes on whether to accuse an official. The senate hears arguments on the charges and votes guilty or innocent. If found guilty, the official is removed from office.

State legislatures also have authority to judge their own members. They may censure members for improper conduct or, in extreme cases, the legislature as a whole can vote to expel a member from office. Neither impeachment nor censure is used very often in actual practice.

REPRESENTING CONSTITUENTS

Whether voting on legislation or exercising other powers, legislators try to best represent the interests of their constituents. Constituents must be reasonably satisfied, or at least not actively unhappy, with what their senators and representatives are doing at the State Capitol if the legislators hope to be reelected.

One way for legislators to keep voters happy is to seek ways to help their home district or its residents. This may include helping individuals who have problems with the state government. Or it may mean sponsoring legislation to allocate more funds for the local college or money to train employees in a local industry. Whatever a legislator does creates a reputation among constituents who, in turn, will vote for or against that legislator in the next election.

Section Review

1. What is a basic feature of the structure of state legislatures?
2. Which state does not have a bicameral legislature?
3. What is the importance of the *Baker v. Carr* decision?
4. What are the requirements for being a state legislator?
5. **Challenge:** Why, do you think, is being a state legislator often a full-time job?

3 State Legislative Process

To carry out their lawmaking function, state legislatures follow certain steps from the moment a bill is introduced until it is signed into law by the governor. The legislatures are organized to try to make complicated lawmaking procedures run smoothly.

Legislative Committees

Due to the number and complexity of issues dealt with by state legislatures, much of their work is done in committees, the basic work unit in the legislature. In these committees, bills are reviewed, citizens and interest groups give testimony, and budgets and policies are drafted for the full legislature's consideration. In all states, committee meetings must be open to the public.

A typical committee has 10 to 12 members, and each legislator sits on several committees. Party affiliation, personal preferences, seniority, loyalty to party leaders, and expertise all are considered when committee assignments are made. In lower houses, the presiding officer, or the leader of the majority party, generally names committee members. In the upper houses, the president of the senate or the majority leader may have this job.

Committees vary in power and influence. The most important usually deal with money, either taxing or spending or both. Other powerful committees deal with education, transportation, crime, or other issues of major importance to constituents. Serving on a major committee may bring a legislator power, publicity, and a high profile with the voters.

As shown in Figure 22-5, state legislatures have several kinds of committees. Each house has its own standing committees dealing with specific topics. There may be a standing committee, for example, on wildlife, agriculture, or health. The number of standing committees varies among the states, with 15 to 25 per house being typical.

Whenever bills are introduced in the legislature, they are referred to the appropriate standing committee for study. Thus, a bill affecting public schools goes to the education committee, and a bill concerning hospitals goes to the health committee. The committee then decides the bill's fate: to be passed, amended, or killed.

Joint committees are standing committees made up of members of both houses. Working together on common problems saves time, effort, and money. Today, joint committees are used in 17 states.

Often the two houses pass different versions of the same bill. In such cases, a temporary conference committee works on settling the differences. The agreed-upon version is then sent back to both houses for a new vote.

Many problems need more study than can be accomplished during regular sessions. In these instances, special **interim committees** may be set up, usually in the summer or fall, to receive testimony as other committees do. Proposed legislation may be developed, which is presented to the entire legislature during the regular session.

Leaders

All state legislatures have leaders who help direct the work of the house through a legislative session. This leadership is organized along party lines. The political party with the most members in a house is the majority party, and the one with less than half is the minority party.

In the lower house, the most important leader is the speaker of the house. The speaker usually is chosen by majority party members at the beginning of the session. He or she presides over the full house, interprets rules, and often gives legislators their committee assignments.

In many states, a prominent leader is the president of the senate. In the

interim committees committees that meet when the legislature is not in session

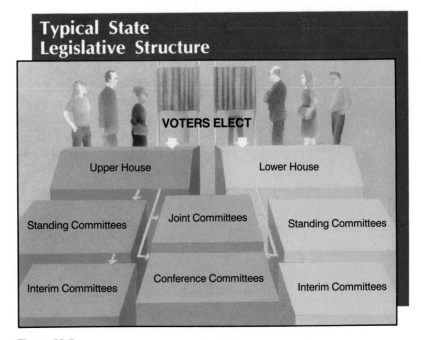

Typical State Legislative Structure

VOTERS ELECT

Upper House

Lower House

Standing Committees

Joint Committees

Standing Committees

Interim Committees

Conference Committees

Interim Committees

Figure 22-5

past, the lieutenant governor has served in this position, as is true today in 28 states. In the other states, the senate elects one of its own members to that office. The president of the senate schedules legislative floor action and may vote to break a tie.

Other important legislative leaders are the majority leader of the dominant party and the minority leader of the other party. Elected by their parties at the beginning of the session, they make sure issues of interest to their parties receive attention and support. They often are assisted by other leaders, such as party whips, who help schedule legislation, maneuver bills on the floor, and gather support for a party's proposals.

Passing Legislation

Only a legislator may introduce a bill in the house or senate of a state legislature. Legislators themselves may develop ideas that they want to see become law, but ideas for bills also come from other sources. Members of the executive branch, such as the governor, an agency head, or local officials may make suggestions. Other bills are the ideas of special interest groups.

Legislators depend on both professional and volunteer staff to help them create good legislation. Nationwide, over 20,000 permanent staff members, as well as interns and other unpaid workers, assist legislators.

For a bill to become law, it must go through elaborate steps, comparable to the way Congress passes a federal law. A bill travels to the first house committee and then to the whole house for a vote. From there it goes to the second house committee and a vote by that full house. Then it lands on the governor's desk for his or her signature. But just as in Congress,

there are many twists along the way and few bills have an easy time from start to finish. In fact, most are killed en route.

Thousands of bills may be introduced during a legislative session. In any two-year period, state legislatures combined are likely to see almost 200,000 bills, although the number per state varies widely. In general, states with large populations, such as New York and California, discuss more bills than small states.

What happens to a bill by the end of an annual session also varies. It may have been killed or "postponed indefinitely." In some states it may roll over into the next session. Or the bill may have been passed by the legislature and sent to the governor.

If the governor signs the bill, it becomes law. But, in every state except North Carolina, the governor may choose to veto a bill. If this happens, the legislature may try to override the veto by passing the bill again, usually with a two-thirds majority of each house. Vetoes, however, usually win. For example, only about five percent of vetoes nationwide are overridden each year.

Section Review

1. Why are committees important in the work of state legislatures?

2. What are four kinds of committees that operate in most state legislatures?

3. Who are the main legislative leaders in most state legislatures?

4. Who may introduce a bill in the state legislature?

5. **Challenge:** Why do you think so few vetoes are overridden by the state legislatures?

4 State Executive Branch

The executive branch of state government administers and enforces the laws passed by the state legislature. This branch is made up of the governor and other elected and appointed executive officers who provide leadership in carrying out public policy within the state.

The Governor

The governor heads the executive branch on the state level, a position comparable to the President's on the national level. But governors do not have as much power within their states as the President has within the national government.

QUALIFICATIONS

Candidates for governor must meet formal and informal qualifications for the office. The formal requirements are described in each state's constitution. In most states a candidate must be at least a specified age, usually 25 or 30. Ordinarily, only American citizens who also are state residents can run. Sometimes the person also must be a qualified voter.

Equally important are the many informal requirements that a candidate for governor is expected to meet. The candidate generally is active in a major political party and often has held another state elective office. Many governors previously served as state legislators, mayors of large cities, or even members of Congress. It is interesting to watch which current officeholders are trying to gain enough statewide popularity to make a future bid for the governor's office.

Because campaigns are very expensive, having access to funds is certainly helpful in one's race for gover-

Governors, such as Don Sundquist of Tennessee, are the executive heads of their state governments. How do their powers compare and contrast with those of the President of the United States?

nor. Many gubernatorial candidates have spent personal fortunes seeking that office. The 1990 race in Texas set a record for the most money spent: $57.9 million between the candidates.

ELECTION

The first step toward the governor's office is nomination by a major party. Most states hold primary elections, although some use caucuses and conventions for nominations.

In the general election, 46 states simply require a plurality of votes to declare a winner. The four other states require a majority to win, which if not achieved, results in a further election. In Georgia and Louisiana, the top two vote-getters meet in a runoff. Mississippi's winner is elected by the state house of representatives, while in Vermont this decision is made by both houses.

In most states, the governor serves a four-year term. As shown in Figure 22-6, however, the governors in New Hampshire, Rhode Island, and Vermont serve two-year terms. Over half of the states limit the number of times a governor may be elected.

State Government   547

STATE GOVERNORS, 1993

States	Term in Years	Annual Salary
ALABAMA	4	$ 70,223
ALASKA	4	92,988
ARIZONA	4	75,000
ARKANSAS	4	60,000
CALIFORNIA	4	114,000
COLORADO	4	70,000
CONNECTICUT	4	78,000
DELAWARE	4	95,000
FLORIDA	4	103,909
GEORGIA	4	92,088
HAWAII	4	94,780
IDAHO	4	75,000
ILLINOIS	4	100,681
INDIANA	4	77,200
IOWA	4	76,700
KANSAS	4	65,000
KENTUCKY	4	81,647
LOUISIANA	4	73,400
MAINE	4	70,000
MARYLAND	4	120,000
MASSACHUSETTS	4	75,000
MICHIGAN	4	112,024
MINNESOTA	4	109,053
MISSISSIPPI	4	75,600
MISSOURI	4	90,312
MONTANA	4	53,006
NEBRASKA	4	65,000
NEVADA	4	90,000
NEW HAMPSHIRE	2	79,542
NEW JERSEY	4	130,000
NEW MEXICO	4	90,000
NEW YORK	4	130,000
NORTH CAROLINA	4	91,938
NORTH DAKOTA	4	68,280
OHIO	4	105,000
OKLAHOMA	4	70,000
OREGON	4	80,000
PENNSYLVANIA	4	105,000
RHODE ISLAND	2	69,900
SOUTH CAROLINA	4	99,960
SOUTH DAKOTA	4	72,475
TENNESSEE	4	85,000
TEXAS	4	93,432
UTAH	4	77,250
VERMONT	2	85,977
VIRGINIA	4	110,000
WASHINGTON	4	121,000
WEST VIRGINIA	4	72,000
WISCONSIN	4	92,283
WYOMING	4	70,000

Figure 22-6

COMPENSATION

Unlike the job of most state legislators, the governorship is a full-time position in all states. Governors' salaries range from $60,000 in Arkansas to $130,000 in New York. Most states also provide the governor with an official residence, a travel allowance, and one or more means of transportation. Governors also have a staff for their office.

Besides salary and benefits, governors receive intangible rewards such as prestige and public exposure. The fact that many governors use their office as a political stepping stone is shown by the 16 Presidents who had previously served as governors.

SUCCESSION

Each state constitution has provisions for a successor if the office of governor becomes vacant. In most states the lieutenant governor fills the position, while in a few states, the secretary of state or the president of the senate takes over.

The office of governor may become vacant for a number of reasons. The governor may die or become a member of Congress or even President. Or the office may become vacant because the incumbent has been impeached by the state legislature.

In every state but Oregon the governor can be impeached, yet this has only happened eight times. The most recent case occurred in 1988 when Evan Mecham, governor of Arizona, was impeached and convicted on criminal charges of campaign finance mishandling and lending $80,000 of state money to his car dealership. Upon his conviction, the Arizona secretary of state assumed the office.

In 15 states, the governor also may be recalled from office by the voters. In fact, the momentum to remove Governor Mecham began when a citizen recall effort gathered 400,000 signatures and forced a recall election to be scheduled.

Roles of the Governor

A state governor has many roles, which are similar in some ways to those performed by the President.

CHIEF ADMINISTRATOR

Perhaps the most important role of a governor is that of chief administrator. As such, the governor coordinates the policies and day-to-day work of the various agencies and departments of a state's executive branch. When conflicts arise between these agencies, or when policies fail, the governor must step in to help resolve the situation.

As head of the state administration, the governor is ultimately responsible for thousands of state employees, from social workers to state troopers to janitors. When their work goes well and the public is pleased, the governor often gets credit. But if there is a problem, the governor is most likely to receive plenty of blame.

In 1988, Arizona's Secretary of State Rose Mofford became governor of the state following the impeachment of Governor Evan Mecham. In most other states, what official fills the governorship if the office becomes vacant?

STATE SPOKESPERSON

A governor frequently speaks in an official capacity, representing the state at various public functions and ceremonies. For example, he or she may welcome important people from other states or countries. The governor also works with other leaders at the local and national levels of government. For instance, the governor may testify before Congress or work with the state's congressional delegation to develop specific legislation benefiting the state. And as a member of the National Governors' Association, each governor has an opportunity to work with other governors to debate issues and recommend policies on issues facing all states.

POLITICAL PARTY LEADER

Governors are looked upon as the leaders of their political parties. They push for party goals by speaking at fund-raising dinners and campaigning for party candidates. As party leader, the governor also can call on party loyalty from state legislators or congressional members in order to further his or her own goals.

POLICY LEADER

As policy leaders for their states, governors identify problems and propose goals and programs. If, for example, the governor feels there are too many homeless families, he or she may request funds to provide housing and jobs for these families.

When governors run for office, they often propose changes for the state during their campaigns. Once in office, they must try to influence the legislature to implement these proposals. This always sounds easier on the campaign trail than it is in reality.

The governor also is expected to establish policies for the executive branch. Assistance in this process is provided by the governor's staff and other members of the executive branch. For instance, if there is a growing need for drug abuse clinics, the governor might ask the staffs of the budget and health departments to study the problem and make recommendations. Based upon staff ideas, the governor can then set a course for action. This may mean shifting existing resources to set up clinics or going to the legislature for more funding.

Arkansas Governor Jim Guy Tucker promotes tourism in his state at a press conference. What other tasks does a governor carry out in the role of state spokesperson?

Powers of the Governor

To perform the role of chief executive of the state, the governor has various powers. These can be viewed as executive, legislative, and judicial in nature.

EXECUTIVE POWERS

Laws passed by the state legislature must be carried out fairly, efficiently, and effectively. To put these laws into effect, governors are given certain executive powers, including the important powers of appointment and removal. In recent years, there has been a trend toward reorganizing state government and giving the governor more say in running the executive branch. This generally includes the power to hire and fire more executive leaders. Governors who may appoint many of their own department and agency heads are better able to coordinate policies and accomplish their goals.

Governors in all 50 states also are given some power regarding money. In all but five states, the governor prepares a budget based on requests by state agencies, which is then presented to the state legislature. In the other states, the governor works with a special commission that makes the budget requests to the state legislature.

Budget decisions are important because they are the heart of what gets accomplished by the state. The power to create the budget allows the governor to set priorities for using state money. Although the legislature may make changes in the governor's budget, the original requests carry a lot of weight in most states.

Another executive power is military, though this is more symbolic than vital. The governor acts as commander in chief of the state's National Guard, which can be called out to deal with emergencies such as floods, earthquakes, or riots.

LEGISLATIVE POWERS

Along with their executive powers, governors also have legislative powers. Specific requests for new or improved state laws may be made in the recommended budget, a speech, or an outlined bill. Informally, governors also may use their party influence and public opinion to get their programs passed.

In each state, the governor also may call the legislature into special session. This may be needed to deal with state emergencies, such as shortfalls in school funding or drought relief for farmers.

Lastly, in every state except North Carolina, the governor may veto bills passed by the state legislature. In 43 states, the governor also has the power of a line-item veto, which allows him or her to veto only *parts* of a bill without rejecting the whole bill. This type of veto usually applies to spending bills. Certain legislative projects may be singled out by the governor to be axed without jeopardizing funding for all the state's agencies. Often even the threat of a gubernatorial veto is enough to get the legislature to change offending portions of a bill.

JUDICIAL POWERS

In every state, the governor has powers that are judicial in nature. Some governors appoint certain state judges to office. Most governors also have "executive clemency" powers, which allow them to show mercy to persons already found guilty of crimes. The governor may grant pardons, reduce prison sentences or fines, or parole prisoners early. But these powers are usually used only in exceptional cases.

PARTY AFFILIATION OF GOVERNORS AND STATE LEGISLATURES, 1995

State	Governor	Upper House	Lower House	State	Governor	Upper House	Lower House
Alabama	D	R	R	Montana	R	R	R
Alaska	D	R	R	Nebraska	D	**	**
Arizona	R	R	R	Nevada	D	R	*
Arkansas	D	D	D	New Hampshire	R	R	R
California	R	D	*	New Jersey	R	R	R
Colorado	D	R	R	New Mexico	R	D	D
Connecticut	D	D	R	New York	R	R	D
Delaware	D	R	D	North Carolina	D	D	R
Florida	D	R	D	North Dakota	R	R	R
Georgia	D	D	D	Ohio	R	R	R
Hawaii	D	D	D	Oklahoma	R	D	D
Idaho	R	R	R	Oregon	D	R	R
Illinois	R	R	R	Pennsylvania	R	R	D
Indiana	D	R	R	Rhode Island	R	D	D
Iowa	R	D	R	South Carolina	R	D	***
Kansas	R	R	R	South Dakota	R	R	R
Kentucky	D	D	D	Tennessee	R	D	D
Louisiana	R	D	D	Texas	R	D	D
Maine	I	D	*	Utah	R	R	R
Maryland	D	D	D	Vermont	D	R	R
Massachusetts	D	D	D	Virginia	R	D	D
Michigan	R	R	R	Washington	D	D	R
Minnesota	R	D	D	West Virginia	D	D	D
Mississippi	D	D	D	Wisconsin	R	R	R
Missouri	D	D	D	Wyoming	R	R	R

*Evenly divided between Democrats and Republicans.
**Unicameral body elected on a nonpartisan ballot
***Because of three Independents, there is not a majority party.

Other State Executive Officers

Some leaders in the executive branch are elected by the voters; others are appointed by the governor or the legislature.

ELECTED OFFICIALS

In 47 states, the people elect at least some members of the executive branch besides the governor. In Maine, New Jersey, and Tennessee, the governor is the single official elected on a statewide basis.

The offices that are filled by public vote differ from state to state. Some states have executive power concentrated in the governor's hands so that citizens may readily know who is responsible for executive decisions. Other states want more publicly elected officials to ensure that their leaders are responsible to public wishes. Each state has determined which officials are elected and which are appointed.

Forty-three states have a **lieutenant governor** who acts as chief executive when the governor is out of the state or if the office is vacated. In about

lieutenant governor person who acts as chief executive when the governor's office becomes vacant

half the states, he or she also presides over the state senate. Although elected to this high state office, the lieutenant governor usually is not a powerful leader. In only 22 states are the governor and lieutenant governor elected as a team. In the other states, where the two offices are totally separate on the ballot, these two people may even be from different political parties.

Another elected executive leader is the attorney general. Forty-three states have decided that the top lawyer for the state should be independently accountable to the people. This officer is the state prosecutor, who decides which crimes should be prosecuted. He or she also is charged with defending the state's interests in any lawsuits brought against it. The attorney general may be requested to give legal advice to the governor, other executive leaders, legislators, and sometimes local officials. With the growing importance of lawsuits and legal conflicts, this office continues to grow in strategic importance in state government.

Keeping the public money safe is the job of the state treasurer in over two-thirds of the states. This person accounts for the various state funds: receiving them from taxpayers, investing them, and paying them out as the legislature directs.

Every state except Alaska, Hawaii, and Utah has a secretary of state. In those three states, the lieutenant governor carries out the duties of this office. The main role of the secretary of state is to be the state's chief recordkeeper, publisher of the state laws, and head of state elections. Yet, in only 36 states does the public elect the secretary of state. In the other states, either the governor makes the appointment or the legislature determines who should fill the position.

Numerous other state officials are also elected across the country. These may include auditors, public utility commissioners, tax officers, and members of various state boards. Each elected official brings a slightly different perspective and political agenda to the State Capitol. In cases where there are many elected officials, the direction of the executive branch often becomes unclear because so many people are pulling on the steering wheel.

APPOINTED OFFICIALS

In all states there are many more appointed officials than elected ones. Some appointed officials are on the governor's staff, offering technical and political advice. Others are the highly visible department heads, who are part of the governor's cabinet and responsible for the day-to-day decisions of running state agencies. These people usually are appointed by the governor with confirmation by the legislature.

Which departments are headed by appointed officials depends on the state, and may include such departments as health, revenue, and commerce. The head of the health department, for example, might be charged with regulating state hospitals and clinics to ensure patient health. This department often is responsible for tracking and cleaning up polluted air and water, and may even run alcohol and drug treatment centers.

The appointed head of the state's revenue department has broad powers over another state government function. This is the unpopular job of collecting taxes and fees. The revenue department also may issue drivers' and vehicle licenses, and may direct the state lottery if there is one.

The head of the state prisons department has an extremely difficult

Food and health inspectors are among the vast number of state government employees who are part of the civil service. What is the purpose of the civil service system?

job, but one that is vital to public safety. The state prison system is responsible for inmates 24 hours a day. Prisoners' work, treatment, family visits, court dates, health, and education all must be closely supervised. In addition, the head of prisons must prepare for the possibility of prison riots or breakouts. Few jobs in the state are more stressful.

STATE GOVERNMENT EMPLOYEES

At one time, many jobs in state government were handed out as political favors by victorious political parties. But a reform movement begun in 1883 led to a hiring system based on merit that is used in most states. The merit system, also called civil service, determines how people are to be hired, promoted, or fired based on tests and job performance.

Civil service covers the vast majority of state jobs today. Over 4 million people worked for the 50 state gov-

ernments in 1986. Of these, about 58 percent were men and 73 percent were white. These workers are found not only in the state capitals, but in cities and rural areas, too.

Section Review

1. What formal qualifications must be met by candidates for governor in most states?

2. What are four roles of a state governor?

3. What are the executive powers of most state governors? What other kinds of powers do governors have?

4. What four executive officials are elected in most states?

5. **Challenge:** In your opinion, what are one advantage and one disadvantage of having a lieutenant governor and a governor from two different political parties?

ISSUE: PUERTO RICO

THE FIFTY-FIRST STATE?

Many Americans are in favor of it. Others oppose it, while many other Americans probably have not thought about it at all. What is "it"? Statehood for Puerto Rico, the Spanish-speaking island that now is governed by the United States but has wide powers of self-rule.

In 1993 Puerto Ricans narrowly defeated a vote on statehood, choosing instead to remain a commonwealth of the United States. Even if voters had approved statehood, the territory might not have become a state. It is up to the Congress of the United States to make the final decision.

The close vote ensured that the issue of statehood was still alive. And Puerto Ricans continue to debate it.

Supporters of statehood argue that statehood is the only way for Puerto Ricans to enjoy full equality with other American citizens. They also claim that statehood would give Puerto Rico an equal say with other states in the making of American domestic policies. Among the backers of statehood are many of the Puerto Ricans who have moved to the United States mainland since World War II.

Opponents of statehood, however, claim that statehood could have negative effects on the island. Puerto Ricans would be required to pay federal income taxes, and their businesses could lose important tax breaks they now enjoy. In addition, Congress, which sets conditions for statehood, might require that English become the island's only official language. Today, both English and Spanish are official languages.

Wanting to avoid these problems, many Puerto Ricans prefer keeping the present relationship with the United States; however, they support more freedoms for Puerto Rico. For example, they believe Puerto Rico should be able to set local pollution standards, control the island's immigration policy, and influence American foreign policy.

Other Puerto Ricans opposed to statehood favor complete independence. They believe that the United States has no legal right to rule the island. Some proindependence groups have used violence to advance their cause. For example, in January 1981 a group

supporting independence blew up 11 jet fighters belonging to Puerto Rico's National Guard.

Linked to Puerto Rico by language and culture, many Latin American countries support Puerto Rican independence. They have sponsored international conferences on the topic and have sought support for independence in the United Nations. In 1982 the Foreign Minister of Venezuela summarized the feelings of many Latin Americans when he said, "Among Venezuelans there is a deep sentiment . . . that Puerto Rico should be a member of the Latin American family."

Those opposing independence point to Puerto Rico's economic dependence on the United States. Ninety percent of the island's food comes from the mainland United States. A majority of Puerto Ricans use food stamps.

Despite their differences on the island's future, Puerto Ricans agree that the decision should be theirs.

1. Why might Congress want to require that English be the official language of all states? Why would this be a problem for Puerto Rico?
2. Which of the three options for Puerto Rico's future do you favor? Give reasons to support your answer.

5 State Judicial Branch

The judicial branch of state government interprets state law and settles legal disputes involving the state constitution. In general, the state judiciary does at the state level what the federal judiciary does at the national level. But the 50 state court systems are responsible for many more cases than the federal courts. State courts interpret and apply state and local laws, involving everything from speeding tickets and littering to assault and murder.

In criminal cases heard in state courts, such as this one in Florida, the government itself brings suit against the offender, because a specific law has been broken. How are civil cases brought into state courts?

Civil and Criminal Cases

State courts deal with both criminal and civil cases. The breadth of state responsibility is all-encompassing regarding state and local laws.

CRIMINAL CASES
In a criminal case, a person or group is accused of breaking the law. State laws specify what exactly is against the law. If the law is broken, the government itself brings suit against the offender. The way a murder case is labeled, for example, shows this: *State of Ohio v. J. Smith.*

There are two categories of criminal offenses. A misdemeanor is a minor crime such as disorderly conduct or illegal trash dumping. These acts generally are punished with fines, short jail terms, or probation. A felony is a serious criminal offense and includes murder, arson, or bribing government officials. Punishment may be stiff fines, imprisonment, or even death. State laws define categories of misdemeanors and felonies, and spell out what the punishment should be for each crime.

CIVIL CASES
Whenever two or more people get into a major dispute, they may file a civil suit with the state courts. A person or group also may bring suit against the government. In either case, the party with the complaint is not the government. For example, a dispute may occur when two businesses disagree over the boundary line between their properties. Or a civil suit may be raised by a rancher whose horse was shot by a nearsighted hunter. Other civil cases include divorces, child custody battles, and traffic accidents. Civil cases jam virtually every state court in the nation, sometimes resulting in a several-year delay before a case is heard.

State Court Structure

In all states, there are two levels of courts, trial courts and appellate courts. Trial courts are where civil and criminal cases first enter the court system. For this reason, trial courts are said to have original jurisdiction.

Appellate courts hear appeals of cases already decided in trial courts. There are strict limits on the reasons a trial court decision may be appealed. Thus, appellate courts hear only a fraction of the cases heard by trial courts.

The structure of each state's court system is outlined by the state's constitution. But states usually have organizations similar to that shown in Figure 22-8.

LOCAL TRIAL COURTS

As their name implies, **local trial courts** are found at the local level of government. Their jurisdiction is limited to whatever the state government has authorized. Local courts are restricted to misdemeanors and civil cases involving small sums of money. In various states the local trial courts are known as minor trial courts, inferior trial courts, or simply, lower courts.

There are several kinds of local trial courts. For instance, justice courts can be found in small towns and rural areas of about half the states. In these courts a **justice of the peace** usually hears cases without a jury present. They are commonly elected and may or may not have had legal training.

Minor legal matters also are handled by other local courts such as police courts, magistrate's courts, or municipal courts. Sometimes special courts are set up to deal with such matters as family violence, juvenile delinquency, or traffic tickets. In most states, judges in these courts have legal training.

Typical State Court System

STATE SUPREME COURT

INTERMEDIATE APPELLATE COURTS

GENERAL TRIAL COURTS

LOCAL TRIAL COURTS

Municipal Courts

Special Courts

Police Courts

Justice Courts

Magistrate's Courts

Figure 22-8

GENERAL TRIAL COURTS

The next level in the state court system is the **general trial court.** Most trials at this level are decided by jury. General trial courts also may hear appeals from lower courts, although most appeals are heard in appellate courts.

Each state is divided into several judicial districts, or circuits, with each having at least one general trial court. But some have two; one for criminal cases and the other for civil cases. Other common names for general trial courts are district courts, circuit courts, or superior courts.

States vary in how many general trial courts or judges they have. The judges usually are required to be lawyers or, as some states say, "learned in law." Some states also

local trial courts first level of courts in a state judicial system

justice of the peace official of a justice court who hears small local cases

general trial court court with original jurisdiction for major civil and criminal cases

state supreme court
highest court of appeals in a state system

set a minimum age for these judges, usually 30, and other requirements such as citizenship or residence in the judicial district.

INTERMEDIATE APPELLATE COURTS

intermediate appellate courts first court of appeals in a state judicial system

Intermediate appellate courts are courts of appeals that are above the trial courts but below the state's supreme court. Appellate courts do not hear facts in a case; trial courts have done that already. But any questions of what the law is and how it applies to a case can be dealt with by an appellate court. In other words, an intermediate appellate court is concerned with such things as whether the judge in the lower court has interpreted the law correctly and applied it fairly. Because there are many fine points of law, and sometimes competing understandings of the law, the appellate function is very important in ensuring justice, both in civil and criminal cases.

Appellate cases are heard by a panel of judges rather than by a jury. The number of judges on the panel varies from three to nine in different states. Judges at the appellate level, in general, must meet the same legal qualifications as judges of the trial courts. In practice, intermediate appellate judges usually are more experienced and may have served as judges at the lower levels first.

Instead of hearing the testimony of witnesses, appeals judges hear oral arguments presented by the attorneys and study the legal documents and records in the case. Decisions in these cases are made by a majority vote of the judges.

STATE SUPREME COURT

Above the intermediate courts is the **state supreme court.** It hears appeals of decisions from lower courts and, in most cases, has the final decision. Only cases involving federal law or constitutional rights can be further appealed to the United States Supreme Court. For this reason, the state supreme court sometimes is called the court of last resort. It may have original jurisdiction in a few cases

Supreme courts are the final courts of appeal in each state. For example, Maryland, whose state capitol is shown here, has a supreme court that hears civil and criminal appeals. What appeals can be sent from a state supreme court to the U.S. Supreme Court?

where the government itself is being sued or where one branch of government has a legal dispute with another.

Like the intermediate appellate courts, cases at the state supreme court level are heard by a panel of judges. The size of the court, as set in the state constitution, is most often seven, but varies from three to nine across the states. One member of the supreme court serves as chief justice, while the other judges are referred to as associate justices. Qualifications are the same as for other appellate judges. And usually the justices have served in other judicial positions.

The procedures in the state supreme courts are similar to those in the intermediate courts of appeals. The justices hear oral arguments and study court records before reaching a majority decision. The impact of these decisions may be far-reaching, because all lower courts in that state must adjust their understanding and application of the law according to what the justices declare to be correct.

Selecting and Evaluating State Judges

The most troubling, unresolved issue concerning state judiciaries is how to select state judges. Should they be elected, thus allowing them to be voted out of office for unpopular decisions? On the other hand, if they are appointed by the governor or legislature, is the judiciary truly independent? Each state has wrestled with these questions, and many different approaches are being tried.

Who becomes a judge, and for how long, is important because the opinions of state judges are final. The legislature may write the law and the executive may apply it, but the final say about a law comes from the

Here, a state judge in Illinois is seated at the bench of his courtroom. In the early days of the United States, judges were chosen by state legislatures. What methods are used to choose state judges today?

judiciary. A judge's rulings will remain public policy unless the legislature passes new laws. These, of course, can then be declared unconstitutional by the state judiciary.

In colonial days, judges were selected by the governor. Following independence and the creation of the states, this responsibility fell to state legislatures. Since the mid-1800s, due in part to legislative corruption, more judges have been elected by the public. Today, the manner by which judges are chosen varies widely, but most states use one or more of the following methods.

POPULAR ELECTION
The most common method of selecting state judges is popular election. At least some judges are chosen by this process in the majority of states. The elections may be either on partisan or nonpartisan ballots. For instance, in Kentucky all judges are elected on nonpartisan ballots, while in Arkansas

all are elected on a partisan basis. The main argument against popular election is that voters may not know enough about either judges or the law to decide rationally. Supporters of elections, however, say that judges should reflect public opinion and be just as accountable as other government officials.

EXECUTIVE APPOINTMENT

Another method of choosing judges is to have the governor appoint them. Those who favor this method believe that the governor may look more at candidates' legal qualifications than at their popularity. But opponents fear the governor may select only members of his or her political party. In some states these appointments are subject to approval by the state legislature or, at times, by popular vote. Often there is a nominating committee that recommends names to the governor for final selection.

LEGISLATIVE APPOINTMENT

The state legislature also may hold appointive powers. In Virginia all judges are elected by the legislature. In a few other states, such as Connecticut, Rhode Island, and South Carolina, the legislatures select some of the state judges. The pros and cons of legislative appointment are similar to those of gubernatorial appointment.

APPOINTMENT AND ELECTION

In Missouri, a major compromise plan on judicial selection was worked out in 1940. Since then, this plan has gained favor in about one-third of the states. The plan calls for judges to first be appointed by the governor. After they have been in office for a certain time, the judges must run in an election to retain their position. This method allows the voters to decide on the basis of the judges' records.

EVALUATION AND REMOVAL

Nearly all state judges are elected or appointed to office for a fixed term, usually six or twelve years. When their terms are over, most judges are reappointed or reelected.

Laws concerning *removal* of judges are highly complex and depend not only on the state but also on the level of the judges. One rarely used method of removal is impeachment by the state legislature. Sometimes the governor acting alone may remove lower court judges. And in some states, citizens have the right to initiate a special recall petition and force an election.

In the past few decades, most states have taken steps to establish more effective methods for the evaluation and removal of judges. In 1960 a Commission of Judicial Performance was established in California. This commission consists of several judges, attorneys, and private citizens who investigate complaints about judges. They hold hearings for judges accused of improper or unfair conduct. Today, almost all states have a judicial evaluation committee to make sure that judges are performing their duties as required.

Section Review

1. What two general types of cases do state courts decide?

2. What two types of offenses are included under criminal law?

3. What are the two general levels of courts in a state court system?

4. Why is the state supreme court sometimes called the court of last resort?

5. **Challenge:** Why, do you think, is the right to appeal a case important?

1. Since the original 13 colonies became states, 37 others have been admitted to the Union.

2. State constitutions are similar to the national Constitution in that they set up representative governments with three branches and a system of checks and balances.

3. State legislatures, except in Nebraska, are bicameral. Usually, the two houses are called the senate and the house of representatives.

4. Most Americans live in two state legislative districts—one for the upper house and one for the lower house.

5. The main function of state legislatures is making public policy.

6. In addition to their legislative powers, state legislatures also have executive and judicial powers.

7. Most of the work of state legislatures is done in committees. Among these are standing, joint, conference, and interim committees.

8. Some of the important leaders in state legislatures are the speaker of the house, the president of the senate, and the majority and minority leaders.

9. For a bill to become a state law, it must pass through several steps in both houses of the state legislature.

10. The executive branch of state government administers and enforces the laws passed by the state legislature.

11. A state's governor serves as chief administrator for the state, state spokesperson, political party leader, and policy leader.

12. Governors have many executive powers, including appointment and removal powers, budget-making powers, and military powers. Governors have legislative and judicial powers as well.

13. States have many high-level officials appointed by the governors. Most of these appointed officials head departments within the executive branch. The top appointed officials form the governor's cabinet.

14. The judicial branch of state government resolves legal disputes and interprets the laws of the state.

15. State courts deal with legal cases of two general types—civil and criminal.

16. Both civil and criminal cases enter the judicial system in trial courts. In some cases the decision of a trial court is appealed to an appellate court. A further appeal can sometimes be made to the state supreme court.

17. Depending upon the state, state judges may be elected by popular vote; or selected by the governor, the state legislature, or by an alternative selection plan.

Chapter 22 Review

★ Building Vocabulary

Use terms you have read about in this chapter to complete the following statements.

1. A(n) _____ _____ _____ is a bill that formally allows an area to become a state.
2. The executive power of reviewing public policy is _____ _____.
3. _____ _____ _____ are the first courts of appeals in a state judicial system.
4. The person who acts as chief executive when the governor's office becomes vacant is the _____ _____.
5. The _____ _____ _____ is the highest court of appeals in a state system.
6. The first level of courts in a state judicial system is _____ _____ _____.
7. A(n) _____ _____ _____ _____ is an official of a justice court who hears small local cases.
8. The method of proposing amendments in which a petition describing the change must be signed by a certain number of the state's voters is called a(n) _____ _____.

★ Reviewing Facts

1. How is a territory admitted to the United States to form a new state?
2. What two general steps are used to amend a state constitution?
3. How do state legislatures differ among the states?
4. In what ways do state legislators represent their constituents?
5. What are the duties of a state governor as chief administrator? state spokesperson? political party leader?
6. Besides the governor, what other state executives commonly are elected?
7. What state officials frequently are appointed by the governor?
8. What kinds of cases can be appealed from state supreme courts?

9. What four methods are used in different states to select state judges?
10. What methods do states use to evaluate and remove state judges?

★ Analyzing Facts

1. How do you think the rights of state residents would change if their state constitution had no bill of rights? Explain.
2. In your opinion, should all states have fulltime legislators? Why or why not?
3. When do you think a legislator should vote the way the majority of his or her constituents would want? When do you think a legislator should vote according to his or her own opinion? Explain.
4. Which method for selecting judges, in your opinion, is least partisan? Explain.
5. What do you think are the advantages of a state governor having strong political power? What might be some disadvantages? Explain.

★ Evaluating Ideas

1. If you were a lobbyist wanting to change a state law, whom in the legislature would you contact? Why?

Using Your
Civic Participation Journal

Review the entries you made in your Civic Participation Journal about your state's constitution. Use the information to write a persuasive essay trying to convince state legislators to call a convention to write a new state constitution.

2. Argue the case for a unicameral legislature.

3. In your opinion, how might the right of appeal conflict with guarantees of a fair and speedy trial and with the requirement that the guilty be punished?

4. Do you think state legislators should reapportion their own state's legislative districts, or should a separate commission be formed to make such changes? Explain.

5. Why do you think all legislative committees in all state legislatures are not joint committees?

★ Critical Thinking
Cause and Effect Relationships

Identifying relationships involves looking for connections between things. Everything that happens does so because something makes it happen. What happens is called the effect. The cause is what makes it happen. Identifying relationships between causes and effects is a part of good thinking skills.

Explanation An effect frequently will have more than one cause. In addition, the effect of one cause, or set of causes, can become a cause of another effect. For example, the new faculty advisor could be the cause for the change in the way the yearbook editor is chosen. That effect, in turn, can be a cause of declining yearbook sales, although there are likely other causes as well.

Seeing cause and effect relationships under such circumstances can sometimes be difficult. The following guidelines will help you identify cause and effect in written or spoken material.

1. Statements often contain "clue words" that will alert you to cause and effect relationships. Look for words and phrases such as *because, since, therefore, produced, consequently, thus, so that, resulted in, brought about, led to, if. . . then.*

2. Sometimes, because of writing style, there are no "clue words." Instead *and* or a comma may appear. When no "clue words" exist, you can test for the presence of a relationship by putting clue words into the passage to see if it still makes sense.

3. Cause and effect may not always appear in the same sentence or even in the same paragraph. Sometimes it may take several sentences or paragraphs to explain the cause or causes and to state the effect.

4. Be aware that events can have more than one cause and that, in turn, they can cause other effects.

Practice The following passage illustrates the presence of cause and effect relationships. *Compared to other professions, legislative salaries remain low.* [cause] *For this reason, legislators in some states continue working at their regular jobs, taking time off to attend sessions.* [effect] *As legislative sessions run longer, though,* [cause] *being a state legislator has essentially become a full-time job.* [effect]

Two cause and effect relationships are present in this excerpt. In the first one, the clue words *for this reason* should alert you that there is a relationship between low legislative salaries and the fact that some legislators work at other jobs. However, no such clue words signal the second relationship between longer legislative sessions and the full-time nature of the state legislator's job. Had the author stated the relationship directly, it might have read, "Legislative sessions run longer. Therefore, begin a state legislator . . ."

You might also find it useful to use the following diagram when you are determining cause and effect.

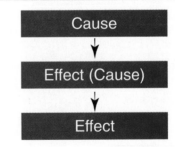

Independent Practice Find three examples of cause and effect relationships in the material in this chapter. In each case, identify the cause and the effect, and identify on what you based your decision.

Chapter 23

State Finance and Issues

See CD-Rom and videodisc correlations beginning on page T26.

How effective a state government is in dealing with important issues is largely influenced by the amount of money a state has and the way in which that money is spent. The questions asked over and over by the people and by state legislators are "who pays?" and "who benefits?" In this chapter, you will learn what the sources of state money are and how states spend their money.

Chapter Preview

TERMS TO KNOW

state revenue, state taxes, general fund, general sales tax, individual income tax, corporate income tax, selective sales tax, excise tax, severance tax, state income tax, intergovernmental revenue, property tax, state expenditures, state budget

READ TO DISCOVER

- what are the sources of state revenue.
- what expenditures state governments make.
- how state budgets are developed.
- what are the important issues facing state governments today.

★ ★ ★ ★ ★

Civic Participation Journal

Property taxes are one of the ways that local communities help fund education. Contact your local tax assessor's office to learn the property tax rate in your community. Also find out if there are any proposals to ask the voters to increase the tax to fund education. If so, you might volunteer to work either for or against the proposed increase. Record your findings in your journal.

COMBINED STATE GOVERNMENT REVENUE, 1992		
SOURCE	**IN MILLIONS**	**PERCENT OF TOTAL**
Taxes		
Sales and Gross Receipts	$162,308	21.9
Individual Income	104,401	14.1
Corporate Income	21,566	3.0
Licenses	21,691	3.0
Property	6,594	0.9
Miscellaneous	11,262	1.4
Federal Government	159,041	21.4
Local Government	10,861	1.4
Insurance Trust Revenue	129,940	17.5
Utility and Liquor Store Revenue	6,579	0.9
Charges and Miscellaneous General Revenue	107,610	14.5
TOTAL	**$741,853**	**100%**

Source: U.S. Department of Commerce, Bureau of the Census
Figure 23-1

general fund   state money collected through various state sources to pay most of a state's expenses

1 State Revenue

Every state needs money to carry out its activities. States receive **state revenue** from a variety of sources ranging from state taxes to federal grants. Figure 23-1 shows the breakdown of revenue by source, and lists the dollar total from each source.

Tax Revenue

About half of the revenue collected from state governments comes from **state taxes.** Dollars collected through taxes make up a state's **general fund.**

Decisions about which types of taxes to levy raise very important issues. For example, some people feel that most of the tax burden should be

on those who gain from state government programs. Others argue, however, that the tax burden should be carried by those citizens best able to afford it. The taxes collected by the states are of three kinds: progressive, regressive, and proportional. A progressive tax is one in which the proportion of income paid in taxes rises as income rises. That is, the higher one's income, the higher the tax rate that is paid. For example, a person making $100,000 a year might pay 40 percent of his or her income in taxes, whereas a person making $20,000 a year might pay only 10 percent.

In contrast, a proportional tax takes the same percentage of all incomes. As income rises, the amount of tax rises. The percentage of income paid in taxes, however, remains the same. A regressive tax is one in which the percentage of income paid as taxes decreases as income rises. For example, sales taxes are regressive because everyone pays the same rate.

GENERAL SALES TAX

All states except Alaska, Delaware, Montana, New Hampshire, and Oregon have a statewide **general sales tax,** which is the tax consumers often pay when buying anything from socks to televisions. Only certain items, such as food, medicine, and newspapers are often exempted from the tax. Sales tax is added to the price of an item by the stores, which in turn submit the money to the state. Each state sets its own rate of taxation, ranging from 3 percent in Wyoming to 7 percent in Rhode Island.

For most states with a general sales tax, this is the most important source of revenue. The sales tax is popular because it is easy to collect and is a steady, dependable source of income.

SELECTIVE SALES TAX

A special kind of sales tax is the **selective sales tax.** For instance, all states place special taxes on gasoline, cigarettes, alcohol, and insurance. In addition, 40 states place a special tax on public utilities, such as telephones and electricity. Sometimes the selective sales tax is referred to as an **excise tax.** Excise tax rates vary from state to state and from item to item.

It is becoming increasingly common for states to use selective sales taxes to pay for a related state program. For example, in North Carolina, taxes on alcohol are used to support alcohol treatment programs.

INCOME TAX

The **state income tax** is another valuable source of revenue for states. There are two kinds of income taxes: the individual income tax and the corporate income tax. Combined, these two taxes brought the states about $126 billion in revenue in 1988.

The **individual income tax** is a progressive tax, so the higher a person's income, the higher the tax rate. Rates vary from state to state, but in most states with an individual income tax, persons with incomes below a certain level pay no taxes. Only Alaska, Florida, Nevada, South Dakota, Texas, Washington, and Wyoming have no individual income taxes. In 1992 workers and other persons with sufficient incomes paid states some $105 billion.

All states, with the exception of Nevada, Texas, Washington, and Wyoming, have a **corporate income tax.** The corporate tax rates differ from individual tax rates and also vary from state to state. In most states, corporations are taxed at a uniform rate regardless of income.

The corporate income tax has always been a source of controversy. Critics have argued that the tax burden is often passed on to consumers through higher prices, to employees through lower wages, and to stockholders through lower dividends. States looking to attract new businesses may lower the corporate tax rate to make it more profitable for businesses to operate in that state.

BUSINESS TAXES

In addition to income taxes, businesses may be required to pay other types of taxes. For example, certain kinds of companies, such as amusement parks and taverns, must buy a license before they may open for business. This license is considered a business tax. Another form of special business tax is the **severance tax.** Thirty-three states impose a severance tax on oil and gas, mining, and timber companies.

general sales tax tax paid by consumers on the sale of various commodities

individual income tax tax on the amount of money a person earns

corporate income tax tax on business income

selective sales tax sales tax levied on selected items

excise tax a selective tax on the sale of certain items

severance tax tax imposed on companies that remove and use a state's natural resources

state income tax tax levied on the money a person or business earns

PERSONAL TAXES

States also impose various personal taxes on their citizens. The most widespread is the tax on motor vehicles, which a person pays whenever he or she gets a driver's license or registers a car or motorcycle. Other personal taxes are levied on marriage licenses, hunting and fishing licenses, boating licenses, and so on. Over half the states also impose fees for registering mortgages, stocks, deeds, and other official documents. In addition, all states but Nevada have either a gift tax or an inheritance tax. A gift tax is charged to a person donating a sum of money to another person or organization. An inheritance tax is levied on the amount of money people inherit from an estate.

PROPERTY TAX

Property tax is charged on tangible property a person owns, mostly real estate, although other expensive items such as farm equipment or boats may be included. Tax payments are based on the value of the item and the rate is set by each state.

Historically, when the country was largely agricultural and most people held their wealth in the form of real estate, the property tax was the foremost source of state revenue. As commerce and manufacturing grew, however, many people began to put some of their wealth in stocks, bonds, or businesses. As a result, the less affluent began to assume a greater share of the property tax burden, and the tax became unpopular. In the 1970s and the 1980s, voters in several states began to rebel against property taxes. California residents passed an initiative called Proposition 13 that severely limited the amount of property taxes the state could collect. Massachusetts voters also placed strict limits on property taxes. Other states, fearing similar reactions from their voters, began to look to other taxes and revenue-raising measures as an alternative to property taxes. Today, although 42 states still have some form of property tax, the significance of this tax as a source of revenue has declined.

Nontax Revenue

As noted previously, taxes bring in about half of a state's revenue. The other half comes from various nontax sources, which in 1992 brought in over $415 billion to the states.

INTERGOVERNMENTAL

The largest nontax source of income for states is **intergovernmental revenue,** most of which flows from the national government to state governments. In 1992 this stream of money amounted to over $165 billion.

The states receive funds from the national government in the form of grants-in-aid and cost-sharing funds, which are spent on diverse programs ranging from public welfare to water pollution cleanup to wildlife studies. Figure 23-2 shows how these funds are used. Some federal funds have been more scarce in the 1990s than in previous decades. There are two main reasons for this decline: the continuing shift of responsibilities to the states and the desire to limit the federal deficit. The decline in federal funds began during the Reagan administration when in 1982, for the first time since 1948, federal funds were lower than for the previous year. In 1978 federal funds made up over 26 percent of state revenues, but by 1992 they dropped to only 23 percent. To make up for the losses, states either cut programs or raised taxes, or did both.

Local governments also give money to state governments, but this

intergovernmental revenue money given by one level of government to another

property tax tax paid by owners of certain kinds of property according to the valuation of the property

is generally for accounting purposes, as when local governments repay the states for services the state provided, or when they share the costs of a local project with the state. Far more money goes from states to local governments than in the other direction.

INSURANCE AND RETIREMENT

Another source of nontax revenue comes from insurance and retirement programs that the states operate. People and businesses pay billions of dollars annually into these programs and, in turn, receive benefits. Among these programs are Worker's Compensation, in which workers injured on the job receive benefits; Unemployment Compensation, which pro-

vides benefits for people who have lost their jobs; and retirement funds, which provide benefits to retired state employees. With the first two programs, employers pay the state to manage the programs. The retirement program is funded by state employees. Any profits from any of these funds are usually set aside to support specific programs and are not part of the state's general fund.

BUSINESS ACTIVITIES

States have always been involved in various activities for which they charge fees. For example, they may lease state lands or sell state forests for lumbering. In other instances, the states become involved when a service is needed but no private company

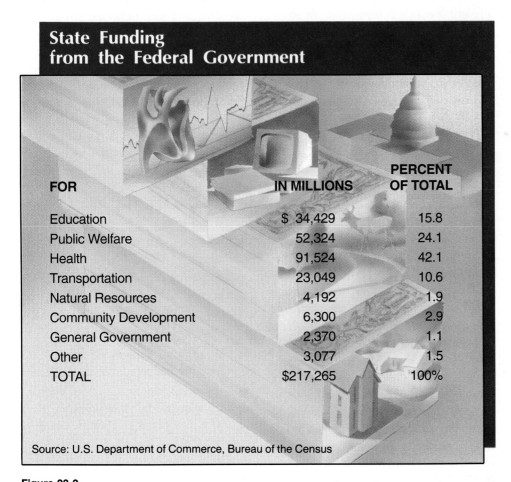

State Funding from the Federal Government

FOR	IN MILLIONS	PERCENT OF TOTAL
Education	$ 34,429	15.8
Public Welfare	52,324	24.1
Health	91,524	42.1
Transportation	23,049	10.6
Natural Resources	4,192	1.9
Community Development	6,300	2.9
General Government	2,370	1.1
Other	3,077	1.5
TOTAL	$217,265	100%

Source: U.S. Department of Commerce, Bureau of the Census

Figure 23-2

is willing or able to do the job. For instance, states may build toll roads or bridges or operate ferries. To recover their costs, they charge user fees, such as tolls and parking fees. The tuition fees paid by students at state colleges and universities also comprise part of state nontax revenue.

After Prohibition ended, some states decided to regulate alcohol by running state liquor stores. Indeed, states have become involved in various business endeavors, as this account from 60 years ago illustrates:

North Dakota has embarked on the construction and operation of grain elevators. New York must administer a great canal with numerous terminals. Two states, South Dakota and Tennessee, have public coal mines, the latter using prison labor in exploiting them. . . . As an adjunct in constructing highways and other public works, states sometimes operate cement mills. A few have power plants.

Yet for the most part, state governments prefer to leave business to private enterprise.

Another rapidly growing source of nontax revenue is the state lottery. As recently as 1980 only 14 states had lotteries. Now, 32 states raise money by legal lotteries, and most other states are considering them. For every dollar spent on a lottery ticket, a state gets from 27 to 72 cents; the rest goes for prizes and administration. Yet, states are raising billions of dollars through this legalized form of gambling. In most states the revenue goes directly into the general fund, but in the rest, it is dedicated to a single purpose. In Florida, for example, lottery proceeds go toward education; in Arizona, profits go toward transportation.

BORROWING

Another source of nontax funds for states is borrowing. Since borrowed money must be repaid, loans are different from other sources of state finance. Borrowing money, however, is a common way for states to push today's costs into the future. Borrowed money usually finances long-range projects, such as building public offices, highways, and bridges, all high-cost items that cannot easily be paid for in one year.

Most states borrow money by selling bonds. Investors buy the bonds to get future interest payments, and the states get the funds for immediate use. Most states have strict limits in their constitutions on the amount of borrowing allowed. In earlier days, when there were no such limits, many states went deeply into debt and some even went bankrupt. Indiana, for example, now prohibits any state debt, because under its first constitution it went bankrupt building canals. Another common check for keeping state debt under control is the requirement for voter approval of such debt.

Section Review

1. What is the most important source of tax revenue in most states?

2. What other kinds of taxes are important to the states?

3. What is the largest source of nontax revenue for states?

4. What other sources of nontax revenue are available to the states?

5. **Challenge:** In your opinion, which is better—a single state income tax rate or a progressive state income tax for individuals? Explain.

2 State Expenditures

Every year, state governments spend billions of dollars providing services that their citizens expect, even demand. In 1992, $700 billion were spent in **state expenditures** to pay for all the activities of state government. These costs have been rising annually in recent years, the result of population growth, inflation, and people's expectations. This last reason is especially significant because at the same time people are expecting more from the states, the national government has stopped funding some programs, leaving states to pick up those costs.

Spending Patterns

States must choose how to invest their time, effort, and financial resources. So the details of state spending vary over time and from state to state. Yet, states follow some general patterns in how they spend their money, with two expenditures standing out as the most costly—education and social services. Other activities, such as state insurance programs, transportation, and public safety, are important also. Figure 23-3 shows the percentage of state spending in each of these areas.

Education

One-third of all state expenditures go to support public education. Education is the largest category of state expenses in every state except New York and Massachusetts, where it is a close second to public welfare.

About two-thirds of education dollars go to elementary and secondary schools to pay for textbooks, teachers' salaries, and so forth. States also support higher education, with at least

one state college or university found in every state. State payments help keep down the cost of higher education, thus making college accessible to more students. Despite higher payments by the states, tuition costs continue to rise.

Social Services

Another major cost to state government is the system of social services provided to persons in need. Indeed, in 1992 alone states spent over $126 billion for social services for their residents. Most of these programs are mandated by the federal government. For example, Aid to Families with Dependent Children (AFDC), Medicaid for the ill, and Old Age Assistance are all programs the states are required to provide. The states receive federal funds for some of these programs, but they are also expected to contribute to these programs through the general revenue.

state expenditures monies spent by a state government

Public education is an important category that is supported by state expenditures. How much state money does public education receive in comparison with other categories?

States also have public health responsibilities and expenditures. They regulate hospitals and toxic wastes; license medical professionals; and conduct health inspections in restaurants, meat-packing plants, grocery stores, and other food sources. For those who are sick, states often operate hospitals or pay private hospitals to care for persons who are the most needy.

Additional state responsibilities include taking care of persons who are unable to receive adequate care other-

COMBINED STATE GOVERNMENT EXPENDITURES, 1992

TYPE	IN MILLIONS	PERCENT OF TOTAL
Education		
Elementary and Secondary Education	$ 2,221	0.4
Higher Education	70,904	14.2
Other	13,525	2.7
Social Services and Income Maintenance		
Public Welfare	125,500	25.2
Hospitals and Health	41,643	8.4
Highways	40,266	8.1
Public Safety		
Police Protection	4,863	1.0
Corrections	13,306	3.7
Environment and Housing		
Natural Resources	9,022	1.8
Parks and Recreation	2,688	0.5
Housing and Community Development	1,606	0.3
Sewerage	2,235	0.4
Insurance Trust	79,895	16.0
Government Administration	19,847	4.0
Interest on General Debt	24,622	4.8
Other Expenditures	41,497	8.4
TOTAL	$498,640	100%

Source: U.S. Department of Commerce, Bureau of the Census

Figure 23-3

This highway in Louisiana was built in part with state funds. Why is state funding of transportation so important?

wise. Among this group are people who are severely mentally handicapped or seriously mentally ill, orphans, abused children, and others who cannot care for themselves.

Other Responsibilities

Each year, states must invest in their transportation systems. Roads must be repaired or widened, bridges maintained, airports updated, and waterways kept open. Transportation is important to public health, safety, employment, and commerce.

Another state duty is ensuring public safety. One of the most visible public safety occupations is the state patrol, which polices state roads and highways. Then there are the thousands of prison cells operated by the state. Prisons cost millions of dollars to build and thousands per prisoner per year to operate. As prison populations grow, the cost to the public to house convicts has skyrocketed.

There are many other areas to which states must allocate funds. States pay for such items as state parks, housing projects, and safe water. In addition, the state governments must pay for state buildings, vehicles, and employees. On the whole, state governments must juggle their responsibilities while keeping the costs within the range taxpayers are willing and able to bear. These decisions are focused in the state budget process.

Section Review

1. What are two reasons for the growth in state government expenditures?

2. What is the largest area of expenditure for state governments?

3. **Challenge:** If you were responsible for developing a state budget, what would be your number one budget concern? Why?

3 State Budgets

state budget the financial plan of a state government

The **state budget** specifies how much revenue the state expects to take in and how much money the state may spend. Because all areas of state governments require money to operate, the budget reflects the state's public policy and priorities. It declares which programs will grow, which will shrink, and which will disappear altogether.

In 29 states, a new budget is adopted each year; in the remaining 21 states, the budget is created on a two-year basis. The fiscal year for a state usually begins on July 1 and ends on June 30. Since most legislative sessions begin at the first of the calendar year, this gives the legislature several months to consider and adopt a new budget before the budget must go into effect. Figure 23-4 shows a typical annual budget cycle, from the beginning to the end of a fiscal year.

Balancing the Budget

Unlike the federal government, states generally cannot go very far into debt. Sometimes they may borrow by issuing bonds for special

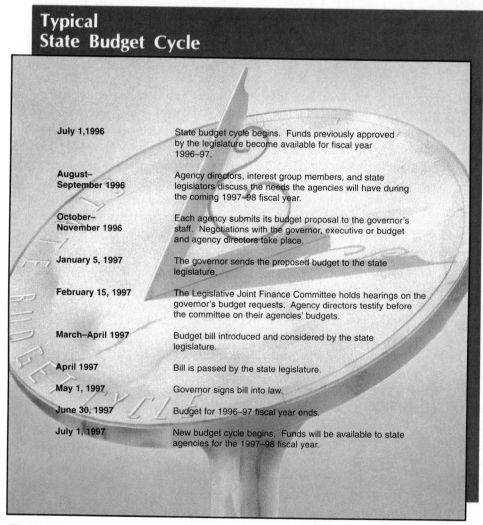

Typical State Budget Cycle

July 1, 1996	State budget cycle begins. Funds previously approved by the legislature become available for fiscal year 1996–97.
August–September 1996	Agency directors, interest group members, and state legislators discuss the needs the agencies will have during the coming 1997–98 fiscal year.
October–November 1996	Each agency submits its budget proposal to the governor's staff. Negotiations with the governor, executive or budget and agency directors take place.
January 5, 1997	The governor sends the proposed budget to the state legislature.
February 15, 1997	The Legislative Joint Finance Committee holds hearings on the governor's budget requests. Agency directors testify before the committee on their agencies' budgets.
March–April 1997	Budget bill introduced and considered by the state legislature.
April 1997	Bill is passed by the state legislature.
May 1, 1997	Governor signs bill into law.
June 30, 1997	Budget for 1996–97 fiscal year ends.
July 1, 1997	New budget cycle begins. Funds will be available to state agencies for the 1997–98 fiscal year.

Figure 23-4

projects, but for day-to-day operations, most states require a balanced budget. In other words, authorized state spending may not exceed state funds.

The requirement for a balanced budget is found in virtually all state constitutions or state statutes. Only Vermont and Wisconsin are silent on this issue. Usually, not only must the executive branch ask for a balanced budget from the legislature, but the legislature must pass a balanced budget as well.

The requirement for a balanced budget at the state level is a twentieth-century development. One political writer noted that until 1920 the budget process was very haphazard, as legislators took no responsibility for fiscal restraint:

Finally at the very close of the session, scores of appropriations were rushed through at lightning speed and thrown upon the governor's table for his approval or veto. If the governor had the power to veto single items, he could cut and slash the bills at his pleasure. Not until the governor was through with his review was it possible to know how much money had been actually appropriated at the legislative session and how much revenue had to be raised to pay the bills.

Achieving a balanced budget is difficult, especially during economic recessions, when revenues are falling. If cuts are needed, there are only certain areas of the budget that may be cut. For instance, education often cannot be cut since public schools statewide have been promised certain funds, usually by law. Similarly, federal programs mandate certain public welfare expenses. There are only a few optional items that can be eliminated. However, these are often the favorite project of some powerful politicians or interest groups, so the pressure to keep them may be strong. Some people argue that the most creative and helpful state programs are the first to be cut whenever there is a funding shortfall.

One additional legal provision in most states makes the task of balancing the budget a full-time job. Most states require that the budget year finish "in the black," or with a surplus. So if state revenues do not come in as expected during the year, the budget must be cut midyear, since deficits may not be carried over from one fiscal year to the next.

Budget Adoption Process

In all states except Mississippi, South Carolina, and Texas, the budget is drawn up by the governor. In those three states, the governor shares power with a legislative committee that has the job of proposing a budget to the legislature. In all states the budget process has many steps, and each state is somewhat different in how the budget process works. Most states, however, follow a pattern.

The first step in the budget adoption process is for each state agency and department to estimate its needs for the upcoming fiscal year. This is not as easy as it sounds, since the demand for government services may vary and may not be easy to predict. For example, when unemployment rises, there is increased call for public welfare services. But, when unemployment drops, more businesses apply for state licenses, and the accountants in the Department of Revenue have more tax forms to handle. Who can accurately predict over a year in advance which way the unemployment numbers will go? Other factors must also be weighed. For example,

These barges are traveling on the Mississippi River, one of the nation's busiest waterways. State budgets usually provide funds for cleaning up and maintaining waterways. How does the state budget process work?

is there any new legislation, state or federal, taking effect? Is there a waiting list? Have computers eased the work load?

In most states, the estimates and requests from all the agencies are submitted to a special department within the executive branch for collation and review. This department, often a division of budget or finance, then analyzes the proposals and makes recommendations to the governor. The governor and key advisers debate how to allocate state resources among the agencies. Because state revenue is limited and because agency needs always seem to exceed those revenues, the difficult job of budgeting is deciding where to cut.

The proposed budget is then submitted to the state legislature, usually in bill form. Once presented, the bill is assigned to a legislative committee,

which may be a special committee that deals with budget issues. California and Kansas have a Legislative Budget Committee, whereas Idaho has a Joint Finance-Appropriations Committee. The budget bill follows the route of all bills on its way to becoming a law. How much change the legislature makes to the budget depends on the state. In some states with a stronger executive branch, the governor's proposed budget is hardly changed. In a few states, the governor's proposed budget is largely ignored. But most states fall somewhere in between; that is, the executive's recommendations are seriously considered but are not the final word.

Once the budget bill has been considered, revised, and passed by the state legislature, it is sent to the governor for signature. In most states, the governor has the legal right to choose among the budget items, vetoing or accepting the items as he or she sees fit. Once signed, the approved items in the budget bill become law. Then, when the new fiscal year begins, those funds are available to the state government.

Influences on the Process

Since the budget is a highly charged political document, many hands want to sculpt it. As a state budget goes through the formal adoption process, many people and factors influence its progress. First is the status of the governor. When the governor is a powerful or popular figure, his or her priorities carry great weight. They carry even greater weight when the legislature is controlled by his or her political party. When the governor is a weaker figure, or of a different political party than the legislators, however, there are often conflicts between the two branches. These antagonisms can make for poor budgeting, as power struggles interfere with objective needs.

Federal decisions also may play a significant, though indirect, role in setting state budgets. When the federal government legislates certain standards—for example, water pollution standards—state governments may have to put more money into cleaning up waterways than they would have otherwise. Or when the federal government authorizes funding for a special project, such as a grant to set up a rural clinic, a state will be pressured to assume the additional financial obligations when the federal funding ends.

Judicial decisions, at the federal or state level, may also dictate what the state may or may not do. The state courts might say that the legislature may not use money in certain ways. Perhaps the court ruled that toll road funds may not be used to pay for highway signs; then the budget must be changed to reflect this ruling. Sometimes the use of millions of dollars is at stake in various lawsuits. In several states, for example, the federal courts have ruled that prison overcrowding is cruel and unusual punishment prohibited by the Bill of Rights. As a result, under court order, the states have had to appropriate funds to build new prisons.

The impact of special interest groups cannot be overemphasized. As state power has grown, so have the lobbying efforts of state-level interest groups. Since the 1980s, almost any issue lobbied on the national scene has state counterparts. While Congress considered raising the federal minimum wage, states also were considering the same issue. The most controversial issues of our times, from gun control to abortion to censorship, are argued by lobbyists in all 50 states, and all of these issues have their costs. Depending on the state budget process in their respective states, these groups may pressure the governor, the executive branch managers, the legislative committees, or individual legislators.

Section Review

1. What part does the governor play in drawing up the state budget?

2. What is meant by a balanced budget?

3. Name four factors that influence the state budget-making process.

4. **Challenge:** In your opinion, should states require their budgets to be balanced? Why or why not?

4 Policy Issues

State governments today are concerned about how society should be shaped, regulated, and protected. It is a safe bet that there is no human activity or need which cannot be or has not been debated in a state legislature. Some of their concerns cross state and even national boundaries, so it is not surprising that state legislatures have gone on record as condemning repression in China or apartheid in South Africa. Yet many of their concerns are closer to home.

In looking at a few examples of the sorts of issues, small and large, that confront states, we can see that state decisions are not easily reached. There are trade-offs, compromises, and raging debates on thousands of state issues. Finding an acceptable state policy on controversial issues is the legislative goal, but there is no guarantee that this is possible. Where emotions run high, this is particularly difficult. Many issues are like a jagged rock that gets banged around each session, until the sharp edges are worn off. The rocky issue does not simply disappear, but it may become manageable over time.

Crime and Punishment

Each year crime rates, especially for violent crimes, are on the rise. In 1992, for example, 22,540 Americans were murdered. This represents a 3.9 percent increase over 1991. Aggravated assaults totaled 1,127,000 in 1992. In fact, more than 1.9 million violent crimes were committed that year.

Given these statistics, is it any wonder that in every community crime is on the minds of citizens? In addition, the people are expressing their concerns about such related issues as: What can be done to stop crime from growing? Are the police doing a good job? Should criminals be punished or rehabilitated? These are emotional, personal issues to most citizens, and every state is deeply involved in seeking solutions.

Solutions may vary because ideas about what is legal and illegal vary from state to state. In some states, for example, motorcycle riders must wear helmets, while in other states such helmets are optional. Similarly, seat belt usage is mandatory in some states and optional in others. In addition, each state sets its own consequences for breaking the law. For example, a driver going 85 miles per hour in a 55-mile-per-hour zone could be fined up to $101 in Idaho, $113 in Tennessee, $180 in Washington, and $260 in Maryland. In other states, drivers

Because today's world is so interdependent, state legislatures have often expressed opinions on global issues, such as apartheid in South Africa. How do state governments reach decisions on important issues both at home and abroad?

caught going that fast would face an automatic date in court, where the judge would decide the punishment.

One issue that continues to trouble legislators in all states is the death penalty. Although most states have some sort of death penalty for persons convicted of committing certain crimes, every state has its own standards as to what constitutes such a crime. In addition, not all legislators agree that a death penalty should exist.

Opponents believe that civilized society cannot condone murder, regardless of whether it is of innocent victims or their convicted killers. In addition, they argue that the poor, especially minorities, are more likely to be sentenced to death. Supporters of the death penalty argue that it deters people from committing crimes. Besides, they argue, because violent criminals are sentenced to life in prison, why should taxpayers pay over $20,000 a year to support a prisoner who will never get out? Since the Supreme Court has ruled that the death penalty is constitutional, the states will continue to wrestle with this thorny issue.

Throughout the 1990s, state legislators have reacted to several decades of rising crime by increasing the penalties for many crimes. For some crimes, this has meant mandatory prison sentences; for other crimes it has meant longer sentences. The result nationwide has been a dramatic surge in the number of people in state prisons. In 1970, for example, only 97 out of every 100,000 people were imprisoned. This figure was 142 in 1980 and 330 in 1992.

Prison systems are tremendously expensive. Construction costs; guards; food and clothes for prisoners; and work, education, or therapy programs for prisoners who will be released, all add up to billions of dollars nationwide. Yet because each prison is filled with society's lawbreakers, some states have been reluctant to spend even the minimum amount required to keep prisons humane or safe. As a result, the courts have had to intervene in 38 states to ensure that at least certain standards of space, cleanliness, and reasonable treatment are implemented.

All states are examining alternatives to continued imprisonment of large numbers of people. Some are looking at a "boot camp" for first-time offenders to instill discipline in them. Other states are looking at probation or community halfway houses where offenders, under supervision, are allowed to work in the community. Regardless of the alternatives, however, 63 percent of those released from prison will be rearrested for serious crimes within three years. Young offenders are far more likely to "reoffend" than older prisoners. As a result, crime and punishment issues will continue to face citizens and states.

The Economy

Economic health is a primary concern for every state. Both the executive and legislative branches keep close watch on the local economies, focusing on such issues as the number of people working, the profitability of businesses, and the direction of the economy. It is not clear what a state can or should do to maintain its economic well-being, but most are actively trying to do something.

States enact many policies that affect the well-being of their economies. In education, states decide whether or not to fund colleges, provide student loans, or offer scholarships. Similarly, every state sets tax policies for corporations and individuals. Corporate taxes, along with other business regulations, either encourage or discourage businesses to stay or move to another state. North Carolina, for example, passed favorable banking laws that attracted major regional banks. This has, in turn, brought money and employment to the state.

States try to diversify their economies so that no one industry dominates. Economies based on single industries are vulnerable if that industry takes a downturn, which happens all the time. The auto industry has declined, family farming has declined, steel plants have closed, and so on. States that were dependent on oil and gas businesses, such as Texas, Wyoming, and Louisiana, were devastated when oil prices dropped from $35 to $16 a barrel. Thousands of workers were laid off, and hundreds of companies went bankrupt. Learning a lesson, Texas passed various laws to encourage development of research and computer industries. Texas taxpayers also subsidize businesses moving to the state.

State natural resources also are under state legal supervision. Mining laws may be flexible or unyielding, water and air pollution may be strictly regulated or ignored, and wilderness areas may be preserved or destroyed.

Alaska is an interesting example of the issues. Its economy is highly dependent on oil production, and taxes on the oil business make up most state revenues. Yet when the ship *Exxon Valdez* ran aground and spilled 10 million gallons of oil fouling 800 miles (1280 kilometers) of pristine shoreline, many people began to question that dependence on oil. Alaska, like every other state, is looking at its options and planning its future economy.

Environment

In recent years, states have assumed greater responsibility for managing the environment—for dealing with radioactive wastes, plastics that do not decompose, overflowing landfills, acid rain, smog, disposal of medical wastes, and the dumping of garbage in the oceans, to name just a few issues. Often states tackle these problems before the national government has acted. For example, Pennsylvania approved a tough strip-mine reclamation law long before a similar federal law was passed. With firsthand knowledge of local problems, states can often implement safeguards more efficiently than can the federal agencies. The question is, *will* they?

In the 1990s, states paid more attention to safeguarding the environment. States no longer avoided or ignored environmental problems. They realized that many of the choices about economies, wealth, and employment directly affect our air, land, and water. For decades many industries argued that pollution controls were so costly that businesses would go bankrupt and salaries would have to be cut to implement such controls. Yet pollution usually affects the health, comfort, and surroundings of residents.

The environmental issue affects virtually every community. One example illustrates the complexity of many situations. The Pigeon River in North Carolina is a pristine stream until it reaches a paper mill, which has been dumping wastes there for over 80 years. Down river, it is just a sewer:

. . .*the Pigeon has been transmogrified into a sludgy mess that looks like coffee and smells as bad as rotten eggs. The cause of this revolting change: industrial wastes.*

But the polluting paper mill provides employment for 2200 families in an area of high unemployment. So, repeatedly, the state has given the mill approval to discharge industrial wastes into the river. When some downstream residents went to court to force a cleanup, the paper company warned that it would shut down the mill instead. Added to this controversy was some additional evidence that the mill's wastes included cancer-causing dioxin.

The pros and cons of allowing environmental damage are argued vehemently in every state, but there are no easy answers. Some states, however, have come to believe that there is no conflict between jobs and environmental protection. They feel that to attract and retain businesses and skilled workers, they must offer a positive quality of life.

Education

The question of who should pay for whose education is an ongoing issue for every state. In the past, money to support public schools came only from local property taxes. But, increased enrollments, higher teacher salaries, expensive equipment, and inflation brought about sharp rises in costs that could not be met through property taxes alone. And given the decline in property taxes as a source of revenue, states must now determine how to raise the needed funds and how to distribute them equitably to school districts throughout the state. In 1960 public education cost taxpayers almost $16 billion, but by 1992 states alone were spending $212 billion.

Even more important, states must decide what they expect public schools to do. The answer is not as easy as it once appeared to be. For

example, schools have been asked to teach basic education; instill moral values and appreciation of the arts; prevent school dropouts; sponsor sports teams; detect child abuse; provide sex education; dispense health advice; counsel students with alcohol and drug problems; identify visual, hearing, and learning problems; teach students social skills; and ensure that students develop good work skills and attitudes. Educators ask how they can accomplish these tasks in a lifetime, much less in a few school years. Yet, each state has placed a set of expectations on its schools.

One key word now in education is *excellence*. States have tried to achieve this goal in various ways. A growing number of states require students to pass competency tests to advance to the next grade. And some states require teachers to pass state tests as well. Some states have considered increasing the school day or school year to give students more time in the classroom. Many states are also raising graduation requirements.

States expect schools to provide services, such as sports events, so that students will have a well-rounded education. What requirements have states set to achieve excellence in education?

Providing affordable housing is a responsibility that involves federal, state, and local governments as well as private enterprise. What other kinds of social services are jointly funded or administered by state and federal governments?

Social and Health Issues

The states are usually held responsible for the health and well-being of their residents. But, because of the size of this task, states can assume only certain aspects of safeguarding citizens. Poverty, affordable housing, discrimination, homelessness, lack of emergency medical services, and dozens of other issues can never be resolved solely by a single layer of government.

Many vital social welfare programs are jointly funded or administered by the state and federal governments. Aid to Families with Dependent Children (AFDC) and Medicaid, both mentioned earlier, are examples of joint programs. While the federal government may set certain requirements, such as who may qualify for AFDC, the states are responsible for ensuring that services get to the needy.

Social issues do not pertain only to the poor or disadvantaged. Increasingly, states are called upon to address such individual and family problems as teenage pregnancy, drug and alcohol addiction, and child abuse, which know no boundaries of income or class.

At the same time, the states are unsure about how to handle such problems. For example, about 1200 children die annually from neglect or physical abuse. Half of the cases had been previously reported to state agencies. Sometimes the state will remove children from abusive homes, such as where both parents are alcoholics, only to have the child wind up in one foster home after another. At any one time, a single social worker may be handling 70 to 80 cases, so it is difficult to decide how best to serve each child's needs.

The state hires, trains, and supervises social workers and is ultimately responsible for administering many social and health care agencies. But, state legislators, administrators, and the courts are continually wrestling with the issue of what the limits of the role of the state government in this area should be.

States also make other decisions that set out how society is conducted. For example, the state sets the "age of majority," that is, the minimum age for entering a legally binding contract. In most states that age is 18, but in Alabama, Nebraska, and Wyoming it is 19, and in Pennsylvania it is 21.

States also set the age at which one can marry, either with or without a parent's consent. Without parental

ISSUE: INITIATIVES VS. STATUTES

SHOULD VOTERS MAKE LAWS?

Imagine walking into a voting booth with a ballot that asks you not only to vote on national and state offices but also to decide on 54 separate issues. Voters in San Francisco faced that situation in the fall of 1988, causing one political writer to suggest that voters bring a sleeping bag and food to the polls! The 54 issues that San Francisco's voters had to consider included a number of initiatives related to local and state financial matters.

San Francisco was not the only place where voters faced such initiatives. A sample of questions that voters across the nation were asked to decide included: Should state governments be required to roll back taxes? Should state money be used to pay for abortions for underprivileged women? Should gambling be legalized? Should a deposit be required on all beverage containers?

As the popularity of initiatives grows, so does controversy regarding the process. The initiative, a product of the Progressive movement of the 1890s and early 1900s, was designed to give people a more direct voice in lawmaking. State legislatures at the time were often controlled by special interests, such as mining or railroad companies. Today, 21 states have provisions for using the initiative as a means of amending state constitutions, enacting state laws, or both. Since 1980, 21 more states have considered the idea.

The most basic reason why people like initiatives is that they represent "government by the people." Some people say initiatives allow the people to overturn laws they do not like without having to convince the legislature, which wrote the laws in the first place. Others argue that initiatives can deal quickly with issues the legislature cannot or will not decide.

Opponents of initiatives claim that while the theory is good, the practice leaves much to be desired. In most states, it is relatively easy for an organized interest group to gather enough signatures to get an issue on the ballot. Initiative issues are never discussed in a public forum, such as the legislative process of hearings and floor debates. Voters can only say yes or no, and changes

are not possible. Despite the fact that a successful initiative becomes law word-for-word, there is no check before that it is clearly written. In fact, many initiatives have later been struck down by the courts as unconstitutional.

In response to these criticisms, reformers of the initiative process have proposed a number of changes. They suggest that the initiative procedure be changed to make it more difficult to get an issue on the ballot. They also propose that initiatives be sent first to the legislature for discussion and possible action. Finally, they believe that campaign contributions to legislators from special interest groups should be limited. In this way, legislators would be able to better deal with the public issues that become initiatives.

In considering the value and proper use of initiatives, difficult questions must be asked: Where do voters get information to make sound decisions? Does an initiative destroy the foundation of representative democracy? If the initiative were abolished, what recourse would citizens have if they cannot get government to respond to their concerns? Public debate over these questions is likely to continue for years.

1. Why have initiatives become popular in recent years?
2. What are some criticisms of initiatives? What changes in the process have been suggested?

States set standards and provide tests for driving. They also decide on the minimum age (usually between 16 and 18 years of age) for obtaining a driver's license. In what other areas do states set age requirements?

approval marriage partners must be at least 18, except in Mississippi where they must be 21 and Wyoming where they must be 19. With the consent of a parent, the range is usually 13 to 17. Similarly, states decide on the minimum age for obtaining a driver's license, drinking alcohol, leaving school, and sitting on a jury.

Other types of social issues surface regularly in states. For example, Idaho and Oregon have spent years trying to reach fair agreements over Native American land and water rights, which have too often been trampled in the name of progress. Other states are struggling with deciding what languages should be officially recognized for government business. Seventeen states, including Florida and California, which have large Hispanic populations, have adopted English as the official language prompting outcries from some ethnic minorities. No aspect of the social relations of individuals and groups is exempt from controversy and state legislation.

Federal Relations

State problem-solving abilities are closely tied to federal government actions. That is the beauty and frustration of a federal system of government. Three examples will illustrate this point.

First, a glance at federal immigration policies shows that states must be able to react to whatever policies are set. If immigration from Latin America is encouraged, southern border states from Florida to California must be able to absorb new Spanish-speaking immigrants. Similarly, if the United States reaches new agreements with Russia on Jewish emigration, New York and other large cities may expect large numbers of new Russian-speaking residents.

Another example of the federal role in state projects is the proposed Two Forks Dam on the Platte River in Colorado. The federal Environmental Protection Agency (EPA) vetoed the construction of this project, which would have provided water for new Denver suburbs. Even though water users, not the federal government, would have paid for the dam, the EPA felt that flooding a scenic canyon and potentially drying up the Platte as it flowed into Nebraska was unacceptable. As a result, the Denver suburbs had to change their water plans due to a federal decision.

Another type of state issue centers around the location of federal facilities. A nuclear weapons construction plant may not make a good neighbor if it generates hazardous waste, but the federal government has to locate the plants somewhere. Other states find ''clean'' federal facilities, such as federal research laboratories, naval ports, or communications centers, to be highly desirable, so interstate competition for these facilities is fierce. The states are also affected when the federal government closes federal facilities. In 1993 the military closed or cut back 165 bases, affecting the majority of states coast to coast. While from the federal perspective this saves $3 billion a year in expenditures, from the states' viewpoint they are losing the revenue that these bases generate for local economies.

Section Review

1. What issues must states deal with concerning crime?

2. On what economic issues do most states focus?

3. What are three environmental issues facing most states today?

4. **Challenge:** Do you feel that students should be required to pass minimum competency tests? Why or why not?

Summary

1. State governments depend on state taxes for nearly half of their total revenue. Money received from state taxes goes into a general fund.

2. Other major sources of state revenues are intergovernmental funds, insurance and retirement programs, government business activities, and borrowing.

3. Population growth, inflation, and increased demand for state services have caused state spending to grow.

4. States spend most of their money on education and social services, followed by state insurance programs, transportation, and public safety.

5. Each state has a budget to determine how to spend money. More than one-half of the states adopt a new budget every year; the other states adopt a new budget every two years.

6. State budgets are adopted by a formal process that involves the governor, state legislature, certain special interest groups, and often the courts and federal government.

7. State budget problems are related to the priority given to certain programs, the need for a balanced budget, spending limits, and earmarked funds for specific programs and projects.

8. Most states deal with the disagreement as to who should carry the tax burden by levying different kinds of taxes.

9. State tax reforms have led to limits on state revenue and state spending.

10. Changes in the economy and decreases in federal funds to states have significantly affected state revenues.

11. In addition to state budget issues, state governments are also concerned with policy issues such as crime and punishment, ensuring quality education, protecting the environment, and ensuring residents' health and well-being.

12. Other issues facing each state are such intergovernmental issues as its relations with the federal government, other states, and with local governments.

Chapter 23 Review

★ Building Vocabulary

Several of the new terms introduced in this chapter appear below. Use each word correctly in a sentence. You may use more than one of the terms in the same sentence.

1. state revenue
2. general fund
3. selective sales tax
4. state income tax
5. corporate income tax
6. property tax
7. state expenditures
8. state taxes
9. general sales tax
10. excise tax
11. individual income tax
12. severance tax
13. intergovernmental revenue
14. state budget

★ Reviewing Facts

1. What are six sources of state tax revenue?
2. How do states generate nontax revenue?
3. What are the five major categories of state expenditures?
4. What procedure do states use to borrow money?
5. What are the usual steps in adopting a state budget?
6. In what ways do special interest groups try to influence the budget adoption process?
7. What types of taxing and spending issues cause problems for state governments?
8. What factors often affect state spending limits?
9. What kinds of policy issues concern state governments?
10. On what kinds of issues might a state and the federal government differ?
11. What alternatives are available to states when revenues decline?

★ Analyzing Facts

1. If you were a governor or legislator, how would you decide which state programs to fund and which ones the state could not afford?

2. Education is the largest state expenditure. Yet, the public is concerned about school performance and educational standards. At the same time, many states have adopted public spending limits. How would you solve this conflict?

3. Environmental issues have become increasingly important for states in recent years. What are some environmental issues in your state and how is your state dealing with them?

4. What advantages or disadvantages do you see in 50 states proposing 50 different standards for a policy issue such as punishing armed robbers or licensing hazardous waste disposal?

5. How has the decline in federal funds to states affected your state's budget?

★ Evaluating Ideas

1. Compare your state's budget to the information in this chapter. How do they differ? Why do you think this happens?

2. You are a lobbyist for a program whose funds have been cut. Pick a program and develop an argument to present to the legislature that will persuade the policymakers to restore the program's funding.

Using Your
Civic Participation Journal

Review the information about local property tax rates that you recorded in your Civics Participation Journal. Use the information to calculate how much the owner of a home valued at $50,000 would pay in taxes each year. Then write an essay either favoring or opposing a 10 percent increase in the property tax rate.

3. Which, do you think, is a better source of state revenue—sales taxes or income taxes? Why?

4. In your opinion, what are possible solutions that states might follow in order to solve the problem of fair water use rights?

5. Besides the methods proposed in this chapter, what possible solutions would you offer to states struggling with the problem of overcrowded prisons?

★ Critical Thinking
Supporting Generalizations

As you learned in the Critical Thinking Skill for Chapter 15, a generalization is a broad statement, without any details or evidence, about a certain topic. For generalizations to be useful, evidence that supports them must exist.

Explanation As previously indicated, the usefulness of a generalization is based on the evidence available to support it. To truly support a generalization, that evidence must meet these standards.

1. Statements of evidence must relate directly to the generalization.

2. The evidence must have a basis in fact.

You can apply these standards to generalizations you are tempted to make or to evaluate generalizations that you read or hear.

Practice The following example applies the above standards to evaluate a generalization by examining all of its supporting evidence.

Generalization:

No other country has had such a clearcut policy for growth as the United States.

Supporting statements:

1. *The original 13 states have been joined by 37 others over the past 200 years.*

2. *The United States has added territory through negotiation, purchase, and war.*

3. *The Constitution does not limit the number of states that may be admitted to the Union.*

4. *Even before the Constitution, Congress established the methods and conditions for new states to come into the Union.*

5. *The philosophy of Manifest Destiny, or expansion from Atlantic to Pacific, influenced American foreign policy through most of the nineteenth century.*

The generalization is poorly supported. The statements are logical and each as a good basis in fact. But statements 1 and, possibly, 2 are not directly related to the generalization. While they certainly prove a *history* of growth, they do not support the claim of a *policy,* or plan, for growth. Statement 3, although a fact, really has almost nothing to do with the generalization. Only statements 4 and 5 directly support it by providing evidence of a policy for growth.

Independent Practice Study the cartoon about special interests in Congress at the bottom of this page. Decide whether each of the following statements supports the generalization that Congress is subject to special interests.

1. Congress voted down reforms that would limit campaign contributions.

2. Special interests provide most of the contributions to congressional campaigns.

Chapter 24

Local Government

Long before the states were formed, some cities and towns were providing government services for their citizens. Today, local units continue to play unique roles in the American governmental system. In this chapter you will learn what the various types of local governments are, how they are administered, and how they directly affect the lives of all citizens.

★ ★ ★ ★ ★

Chapter Preview

TERMS TO KNOW
local governments, counties, boroughs, parishes, county seat, county board, townships, county commissioners, ordinances, board-manager plan, board-chief executive plan, municipalities, metropolitan area, home rule, incorporation, charter, mayor-council form, wards, weak-mayor plan, strong-mayor plan, council-manager form, commission form, New England town, special district

READ TO DISCOVER
- what the foundations of local government are.
- how county governments are organized and how they function.
- how municipal governments are organized and how they function.
- how other types of local governments are organized and function.

Civic Participation Journal

Contact your local law enforcement agency to find out what programs they have that enlist citizen support to help combat crime. If you have time, you may wish to volunteer to help with one of these programs. Record your findings in your journal.

1 Foundations of Local Government

Today, the importance of local governments is highlighted by their vast numbers and the many services they provide for the people of their communities.

What Are Local Governments?

local governments units of government found within a state

During its eruption in 1980, Mount Saint Helens caused many deaths and tremendous damage in the southern part of the state of Washington. Local communities in the devastated area sought emergency state aid. In what other ways do local communities depend on state government to meet their needs?

There are many different kinds of **local governments,** including cities, towns, and counties. They often are described as being "closest to the people," because they provide many of the services people rely on every day: water, schools, hospitals, libraries, street maintenance, and airports, to name just a few. It takes thousands of people to keep local governments operating.

LEGAL STATUS
The relationship between local governments and the states is different than that between the states and the national government. The state-national relationship is a federal one, which means that each level of government derives its powers from a source legally superior to both, the United States Constitution. In cases of conflict, the authority of the national government generally takes precedence over the authority of the states. But the states and the national government exist and operate in parallel fashion.

The relationship between local governments and the states, on the other hand, is unitary. In a unitary government, the ultimate power to govern is held by a central government, or in this case, the state. All units of local government, whether cities, counties, or special districts, are legally inferior to the state government. They are created by the state either through law or through constitutional provision. Local governments derive their authority from the state. States impose duties and limitations upon local units and can legally abolish any local government.

As a result of this unitary relationship, decisions made at the state level directly affect local governments. States often depend on local units to implement state policies and programs. Similarly, local governments depend on the states to meet their needs. In times of emergency brought about by fire, flood, or drought, for example, local governments may seek emergency state aid. Or to attract more business to a community, local leaders may lobby the state government to build a new highway near or through their area.

NUMBER
The United States has one national government and 50 state governments. The number of local govern-

ments, as you might expect, is huge in comparison. As shown in Figure 24-1, there were 86,743 local governments in 1992, and this number is constantly changing. Between 1972 and 1992, as you can see, the number of every kind of local government changed in some way. However, they were numbers not evenly distributed throughout the country. For instance, as of 1992 there were 6810 local governments in Illinois, while Hawaii had only 21.

Many different local governments may cover a single area. How is this possible? Most American citizens are governed by a county, a city, and other special district governments at the same time.

GOVERNMENTS IN THE UNITED STATES, 1972–1992

TYPE OF GOVERNMENT	NUMBER OF UNITS 1972	NUMBER OF UNITS 1992
National	1	1
State	50	50
Local		
Counties	3,044	3,043
Municipalities	18,517	19,296
Townships	16,991	16,666
Special Districts	39,666	47,687
Total	78,269	86,743

Source: *Statistical Abstract of the United States,* 1980 and 1994
Figure 24-1

Local Government Services

Local governments provide many of the same services as state governments. They keep records, repair roads and bridges, care for the environment, provide health care, and give public assistance to people who are needy. But some services can be provided more efficiently in a local setting than by the state. These include fire and police protection, public transportation, public education, and recreational facilities.

The services local governments must provide are described in a state's constitution and in various state laws. These services vary from one area to another, depending on many factors. Population is one. A city the size of Miami or Detroit has far more needs than a town so small it has only one stoplight. Other factors, such as location, physical geography, climate, and wealth also influence the kind and number of services provided by local governments.

Who actually provides these services? Tens of thousands of women and men are needed to do the daily work of local governments. Local governments employ far more people than state and federal governments combined. Currently, local employees number over 11 million coast to coast, or about 59 percent of all civilian workers at all levels of government. Local employees include librarians, school teachers, street maintenance workers, bus drivers, nurses, and office clerks. Nationwide, one of every 6 people who work do so for a local government.

Section Review

1. What form of government describes the relationship between local governments and the states?

2. What kinds of services do local governments provide?

3. **Challenge:** What services of local government have you used so far today?

2 County Government

counties local units of government originally designed to govern rural areas

boroughs county governments in Alaska

parishes county governments in Louisiana

county seat town in which county business is conducted

There are 3042 **counties** in the United States. Counties are established by a state to serve its administrative needs. Only Connecticut and Rhode Island do not have organized county governments. In Alaska these local governmental units are known as **boroughs,** and in Louisiana they are called **parishes.**

The first American county governments were organized by English settlers who had similar forms of local government in their homeland. A town that was geographically centered in the county usually was made the **county seat.** Most day-to-day business, such as record-keeping and court operations, takes place there.

Counties in America were originally designed to govern rural areas, and there they remain the most important units of local government. But many counties also contain large urban areas, and therefore must provide services similar to those provided by cities elsewhere. In fact, some counties are made up of one large city, such as Denver County in Colorado.

Number and Size

The number of counties differs in each state. Delaware and Hawaii have only three counties each, while seven states have 100 or more. The number is determined by that state's legislature and does not necessarily depend upon the state's size. Alaska, the largest state, has only eight counties. The second largest, Texas, has 254. Although part of this difference is accounted for by population density, this is only one factor a state uses to set up counties.

Counties can be large or small, again depending on how the state legislature chooses. New York County, New York, covering only 22 square miles, is the smallest county in the United States. The largest, San Bernardino County in California, is more than 900 times that size, covering 20,102 square miles.

County Government Services

There are a number of services that county governments typically provide. As official record-keepers for their communities, counties keep

Seattle, in the state of Washington, is an important manufacturing and trading center of the Pacific Northwest. In addition to being Washington's largest metropolitan area, Seattle also is the seat of King County. Why do states have county governments?

Public libraries are among the services provided by county governments. What other services do county governments make available to local citizens?

track of birth and death certificates, deeds, mortgages, marriage licenses, and other official documents.

Most counties also provide certain police and regulatory services. In some areas, police protection is supplied through the county sheriff's department. Many counties have their own court systems and help administer state trial courts as well. In addition, counties may control the issuing of certain licenses and permits. For example, the county may determine business zones, or areas where industry may locate. Often, too, the county enforces health and safety regulations, such as inspecting restaurants for cleanliness.

Counties also play an important role in the election process. They are responsible for registering voters, preparing ballots, supervising elections, and keeping election records on behalf of state governments. This is an example of a state function delegated to local units because they are closer to the people. Finally, counties provide a wide range of other services. These include constructing and maintaining roads; assessing and collecting taxes; maintaining parks, libraries, airports, and hospitals; and administering welfare programs.

County Government Structure

Because state laws and needs differ, the organization of county governments varies from one state to another. Generally, there is no central administration or executive officer that coordinates county functions. Elected board members and appointed officials direct most county operations without strong central leadership. And, it is not uncommon for certain county officials, whether elected or appointed, to hold both executive and legislative powers. For example, county officials sometimes make laws as well as enforce them. This arrangement often leads to confusion when such powers and responsibilities overlap, due to limited governmental checks and balances.

COUNTY BOARDS

The men and women elected to carry out county business serve on a **county board.** These are also called boards of commissioners or, in some states, boards of supervisors. While most county boards hold public meetings at least once a month, special meetings may be called when necessary, such as around budget time.

county board group of citizens elected to carry out the county's business

County boards pass
ordinances on such
matters as the
vaccination of pets.
What other powers do
county boards have?

Most counties are divided into
smaller units of government called
townships. Voters from each of these
districts usually elect members of the
county board. However, in some
counties the members are elected at
large, depending on state law. The
number elected to serve on a board
usually is three to seven, although
counties that include large cities may
have as many as 100 board members.
Once elected, **county commissioners**
serve two- or four-year terms. Since
formal requirements to run for the
position are few, commissioners tend
to reflect a wide variety of backgrounds.

One commissioner commonly is
elected chairperson to sign papers on
behalf of the board and to run the
meetings. The board has the legislative power to enact **ordinances,**
which may cover a wide range of
subjects. Ordinances may be passed,
for instance, to regulate traffic, vacci-
nate pets, or provide penalties for
public drunkenness. Boards also levy
taxes to pay for their work and fix the
amounts to be spent for each county
function in their annual budget.

The county board often serves as
the county's executive branch as well.
It supervises the purchase, maintenance, and sale of county property,
such as buildings, emergency vehicles, or land. But as the number and
complexity of issues facing county
governments has grown, some counties have attempted to separate executive and legislative functions. As a
result, two new types of governmental
structures have appeared.

The **board-manager plan** leaves
legislative and policy-making powers
in the hands of the board, but gives
some executive duties to a manager.
This person is hired by the board and
can be fired at any time for any
reason. He or she is responsible for
carrying out the board's policies and
making sure that daily county operations run smoothly. This plan is used
in over 500 counties across the nation.

The **board-chief executive plan**
also leaves legislative and policy roles
with the board, but gives administrative duties to a more powerful chief
executive officer. The difference between this plan and the board-
manager plan is that the executive
officer is elected by the people, not
appointed by the board. Chief executives are granted power to prepare the
county budget, supervise county employees, suggest policies to the board,
and act as the county spokesperson.
These powers are limited, however,
by the veto power of the board. About
60 relatively large counties, such as
Cook County, Illinois, use this division of duties.

SPECIAL BOARDS

In some counties, special boards are
created to perform specific tasks.
Members of these boards may be
appointed by county commissioners,
judges, or state officials. Or they may
be elected by the people.

One example of a special board is a county board of health. It may make or recommend health and sanitation regulations. It also may administer a county hospital or clinic, or may carry out such state health programs as inoculation programs for children. Another special board is the board of elections, which handles voter registration and election procedures.

Some counties have their own public school systems. In these areas, a county board of education oversees the administration of the schools. The board may be appointed by the local governing body or may be dependent on it for funds. In most places, however, the county board of education is independent of other local governments. The school board then usually is elected by the people, can draw up its own budget, and may even collect its own taxes.

Other County Officials

Besides board members, a number of other officials serve in most county governments. Usually directly elected by the voters of the county, these officials and their departments do much of the daily county work. Some of the main officers are the sheriff, the prosecuting attorney, and county court judges. Others include the county treasurer, coroner, clerk, auditor, and county assessor.

A variety of other county officers are found across the United States. Some counties may have an engineer who oversees the location, design, and construction of county roads and bridges. A surveyor may be hired to determine property boundaries. In more than half the states, a county superintendent of schools manages the development of education programs, oversees school property, and keeps personnel records.

The judicial branch of government in the county is the county court. County judges may address questions of both local and state law. County courts generally are trial courts, hearing both civil and criminal cases. They also may handle appeals from lower courts. Usually, county courts are funded and administered by the county and are presided over by paid judges who are elected by the voters.

Surveyors are hired by county governments to determine property boundaries. What county officials are elected by voters?

Section Review

1. What determines the number and size of counties in a state?

2. Name four services provided by county governments.

3. What is the main difference between a board-manager plan and a board-chief executive plan?

4. Who are some of the main officers of county government?

5. **Challenge:** What services are provided by your county government?

3 Municipal Government

In 1990, 75 percent of the American people lived in urban, or highly populated, areas. To be classified as urban, an area generally has at least 50,000 persons in the central city or the city plus adjacent suburbs. Over the years, more and more people have moved from rural to urban areas because that is where the jobs are. In 1790 only 5 percent of Americans lived in cities. This number had increased to 40 percent by 1900.

Urban areas with their own units of government are called **municipalities.** The forms of government for municipalities are defined in state laws. There are 19,290 municipal governments in the nation today. While an overwhelming number of cities have less than 50,000 people, several cities may run together to form a **metropolitan area.** Officially, there are 323 metropolitan areas in the country. They range from Lewiston, Maine, in the East to Honolulu, Hawaii, in the West; and from Anchorage, Alaska, in the North down to Brownsville, Texas, in the South. Altogether more than 187 million Americans live in metropolitan areas.

In most states, the more populous municipalities are called cities. New York City, with 7 million inhabitants, is the largest city in the nation. Municipalities with smaller populations often are called towns, villages, or boroughs.

Regardless of their size or type, all municipal governments provide similar services to their communities. Some of these are police and fire protection, garbage collection, snow removal, and street repair. In addition, municipal governments provide and maintain street lights, water supplies, parks, museums, and libraries.

Legal Status

Because of the unitary nature of state government in America, states have complete control over all local governments within their borders.

municipalities urban areas governed by their own units of government; include towns, cities, and villages

metropolitan area urban community that includes a large central city with nearby suburbs, towns, and villages

With more than 3 million works of art, the Metropolitan Museum of Art in New York City is the largest art museum in the United States. In addition to museums, what other kinds of services are provided by municipal government?

While counties are established to serve the administrative needs of the state, the creation of municipalities is based on the needs of the people. Wherever there are concentrations of people, public services must be provided. Municipalities provide those services.

INCORPORATION

As population in an area increases, residents may find that their county government cannot keep up with the demand for services. When this happens, the people must decide whether they wish to form a municipality. Since 1980, hundreds of cities have come into existence. The vast majority of these were in Texas.

A municipality is formed and given legal status by a process called **incorporation.** Each state's constitution or statutes set out what a community must do to become an incorporated municipality. Most states require a certain number of persons to live in an area before incorporation is possible. Then a specified number of that community's residents must sign a petition asking for incorporation. Usually an election is held to obtain voter approval or rejection of the petition.

MUNICIPAL CHARTER

A **charter** is the fundamental law of a municipality. In effect it is its constitution. Most charters give a municipality its name, describe its boundaries, and explain its powers and organization. With a charter, a municipality becomes a municipal corporation, with the right to sue and be sued in court, to borrow and lend money, to enter into contracts, and to own and manage property.

Over the years, many different kinds of municipal charters have been developed. Some states create a special charter for each new municipality, while others draw up a single charter for all municipalities. Still other states provide similar charters for all municipalities of comparable size or allow new cities to choose from among several standard charters.

In 40 states, the people of an area are allowed to draft, adopt, and amend their own municipal charter. Known as **home rule,** this plan allows the people to choose their own governmental structure and set guidelines for their local ordinances. Home rule is important because it allows cities a greater degree of control over their own fate. Home rule cities, then, are more powerful than those without such status.

Home rule charters usually are written by an elected charter commission. Once written, the charters must be approved by the voters. In some states, the state legislature must ratify the charter as well. The extent of home rule varies among the states, depending on how much responsibility each state wants its cities to have. In several states, home rule is granted and may be retracted by the state legislature on a case-by-case basis. In some states any municipality may write and adopt its own charter, while in others only those with a certain size population may do so.

Depending on their charters, municipalities may have one of three forms of municipal government. These are the mayor-council form, the council-manager form, or the commission form.

Mayor-Council Government

The oldest and most widely used form of municipal government is the **mayor-council form.** In it, the most important municipal leaders are the mayor and the members of a council. The mayor is the chief executive,

home rule plan that allows the people of an area to write and amend their own charter

incorporation process of establishing a municipality by receiving a state charter and being voted upon by the people

charter plan of government a state authorizes for a municipality

mayor-council form municipal government in which the mayor is the chief executive and the city council is the legislative body

Here, Philadelphia's mayor, Wilson Goode, (right) debates a rival Democratic candidate. What duties does a mayor have in a mayor-council government?

while the council is the legislative body.

The mayor administers the municipal government on a daily basis. He or she oversees the operation of most city agencies and departments, appoints department heads, and serves as the city's spokesperson. He or she, for instance, may meet with business leaders to attract new employment. The mayor also might represent the city in negotiations with state or federal officials to obtain funding for cleaning up a hazardous waste site.

wards geographical areas into which some cities are divided for voting purposes

Qualifications for mayor, such as age or residency requirements, usually are set by the municipal charter. Thus, they vary considerably. Most mayors are elected by the voters for either two- or four-year terms.

The city council generally is a unicameral body. It passes ordinances, sets local tax rates, and adopts the municipal budget. In addition to lawmaking, the council may have other duties. Like the state legislature, a council must review projects and policies to determine how well the municipal government is being run. It is expected to make long-range plans to meet the future needs of the community. And as representatives of the people, the council also must consider requests and petitions from the public.

Councils vary greatly in size. Most have nine or fewer members, but larger cities may have more. Chicago has the largest council with 50 members. Council members are usually elected in at-large elections. Some cities, however, are divided into **wards,** whose residents elect one or more council members to represent them. In some cities, certain members are elected from districts and others at large. Council terms vary from one to six years, with four-year terms being the most common. Members usually meet on a regular weekly or monthly schedule.

There are two kinds of mayor-council governments, depending on state laws and municipal charters. The amount of power given to the mayor under the charter determines if the government is the weak-mayor or strong-mayor plan.

PROFILE: TOM BRADLEY

A CONSENSUS BUILDER

Tom Bradley, former mayor of Los Angeles, set a remarkable record. Bradley was mayor of the nation's second largest city longer than anyone else. First elected in 1973, Bradley became one of America's most important politicians and led Los Angeles until 1993.

Bradley was born on a Texas cotton plantation in 1917, the son of sharecroppers. Raised in Los Angeles, he graduated from the University of California at Los Angeles in 1940. After college, he became a police officer, while studying law at night. Upon leaving the police force in 1961, he practiced law. He then served on the Los Angeles City Council until his election as mayor in 1973.

Bradley's victory was a major achievement, considering the diverse population of Los Angeles, a mix of whites, blacks, Hispanics, and Asians that Bradley calls an "ethnic and cultural mosaic."

Los Angeles, like other large cities in the United States, has many problems—pollution, lack of affordable housing, and gang violence. The people of Los Angeles are concerned about improving their quality of life. Bradley and other mayors have shown that, with good leadership and the efforts of many people, the quality of life in American cities can be improved.

Mayor Bradley is especially proud of the city's economic growth during his administration. In his victory speech in 1989, he also cited as accomplishments strengthening the police, improving education, and working to curtail pollution. Throughout his years as mayor, Bradley was praised by both opponents and supporters for his skills in consensus-building—reaching a solution to which groups with varying viewpoints can agree.

Reelected in 1989, the mayor hoped to make his next term his most productive. Tragedy, however, marred his term. In the summer of 1992, the city erupted in violence. In depressed south central Los Angeles, residents took to the streets to vent their anger. The riots began in reaction

to a not-guilty verdict in the widely publicized trial of four white police officers who were videotaped savagely beating an African American motorist. African Americans had focused on the trial of the officers as a way to redress the police brutality that many African Americans believed plagued their community.

When a jury acquitted the police officers, some African Americans reacted by burning and looting stores and businesses. Thousands of people of all colors joined in. The loss of stores and businesses in Los Angeles was devastating. Once order returned to the area, community residents, people from other neighborhoods, and business owners came together to clear the rubble. People of all ethnic groups, businesses, and the federal government began to rebuild the community and improve the conditions that led to the riot.

A saddened Mayor Bradley, helped restore peace before he vacated the mayor's office in 1993. He left it to his successors to continue trying to build the consensus that he had so desperately tried to achieve over 20 years in office.

1. What is consensus-building? Why might consensus-building be an important skill in a city like Los Angeles?
2. What characteristics must a large city have to offer people a good quality of life?

WEAK-MAYOR PLAN

The **weak-mayor plan** is used by most small cities, towns, and villages. As shown in Figure 24-2, it is one in which the mayor of a municipality has limited powers. His or her role is to be the ceremonial head of government. Often elected from among city council members, the mayor shares power with the council. Council members, rather than the mayor, direct the work of the city departments as well as appoint and dismiss department heads. The mayor rarely has the power to veto acts of the council.

STRONG-MAYOR PLAN

The plan used by most larger cities is a sharp contrast to the weak-mayor plan. In the **strong-mayor plan,** shown in Figure 24-3, an elected mayor has full executive powers, while a council retains a separate legislative role. Under this plan, the mayor is a highly visible figure. And since the mayor is elected directly by the voters, he or she has a power base independent of the council.

In the strong-mayor plan, the mayor appoints and dismisses department heads and administers the daily activities of the city bureaucracy. The mayor's priorities are reflected in his or her allocation of current funds as well as the prepared budget for the next fiscal year. The mayor also suggests legislation to the council and plays an important policy-making role. While the council itself passes acts or ordinances, these may be vetoed by most strong mayors.

Council-Manager Government

Another type of municipal government, the **council-manager form,**

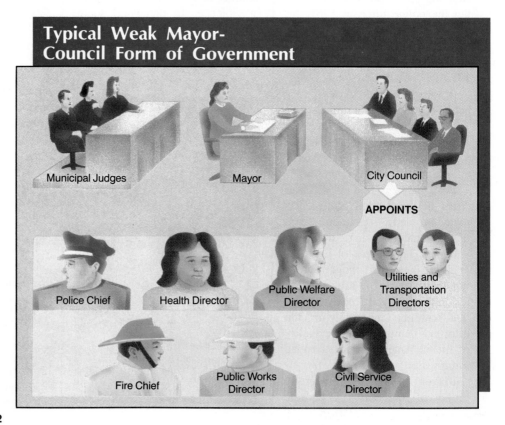

Typical Weak Mayor-Council Form of Government

Municipal Judges

Mayor

City Council

APPOINTS

Police Chief

Health Director

Public Welfare Director

Utilities and Transportation Directors

Fire Chief

Public Works Director

Civil Service Director

Figure 24-2

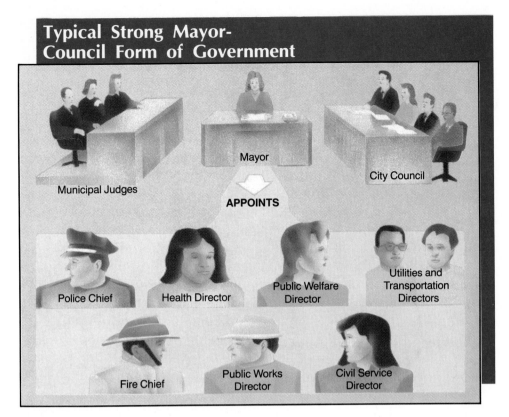

Typical Strong Mayor-Council Form of Government

Municipal Judges

Mayor

City Council

APPOINTS

Police Chief

Health Director

Public Welfare Director

Utilities and Transportation Directors

Fire Chief

Public Works Director

Civil Service Director

Figure 24-3

is growing in popularity. It features five to seven elected council members who are the legislative body, and a manager who is hired to take care of the daily administrative duties. Outlined in Figure 24-4, the council usually hires the manager as an employee of the city. And depending on the city, either the voters or the council then elect a weak mayor who performs mostly ceremonial duties.

The city manager often is a professional with a degree in public administration. In most cases, he or she appoints department heads, prepares the budget, and suggests legislation to the council. In other words, the manager carries out many executive duties, but without the independence a strong mayor has. Instead, the manager conducts city business as directed by the council. If it is not satisfied with the work, the council may fire the manager. With no direct

public support, the manager, unfortunately, is sometimes a convenient scapegoat.

The council-manager form of government is based on the model of a private company. Just as stockholders elect a board of directors to oversee a corporation, voters elect a city council to direct the government. In place of a general manager hired to direct the business, the city council hires a city manager.

The council-manager form began in the early 1900s as part of a reform movement. It was hoped that such a plan would remove partisan politics and corruption from city government. Staunton, Virginia, hired a city manager in 1908. The first large city to adopt the plan was Dayton, Ohio, in 1914. Today, the council-manager form is used in over half the cities that have populations of more than 25,000.

Typical Council-Manager Form of Government

Municipal Judges

Mayor

City Council

APPOINTS

City Manager

APPOINTS

Police Chief

Health Director

Public Welfare Director

Fire Chief

Public Works Director

Civil Service Director

Utilities and Transportation Directors

Figure 24-4

The major weakness of this plan is the same as its strength: the chief executive is, by design, a technician. There is no central political leadership to propose innovative solutions or to win voter support for change or difficult decisions.

Commission Government

commission form municipal government that combines legislative and executive power in a group of elected commissioners

The least common form of municipal government is the **commission form,** which combines legislative and executive authority in an elected group of commissioners. Three to nine commissioners usually are elected on a nonpartisan basis from the city at large. They serve for two- or four-year terms.

Under a commission plan, then, there is no separation of powers. In this sense, it is similar to many county boards. The commission sets public policy and prepares the budget. In addition, each commissioner is the head of one or more city departments, such as police, public works, and so on. Either the commission or the voters choose one commissioner to serve as chairperson. As well as heading one of the city's departments, that person may run council meetings and sometimes serve as mayor for ceremonial occasions.

The commission form of municipal government was developed as the result of a natural disaster in Galveston, Texas. In 1901 a tidal wave and hurricane swept Galveston, killing more than 6000 people and laying much of the city to waste. The weak-mayor government in power at the time was unable to cope with the emergency. In the wake of the disorder that followed, the Texas legislature provided Galveston with a new charter that established a board of five commissioners charged with making and enforcing laws necessary to restore order to the city. Their activities were so successful that the decision was made to continue the plan permanently. In 1907 Des Moines, Iowa, also adopted the commission form. By 1917 about 500 cities had switched, although many, including Galveston and Des Moines, later abandoned the form. Today, fewer than 200 American cities use a commission form of government.

Departments of Municipal Government

Residents expect many services from their cities, and most municipalities have departments set up to handle those services. Just as municipalities differ in the services they provide, they also differ in the number and organization of their departments. But most municipalities have at least eight departments: public safety, public works, public utilities, health, welfare, finance, law, and personnel.

PUBLIC SAFETY
Some of the most important activities of municipalities are their public safety services. Many cities have combined their police and fire protection services into a single department of public safety. Sometimes this department includes a traffic bureau, which may be established to study traffic snags and plan for future traffic needs. Also reporting to this department may be a city building inspector who reviews construction plans and inspects construction sites for new or renovated buildings.

PUBLIC WORKS
The public works department usually is the largest department in a municipal government. There often are many divisions within it, each having its own specialty. For instance, the street maintenance division repairs streets and keeps them clear of snow and ice. Cleaning the streets and disposing of garbage is the job of the division of sanitation. The sewer maintenance division properly disposes of and

Typical Commission Form of Government

Municipal Judges

Commissioner/ Department Head

Commissioner/ Department Head

Commissioner/ Department Head

Figure 24-5

Washington D.C.'s metro, shown here, is one of the newest subways in the nation. Many cities have a department of public utilities that owns and operates subway systems. What other departments are found in many municipal governments?

treats human and household wastes removed by water. All of these services are essential to the residents' health and the livability of the city.

PUBLIC UTILITIES

Many cities own and operate public utilities, which may include electricity, water, gas, airports, auditoriums, port facilities, and parking lots and garages. Many cities also operate bus and subway systems. These utilities are organized like a business; cities sell the services to consumers and collect money, which goes to the city treasury.

PUBLIC HEALTH

Municipalities always have played an important role in protecting the health of their citizens. Cities establish and enforce basic rules of cleanliness and sanitation for safe water and food supplies. City health departments inspect restaurants, nursing homes, and other public places to make sure they

obey state and local sanitation rules. Other divisions within the department may control insects, stray animals, and smoking in prohibited places. They also may operate medical clinics and treatment centers. And records of births, deaths, and contagious diseases usually are kept in the local health department.

PUBLIC WELFARE

Responsibility for the welfare of people who are unemployed or underprivileged is shared by all levels of government. Municipal governments spend millions of dollars each year on various welfare programs. These programs include aid to dependent children and aid to people who are disabled, elderly, or blind. Medical care and foster home care also fall in this category. Most of the money for these programs comes from state and federal governments, although funds sometimes are allocated to cities through county governments. In some cases, the local government is required by federal and state law to provide additional funds. Whatever the source of the funds, local officials set guidelines and actually run the programs.

FINANCE

The department of finance takes care of money matters for the municipal government. The director of finance supervises the collection of taxes and pays the city's bills. The finance department also sees to it that other municipal departments keep within their budgets. In addition, some cities have an auditor who makes sure city agencies are spending money only in ways authorized by the city council or commission.

LAW

The law department helps draw up the city's ordinances, contracts, deeds, and other legal papers. The city attorney, sometimes called the city solicitor, heads this department. He or she gives advice to council members, department heads, and other municipal officials about the legality of their actions. In addition, the attorney defends the city in lawsuits, files suits on behalf of the city, and helps to assure that city ordinances are enforced.

The law department is a separate entity from municipal courts, which are part of the judicial branch of government. As discussed in Chapter 23, municipal courts handle lesser legal matters, such as misdemeanors, traffic cases, and some civil suits.

PERSONNEL

Today, almost all cities and counties use merit systems to hire employees at all levels below department heads. Any hiring, promoting, or firing of people is based on their experience and competence rather than on personal politics. Such merit systems are run by a personnel board or civil service commission.

Section Review

1. Why are municipalities formed?

2. How do municipalities attain legal status?

3. What are the three major forms of municipal government in the United States?

4. What is the major difference in the two mayor-council plans of government?

5. **Challenge:** If you lived in a large city that was facing serious economic and social problems, which form of government do you think would be most effective in governing your city? Explain.

4 Other Local Governments

Along with county and municipal governments, many other units of local governments are found in the United States today. Such units may exist side-by-side with or overlap county and municipal boundaries.

New England Towns

The **New England town** is one of the oldest forms of local government in the United States. In colonial times, a town consisted of a village plus the surrounding rural areas of forests and farms. Today, as then, New England towns include both rural and urban areas. But, they should not be confused with small municipalities or towns found in other parts of the country. Elsewhere, small cities and towns do not include rural areas. And while county boundaries are found in all six New England states, the important units of government are the towns within those counties.

A New England town provides the same public services that county and municipal governments in other regions do. But that is where the similarity ends. As in colonial times, traditional New England town governments practice direct democracy. The people themselves govern the town through a traditional town meeting, usually held once a year, which all qualified voters may attend. There, everyone is allowed to speak and vote on topics of importance.

The people themselves pass laws, prepare the budget, and set taxes for the town. In short, the townspeople, not mayors, councils, or managers, decide local policies. During an annual town meeting, the people also may elect a town clerk, a school

New England town form of local government combining rural and urban areas

Special districts provide services, such as fire protection. What is the most common special district?

board, police officials, a tax assessor, and a group of selectmen and selectwomen. It is the duty of the latter to administer the government between town meetings.

Over the years, growing populations and greater complexity of the services provided by local governments have forced many New England towns to change the way they are governed. In some towns, the voters now elect representatives to attend town meetings and make decisions for them. Some towns hire town managers who have duties similar to those of county or city managers.

Townships

Townships, a variation of the New England town, developed in the northern and central states. These small units of government originally were formed to govern rural areas. After the Land Ordinance of 1785, many midwestern states were divided into six-mile-square townships, which were further divided for homesteading.

Today, 16 states have township governments, although their importance has declined substantially. Some townships administer county government services to rural areas, handling functions such as road maintenance, police protection, and health care. But, more often these functions have gone to the county governments. And, the expansion of metropolitan areas have further overshadowed townships. Yet townships in some heavily populated areas, such as New Jersey, Pennsylvania, and New York, have taken on the job of delivering more municipal-type services.

In most states having townships, the township is governed by an elected board of trustees or a board of supervisors. Or, voters may elect

individual township officers, such as a clerk, treasurer, assessor, and police official, who form the governing board of the township.

Special Districts

A **special district** is a unit of local government that provides a service not supplied by other units of government. The service may deal with education, police and fire protection, water or sewage treatment, housing, or transportation. A special district also may provide recreation facilities, hospitals, libraries, cemeteries, or pest control. Special districts, then, provide an area-wide approach to a particular problem or service.

Depending on the services provided, the budget of a special district may range from a few hundred dollars to tens of millions of dollars. To raise money, the districts may levy taxes, borrow money, or charge fees to consumers of their services. The rules under which special districts operate are set by each state.

In general, most special districts are found in urban areas. Some districts may have boundaries identical to those of a county or municipal government. Others, such as an urban transportation district or a rural irrigation district, may have responsibility for a number of cities or counties. One of the largest and most successful special districts is the Port Authority of New York and New Jersey. It crosses state lines to handle port development and transportation within 25 miles of New York City. Another example is the Metropolitan Water District of Southern California, which serves over 13 million people in 130 cities, including Los Angeles.

Special districts are by far the most common form of local government in

America. In 1992 there were 48,712 special districts nationwide. Illinois and California both have over 2800 such districts, mainly because of the many school districts such heavily populated states need.

Indeed, the most common special district is the local school district. Over half the states have school districts to oversee public education. As the governing body of the school district, the school board may levy taxes, hire teachers, borrow money, and set some policies, such as the length of the school year. Though all their decisions must conform to state law, local school boards have wide latitude in running the schools. In most states, the school board is elected by the voters of their district, and its members may or may not have a salary. Most boards hire a superintendent to direct the school district's work.

Section Review

1. Why is a traditional New England town unique in the way it is governed?

2. Why were townships first formed?

3. What is the role of special district governments?

4. **Challenge:** What are some advantages of a direct democracy style of government like that found in traditional New England towns? disadvantages?

Summary

1. Local governments are the building blocks of America's system of representative government.

2. The relationship between state and local governments is unitary. Local governments exist when and where state law allows.

3. Counties (also called boroughs and parishes) are a form of local government and differ in number, area, and population from state to state.

4. Counties usually are governed by a county board, which has both executive and legislative powers.

5. Various plans separate executive and legislative powers in county governments.

6. To cope with increasing problems, counties often create special boards.

7. Most Americans live in urban areas of varying size. These areas are governed by a variety of municipal governments that provide public services to the community.

8. In order to become a municipality, an urban area must incorporate and draw up a charter, which must be approved by the state.

9. Municipal governments may take different forms. Among these are the mayor-council, council-manager, and commission forms.

10. Other kinds of local governments include New England towns, townships, and special districts.

11. Special districts are the most common form of local government. Most special districts are set up to provide a single service, such as education or police and fire protection.

Chapter 24 Review

★ Building Vocabulary

All of the following terms relate to local governments. Explain the difference between each of the following pairs of terms by using each pair in a sentence.

1. counties
   municipalities
2. county seat
   county board
3. strong-mayor plan
   weak-mayor plan
4. council-manager form
   commission form
5. New England town
   townships

★ Reviewing Facts

1. Why is the relationship between state and local governments a unitary one? Why is this relationship important?
2. What factors might influence the type of services provided by local governments?
3. What general statements can be made about county government organization?
4. What is the structure of a typical county government?
5. What types of power do county boards have?
6. Why are special county boards created?
7. What is one reason for citizens to establish municipalities?
8. What are the major parts of a municipal charter?
9. What are eight departments found in most municipal governments?
10. How are New England towns governed?
11. What are some services provided by special districts?

★ Analyzing Facts

1. Many people believe that the rapid growth of municipal governments has made county governments obsolete. Do you agree? Why or why not?

2. How do you think county governments could best be redesigned in order to separate more efficiently the legislative and executive funtions?
3. What, do you think, are some advantages that home-rule municipalities have over nonhome-rule municipalities? Explain your response.
4. Many people are unaware of special districts, though these districts provide many services. Why do you think this is so?
5. Imagine that you live in a small but fast-growing community. Which type of government leader would you prefer, a mayor or a manager? Based on what you learned, what do you think are the advantages of each? What might be some disadvantages?

★ Evaluating Ideas

1. Compare the three types of city government. In your opinion, which one is the most efficient for very large cities and for very small ones?
2. The traditional New England town government has been called the most democratic of all forms of local government. Why, then, are all units of local government not run this way? Why have many towns turned to a representative town meeting?

Using Your
Civic Participation Journal

Review the information on citizen involvement to combat crime that you recorded in your Civics Participation Journal. Work with five of your classmates who live close to you to work with the local police to set up a program in your neighborhood. Report your activities and findings to the class.

3. In reality, all of the various types of local govern-ment are formed by the state. Imagine, however, that local governments had the same role in form-ing state governments as state governments have now in forming local governments. How, do you think, might state governments be different from what they are now?

4. The most common special district in the United States is the local school district. Would you pre-fer to attend school in a large school district or in a small one? Explain.

★ Critical Thinking
Supporting a Viewpoint

A viewpoint is a postition or opinion that someone has on a topic. If someone asks for your viewpoint on something, he or she probably will expect you to sup-port it—especially if your viewpoint differs from their own.

Explanation Use the following guidelines to present and support your viewpoints clearly and persuasively.

1. Before stating your viewpoint on a topic, think about it carefully. Find out others' viewpoints on the same topic and why they hold those view-points.

2. Develop as many supporting statements as you can to support your viewpoint. Make sure that each statement relates directly to the topic, to other sup-porting statements, and to the viewpoint you want to defend.

3. Arrange your statements in a logical order so that they support your point of view in a clear way that is easy for oth-ers to follow. Your statements should define, clarify, explain, and give rea-sons for holding your views.

4. State your position and then present your supporting statements. Save your most impressive supporting statement for last, when it will have the most impact. Your last statement can also restate your views, but in different words than your opening statement.

Practice Read the viewpoint presented below and note the references to the guidelines that accompany each statement:

Statement of viewpoint: *I believe local govern-ment is unimportant.* Supporting statements: *I mean, American cities and towns have less power than nation-al or state governments, so they are less important in our lives.* [defines and clarifies viewpoint] *They are unimportant because they are legally inferior to the states. They are required to carry out state duties, and they depend on the state to meet their needs.* [reasons for viewpoint] *They depend on the state for highways to bring business and tourists to their towns and for emer-gency disaster relief.* [examples] *But a state can totally abolish any of them at its pleasure, and I think that shows how really unimportant they are.* [final sup-porting statement and restatement of viewpoint]

All supporting statements were directly related to the viewpoint expressed and were presented in a logi-cal order that was easy to understand. But the speaker did not anticipate arguments from local government supporters that likely would focus on all the services such governments provide.

Independent Practice Study the cartoon below. The cartoonist is commenting on the many corporations that have begun to take over and run public schools in some communities. First, what is the artist's view-point? Second, what information might someone use to support the viewpoint?

Chapter 25

Local Finance and Issues

From the moment you wake up until you go to sleep, and even when you are sleeping, your local government is touching your life. The electricity that causes your alarm clock to ring, the water you drink, the roads you drive on, the police sirens that scream through the night—all these are services of or indicators that your local government is at work.

How do local governments decide which services to provide? And where do they get the money to fund these activities? This chapter will reveal how your basic governing body answers such questions.

★ ★ ★ ★ ★

Chapter Preview

TERMS TO KNOW

local revenue, local taxes, assessed value, tax base, bonds, local expenditures, tax exemptions, annexation, intergovernmental service agreement, consolidation, councils of government, planning commissions, master plan, zoning, zoning ordinances, urban renewal

READ TO DISCOVER

- where local governments get their monies.
- how local governments spend their funds.
- the complexity and variety of public issues facing local governments.

Civic Participation Journal

Local government budgets are perhaps the government budgets that affect your daily life the most. Contact the mayor's office to get a copy of the budget for your community. Assume the role of a budget cutter and describe in your journal what programs you would cut to lower the budget by 10 percent.

1 Local Revenue

As shown in Figure 25-1, **local revenue** comes from both tax and nontax sources. This figure has grown rapidly in recent years as local governments have assumed responsibility for funding more services, and state governments have increased funding for education.

Tax Revenue

Local governments depend upon **local taxes** for a third of their overall funds. Most local tax revenues come from property, sales, and income taxes.

Local governments receive their power to tax from the states. Therefore, their taxing power is limited by state constitutions and laws, as well as by restrictions of the federal Constitution. For example, some states regulate the amount of property taxes that local governments may collect. A constitutional restriction prohibits the taxing of imports or exports.

PROPERTY TAXES

For local governments, the largest stream of tax revenue comes from property taxes, or taxes paid by owners of certain kinds of property. Property taxes are generally levied on real property; that is, land, homes, and other buildings. The value of this real property is usually set by officials

COMBINED LOCAL GOVERNMENT REVENUE, 1992

SOURCE	IN MILLIONS	PERCENT OF TOTAL
Federal Government	$ 20,047	3.4
State Government	195,539	33.2
Local Taxes		
Property	171,863	29.2
Sales	23,073	3.9
General Motor Fuels and Motor Vehicle Licenses	1,524	0.3
Individual and Corporate Income	12,591	2.1
Other	10,348	1.8
Current Charges		
Education	10,201	1.7
Hospitals	25,023	4.2
Other	15,531	2.6
Utility and Liquor Store Revenue	55,852	9.4
Interest and Miscellaneous Revenue		
Interest Earnings	28,746	4.9
Other	780	0.1
Insurance Trust Revenue	18,296	3.2
TOTAL	$589,414	100%

Source: Bureau of the Census

Figure 25-1

called tax assessors. Nationwide, there is trillions of dollars' worth of taxable real property.

Every few years, assessors determine a property's market value, or the value of the property if it were sold. Next, the tax assessor sets an **assessed value** which, by custom, is a certain fraction of the market value. Let's say, for example, that the assessed value for property in your community is one-third of the actual market value. A $90,000 home would then be taxed on its assessed value of $30,000.

How much tax would you pay if you owned this house? The tax each property owner is actually charged depends on the tax rate set up by the local government. Tax rates are measured in mills, with one mill equaling one-tenth of 1 percent. In actual money, one mill equals one-tenth of one *cent*. A tax rate of *10* mills, then, would equal 1 percent, or one penny.

The amount of taxes owed on a piece of property is determined by multiplying the local tax rate by the property's assessed value. Thus, if your house is assessed at $30,000 and you have a tax rate of 10 mills, the taxes on your house would be $30,000 times 1 percent, or $300 per year.

The property **tax base** varies among different local governments. For example, a city with many industries and large factories would have a high tax base because the value of commercial property is high. On the other hand, a city with many low-income housing units would have a low tax base and collect low amounts of tax revenues. In this case, the city also might have difficulty providing adequate services due to a lack of funds. Therefore, local governments work hard to ensure a high enough tax base to pay for their services.

SALES TAXES

In 1992 local sales taxes provided over $23 billion, or about 10 percent of local tax revenues. Many cities and counties, and even some special districts, levy their own local sales taxes in addition to the state sales tax. For example, the *state* sales tax in Ohio is 5 percent. Franklin County, Ohio, adds a ¾ percent sales tax, making the total tax rate 5¾ percent in the county. Many local governments also charge selective sales taxes for such items as tickets to sporting or cultural events. Cities may charge tourists taxes on hotel rooms to extend the tax burden to nonresidents.

The sales tax is widely used by local governments for the same reason that it is used by state governments. It is easy to collect and may produce a steady and dependable amount of revenue. In fact, the sales tax is growing in importance as a substitute for property taxes. Sometimes a sales tax is voted on by the public, usually when the tax proceeds are to be used for a single purpose, such as the city symphony. Otherwise, the governing board of the local government may set the tax rate within bounds allowed by the state.

INCOME TAX

Eleven states currently allow their local governments to use income taxes to raise revenues. In 1992 more than $12 billion were paid by individuals and corporations in income taxes to local governments. Local income taxes are a steady source of revenue, especially for inner cities with many businesses.

Many people who live in a suburb but work in the city must pay some type of city income tax to help fund the services from which they benefit. Commuters use such services as transportation, sanitation, and police and

assessed value value to be used for tax purposes

tax base total value of all taxable property within a local government's boundaries

fire protection. Without a city income tax, only city residents would pay for these.

OTHER TAXES

Local property taxes, sales taxes, and income taxes provide most of the tax revenue for local governments. But other taxes, including taxes on gasoline and on motor vehicle licenses, accounted for $18 billion of local revenue in 1992.

Nontax Revenue

Approximately two-thirds of the income of local government comes from sources other than local taxes. In 1992 local governments received more than $420 billion from nontax sources.

INTERGOVERNMENTAL REVENUE

Funds from the state and national governments account for the largest chunk of nontax revenue. Together, they provided one-third of all local revenue, or about $216 billion, in 1992. While federal funds dwindled during the Reagan years, state funds soared. This loss of federal funds hit cities very hard. Terry Goodard, mayor of Phoenix, Arizona, hoped that the Bush administration would be more helpful:

We have not fared well under the prior [Reagan] management, and it's no secret that cities were basically devastated in terms of their relationship with the federal govern-

State and Local Taxes for a Family of Four, 1992

CITY	INCOME LEVEL		
	$25,000	$50,000	$75,000
Albuquerque, NM	1,478	3,434	5,943
Baltimore, MD	4,068	8,246	12,791
Bridgeport, CT	4,519	9,416	16,270
Charleston, WV	1,691	3,542	6,373
Columbus, OH	2,151	4,713	7,712
Detroit, MI	4,723	9,680	14,773
Indianapolis, IN	2,017	3,703	6,268
Louisville, KY	2,439	5,100	8,099
Memphis, TN	1,718	2,896	4,506
Newark, NJ	5,853	11,445	17,696
Portland, OR	2,428	5,369	8,623
Salt Lake City, UT	2,038	4,682	7,564
Virginia Beach, VA	2,089	4,423	7,521
Median	1,970	4,306	7,253

Figure 25-2

ment. A whole lot more went from us to the feds than came back. . . . Let's not. . .get the kind of rogue federalism that seems to be afoot today, which says, ''We're going to cut off all your funds and everything we ever gave you, whether it was justified or not.''

Despite Goodard's hopes, the loss continued during the Bush and Clinton administrations.

Grants to local governments from states and the national government target virtually any purpose for government. Figure 25-2 shows the distribution of state funds to local governments. While funds for education head the list, other items, such as vaccinations, parks, street paving, and mental health care, are included as well. Many grants are only partially funded with state or federal money. The local government must supplement the funding in order to meet grant requirements. Whether or not they receive any grants, very often local governments are mandated by either state or federal laws to provide certain programs.

GOVERNMENT ACTIVITIES
Many of the activities of local government generate revenue, either as money-raisers or to just cover the cost of providing the service. For example, they raise money by charging fees, levying fines, and earning interest on money they have on deposit in banks. Local governments earn money by operating businesses, such as parking garages, ferries, and toll roads. Another source of revenue is the profits earned from local government-owned liquor stores and public utilities; that is, water, electric, and gas services. In 1992 these businesses brought local governments more than $56 billion. All of these revenue sources make up about one-third of the total local government income, but the way this revenue can be spent may be restricted by law. It may not be available for general government purposes.

Borrowing Money

Most local governments find that tax and nontax revenues alone are not enough to fund major long-term projects, such as the construction of government buildings, highways, schools, museums, and auditoriums. And even if these revenues were enough, sometimes money for these projects will not be available until a future date, even though the need for the service or facility is immediate. As a result, local governments are forced to borrow money. In 1992 local governments had an outstanding debt of about $599 billion. This figure is far higher than for state governments, in part because some states are prohibited from such borrowing.

Most local governments are also limited by state constitutions or statutes as to how much they may borrow. In a few states, local governments must secure voter approval to borrow money for certain purposes or over certain amounts.

The most common way local governments borrow money is by issuing **bonds.** Like bonds sold by state governments, the local government promises to pay back the original amount plus interest to the buyer. Meanwhile, the government may use the money to begin needed projects. Because these bonds are considered safe, they are attractive to investors. But local governments must be careful not to overload their budgets with payments for bonds. Nationwide, almost $40 billion of local government spending is for interest on debt.

bonds certificates that individuals may purchase in order to lend money to a government

Section Review

1. What are three kinds of taxes collected by local governments?

2. How do local governments determine property taxes?

3. What is the largest source of nontax revenue collected by local governments?

4. **Challenge:** Do you think the loss of federal revenue-sharing funds has affected your local community? Explain.

local expenditures monies spent by local governments

Providing electricity is very expensive for local governments. What are the six major areas of local government expenditures?

2 Local Expenditures

The billions of dollars of tax and nontax revenues collected annually by local governments are used to provide many services to the public. In 1992 **local expenditures** amounted to about $611 billion and, as shown in Figure 25-3, cover a wide variety of activities and programs.

Local spending patterns vary, with differences depending largely on the type of local government involved and the needs of each community. For instance, a school district spends 100 percent of its budget on education, but cities divide their budgets among many types of services.

Yet there are generalizations that can be made about local government spending. Figure 25-3 shows the major areas of expenditures. The figure gives details about these spending areas, along with appropriate dollar amounts.

Education

As is true at the state level, local governments place a high priority on providing education. It is often their largest area of expenditure. In fact, $240 billion, or almost 40 percent of local budgets, was spent for schools, teachers, books, and educational supplies in 1992. The vast majority of these funds go toward elementary and secondary education. Additional local government funds go to support public libraries, which are important for the education of people of all ages.

Utilities

In many instances, local governments have entered the utility business. This may include heating public buildings, lighting streets and highways, and maintaining a water system for the public. Providing these services is very expensive, and utilities comprise a large category of government expenditures.

Social Services

Another large expenditure of local governments is for social services for the needy. In 1992 about $75 billion was spent by local governments for health care and public welfare pro-

COMBINED LOCAL GOVERNMENT EXPENDITURES 1992

TYPE	IN MILLIONS	PERCENT OF TOTAL
Education		
Support of		
Local Schools	$226,696	37.1
Higher Education	13,424	2.2
Social Services		
Public Welfare	28,734	4.7
Health and		
Hospitals	46,469	7.6
Highways	26,211	4.3
Public Safety		
Police Protection	29,682	4.9
Fire Protection	14,358	2.3
Corrections	10,300	1.7
Environment and Housing		
Natural Resources, Parks and		
Recreation	16,167	2.6
Sewerage and		
Sanitation	30,163	4.9
Housing and Community		
Development	15,461	2.6
Government Administration	30,488	6.0
Intergovernmental Expenditures	7,355	1.2
Other Expenditures		
Interest on		
General Debt	30,633	5.0
Insurance		
Trust Fund	10,381	1.9
Liquor Store		
and Utility	74,748	12.2
TOTAL	$611,270	100%

Source: Bureau of the Census

Figure 25-3

grams. These expenditures are the result of both public demand and federal and state requirements.

In general, the need for social services is greater in urban areas than in rural areas. In the urban setting, there is more likely at least an organized system to deliver needed services. For these reasons, local governments in urban areas often spend as much money for health and welfare as they do for education.

State and local governments share the responsibility of inspecting public restaurants. In what local government expenditure area are inspections included?

Environment and Housing

Spending for environment and housing services comprise a variety of activities. These include maintaining parks and recreation areas, protecting air and water from pollution, and providing sewage and sanitation services. This spending category also includes low-cost housing and urban renewal projects. In 1992 local governments spent 10 percent of their budgets for these programs.

Public Safety

Public safety is a growing part of many local governments' activities. For instance, local governments spent 28 percent more money for public safety in 1992 than in 1988. These services include police and fire protection, jails, and safety and health inspections of businesses.

Because most crime occurs in urban areas, municipal governments are forced to spend more to maintain public safety than rural units of government do. In fact, some cities spend more for public safety than for social services.

Highways

In 1992 local governments spent more than $26 billion on highways. Most of the local transportation costs are for road and bridge construction and repair.

Other Expenditures

There are many other areas to which local governments must allocate funds. The costs of running the government itself include construction and upkeep of government property, buildings, and vehicles. Paying interest on bonds is also expensive for many local governments. And sometimes local governments must reimburse the state government for expenses incurred on their behalf. Localities also spend a great deal of money on regulating the sale of alcoholic beverages.

Section Review

1. What two reasons may explain why spending patterns vary among local governments?
2. What is the largest expenditure area for local governments?
3. List the major areas of local government expenditures.
4. **Challenge:** How, do you think, might government spending patterns in large cities differ from those in smaller municipalities?

3 Local Government Issues

Each of the more than 86,000 local governments in the United States has its own unique problems, opportunities, and issues. Each faces challenges and changes in its own political and social setting. Yet local governments share some of the same complex problems and face even more difficult public policy decisions. We increasingly look to our local government to reclaim, protect, and enhance our quality of life. But to make any difference, local governments need money, effort, and public support.

Taxing and Spending Issues

The crucial issues that local governments face revolve around what programs and services to provide, for whom to provide them, and how to pay for them. While state and federal governments may ponder large-scale or abstract policies, local governments have the hands-on duty to actually implement programs.

BUDGET ISSUES

The budget process at the local level is similar to the process at the state level. For most local governments, the budget covers a one-year period and reflects the government's policies and priorities for that year. Major agencies and departments judge what services are needed by the public. They then calculate the costs and present their budget requests for the coming year to either the city manager, the district officers, the mayor, the city council, or the county board for approval. Lobbying by the agency, special interest groups, or the general public is always influential in helping to set budget priorities.

Because almost no government activity can proceed without funding, all activities vie for the limited revenue available. Budget conflicts often arise when either demands for services increase or available revenues decrease. For example, suppose a city council increases the public safety budget to hire more police. Funds may have to be taken from another budget area, such as park maintenance or health care. The park or health program directors then must seek funds from other sources, cut their staffs, convince budget-makers to cut funds elsewhere, or persuade the public to raise taxes to support *all* the programs.

Limited budgets are a fact of life for cities and most other local governments. In 1975, New York City found itself facing bankruptcy. City officials had borrowed heavily to meet basic city expenses and lacked money to pay the bills. The state and national governments loaned the city even more money, but New York had to take drastic measures, such as major cutbacks in services, increased taxes, and employee layoffs, to return to solid financial ground.

In recent years, public safety needs have required local governments to hire more police. What problems do local governments face when the demand for services increases?

New York City is just one dramatic example of a common problem. Other local governments run up against major funding problems every year as they face increasing demands to repair crumbling bridges and streets, fight drug-related crime, support better education, care for AIDS patients, and ensure housing for all residents.

TAX ISSUES

As noted earlier, local taxes provide a significant portion of local revenues. There are, however, several restraints on the ability of local governments to raise revenues through taxes. First, the Constitution of the United States prohibits state and local governments from taxing the federal government. As a result, in cities such as Boston, Massachusetts, and Kansas City, Missouri, there are many government buildings that escape property taxes. Nor can United States military bases, which may cover thousands of acres, be taxed by local governments.

A second limit on the power of local governments to raise revenue through taxation comes from the states. These limits may involve **tax exemptions.** State constitutions or statutes may give tax exemptions to various private institutions, such as museums, churches, charitable organizations, and not-for-profit companies. Taken together, these exemptions are large, so other organizations and citizens pay a proportionately higher share of taxes. The states also restrict the kind and amount of taxes that local governments may levy.

Finally, the ability of state and local governments to raise revenue through taxation is affected by the amount of wealth and income within their borders. Some states and communities cannot raise enough funds to provide the same level of services that wealthier areas have.

tax exemptions freedom from obligation to pay taxes on certain kinds of income

Other tax issues for local governments center on the property tax. One criticism is that it is difficult to determine the true value of land or buildings. Many factors, such as inflation, neighborhood decay, and local improvements to streets and sewers, can cause property values to go up or down. This means that property taxes also vary.

Another problem stems from the idea that property that is worth more should be taxed more. This has a harmful result in instances where the value of a house increases while the owner's income does not. Although the house is worth more, the owner may not be able to pay the higher taxes and may be forced to sell the house. This is especially true for the elderly who are on fixed incomes.

Property taxes also raise other issues. For example, because property taxes vary from city to city, families and businesses often move from one location to another to take advantage of a lower tax rate. In the past few decades, the property tax base has declined in many cities as people and businesses have moved to the suburbs. Yet many older suburbs are now forced to raise property taxes to meet their citizens' needs just as the central cities do.

FEDERAL FUNDING ISSUES

Although the federal government has cut back on many of the funds that once flowed to local governments, there is still a sizable revenue stream. By and large, these funds are earmarked for specific projects and most cover only a portion of project costs. Federal funds typically are then matched by either state or local funds.

Federal funding, however, is accompanied by numerous federal regulations, on everything from how to order supplies to antidiscrimination provisions to the proper wages for construction workers. Complying with these regulations requires much labor, money, and time. New York City's former mayor, Edward Koch, once estimated that his city spent $1.75 million a year to fill out forms, make reports, and keep records to meet federal requirements.

At times, federal regulations fail to take into account regional differences. To receive federal funds, a small town may be required to meet the same standards as a large city. For example, a rural town of several hundred residents probably would not need, nor have the property tax base for, a water-treatment system of the same quality as that for a large city. Yet to receive federal funds for a new system, small towns are expected to follow the same antipollution laws as a large city that has many waste-producing industries.

Changing Local Government Services

Some local governments are tiny, such as a rural water district, and others are huge, such as the city of Chicago. But large or small, these local units are always seeking better ways to provide the services demanded by their citizens.

Small units of government may be inefficient in terms of how they spend their time and money. Yet huge governments may also lack the closeness to a community to fill its needs well. Pushed and pulled between these extremes, local governments change: they form, grow, merge, divide, and cooperate with one another.

FORMATION
There are specific legal procedures in each state for how a local unit of government may be created. Resi-

dents, land owners, developers, or a government agency itself may seek to form a new local unit. Petitions or public votes may be necessary, as well as the approval of the state.

The reasons for forming new units of local government vary and depend on circumstances. A new subdivision built outside of the city limits may need water, so a new water district is formed. If the residents want their own police department, a town may be incorporated as well. In an existing city, local merchants may decide they want better sidewalks and curbs in their neighborhood. Rather than wait for the city to act, the business owners form a new local improvement district and essentially tax themselves for the improved sidewalks.

Special districts can be quite fragmented and often overlap or leave out certain areas. Small towns may take on odd shapes due to local politics and patterns of land ownership. One of the most difficult problems faced by areas experiencing population growth is planning and controlling the formation of new local governments.

In many urban neighborhoods, residents have formed special districts to tax themselves and to make improvements. In what other ways are local government services changing?

ANNEXATION

annexation addition of territory to a municipality

Traditionally, municipalities have grown through **annexation.** Most of the large cities in the nation were formed this way. Today, most annexations add unincorporated lands into an adjacent city. Methods for annexation are often described in a state's constitution. Generally, both the residents of the area to be annexed and the people of the city must approve the annexation proposal.

Annexation issues can become very complicated. Suburbs or rural areas often resist annexation, fearing a loss of their identity. They also fear a decline in services; an increase in problems usually associated with cities, such as crime, poverty, and drugs; and higher taxes. Some *city* dwellers also may be hesitant about annexation, even though the city may need the tax base that annexation of more land would bring. They may be reluctant to assume the cost and responsibility of providing services, such as paving streets, building parks, and laying water and sewage lines, for thousands of additional citizens.

intergovernmental service agreement contract between governments to provide services across boundaries

CONSOLIDATION

consolidation merger or joining of several units of government

Consolidation takes place when small units of government decide to merge, thus forming a single government. For instance, many school districts have merged so that educational services can be improved. Years ago, the cities of Boston, New York, and Philadelphia were each formed by consolidating previously independent cities into one.

Also, city-county mergers exist to some degree in several of the nation's major metropolitan areas, such as Nashville-Davidson County, Tennessee; Jacksonville-Duval County, Florida; and Lexington-Fayette County, Kentucky. One variation on consolidation is a form of county government, such as that created in Dade County, Florida, in 1957. In Dade County, over 20 municipalities, including Miami, formed a county government called Metro.

The purpose of city-county consolidation is to allow for more efficiency in government. Together, one set of taxes is collected, offices and buildings are shared, there is a single decision-making process, and so forth. Consolidation must be approved by the residents before it can take effect. Such change, however, is often not popular with voters, who perhaps fear a larger government entity.

OTHER FORMS OF CENTRALIZATION

One of the most common solutions to the problems of relatively small governments is for units of government to cooperate by contracting with one another for some services. For example, one government may sell water or electricity to another under an **intergovernmental service agreement.** Such agreements are often entered into in order to share the operation of airports, jails, libraries, and hospitals. Most cities, in fact, have some agreements with other cities. Counties may also find it useful to contract with each other to share a service, perhaps an emergency medical facility, which each alone could not afford. Most contracts do not involve voter approval, but they may require authorization by the state legislature.

One of the most extensive instances of intergovernmental service contracts is found in southern California. Los Angeles County sells over 50 types of services to the 77 cities within its boundaries.

councils of government cooperative effort by representatives of several governments to deal with common problems

Councils of government (COGs) are another type of cooperative effort. Made up of representatives from the member local governments, COGs study area-wide problems and provide a place for communication and coordination between government officials, business leaders, and citizens at large. Within the council, members can address such problems as unemployment or air pollution, which overlap many government boundaries.

COGs began in the 1950s as part of a metropolitan reform movement. During the 1960s and 1970s, federal and state governments encouraged COGs by mandating that many federal grants be reviewed by such bodies.

Yet COGs rarely have final authority to make decisions. Local governments keep their structure and independence and choose whether to act as the COG recommends. One of the most successful COGs is the Twin Cities Metropolitan Council of Minneapolis and St. Paul, Minnesota. This council has dealt with such problems as sewage and water pollution, garbage disposal, and traffic. On the whole, however, COGs have not performed up to expectations. In some cases, local governments, fearful of appearing as if some other body is making decisions for them, have prevented COGs from achieving success.

City Planning Issues

Physical planning for American cities dates from colonial times. Early planned cities include Williamsburg, Virginia; Savannah, Georgia; and Washington, D.C. Today, as our nation has become more urban, cities find that planning is a crucial duty of government.

Most cities with a population of 10,000 or more have established groups, often called **planning commissions,** to study future needs. Planning commissions usually are com-

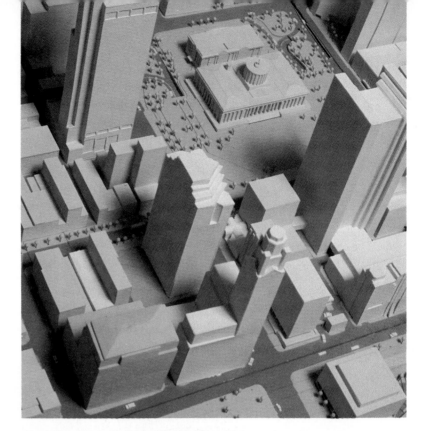

This model shows the expansion plans of a large American city. What factors do city planners take into account when preparing for future urban needs?

posed of local leaders; specialists, such as architects and engineers; and private citizens. Other municipalities have a full-time city planner and sometimes hire an entire planning department.

City planning must take into account not only the physical needs, but also the social and economic needs of a community. For example, planners predict changes in area population. Based on these predictions, a municipality can make sure it has adequate facilities for residents. An increase in the number of young couples, for instance, might suggest a future need for more schools, whereas an increase in the number of elderly might mean a need for more medical services. Either increase might require more recreational facilities or more roads and public utilities for residents.

planning commissions
groups formed by a community to study and plan for future needs

master plan description of a land area and its present use, with an outline of its proposed uses

zoning practice of dividing a city into a number of districts, or zones, and regulating the uses of property in those districts

zoning ordinances laws that regulate the use of land and buildings

One of the most important jobs of city planners is to draw up a **master plan** that describes a current land area and outlines future uses of that land. Once a city adopts a master plan, it can be changed only by a vote of the governing body. Therefore, roads, buildings, parks, or public utilities that do not follow the plan cannot be built without special approval by the planning commission or city council.

One of the most important tools used by planners is **zoning.** In theory, zoning will group together similar types of land use. For example, factories will be grouped in one area and houses will be grouped in another.

Experience has shown that most residents and businesses want this type of separation. Zoning is practiced in almost every city in the United States except Houston, Texas, where it was rejected by voters.

There are four major types of zones: residential, commercial, industrial, and recreational. Each type may be divided into even smaller areas, or sub-zones. For example, a residential zone may have some areas designated for apartments and some set aside for single-family houses. Figure 25-4 shows a typical zoning map.

A master plan is implemented through **zoning ordinances.** Most

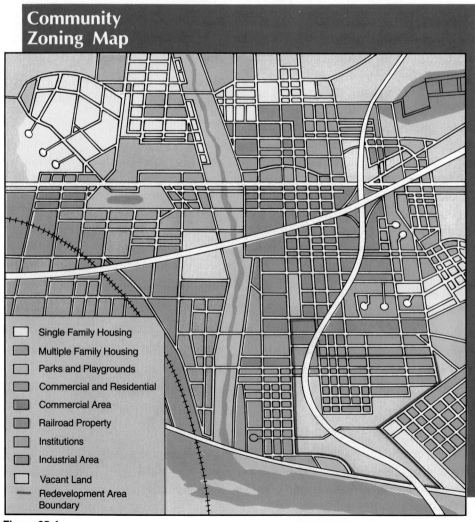

Community Zoning Map

- Single Family Housing
- Multiple Family Housing
- Parks and Playgrounds
- Commercial and Residential
- Commercial Area
- Railroad Property
- Institutions
- Industrial Area
- Vacant Land
- Redevelopment Area Boundary

Figure 25-4

PROFILE: THE NADERS

A FAMILY OF ACTIVISTS

Family traditions are an important part of American life. For the Nader family of Winsted, Connecticut, a significant family tradition is civic activity. Although Ralph Nader is the family's, and perhaps the nation's, best-known activist, he is far from being its only one.

The Naders settled in Winsted, a small town in western Connecticut, when they came to the United States from Lebanon. Nathra Nader ran a bakery-restaurant, described by one customer as "no place to eat in peace. Mr. Nader would always try to heat everybody up about wrongs and injustices."

Nader challenged his children to think and take action. When the telephone company made small businesses pay rent for pay phones, Nader took the case to AT&T and won. Mrs. Nader reinforced the lesson, telling her children, "If you love your country, you want to work to make it more loveable." The children took these lessons seriously.

As a young attorney, Ralph Nader wrote a best-selling book, *Unsafe at Any Speed,* which linked highway deaths to defects in cars, particularly in the Chevrolet Corvair. When General Motors, the maker of the Corvair, hired a detective to spy on Nader, Nader sued and won a $280,000 settlement.

The settlement money helped start Public Citizen, Inc., a consumer advocacy group. Nader and Public Citizen's staff—often called Nader's Raiders—took on not only the automobile industry, but many other industries, Congress, and the Federal Trade Commission. Nader's activities have changed many industrial practices and brought about a number of consumer protection laws. Early in 1989, however, Nader left Public Citizen, Inc. and returned to Winsted. One of his reasons for going back to his hometown was to carry on the work of his brother, Shafeek. Shafeek, who died in 1986, had undertaken many community improvement projects—bringing the Northern Connecticut Community College to Winsted, setting up small businesses, and starting a farmer's market and a radio station.

Claire Nader, Ralph and Shafeek's sister, also has been a local activist. She was one of the leaders in a campaign to save the town's old elementary school. Although this effort failed, she has not given up on preserving small town life.

One of Ralph Nader's first strategies for his Winsted project was to involve teenagers—to turn Winsted into a "hotbed of teenage civic involvement." Nader's first action was to distribute a survey to find out about the concerns of Winsted's citizens. To help people resist "burnout" when their efforts failed, Nader started a group that helped citizens "fight city hall in their spare time."

Right now, Nader says, Americans "are psychologically very susceptible to disappointment and depression once they make an effort and nothing happens—whether they are trying to improve a local hospital or clean up city hall or take on toxic waste." What they should understand, he says, is "whenever you are up against an obstacle the response is, how do you find a creative way to overcome it?"

1. What issues concerned the Naders? List three of them and give an example of each kind of issue in your own community.
2. What difficulties might an activist face in community affairs? How can these difficulties be overcome?

zoning ordinances describe building restrictions as well as establish the zones of a city. These restrictions might include building use and such physical dimensions as height, area of lots, and distance from the street and other buildings. In certain developments, sometimes called planned unit developments, the builders are also required to include such amenities as open spaces or parks to make the area more livable.

Issues often arise when individuals or groups disagree over zoning decisions. Some see zoning as an infringement of their rights as property owners. For example, a homeowner who wants to create and rent out a basement apartment may request a zoning change. In most cities, zoning boards review cases involving zoning exceptions. In this instance, some neighbors might feel the change would create too much noise and traffic. They can air their feelings at a hearing before a zoning board, which then must make a decision. In some cases,

millions of dollars of profit may depend on the zoning board's decision. Sometimes, zoning issues must be resolved in court.

Local Issues

Housing shortages, crime, poverty, and the crisis in public education are problems that affect all Americans either directly or indirectly. Although they are often considered urban issues, they go way beyond that simple label. Suburban and rural areas are far from immune to these same problems. In addition, everyone's tax dollars are used to seek solutions.

HOUSING

There is a massive shortage of affordable housing in virtually every corner of the United States. There are three components to the national housing crisis: homes for the homeless, decent shelter for low-income families, and affordable housing for potential homeowners.

Homelessness has recently been recognized as a problem not just of derelicts and the mentally ill, but of families as well. An estimated one-fourth of all homeless people are children. As President Bush told Congress, "The moral imperative is clear. We must confront this national shame." Few cures, however, are readily available. Shelters are necessary stopgap solutions, but permanent homes are needed.

Decent housing for low-income families is also a problem. Part of the problem stems from the fact that federal funding for building low-cost housing has virtually been eliminated. In 1980, before the Reagan administration, 36,365 units of public housing were built. In 1992 there were only 7200 built. With one respected national association estimating that

Donna Shalala, head of Health and Human Services (HHS), inspects a day care center. How effective has HHS been in solving the housing crisis?

the United States will need 8 million more low-income units by the year 2000, the problem is likely to intensify. Today, many families are unable to find a place to live and are literally forced onto the streets. Others become homeless as a result of turbulent employment conditions. As one homeless man told a reporter, "The difference between me and you is two paychecks."

The Housing and Urban Development Department (HUD) under the Bush administration faces the enormous task of helping local governments find answers. It does not help that HUD has been rocked by scandals concerning enormous waste, influence peddling, and corruption from the Reagan years. In some cases, local governments are turning to private developers, but the market for middle- and upper-income housing is far more profitable. One private organization, Habitat for Humanity, may offer a possible solution: volunteers help low-income workers build their houses, and the new homeowners then help build other modestly priced housing for others.

Finding affordable housing, especially for young families, is another problem. The average price for a starter home rose to an all-time high of nearly $76,000 in 1988. In some states, such as California, housing is even more costly. In San Francisco, the average is $230,000, a price few can afford.

Complicating the housing issue is **urban renewal.** Some cities, such as Paterson, New Jersey; Cincinnati, Ohio; St. Louis, Missouri; and Baltimore, Maryland, have mounted successful urban renewal efforts. But, in other cities, urban renewal has raised many issues. Older buildings, admittedly in terrible condition but home to thousands of poor people, have been torn down and replaced by expensive apartments. Small shops in many areas have been replaced by upscale malls. Another issue raised by urban renewal is the destruction of whole communities and the loss of a sense of identity for their residents.

CRIME

Urban areas, especially the centers of major metropolitan areas, have the highest crime rates. The risk of violent crime in the center of cities is four times as great as in small communities or rural areas. Yet suburbs, towns, and the countryside are far from being crime free. Every year, 25 percent of American families are personally touched by crime, ranging from assault to theft.

The crime problem raises important issues for local governments. Many people feel that crime is related to other social issues, such as poverty, unemployment, and lack of education. But perhaps an even more troublesome cause of crime is drugs, which may lead to crime in at least three ways. Rivalry in the drug trade among dealers result in some deaths. In addition, drug addicts are often forced to turn to crime to be able to support their habits. Moreover, other senseless crimes are committed by drug users who, under the influence, become irrational.

Local communities differ in the degree of crime they face. Some areas, most notably sections of New York, Los Angeles, Chicago, and Washington, D.C., are war zones where street gangs and drug dealers pose a deadly threat. Community leaders have yet to find ways to retake the streets and make them safe for all residents.

Communities, rural and urban, are trying to cut the crime rate by sponsoring job training, encouraging

urban renewal process of tearing down city slums and replacing them with new shops, office buildings, and housing

At day care centers, children learn basic skills before they enter school. What other steps are being taken to improve education at the local level?

business opportunities, improving schools, and providing drug and alcohol treatment. Of course, these programs cost money, which must come from already tight budgets. Yet communities realize that law enforcement may be even more costly. Investigating crime, financing trials, and paying to house inmates in jail all put a strain on local budgets.

POVERTY

One of the continuing major problems in America is poverty. While most of the poor are likely to have jobs, their income does not provide a minimum standard of living. Persons earning only the minimum wage fall below the poverty level as defined by the federal government. For a family of 4, the poverty line in 1993 was an income of $14,763 or less per year.

The same percentage of poor people live in rural areas as in urban areas, but certain groups are harder hit than others. Many of the poorest Americans are women and children in single-parent families. More than one-third of all such households live in poverty. Although poverty strikes all ethnic groups, a larger percentage

of blacks and Hispanics are classified as poor. In terms of total numbers, however, whites comprise two-thirds of all persons living in poverty. Of the estimated 45.2 million poor Americans in 1993, 26.2 million were white, 10.9 million were African Americans, and 8.1 million were Hispanic.

Local governments are trying to end the cycle of recurring poverty by sponsoring education, literacy programs, job training, and social services to those most in need. Private organizations are also helping, working with local government or acting independently. Churches, businesses, and volunteer groups assist in many communities by offering tutoring, day care, food kitchens, shelters for the homeless, and referral services.

EDUCATION

No other function of local governments is as vital as providing schools and basic education. But how well local governments are fulfilling this responsibility is a major issue. The charges brought against public education include failure to teach basic skills; widespread drug and alcohol abuse among students; high dropout rates, especially among minority students; and low budgets for buildings, supplies, and teacher salaries.

But what some call a "crisis" in public education has not gone unnoticed. Public awareness of the need for school reform has been building for over a decade. Most states and localities are dedicating more money to education, but the solutions go well beyond money alone. Many of the proposed changes focus on young children and include providing programs such as Head Start, day care, and before-and-after-school care.

Other localities are trying to create better schools by operating them year round, or at least extending the school year. In some cities, a radical experiment is being attempted. There, the powers of the school board have been dismantled and distributed to private for-profit corporations. The corporations have contracts to administer all the communities' educational facilities. Rochester, New York, is also experimenting with giving more power to local schools. Businesses and teachers are working together to ensure higher quality education in that community. In Colorado, several small towns have decided to "guarantee" that their high school graduates will achieve certain levels of competency. If they do not, the school system will work with employers to bring the students up to an acceptable level of competency.

Section Review

1. What are three money issues that local policymakers often are faced with today?

2. What are three restraints on the ability of local governments to raise revenues through taxes?

3. What is the difference between annexation and consolidation?

4. Why is planning an important issue for local governments?

5. What are four major issues faced by many local governments today?

6. **Challenge:** Which local issue do you think is the most urgent in your community? How would you solve this problem?

Summary

1. Local governments provide a variety of services for which they need revenue. They raise this revenue from taxes, state and federal funds, fees and service charges, and borrowing.

2. Local governments receive their power to tax by permission of the states.

3. For many local governments, their most important source of tax revenue is the property tax. Their largest source of nontax revenue is state and federal funds.

4. There are six major areas of local government expenditures: education, utilities, social services, environment and housing, public safety, and transportation.

5. Budget issues for local governments are similar to those for the states and national government. They revolve around the ability of government to raise revenues and to decide which programs and services to fund.

6. Local governments change by forming new units, annexing adjacent lands, and consolidating.

7. Other forms of centralization include entering into intergovernmental service agreements and forming councils of government.

8. Local units of government try to control their future growth through planning and zoning.

9. Local governments are faced with housing shortages, crime, poverty, and the crisis in education, and there are no easy solutions for any of these issues.

Chapter 25 Review

★ Building Vocabulary

Study the following vocabulary terms and write two paragraphs about local finance and issues. All 10 terms should appear in your paragraphs.

1. local revenue
2. tax base
3. bonds
4. annexation
5. consolidation
6. planning commissions
7. zoning
8. urban renewal
9. master plan
10. local expenditures

★ Reviewing Facts

1. What are three major sources of tax revenue for local governments?
2. Besides levying taxes, how else do local governments raise revenue?
3. Why is a property tax base critical for local governments?
4. How do local governments borrow money?
5. What general categories account for most local government expenditures?
6. What causes much of the conflict surrounding local government budgets?
7. How does federal funding both help and hinder local governments?
8. How are local governments limited in their ability to control their tax income?
9. In what ways may local governments coordinate services?
10. Describe the purpose of zoning ordinances.
11. How has rapid population growth affected urban areas?
12. Why are urban renewal plans controversial in many cities?

★ Analyzing Facts

1. In what areas do you think local governments spend too much money? too little money? Explain.
2. Do you think city planning should be eliminated? Why or why not?
3. Some people believe that the areas with the greatest problems soon will be the suburbs and rural areas rather than the cities. Do you agree or disagree? Explain your answer.
4. Who do you think would be helped if property taxes were eliminated? Who would be hurt? Explain.
5. Do you think local governments should depend on money from the states? Why or why not?
6. What, in your opinion, is the most effective way for local governments to raise money? Explain.
7. What local government issue is involved in the statement, "Everybody wants you to pick up their garbage, but nobody wants you to put it down"? What solution would you offer to help communities solve this problem?

★ Evaluating Ideas

1. Compare your city or county budget with the revenue and expenditure tables in this chapter. Are there any differences? If so, what do you think causes the differences?
2. Select a budget or policy issue facing a local government in your community. How did the issue arise? Who is affected by the issue? How would you solve the issue?

Using Your
Civic Participation Journal

Review the budget cutting suggestions you entered in your Civics Participation Journal. Work with five of your classmates to come up with composite ideas for cutting the local budget. Present your findings to the class and compare your results with those of the other groups in your class.

3. Has your city or county been experiencing population growth or decline? What effects has this had on local government services?

4. How has the general decline in federal funds affected local government services in your city of county?

5. Based on what you have learned in this chapter, what arguments would you give in favor of an area being annexed by a municipality? In favor of consolidation? Explain.

★ Critical Thinking
Determining Reliablity

Reliability is the quality of dependability. It means that you can rely on what you hear or read as being accurate.

Explanation   To judge the reliability of a source of information, be it a person or written material, you can use the following guidelines.

Consider the background and qualifications of the person providing the information. Just because someone is an expert in one area does not mean that he or she is an expert in another. In addition, does the speaker or writer have any *biases,* or reasons to distort the truth?

Consider the information presented. Is the information a *primary* or *secondary source?* Are the viewpoints and arguments expressed clearly, or does the information contain *ambiguous statements?* Does the speaker or writer present any *value claims?*

Consider the supporting evidence. Is the information merely a series of emotional statements or is it supported by evidence? Is the evidence based on opinions of other people or is it mostly fact? If most of the evidence is *relevant,* or directly related to the topic, if its accuracy can be proven, if most of it supports the topic and no significant counter-evidence can be found, then we can have some confidence that what we have read or heard is reliable.

Practice   You can apply the above guidelines to determine the reliablility of the following statement made by Ronald Reagan while he was President. He was advocating reduction or elimination of revenu-sharing programs:

It doesn't make sense for a federal government running a deficit to be borrowing money to be spent by . . . local governments that are now running a surplus.

In determining the reliablility of this information you would want to consider Mr. Reagan's strong biases about the federal government's involvement in people's lives. Knowing this should cause you to question the accuracy of his position. Before accepting his statement as reliable information, you would first want to know more about the federal deficit. You also need more information about his "fact" that local governments are running surpluses.

Independent Practice   Study the cartoon below. The cartoonist shows President Clinton and Secretary of State Warren Christopher cautioning the President of Iraq. The cartoonist has the President saying that he will pay his rent if the United States ousts him from Iraq. The cartoonist is referring to the American decision to pay the rent of exiled Haitian military leader Raoul Cédras when he fled to Panama. Would you consider this cartoon a reliable source for predicting future United States policies? Why or why not?

SEVEN REVIEW

REVIEW QUESTIONS

1. What do you think are the advantages of having separate state and national governments? What are some disadvantages?

2. Most state constitutions are longer and more detailed than the United States Constitution. In your opinion, why is this so?

3. How do state governments differ from local governments in their sources of revenue?

4. What are the important features of the unitary relationship between states and their local governments?

5. Why do you think the problems of American local government tend to center on the metropolitan areas?

6. Based upon your reading of the unit and your knowledge of your own state and community, what changes would you most like to see in state government? What changes would you most like to see in local government? Explain.

SUGGESTED READINGS

1. *The Book of the States*. Lexington, KY: The Council of State Governments. Published annually. Provides statistics on structures, working methods, financing, and activities of state governments; summarizes the three branches of government in each of the 50 states.

2. Burns, James MacGregor, J. W. Peltason, and Thomas E. Cronin. *State and Local Politics*. Englewood Cliffs, NJ: Prentice-Hall, Inc., 1984. Examines the political systems of the states and local communities.

3. Elazar, Daniel J. *American Federalism: A View from the States*. New York: Harper & Row, Publishers, 1984. Examines federalism from the perspective of the states.

4. Gay, Kathlyn. *Cities Under Stress: Can Today's City Systems Be Made to Work?* New York: Watts, Franklin, Inc., 1985. Examines the urban crisis.

5. Henig, Jeffrey R. *Public Policy and Federalism*. New York: St. Martin's Press, 1985. Presents and analyzes policy issues in an intergovernmental context.

6. Hyman, Dick, compiler. *The Trenton Pickle Ordinance: And Other Bonehead Legislation*. Lexington, MA: Stephen Greene Press, 1984. Collection of state and local laws that shows how far some lawmakers will go.

7. Judd, Dennis R. *Politics of American Cities: Private Power and Public Policy*. Boston, MA: Little, Brown & Company, 1983. Focuses on the close relationship between public authority and the private sector.

8. Liston, Robert A. *Getting in Touch with Your Government*. New York: Messner, 1975. Explains which level of government one can approach for solutions to problems.

9. Mason, Alpheus T. *States Rights Debate: Anti-Federalism and the Constitution*. New York: Oxford University Press, 1972. Discusses the long struggle over federalism.

10. *State Government: CQ's Guide to Current Issues and Activities 1987-88*. Thad H. Beyle, ed. Washington, D.C.: Congressional Quarterly, Inc., 1987. Addresses recent issue developments in all 50 state governments.

11. Straayer, John A. *American State and Local Government*. Columbus, OH: Merrill Publishing Company, 1983. Describes the basic structure and functions of state and local governments, with special emphasis given to political participation and public policies.

12. Warren, Robert Penn. *All the King's Men*. New York: Random House, Inc., 1960. Pulitzer Prize winning novel about the rise and fall of a ruthless Southern politician.

MAKING DECISIONS

Making good, or effective, decisions is an important part of citizenship. It involves making a suitable choice from among several alternatives, as well as weighing the values that support each alternative. In addition, you must consider the impact of each alternative on yourself and on others.

Citizens and political leaders make countless decisions each day. Children require decision-making competence when they choose a leader for a playground activity. Teenagers must decide whether to abide by family rules or to submit to peer pressure. Adults must decide whether or not to vote. As a student, you may already be trying to decide what kind of job to pursue during summer vacations or what career you want to follow after graduation.

Often, bad or ineffective decisions happen when you do not get all the facts, do not think through the alternatives, or are simply not being thoughtful. Your decisions can have tremendous impact not only on your own life, but sometimes on your family and friends as well. Poor decisions in the political arena can have serious consequences for thousands of people.

As you follow the decision-making exercise below, ask yourself these questions:

1. What are the facts in this case?
2. What appear to be the alternatives that are proposed?
3. What values does each alternative seem to support?
4. Who has these values?
5. What would be the impact of each alternative on me, on my family, on my friends, on my community?
6. Which alternative seems best?
7. What compromises might be reached?
8. What values am I supporting?

Imagine that the city council in your town must make a decision whether or not to ban swimming in the lake located in a city park. Although there are signs warning children not to swim there unless an adult is present, two children recently have drowned. There also have been complaints from some people about the noise created by young people congregating on the beach at lake side. Litter has become a growing problem. And since the city already is facing significant budget-ary constraints, hiring lifeguards or additional police does not seem very likely.

Many in the community are appalled at the idea of closing the lake to recreational swimming. These people contend that teenagers need a place where they can engage in healthy, physical activity. They point out, also, that during warm weather, many families have picnics along the shore. In addition, concessionaires—those who sell soft drinks, hot dogs, and hamburgers —would be forced to close down if swimming were banned. These people point out that life-guards and extra police patrols would help reduce many of the problems that have been identified. They maintain that city officials could easily reduce funds in other areas of the city budget in order to cover the additional expenses. How would you recommend the city council to vote?

Unit 8

THE GLOBAL COMMUNITY

As you read newspaper articles and watch television news programs, you are undoubtedly aware of the significant changes that are sweeping our world. Although many of these events occur in foreign countries, they have a profound impact on us Americans. Increasingly, we in the United States are becoming aware of the fact that we live in a global community in which people are very different from each other but also have many things in common.

One characteristic that people throughout the world share is a love of freedom. As the photo of Berlin on the facing page reveals, the city is once again the capital of a united Germany. It was named the capital after communism collapsed in Europe in the early 1990s.

We have no idea what our world will be like by the year 2000, but it will certainly be one that will challenge you and your children to make life better for all people everywhere.

Chapter 26

Comparative Governments

Our country's track record of over 200 years of stable, constitutional government is truly remarkable. Few other countries have had such consistency in government over such a long period. In this chapter, you will look at a wide array of nations and their governments. Some, like the United States, are firmly committed in their approach to government. Others still search for a workable system.

★ ★ ★ ★ ★

Chapter Preview

TERMS TO KNOW
minister, apartheid

READ TO DISCOVER
- the diversity of forms of government around the world and how they compare to our government.
- which governments are stable and which are not.

Civic Participation Journal

Choose a nation of the world and use the school or public library to learn more about that country's form of government. Write a paragraph in your journal detailing the government and the challenges it is now facing.

1 Stable Systems

While all nations face pressures to change their governments, in *stable* systems there is an agreed-upon nonviolent process that allows such change. In such governments there also is widespread agreement on the rules of governing, such as who makes decisions, what may be decided, and how citizens relate to their government. The United States is fortunate to have a stable system of constitutional federalism. Other stable government systems also exist in the world today.

Some nations, like Great Britain, France, and Saudi Arabia, have had years of experience with their current arrangements. Others, like Japan and Mexico, have undergone significant changes in this century to reach a relatively stable system.

Great Britain

The United Kingdom of Great Britain and Northern Ireland, commonly called Great Britain, occupies most of the British Isles. Although politically united for decades, Scotland, Northern Ireland, England, and Wales still hold their separate identities. As evidence, even though the English language predominates, some people still speak Welsh or Gaelic.

So much of American government is rooted in the history of Great Britain that it is easy to assume our systems are the same. Yet there are some notable differences. Great Britain is a constitutional monarchy with a parliamentary government. And although other religions flourish, the Church of England is England's established church and has close ties to the monarchy. The *separation* of church and state, on the other hand, has been instituted in the First Amendment of our Constitution.

CONSTITUTIONAL MONARCHY

The British government has evolved from a monarchy with few restrictions to a monarchy that is fully limited in its actions. The laws and customs that define what the monarchy may and may not do have developed over the centuries. The Magna Carta, as you learned earlier, was the first such document to set certain legal restraints on the monarch's actions.

The monarchy is hereditary, falling to the oldest son of the current monarch. If there are no sons, the oldest daughter reigns. Queen Elizabeth II, Britain's present monarch, has many functions related to governing, but these are not real political powers. For example, she appoints the prime minister, but only after the House of Commons first elects the person to the post. Other symbolic roles of the queen include "opening" the sessions of Parliament and giving her royal assent to any bills and treaties that

This peaceful English village reflects the British love of tradition. What role does tradition play in the British political system?

have passed through Parliament. The monarch is not allowed independent judgment on these matters.

Why, then, do the British pay for the vast expenses of a monarchy, including the queen's entire family, the palaces, and the royal lifestyle? The monarchy is a cherished symbol of national unity and continuity. Politicians, policies, wars, and even an empire may come and go, but the monarchy represents stability. We find this stability in our Constitution.

The British have no ''constitution'' the way we do. Rather, theirs is a body of agreements, both written and unwritten, which define proper roles for all participants, including the monarchy. It is based on the 1689 Bill of Rights, the Reform Bill of 1832, and on laws passed by Parliament. The constitution also incorporates the common law of Britain, based on judicial decisions through the years.

Underlying even these sources, however, is the principle of usage. This means that the constitution includes everything that citizens customarily agree should be included. Thus, the constitution changes as needs change, but at any one time there is a single, binding rule.

PARLIAMENT

Government in Great Britain generally is directed by the two houses of Parliament. The stronger of the two is the House of Commons. It has 650 members elected from geographic districts by British subjects over age 18. The House of Lords is composed of more than 1000 peers, but only about 200 actually participate. Peers primarily are persons who have inherited titles of nobility, such as duke, earl, or baron. Other peers are appointed by the queen or have had titles bestowed upon them. The House of Lords is weak, which clearly reflects

Here, Queen Elizabeth II (left) and her family watch a sports competition near their summer home in Scotland. In Great Britain, it is said that "the Queen reigns, but does not rule." How is Great Britain actually governed?

that power in Britain today rests not with titled nobility, but with the common citizen.

Unlike the United States Congress, Parliament manages *both* the legislative and executive functions of the British government. Almost all bills are introduced in the House of Commons. When passed by the Commons, the House of Lords may accept or delay the bill, but may not kill it.

Parliament also has the power to change any and every law or to alter any element of the constitution. Why would citizens give such great power to one group? According to British tradition, Parliament embodies the will of the people and is, therefore, supreme. Plus, the odds that Parliament would act radically are very small. But the legal possibility points out the difference between our legalistic American system and the tradition-based British one.

Prime Minister John Major holds a press conference. How are governments formed in Great Britain?

THE GOVERNMENT

The political party with the most votes in the House of Commons elects one of their members to be prime minister. He or she, in turn, forms the "government," a term equivalent to the American term "administration."

Great Britain's government, then, is headed by the prime minister and the people chosen by him or her to be the cabinet. The cabinet is made up of 15 to 25 other members of Parliament, mostly from the Commons. Like the American Cabinet, each **minister**, such as the foreign secretary or the secretary for the environment, is responsible for a department of government. A significant difference, however, is that these ministers also are members of Parliament who have been elected to legislate.

Local government is organized under a unitary system, which makes the national law supreme. Local units such as cities serve only the purposes laid out for them by Parliament. But there are numerous locally elected officials, such as mayors and city councils, who serve the specific needs of their locales.

minister head of a government department

PARTIES AND ELECTIONS

Like our Congress, Parliament is organized according to political party. But Britain's parties and their platforms are more clearly defined, usually appealing to specific segments of British society. Two major parties now dominate British politics: the Conservatives (Tories) on the right and Labour on the left.

The party that wins the most seats in parliamentary elections gets to form the government; the next largest party is called the opposition. Other smaller parties choose whom they will back. While Margaret Thatcher and John Major led Tory majorities from the 1980s through the mid-1990s, the Labour party gained significant strength to challenge continued Conservative leadership.

Elections for Parliament are held at least every five years, but they may be called at any time. For example, the party in power may call for elections whenever it feels it is in a position to win. But if it misjudges the voters, it may become the opposition.

Occasionally, elections are called when the government receives a vote of "no confidence" in Parliament. That is, if a major bill sponsored by the government is voted down by the House of Commons, the government "falls." Elections are then held for members of the Commons, who, again, form a new government. While this election process is more unpredictable than our elections, which are held every two and four years, the British feel it is accountable and responsive to public demands.

France

The French Republic is a long-standing democracy, tracing its origins to the French Revolution and its resulting Declaration of 1789. The motto of the Revolution, "Liberty, Equality, Fraternity," is still the national motto today.

The French, however, have a mixed track record on government over the decades. While they agree on the underlying principles of representative democracy, history shows a string of failed attempts to put those principles into practice.

The French Constitution, rewritten in 1958, formed the Fifth Republic. This means that just as America tossed aside the Articles of Confederation in 1781, France is into its fifth major reorganization since the same era. And scattered between these republics were other governmental systems, such as Napoleon's Empire and the German occupation during World War II.

But democracy keeps returning, for better or for worse. The Fourth Republic, for instance, had 26 governments from 1946 to 1958. Its major problem was a weak chief executive office unable to lead the many fragmented political parties. The Fifth Republic, therefore, was designed to have a powerful central executive official, the president. France's written constitution details the division of responsibilities for the government, combining a strong president with a parliamentary system.

PRESIDENT

The president is directly elected by a nationwide vote for a seven-year term. The constitution has some remarkably strong words for the duties of the president: "He shall ensure. . .functioning of the public powers, as well as the continuity of the State. He shall be the guarantor of national independence."

In addition, the president has some powers far exceeding those of our President. For example, France's chief executive may send a bill directly to the voters for approval in a national referendum, thus avoiding Parliament. The president may dissolve one chamber of Parliament known as the National Assembly and call for new elections. He or she also may take whatever measures are necessary to govern single-handedly in times of emergency.

France's President Francois Mitterand enjoys a stroll through a park. Mitterand, a socialist, was elected to office in 1981. What powers does the French president have?

PREMIER AND CABINET

The French president appoints a premier who directs the operation of the "government;" that is, the administration. The premier, in turn, appoints cabinet ministers to head each department of government, such as Agriculture, National Education, or Local Government. Since French government is unitary and highly centralized, these are powerful positions that establish local as well as national policies. Unlike the British system, cabinet ministers are not members of Parliament, but experts in their given fields.

Along with their executive roles, the premier and cabinet control the operations of the legislature, called the National Assembly. The premier and cabinet can and do introduce bills and sit in the Assembly. In fact, all bills concerning taxing and spending must come from the government. But the premier and cabinet have no vote in the Assembly. Rather, they push the president's policies through that body.

Many old buildings, such as this palace, line the banks of the Seine River in Paris, France's capital. Paris has been the seat of French government since the Middle Ages. What form of government does France have today?

The National Assembly is not powerless, however. It may vote "no confidence" in the government, which forces both the premier and cabinet to resign. Thus, they are at times caught in the middle, appointed by the president but accountable to the Assembly. But since the president is the stronger of the two, the scales often tip in that direction.

PARLIAMENT

There are two chambers in the French Parliament, the Senate and the National Assembly. The Senate is a weak body of 319 representatives indirectly elected from the 96 units of local government and from France's overseas territories.

The National Assembly is the principal legislative body. Its 577 deputies are elected directly by universal suffrage from single-member districts. The deputies serve five-year terms, unless new elections are called sooner.

Parliament's powers are strictly limited by the constitution, which specifically outlines the subjects that may be legislated. These include education, crime, civil rights, tax rates, administration of local communities, and other national concerns. Those items not listed belong solely to the government. This split in powers somewhat resembles that between the executive and legislative branches in our system. But unlike the United States Congress, the French Parliament is more restricted in some national matters and more powerful over local matters.

PARTIES

The French feel strongly about their politics, but to a lesser degree about their parties. Thus, they are organized into myriad political parties at both the local and national levels. These parties tend to split and regroup trequently. Currently there are four major parties covering a broad spectrum from right to left. These are the Gaullists, the Socialists, the Independent Republicans, and the Communists. You may be surprised to know that Communists are regularly elected to public office, including to the National Assembly.

Saudi Arabia

The Kingdom of Saudi Arabia occupies most of the desert lands of the Arabian Peninsula. The official language is Arabic and the official religion Islam, which originated in Arabia. Despite its great wealth from oil production, Saudi Arabia has an extremely traditional Islamic society. The national flag has the words "There is no God but God and Muhammad is the prophet of God."

For centuries the lands of Arabia have been governed by dizzying parades of dynasties, sultans, and kingdoms. In the early 1900s, two great families, the Hashimi and the Saud, vied for power and the ultimate prize—control of the holy city of Mecca. The Saudis proved the victors. In 1932 the various Arabian states merged into the Kingdom of Saudi Arabia.

ABSOLUTE MONARCHY

In an absolute monarchy, no opposition to the ruler, either social or political, is tolerated. All power rests with the king, who governs by royal decree. Saudi Arabia's first king was Ibn-Saud, and each subsequent king has been one of his sons. All important posts are held by male members of the royal family.

This absolute monarchy is both the cause and effect of the great stability in Saudi Arabian government. The rules are well-known and accepted by

the citizenry. For instance, only men may have political roles. All know that the king rules in strict accord with the Shari'a, the sacred law of the Islamic religion. The king, in fact, is the supreme religious leader as well as the head of state.

The particular style of Islam practiced by the Saudi rulers is extremely conservative. Changes in governing are minuscule; changes in policies, infrequent. Even if the Saudi family were overthrown, the odds are high that the new rulers would assume the same style of government—an absolute monarchy.

GOVERNMENT

There is no legislature in Saudi Arabia, nor are political parties permitted. The king has a Council of Ministers who carry out executive and legislative functions. The ministers serve at the pleasure of the king, and they hold power that is strictly personal rather than institutional. Each of the important ministers are princes in the Saudi family.

Local government is organized around tribes and cities. Chiefs, or

This street scene is in Riyadh, the second major city of Saudi Arabia. The most important city, Mecca, is a leading center of Islam. What influence does Islam have on the government of Saudi Arabia?

sheikhs, head local councils, which carry out the law.

Law in the nation is largely rooted in the centuries-old writings of Islam, but also is coupled with royal decree. For instance, in 1962 a series of administrative reforms were passed by the king, including one that abolished slavery. While still very traditional, then, Saudi Arabian life has been affected by modern values.

Japan

Just east of the coast of Asia lie the 3000 islands that make up Japan. Japanese is the language spoken by its 125 million residents, while Shintoism and Buddhism are their main religions. The Japanese identity spans 2000 years, so the people share strong traditions and values.

Before the mid-1800s, Japan resembled medieval Europe in its power structure. Emperors ruled by divine right. Local lords who owned vast tracts of land were defended by warriors known as samurai. After contact with the West was made, however, changes were introduced. By the late 1800s Emperor Mutsuhito saw advantages to modernization.

Under his rule, which lasted from 1868 to 1912, a constitution was adopted, which was a radical idea for a monarchy. A legislature was formed, but most power remained with the emperor and his cabinet. Other reforms led to adapting Western ideas to Japanese culture.

But for many reasons, twentieth-century Japan turned away from democracy toward zealous militarism. Political power was usurped by the military, which led the nation into campaigns of conquest against Asia and, ultimately, against the United States in World War II. After Emperor Hirohito surrendered in 1945, his nation was occupied by American forces. Japan eventually regained its sovereignty in 1952.

JAPANESE CONSTITUTION

While occupied by the United States, a new democratic constitution was written, which went into effect in 1947. It set up a constitutional monarchy with a parliamentary system similar to that in Great Britain. The emperor remained a symbol of national unity but held no political power. Political power is drawn from the people according to the new tenets of Japanese governance.

The constitution has not been in effect long, but there is ample evidence that it has brought stability to Japan. The former power elite, the military, has lost its influence. As the constitution states: "The Japanese people forever renounce war as a sovereign right of the nation." Only self-defense forces are allowed. The military, as we know it, is prohibited.

THE DIET

Japan's Parliament, called the National Diet, has two houses. Together, they hold the highest state power. The

Emperor Akihito, shown here with Empress Michiko, is Japan's ceremonial head of state, but, like Britain, Japan is a constitutional monarchy. What role does the prime minister have in the government of Japan?

House of Representatives has 511 seats; the House of Councilors has 252 seats. All members are elected by the people. Representatives are elected from multimember districts, and councilors are elected either from districts or from the nation as a whole.

The House of Representatives is by far the more powerful body. It has the exclusive power to bring down the prime minister and government through a vote of ''no confidence.'' It, alone, passes the budget and makes treaties. On other bills, however, the House of Councilors becomes involved, basically providing a check on hasty, ill-advised actions of the representatives. But a bill vetoed by the councilors may still be passed if the House of Representatives reapproves it by a two-thirds majority.

PRIME MINISTER AND CABINET

The prime minister is selected from the Diet by its majority party. Administrative duties of national government are carried out by a cabinet, which is appointed by the prime minister. Cabinet members, the majority of whom must be Diet members, head twelve departments, including Justice, Labor, and Finance. The cabinet functions as a unit, due to the strong Japanese value on consensus and unity. Dissent is not tolerated. This solidarity approach causes policy changes to be long in coming as agreement is slowly worked out.

The prime minister and cabinet both are responsible to the Diet and direct most of the legislative work there. Most bills, in fact, originate with the government and are shepherded through the Diet by the cabinet. The prime minister may even dissolve the House of Representatives and call for new elections.

JAPANESE POLITICS

Since its formation in 1955, the Liberal-Democratic party (LDP) has been the dominant force in Japanese politics. Within the LDP itself are factions headed by powerful leaders. When a factional leader becomes prime minister, his closest followers will be the new cabinet. Although the constitutional system allows multiple parties, every prime minister since 1955 has been from the LDP.

Other parties, however, are represented in the Diet. The second largest party is the Socialist party (JSP). The only prominent female politician in Japan, Takako Doi, ranks high in the party. Minor parties represented in the Diet also include the Clean Government party, the Communist party, and the Democratic Socialist party.

In Japan, just as in our country, there are many connections between power and money. For instance, elected politicians are expected to give their constituents substantial gifts of money at weddings or funerals. To finance this practice, as well as their political campaigns, politicians expect businesses to hand over huge contributions. But then the government also works closely with industrialists, which accounts in part for the tremendous economic recovery of Japan after World War II.

Currently, politics in Japan is under pressure to reform. With opposition parties becoming stronger, LDP leaders must consider changes. Many people feel that consumers' needs have been sacrificed for business interests long enough. And financial scandals in the late 1980s, implicating all leaders of the government, have given pause to even the most traditional-minded politicians. In addition, Japanese women may emerge as a major force of reform if recent elections are an indication. But whatever

Takako Doi

Mexico City, shown here, is the capital of Mexico. With about 20 million people, it is the world's largest city in population. What political party, based in Mexico City, has ruled Mexico since the 1930s?

reforms are instituted, it is clear that they will come through Japan's constitutional system.

Mexico

The United Mexican States share a long border with our southern states. Mexico's principal language is Spanish, although about one in ten Mexicans speak a native Indian language. Almost all Mexicans are Roman Catholic, but the government itself is secular.

Since its conquest by Spain in the 1500s, Mexico has been ruled by virtually every style of government. Long an exploited colony, Mexico was torn by wars for independence from 1810 to 1821. Civil war ensued in the 1860s as democratic reforms were attempted. Then France tried to install one of Europe's nobles, Maximilian, as emperor of Mexico. He was executed there in 1867. A ruthless dictatorship under Porfirio Diaz lasted from 1876 until the Revolution of 1910. Throughout the history of this nation, the forces of democracy have struggled with authoritarianism.

MEXICAN CONSTITUTION

The current Mexican constitution went into effect in 1917. It reflects the goal of the Revolution: to remove the concentration of power from the hands of the wealthy landowners and the Catholic church. The constitution also includes a labor code to protect workers from exploitation. And education is guaranteed to all.

While it is not antireligious, the constitution clearly outlines the role of the church. No churches may own real estate; instead, churches are the property of the nation. Religious leaders are forbidden to criticize laws, to vote, to organize political associations, or to hold political meetings in churches. This sharp line between church and state grew out of the Mexican experience in which the Church had been intricately involved in the government.

Many Socialist principles also are incorporated in the constitution. Minimum wages are set for farm and industrial workers, and these workers have the right to strike. Small communal landholdings are encouraged, and large estates are to be broken up into small farms. All minerals, including oil, belong to the government. And foreign investors, including Americans, are seriously restricted in what they can own and what they can do in Mexico.

GOVERNMENT

The Mexican government is a federal republic. The highest executive authority rests with the president, who is elected for a six-year term. He or she appoints a Council of Ministers who, in turn, guide the various national departments, such as Interior, Foreign Affairs, and Agriculture.

Legislative power resides with the Mexican Congress, which has two houses: the Chamber of Deputies and the Senate. Similar to our Congress, the deputies represent the population while the senators represent the states.

There are 31 states plus the Federal District that encompasses the capital, Mexico City. Each state has its own constitution, a governor, and a Chamber of Deputies. State governments have the right to legislate on specific matters and to levy their own taxes.

POLITICS

The early years of the government were filled with violence, corruption, and political scandal. Major political power eventually fell to the Institutional Revolutionary party (PRI). Since its organization in the early 1930s, the PRI has led Mexico in a virtual one-party system, although this often was the result of election fraud. The hold of the PRI has been so firm that all leaders and policies have emerged from the party.

The ideals of the constitution and the revolutionary slogan "Land and Liberty" still have not been realized. Yet, over the years, many leaders have struggled to bring honest public participation to Mexican government. In 1987 the PRI publicly announced its candidates for president. This was a major event since previous selections were made secretly. In 1989 an opposition party, the National Action party (PAN), won an election for governorship of a state for the first time. Also in the 1980s, President Miguel de la Madrid pushed through new legislation against misuse of public funds.

Mexico and its constitution, then, have achieved at least some measure of stability. Elections, even if flawed, are expected to be held and conducted freely. Opposition, even if unpopular, is tolerated. And change is accomplished via constitutional methods.

Section Review

1. What are two characteristics of a stable government system?

2. What role does the monarchy play in British government?

3. What happens when the French National Assembly votes "no confidence" in the government?

4. What roles do the legislature and political parties play in the government of Saudi Arabia?

5. How are the prime minister and the cabinet selected in Japan?

6. What form of government operates in Mexico today?

7. **Challenge:** Based on what you have learned in this section, how do you think the governments discussed are most similar? What major differences do you think exist?

2 Countries in Search of Stability

Political change is always occurring. How well the people of any nation handle such change depends on their acceptance of the fundamental rules of governing. Many countries lack these rules. They are still looking for answers to such basic questions as "Who is a citizen?" "What powers do citizens hold?" "Who can speak for the public—a dictator? A party? The military?"

This section looks at three nations searching for stable governments. Included are Russia, Cuba, and South Africa. Each is unique, but all face strong pressures to change.

Russia

First chieftains, then czars, and finally dictators ruled Russia; until very recently, authoritarian government was all the people had known. They had had no experience with democracy or freely chosen representative government until the 1990s. Before then, Russia led the powerful Soviet Union, which was the essence of a totalitarian communist regime.

But in the late 1980s and the 1990s, phenomenal changes took place in Russia. Political, social, and economic reforms were dramatic and continue to evolve. Individuals and whole nationalities that had been part of the Soviet Union declared their independence, and Russia worked toward building a democratic society.

As the world's largest country, Russia spreads from Europe eastward through the arid deserts and vast Siberian forests of Asia. The population of about 149 million includes 120 different ethnic groups, but ethnic Russians make up 82 percent of the population. Other large ethnic groups include Tartars (4 percent), Ukrainians (3 percent), Belarusians (less than 1 percent), Udmurts, and Kazakhs. Russian is the official language although regional languages are often taught in schools.

When the Communists ruled Russia, the government officially discouraged religion. Nevertheless, many Russians continued to follow the Eastern Orthodox religion. Under the new regime, people have the freedom to practice whatever religion they choose. The Russian Orthodox church remains the dominant religion. In rural areas, the Orthodox church is often the only religious institution. In urban areas, however, most of the world's religions are practiced.

RUSSIAN ATTITUDES

Russia's long history of totalitarian rule limited opportunities for people to make their own decisions. First the

The old Russian style of architecture dominates the center of Moscow, the capital of Russia. How were the peoples of Russia governed before the Communist Revolution of 1917?

czars and then the Communists tried to stifle personal initiative and responsibility and tried to make every citizen conform to officially sanctioned opinions and behavior.

Now that the nation is experimenting with democracy, Russia often seems chaotic. Many Russians are not happy with the rapid pace of change, which has resulted in high prices, increasing crime, unemployment, and a reduced standard of living. Many Russians are unsure that they want to pay such a high price for economic and political freedom. Almost all Russians, however, realize that the communist experiment that began with the Revolution of 1917 was a failure.

Communist ideology called for a total reorganization of the way citizens related to the government. The absolute monarchy of the czars was gone, replaced by a "dictatorship of the proletariat." On paper, this means government by the people, who believed they could trade their shackles, plus a measure of personal freedom, for equality and prosperity. In reality, the Soviet Union's dictatorship was even harsher than that of the czars.

TRANSITION FROM COMMUNISM

In the early 1980s, few people guessed that the days of the Soviet Union were numbered. The Communist party had a firm grip on the nation, and reform seemed out of the question.

In 1985, however, Mikhail Gorbachev became the new leader of the Soviet government. When Gorbachev took over, the Soviet economy was on the verge of collapse. For years the Communists had relied on central planners to decide what products would be produced. As a result, the economy had concentrated on developing heavy equipment and the weapons industry at the expense of consumer goods. Shortages of vital products such as clothing, shoes, and even food had become commonplace in Soviet life. Believing that reform was necessary, Gorbachev launched *perestroika,* or restructuring, to bolster the Soviet economy. Under the old system, the government had owned all the nation's factories, stores, farmlands, and homes. Under *perestroika,* the government gave the people the right to own private property and to start small businesses. New laws allowed farmers to own their own land.

Another part of Gorbachev's policies called for *glasnost,* or openness. For the first time in Soviet history, people were allowed to criticize the government openly and even to hold public demonstrations. Gorbachev also freed thousands of political prisoners, and he relaxed censorship rules on books and films.

The reforms that Gorbachev set in motion seemed unstoppable, and the people clamored for even more reforms. In 1989 the Soviet Union had its first free elections since 1917 to elect representatives to the Congress of People's Deputies. Many of the newly elected deputies were not Communists, and they openly criticized the government. By 1990 new political parties that challenged traditional communist power had sprouted and become powerful.

THE END OF SOVIET RULE

In 1991 a rapid succession of events brought an end to the 74-year communist regime. First, a group of communist hardliners who wanted to halt Gorbachev's reforms ousted the Soviet president and proclaimed a

COMPARISON: VOTING

THE UNITED STATES AND RUSSIA

Most American citizens over the age of 18 take the right to vote for granted. While they may not vote (39 percent did not in the 1992 presidential election), they know they can cast their ballot on a wide range of issues and for local, state, and federal offices. They expect that there will be meaningful choices for most—if not all—of the offices.

Such complacency about voting was not seen in the Soviet Union, where March 26, 1989, marked the first freely contested elections in more than 70 years. At that time, voters elected members to the Congress of Deputies. For the first time, the voters could choose between several candidates for each position.

The new Congress was instrumental in the democratic reforms that took place in the early 1990s, including the breakup of the Soviet Union. Today Russia occupies most of the territory of the former Soviet Union, and reforms are continuing.

The reforms and the elections that are taking place in Russia today are a far cry from government under the Soviet dictatorship. While the Soviet press always reported high voter turnout in elections, only candidates with Communist party approval were allowed to seek office. As part of the reforms begun under President Mikhail Gorbachev and continued under President Boris Yeltsin of Russia, freely contested elections have been commonplace since that first free election in 1989.

Although many Soviets were skeptical about the real willingness of the party leadership to allow dissenters a role within the government, they eagerly took part in the electoral process in 1989. Criticism of the system that would have been unheard of a few years before was openly voiced during the campaign. A wide range of issues echoing those of concern to many Americans also was debated. These issues included poor housing, ethnic questions, the environment, nuclear power, the economy, and national defense.

The way Soviets voted also indicated that they took the election seriously. The result in districts where real opposition was available was an overwhelming victory for reform. Boris Yeltsin, who had been booted from party leadership by Gorbachev just two years previously, beat the Communist party candidate by a 9 to 1 margin. Candidates who represented the military did poorly, as did many Party leaders. Even some unopposed party candidates failed to win a majority, since voters were allowed to cross off an unopposed candidate's name.

The Communists have continued to lose ground in the elections since 1989. In 1991, for example, Boris Yeltsin, campaigning as a political independent, won the Russian republic's first presidential election.

President Yeltsin oversaw more free elections in the 1990s. In 1993, elections for a new parliament were held. Voter turnout in this election, however, was much lower than in the previous free elections. Only 55.5 percent of eligible voters cast ballots. The percentage was roughly the same as that in American elections.

Observers are uncertain whether Russian voter participation will return to the highs set in the first free elections. Only future election results will reveal if voter apathy is becoming common in Russia as it is in the United States.

1. How did Americans and Soviets differ in their attitudes toward voting?
2. How do you account for the low voter turnout in Russia's 1993 elections?

new government in the old communist tradition.

The hardliners, however, failed to take into account Russian president, Boris Yeltsin, who rallied the Russian people against the new leaders. When the coup collapsed and Gorbachev returned to Moscow, everything had changed: Yeltsin, not Gorbachev, was in charge.

Gorbachev resigned as head of the Communist party and urged that it be abolished, but nothing could stem the tide of change. First, the Baltic republics won their freedom, and then the remaining 12 republics of the Soviet Union proclaimed their independence. By the end of 1991, 11 of the former Soviet republics had joined in a Commonwealth of Independent States. Russia and Yeltsin were dominant.

On December 25, Mikhail Gorbachev resigned the Soviet presidency. Following Gorbachev's resignation, the red hammer and sickle Soviet flag that had flown over the Kremlin for 74 years was lowered and replaced with the white, blue, and red flag of Russia. While signaling the end of Gorbachev's presidency, the formation of the Commonwealth confirmed Yeltsin's rise to power. As leader of the largest nation in the world, Yeltsin became an international figure.

Eager to bolster Russia' move toward democracy, the Western democracies, such as the United States, Great Britain, and France, pledged support. Nevertheless Russia's move away from communism has been difficult.

Yeltsin has had to assume responsibility for Russia's problems: a shattered economy, deteriorating public services, and ethnic strife. Many Russian citizens became disenchanted during the transition and wanted to

oust Yeltsin. Some even longed for a return to communist rule when the government made decisions for everyone. Nevertheless, Yeltsin remained in control, and the country continued to move reforms forward.

In 1993 a new constitution went into effect. Under the new government, a president is head of state and a prime minister is head of government. The president is strong and has power to dissolve parliament and set foreign policy, as well as appoint the prime minister. The parliament has two houses: the Federation Council and the State Duma.

AN UNCERTAIN FUTURE

As Russia moves into the twenty-first century, the nation faces an uncertain future. Throughout the early 1990s, the government continued to turn over land and factories to private investors. This change often caused economic disruption. In particular, workers often lost their jobs when private owners streamlined the operations of formerly inefficient businesses.

Inflation also became a serious problem in the newly free economy.

Russian President Boris Yeltsin has overseen his country's rapid move toward democracy. What are some of the changes that have taken place?

For years the Soviet Union had set prices on everything. Under a market economy, however, the forces of supply and demand set prices. Because so many goods in Russia were in short supply, prices soared. Suddenly people who thought that their incomes were adequate for life did not have enough money to live.

Faced with the sudden jump in unemployment and soaring prices, many Russian workers longed for the days of communist rule. Nevertheless, Boris Yeltsin retained his position as president, and the pace of reform continued.

Predictions about the future of Russia vary. Pessimists conclude that continuing economic distress might deepen into famine. Such a situation, they say, might lead to riots, civil war, and the return of dictatorship in the fragile democracy.

Optimists, while acknowledging the critical economic situation, do not expect widespread famine. They predict continued shortages, long lines of dissatisfied shoppers, and perhaps pockets of poverty at the mercy of the decaying transportation system. They do not necessarily believe that Russia is headed back to dictatorship.

Whether pessimist or optimist, experts agree that Russia's job of converting to a free market economy will be long-term and will not bring prosperity for many years. During the transition, unemployment will rise as more inefficient industries close. Inflation will continue as prices fluctuate.

Cuba

Cuba, an island nation just 90 miles south of Florida, was ruled by Spain from the 1500s until 1898. Not surprisingly, then, Cubans speak Spanish, and most are Catholic.

Fidel Castro

The United States ruled the island for four years, granting it limited independence in 1902. Although Cuba became fully independent in 1934, we retained major economic, political, and social ties with it. To this day, we have a military base there.

The governments of Cuba in this century have been a series of dictatorships. An armed rebellion, led by Fidel Castro, overthrew the repressive, corrupt dictatorship of General Fulgencio Batista in 1959. Castro then instituted a Communist dictatorship with himself as the center of power.

GOVERNMENT

In any personality dictatorship, all important decisions are made by a single, powerful person. In this case that person is President Fidel Castro. But the rest of the Cuban government is organized as a traditional Communist state. In theory, all power belongs to the workers. The Communist party (PCC) is the "leading force of society and the state." It is the sole legal party and has very little organized opposition.

An elected National Assembly of People's Power meets to ratify the measures adopted by the PCC Congress. Thus, in name the government is representative of the public, but, in fact, decisions are made within the party. Ultimate power is held by the party's politburo, modeled after that body in the Soviet Union. Other levels of government bureaucracy ensure that the policies of Castro and his party allies are carried out.

According to Cuba's written constitution, the state organizes and directs the economic life of the nation. The document also guarantees basic rights such as the right to work, to receive an education, to assemble, and to demonstrate. But as in the former Soviet Union, these rights are seriously limited in actual practice. Cuban jails hold hundreds of political prisoners, and thousands of other Cubans have fled the country to escape Castro's repression.

POLITICAL CHANGE

Until the collapse of the Soviet Union, Cuba relied on billions of dollars in Soviet aid each year. Rather than using this aid to help the economy, however, the Cubans spent most of it on foreign military ventures. When the Soviet Union was disbanded and Russia moved toward democracy, this aid suddenly stopped. The results were disastrous for the Cuban economy. Shortages of everything from consumer goods to gasoline to food plagued the already weak economy. Although many people predicted that the shortages would topple the government, Castro remained in power.

With most other formerly communist nations moving toward free enterprise and democracy, it is quite possible that the same fate will befall Cuba. The Cuban people are not completely isolated. Information about the changes occurring worldwide has filtered into the nation through limited contact with the thousands of Cubans living in our country. More news comes across the airwaves from Radio Marti, a propaganda station beamed from the United States to Cuba.

The Castro government was shaken in 1994 when thousands of people wanted to flee. The government allowed them to leave, often to go to the United States. Another source of stress in the Cuban political system will come when Castro dies. Since he has held firm control in his own hands, there will inevitably be a difficult power struggle before a suc-

cessor emerges. When this happens, the will of the Cuban people may perhaps become more evident.

South Africa

The Republic of South Africa is the southernmost country on the African continent. Most of its people are black Africans, with minorities of Europeans and Asians. The official languages are Afrikaans (a Dutch dialect) and English.

The Union of South Africa was formed in 1910 by the merger of four British colonies. In 1934 the Union was given its independence, and in 1961 it became the Republic of South Africa. From 1910 until minor reforms were made in 1984, all government was the exclusive right of the Europeans. And yet whites made up only 17 percent of the population. A new constitution written in 1984 allowed partial self-government by the Coloureds (people of mixed race) and the Asians. But the black majority had no political power.

THE OLD GOVERNMENT

Due to their English and Dutch heritage, white South Africans leaned

Nelson Mandela and his wife, Winnie, greet crowds after Mandela's release from jail. Mandela had been imprisoned by the South African government for 27 years. What changes does Nelson Mandela favor for South Africa?

toward constitutional government. How they viewed the relationship of citizens to government was clearly stated in their constitution. Laws were enacted by the designated powers, and the courts enforced duly adopted laws. Thus, the government was highly constitutional, but with a major omission. It ignored the wishes of the black majority. The constitution specifically outlined that rights were withheld from blacks. The 1984 constitution, ratified by the white voters, continued the policy of **apartheid,** the theory of separate but equal development of racial groups. In practice, it meant white supremacy.

The constitution set up three houses in Parliament: the House of Assembly for Whites, the House of Representatives for Coloureds, and the House of Delegates for Asians. All members were elected by their own racial groups, and each house governed matters pertaining solely to its own race. A Minister Council in each house handled executive matters.

apartheid separation of the races

Members of the three houses, dominated in numbers by the white Assembly members, elected a powerful state president. The president, in turn, selected a cabinet, which was responsible for all national affairs. In addition, any legislation that was not passed by all three houses was referred to the President's Council, a body made up primarily of white Assembly members or presidential appointees. The government, needless to say, was in the hands of whites, except for very narrow Coloured or Asian affairs.

BEGINNINGS OF CHANGE

When Frederik Willem de Klerk became president in 1989, he implemented a series of reforms designed to move the nation toward democracy. De Klerk freed political prisoners, desegregated hospitals and other public facilities, lifted the state of emergency that the government had decreed, and gave the African National Congress—a black political party—legal status. De Klerk also began talks on power sharing with black Africans.

Throughout the early 1990s, de Klerk continued his policy of reform. In late 1991 he outlined his proposals for a new constitution that would provide suffrage to the black majority for the first time. In 1992 South African whites overwhelmingly endorsed de Klerk's reform policies in a referendum. The voters approved negotiations to end white minority rule through talks with the black majority.

The pace of reform quickened throughout 1993. In February the government and the ANC, headed by Nelson Mandela, agreed on a transitional "government of national unity" in which both parties would be partners. In July the date for the country's first universal suffrage elections was set for April 26-29, 1994. In November 1993, a new majority-rule constitution that provides fundamental human rights to all South Africans was approved.

FREE ELECTIONS

In April 1994, South Africans went to the polls. For most voters, it was their first experience with a democratic election. At stake was the future of their country.

In national and provincial elections, the voters chose delegates to the national parliament—a 400-seat national Assembly and a 90-seat Senate. The parliament selects the president who is head of state and head of the government. Two vice presidents, one from the majority party and one from the strongest opposition party assist the president. After the 1994 elections, Nelson Mandela became president. The two vice presidents were Thabo Mbeki and F.W. de Klerk.

Despite the progress that South Africa has made toward majority rule, several questions remain. Will the new government be able to ensure equal rights for all? Will the white minority try to resist the new changes with violence or mass emigration? No one knows for sure. But everyone is certain that the new government will do everything within its power to ensure a peaceful transition until parliament drafts a permanent constitution in 1999.

Section Review

1. What changes have taken place in Russia in the early 1990s?
2. What role does the Communist party hold in Cuba today?
3. What major omission has been corrected in South Africa's new constitutional government?
4. **Challenge:** What plan would you offer for the citizens of South Africa to achieve a stable, democratic government?

Summary

1. Few countries besides the United States have been consistent over a long period of time concerning the rules of how they would be governed.
2. Pressure for political change can come from a wide variety of internal and external sources. One powerful source is the knowledge of other forms of government.
3. Stable governments are marked by having an agreed-upon, nonviolent process for allowing change. They also have widespread agreement on the fundamental rules of governing.
4. Great Britain is a constitutional monarchy with a parliamentary government.
5. France has combined a strong president with a parliamentary system.
6. An absolute monarchy exists in Saudi Arabia and has contributed to the stability of the nation.
7. Japan, like Great Britain, is a constitutional monarchy with a parliamentary government.
8. Similar to our country, Mexico has a federal republic. Pressure to allow more competition between political parties is increasing.
9. In unstable governments, the fundamental rules of governing are not accepted by the majority of people, or the rules are nonexistent.
10. Russia, long a part of a totalitarian communist regime, has recently seen major political, social, and economic reforms.
11. A Communist dictatorship under Fidel Castro has ruled Cuba for 30 years. This may change when Castro dies.
12. The white minority government of South Africa has yielded to change and allowed the black majority a say in government.

Chapter 26 Review

★ Building Vocabulary

Based on what you have learned in this chapter, write at least two paragraphs on comparative governments. Be sure to include the following vocabulary terms in your paragraphs: minister, apartheid.

★ Reviewing Facts

1. What is the most powerful force for political change nationwide?
2. Who will ultimately decide how a particular nation is governed?
3. What is the basis of Great Britain's system of government?
4. Who selects the British prime minister?
5. How is local government organized in Great Britain?
6. How does the 1958 French constitution strengthen governmental stability?
7. Describe two differences between the powers of the president of France and those of the American President.
8. According to France's constitution, what subjects may the Parliament legislate?
9. What four major political parties have been active in recent French history?
10. What has brought about the great stability in the Saudi Arabian government?
11. On what is national law based in Saudi Arabia?
12. What kind of government was set up by Japan's constitution in 1947?
13. What exclusive power is held by the Japanese House of Representatives?
14. What is causing pressure on current Japanese leaders to initiate political reforms?
15. Describe the role of the Catholic church and Church leaders as outlined by the current Mexican constitution.
16. If the Mexican PRI party dominates politics, why is the system considered stable?
17. How would you describe the present political and economic situation in Russia?
18. What was the role of the Communist party in the former Soviet Union? How has this changed?
19. What are the goals of the newly formed government in South Africa?

★ Analyzing Facts

1. What is the difference in the process of political change between stable and unstable government systems?
2. If the French are on the Fifth Republic, why is the French government considered stable?
3. Why is growing global awareness a force for change in many countries?
4. How do the government systems of Japan and Great Britain compare?
5. What are the differences between the Soviet government and the Russian government?
6. Describe the changes in the Cuban government you think would occur if Castro dies.

★ Evaluating Ideas

1. To what degree should American economic and foreign policies support the forces of change in other countries? Explain.

Using Your
Civic Participation Journal

Review the information on a foreign government that you entered in your Civic Participation Journal. Work with five of your classmates who compiled information on other countries. Construct a chart comparing the six nations and present the chart to the class.

2. Do you think that the increasing global awareness developing in the world today will increase the forces for political change worldwide? Why or why not?

3. In your opinion, in what instances would political change in a country not be desirable? Explain.

4. What are the challenges to democracy in South Africa?

★ Critical Thinking Classifying

To classify things is to sort and arrange them into groups on the basis of shared or common characteristics. Classifying can help you manage and understand material that is complicated or large in volume. It also can help you to find new meanings in data.

Explanation When attempting to classify things, scan the material and look for ways to arrange it into related groups. First, pick a category that you think will include many of the items and fit what you can into it. Then choose a second category that is related to the first one and place into it as many of the remaining items from the material as meet the requirements of the category. Continue this process until as many items as possible have been separated from the general material and sorted into specialized groups of items that share common characteristics. When the process is complete, the items from the general material will be contained in one of several related smaller groups.

The requirements that you establish for your classification scheme, and for each category within it, will depend on what use you wish to make of the material. The same set of data often can be sorted and classified in more than one way. For example, in doing your laundry, you would not create a separate category for black socks. Unless you had enough of them for a complete load of wash, you probably would include them in the larger category of dark colors. But later a separate category for black socks would help you sort your clean laundry and put it away.

One way to classify material is to put it into a table or chart. Tables and charts are graphic representations of written information set up in columns and rows. Major categories are written across the top of the chart and then each item of information is placed under the proper heading.

Practice The following list of nations has little in common. However, depending on how you intend to use the information, there are several ways to sort and classify the nations.

1. Afghanistan	12. Madagascar
2. Austria	13. Malaysia
3. Brazil	14. New Zealand
4. Chad	15. Philippines
5. Chile	16. Saudi Arabia
6. China	17. South Africa
7. Denmark	18. South Korea
8. Italy	19. Russia
9. Japan	20. United States
10. Laos	21. Zambia
11. Libya	

If you were interested in their geography, you might notice that while some have coastlines, others are landlocked. One way to classify these nations is on that basis.

Island Nations: 9, 12, 14, 15
Peninsula Nations: 7, 8, 13, 16, 18
Nations with Coastlines: 3, 5, 6, 11, 17, 19, 20
Landlocked Nations: 1, 2, 4, 10, 21

You could show this classification system even better if you created a chart with the categories across the top and then listed the nations in columns under each category.

Independent Practice Classify the nations on the above list in at least three more ways, including at least one system based on their governments. Make a chart for each classification system.

Chapter 27

International Organizations

Think about your role in your school environment. First, you are a member of the entire school population. Next, you are a member of your grade level. And within these two categories are a number of smaller organizations you may have joined.

The nations of the world have a similar breakdown of roles. Our country is a member of the global community. We are also a member of an international organization—the United Nations. Further, we belong to various "clubs" whose members share common interests. This chapter will show you how such alliances impact the global scene.

Chapter Preview

TERMS TO KNOW
interdependent, per capita GDP, third world, visas, international organization, alliances, collective security, balance of power, common markets, free trade associations

READ TO DISCOVER
- the role of the United States in an interdependent world.
- the structure and activities of the United Nations.
- the role of defense organizations.
- the role of economic and political organizations.

★ ★ ★ ★ ★

Civic Participation Journal

We live in an interdependent world that relies on world trade. Make a list of 10 items that you would like to purchase. Note the items in your journal. Visit area stores to look at the products and note where they were produced. Record your findings in your journal.

1 Global Interdependence

Throughout this century, the nations of the world have become increasingly **interdependent.** This interdependence increases as nations rely ever more heavily on other nations' resources, manufactured goods, services, and markets.

American foreign policymakers look out for the best interests of the United States, but at the same time they understand that our actions can affect other nations and vice versa. Moreover, in dealing with American allies, our leaders realize that these nations may have different interests and goals than we do.

France and Germany, for example, have a greater dependence on oil and gas imports than we do because they have no internal supply of these vital resources. As a result, their foreign policy toward Russia, an energy supplier, might differ from our foreign policy toward that nation and might even cause conflict with the United States.

This, indeed, happened. France and West Germany signed an agreement with the Soviet Union in the 1980s to build a $25 billion natural gas pipeline from Siberia to Western Europe. The project was financed with French and West German funds and included an agreement by which those two nations would sell high-technology equipment and supplies to the Soviet Union.

Our nation opposed the deal, believing it would make our Western European allies too dependent on Soviet energy and, thus, too open to Soviet pressure on other issues. The United States also felt that selling equipment to the Soviets was helping an opponent of democracy. But France and West Germany believed that their energy needs outweighed possible Soviet threats and went forward with the agreement.

Many factors have led to an increase in global interdependence. Increases in world trade and travel; international mail, telephone, and facsimile service; and even exchange of movies, music, and television programs have brought nations closer together. American interdependence is dramatically shown by its increased international investments. In 1950, for instance, the United States invested $10 billion in the economies of other nations. This figure had climbed to $487 billion by 1992.

The Global Community

The global community is made up of more than 170 independent nations. In the process of becoming more interdependent, these nations have often come into conflict with one another. At the same time, however, most leaders realize that cooperation is required to achieve peace and economic well-being.

There are many factors that affect the role a nation plays in the international community. Nations differ widely, for instance, in geographic size and population, language and culture, type of government, and economic wealth. Measured by gross domestic product (GDP), the United States is the wealthiest nation in the world. But if you look at **per capita GDP,** Americans are poorer than citizens of Switzerland and Sweden or such oil-rich nations as Kuwait and Saudi Arabia. Equally stark differences among nations can also be found by comparing military strength, natural resources, agricultural or industrial production, energy consumption, and a variety of other factors.

One way that scholars who study global interactions often group na-

interdependent tied to one another because decisions and actions in one country have a direct impact on other countries

per capita GDP amount of a country's GDP produced per person; average yearly income

Paris Stock Exchange

tions is in terms of economic development. Countries are classified in terms of developed, newly developed, and developing nations. **Developed nations** are the rich, strong, industrialized states. The key developed nations are the United States, the western European nations, Japan, and Australia.

Newly developed nations are middle-income states with some industrial base. These include countries of eastern Europe, several Middle Eastern states, and countries like South Korea, Mexico, and Argentina.

Developing nations are states with little or no industry. The great majority of these countries, like Haiti or Ethiopia, are very poor. A few, such as Saudi Arabia and Kuwait, are rich, usually because of oil. Most were former colonies of western European nations and gained their independence after World War II. More than 75 percent of the world's population lives in developing nations.

Developing nations have tried to present a common front on global issues, especially on international economic issues. On such issues developing nations often demand policies they believe would correct injustices they suffered when they were colonies of the European nations. On other issues, such as the environment, they may resist policies that developed nations advocate. For example, developing nations might argue that pollution regulations would limit their ability to open new factories and promote economic growth.

No matter what the economic status of any nation, its actions often affect other nations of the world. Developments in Cuba in mid-1994 provide one example of such global interaction.

Civil unrest in Cuba led the Communist dictator, Fidel Castro, to stop interfering with Cubans who wanted to flee to the United States. Thousands of hopeful refugees piled into rickety rafts for the voyage across the Straits of Florida. Faced with a sudden influx of immigrants, President Clinton changed the decades-old American policy that automatically granted refugee status to people fleeing the Communist island. Instead, the United States would detain refugees in camps until their status was confirmed. Most of the Cubans arrived with no legal documents, including **visas.** The American government spent millions of dollars to set up relocation camps for the aliens. By his action, Fidel Castro forced the United States to change its immigration practices and spend millions of unbudgeted dollars.

developing nation state with little or no industry

visas government permits that allow aliens to enter the United States

Section Review

1. What are three factors that have led to an increase in global interdependence?

2. What are some factors that can affect a nation's role in the world?

3. What are some shared characteristics of developing nations?

4. **Challenge:** In your opinion, should the United States continue to increase investments in foreign economies? Why or why not?

2 The United Nations

In the 1900s, attempts have been made to establish an **international organization** whose purposes are to maintain peace and help solve economic and social problems. The League of Nations, established at the end of World War I, was one such attempt. It was established to provide collective security on a global scale. But the League failed to achieve its goal, partly because the United States never joined. Why?

Following the war, Americans were not willing to accept a major role as a leader in the international community. The League also failed because member nations did not cooperate to prevent military aggression by Germany, Italy, and Japan in the 1930s.

With the end of World War II, the nations of the world again saw a need for an international organization to peacefully resolve global differences. Accepting its role as a major economic and military power, the United States was a key player in establishing the United Nations.

The UN Organization

The United Nations (UN) was established at the close of World War II by the Allied nations—headed by the United States, the Soviet Union, Great Britain, France, and Nationalist China. These nations hoped that the new international organization would help to prevent future world wars.

In April 1945, delegates from 50 nations met in San Francisco to work out the principles and basic structure of the UN. The final result of their efforts, the United Nations Charter, established the UN as an organization that would maintain international peace and security, develop friendly relations among all nations of the world, and promote justice and cooperation in resolving conflicts among nations. Today, issues of economic development and security and the environment also are concerns of the UN.

Originally, membership was open to any ''peaceloving'' nation that accepted the obligations of the UN Charter. The United States was the first nation to approve the Charter and become a member. By October 1945, 51 nations had accepted the charter and joined the UN. Since then, other nations have been admitted by a two-thirds vote of the General Assembly. Today, membership has grown to 184 nations. Many new members, such as nations from Africa and Asia, were once European colonies. Member nations are identified in Figure 27-1.

The United Nations is divided into six major units, each assigned various duties and responsibilities by the UN Charter. The organization of the UN is shown in Figure 27-2.

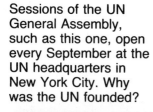

international organization
organization to which many, if not all, independent nations of the world belong

Sessions of the UN General Assembly, such as this one, open every September at the UN headquarters in New York City. Why was the UN founded?

UNITED NATIONS

Afghanistan (1946)
Albania (1955)
Algeria (1962)
Angola (1976)
Antigua and
  Barbuda (1981)
Argentina
Armenia (1992)
Australia
Austria (1955)
Azerbaijan (1992)
Bahamas (1973)
Bahrain (1971)
Bangladesh (1974)
Barbados (1966)
Belarus (1945)
Belgium
Belize (1981)
Benin (1960)
Bhutan (1971)
Bolivia
Bosnia and
  Herzegovina (1992)
Botswana (1966)
Brazil
Brunei Darussalam
  (1984)
Bulgaria (1955)
Burkina Faso (1960)
Burundi (1962)
Cambodia (1955)
Cameroon (1960)
Canada
Cape Verde (1975)
Central African
  Republic (1960)
Chad (1960)
Chile
China
Colombia
Comoros (1975)
Congo (1960)
Costa Rica
Côte d'Ivoire (1960)
Croatia (1992)
Cuba
Cyprus (1960)
Czechoslovakia
Czech Republic
  (1993)

Denmark
Djibouti (1977)
Dominica (1978)
Dominican Republic
Ecuador
Egypt
El Salvador
Equatorial Guinea
  (1968)
Eritrea (1993)
Estonia (1991)
Ethiopia
Fiji (1970)
Finland (1955)
France
Gabon (1960)
Gambia, The (1965)
Germany, (1973)
Ghana (1957)
Greece
Grenada (1974)
Guatemala
Guinea (1958)
Guinea-Bissau
  (1974)
Guyana (1966)
Haiti
Honduras
Hungary (1955)
Iceland (1946)
India
Indonesia (1950)
Iran
Iraq
Ireland (1955)
Israel (1949)
Italy (1955)
Jamaica (1962)
Japan (1956)
Jordan (1955)
Kazakhstan (1992)
Korea, N. (1991)
Korea, S. (1991)
Kenya (1963)
Kuwait (1963)
Kyrgyzstan (1992)
Laos (1955)
Latvia (1991)
Lebanon
Lesotho (1966)

Liberia
Libya (1955)
Liechtenstein (1990)
Lithuania (1991)
Luxembourg
Macedonia (1993)
Madagascar (1960)
Malawi (1964)
Malaysia (1957)
Maldives (1965)
Mali (1960)
Malta (1964)
Marshall Islands
  (1991)
Mauritania (1961)
Mauritius (1968)
Mexico
Moldova (1992)
Monaco (1993)
Mongolia (1961)
Morocco (1956)
Mozambique
  (1975)
Myanmar (Burma)
  (1948)
Nambia (1990)
Nepal (1955)
Netherlands
New Zealand
Nicaragua
Niger (1960)
Nigeria (1960)
Norway
Oman (1971)
Pakistan (1947)
Panama
Papua New Guinea
  (1975)
Paraguay
Peru
Philippines
Poland
Portugal (1955)
Qatar (1971)
Romania (1955)
Russia (1945)
Rwanda (1962)
St. Kitts
  and Nevis (1983)
St. Lucia (1979)

St. Vincent and
  the Grenadines
  (1980)
Samoa (Western)
  (1976)
San Marino (1992)
São Tomé and
  Príncipe   (1975)
Saudi Arabia
Senegal (1960)
Seychelles (1976)
Sierra Leone (1961)
Singapore (1965)
Slovakia (1993)
Slovenia (1992)
Solomon Islands
  (1978)
Somalia (1960)
South Africa
Spain (1955)
Sri Lanka (1955)
Sudan (1956)
Suriname (1975)
Swaziland (1968)
Sweden (1946)
Syria
Tajikistan (1992)
Tanzania (1961)
Thailand (1946)
Togo (1960)
Trinidad and
  Tobago (1962)
Tunisia (1956)
Turkey
Turkmenistan (1992)
Uganda (1962)
Ukraine (1945)
United Arab
  Emirates (1971)
United Kingdom
United States
Uruguay
Vanuatu (1981)
Venezuela
Vietnam (1977)
Yemen (1947)
Yugoslavia
Zaire (1960)
Zambia (1964)
Zimbabwe (1980)

The charter members of the UN do not have dates after their names. Other nations are listed with their years of admission.

Figure 27-1

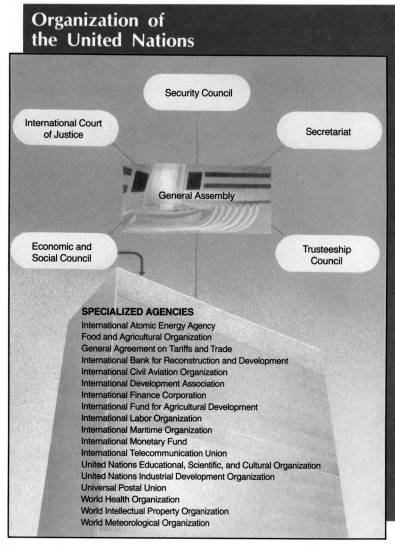

Organization of the United Nations

Security Council

International Court of Justice

Secretariat

General Assembly

Economic and Social Council

Trusteeship Council

SPECIALIZED AGENCIES
International Atomic Energy Agency
Food and Agricultural Organization
General Agreement on Tariffs and Trade
International Bank for Reconstruction and Development
International Civil Aviation Organization
International Development Association
International Finance Corporation
International Fund for Agricultural Development
International Labor Organization
International Maritime Organization
International Monetary Fund
International Telecommunication Union
United Nations Educational, Scientific, and Cultural Organization
United Nations Industrial Development Organization
Universal Postal Union
World Health Organization
World Intellectual Property Organization
World Meteorological Organization

Figure 27-2

GENERAL ASSEMBLY

The General Assembly is the major unit of the UN. By joining, all nations automatically became members of the General Assembly. Each nation may send five delegates, five alternate delegates, and as many advisers as it wishes to the General Assembly. However, each nation has only one vote in the Assembly meetings.

Most issues brought before the General Assembly are decided by a simple majority, although major issues require a two-thirds majority. By charter, however, the only decisions of the General Assembly that members must obey are votes on the UN budget.

The General Assembly holds one regular session each year, traditionally at the New York headquarters, beginning on the third Tuesday in September. Originally, sessions were three months long, but they are now often longer because of a heavy agenda of issues. An emergency session can be called by a majority of member nations or the Security Council to deal with an immediate threat to international peace and security. Special sessions have been called to address disarmament and UN finances.

Until the 1960s, the General Assembly was dominated by the western bloc, consisting of the United States and non-Communist nations in Europe, the Americas, and the Pacific. Issues at that time centered on the cold war between the two superpowers and their allies. Since then, newly independent nations of Africa, Asia, and the Middle East have had increasing influence on issues addressed by the UN. In addition to concerns about war, they have presented to the General Assembly such issues as their mounting international debts and growing deficits, increasing populations, and poverty.

A number of specialized organizations report to the General Assembly. They include the UN Children's Fund (UNICEF), the World Food Council, the UN Conference on Trade and Development, the UN Environment Program, and others. Three commissions also report to the General Assembly—the commissions on international law, international trade, and disarmament. Finally, two autonomous organizations are affiliated with the UN. They are the General Agreement on Tariffs and Trade

(GATT) and the International Atomic Energy Agency, which promotes the peaceful use of nuclear energy.

SECURITY COUNCIL

According to the UN Charter, the Security Council has primary responsibility for maintaining international peace and security. The Council is composed of 15 member nations, each represented by one delegate. The United States, United Kingdom, Russia, China, and France are the five *permanent* members of the Council. The other 10 are nonpermanent members, each selected by the General Assembly for 2-year terms.

On routine matters, the Security Council can act with the approval of any nine members. On important issues, such as whether to sanction a member nation, all five permanent members must be included in the nine-member majority favoring the proposal. If any permanent member opposes and casts a veto, the Security Council cannot approve the proposal.

The Security Council has the power to decide the course of action the UN should take in settling international disputes. It meets at the request of UN members to consider any serious confrontation between nations that may lead to war. In responding to such a situation, the Security Council may take a number of steps, including calling on the disputing nations to seek peaceful solutions to their problems; suggesting ways to resolve issues, such as going before the World Court; and asking nations not involved in the dispute to assist in efforts to find a peaceful settlement.

In clear-cut cases of aggression, the Security Council may call for forceful action, such as asking UN members to impose a trade ban on a nation violating UN principles. As a final measure to end a dispute, the Council may ask UN members to contribute military forces to a UN action. The Council, however, cannot force nations to obey its rulings. Instead, it must rely on moral persuasion by the global community to put its recommendations into effect.

In addition to its peacekeeping responsibilities, the Security Council approves applications for membership to the UN and also selects the candidate to head the Secretariat.

SECRETARIAT

The Secretariat carries out the daily business of the UN. It is staffed by about 14,000 international civil servants—citizens of member nations. Some work at the UN headquarters in New York City, while others work at the UN European offices in Geneva, Switzerland, or in UN agencies throughout the world.

The Secretariat is headed by the Secretary-General, who is appointed by the General Assembly for a five-year term. As chief administrative officer, the Secretary-General oversees the staff of the Secretariat and reports to the General Assembly on UN business and activities.

Since the UN's creation in 1945, a number of diplomats have served as Secretary-General. Trygve Halvdan Lie of Norway was the first, and others include Dag Hammarskjold of Sweden (1953), U Thant of Burma (1961), Kurt Waldheim of Austria (1972), Javier Perez de Cuellar of Peru (1982), and Boutros Boutros-Ghali, who took over in 1992.

ECONOMIC AND SOCIAL COUNCIL

The Economic and Social Council plays an important role in UN efforts to advance human rights and improve standards of living worldwide. It promotes cooperation among nations in

This American trawler harvests its catch of fish in the Puget Sound near the Canadian border. Nations involved in disputes over fishing rights often appeal their cases to the International Court of Justice. What other kinds of international disputes are handled by the Court?

the areas of health care, education, housing, human rights, and cultural development.

The Council's 54 member nations (elected to three-year terms) meet twice a year and also sponsor a variety of conferences and publications. The Council also issues recommendations on social and economic programs to individual nations, the General Assembly and Security Council, and other UN organizations. Another function of the Council is coordinating the work of the UN's many specialized agencies that deal with such areas as transportation, narcotics, labor organizations, and civil aviation.

INTERNATIONAL COURT OF JUSTICE

Sometimes referred to as the World Court, the International Court of Justice handles the judicial and legal affairs of the UN. Located in The Hague, Netherlands, the Court is made up of 15 judges, each from a different nation, selected by the General Assembly and Security Council for nine-year terms.

The Court generally tries cases between nations, and any UN member can bring a dispute before the Court, although none is required to do so. Nations may accept the Court's jurisdiction over their cases with or without preset conditions.

Most disputes handled by the Court involve such matters as fishing rights, national boundary lines, and financial claims. If either party fails to obey the Court's decision—reached by a majority vote—the other party may take the issue to the Security Council.

TRUSTEESHIP COUNCIL

The five permanent members of the Security Council are also members of the Trusteeship Council. This council sets policies for handling the affairs of trust territories, those special colonial territories placed under UN direction. The Council's goal is self-government for all dependent territories. Certain UN member nations serve as trustees, or administrators, of the territories to prepare them for independence. Today, only the United States administers a trust territory—the Palau Islands in the Pacific.

ISSUE: UNITED NATIONS

WHO PAYS THE BILLS?

Any large organization must deal with a very basic question—"Who will pay the bills?" For the 184-member United Nations, this question continues to be one of heated debate. The issue has intensified as the UN budget climbed from $178 million in the early 1970s to over $2.7 billion in the 1990s. Such huge budgets have led many member nations to question the amount they pay toward the UN budget and how the international organization spends their contributions.

Contributions from member nations are the primary source of UN funds. The 18-member UN Committee on Contributions decides how much a nation pays based on the total income of that nation as shown in its gross domestic product. Over one-half of the member nations pay between .01 and .03 percent of the total UN budget. Eight nations, including the United States, Japan, Germany, Russia, France, Great Britain, Italy, and Canada pay 70 percent of the UN's annual operating budget.

UN members contributing the most money question the use of a nation's total income as a basis for contributions. Some nations, for example, have a higher per capita income than the United States, but may pay much less toward the UN budget.

Nations paying large dues also question how the money is spent. The budget is allocated in the General Assembly, where all member nations get one vote. Developing nations hold a majority in the General Assembly and thus can push through programs they support with little concern for the costs.

In 1985 the United States Congress revolted, withholding half of its dues—about $100 million. A special UN committee then made a series of recommendations for changing the way the budgeting is done to give countries paying more money more control. The recommendations also included ideas for cutting some costs, such as reducing the number of people employed at UN agencies throughout the world. The recommendations were passed by the General Assembly.

Although the changes in budgeting procedures were not to take effect until 1989, the UN began immediately to put some of the cost-cutting measures into effect. By 1988, for example, the UN had cut its worldwide staff by 13 percent, a significant reduction in the large workforce.

Despite these efforts, UN costs have skyrocketed, especially for UN peacekeeping efforts in Africa, Central America, the former Yugoslavia, and Southeast Asia. The United States has continued to be the organization's largest contributor, paying more than twice as much as the second largest contributor, Japan. The United States' share in 1994 was $300 million, as well as millions in special assessments. Many Americans, however, continue to question why the United States must shoulder so much of the burden.

The future of the UN, in a time that Secretary General Boutros Boutros-Ghali describes as one of promise depends on its ability to convince member nations to continue paying the costs of running an international organization with many functions.

1. How are member nations assessed their contributions to the UN budget?
2. Do you think the United States should continue contributing so much to the United Nations?

UN Issues and Problems

The United Nations has been relatively successful in its social, economic, and humanitarian work. Through its specialized agencies and organizations, the UN has provided a way for countries to work together to decrease some of the world's social and economic problems. It has provided a place for nations to discuss and debate their differences, rather than engage in military conflict, and has also helped solve or ease disputes among smaller nations.

Yet, the United Nations has had only partial success in its peacekeeping efforts. It has little power to solve disputes.

Since the UN has no sovereignty, it cannot force members to abide by the UN Charter. UN members, for instance, have failed to agree on establishing a permanent police force to handle international disputes, and, as a result, the UN must rely on persuasion or temporary forces donated by member nations. UN troops were able to stop North Korean aggression against South Korea. More recently, however, they were unable to halt fighting between Christian and Islamic forces in Lebanon. In 1994, in Bosnia, the warring factions in the region openly scorned the UN forces that had been sent to restore peace. Serbian insurgents even took some peacekeeping forces hostage. In the face of mounting hostility, the United Nations withdrew all forces from the wartorn land.

The United Nations also faces financial problems. Each UN member is responsible for paying a portion of the organization's operating expenses, with contributions based on a nation's ability to pay. Today, the United States pays the highest rate of any nation—25 percent of the regular annual budget. Some smaller nations pay the minimum of 1/100 of 1 percent, and other nations' contributions fall somewhere in between. Russia, for instance, pays 6 percent. Compounding the problem is the failure of many nations to keep up with their payments. In addition, other nations have failed to pay special assessments for such operations as peacekeeping forces.

Despite these limitations, most countries still view the United Nations as both necessary and useful. UN membership gives all nations a forum where they can bring their concerns to the attention of the global community. It also provides developing nations with opportunities to benefit from UN social and economic assistance programs.

For all of its failings, the United Nations is the only world organization that promotes world peace through a global effort. It also enables nations to join together to combat threats to the environment. As former astronaut Wally Schirra remarked: "We've definitely got to get concerned about Spaceship Earth. It's where we live."

Section Review

1. Why was the United Nations formed?

2. What are the six main bodies of the United Nations?

3. With so many member nations, why does the United Nations face financial problems?

4. **Challenge:** Do you think the United Nations has been successful in meeting its goals? Why or why not?

3 Military Organizations

Throughout history, nations have joined together in **alliances** to solve problems. Even though nations may disagree on some issues, alliances allow them to work together on broad areas of common concern. In the past, military alliances for defense were the most common type of alliance. But recently, economic and political alliances have developed as well. It is important to note that these three categories are hard to separate. Some alliances are strictly military, whereas others may also include economic and political goals. Also, just as nations change their goals, alliances may change *their* objectives over time.

The United States is a member of several alliances. It also interacts with alliances that it does *not* belong to. And, like other nations, the United States is involved in many international activities that do not involve alliances. Although the United States is a leader in world trade, for example, it does not belong to any major economic alliance.

When nations form military alliances, members pledge to attack or defend themselves jointly against a common enemy. The Delian League, a military alliance formed by Greek city-states nearly 1,500 years ago, was a forerunner of today's military alliances. Military alliances may be established between only two nations, as well as between groups of nations joining for **collective security.** That is, alliance members agree to take action against any outside nation that commits a hostile act against an alliance member.

The formation of one military alliance often results in the formation of another by the opposing side. This is often done to maintain a **balance of power,** or a situation in which no single nation or group of nations dominates the others. While prepared for military conflict, alliances generally try to avoid war through strength of arms.

alliances voluntary agreements by nations to work together to solve problems

collective security group action taken against any outside nation that commits an act of aggression against a member of the group

balance of power arrangement of power in which peace and security are maintained because no one country or group of nations dominates

The United States and Canada work together for the defense of North America. The continent's air and missile defense is the responsibility of the North American Aerospace Defense Command (NORAD), which is located under this mountain in Colorado. What kinds of alliances have been formed by the world's nations?

As President Truman looks on, Secretary of State Acheson signs the North Atlantic Treaty. What is NATO's goal?

Since World War II, the United States has formed military alliances with more than 40 nations. In these agreements, we and our allies promise to defend one another in case of an enemy attack. Some alliances are formal organizations with rules for making and carrying out defense policies. Others are less formal and promise cooperation only in times of emergency.

North Atlantic Treaty Organization

The original purpose of the North Atlantic Treaty Organization (NATO) was to provide for the common defense of Western nations against attack. Historically, the Soviet Union and its allies were seen as the most likely aggressors. Article V of the North Atlantic Treaty states:

The parties agree that an armed attack against one or more of them in Europe or North America shall be considered an attack against them all.

NATO was formed during the early days of the cold war. The Communist takeover of Czechoslovakia and the Berlin blockade prompted 12 Western nations to sign the North Atlantic Treaty in Washington, D.C., in 1949. During the cold war, four more European nations joined the alliance.

The rapid changes of the 1990s transformed NATO. The alliance no longer binds together the United States and its allies as it once did. Differing defense goals and changing economic policies and political realities weakened the alliance even before the end of the cold war. As defense costs soared, our nation was also calling on its allies to shoulder a greater share of the defense burden. In addition, some American leaders wanted our allies to regard the Soviet Union's various peace initiatives with skepticism and proceed with caution.

During the cold war, the forces of NATO squared off against a rival Communist alliance, the Warsaw Pact. Both alliances raced to develop weapons that would thwart an attack by the other. As the cold war drew to a close, both alliances agreed to reduce their armaments and continued to do so. Finally, in the summer of 1991, the Warsaw Pact formally disbanded. Arms reductions talks, however, continued because forces were already in place. Throughout the early 1990s, the former foes worked to ensure continued peace and goodwill.

In 1994 NATO leaders endorsed a proposal offering the former members of the Warsaw Pact limited association within NATO. The Czech Republic, Slovakia, Poland, Hungary, Romania, Bulgaria, and the republics of the former Soviet Union would be eligible to become "partners in peace." NATO leaders hoped that the new alliance would help promote European security.

Many leaders thought that the partnerships would lead to full-scale alliances between the former foes.

Eastern European leaders were quick to accept the invitation. Within a few months of the formal proposal, Romania, Estonia, Lithuania, Ukraine, Kazakhstan, Russia, Finland, Hungary, the Czech Republic, Slovakia, and Poland had applied for membership. Although each eastern nation had hoped for full status in NATO, each was content to begin as a part of the partnership for peace.

Inter-American Treaty

The Inter-American Treaty of Reciprocal Assistance, known as the Rio Pact, provides for the common defense of the Americas. Signed in 1947, the pact reflects the importance we place on the defense of the Western Hemisphere. Under this pact, member nations have pledged to aid one another in case of attack. Members have also agreed to negotiate peaceful settlements to their disputes.

Acting with the support of Rio Pact members in 1962, President John F. Kennedy imposed a naval blockade of Cuba to prevent the Soviet Union from setting up missile bases there. This success in preventing outside aggression, however, has not been matched in resolving internal problems. For example, members have been unable to halt the armed conflicts in Central America.

Asian and Pacific Alliances

Our country maintains a number of military alliances in other parts of the world. In Asia, for example, the United States has mutual defense ar-rangements with the Philippines, South Korea, and Japan. In these alliances, American military forces protect allied nations as well as guard our economic and political interests. Recently, however, several member nations have begun questioning their roles, the cost of membership, and the continuing need for such alliances.

The ANZUS Pact, signed in 1951, joined the United States, Australia, and New Zealand in a defensive alliance that covered the South Pacific. But changing political and economic priorities strained this alliance. In 1985, for example, New Zealand prohibited American warships carrying nuclear weapons from entering New Zealand ports. Amid increasing disputes over this issue, New Zealand withdrew from the alliance in 1989.

As with ANZUS, military alliances exist only as long as the conditions that spawned their creation continue to exist. As nations' economic, military, and political interests change, so, too, do alliances. In 1954, for example, the United States pledged to protect Taiwan in case of attack by the People's Republic of China. This pact was dissolved in 1979, after the United States established diplomatic relations with the People's Republic.

Section Review

1. Why do nations form alliances? What kinds of alliances exist in the global community?

2. What was the role of NATO during the cold war?

3. What strains are placed on military alliances today?

4. **Challenge:** In your opinion, have military alliances been effective in protecting the United States? Explain.

4 Economic and Political Alliances

Economic alliances are formed to promote greater economic cooperation and profit among member nations. Some of these alliances take the form of **common markets,** in which member nations unify their economies. Others take the form of **free trade associations.** These alliances are more limited in their economic goals: while freer trade among member nations is sought, each nation's economy remains independent. Finally, some economic alliances try to agree on a common trade policy for a single export product, such as oil.

The United States has only recently joined in a major economic alliance. We trade extensively with members of other economic alliances. Our economic and trade policies, however, are affected by actions and decisions taken by these alliances.

Political alliances are frequently formed to promote cultural, social, or other ties that member nations have in common. Members of such alliances often share common foreign policy goals, too. These nations may also be joined together in economic or military alliances.

European Union

Created in Rome, Italy, in 1957, as the European Economic Community (EEC), the European Union (EU) is slowly moving toward forming one European common market out of the separate economies of its 12 member nations. Despite continuing policy differences among its members, the EU is one of the world's most successful economic alliances. Tariffs among member nations have been abolished, and a common tariff has been established for all nonmember nations.

The EU has removed all economic restrictions so that resources, workers, and goods move almost as freely through western Europe as they do within our 50 states. As a result of greater economic union, member nations have also reached new political and military agreements. As more

common markets
economic unions in which nations unify their economies to increase production, trade, and employment

free trade associations
economic unions that provide free trade among member nations without merging their economies

This port in Italy reveals the importance of sea trade in the economies of the EU countries. What goals do the EU countries plan to achieve in the future?

nations clamor to join, the influence of the EU is expected to grow even more.

NAFTA and GATT

Two economic alliances that involve the United States are the North American Free Trade Agreement (NAFTA) and the General Agreement on Tariffs and Trade (GATT). American participation in both these alliances came about after much debate.

Ratified in 1993, NAFTA provides for a free trade zone among Canada, the United States, and Mexico. Before NAFTA, United States goods entering Mexico faced an average tariff of 10 percent. At the same time, many goods entering the United States from Mexico were taxed at 4 percent. NAFTA aims to eliminate these taxes altogether.

The 103rd Congress approved GATT as its last official act in December 1994. Unlike NAFTA, GATT is a worldwide agreement. Begun in 1947, GATT has been revised several times. The most recent revision pledges member nations to work to reduce many nontrade barriers that interfere with world trade.

Latin American Free Trade Association

The Latin American Free Trade Association (LAFTA) is an economic alliance of Central and South American nations. Established in 1960, LAFTA was set up to promote regional trade, to coordinate agricultural and industrial development, and to reduce tariffs among member nations. In 1980, LAFTA was reorganized as the Latin American Integration Association, with the same

The Organization of Petroleum Exporting Countries (OPEC) is an economic alliance that provides a common oil market policy for its members. Policy making occurs at meetings such as the one above. How does OPEC carry out its responsibilities?

economic goals. These goals will be difficult to achieve, however, given the political turmoil, military conflict, and drug-related problems troubling Latin America.

Organization of Petroleum Exporting Countries

The Organization of Petroleum Exporting Countries (OPEC) is an economic alliance of 13 oil-producing nations. Formed in 1960, OPEC attempts to provide a common oil policy for its member nations. The alliance is responsible for setting members' production rates, as well as prices and taxes on oil exported by OPEC members. It also sets various trade rules that OPEC members must follow.

In the early 1980s, OPEC members began to have difficulty reaching agreement on oil prices. Iran, for example, wanted to continue charging

Students and teachers gather for a ceremony outside their school in Zimbabwe. The Organization of African Unity (OAU) seeks to improve educational standards among member nations. What are the other goals of OAU?

promote policies that would improve economic and social development in the region. Its activities include promoting regional cooperation among its members in the fields of housing, health, and education and working to boost agriculture, industry, and trade.

The OAS has often been called on to deal with difficult issues, such as how to restrict the influence of Communist Cuba, how to remove Panamanian dictator Manuel Noriega from power, and how to halt widespread conflict in Central America. This alliance has had only limited success in dealing with these issues.

Organization of African Unity

An alliance of African nations, the Organization of African Unity (OAU) was formed in Addis Ababa, Ethiopia, in 1963. Similar to the OAS, the OAU seeks to improve economic, educational, and social conditions among its members. The organization also works for the peaceful settlement of disputes among member nations.

One goal of the OAU is unique, however, as most of its members were at one time European colonies. As a result, the alliance works to eliminate all aspects of colonialism in Africa. To a great extent, it has succeeded, and today OAU members are independent nations playing an important role in world affairs.

Arab League

The Arab League is a political alliance of Arab nations in the Middle East and North Africa. Organized in Cairo, Egypt, in 1945, the league was formed to foster unity among newly independent Arab nations. Almost half a century later, this goal of unity is still being sought. The alliance

the highest possible prices for its oil. But some alliance members, such as Saudi Arabia, favored keeping price increases to a minimum. The 1980s and 1990s also saw an oil glut, or an overproduction of oil, partly as a result of a world recession and fuel conservation. As world oil prices began to fall, OPEC had difficulty convincing members to limit production in order to stabilize prices and to protect earnings. Today, the alliance continues to have trouble getting such cooperation from its members.

Organization of American States

The Organization of American States (OAS) is a political alliance of nations from North, Central, and South America, most of which also belong to the Rio Pact. The alliance was created by the Act of Bogota (Colombia) in 1948, and it has tried to

members have also tried to coordinate national policies and to speak as a united group in world affairs. But disagreements among members have reduced the league's effectiveness.

The major source of unity among alliance members formerly came from longstanding opposition to the Jewish nation of Israel. The Arab League claimed that Israel occupied territory belonging to Palestinian Arabs. Peace agreements between the Palestinians and the Israelis in the 1990s, however, eliminated this issue as a unifying factor for the Arab League.

Section Review

1. What is the purpose of economic alliances? political alliances?

2. What is a unique characteristic of the Organization of African Unity?

3. In what way has the effectiveness of the Arab League been reduced?

4. **Challenge:** Why, do you think, is it often difficult for alliances to achieve their goals?

Summary

1. The nations of the world have grown more interdependent because of such factors as increased world trade and communications.

2. The global community consists of more than 160 nations that differ in size, population, resources, government, and culture.

3. Since World War II international politics has been dominated by three major blocs—the western bloc, the eastern or largely Communist bloc, and the developing nations. These blocs broke down with the collapse of communism.

4. The United Nations (UN), an international organization created to maintain world peace, consists of six main bodies: the General Assembly, the Security Council, the Secretariat, the Economic and Social Council, the International Court of Justice, and the Trusteeship Council.

5. Nations form alliances to promote economic, political, or military/defense goals.

6. After World War II, the United States formed military alliances with more than 40 nations. These alliances included the North Atlantic Treaty Organization, the Rio Pact, and the ANZUS Pact.

7. Since the end of the cold war, NATO has worked to forge closer ties with the nations of eastern Europe.

8. As the cold war subsides, so does the importance of both NATO and the Warsaw Pact.

9. Economic alliances promote economic cooperation among member nations. The European Union and the Organization of Petroleum Exporting Countries are examples of economic alliances.

10. The United States has only recently joined a major economic alliance. It joined NAFTA in 1993.

11. Political alliances strengthen cultural, social, and other ties among member nations. The Organization of American States, the Arab League, and the Organization of African Unity are examples of political alliances.

Chapter 27 Review

★ Building Vocabulary

Match each of the following numbered definitions with the correct lettered vocabulary term.

1. nations of Africa, Asia, Latin America, and the Middle East that are experiencing economic development

2. voluntary agreements by nations to work together to solve problems

3. arrangement of power in which peace and security are maintained because no one country or group of nations dominates

4. economic unions that provide free trade among member nations without merging economies

5. economic unions in which nations unify their economies to increase production, trade, and employment

6. group action taken by nations against any nation that commits an act of aggression

7. organization to which many, if not all, independent nations of the world belong

8. tied to one another because decisions and actions in one country have a direct impact on other countries

A. interdependent
B. developing nations
C. international organization
D. alliances
E. collective security
F. balance of power
G. common markets
H. free trade associations

★ Reviewing Facts

1. Why and how has global interdependence grown?

2. How do nations differ? How do these differences affect their roles in the global community?

3. What are the major groupings of nations according to economic development?

4. How has the membership of the United Nations changed since 1945?

5. What are some differences between the United Nation's Security Council and the General Assembly?

6. How may the Security Council settle international disputes?

7. Why is it difficult for the United Nations to maintain world peace?

8. To what political alliance does the United States belong? What is the purpose of this alliance?

★ Analyzing Facts

1. What are the advantages and disadvantages a nation faces as a member of an alliance?

2. Do you think Latin American nations need a political alliance (OAS), a military alliance (Rio Pact), and an economic alliance (LAFTA), or would one general alliance do? Explain.

3. Numerous conflicts have occurred between different members of the United Nations. Do you think this means that the United Nations is a failure? Why or why not?

★ Evaluating Ideas

1. The United States left UNESCO, a United Nations agency, because the organization let politics influence its actions. Do you think the United States should leave the United Nations for the same reason? Why or why not?

Using Your
Civic Participation Journal

Review the list of items that you recorded in your Civic Participation Journal. Work with two of your classmates to compare lists. Write an essay explaining the importance of world trade in your everyday life.

2. Are your community and state part of an interdependent world? Explain.

3. The United Nations General Assembly has been called the "town meeting of the world," yet it has little formal power. Do you agree or disagree? Explain.

4. What single factor do you think is most important in determining a nation's power? Explain.

★ Critical Thinking
Determining the Strength of an Argument

An argument is a series of reasons supporting a point of view. The strength of an argument largely depends on the evidence presented to support it.

Explanation   Just presenting an argument to your readers or listeners is no guarantee that they will accept your point of view. Convincing them probably will depend on how strong an argument you present. Similarly, you should not necessarily change your own viewpoint just because someone else presents an argument. You might be swayed, however, if it is a good, strong argument.

The following steps will help you determine the strength of an argument.

1. To make sure that you understand the argument, restate it in the clearest terms possible.
2. Identify the reasons presented in the argument and determine if each reason is truly related to the issue under discussion.
3. Whenever possible, check the accuracy of any evidence used to support the argument.
4. Ask yourself, would an unbiased person reviewing this evidence come to the same conclusion as the person who is making the argument?

Practice   You can use these steps to determine whether the argument presented in the passage on pages 659 and 660 of this chapter is a strong one.

1. The argument is that as the nations of the world become increasingly interdependent, an American foreign policy that both protects our national interests and satisfies our allies is difficult to achieve.

2. Several reasons for this argument are provided. Growth in international trade and investment, cultural exchange, world travel, communications improvements are cited as reasons for increasing global interdependence. Our foreign policy difficulties are credited to the differing motives, interest, and needs of our allies.

3. International investment figures are cited, and examples of cultural exchange and communication improvements are provided. A case study of German and French energy needs is used to show foreign policy difficulties. The accuracy of all supporting evidence is verifiable.

4. An unbiased person would likely reach the same conclusion from this argument.

Independent Practice   Study the cartoon below and review the material on UN Issues and Problems on page 668. Using the steps above, determine the strength of the argument that "most countries still view the United Nations as both necessary and useful."

Chapter 28

International Policy and Issues

Political unrest, economic rivalry, environmental destruction, terrorism, and the gap between rich and poor nations are but a few of the challenges our government must confront. America's foreign policy guides our nation's response to such issues in ways intended to guard our national interests. But as a result of increasing global interdependence, our foreign policy decisions must be made only after careful consideration of their possible impact on our friends and enemies. This chapter will examine some of these issues and decisions.

Chapter Preview

TERMS TO KNOW
draft, disarmament, developing nations, foreign aid, global economy, international trade, terrorism

READ TO DISCOVER
- the relations between the United States and its allies.
- the United States' role in Eastern European affairs.
- how our country relates to developing nations.
- how international issues affect our government and you.

★ ★ ★ ★ ★

Civic Participation Journal

Choose one of the regions described in this chapter. For one week watch television news reports and read your local newspaper and note any reports about American relations with that region. Record your findings in your journal.

1 Relations with Western Europe

The United States has economic, military, and political relations with many countries around the world. Those nations with whom the United States shares the greatest number of common interests and goals are called allies. Yet despite their similar positions on many issues, even allies have differences that must be resolved if they are to *remain* allies.

Solving trade problems is an issue the United States faces with both Japan and the western European nations. We will look at our relations with western Europe as an example.

North Atlantic Treaty Organization

Founded in 1949 to combat Communist aggression in Europe, the North Atlantic Treaty Organization (NATO) celebrated its forty-fifth anniversary in 1994. The collapse of communism has profoundedly altered both the organization and the purpose of the alliance. Instead of existing to safeguard democratic western governments against a Communist invasion, the alliance now concentrates on ensuring stability throughout post-cold war Europe.

During the cold war, the forces of NATO squared off against a rival Communist alliance, the Warsaw Pact. Both alliances raced to develop weapons that would thwart an attack by the other. As the cold war drew to a close, both alliances agreed to reduce their armaments and continued to do so. Finally, in the summer of 1991, the Warsaw Pact formally disbanded. Arms reductions talks, however, continued because forces were already in place. Throughout the early 1990s, the former foes worked to ensure continued peace and goodwill in Europe.

With the end of the cold war, American troops withdrew from a newly united Berlin.

This tank force was part of the American military presence in West Germany. From the 1940s to the 1990s, American troops were stationed in Europe to defend NATO allies. Why did many people call for a reduction of U.S. troops in Europe?

In 1994 NATO leaders endorsed a proposal offering the former members of the Warsaw Pact limited association within NATO. The Czech Republic, Slovakia, Poland, Hungary, Romania, Bulgaria, and the republics of the former Soviet Union would be eligible to become "partners in peace." NATO leaders hoped that the new alliance would help promote European security.

Many leaders thought that the partnerships would lead to full-scale alliances between the former foes.

Eastern European leaders were quick to accept the invitation. Within a few months of the formal proposal, Romania, Estonia, Lithuania, Ukraine, Kazakhstan, Russia, Finland, Hungary, the Czech Republic, Slovakia, and Poland had applied for membership. Although each eastern nation had hoped for full status in NATO, each was content to begin as a part of the partnership for peace.

A New American Role?

Because the cold war had ended and the Warsaw Pact had disbanded, many Americans believed that the American presence in Europe should be reduced. These critics pointed out that the dollars the United States was spending in Europe could be better used to help solve domestic problems.

The United States did withdraw most of its troops that had been stationed in Europe, but the government continued to aid the Europeans. Throughout the mid-1990s, the United States debated what its role in a Communist-free Europe should be.

Similar issues are faced in our other alliances as well. For example, why should millions of U.S. tax dollars be paid to rent military bases in foreign nations when those bases protect that nation as well as serve American defense needs? Similar questions arise regarding United States defense spending on behalf of Japan. Since the Japanese economy is so strong, why shouldn't the Japanese pay for their own defense rather than depending on the American taxpayer? It remains to be seen whether our nation will continue to act as a global police officer.

ISSUE: FOREIGN POLICY

A UNIFIED EUROPE?

When World War II ended, the United States was clearly the strongest power in the world. As Soviet takeovers in Eastern Europe heightened fear and confusion, the U.S. government gladly took on the role of defending Western Europe from Communist expansion.

More than 40 years later, times had changed. The United States, deeply in debt, faced stiff economic competition from a powerful western Europe. At the same time, the Soviet collapse helped cement the collapse of communism in eastern Europe. Suddenly, the American role in the defense of Europe from the Communist threat seemed unnecessary.

Soon after the end of the cold war, the United States began pulling forces out of Europe. Now, however, it seemed that all of Europe was competing with the United States economically.

The newly democratic nations of eastern Europe were forging economic and political ties with the European Union. The European Union offered aid and resources to the new democracies.

The European Union also encouraged other European countries to join the trade organization. Although some Europeans feared that joining the union would decrease their own country's economic strength, most agreed that economic cooperation would be beneficial. By 1994 Austria, Cyprus, Finland, Malta, Sweden, Switzerland, and Turkey had applied for membership. Norway also applied, but the Norwegian voters rejected membership in November 1994. Norwegians in rural areas feared that the absence of tariffs would lower prices for their products.

Although Norway did not join the union, the members continued their plans for a unified Europe. Plans called for a European currency, known as the ECU or European Currency Unit, to replace national currencies by 1998.

A sure sign that the cooperative spirit among union members was strong was the completion of the Eurotunnel. The tunnel under the English Channel provided a land link between Great Britain and its European neighbors for the first time in history. The tunnel cut travel time between Great Britain and France from more than 3

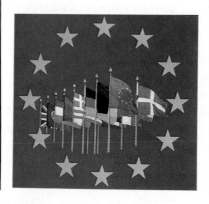

hours to a mere 35 minutes. Inaugurated in the summer of 1994, the tunnel was simply one more symbol of a more unified Europe.

Will Europe, with all its different nationalities and languages, ever become completely unified? The Europeans have made great strides in unifying a continent that has been the scene of the bloodiest wars in the history of humankind. Nevertheless, many experts doubt that there will ever be complete unification. They point out that Europeans are fiercely proud of their national heritages. The French, for example, point to their impressive history as an arts center. The British take pride in their history of empire and civilization. Experts doubt that such nationalism could ever be replaced by loyalty to Europe as a whole. Also, each nation is fiercely proud of its language. If unity were to be achieved, wouldn't the entire continent have to speak the same language?

Whatever the results of the move toward European unity, one point is certain. The continent is far more unified today than ever before in history.

1. How has Europe changed since the end of the cold war?
2. What are the prospects for the creation of a United States of Europe similar to the United States of America?

European Union

Established as an economic alliance, the European Union (EU) was previously known as the European Economic Community. With the end of the cold war, the EU has increasingly affected the internal politics of its member nations. Meeting in Strasbourg, France, the EU Parliament must be consulted on a number of health, safety, environmental, and technological issues before economic changes can be made within EU nations. Political parties that contend for power at home also compete for their nation's seats in the EU Parliament. While guiding the alliance toward greater economic unity, they also are changing the face of European politics. Although national interests still predominate, party members are finding they have similar interests with parties in other countries.

The collapse of communism strengthened the EU's resolve to work toward unity. As non-Communist parties gained power in Poland in 1989, the EU sent about $100 million in food to the Polish people. When Hungary first opened its borders and allowed greater civil and political freedoms, the EU expanded trade ties with that nation. As the rest of eastern Europe abandoned communism, western nations offered to help with their economic and industrial development. Although the amount and type of assistance coming from the EU differs, all members agree on the goal that aid and trade should be given to support the vast changes that have taken place in eastern Europe.

In January 1993, the European Union officially became the single largest unified market—in terms of population and GDP—in the world. It is even larger than the United States. It is a single market because no internal barriers regulate the flow of workers, financial capital, or goods and services. Citizens of the EU hold common passports and can vote in EU Parliament elections, and can travel anywhere in the EU to work, shop, save, and invest.

The EU collects revenues in the form of a VAT (Value Added Tax) and then distributes the funds to its members on the basis of need. Hundreds of billions of dollars have been redistributed in this manner and have been used to build highways, rail systems, and other public goods that will benefit the EU.

Many Europeans hope that the European Union will result in a true "United States of Europe" with a federal system of government similar to that of the United States of America. To date, however, national European rivalries and the patriotism that Europeans feel toward their nation have prevented such a transformation.

Europeans have, however, unified their economies to a great extent. This union has challenged the ability of American businesses to compete in Europe, and one of the goals of American foreign policy has been to ensure that barriers against American goods are not increased. Currently leaders are working on improving trade agreements.

Section Review

1. What are some of the issues NATO has faced since the cold war?

2. What is one of the major goals of the European Union?

3. **Challenge:** In your opinion, how would the creation of a United States of Europe affect the United States of America's economy?

2 Relations with Eastern Europe

The cold war once clearly defined relations between the United States and the Communist nations of Eastern Europe. With the collapse of communism in the early 1990s, however, relations between East and West changed dramatically. Former antagonists, the United States and the newly democratizing nations of eastern Europe sought closer ties. At stake were the results of the generation-long armaments race that had stockpiled enough nuclear weapons to destroy the world many times over.

Many Americans thought that the new governments of eastern Europe were fragile democracies that might not survive. Policymakers feared that tyrants might take over these governments and threaten the world with the vast arsenals of nuclear weapons they had inherited from the Communists. To avoid such a catastrophe, the United States sought arms agreements with the former Communist states.

disarmament reduction in the number of weapons and troops

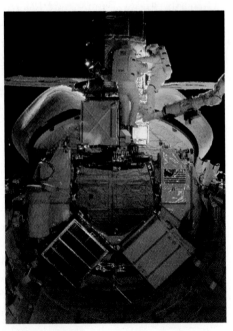

Here, astronauts in space are working outside of a space shuttle, one of the important vehicles in the U.S. space program. As part of their space explorations, the United States and the former Soviet Union also have developed missile systems for use in warfare. What steps have the two countries taken to lessen the arms race?

Armaments

As the United States and the Soviet Union began the cold war, they also started competing in an arms race, or buildup in the number and kinds of weapons in each nation's arsenal. Although the United States was the dominant nuclear power early in the cold war, in later years there was a nuclear balance of power—some would say it was a balance of terror—between the two superpowers. Under the threat of mutual destruction, each nation and its military allies refrained from attacking the other. One noted philosopher commented that:

Atomic warfare saw its first spectacular demonstration in Japan. This ultimate achievement in destructive power has now placed within man's reach the possibility of self-extermination. Whether we shall be wise enough to resist this temptation remains to be seen.

Many felt that the wisest course was the effort to promote arms control, or the regulation of the growth of armaments, and **disarmament.** Various general disarmament treaties were negotiated through the United Nations Disarmament Commission. In 1963 and 1967 the United States, the Soviet Union, and Great Britain signed a Limited Nuclear Test Ban Treaty and an Outer Space Treaty on the peaceful use of space. China and France, both nuclear powers, declined to sign the test ban treaty. The Nuclear Nonproliferation Treaty of 1968 was ratified by over 100 nations, again with the exception of China and France.

In addition to signing general UN-sponsored treaties, the superpowers worked directly with each other to reduce military tensions. In 1969 the United States and the Soviet Union

The Soviet collapse left the nations of eastern Europe with vast nuclear arsenals. Why is it important to reduce armaments?

began negotiating limits on intermediate and long-range nuclear missiles. The Strategic Arms Limitation Treaty (SALT I) of 1972 limited the number of each country's defensive missiles and restricted various offensive nuclear weapons. A SALT II agreement in 1979 was not ratified by the U.S. Senate, which felt the treaty gave too many concessions to the Soviets. In general, both nations have abided by SALT although each has raised questions from time to time about the other's compliance.

In the mid-1980s the superpowers began installing new nuclear missiles in Europe. Faced with yet another round in the nuclear arms race, the American secretary of state and the Soviet foreign minister met in Geneva, Switzerland, to resume arms control negotiations. At a summit meeting in November 1985, American President Ronald Reagan and Soviet General Secretary Mikhail

Gorbachev agreed that both sides desired a peaceful settlement of their differences.

The two leaders signed the Intermediate-Range Nuclear Forces Treaty (INF) in December 1987. Ratified by the U.S. Senate in 1988, the treaty called for the destruction of all American and Soviet intermediate-range nuclear missiles and on-site inspections to verify these results. In June 1989 the Soviets and Americans also agreed to reopen the Salt II talks to reduce long-range nuclear missiles.

The two nations were continuing these talks when the Communist systems collapsed. The United States was quick to negotiate with the new governments to ensure world peace, and in the 1990s several international agreements were reached. Still, however, the very existence of nuclear arsenals is a reminder of the tensions of the cold war and a threat to world peace.

In this scene of Moscow, you can see the brick walls of the Kremlin, an old fortress that now serves as the seat of the Russian government. How has Russia changed since the collapse of Communism?

Russia

During the 1990s, the United States sought to stabilize relations with Russia. The Clinton administration pledged aid to help the nation meet the challenges brought on by the rapid move to a democratic political system and a free market economy.

The challenges often seemed daunting. Inflation had wiped out life savings of elderly Russians. Eager capitalists, operating in an unregulated marketplace, often took advantage of people who had no experience with making their own choices.

In the chaos of the transformation, some Russians longed for the old days of Communist rule. They reasoned that life had been easier when someone else told them what to do. These people, however, constituted a small minority of the population. Most Russians seemed to resign themselves to the idea that the capitalist transforma-

tion would take time and would mean some hardships at the beginning. They also believed that the hardships were worth the price of freedom.

During the period of Soviet collapse, eastern Europe underwent a number of significant changes as well. Nations newly freed from Communist rule experienced many of the same difficulties as their former masters in Moscow.

Poland

In Poland, the Communist party had controlled the country for more than 40 years. It had banned the Solidarity trade union in 1981 and arrested its leaders or forced them into hiding. In 1989, however, the Solidarity trade union party replaced the Communist party and formed a new government. Nevertheless, the Communists retained a good deal of power by keeping the Defense and Interior Ministries, which controlled the armed forces and the police.

As with the rest of the Eastern Bloc, Poland quickly abandoned all vestiges of communism. Free elections were held, and the nation moved quickly toward democracy.

Czechoslovakia

Poland's southern neighbor went through great changes as well. There the transition away from communism resulted in the creation of two new nations—the Czech Republic and Slovakia. Both these nations continued to institute democratic reforms in the 1990s.

One of the most remarkable changes in both nations was the return of property that had been confiscated when the Communists took over in the 1940s. Residents who could prove that the previous regime had taken away family lands had them restored. Often, however, the lands and buildings had suffered years of neglect at the hands of the Communist rulers.

United Germany

One of the staunchest and most conservative Communist nations had been East Germany. The Berlin Wall that ran through the center of the former capital of a united Germany was a symbol to the world of the tensions of the cold war. Yet, it too came tumbling down, just as the Communist rulers did in 1989. The two Germanies reunited and agreed to work together toward democracy and a free enterprise system.

The road to reform has been extremely difficult for the Germans. The eastern residents often resent their western counterparts who have a higher standard of living. Also, under the new regime, many of the inefficient eastern businesses have closed, throwing thousands out of work and adding to the unrest.

Another problem that has cropped up in the united Germany is neofascism. For years, the tensions of the cold war seemed to keep protests against the West German government to a minimum. In the East, the Communist regime stifled all protest. With unity and democracy for the entire nation, however, Germans have been free to express all opinions. One small group of right-wing extremists looks back nostalgically to the Nazi era when Germany was a great power. These neofascists believe that the immigrants that have flooded to Germany in recent years are the cause of many of the nation's current problems.

The neofascists routinely terrorize minorities—including eastern Europeans and Jews—who live in Germany. The German authorities have responded with harsh prison sentences for the offenders. The government, however, wants to make certain that it preserves the freedoms guaranteed in the German constitution while protecting all German residents from terrorist violence.

This medieval gateway in the Polish city of Torun reflects Poland's rich cultural heritage. What role does the Solidarity movement play in Polish politics?

Here, joyous Berliners stand on the remains of the Berlin Wall and celebrate the opening of the barrier that had divided their city since 1961. What developments in East Germany led to the opening of the Berlin Wall?

The Yugoslav Tragedy

Perhaps the most violent and tragic transition away from communism occurred in what had been Yugoslavia. The nation had always included many ethnic groups, but peace had been maintained because of a strong dictatorship. The end of the dictatorship, greeted at first with enthusiasm, doomed the nation. Soon, groups split into warring nation-states. By late 1991 the conflict had become the first full-scale war in Europe since 1945. What had once been peaceful countryside became an unparalleled bloodbath. Moreover, the warring sides seemed unlikely to agree to peace, even when branded international outlaws.

For its part, the world community did little to intervene in the war-torn land. Although international threats were made, the fighting continued throughout the mid-1990s. The costs in property and human terms were staggering.

Section Review

1. Why is arms control an important United States foreign policy issue?

2. What steps have been taken to reduce the spread of nuclear weapons worldwide?

3. What problems are the nations of eastern Europe encountering in the post communist era?

4. **Challenge:** In your opinion, are the hardships facing eastern Europeans worth it? Explain.

3 Developing Nations

Within the global community, some nations are prosperous while others, often called **developing nations,** are poor. One issue facing both the global community and U.S. policymakers is how to narrow the gap between the wealthy and the poor nations of the world. Our political leaders have long believed that as nations become prosperous, they are more likely to adopt democratic politics. Also, they often become better trading partners for the United States. So, a foreign policy that strengthens the economies of the developing nations seems in the best interests of the United States.

Often former colonies of European powers, the developing nations are found primarily in Africa, Asia, Latin America, and the Middle East. Most of these agricultural nations are trying to industrialize, although for the most part they still supply raw materials to industrial nations in exchange for manufactured goods. Many developing nations face the common problems of poverty, hunger, disease, overpopulation, and a lack of educated workers.

United States Foreign Aid

The United States tries to assist developing nations with **foreign aid.** The goal of American foreign aid is to promote economic development, political stability, and military security. This can involve the transfer of money, equipment, or labor to help build the receiving nation's economy or armed forces, or both. For instance, American experts may teach modern agricultural methods to farmers in Africa. The United States may supply military or police equipment to a South American government involved in the "drug war." Or American Peace Corps volunteers may demonstrate new marketing methods to businesspeople in Central America. In the 1950s, American foreign aid under the Marshall Plan helped to rebuild and stabilize Western Europe. In recent years most economic aid has gone to the developing nations of Africa, Asia, and Latin America.

American public support for foreign aid declined in the 1990s. At the same time, government officials recognized that massive foreign aid had not produced many overseas friends for the United States. One issue of American foreign policy currently is how to redefine our foreign aid goals. Is the goal to get nations to support American positions in world affairs, or is it to help nations become politically free and economically strong? Could these two goals sometimes be achieved together?

American foreign aid goes primarily to nations who support our foreign policy goals. The emphasis is on economic aid to help bolster developing nations' economies. And most of the aid is in the form of grants, not loans that must be repaid. In total

developing nations poor countries whose economies depend primarily on agriculture; found mainly in Africa, Asia, Latin America, and the Middle East

foreign aid economic or military assistance that one government provides to another

These busy field workers are among the 120,000 volunteers who have served in the Peace Corps since its founding in 1961. In what other ways does the United States provide assistance to foreign countries?

dollars, the United States gives more foreign aid than any other nation. As a *percentage* of the national budget, however, our foreign aid is not as generous as many of the other industrialized nations of the global community. Other nations with major foreign aid programs are Norway, Great Britain, France, Canada, West Germany, Japan, Kuwait, and Saudi Arabia.

United States Foreign Trade

A nation's economy supports its overall well-being. Since each nation of the world has a different economy, each government must make different economic decisions. Also, government control over economic decisions varies. The economies of all nations make up a **global economy.** This interconnected system of national economies produces and distributes goods and services throughout the world. With growing interdependence, each nation's economy is directly influenced by economic events in other countries. Economic systems are tied together through **international trade.**

America often views its foreign trade policies as a way to help developing nations to expand economically. That is, by purchasing their goods and raw materials, the United States is providing money that can further their economic development. Also, American goods and services that these nations buy will help them achieve their economic and political goals.

However, many developing nations feel that they are not strong enough to compete without additional assistance. They would like to see American trade barriers lowered for their products. Others want to purchase goods and services at reduced rates, thereby combining trade with American foreign aid. In short, developing nations would like preferential treatment until their economies are strong enough to compete in the global economy on more equal terms with the developed nations.

Global Economic Debt

In addition to benefiting from foreign aid and trade, developing nations sometimes borrow money to build their economies. Banks in industrialized nations make loans for projects such as roads and airports, which, in turn, attract foreign investors and international corporations to developing nations.

Even with the best of intentions, some developing countries have gone deeply into debt and have trouble repaying their loans. Some have asked American banks to lower interest rates on their loans or to postpone collection. Others have simply just stopped making payments until their economic situation improves. Some debtor nations have gone to the International Monetary Fund (IMF) for emergency loans. Generally, the IMF requires a nation to take steps to solve its economic problems before a loan is granted. For example, a nation may be required to raise taxes and lower government support of food prices or bus fares before receiving loans.

The worst debt problems are in Africa and Latin America. Argentina, for example, was rocked by food riots in the summer of 1989. Even the middle class of this once prosperous nation could not afford the 500 percent annual rise in the cost of food and other necessities. Such nations could collapse unless drastic steps are taken.

One sign of hope in solving the seemingly impossible debt problem is

global economy interconnected system of national economies

international trade exchange of goods and services between countries

Some of the hottest attractions in Moscow today are Western businesses such as McDonald's. Here, employees wait on long lines of Russian customers eager to try their first hamburger and fries. How does the opening of Western businesses in Russia reflect recent global economic developments?

the Mexican Accord. Mexico had struggled to make the economic reforms demanded by its creditors, yet its economy was stagnant. With the help of U.S. Treasury Secretary Nicholas Brady, an accord was reached with American banks to either cut the Mexican loan balance, reduce interest rates, or provide more credit. To support this accord, Japan agreed to provide new loans and the IMF and World Bank moved to shore up the Mexican economy.

How bad is the worldwide debt problem? In the 1990s a global debt of more than $1 trillion threatened the economic security of many nations and the overall stability of the global economy. The creditor nations, and our own country, have hard choices to make. What is in the best interest of the United States, as well as the debtor nations of the world? Which debtor countries most deserve a fresh start by writing off or forgiving their international loans? Which deserve new loans? At home, who will bear the brunt of failed loans—banks and their owners or the American taxpayer?

Although the United States is itself the world's greatest debtor nation, American banks are heavily involved in loans to developing nations. Many of those loans are at risk. The international debt bomb could explode, wreaking havoc with the American economy. U.S. foreign policymakers must discover how to steer the developing nations toward economic growth and stability—thus saving their economies, and perhaps ours as well.

Section Review

1. What are some common problems faced by many developing nations?

2. What is the main policy goal of United States foreign aid?

3. How does the United States often view trade with the developing nations of the world?

4. **Challenge:** How would you determine which nations should or should not receive United States economic aid?

4 Global Issues

While some foreign policy issues involve the United States and a single nation, such as Russia, or a group of nations, such as NATO, other issues are more global. In addressing them, the United States may be involved with many nations or blocs of nations, or may take such issues before the United Nations.

Terrorism

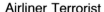

terrorism use of violence to achieve political goals

Terrorism, or the use of violence to achieve political goals, has been called "the ultimate violation of human rights," because terrorist actions are aimed at killing innocent people. Terrorist acts have occurred in every region of the world and, over the past decade, the number of violent attacks has increased. Examples include the assassination in West Germany of a British soldier's wife by the Irish Republican Army, the bombing of a Pan American jetliner over Scotland by Islamic terrorists, and the bombing of the World Trade Center in New York City by Arab terrorists.

TERRORIST TACTICS
The purpose of terrorism is to frighten opponents and force them to accept the terrorists' demands. Hijackings, bombings, kidnappings, murders, and armed attacks on foreign embassies or government buildings are common methods used by terrorists to achieve their goals.

In some cases, terrorists and their actions have the support of large groups of people, or even governments. Palestinians who attack Israel, for instance, have widespread support among Iranians, where they are viewed as freedom fighters rather than terrorists. One Palestinian leader has even compared his followers to the troops of the American Continental Army fighting against Great Britain in the 1770s.

Terrorist groups are believed to be linked through international networks that supply training, weapons, money, and forged documents. For example, a massacre at the Tel Aviv Airport in Israel was carried out by Japanese terrorists, who were trained by radical Arab nations and North Korea and armed by terrorist organizations in Western Europe.

International terrorists hold many different political opinions. Some are anarchists who oppose all forms of government, while others support a new social order based on Marxist ideals. Many terrorists represent ethnic, religious, or nationalist causes, such as Sikh terrorists who want a separate Sikh state in India and Basque terrorists in Spain who want their own country. Nonpolitical, criminal groups have also resorted to terrorism on a large scale.

International terrorism has directly or indirectly influenced the lives of most Americans. Those held captive by terrorists in Lebanon were obviously most directly affected. But their friends, relatives, and coworkers were also hurt, both psychologically and emotionally. Businesspeople and diplomats may be restricted in their work and travel. Political leaders have less access to the public as security measures are tightened. Travelers have encountered delays due to searches of clothing and baggage at air terminals. And tax dollars increasingly are diverted to combat terrorism.

POLICIES TOWARD TERRORISM
Governments deal with terrorism in many different ways. Some have followed a policy of giving in to terrorist

Airliner Terrorist

demands in order to save lives. More commonly, countries refuse to cooperate or negotiate with terrorists. This often involves answering force with force, so many nations have set up special police and army units to deal with terrorists. The general policy of the United States is *not* to negotiate with terrorists.

While most governments want an end to international terrorism, no agreement exists on how to do it. Officials of the world's nations cannot decide whether terrorists should be treated as political revolutionaries or common criminals. Political differences among nations also complicate the issue. The United States is opposed to acts of terror no matter what the terrorists' motives might be. Thus, it seeks international agreements to punish offenders. The western bloc nations have agreed to suspend air traffic to and from countries that refuse to arrest hijackers. Terrorists have also been tried and jailed in the United States, Britain, Germany, and Italy.

But some countries believe that terrorist acts are legitimate if the cause is just. They often view terrorism as a tool of resistance against outside influence and control. Further complicating the search for solutions are terrorist acts supported and encouraged by some governments. Nations said to be engaged in such state-sponsored terrorism include Iran, Libya, and Syria.

Global Drug Trade

The global trade in illegal drugs has become an issue of vital concern for the world community. The problems that drugs, such as cocaine, crack, and heroin, cause for all nations are numerous. In many cases, drug users turn to crime to support their habits. Thus, governments must spend more money on police, courts, and jails. As violence between drug suppliers soars, so does violence directed toward government authorities. And attempted or outright bribery of officials is as destructive to a society as violence. Drug users are more likely than nonusers to miss school or work because of health problems. They also have more personal problems with family, friends, and coworkers. The millions of dollars spent on drugs is not spent in more productive ways and goes untaxed, so a nation's economy and tax base suffer.

Many nations are trying to deal with the international drug trade. Russia has acknowledged that it has a growing drug problem, and has signed a United Nations agreement to cooperate on drug-related problems. European nations and the United States are stepping up treatment programs, education programs, and criminal sanctions. The United States is also supplying desperately needed foreign aid to countries like Mexico and Colombia to help in the fight against drug suppliers.

Drugs also cause problems in countries that supply them. Mexico, Colombia, Bolivia, and Peru all face serious drug-related challenges to their national security. In the 1990s the drug lords of Colombia went on a spree of assassinations and bombings directed at that nation's political parties, police, judges, newspapers, banks—all aspects of Colombian civil authority. In other countries the authorities are quietly or openly bribed. Panama's General Manuel Noriega, finally ousted by an American invasion in 1989, is an example of a government leader who many believe made a personal fortune by helping Latin American drug lords.

In Africa, elephants may face extinction because poachers slaughter them to satisfy an overseas demand for ivory. What efforts are being taken to save the African elephant from destruction?

Under international pressure, some drug-producing countries are trying to reduce the supply, but the job is not an easy one. Many people in countries like Bolivia and Peru have grown and used certain drugs for many years. Now that these drugs are also a valuable cash crop, why, they ask, should they stop growing and selling them? Many also argue that the problem lies in Europe and the United States where the demand is greatest. But whatever the argument, the governments of many drug-producing countries are unwilling to allow the drug lords to become economic, military, and political powers.

When production, sale, and use are taken together, drugs are a massive international problem. Its resolution will take the combined efforts of many nations. For the United States, it is both a major internal problem and an important foreign policy issue.

Environmental Concerns

Elephants may face extinction because poachers slaughter them to sat-isfy a demand in Japan and other nations for items made of ivory. The forests of Brazil, Thailand, and Malaysia are being destroyed to feed a global demand for paper and wood products. Acid rain from air pollution in the United States is killing forests and lakes in Canada. The greenhouse effect may be permanently changing Earth's climate, which will affect all nations. Such environmental issues affect the quality of life for people worldwide. They may even alter the ability of Earth to support life as we know it.

Slowly, the global community is beginning to respond to environmental concerns. Many nations have banned trade in ivory, and assistance goes to countries like Kenya that are working to establish and maintain game preserves. Developing nations like Mexico and Costa Rica are recognized for their efforts to set aside lands for national parks and forests. And industrialized nations are finding ways to reduce pollution and recycle wastes.

But greater efforts are needed to keep ahead of the environmental problems. As an example of how issues are being addressed, in 1992 178 nations meeting in Rio de Janiero, Brazil, signed several environmental agreements. The Rio agreements are just one indication of the willingness of governments to address the environment.

There are stumbling blocks, however. Many developing nations say that the industrialized nations polluted the environment on their road to economic development. Why, they argue, should the developing nations be expected to play by a different set of rules? Many are not willing to do so. Brazil, for example, has claimed that international protests about the destruction of Brazil's Amazon rain forests are foreign interference in its internal affairs. However, the World Bank and the International Monetary Fund now strive to promote economic development that does not come at the expense of the environment. If industrial nations like the United States will work with developing nations, there is still a chance to meet their needs for development while pursuing the global obligation to protect the fragile environment of "Spaceship Earth."

Section Review

1. What is the purpose of most acts of terrorism?
2. How have governments worldwide responded to terrorists?
3. What are some problems caused by the international drug trade?
4. **Challenge:** What can you do to protect or restore the environment in your area?

Summary

1. American foreign policy is influenced by a variety of international issues and the various nations involved.
2. After the cold war, NATO members reached several agreements with the nations of eastern Europe and established the partnership for peace program.
3. United States foreign policy must respond to an economically unified Western Europe.
4. Negotiations to reduce conventional armaments and troop strength are difficult because they involve many nations.
5. The global community has tried to control the development of nuclear weapons through a number of international agreements.
6. During the 1990s, the United States offered aid to Russia in its move toward democracy.
7. As Russia moves toward a free enterprise system, economic problems have plagued the nation.
8. Eastern European nations, like Hungary and Poland, have followed Russia's lead in implementing reforms.
9. Vast differences in wealth exist among the industrialized nations and the developing nations. Developing nations want a larger share of the world's economic resources.
10. The industrialized nations use foreign aid to assist friendly governments and to advance their foreign policy goals.
11. The United States believes that trade and aid together will help developing nations achieve economic growth.
12. Terrorist activity occurs on a worldwide scale despite attempts to halt it.
13. The drug trade has become an international issue, creating crime in Europe and the United States and terrorism in Latin America.
14. Nations are now realizing that by destroying the environment we may be destroying humanity.

Chapter 28 Review

★Building Vocabulary

The vocabulary terms introduced in this chapter appear below. Use each word correctly in a sentence.

1. draft
2. disarmament
3. developing nations
4. foreign aid
5. global economy
6. international trade
7. terrorism

★Reviewing Facts

1. What is the intent of America's foreign policy?
2. What is the original purpose of the NATO alliance and how has it changed?
3. What are the most complex issues faced by the United States with regard to arms negotiations?
4. What should the role of the United States be in a communist-free Europe? Why?
5. What is the primary goal of the EU?
6. How is the European Union transforming Europe? How can the creation of a unified Europe affect the United States?
7. What is the major obstacle to complete unification of Europe?
8. What are the incentives for the United States and Russia to achieve arms control?
9. What recent changes have taken place in Russia, Poland, and Czechoslovakia?
10. What changes have recently occurred in Germany? How are these changes similar and how are they different from those in Russia?
11. What terms or characteristics might be used to describe developing nations?
12. What types of foreign aid does the United States provide to developing nations?
13. Why is the global debt a problem of major concern to the United States?
14. How does terrorism affect the lives of people worldwide?

15. What attempts are being made worldwide to deal with global environmental issues?

★Analyzing Facts

1. Do you think Americans should favor a continuation of arms control talks between the United States and Russia? Why or why not?
2. What, if any, benefits do you see in the United States adopting a protectionist trade policy?
3. In your opinion, what steps could be taken to lessen the economic gap between the developed and developing nations?
4. Do you think the United States should conduct diplomacy with any country regardless of a country's political or economic system? Explain.

★Evaluating Ideas

1. A presidential candidate once noted that "there is no evil in the atom, only in men's souls." How, do you think, does this statement apply to the arms race?
2. In your opinion, how is the United States part of an economically interdependent world? How could the level of interdependence be lowered? Do you think it should be? Why or why not?

Using Your
Civic Participation Journal

Review the entries in your Civic Participation Journal about events in one of the regions of the world. Work with two of your classmates to create a mock newspaper page detailing events in the world during the past week.

3. In your opinion, what steps should the President take to deal with terrorism?

4. Do you think the global environmental problem is one that can be solved? Why or why not?

5. If world population is increasing and natural resources are decreasing, what effect do you think this will have on the global community?

6. Terrorism, global drug trade, and environmental issues all are concerns that face you as an American citizen and as a citizen in the world. Of these issues, which do you think is the most pressing? Explain.

★ Critical Thinking
Determining the Reliability of a Source

Each piece of information you receive has a source, a place from which it came. Determining the reliability of a source of information involves judging whether that source is believable, unbiased, and accurate.

Explanation   The following guidelines will help you determine the reliability of a source of information.

1. Consider the background of your source. What is your source's viewpoint? Could he or she have a reason to be biased?

2. Consider where your source got the information. Does your source have direct, firsthand knowledge of the information being provided? Or does it depend on outside sources?

3. Consider why your source is making the information available. Information provided for private use can sometimes be more accurate than what is produced for public consumption. What could be gained or lost if the information is given wider exposure?

Practice   The following excerpt is from an article that appeared in a Moscow magazine in 1994. You can use the above guidelines to determine the reliability of this source of information.

No transitional leader in modern times has managed to play so many political roles as Boris Yeltsin. In the last 10 years, the Russian president has spent time as a Communist Party official, an anticommunist, a populist, a liberal, a cosmopolitan, and a government official, while keeping in reserve the roles of socialist and unifier of the former U.S.S.R. And he has performed all of these roles in the same ruling style: He is impatient and aggressive and always tries to exacerbate the situation in order to ram through his solution; he is shockingly direct and despises compromise as weakness.

1. You should first learn more about the magazine. Does it have any biases about Yeltsin?

2. While the source has firsthand knowledge, you do not know whether the writer supports or opposes Yeltsin's reforms.

3. Material in a magazine is public information. You should consider what the writer has to gain or lose by making this information available.

Independent Practice   Study the cartoon below. It appeared in a publication in Vienna in 1994. How can you determine whether it is a reliable source?

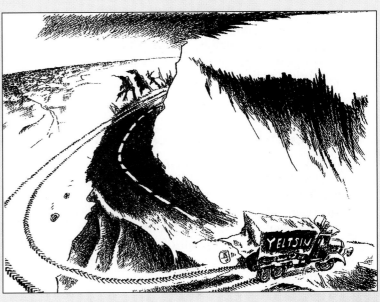

EIGHT REVIEW

REVIEW QUESTIONS

1. Based on what you have learned in this unit, what do you think should be the role of the United Nations in dealing with such global issues as terrorism, third world debt, and the international drug trade? Explain.

2. What factors, do you think, make it so difficult to end or reduce the world trade in military armaments?

3. In your opinion, should the United States have joined the League of Nations? Why or why not?

4. Based on what you have learned in this unit and what you know of global events in the past few years, compare the changes that have occurred in NATO and the EU with the changes that have developed in Russia and in other Eastern European countries.

5. If we do live in an increasingly interdependent world, do you think that interdependence will lead to greater similarity in nations' economic and political systems? Explain.

6. Modern technology has enabled such realities as jet travel to all parts of the world and instantaneous communication of words and pictures by space satellites. What effect do you think this has had on interdependence among the world's nations? Explain.

SUGGESTED READINGS

1. Ambrose, Stephen E. *Rise to Globalism: American Foreign Policy Since 1938*. New York: Penguin Books, 1983. Analyzes the history of American foreign policy, focusing on technological changes, shifts in popular attitudes, external forces, and how all of these variables preceded changes in policy during the rise of the United States to globalism.

2. *A Citizen's Guide to U.S. Foreign Policy: Election '88*. Editors of Foreign Policy Association. New York: Foreign Policy Association, 1988. Explains 18 foreign policy issues that voters and candidates covered in the 1988 election year.

3. Clancy, Tom. *Red Storm Rising*. New York: G. P. Putnam's Sons, 1986. Facing a critical oil shortage brought on by a terrorist attack, the Soviet Union sees a military attack on Europe as a last ditch option and takes it.

4. Drury, Allen. *The Promise of Joy*. Garden City, New York: Doubleday & Co., 1975. With the outbreak of nuclear war between China and Russia beginning, what does an American President do?

5. Forsythe, Frederick. *The Negotiator*. New York: Bantam Books, 1989. The United States must gain control of Middle Eastern oil supplies, or so believes one fanatic. If the President of the United States is in the way—get rid of him.

6. Harrison, Paul. *Inside the Third World: The Anatomy of Poverty, 2nd ed*. New York: Viking Penguin, Inc., 1982. Looks at the problems that make the poor nations of Asia, Africa, and Latin America so susceptible to turmoil.

7. Lederer, William, and Eugene Burdick. *The Ugly American*. New York: W. W. Norton Co., Inc., 1965. Classic tale of the blundering hypocrisy of some top-level American diplomats overseas.

8. Ludlum, Robert. *The Bourne Identity*. New York: Bantam Books, 1984. An American agent takes on the international terrorist, Carlos. Then, the agent finds his own side hunting him.

9. Weiss, Ann E. *The Nuclear Arms Race— Can We Survive It?* Boston: Houghton Mifflin Co., 1983. Relates important events in the nuclear arms buildup.

MAKING JUDGMENTS

Making judgments is an evaluative activity that we do all the time. We make judgments in terms of whether something is good or bad, desirable or undesirable, or appropriate or inappropriate.

Was the high school principal right when she suspended ten students for cheating? Is it appropriate for candidates who are behind in the polls to engage in negative campaigning? Should financial aid be sent to a Marxist government in Ethiopia when there are so many homeless Americans?

Whether we are aware of it or not, when we make judgments about political issues, we do so in terms of standards or criteria that support our own personal values and needs. Sometimes these standards are self-serving; often they have to do with ''American'' values, such as justice, equality, rights, liberty, and morality. The Preamble to the Constitution contains criteria that often can be used as a convenient, ready-made way to judge something. Does a particular law really unite us as a people, or is it divisive? Was a family treated fairly when their application for food stamps was turned down? Will the addition of more prisons reduce drug abuse? Do we need to spend more money on law enforcement personnel? Why should someone be faced with higher taxes to pay for education when he or she has no children in school? Every one of these issues involves reasons for which our nation was established.

Sometimes, however, issues arise for which there are no easy-to-find criteria, and we may be forced to develop new ones. One such issue is the Strategic Defense Initiative. Two criteria that those who oppose the Initiative have used are practicality and cost.

In order to make good judgments, citizens must learn to identify and develop, if necessary, criteria that they will use to evaluate issues and actions. They also must know how to apply those criteria systematically. And they must periodically assess whether the criteria they are using are still appropriate.

The following exercise will help you hone your skills in identifying or developing criteria for making judgments. For each event, tell whether you agree or disagree with the decision that was made, and tell what criteria you based your judgment on.

1. The President authorizes the CIA to use covert action to try to overthrow a right-wing dictatorship.

2. The Congress authorizes the sale of guns and other sophisticated weaponry to Israel.

3. The Immigration and Naturalization Service breaks into a church in San Diego, looking for illegal aliens.

4. The President sends military advisers to a small nation in Central America to support an insurgency movement there.

5. Congress votes to send massive economic aid to Poland and Hungary following the restructuring of their governments.

6. An American ambassador secretly encourages a Warsaw Pact nation to withdraw and join NATO.

THE AMERICAN FLAG

★ ★ ★ ★ ★

Honoring the Flag

A great many rules and customs have grown up about how to use and display the American flag. These rules and customs were incorporated in a flag code passed by Congress in 1942 and amended in 1976. No one is expected to know all of the regulations. The important thing is to treat the flag with respect. Here are some of the rules of the flag code.

★ The flag should be displayed from sunrise to sunset. It should not be flown at night except on special occasions or in certain places.

★ The flag should not be flown in bad weather.

★ No other flag should be flown above the American flag or to the right of it at the same height.

★ The flag should not be used to cover a statue or painting at an unveiling.

★ On Memorial Day, the flag should be flown at half-mast in the morning and at full-mast in the afternoon.

★ The flag may be flown at half-mast to mourn the death of public officials. When it is flown at half-mast, it should first be hoisted all the way up and then lowered.

★ When the flag is used to drape a coffin, it should be placed so that the union (the stars) is at the head and over the left shoulder of the casket.

★ The flag should never touch the ground or floor beneath it.

★ The flag may be flown upside down only to signal distress.

★ If the flag is suspended over a street, the union should face north or east.

★ The flag should never be used as a drapery or displayed in festoons or folds. It should always fall free.

★ The flag should never be used for advertising purposes.

★ The flag should never be dipped to any person or thing.

The Pledge of Allegiance

"I pledge allegiance to the Flag of the United States of America and to the Republic for which it stands, one Nation under God indivisible, with liberty and justice for all."

Francis Bellamy, a magazine editor, wrote the Pledge of Allegiance in 1892 to celebrate the 400th anniversary of Columbus's discovery of America. In 1954, Congress amended the Pledge by adding the words "under God." Over the years, it has become an American tradition to recite the Pledge of Allegiance in school and at many public gatherings.

When you recite the Pledge of Allegiance, you should stand facing the flag and place your right hand over your heart. People in military uniform should give a military salute with their right hand.

APPENDIX

ATLAS KEY

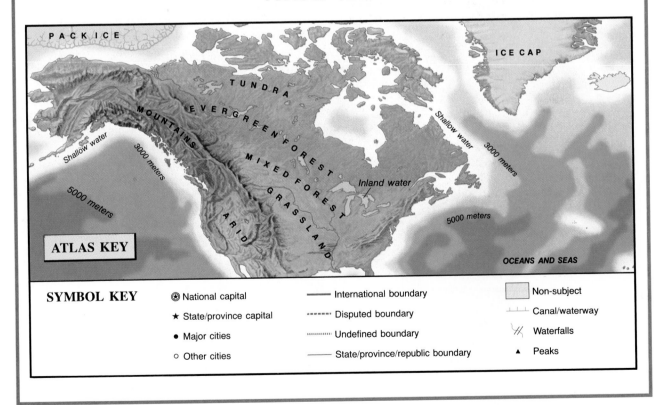

PACK ICE

ICE CAP

TUNDRA

EVERGREEN FOREST

MOUNTAINS

MIXED FOREST

GRASSLAND

ARID

Shallow water

3000 meters

5000 meters

Shallow water

3000 meters

Inland water

5000 meters

ATLAS KEY

OCEANS AND SEAS

SYMBOL KEY

⊛ National capital
★ State/province capital
● Major cities
○ Other cities

—— International boundary
------- Disputed boundary
·········· Undefined boundary
—— State/province/republic boundary

☐ Non-subject
⊥⊥⊥ Canal/waterway
⋎ Waterfalls
▲ Peaks

CANADA

Lake of the Woods

Woods Lake

Lake Superior

MICHIGAN

Duluth

MINNESOTA

Lake Huron

Minneapolis ★St. Paul

Mississippi

Rochester

WISCONSIN

Green Bay○
Appleton○

Lake Michigan

Grand
Rapids○ ○Flint

Lansing
Detroit

IOWA

Dubuque○

Cedar
Rapids○

Davenport○

Madison★

Milwaukee●
Racine○

Rockford○

Chicago●

South
Bend○

Aurora○

Joliet○

Gary●
Hammond●

Toledo○

Ann Arbor○

Fort Wayne○

MICHIGAN

Lake Superior

St. Lawrence River

MAINE

Moosehead Lake

Bangor○

Mt. Washington
6,288 ft.
(1,905 m.)

★Augusta

Lewiston○

Lake Champlain

Burlington○

Montpelier○

VT. **N.H.**

Portland○

ADIRONDACK MTNS.

Hudson

Concord○
Manchester○

MASS.

Cape Cod

Utica○

Rochester○

Syracuse○

Albany★

Springfield○

Worcester○

Boston★

NEW YORK

Lake Ontario

Niagara Falls○ Buffalo●

Binghamton○

Providence★

Hartford★

New Haven★

R.I.

CONN.

Yonkers○

Susquehanna River

Newark●

Allentown○

N.J.

New York●

Council Bluffs

Des Moines★

ILLINOIS

Peoria○

CENTRAL LOWLAND

Springfield★

Decatur○

Muncie○

OHIO

Columbus●

Cleveland●

Youngstown○

PENNSYLVANIA

Akron○
Canton○

Pittsburgh●

Harrisburg★

Philadelphia●

Trenton★

Camden○
Wilmington○

Dover★

DEL.

MD.

DELAWARE BAY

Kansas
City●

Independence○

Jefferson City★

St.
Louis●

East
St. Louis○

Evansville○

Wabash R.

INDIANA

Indianapolis★

Dayton○

Cincinnati○

Wheeling○

WEST VIRGINIA

Baltimore●

Annapolis★

Arlington○

Washington
D.C.

ATLANTIC OCEAN

Harry S. Truman
Res.

MISSOURI

Springfield○

S. Kerr
Res.

OZARK PLATEAU

ARKANSAS

Fort Smith○

North
Little Rock○

Little Rock★

Hot Springs○

Pine Bluff○

Ohio River

Frankfort★

Lexington○

Louisville●

KENTUCKY

Owensboro○

River

Charleston●

Huntington○

Roanoke★

VIRGINIA

Richmond★

Roanoke

Newport
News○

Norfolk○

CHESAPEAKE BAY

Cape Hatteras

Cumberland

Knoxville○

PLATEAU

Mt. Mitchell
6,684 ft.
(2,037 m.)

Winston-
Salem○

Greensboro○

Durham○
Raleigh★

NORTH CAROLINA

Nashville★

TENNESSEE

Chattanooga○

Tennessee River

Memphis●

Huntsville○

APPALACHIAN

Charlotte○

Greenville○

Spartanburg○

Columbia★

Greenville○

SOUTH CAROLINA

Charleston○

CUMBERLAND

Birmingham●

Tuscaloosa○

Atlanta★

Augusta○

Chattahoochee

ALABAMA

Montgomery★

Columbus○

Macon○

GEORGIA

Savannah○

Shreveport○

Meridian○

Jackson★

LOUISIANA

Toledo
Bend
Res.

Hattiesburg○

MISSISSIPPI

Alabama R.

COASTAL

PLAIN

Sam Rayburn
Reservoir

Houston

Mississippi River

Greenville○

Baton Rouge★

Lafayette○

Lake
Charles○

New Orleans●

Lake Pontchartrain

Biloxi○

Mobile○

Pensacola○

Tallahassee★

FLORIDA

Jacksonville○

Orlando●

Cape
Canaveral○

Tampa●

St. Petersburg○

Lake Okeechobee

Palm Beach○

Miami Beach○

Miami●

Cape Sable

Key West○

Strait of Florida

GULF OF MEXICO

↑
N

THE BAHAMAS

CUBA

UNITED STATES

⊛ National capital
★ State capital
● Major city
○ Other city
—— International boundary
—— State boundary

| 0 | 100 | 200 Miles |
| 0 | 100 | 200 Kilometers |

Projection: Albers Equal Area

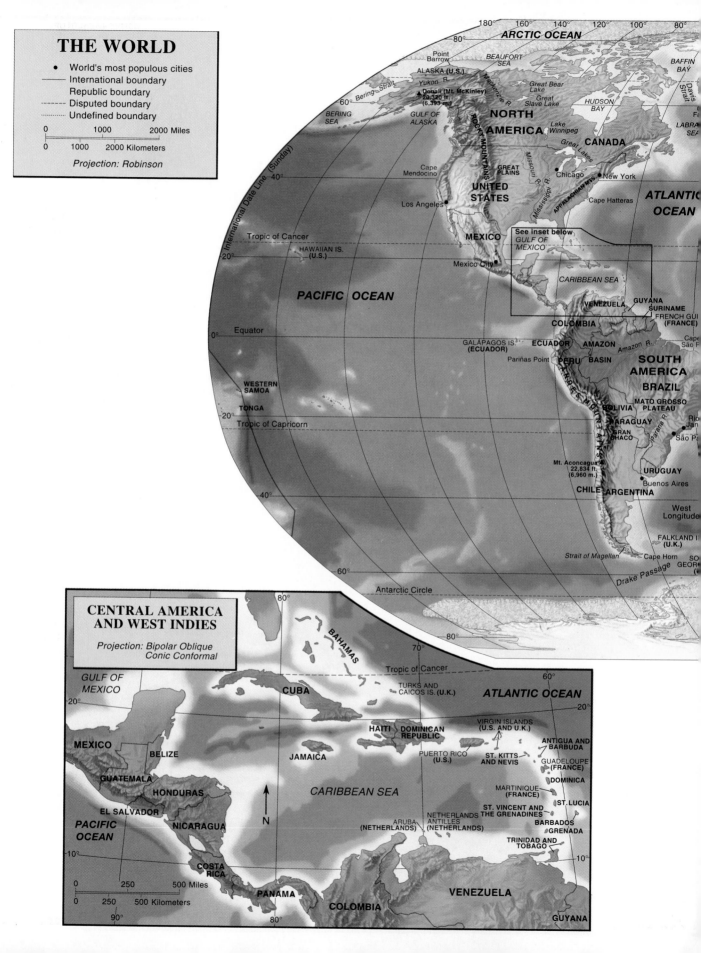

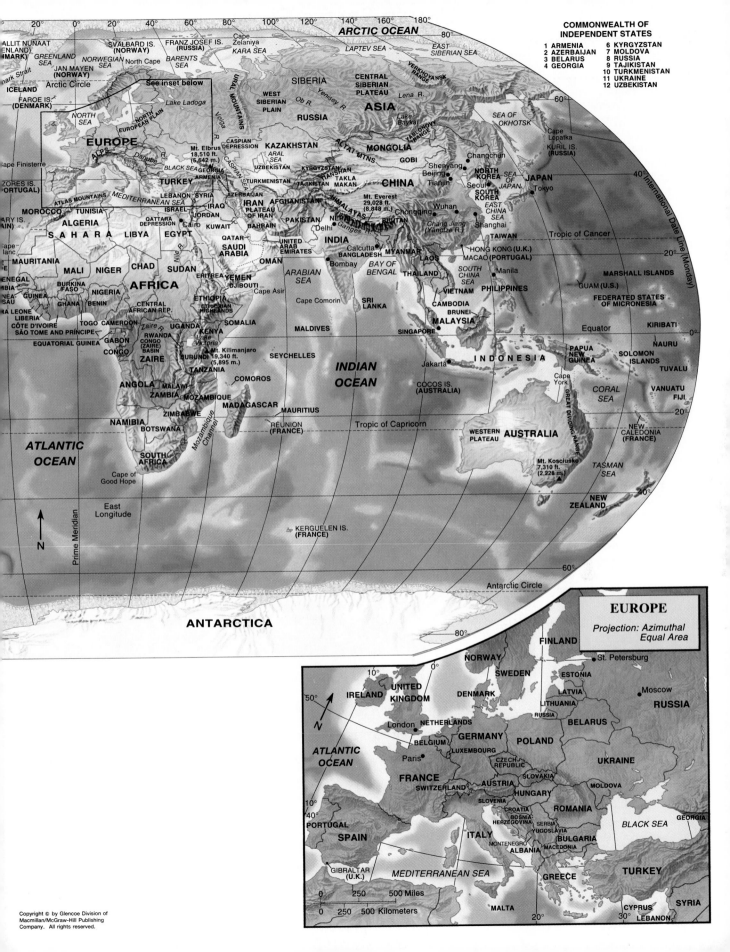

ARCTIC OCEAN

GREENLAND
SEA
ICELAND
FAROE IS.
(DENMARK)
NORTH
SEA
EUROPE
AZORES IS.
(PORTUGAL)
ATLAS MOUNTAINS
MOROCCO
ALGERIA   LIBYA   EGYPT
SAHARA
MAURITANIA MALI NIGER CHAD SUDAN
SENEGAL
GUINEA
SIERRA LEONE
LIBERIA
CÔTE D'IVOIRE
GHANA BENIN
TOGO CAMEROON
SÃO TOMÉ AND PRÍNCIPE
EQUATORIAL GUINEA
GABON
CONGO
ZAIRE

AFRICA

ANGOLA
ZAMBIA
NAMIBIA
BOTSWANA
SOUTH
AFRICA
Cape of
Good Hope

ATLANTIC
OCEAN

ANTARCTICA

SVALBARD IS.
(NORWAY)
FRANZ JOSEF IS.
(RUSSIA)
Cape
Zelaniya
KARA SEA
LAPTEV SEA
EAST
SIBERIAN SEA
BARENTS
SEA
North Cape
Arctic Circle
SIBERIA
CENTRAL
SIBERIAN
PLATEAU
Lena R.
VERKHOYANSK
RANGE
WEST
SIBERIAN
PLAIN
Ob R.
Yenisey R.
Lake
Baykal
RUSSIA
ASIA
SEA OF
OKHOTSK
Cape
Lopatka
KURIL IS.
(RUSSIA)
KAZAKHSTAN
ARAL
SEA
MONGOLIA
GOBI
ALTAI MTNS.
YABLONOVY
RANGE
Changchun
Shenyang
NORTH
KOREA
SEA
OF
JAPAN
JAPAN
Tokyo
UZBEKISTAN
KYRGYZSTAN
TURKMENISTAN
TAKLA
MAKAN
TIANSHAN
Beijing
Tianjin
Seoul
SOUTH
KOREA
TURKEY
ARMENIA
AZERBAIJAN
TAJIKISTAN
AFGHANISTAN
CHINA
Mt. Everest
(8,848 m.)
Chongqing
Wuhan
Shanghai
EAST
CHINA
SEA
LEBANON SYRIA
ISRAEL
IRAQ
JORDAN
IRAN
PLATEAU
OF IRAN
PAKISTAN
NEPAL
BHUTAN
HIMALAYAS
Chang Jiang
(Yangtze R.)
TAIWAN
Tropic of Cancer
Cairo
KUWAIT
BAHRAIN
Delhi
Ganges R.
INDIA
Calcutta
BANGLADESH
HONG KONG (U.K.)
MACAO (PORTUGAL)
QATTARA
DEPRESSION
QATAR
SAUDI
ARABIA
UNITED
ARAB
EMIRATES
OMAN
Bombay
MYANMAR
LAOS
SOUTH
CHINA
SEA
Manila
MARSHALL ISLANDS
YEMEN
DJIBOUTI
ERITREA
Cape Asir
ARABIAN
SEA
BAY OF
BENGAL
THAILAND
VIETNAM
CAMBODIA
BRUNEI
GUAM (U.S.)
FEDERATED STATES
OF MICRONESIA
ETHIOPIA
ETHIOPIAN
HIGHLANDS
CENTRAL
AFRICAN REP.
SOMALIA
UGANDA
KENYA
Cape Comorin
SRI
LANKA
MALDIVES
PHILIPPINES
MALAYSIA
SINGAPORE
KIRIBATI
NAURU
RWANDA
BURUNDI
CONGO
(ZAIRE)
BASIN
Lake
Victoria
Mt. Kilimanjaro
19,340 ft.
(5,895 m.)
TANZANIA
SEYCHELLES
INDONESIA
Jakarta
PAPUA
NEW
GUINEA
SOLOMON
ISLANDS
TUVALU
Equator
COMOROS
MALAWI
MOZAMBIQUE
MADAGASCAR
MAURITIUS
COCOS IS.
(AUSTRALIA)
Cape
York
GREAT DIVIDING RANGE
CORAL
SEA
VANUATU
FIJI
ZIMBABWE
RÉUNION
(FRANCE)
Tropic of Capricorn
WESTERN
PLATEAU
AUSTRALIA
Mt. Kosciusko
7,310 ft.
(2,228 m.)
TASMAN
SEA
NEW
CALEDONIA
(FRANCE)
NEW
ZEALAND
Antarctic Circle

INDIAN
OCEAN

Mozambique
Channel

Prime Meridian
East
Longitude
N
KERGUELEN IS.
(FRANCE)

See inset below
URAL MOUNTAINS
Lake Ladoga
Volga R.
Mt. Elbrus
18,510 ft.
(5,542 m.)
CASPIAN
DEPRESSION
CASPIAN SEA
BLACK SEA
Danube R.
ALPS
NORTH
EUROPEAN PLAIN
MEDITERRANEAN SEA
TUNISIA
PLATEAU
OF IRAN

International Date Line (Monday)

EUROPE
Projection: Azimuthal
Equal Area

FINLAND
St. Petersburg
NORWAY
SWEDEN
ESTONIA
Moscow
IRELAND
UNITED
KINGDOM
DENMARK
LATVIA
LITHUANIA
RUSSIA
RUSSIA
BELARUS
London
NETHERLANDS
BELGIUM
GERMANY
POLAND
ATLANTIC
OCEAN
Paris
LUXEMBOURG
CZECH
REPUBLIC
UKRAINE
SLOVAKIA
FRANCE
AUSTRIA
HUNGARY
MOLDOVA
SWITZERLAND
SLOVENIA
ROMANIA
PORTUGAL
CROATIA
BOSNIA
HERZEGOVINA
SERBIA
YUGOSLAVIA
BLACK SEA
GEORGIA
SPAIN
ITALY
MONTENEGRO
ALBANIA
MACEDONIA
BULGARIA
GIBRALTAR
(U.K.)
MEDITERRANEAN SEA
GREECE
TURKEY
MALTA
CYPRUS
SYRIA
LEBANON
N

0   250   500 Miles
0   250   500 Kilometers

UNITED STATES FACTS

State*	Year Admitted	Population 1990	Area Sq. Mile	Capital	Largest City	House Rep. 1990**
1. Delaware	1787	666,168	2,057	Dover	Wilmington	1
2. Pennsylvania	1787	11,881,643	45,333	Harrisburg	Philadelphia	21
3. New Jersey	1787	7,730,188	7,836	Trenton	Newark	13
4. Georgia	1788	6,478,216	58,876	Atlanta	Atlanta	11
5. Connecticut	1788	3,287,116	5,609	Hartford	Bridgeport	6
6. Massachusetts	1788	6,016,425	8,257	Boston	Boston	10
7. Maryland	1788	4,781,468	10,577	Annapolis	Baltimore	8
8. South Carolina	1788	3,486,703	31,055	Columbia	Columbia	6
9. New Hampshire	1788	1,109,252	9,304	Concord	Manchester	2
10. Virginia	1788	6,187,358	40,817	Richmond	Norfolk	11
11. New York	1788	17,990,455	49,576	Albany	New York	31
12. North Carolina	1789	6,628,637	52,586	Raleigh	Charlotte	12
13. Rhode Island	1790	1,003,464	1,214	Providence	Providence	2
14. Vermont	1791	562,758	9,609	Montpelier	Burlington	1
15. Kentucky	1792	3,685,296	40,395	Frankfort	Louisville	6
16. Tennessee	1796	4,877,185	42,244	Nashville	Memphis	9
17. Ohio	1803	10,847,115	41,222	Columbus	Cleveland	19
18. Louisiana	1812	4,219,973	48,523	Baton Rouge	New Orleans	7
19. Indiana	1816	5,544,159	36,291	Indianapolis	Indianapolis	10
20. Mississippi	1817	2,573,216	47,716	Jackson	Jackson	5
21. Illinois	1818	11,430,602	56,400	Springfield	Chicago	20
22. Alabama	1819	4,040,587	51,609	Montgomery	Birmingham	7
23. Maine	1820	1,227,928	33,215	Augusta	Portland	2
24. Missouri	1821	5,117,073	69,686	Jefferson City	St. Louis	9
25. Arkansas	1836	2,350,725	53,104	Little Rock	Little Rock	4
26. Michigan	1837	9,295,297	58,216	Lansing	Detroit	16
27. Florida	1845	12,937,926	58,560	Tallahassee	Jacksonville	23
28. Texas	1845	16,986,510	267,339	Austin	Houston	30
29. Iowa	1846	2,776,755	56,290	Des Moines	Des Moines	5
30. Wisconsin	1848	4,891,769	56,154	Madison	Milwaukee	9
31. California	1850	29,760,021	158,693	Sacramento	Los Angeles	52
32. Minnesota	1858	4,375,099	84,068	St. Paul	Minneapolis	8
33. Oregon	1859	2,853,733	96,981	Salem	Portland	5
34. Kansas	1861	2,477,574	82,264	Topeka	Wichita	4
35. West Virginia	1863	1,793,477	24,181	Charleston	Huntington	3
36. Nevada	1864	1,201,833	110,540	Carson City	Las Vegas	2
37. Nebraska	1867	1,578,385	77,227	Lincoln	Omaha	3
38. Colorado	1876	3,294,394	104,247	Denver	Denver	6
39. North Dakota	1889	638,800	70,665	Bismarck	Fargo	1
40. South Dakota	1889	696,004	77,047	Pierre	Sioux Falls	1
41. Montana	1889	799,065	147,138	Helena	Billings	1
42. Washington	1889	4,887,941	68,192	Olympia	Seattle	9
43. Idaho	1890	1,006,749	83,557	Boise	Boise	2
44. Wyoming	1890	455,975	97,914	Cheyenne	Cheyenne	1
45. Utah	1896	1,727,784	84,916	Salt Lake City	Salt Lake City	3
46. Oklahoma	1907	3,145,585	69,919	Oklahoma City	Oklahoma City	6
47. New Mexico	1912	1,515,069	121,666	Santa Fe	Albuquerque	3
48. Arizona	1912	3,665,228	113,909	Phoenix	Phoenix	6
49. Alaska	1959	550,043	586,412	Juneau	Anchorage	1
50. Hawaii	1959	1,108,229	6,450	Honolulu	Honolulu	2
District of Columbia (Washington, D.C.)	—	606,900	68	—	—	—
United States of America	—	248,709,873	3,615,124	Washington, D.C.	New York	435

* Numbers denote the order in which states were admitted. ** Number of members in House of Representatives

GLOSSARY

A

acquittal process of being judged not guilty and set free after a court trial

act of admission bill passed by Congress to allow a territory to become a state

actual malice inaccurate, false, or defamatory statements knowingly published with the intent to do harm

adjourn action of ending a session of a legislative body such as Congress; for Congress to adjourn it takes a vote by both houses

administrative law rules and regulations, having the force of law, made by administrative agencies to help them carry out laws passed by the legislature

adversary system legal system in which two opposing sides present their cases before an impartial court

affirmative action programs procedures and regulations implemented to remedy the effects of discrimination by giving special help to those groups who have been discriminated against; programs designed to further employment and education of women and minorities

aliens people who are not citizens of the country in which they live and who owe allegiance to another country

allegiance loyalty and service given to one's country and its government

alliances groups of nations working together on a specific problem or for a specific goal; these goals can be political, military, or economic

amicus curiae legal term meaning "friend of the court" used to describe briefs or testimony by individuals or groups who are not parties to a legal action but who wish to aid or influence the court in reaching its decision

amnesty power of the President to grant a general pardon to all members of a group who have violated a federal law

annexation expansion of a city's boundaries to take in a nearby area

apartheid racial separation; separate development of the races and political and economic discrimination against non-European groups in South Africa

appellate jurisdiction authority permitting a court to hear cases which are appealed from a lower court; this jurisdiction allows the court to review a case, and either agree or disagree with the lower court's decision

apportion to divide seats in a legislative body among the geographical districts represented in that body; for example, Congress ruled there are 435 seats in the House to be divided among the fifty states

appropriations legislative or authorized grants of money for government expenditures

armistice suspension of a war by agreement between the two sides; a truce

arraignment formal court hearing at which the accused is formally charged with a crime

assessed value value placed on a piece of property; used for tax purposes, it is usually a percentage of the market value

B

bail money deposited with a court by an accused individual to allow him or her to remain out of jail while awaiting trial; it is a guarantee the person will appear for trial

balance of power situation that occurs when no one country or group of countries has more power than the others

bankruptcy legal condition, declared by a court of law, stating an individual is unable to pay his or her debts, and whose property will be divided among his or her creditors to pay those debts

bicameral made up of two legislative houses or units

bill of attainder law that determines an individual's guilt and punishment without a judicial trial

bill of rights statement of the fundamental rights guaranteed to the people by government

bills proposed laws that must be passed by a majority vote in both houses

block grant fixed allotment of money given by the federal government to state and local communities for programs, usually has few federal restrictions for spending

board-chief executive plan county plan of government that gives policy-making power to its board, but gives the responsibility to carry out policies to a county executive elected by the people

board-manager plan county plan of government that gives policy-making power to its board, but gives the responsibility to carry out policies to a hired county manager

bonds certificates providing a means for the government to borrow a sum of money, by giving the lender, in return, a written promise to repay the sum plus interest at the end of a specific period of time

boroughs administrative units of local government in the state of Alaska; similar to counties in other states

budget deficit estimate of government spending in which expenditures are higher than revenue

bureaucracy system of administrative agencies that carries out policy on a daily basis using standard procedures and which is based on a specialization of duties; a term often used to refer to the executive branch of government and implying powerful administrative officials, red tape, and resistance to change

bureaucrats members of the bureaucracy; government workers who help executive leaders do their job

C

Cabinet group of advisers appointed to work for the President, a governor, or a mayor

capitalism economic system based on free enterprise with the underlying principle of competition; private citizens own, produce, distribute, and exchange goods and services

capital punishment death as punishment for a crime

case law reported cases that, taken together, form precedents upon which later judicial decisions will be based

categorical grant federal allotment of money granted for a specific purpose to state or local governments

caucus closed meeting of party members from one house of a legislative body to select leaders or decide legislative business

censure majority vote of disapproval by one house of a legislative body against a member for improper conduct while in office

census official count of the people of the United States required by Congress every ten years

charter municipality's law, authorized by a state, indicating its name, boundaries, and governmental powers

charter colonies in colonial America, colonies governed in accordance with a royal charter and without interference from the Crown

checks and balances principle of American government in which each branch of government can check, or limit, the powers of the other branches so no one branch may dominate the others

circuits twelve geographic regions into which the United States is divided; each circuit has one federal district court of appeals

civil liberties individual freedoms the government must not interfere with; includes freedom of religion, speech, press, assembly, and petition

civil rights rights and freedoms guaranteed by the Constitution to all citizens

classified employees government workers hired for certain jobs on basis of merit or ability; civil service tests are taken by these employees to determine those who qualify

closed primary primary elections in which voters choose a candidate from their party to run for office; voters must declare their party membership before they can vote

cloture rule rule allowing limitation of a debate; it is a technique to end a debate so an issue can be brought to vote; also known as *closure*

coalition combination of political parties that agree to cooperate to gain a majority in order to govern

collective bargaining process of negotiation during which employees and management discuss working conditions, pay, and other benefits; usually employees are represented by a union

collective security nations, usually an alliance, taking group action against any nation that makes an aggressive act against one of its member nations

commission form local form of government in which three to nine city leaders are elected to a board of commissions that handles both executive and legislative responsibilities

common law rules or principles derived from judicial decisions that are based on accepted customs and traditions

common markets international economic alliances of countries whose goal is to unify their economies so they will experience a growth in production, trade, and employment

communism economic and political system in which the means of production, distribution, and exchange of goods and services are controlled by society as a whole

complaint brief, formal statement telling the court the facts of a case and requesting some kind of decision

concurrent jurisdiction authority equally shared by federal courts with state courts to try the same type of case

concurrent powers governmental powers that can be exercised by both the national and state levels of government

concurrent resolutions measures passed by both houses of a legislative body with the intention of expressing an opinion or official policy; these resolutions are not signed by the President and do not have the force of law

concurring opinion written statement that explains the position of a Supreme Court justice who agrees with the majority's decision, but for different reasons

confederate government central government that handles matters of common concern; power is delegated to it by member states

conference committee special legislative committee responsible for rewriting the two versions of a bill passed by the two houses creating a single version acceptable to both; representatives from both houses make up this temporary committee

conservation protection and preservation of natural resources

consolidation joining or combining a county government with one or more cities to form one government

constituents citizens represented by an elected official

constitutional initiative petition from voters proposing that a change be made in a state constitution

constitutionalism elected officials of a national or state government abiding by, and governing in accordance with, a constitution

constitutional supremacy principle of American government whereby the U.S. Constitution is superior to state constitutions, state laws, and all other federal laws or treaties

containment policy adopted by the United States after World War II to prevent any further spread of communism

continuing resolution one large bill combining several, or all, appropriations bills

cooperative federalism concept of government whereby national and state levels of government work together

copyrights exclusive legal rights individuals have to perform, sell, and protect their creative work, such as music, inventions, computer programs, written material, or art

corporate income tax tax on the money a business or corporation makes; usually a standard rate regardless of earnings

cost-of-living adjustments increases in benefits, such as salary, to meet the rate of inflation

council-manager form local form of government in which the elected council members determine city policy while an appointed manager carries out those policies and handles the city's daily business

councils of government representatives from several units of government who jointly attempt to solve common problems or concerns

counties local units of government established by a state to carry out administrative responsibilities at local levels; these responsibilities can be the running of schools, maintenance of roads, or law enforcement

county board governing body of a county, elected by the voters to carry out county business

county commissioners county board's elected officials

county seat town or city where county government is administered

currency money, either paper or coins, issued and approved by a government for its use

D

debt ceiling limit set by law to control debt

deductions amounts of money legally subtracted from tax due

de facto segregation segregation that occurs when students living in one social or economic area are assigned to that area's neighborhood schools

defendant accused party; individual or group in a court case who is accused of wrongdoing

de jure segregation segregation mandated or sanctioned by law

delegated powers powers granted by the Constitution to the national government

democracy form of government in which the people hold the final authority to rule

denaturalization legal process of, by court order, revoking the citizenship that a person has acquired by naturalization

deportation legal process by which a nation expels an alien

deposition written testimony taken by an examiner outside the court and certified to the judge

desegregation elimination of barriers that separate people of different racial groups

detente break in the tension of a cold war

developed nation rich, strong, industrialized state

developing nation state with little or no industry

dictatorship government control, usually gained by force, by one person or a small group

diplomacy various methods used to manage relationships between countries

diplomatic recognition official acknowledgement of diplomatic relations between the United States and a foreign government

direct democracy democracy in which the government is ruled by the citizens themselves

disarmament efforts made by a country to reduce its number of weapons

discharge petition request by petition from members of the Senate or the House of Representatives to force a bill out of committee and onto the floor for consideration; bills held by a committee for more than thirty days can be petitioned

discount rate tool in monetary policy to control the supply of money; the Federal Reserve charges its member banks interest whenever they borrow money

discrimination act of treating groups of people differently or unequally

discuss list court list prepared by the Chief Justice listing cases and petitions that will be considered by the Supreme Court

disenfranchised deprived of the privilege of voting, usually by loss of citizenship, conviction of certain crimes, or failure to meet registration or residency requirements

dissenting opinion written argument that explains a Supreme Court justice's reasons for disagreeing with the majority's decision

double jeopardy trying someone in court again for an offense he or she has already been tried and acquitted of

due process of law Constitutional procedures the government must follow in bringing someone to trial; guarantees an individual's rights

E

earmarked also known as *earmarking;* the practice of setting aside certain revenues to pay for specific expenditures

economic system organized way a society chooses to provide for the production and distribution of goods and services for its people

electoral college group of people elected from each state who cast ballots for President and Vice President

electoral votes ballots cast for President and Vice President in the electoral college by persons from each state who are pledged to the presidential ticket that won the popular vote in that state

electorate group of citizens who meet the requirements to vote in an election

engrossed printed after passage by Congress; the bill has been fully debated and amended by the House or Senate

enjoin court order that prohibits some action by an individual or group

entitlement programs sponsored by the government; they provide benefits to eligible citizens; some examples are social security, veterans' benefits, and certain welfare programs

enumerated powers expressed powers of the government clearly stated in the Constitution

equity suit civil case seeking fair treatment when there is no law to remedy the matter

excise tax selective sales tax levied on the manufacture or sale of certain items

exclusionary rule rule stating that evidence obtained illegally and that is in violation of an individual's constitutional rights cannot be used as evidence in a court of law

exclusive jurisdiction power or authority that a court has, to the exclusion of other courts, over a person or case

exclusive powers governmental powers that belong only to the states, or only to the national government

executive agreements written arrangements, such as treaties, made by the President with heads of other countries; these agreements do not need ratification by Congress

executive branch one of the three branches of government; it has the power and responsibility to enforce and administer the laws of the land

executive departments administrative departments that deal with certain areas of government, such as the Department of Treasury, the Department of State, etc; at present the executive branch of the government is made up of 14 major administrative divisions

executive orders rules or regulations issued by a chief executive, such as a President or governor, that have the same authority as laws

executive privilege right of executive officials, especially the President, to refuse to appear before or to provide information to a legislative body or a court

expatriation voluntarily withdrawing allegiance or residence from the country where a person holds citizenship

expel to remove from office or membership

exports goods that a country produces and then sells to other countries

ex post facto law law that provides punishment for a crime although it was not considered a crime when the act was committed

expressed powers powers of Congress that are stated in the Constitution

F

fascism totalitarian form of government in which a dictator and businesses support each other and seek more power for their nation at the expense of human rights

federal budget this financial plan determines and controls the national government's spending; usually designed on a yearly basis

federal bureaucracy agencies of the national government's executive branch that carry out policy on a day-to-day basis

federal government system that avoids a concentration of power by dividing the power of government between the national government and the state or regional governments

federalism system of government where the power to govern is shared by a written constitution between the central, or national, government and the states

filibuster technique of delay in which senators can use their unlimited freedom of debate by talking several hours to prevent a vote on a bill

first budget resolution joint resolution of Congress; it sets targets for government spending, taxing, and the amount of the surplus or deficit that can be anticipated within these targets; it is nonbinding

fiscal policy national government's financial policy concerning taxing and spending

fiscal year financial year; a period of twelve consecutive months used for accounting purposes

foreign aid assistance given by one country to another to help the receiving country build its economic, political, or military stability

foreign policy plan describing a nation's attitudes and actions toward countries in the rest of the world

free trade policy in which trade between countries is unrestricted

free trade associations economic alliances of international countries that allow their member nations economic independence while still providing free trade among them

full faith and credit obligation of each state in its relations with other states to accept the validity of other states' laws and actions

G

general elections statewide elections held so registered voters can decide the state and national officials who will head the government

general fund used by a state government to pay its expenses; this state money is collected through taxes

general sales tax tax levied on most items sold in a state; the tax rate is a percentage of the sale price

general trial court second level of courts in a state judicial system in which major civil and criminal cases are heard

global economy economic system in which the economy of one country can affect, and be affected by, the economies of other countries

government method or system of control, especially of a city, state, or nation; the people who make up a governing body

grants-in-aid direct federal allotments of money to state or local governments to spend on public programs, usually spending conditions are determined in advance

gross domestic product the dollar value of final goods and services created within a country in a year

H

home rule community's right to draft, adopt, and amend its own municipal charter for government

hopper a box; members of the House of Representatives introduce bills by dropping their written proposals into this box

I

immigrants people admitted to a country for the purpose of becoming permanent residents

impeach formal charges brought by the lower house of the legislature, to be tried by the upper house, against a member of the executive or judicial branch for serious misconduct of public business

implied powers powers of the national government indirectly suggested but not stated in the Constitution, particularly in Article I, Section 8

imports goods made by one country and brought into another country for sale or use

inauguration ceremony installing an elected chief executive, such as a President or governor, into office

incorporation process of establishing a local unit of government, such as a city, by receiving a charter from a state; must meet a population requirement and be approved by the residents' vote

incumbents officials who are presently holding office

Independents citizens who do not claim membership to a political party

indictment formal written accusation by a grand jury charging an individual or group with a crime

individual income tax tax levied on the money an individual earns; tax rate is determined by the amount of income earned

inferior courts lower courts in the court system; may have special or limited jurisdiction

inflation phase in the business cycle where the general price level of goods and services increases as the value of money decreases

information accusation made under oath by a prosecuting attorney, before a court, charging a person with a crime; used instead of a grand jury indictment in some states

infringement using copyrighted material without permission of the owner of the copyright

inherent powers powers of the national government, not stated in the Constitution as these powers belong to all national governments simply because they are nation-states

initiative method available to voters for proposing new laws; the first step of which is to collect signatures on a petition

injunctions court orders forbidding or requiring an action by an individual or group

interdependent dependent upon; nations of the world are directly and indirectly affected by the decisions and actions of the other world countries

interest groups organizations that carry out programs to influence public opinion, government policies, and decisions of the legislative, executive, and judicial branches through lobbying, propaganda, and election policies; also called *pressure groups*

intergovernmental revenue nontax source of money distributed from one level of government to another; usually dispersed from the national government to the state level

intergovernmental service agreement contractual agreement between units of government to provide a service; operation of jails, airports, or hospitals are examples of such services

interim committees legislative groups formed to study a problem or issue between legislative sessions, and possibly propose laws on the subject when the legislature meets again

intermediate appellate courts state courts that first hear appeals after a trial court and before a state supreme court

international organization recognized group of world nations often organized to work together for peace on a global scale; some examples are the former League of Nations and the present United Nations

international trade exchange of goods and services among people and businesses in the global community

interrogatories series of written questions prepared by the attorneys in a lawsuit to be answered by the other side

interstate commerce buying and selling of goods between persons or businesses in different states

iron triangles represent a powerful political force created when congressional groups and members of various federal agencies join with interest groups to make their needs known concerning a government program or issue

isolationism foreign policy of avoiding political, economic, or military involvement with other countries

J

joint committees committees made up of members from both houses of a legislative body that work out compromises for a common problem

joint resolutions similar to bills; approved by both houses and the President these proposals have the force of law; an example of a joint resolution would be the authorization of money for a military action overseas

judicial branch one of the three branches of government; it has the power to interpret the laws and apply these laws in court cases

judicial review principle of American government granting the judicial system the power to declare acts of the legislative or executive branches contrary to the Constitution

junkets publicly funded trips taken by members of Congress to gather firsthand information before taking action on an issue or situation or voting on bills

jurisdiction kinds of cases over which a court has legal authority

jus sanguinis Latin phrase meaning ''right of blood''; a principle by which citizenship is determined by the citizenship of one's parents rather than by place of birth

jus soli Latin phrase meaning ''right of the soil''; a principle by which citizenship is determined by one's place of birth rather than by the citizenship of his or her parents

justice of the peace elected official who presides over a local justice court

justiciable situations appropriate for judicial review

L

laissez faire theory of free enterprise economic systems; also means ''to allow to do''

law body of rules or regulations designed and enforced by a governing body and followed by its citizens

law codes organized written lists of laws developed from the unwritten rules of society

legal tender legally valid coins and paper money accepted for goods and services

legislative branch one of the three branches of government; it gives Congress the power to make the laws

legislative oversight executive-type power held by state legislatures to review state executive activities such as money spending for programs

legislative veto provision in a law giving Congress or one of its committees the power to prevent certain actions by the executive branch; declared unconstitutional by the Supreme Court

libel printing lies about someone with the intent to do harm

lieutenant governor state official who acts as chief executive when the governor is absent from the state, becomes disabled, or dies; he or she may act as president of the state senate

limited government government's power is limited by a constitution; the underlying tenet upon which the United States system of government is built

line agencies organizations in the executive branch of the government that operate programs and deal directly with the people; these agencies can do staff or advisory work; an example is the IRS

line-item veto executive branch uses this power when it vetoes individual items in a bill

lobbying organized efforts, usually by interest groups, to contact government officials in an attempt to influence legislation or policies

local expenditures monies spent by local governments to meet the expenses of the services they provide to the public; education, street and highway lighting, water systems, local transportation are examples of such services

local governments governing offices found in cities, towns, and counties within a state

local revenue money acquired by local governments through tax and nontax sources to meet the expenses of their government activities

local taxes monies paid by people and businesses to local governments to carry out general government activities

local trial courts courts in a state judicial system that are at the local level with original but limited jurisdiction over misdemeanors and small civil cases

loose construction interpretation of the Constitution that allows the national government to use its powers broadly, rather than only as expressly stated in the Constitution

M

majority leader individual who leads the majority party in a legislative house; he or she is a member of that legislative body and elected by its members

majority opinion written judgment that announces and explains the Supreme Court's majority vote

margin requirements tool in monetary policy requiring a minimum percentage of cash payment that a buyer of stock must pay

markup session Congressional subcommittees that meet to make recommended and agreed-upon changes in a proposed bill

master plan plan designed and developed by city planners describing present land areas and their future development

mayor-council form local form of government in which the most important leaders are the elected mayor, with executive power, and the elected council, with legislative power

metropolitan area large urban region consisting of a central city and its surrounding suburbs

minister individual in charge of a government or a department within the government

minority leader individual who leads the minority party in a legislative house; he or she is a member of that legislative body and elected by its members

monarchy form of government in which the power is held by a king, queen, or emperor; the title of power is usually inherited

monetary policy money policy; actions of the national government through the Federal Reserve System to control the availability of money and the cost of credit

mortgage transfer of property to a bank or individual when a debt or loan has not been paid

multiparty system electoral system in which voters can cast their vote for issues or candidates representing three or more political parties seeking power

municipalities local units of government with authority to govern urban or city areas

N

national chairperson leader chosen to head the national committee of a political party

national committee group of leaders of a political party who direct party business during the time between national party conventions

national convention allows party representatives from all over the country to meet every four years to select candidates, adopt a platform, and set the party program for the future

national debt total amount of money the federal government owes as a result of borrowing; occurs when the federal government exceeds its budget and spends more funds than it collects

nationalists individuals who support bringing together power in a centralized government

National Supremacy Clause principle found in Article VI of the Constitution stating that state or local laws cannot conflict with the Constitution or with national treaties and laws

nation-state a country composed of people sharing race, a common language, customs, traditions, and religion

naturalization legal process by which an alien becomes a citizen by meeting certain requirements including residency, literacy, and acceptance of the principles of American government

New England town form of local government in which a ''town'' includes a central village and surrounding rural areas, and practices direct democracy

newly developed nation middle-income state with some industrial base

nominate to name an individual to run as candidate for a public office in an election

nonpartisan elections elections usually held at the state or local level; the candidate's party membership is not given on the ballot

O

ombudsman in this role congressional members serve as a link between their home-state constituents and the government; as such, they attempt to resolve problems, investigate concerns, and answer questions voiced by citizens concerning government's actions

one-party systems electoral systems in which only one party is legally recognized in the country

open primary qualified voters are allowed to participate in this type of election regardless of party affiliation; however, voters must choose candidates from only one party

opinion poll method of sampling a large group to determine its attitudes and feelings on an issue, or to forecast the outcome of an election

opinions statements of explanation written by a judge concerning the decision reached in a certain case; these statements usually entail examples of the law and how it applies to the particular case heard

order of succession sequence by which one person after another assumes a title or an office

ordinances laws of a local unit of government such as a city or county

original jurisdiction authority allowing a court to be the first to hear a case when it enters the legal system

P

pardons releases from punishment granted by chief executives to persons accused or convicted of crimes

parishes administrative units of local government in the state of Louisiana; similar to counties in other states

parliamentary democracy type of democratic political system in which governmental authority is under the control of a cabinet, headed by a prime minister and a parliament

partisan elections candidates running for office in these elections—whether state, local, or federal—are identified by their political party

party platforms statements concerning the beliefs and positions held by a political party

patents registrations of ideas with the government so inventors have the exclusive right to use their ideas, or to license them to others for use

patronage system by which elected officials at all levels of government appoint individuals to fill positions on a party basis

per capita GDP obtained by dividing the amount of the total output or gross domestic product (GDP) by the total population in a particular year; the result is the average yearly income per person

petition request made by individuals to the government, through government officials; petitions can concern government policy or an individual may make an official request to become a citizen

pigeonholed term borrowed from the old-time desks in committee rooms of Congress that had small compartments or ''pigeonholes'' for filing papers; used when a bill is filed or put aside for no further action

plaintiff individual or group filing a complaint in a suit

plank one issue or belief presented by a political party as part of its platform

planning commissions departments that plan for the growth of communities

plea bargain agreement between the prosecutor and the defendant whereby the accused pleads guilty to a lesser charge in exchange for a lighter sentence

pleadings formal papers stating the arguments in a court case

plurality this occurs when the largest number of votes has been cast in an election; this can still be less than half the total and a candidate in most states must win only a plurality of votes to be declared the winner

pocket veto power exercised by a chief executive at the end of a legislative session whereby he or she does not sign a bill and it "dies" after a specified time

political action committees interest groups, often called PACs, that raise money from their members and contribute it to political parties or individual candidates

political culture set of knowledge, beliefs, behaviors, and institutions related to the politics or government of a group or nation

political efficacy power to bring about political action or change

political parties voluntary groups created so individuals have input in the running of their government; these citizens organize in an attempt to influence public opinion or policy, win elections, and control government

political socialization process by which young people, through the influence of family, friends, religion, organizations, school, and the media develop views and attitudes about their nation's political system

political system formal or informal ways citizens manage political activities to set about achieving the goals of government

polling place place where qualified citizens go to cast their votes in a local, state, or federal election; sometimes called the "polls"

poll taxes taxes of a fixed amount for each person, formerly paid as a requirement for voting in some states; banned by the Twenty-fourth Amendment to the Constitution

popular sovereignty principle of American government placing limitations on its power by stating that citizens hold the final authority in government

popular vote votes cast by the people in a general or a primary election

precedents previous court decisions used as a basis for later decisions in similar cases

precinct smallest voting district in a city or county; it must contain a designated number of voters and is assigned a polling place

President-elect candidate selected by the electoral college to be the next President

presidential democracy type of democratic political system in which the executive and legislative branches of the government are separate, and the executive is elected for a fixed term

presidential government term used in the United States to describe the trend toward increased power in the executive branch, often at the expense of Congress

president pro tempore sometimes shortened to "president pro tem"; this senator is elected by the Senate to temporarily preside over it when the Vice President is absent

press all types of printed materials including newspapers, magazines, books, as well as radio, television, and movies

price supports guarantees to farmers by the federal government of minimum prices for specified crops by buying up surpluses of those crops

primary elections preliminary elections in which voters choose party candidates to run for office on their party ticket in general elections; sometimes voters also choose convention delegates and party leaders in primary elections

prior restraint censorship of material by the government before the material has been published

private bills proposed legislation affecting an individual or small group of people; examples are bills allowing certain groups to enter the United States

privileges and immunities special rights, exemptions, and privileges granted to citizens in one state that cannot be denied while in another state

probable cause evidence from a reliable source or valid reasons given which justify issuance of a warrant to search an individual, his or her home, or personal possessions

probation time period in which a convicted individual is given freedom but must demonstrate by behavior and action that he or she can reform; usually supervised by an appointed probation officer

progressive tax rate of tax that increases as the amount to be taxed and supposedly the person's ability to pay increases

propaganda communications, whether true or false, that are based on careful selection and manipulation of data, which are intended to influence the thoughts or emotions of a group in hopes of changing its behavior

property tax   tax paid by the owners of a ceratin property; tax rate varies from state to state and is determined by the value of the property

proprietary colonies   colonies ruled by individuals who had been given a royal charter by the king of England to own the land and govern it in accordance with English law

prosecutor   person who begins criminal proceedings; representative of the government in court who presents the government's evidence

public bills   proposed legislation dealing with subjects of interest to the nation as a whole or affecting many people; an example would be a new tax law

public land   land owned and used by the federal government; primarily located in the West

public opinion   attitudes, views, or beliefs of a large group on a variety of issues and usually expressed in a democracy by elections, lobbying, and interest group activities

public policy   outcome of government decision making, resulting in action to address a problem affecting a large number of people

public services   services provided by the government for the general welfare and benefit of business, industry, labor, and consumers

pure speech   freely voiced opinion in one's private home or a public place

Q

quorum   minimum number of members of a legislative body that must be present in order for action to take place; 51 members must be present in the Senate; 218 in the House

quorum call   request to legislators to come to the floor so that business can be conducted

quotas   limited shares of the total number; restrictions enforced by the government limiting the number of goods or aliens allowed into the country

R

ratify   formal approval; such as approval of a treaty

rational basis   determining factor used by the Supreme Court to assure equal protection by the law to individuals who have been classified into groups by the government

reapportionment   redistribution; this occurs when the distribution of legislative seats must be changed based on a new law, formula, or changes in population

recall   election allowing citizens to vote on whether to remove an official from office; this action occurs before the end of the official's term of office

recesses   periods of time during which a legislative or judicial body is not in session

recession   phase in the business cycle where economic activity takes a downturn

recognition   formal acknowledgement of the legal existence of a government or nation, usually accompanied by establishing diplomatic relations

referendum   vote at an election that allows citizens to accept or reject a bill or law that has been proposed by their state or local government

refugees   people who flee for safety, especially to a foreign country

register   to enroll or enter one's name on a list of qualified, eligible, or available individuals, such as for the military draft or to vote

regressive tax   tax rate which is the same for everyone, regardless of ability to pay; falls relatively more heavily on low income groups

regular sessions   periods in which Congress or a state legislature usually assembles to conduct business

remand   to send back a case to the lower court from which it came

repeal   to rescind or do away with legislation

report   send a bill back to the full house with committee recommendations

representative democracy   called indirect democracy because citizens rule "indirectly" through their elected representatives

reprieves   postponements of punishments or penalties granted by chief executives, usually for humanitarian reasons to await new evidence

reprimand   formal mild reproof established by Congress for misconduct by one of its members

reserved powers   powers not granted to the national government by the Constitution or denied to the states

reserve requirement   tool in monetary policy

requiring member banks of the Federal Reserve to set aside a certain percent of every deposit for the protection of the depositor

resident aliens   people who are not citizens of the country in which they live, but who intend to remain there permanently

resident visa   permit given to noncitizens by the government of the country where they live allowing them to remain in that country indefinitely

revenues   funds or monies received by a government on the national, state, and local levels to carry out its programs

reverse discrimination   discrimination that occurs against an individual or group because another person or group, based on their sex or race, is being treated differently in an attempt to remedy past discrimination against them

riders   amendments or additions to a bill not related to the subject of the bill

royal colonies   settlements under control of the king or queen and governed through appointed officials

rule of law   basic government principle accompanying constitutional supremacy; government shall be carried out according to the established law, and both those who govern and those who are governed will be equally bound by this law

run-off primary   second primary election held between two candidates with the greatest number of votes held when no one candidate in the primary election received a majority of the votes

S

search warrant   official order, usually issued by a judge, authorizing law-enforcement officials to search an individual, his or her home, or personal possessions in connection with a crime

second budget resolution   readjusts the target originally set in the first budget resolution

secretaries   official heads of the executive departments such as the secretaries of state, agriculture, or treasury

secular   not under a church's control; not religious or sacred

seditious speech   written or spoken speech inciting rebellion against the government or disregard of lawful authorities

segregate   to keep certain individuals apart based on their race

select committees   committees of legislators appointed or selected to study a specific problem for a limited time

selective sales tax   tax levied on a specific item for sale in a state, such as gasoline or insurance; sometimes known as an excise tax

self-incrimination   providing evidence or testimony against oneself in court

seniority system   long-standing practice in which the majority party member with the longest period of service on a committee becomes the committee chairperson

separation of church and state   idea that the government may not establish an official church, require the practice of a certain religion, or treat people differently because of their religious affiliation

separation of powers   principle of American government in which power is divided among the three branches—executive, legislative, judicial—so that each is checked by the other two

severance tax   tax paid when natural resources, such as oil or gas, are taken from the land or water

simple resolutions   expression of opinion by a single house of Congress, applying only to itself

slander   telling lies about someone with the intent to do harm

slate of electors   list of candidates in a state nominated by a political party to vote in the electoral college for that party's presidential ticket if it wins the popular vote in that state's general election

socialism   economic system in which the government owns and manages certain basic industries

sovereignty   supreme political authority within the boundaries of a nation-state; freedom from external influence or control

special district   unit of local government set up to provide particular services that citizens desire, but cannot receive from other units of government; these services can include police and fire protection, or water and sewage treatment

special election   election held whenever an issue must be decided by the voters before the next regular election is scheduled

speech plus speech that involves or leads to actions such as parades or demonstrations to communicate ideas

staff agencies organizations in the executive branch who are responsible for advising and helping the President and the White House Office by supplying such activities as planning and budgeting

standing situation where a person can show his or her interests are in danger of being denied by law or executive action; must be shown before judicial review can occur; a standing can involve interests addressing an individual's place in the community, reputation, or even social rank

standing committee permanent committees in a legislative body that deal with specific topics

stare decisis Latin phrase meaning ''let the decision stand''; this legal term means a court decision should follow precedents set in earlier and similar cases

state budget financial plan outlining the revenues needed to meet the expenses of running state programs and operations for a specific period of time, usually a year

state expenditures monies spent by a state government to pay for its programs and operations

state income tax revenue collected in a state by levying this tax on individual's earnings and businesses' earnings

State of the Union Address annual January presidential address to a joint session of Congress outlining the administration's legislative program and urging the program's passage

state revenue money acquired by a state through tax and nontax sources to help run its programs and operations

state supreme court highest court of appeals in a state judicial system, whose decision is final in most cases

state taxes monies paid by the people to the state government for general public purposes

statutes laws passed by the national, state, or local legislature

strict construction interpretation of the Constitution to allow the national government to use its powers narrowly; primarily to follow what is expressly stated in the Constitution, Article I, Section 8

strong-mayor plan mayor-council form of local government in which the mayor has full executive power while the council has separate legislative power

subcommittees divisions of a committee, to study or carry out portions of the committee's work

subpoenas official written orders requiring the presence in court of witnesses or documents

subsidies financial aids given by the government to business, agriculture, or individuals in support of a public goal

suffrage citizen's constitutionally guaranteed right to vote

suspect classification test used by the Supreme Court to determine if the classification of individuals based on race, national origin, or sex has in any way denied those individuals equal protection by the law

symbolic speech symbols or objects, such as flags, buttons, or armbands, used to nonverbally communicate one's ideas or feelings

T

tariffs custom duties or taxes charged by a government on items of overseas trade

tax base total value of all property that may be taxed located within a local government's jurisdiction

tax exemptions individuals or businesses may be free of obligation to pay taxes on certain kinds of property or income

tax returns yearly earnings reports filed with the IRS and with state and local governments where required

temporary visitors noncitizens who intend to stay in a country only for specific period of time

terrorism violent acts committed by individuals or groups for political ends

third parties minor parties presenting a single idea, issue, or personality; these parties win fewer votes than either major party, substantially more votes than other minor parties, and sometimes enough votes to influence, but not win, an election

totalitarianism authoritarian form of government that tries to exert total control over the lives of its citizens

townships small units of local government, usually a subdivision of a county; provide services similar to a county for the people of a certain area

trademarks distinctive names, symbols, words, or phrases used on products or advertisements for them, to identify them and their company; registered trademarks with the Patent and Trademark Office are legally protected

treason disloyal act against one's country, such as aiding the enemy of one's country

trust illegal combination of companies to insure uniform behavior, usually price fixing or other agreements, to restrict competition

two-party systems electoral systems in which two major parties in a country compete for leadership

U

unanimous consent agreements time-saving procedures used by the Senate to speed up debate and call for a final vote; agreements must be accepted by the full Senate; debate continues with one ''nay'' vote

unanimous opinion one written statement representing a court decision reached by all the Supreme Court justices

unclassified employees government workers who do not have to pass the civil service tests to be hired for a government position

unconstitutional actions or laws contrary to the Constitution that make them illegal or invalid

unicameral made up of only one legislative house

unitary government system of government in which the central government holds all powers it does not choose to delegate to local or provincial governments

urbanization process of changing from a country or rural way of life to a city way of life

urban renewal programs to rebuild urban areas by removing city slums and replacing them with new businesses and residential buildings

user fees charges paid for the use of public services

V

verdict decision of a court jury

veto refusal by an official, such as a President or governor, to approve a law

visas entrance permits issued by government officials of one country allowing a person from a foreign country to visit for a designated period of time

W

wards governmental and geographical divisions of some cities for the purpose of voting, particularly in city council elections

weak-mayor plan mayor-council form of local government in which the mayor has limited executive power while the city council members make major decisions

welfare programs established by the government to provide people experiencing hardships, or in need, with money, food, and other necessities

write-in nomination procedure in which a candidate's supporters write in his or her name on the ballot on election day

writ of certiorari written order allowing the Supreme Court to review a case from a lower court, it will order the lower court through ''writ'' to send up the record of that case

writ of habeas corpus formal court order requiring a jailed person to be brought to court to decide whether or not he or she is being held in jail legally

writ of mandamus written order issued by a superior court commanding an official of the government to perform a specified lawful duty or act

Z

zoning method of dividing a city into similar types of areas, such as residential, commercial, industrial, or recreational

zoning ordinances regulations restricting how land or buildings may be used

INDEX

A

Abington School District v. Schempp **1963,** 100
abortion,
  proposed constitutional amendment, 170
  rights, 200, 577, 583
accused, rights of, 26, 36, 60, 62, 107, 115–122, 493, 496, 500, 557
acid rain, 580, 694
Acquired Immune Deficiency Syndrome (AIDS), 417, 620
acquittal, 501
ACTION, 397
Act of Bogota 1948, 674
Adams, John, 29, 179, 348, 467
Adams, John Quincy, 278, 318, 348
Adams, Samuel, 42, 46
adjournment, 248
Administration for Children, Youth, and Families, 394
Administrative Office of the United States Courts, 476
adversary system, 465
advice and consent by Senate, 279
Aerospace Industries Association, 199
affirmative action, 481
Africa, 689, 690
African Americans,
  in Congress, 248
  elective officials, 599
  right to vote, 144, 518
  South Africa, 653–655
  on Supreme Court, 479
African National Congress (ANC), 654
Agnew, Spiro, 332
Agricultural Cooperative

Service, 387
Agricultural Marketing Service, 387
Agricultural Stabilization and Conservation Service, 387
agriculture, 199
Aid to Families With Dependent Children (AFDC), 394, 415–416, 524, 571, 582, 604
Air Force One, 315
Air Force Two, 329
air pollution, 580
air travel safety, 371
Albany Plan, 28
Alcohol, Drug Abuse, and Mental Health Administration, 394
aliens, 149
Allegheny County v. Greater Pittsburgh ACLU **1989,** 101
alliances, 10, 518
alternative dispute resolution (ADR), 502
ambassadors, 321
ambassador to United Nations, 355
ambiguous statements, 157
American Association of Retired Persons (AARP), 200
American Bar Association (ABA), 197, 205, 206, 475, 480
American Cattlemen's Association, 197
American Civil Liberties Union (ACLU), 101, 110, 200, 204, 480
American Farm Bureau Federation, 199
American Federation of Labor-Congress of Industrial Organizations (AFL-CIO), 188, 198

American Independent party, 182, 183
American Medical Association, 197, 198
American nationals, 149
American Nazi party, 110
American Printing House for the Blind, 395
American Revolution, 27–35, 38
American Samoa, 251, 277
American territories,
  citizenship status, 141
amicus curiae **briefs,** 205, 483
Amish, 102
amnesty, for Vietnam years, 327
analysis, 307
Anderson, John, 226
Animal and Plant Health Inspection Service, 387
Anthony, Susan B., 144–145
Anti-Federalists, 41, 46, 179, 180, 464
Antitrust Division, 386
ANZUS Pact 1951, 671
apartheid, 578, 654–655
appellate jurisdiction, 465
apportionment and reapportionment, 251–254
Arabian Peninsula, 643
Arab League, 674–675
Argentina, debt, 690
arguments,
  identifying, 489
  strength of, 677
Arkansas National Wildlife Refuge, 205
armaments, 684–685
Armenia, 648, 686
arms control, 680–681, 685
arraignment, 500–501
Arthur, Chester A., 348
Articles of Confederation, 10, 28, 36–38, 41, 42, 43, 242, 268, 641

Koch, Edward, 621
Korean Business Committee, 206
Korean War, 324, 446
Ku Klux Klan, 161
Kuwait, 660, 690

L

labor unions, 163, 198, 420
Labour party, 640
LaFollette, Robert, 182, 226
laissez faire, 16
Lame Duck Amendment, 64
"lame ducks," 245
Land and Natural Resources Division, 386
Landon, Alf, 170
Land Ordinance 1785, 38
Latin America, 689, 690
Latin American Free Trade Association (LAFTA), 673
Latin American Integration Association, 673
Latvia, 648, 686
law,
   administrative, 497
   binding on all persons, 7
   case, 497
   civil, 498–500
   and crime, 493–494
   criminal, 500–501
   equity, 499–500
   function of, 491–494
   good, 494–495
   history, 496
   limit on government, 492–493
   nature of, 491
   other cultures, 130
   Roman, 496
   and social goals, 493
   statutory, 497
Lazarus, Emma, 151, 153
League of Nations, 662
League of United Latin American Citizens, 199
League of Women Voters, 200
Lebanon, civil war, 668
Lee, Richard Henry, 30, 42
legal system, U.S., 491–505
   juveniles, 503–504
legal tender, 270

legislative agencies, 262–263
Legislative Reorganization Act 1946, 261
Lemon v. Kurtzman 1971, 99, 101
lend-lease, 323
letter writing, 167
Liberal-Democratic party (LDP), 645
Libertarians, 182, 183
"Liberty, Equality, Fraternity," 641
Library of Congress, 262, 271
Libya, 693
Lie, Trygve Halvdan, 665
Liechtenstein, 6
life, liberty, and property, 25, 29, 62, 64, 95
life, liberty, or property, 123, 518
Limited Nuclear Test Ban Treaty, 684
Lincoln, Abraham, 5, 66, 180, 359
   great President, 348
   and habeas corpus, 343
   loose constructionist, 346
   as President, 341
   and strong central government, 527
   war powers, 324, 341, 343
line agencies, *See* federal agencies
literacy tests, 145
Literary Digest poll, 170
Lithuania, 686
Little Rock, AR, 325
lobbying, 203–204, 297
   in conference committee, 304
Locke, John, 8, 25, 492
logrolling, 297
Los Angeles, CA, 599
lotteries and gambling, 570, 583
"loyal opposition," 178
Luxembourg, 6
Lynch v. Donnelly 1984, 101

M

MacArthur, General Douglas, 324
McCollum v. Board of Education 1948, 99

McCulloch v. Maryland 1819, 57, 468, 520
McFarlane, Robert, 364
McKinley, William, 343, 348
Madison, James, 40–42, 61, 348, 467, 513
   and Bill of Rights, 41
   Framer of Constitution, 41
   notes on Constitutional Convention, 42
   and power of states, 533
   strict constructionist, 346
   a writer of *Federalist* papers, 46, 195–196
magistrates, federal, 476
Magna Carta, 496, 638
majority leader, 250
Mandela, Nelson, 654
Mapp v. Ohio 1961, 117–118
Marbury v. Madison 1803, 57, 467–469, 489
margin requirements, 410
Marines, 432
Maritime Administration, 392
markup session, 298
Marshall, George C., 430
Marshall, John, 51, 133, 489, 527
   and judicial review, 467, 469
   profile, 57
   and strong central government, 527
Marshall, Thurgood, 479
Marshall Plan, 430, 689
marshals, United States, 476
Marsh v. Chambers 1983, 101
Marx, Karl, 18, 507
Mason, George, 46
Massachusetts ballots, 232
Maximilian (emperor of Mexico), 646
Mayflower Compact, 24
Mecham, Evan, 549
media, 162, 163, *See also* press; radio; television
media events, 162
Medicaid, 415–416, 441, 454–455, 571, 582
Medical Training, veterans, 396
Medicare, 415–416, 440, 454–455
Meese, Edwin, 363
Meet the Press, 162, 229
mercantilism, 27–28

O

SUPREME COURT CASE INDEX

PHOTO CREDITS

327, P.F. Gero/Sygma; 328, Rick Friedman/Black Star; 329, Tannenbaum/Sygma; 331, AP/Wide World Photos; 332, J.L. Atlan/Sygma; 335, James Larrick/The Columbus (OH) Dispatch; 336, Stephen Ferry/Gamma-Liaison; 338, Scott Eklund/ Gamma-Liaison; 340, file photo; 341, Keystone Press Agency; 343, National Park Service; 344, 345, AP/Wide World Photos; 346, Washington Star Syndicate, Inc.; 347, United Press International Photo; 348, National Gallery of Art, Washington D.C., Andrew W. Mellon Collection; 349, Arthur Grace/Sygma; 350, AP/Wide World Photos; 353, Harry S. Truman Library; 354, file photo; 357, Stock Montage, Inc.; 358, (l) Terry Ashe/ Gamma-Liaison, (r) Ira Wyman/Sygma; 359, Stock Montage, Inc.; 360, 363, Cynthia Johnson/Gamma-Liaison; 365, AP/Wide World Photos; 370, Ron S. Mellott; 371, Dallas Morning News/Gamma-Liaison, (inset) Hank Morgan/Photo Researchers; 372, NASA; 373, Aaron Haupt; 376, U.S. Postal Service; 379, Toles/The Buffalo News/Universal Press Syndicate; 381, Ruth Dixon; 382, Aaron Haupt; 383, Wally MacNamee/Woodfin Camp & Associates; 384, Aaron Haupt; 385, file photo; 386, Robert W. Kelley; 387, Tracy I. Borland; 388, Frank Balthis; 389, 390, David R. Frazier Photolibrary; 391, Cincinnati Convention and Visitor's Bureau; 392, Doug Martin; 393, George H. Matchneer; 394, courtesy American Cancer Society; 395, Tim Courlas; 396, file photo; 397, NASA; 398, Tim Courlas; 399, Aaron Haupt; 401, P.F. Gero/Sygma; 402, P. Chauvel/Sygma; 404, file photo; 406, Joseph DiChello; 407, courtesy Department of Navy; 408, Elaine Shay; 412, Yvonne Hemsey/Gamma-Liaison; 413, Mike Yamashita/Woodfin Camp & Associates; 414, Barbara Stevenson/Smithsonian Institution; 416, Aaron Haupt; 418, Peress/Magnum; 421, file photo; 423, Joseph DiChello; 424, Stephen J. Krasemann/DRK Photo; 426, Kurt Thorson; 427, NASA; 428, Kurt Thorson; 429, The Nixon Project; 430, D. Hudson/Sygma; 431, T. Orban/Sygma; 435, Bob Daemmrich/Stock Boston; 436, Doug Martin; 439, Cobalt Productions; 441, Gary Knight/Saba Press Photos; 444, U.S. News and World Report/Gary L. Kieffer; 448, Dennis Brack/ Black Star; 449, Bob Daemmrich/Sygma; 450, AP/Wide World Photos; 451, Costa Manos/Magnum; 452, Don Jones/Gamma-Liaison; 453, file photo; 454, Doug Martin; 457, Bob Daemmrich/Stock Boston; 459, D.C. Walker; 460, Richard Laird/FPG International; 462, Wally McNamee/Woodfin Camp & Associates; 464, Stephen Ferry/Gamma-Liaison; 465, U.S. Postal Service; 466, Alex Webb/Magnum; 467, Bruce Hoertel/ Gamma-Liaison; 469, Cynthia Johnson/Gamma-Liaison; 470, Diana Walker/Gamma-Liaison; 471, Supreme Court Historical Society; 474, Jeffrey D. Smith/Woodfin Camp & Associates; 477, AP/Wide World Photos; 478, Dennis Brack/Black Star; 479, AP/Wide World Photos; 481, Joe Traver/Gamma-Liaison; 482, 483, AP/Wide World Photos; 484, Martin Simon/Saba Press Photos; 485, AP/Wide World Photos; 489, Dana Summers, The Orlando (FL) Sentinel/The Washington Post Writers Group; 490, Michal Heron/Woodfin Camp & Associates; 492, Russ Lappa; 493, Tim Courlas; 495, James N. Westwater; 496, file photo;

501, Bob Daemmrich/Texas Stock; 502, W.H. Hubbell/Woodfin Camp & Associates; 503, First Image; 507, Peter Blakely/Saba Press Photos; 509, AP/Wide World Photos; 510, Timothy Eagan/Woodfin Camp & Associates; 512, file photo; 514, Steve Lehman/Saba Press Photos; 515, Dennis Stock/Magnum; 516, AP/Wide World Photos; 517, Elliott Erwitt/Magnum; 520, Aaron Haupt; 521, Joseph DiChello; 522, file photo; 524, Paul Brown; 526, F.R.C.; 531, James Larrick/The Columbus (OH) Dispatch; 532, David R. Frazier Photolibrary; 534, file photo; 539, © 1990 Lightscapes/The Stock Market; 541, Allen Zak; 547, Inauguration Committee of Don Sundquist; 549, Don B. Stevenson/Uniphoto; 550, Mark Wilson/Arkansas Democrat Gazette; 554, Cobalt Productions; 555, First Image; 556, Shenandoah Photo/Gamma-Liaison; 558, George H. Matchneer; 559, file photo; 564, Aaron Haupt; 571, Costa Manos/Magnum; 573, Larry Hamill; 576, Chuck O'Rear/Woodfin Camp & Associates; 578, Joseph DiChello; 581, 582, 583, file photo; 584, Bob Daemmrich; 587, Jimmy Margulies, The Record (Hackensack, NJ)/North America Syndicate; 588, George Hall/Woodfin Camp & Associates; 590, Collier/Condit; 592, Aaron Haupt; 593, file photo; 594, Doug Martin; 595, Aaron Haupt; 596, Steve Lissau; 598, Dan Miller/Woodfin Camp & Associates; 599, Gamma-Liaison; 604, David R. Frazier Photolibrary; 606, Joseph DiChello; 609, Jeff Stahler, The Cincinnati Post for USA TODAY; 610, file photo; 616, James N. Westwater; 618, Michal Heron; 619, Aaron Haupt; 621, Elaine Shay; 623, Columbus Convention Bureau/Doug Martin; 625, Brad Markel/Gamma-Liaison; 626, Larry Downing/Sygma; 628, courtesy Victorian Park Kindergarten Preschool and Nursery/First Image; 631, Mike Keefe for USA TODAY; 633, Michael Abramson/Woodfin Camp & Associates; 634, Travelpix/FPG International; 636, Sepp Seitz/Woodfin Camp & Associates; 638, file photo; 639, J. Parker Spooner/Gamma-Liaison; 640, AP/Wide World Photos; 641, Archives © Gigile Freund/Photo Researchers; 642, file photo; 643, Allen Green/Photo Researchers; 644, Sygma; 645, Mitsuhiro Wada/Gamma-Liaison; 646, Jules Bucher/Photo Researchers; 648, file photo; 650, (t) Sovfoto, (b) Allen Green/Photo Researcher; 651, Malcolm Linton/Black Star; 652, Wide World Photos; 653, Eric Bouvet; 658, Jim Anderson/Woodfin Camp & Associates; 660, B. Bisson/Sygma; 661, Leif Skoogfors/Woodfin Camp & Associates; 662, Carl Frank/Photo Researchers; 666, Kurt Thorson; 667, Larry Hamill; 669, Tim Riber/Uniphoto; 670, UPI/Bettmann; 672, Don C. Nieman; 673, Udo Schreiber/Gamma-Liaison; 674, file photo; 677, Roman Genn/Easy Reader; 678, Wally McNamee/Woodfin Camp & Associates; 680, Chris Niedenthal/Black Star; 681, Leif Skoogfors/Woodfin Camp & Associates; 682, Sygma; 684, NASA; 685, Shone/Gamma-Liaison; 686, Gamma-Liaison; 687, file photo; 688, Orban/Sygma; 689, file photo; 691, Ulastimer Shone/Gamma-Liaison; 692, A. Nogues/Sygma; 694, Roger K. Burnard; 697, Oliver/Der Standard/Vienna; 699, Joseph A. DiChello.

'94 ELECTION

"It's a revolution that happened without any bullets."

—-James Thurber, director of congressional studies, American University, commenting immediately after the election

On November 8, 1994, Americans went to the polls. The economy was growing, inflation was under control, hundreds of thousands of jobs had been created. Yet, the public mood was angry. Many Americans believed that the government, under the leadership of President Clinton, was out of touch with the people. They showed their anger in the time-honored traditions of representative democracy—with ballots. They ousted Democrats in historic numbers. The backlash against the Democrats continued until the Republicans had gained 52 House seats, 8 Senate seats, and 11 governorships. It was the best showing for the Republican party in 48 years. Republicans were jubilant, Democrats downcast. Throughout it all, however, the American system of representative democracy worked.

GLENCOE

McGraw-Hill

CONGRESS

Changes in House Seats, 1974-1994

Democratic Gain

GOP Gain

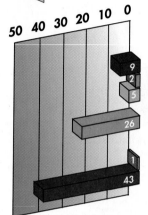

50   40   30   20   10   0

Clinton 1994
Bush 1992
Bush 1990
Reagan 1988   9
Reagan 1986   2
Reagan 1984   5
Reagan 1982
Carter 1980   26
Carter 1978
Ford 1976   1
Nixon 1974   43

0   10   20   30   40   50

52
10

14

33
11

DEMOCRATIC LEADERS VOTED OUT
- Speaker of the House Thomas Foley
- Texas governor Ann Richards
- Tennessee senator Jim Sasser
- New York governor Mario Cuomo
- Illinois representative Dan Rostenkowski

BIGGEST SPENDERS
- In the Senate race in California, Republican Michael Huffington outspent Democrat Diane Feinstein—$27.5 million to $14 million. Huffington spent $25 million of his own money but lost the election.
- Oliver North spent $20 million in his bid to oust Democratic Virginia Senator Robb. Robb won by a narrow margin.
- Houston physician Eugene Fontenot topped the list of big spenders in House elections, using $2.6 million of his own money. He lost.
- Democratic Representative Richard Gephardt of Missouri spent $2.3 million. His fund-raising paid off.

DEMOCRATS   **REPUBLICANS**

The House
All 435 Seats were at stake.

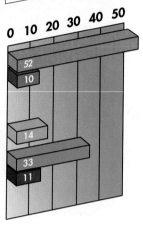

Before the election

100   200   300   435

OLD PARTY DIVISION
256   **178**
1 Independent

Republicans gained 52 seats

100   200   300   435

NEW PARTY DIVISION
204   **230**
1 Independent

Source: Columbus Dispatch

DEMOCRATS   **REPUBLICANS**

The Senate
There were 35 of 100 Senate seats up for election in 34 states.

Before the election

25   50   75   100

OLD PARTY DIVISION
56   **44**

Republicans gained 9 seats

25   50   75   100

NEW PARTY DIVISION
47   **53**

Source: Columbus Dispatch

CONGRESS

	103rd Congress		104th Congress	
	Senate	House	Senate	House
Democrats	56	256	46	204
Republicans	44	177	54	230
Independent/others	0	2	0	1
Women	7	47	8	49
Men	93	388	92	386
Whites	96	376	96	372
African Americans	1	38	1	39
Hispanic Americans*	0	17	0	18
Asian Americans/Pacific Islander	2	4	2	6
Native Americans	1	0	1	0

* Can be of any race

Source: *USA Today*

THE REPUBLICAN AGENDA FOR THE 104TH

- Pass balanced budget amendment
- Limit congressional terms
- Revise the 1994 Crime Bill to emphasize prison building rather than crime prevention
- Cut taxes
- Reform welfare to require able-bodied recipients to work
- Raise defense spending
- Reform health care

WAVES OF CHANGE

- Not one Republican incumbent lost a House, Senate, or governor's race.
- Tom Foley, Speaker of the House in the 103rd Congress, was the first Speaker to lose an election since the Civil War.
- Republicans won 56% of the contests in the South compared to 47% in the 1992 election.
- Republicans won a majority of House seats in the South for the first time since Reconstruction.
- Representative Jamie Whitten of Mississippi retired, ending his 52-year career in Congress.
- The day after Republicans swept the election, Senator Richard Shelby of Alabama announced that he was switching parties—from Democratic to Republican.

Minorities in Congress

(Totals do not include non-voting delegates)

- Hispanic Americans
- African Americans
- Asian Americans

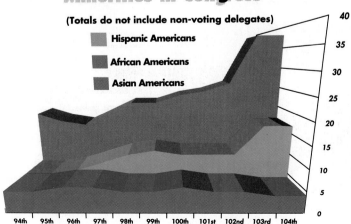

GOVERNORS

Pre-Election

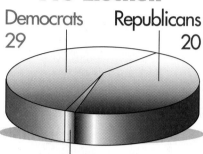

Democrats 29   Republicans 20

Independents 1

BIGGEST REPUBLICAN WINNERS

- George Voinovich, governor of Ohio—72%
- William Weld, governor of Massachusetts—71%
- Tommy Thompson, governor of Wisconsin—66%
- John Engler, governor of Michigan—63%
- Pete Wilson, governor of California—61%

Post-Election

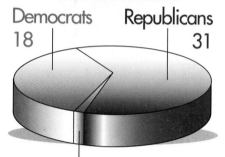

Democrats 18   Republicans 31

Independents 1

YOUR VOTE COUNTS!

- Representative Sam Gejdenson, Democrat from Connecticut, won a recount by a margin of 21 votes—79,188 to 79,167.
- In Alaska's governor's race, Democrat Tony Knowles defeated Republican Jim Campbell by 536 votes out of 339,000 ballots cast.
- Republican Susan Brooks of California led by 93 votes but lost a recount to Jane Harmon.

Sources: National Govenors' Association: *The Associated Press*

WAVES OF CHANGE

- Alabama elected its second Republican governor since Reconstruction— Fob James.
- Former President George Bush had two sons running in gubernatorial races—George Jr. in Texas and Jeb in Florida. George won. Jeb lost.

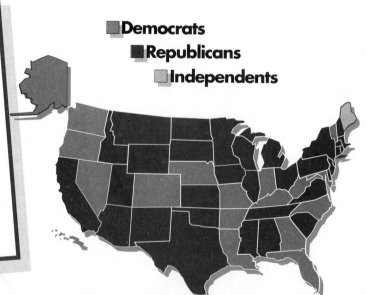

Democrats
Republicans
Independents

Changes

To Republican from Democrat

Alabama
Idaho
Kansas
New Mexico
New York
Oklahoma
Pennsylvania
Rhode Island
Tennessee
Texas
Wyoming

To Republican from Independent

Connecticut

To Independent from Republican

Maine

Source: *USA Today*

All data based on preliminary election results available November 1994.

P/N G34162.01